Europe
in the
Twentieth Century

Europe in the Twentieth Century

ROLAND N. STROMBERG

University of Wisconsin

PRENTICE-HALL, INC., ENGLEWOOD CLIFFS, N.J. 07632

Library of Congress Cataloging in Publication Data

Stromberg, Roland N (date).
    Europe in the twentieth century.

    Bibliography: p.
    Includes index.
    1. Europe—History—20th century. I. Title.
D424.S77   940.5   79–11320
ISBN 0–13–291906–0

Printed in the United States of America

10 9 8 7 6 5 4 3 2 1

Editorial/production supervision by Marina Harrison
Cover design by Lana Giganti
Manufacturing buyer: Ed Leone

Prentice-Hall International, Inc., *London*
Prentice-Hall of Australia Pty. Limited, *Sydney*
Prentice-Hall of Canada, Ltd., *Toronto*
Prentice-Hall of India Private Limited, *New Delhi*
Prentice-Hall of Japan, Inc., *Tokyo*
Prentice-Hall of Southeast Asia Pte. Ltd., *Singapore*
Whitehall Books Limited, *Wellington, New Zealand*

Contents

6

THE DISSOLUTION OF THE ANCESTRAL ORDER: CULTURE AND THOUGHT IN THE 1920s   168

7

THE YEARS OF THE GREAT DEPRESSION   197

8

THE TOTALITARIAN REGIMES   225

9

THE BACKGROUND OF THE SECOND WORLD WAR   250

10

THE SECOND WORLD WAR, 1939–1940 274

11

EUROPE AND THE COLD WAR, 1945–1956 314

12

THE RECOVERY OF WESTERN EUROPE, 1948–1963 343

13

SOVIET COMMUNISM AFTER STALIN 373

14

THE CRISIS OF THE LATE 1960s   402

15

EUROPE AND THE WORLD IN THE 1970s   433

Preface

I have tried in this book to present a historical account of the century in which we live, which is succinct, yet includes the essentials; which is readable, bringing out the excitement and drama of this most turbulent, tragic, and creative of centuries; up-to-date in its scholarship, and judicious in its judgments as well as in its apportioning of space to the varied events and processes of human affairs. The reader will have to judge how well this program has been carried out. I have published a number of previous books, most of them in modern European intellectual history, one at least in international relations; but I have tried not to weight the subject matter overly in favor of my specialties, a common enough textbook ailment.

Obviously much must be left out of a work this short that tries to encompass such a mighty area—on this see some further remarks in the Introduction. The student should get from these pages a solid foundation, on which he or she can build through further readings. (See Reading List at end of book.) From the whole experience the student will, I hope, acquire a sense of understanding of and participation in the amazing human experiment of our times. If students have reactions or questions, I wish they would write to me. This is the first edition. To forestall one criticism: I wish that we had had room for more pictures. Perhaps more next time.

One danger in dealing with matters so near to us in time—this applies especially to the later chapters—was pithily put long ago by Walter Ralegh: "Whosoever in writing a modern history shall follow truth near the heels, it may haply strike out his teeth." Anyone rash enough to venture judgments on what is likely to come next in today's world stands to suffer a few chips, at the least. It is more than likely that at this very moment the world stands at a critical juncture of its long history. If I were teaching the course in twentieth century European or world history, I would ask each student to keep a record of current events in the news which relate to the topics discussed in this book. The student will find quite a few, for we are living in the shadow of the violently disruptive history of the years since 1900.

Acknowledgements and thanks? To too many students, scholars, and libraries to mention, but especially to the staff at Prentice-Hall, to the University of Wisconsin, and to my family. Professor Thomas Hachey of Marquette University was an especially helpful critic, while Jean Chepp was an expert typist and Marina Harrison a skillful editor. I improved my understanding of twentieth century Europe during a period in 1974 spent at the Woodrow Wilson International Center for Scholars in Washington, D.C., as Fellow of that institution directed by a fellow historian, James Billington.

R. N. S.

Introduction

People read history for enjoyment, instruction, orientation, stimulation, inspiration, even therapy; they study the record of past events to broaden their horizons, sharpen their critical sense, find their roots, strengthen their pride, criticize their society, discover other societies; they turn to history out of boredom, curiosity, discontent, piety. Many are seeking to discover the causes or the origins of success, progress, and power or failure, decay, and dissolution. The uses of the past are thus manifold and even contradictory. So is the past itself, encompassing as it does not only the record of public events but also the deeper, often silent processes of social change. It includes scientific, technological, and economic development; artistic and literary achievement; labor and leisure—all the varied activities of all kinds of people. "History is nothing but the activity of men in pursuit of their own ends," Karl Marx once wrote. Such a subject is obviously immense, there being many men and women.

The nitpicker will add that history is the sum of human activities that are both recorded in some way (the overwhelming majority are not) and significant enough to deserve being remembered and studied. The latter qualification is troublesome, for it must be somewhat subjective. A people with a high level of cultural unity, sharing the same traditions and experiences—a small, isolated society, say—might substantially agree on what is important and on the symbolic terms used to describe it. The more diverse, complex, and dynamic a society becomes, the less agreement there will be. We may be sure that the books of two historians on the same subject will differ markedly. All historians writing about the twentieth century will doubtless discuss some of the same things. It is hard to imagine any textbook leaving out the two world wars, the Great Depression, the Russian Revolution, Stalin, or Hitler. But one scholar will omit some matters found in another's book and include matters omitted in other histories. Each will vary in the space he or she devotes to issues, and each will interpret them differently. When an historian interprets history, he or she selects particulars, assigns causation, and judges the wisdom or virtue of decisions that were made.

This is no place to embark on a discussion of such issues; we wish only to warn the reader that there is no one history in the sense that there is one accepted electrical engineering. There are as many histories as there are historians, and the interests of historians change not only from person to person but from generation to generation. Thus the writing of history is an argument without end. The study of history as a profession, itself a chapter of the fairly recent past, has generated some common standards of research and a large body of valuable data, but it has provided little consensus on interpretation or even the methods of interpretation. If it did, this consensus would still be suspect on the grounds of a situational bias.

Selection is a special problem for anyone seeking to cover the entirety of the multitudinous twentieth century in a fairly short volume. Our century has certainly not been lacking either in action or in dynamic development in all phases of human activity. Change has become more rapid, and the total of human knowledge has increased explosively. We can easily argue that there has been more history in this century than in all previous ones combined, just as there have been more books published, more knowledge engendered, more wealth produced, more movements of people. More and more of humanity participates in social processes and is aware of an historical perspective. "The whole immense multitude of men enter finally into the light," that optimistic pre-1914 socialist Jean Jaurès declared. When at about the same time H. G. Wells announced that "history will have to tell more about clerks and less about conquerors," he was noting the fact that clerks, peasants, and workers were ceasing to be merely the inert and passive materials of history and were beginning to play an active, conscious part in human affairs. Certainly a part of the ever accelerating dynamism of Western society is this movement of once almost silent populations into the "light" of consciousness and change—for better or for worse.

The student will do well, then, to take this exercise in historical writing as only one man's opinion and to supplement it with others. Much historical research is being done today, shedding light on numerous neighborhoods in the huge city of modern humanity. To begin to read this rich literature is to enter an exciting world.

Nevertheless I have sought not to be startlingly novel in selecting and interpreting material but rather to include those actions and processes that we should all understand because they have so deeply influenced our lives. In the last analysis history's chief justification is its grasp of the cultural whole. We may, after all, learn about literature, economics, sociology, military science, and so forth in the departments or schools dedicated to these special subjects. Only the historian looks at the movement of whole societies. He or she alone relates the particulars to the big picture. History discusses common experiences affecting the greatest number of people.

Awareness of these shared experiences binds us together in a society; knowledge of the continuity of historical change orients us to our cultural surroundings and makes us more human. Such is the historian's credo. "History is the only true way to attain a knowledge of our condition," Savigny declared. And Lord Acton added, "understanding the present is the prize of all history."

The Peoples and States
of Europe
on the Eve of 1914

Europe in the World

For the sake of an initial perspective, we might make a brief comparison between Europe as it stood at the beginning of the twentieth century and as it stands today. In terms of absolute wealth and power, the peoples and the states of Europe were then much less well off than they are today, for wealth and power have grown enormously through this century, even with all its troubles. The average citizen of England or France, Germany or Italy, Russia, or Hungary has many more material goods today than he did in 1900 or 1914; and governments dispose of far greater resources. But in relative terms, Europe as a whole was then much more dominant in the world. She had fewer rivals, and she was farther ahead of Asia, Africa, and even the Americas in economic, political, and military development.

Prior to 1914 Europe was the undeniable center of world civilization and power. No other region could compare with Europe in military power and political influence; only the United States was comparable in wealth and productivity. The United States had yet to enter the arena of world politics, and though she was rising rapidly, she was not yet the technological colossus she later became. The same holds true for that half-European or doubtfully European giant that links Asia to Europe; Mother Russia was still a giant with feet of clay, extremely backward by European standards in her social structure and economic level of efficiency.

No one else could match Europe, either, in scientific research and discovery, in the brilliance of philosophic thought, and in literature. At least, her material superiority gave her cultural products great prestige, so that other peoples, looking at the power that had subdued them, were inclined to assume that the culture, the ideas, the life style of these Europeans must be superior, too. For at this time, non-European peoples stood in considerable awe of a force that had recently reduced most of them to the position of subjects or satellites. In the 1880s and 1890s, nearly every part of Asia and Africa had been made subservient to the aggressive and competent Europeans. Some territories were annexed and governed directly, others made into protectorates or spheres of interest that though maintaining a nominal independence, had to grant various kinds of special economic and political privileges to the white foreigners.

This subjugation had not happened without resistance. The almost innumerable tribal revolts in Africa testify to this, as do uprisings on the frontier of India; the Boxer Rebellion in China at the turn of the century; and the 1881 riots in Egypt, which brought British troops into the Suez Canal area, not to leave for seventy-three years. Wars with the Afghans, the Zulus, and the Dervishes of Sudan added a touch of glamor to English schoolboy reading. But the British always won, or, if they did not, they returned to gain the final victory, as they did at Khartoum in 1898. Native resistance was futile. Sabers could not defeat carbines:

> *Whatever happens, we have got*
> *A gatling gun and you have not.*

Great Britain led in this wave of imperialism, followed at no great distance by France and, later, by Germany and the United States. Meanwhile, Russia pushed her own borders into the Far Eastern periphery. With a big appetite but small teeth, Italy tried to take part; of the greater powers of Europe, only Austria-Hungary forebore, from lack of naval power. In compensation, little Belgium and the Netherlands acquired very considerable empires, Belgium in Africa and the Netherlands in Southeast Asia. Long ensconced as traders in the East Indies, today Indonesia, the Dutch pushed into the interior of the islands at this time.

Sometimes the European powers stumbled over each other in their haste to seize, exploit, destroy, develop, or civilize the "lesser breeds," and they became involved in conflict or the threat of it. This happened in 1885 between Russia and Britain, in 1898 between France and Britain, in 1905 between France and Germany, and on other occasions as well; but these encounters seldom led to war. It was easy enough to divide up someone else's property. The one great exception occurred in 1904 between Russia and the Westernizing Asian country of Japan, a major, straight-out imperialist war for domination of Manchuria and Korea. It was, however, not between two European powers. And it gave notice, among other things, that the European monopoly of military power might soon end as non-Europeans learned to master the arts and sciences of the West.

That monopoly was not yet under serious threat prior to 1914. As the century turned, the British were engaged in a colonial war that badly shook the country; "we have had no end of a lesson," Rudyard Kipling observed. But this was a fight with another people of European origin, the Dutch settlers on the frontier of British South Africa, who had been aroused to resistance by the aggressive extension of British rule outward from the Cape. French and German opinion, and in fact world opinion generally, cheered for the Boers and chided the British bully in this David-and-Goliath encounter, which the British won only after early setbacks. When newly crowned King Edward VII visited Paris in 1903, he met boos and cries of "Vive les Boers!"; only later did he win the hearts of the French.

But this antipathy did not stop the French and Germans from joining with the British and Russians in organizing an expedition to punish the Chinese for having the insolence to dispute European control of the Celestial Empire. In revenge for antiforeign riots mounted against the White Devils by the "Boxer" societies, much of Peking was burnt and looted in a disgraceful orgy that scarred a proud people too deeply for Europe's future comfort. At the time, it seemed a mere incident in the relentless march toward world hegemony of Europeans, who, their reigning scientific doctrines assured them, had a right to take over from the yellow and brown and black peoples because Europeans were indeed the "fittest." Although some European liberals and socialists protested against inhumane methods of imperial rule, not even they questioned the mission of Europe, by virtue of its higher civilization, to impose its economic and social system on the more "backward" peoples.

For all that, imperialism was not an essential component of Europe's strength. The theory developed by a few socialists, and later exploited by Lenin, that colonies were vital to the capitalistic economy, supplying essential outlets for capital investment at high rates of profit, cannot stand criticism. In general, markets and investments in their colonies or protectorates were neither very extensive nor very profitable to European countries. Empire flatttered the pride of Europe more than it sustained her economy. It was more often pushed by politicians than by businessmen, by military or naval leaders than by capitalists.

The French acquired a huge area of African land that looked impressive on the map but was largely worthless desert. The Russians were building the longest railroad in the world across Siberia in 1900, but it was a government prestige and military project, not an investor's dream. Finding African natives uninterested in the work ethic, Belgians practiced such inhumane treatment that the Congo became an international scandal (it was exposed by British journalists in 1906), but forced labor did not make for great profits except in a few areas. Exposure of the seamy side of imperialism generally led to the need to supply more services to the "natives." Ill-conceived though her plans might be, Europe spent more money on the colonies than she received in profits, favorable prices on raw materials, or other benefits.

Making acquaintance with alien cultures more thoroughly than at any time in the past, some European artists, poets, and philosophers responded to them. In the 1900s, both Japanese and African styles in sculpture and painting influenced avant-garde art in such centers as Paris and Munich. Oriental philosophy, vaguely influential since the middle of the nineteenth century, continued to find a few disciples; the Pacific islands, to which painter Paul Gauguin had fled, functioned as a symbol of some unspoiled spiritual realm to which one might turn for relief from a disgustingly materialistic, philistine, bourgeois Europe. India in Herman Hesse's 1914 novel, *Rosshalde*, and the exotic settings in Joseph Conrad's pre-1914 tales, *Heart of Darkness*, *Lord Jim*, and *Nostromo*, were fascinating to their readers. "Europe bores me," André Gide declared; boredom with a commercialized culture affected a tiny but talented minority of alienated artists and intellectuals in these restlessly innovative *fin de siècle* years.

But the vast majority of Europeans, complacent about their great success, had no interest in cultures other than their own except an occasional amused curiosity. French premier Jules Grévy, an enthusiastic imperialist, grumbled, as he watched certain exotic creatures at the 1889 Paris international fair, that belly-dancers were all the people knew of imperialism. Except, of course, the adventure stories of exploration, intrigue, warfare in the Dark Continent or Kipling's India, exciting reading for the urban masses.

Non-Europeans, by contrast, had to take seriously these Europeans who impinged so forcefully on them. They might react with hatred, anger, and what resistance they could manage; but they might also decide that so formidable a power was worth imitating. "Resistance to the flood-tide of Western civilization is vain," Kemal Ataturk of Turkey decided; marvelling at these people who "pierce the mountains, soar in the skies, see and illuminate all things from the invisible atoms to the stars," he determined to turn his country completely around and Westernize it, a strategy Japan had already practiced with much success. India's Jawaharlal Nehru, who thought that "the very thing India lacked, the modern West possessed and possessed to excess," hoped to inject some but not too much of this dynamic outlook into the somnolent body of Mother India. What historian Arnold J. Toynbee characterized as the "zealot" and the "herodian" reactions to foreign rule (resistance and adaptation), as well as all shadings in between, thus could be found in the attitudes of Asian, African, and Latin American victims of imperialism.

Even the proud Chinese admitted they had much to learn about ships and guns from those they considered barbarians. At the very least, Western technology had to be acquired. But political ideas of democracy, liberalism, socialism, and nationalism seeped into non-Western places, often carried by those educated in the West. In the early years of the century a young Indian named Mohandas Gandhi was studying law in London; a Chinese, Hu Shih, imbibed American political and philosophical ideas at Cornell and Columbia Universities; and Nguyen That Thanh, better known later as Ho Chi Minh, left his native Indochina for France, there to encounter Marxian socialism. All would return to lead movements that rebelled against Western rule in the name of Western ideas. Gandhi's famous philosophy of the simple life, handicraft industries, and militant pacifism absorbed elements of the Hindu tradition, but it also owed a great deal to such nineteenth-century Europeans as John Ruskin of England and Leo Tolstoy of Russia.

In 1900 there were some 400 million people in Europe, about double the number there had been in 1800; counting Russia as far as the Urals, there would be 650 million in 1970. But Europe's percentage of the world total was higher in 1900, amounting to about 1/4 of the world total then, as compared to less than 1/5 today. This despite the fact that over 30 million people emigrated from Europe between 1880 and 1914, the great majority of them to the new world of the Western Hemisphere. In 1890 a list of the most populous twenty cities in the world contained ten European ones, eleven if Constantinople is counted, including the first, third, fourth, and sixth largest. By 1975, only four or five European cities were in the top twenty, and the four largest cities of the world were outside Europe.[1] Europe's share of the world's

---

[1] These are Mexico City, New York City, Tokyo, and Shanghai. Urban population counts are difficult, since they depend on whether the whole metropolitan area or the city limits proper are used, and today they are also subject to rapid

population has declined in this century and is still declining; at the start of this century it was higher than it had ever been or would be in the foreseeable future. This was true also of her wealth. In 1900 Europe as a whole produced some 60 percent of the world's manufactured goods. The three leading industrial countries, Great Britain, Germany, and France alone accounted for a little over 40 percent of the world total. Since these three countries had less than 10 percent of the world's population, they were more than four times as economically productive as the average. Never again would Europe exercise such ascendancy. Powerful competitors would emerge, especially the United States and Japan. The great war of 1914–1918 would set Europe back. Her technological skills did not end, but they never again shone quite so brightly as at the century's turn.

The Divisions of Europe

One could speak of "Western civilization," of "European society," of "Europe"; but Europe, Otto Bismarck once declared (and Charles de Gaulle later repeated) does not exist. Politically, this was obviously true, in that no one government ruled over the Continent; rather it consisted of a number of sovereign states, which had in fact often waged war with each other in the past and were soon to do so again. In 1910, however, there had been no European war since 1871, and the hope was growing that there never would be again. Nevertheless the sovereign states showed no inclination to relinquish their powers to any superstate. A United States of Europe movement can hardly be said to have existed before 1914, despite some internationalisms, among which the socialist International Workingmen's Association, the so-called Second International, was the most important.

Nationalism was everywhere in the ascendancy. It was found among intellectuals, common folk, and even among the socialists, many of whom said that the *Sonderleben*, the special life or culture of each nation, would continue even after the Social Revolution. Nationalism could be found on the Right, on the Left, and in the center; in the pub, the pulpit, and the palaces of the rich. The French truth, French novelist-politician Maurice Barrès declared, is not the same as the English or the German truth. Philosophers affirmed that the thrust of history, which

---

change. The chief European losses appear to be London, first in 1900 and a precarious ninth in 1975; Vienna, which has fallen far out of the top twenty; and Berlin, twentieth or twenty-first even counting both of its divided halves today.

was the Absolute Spirit or God in motion, used the nation as its tool or vessel. Statues were built of Germania; Joan of Arc became a sacred symbol; and many less august peoples, discovering for the first time that they were national peoples, revived ancient languages and sagas.

Popular nationalism rested in part on instinctual attachment to the group, transferred now from the tribe or region to the national community. It rested in part on the success these national communities seemed to have. In such countries as England, France, and Germany, the nineteenth century had brought a steady integration of the masses into the nation, by both action and propaganda. Other peoples, lacking their national independence, dreamed that all would be well if the foreign oppressor was overthrown. From Ireland to Poland, Catalonia to Finland, such unredeemed national groups, real or imaginary, found a beacon of hope in their ethnic solidarity.

Such solidarity is, after all, much older and more deeply rooted than the loyalty to social class, which the Marxists proclaimed and which was merely a matter of economic interest—a cerebral matter, not one felt in the blood. Nation making is one of the fundamental European processes, one of Western civilization's inventions, if you like; it had been going on slowly for centuries. We cannot here describe it fully; nationalism must be taken for granted in any discussion of European history. It was being exported to non-European peoples as one of the chief byproducts of imperialism. But we may note that in many ways the period from about 1880 to 1914 marked its peak.

One reason for this was technology's knitting together larger areas in a transportation and communication network, encouraging the breakup of regional isolation. Urbanization uprooted people from the localities they had long occupied. Greater geographical and social mobility had the same effect. We must be careful not to exaggerate the extent of this process, which was by no means complete. But by 1900 technology, in the form of railways, telegraphs and telephones had made possible a larger locale of loyalty, rendering obsolete Voltaire's eighteenth-century judgment that it is not possible to love anything bigger than one's home, village, city, or province. Millions loved, or thought they loved, Marianne or John Bull or Uncle Sam; they sang hymns to *Deutschland über alles* or called on God to save the King.

Democratization had assisted mightily in this process of nation making. By 1900 most of western Europe had evolved systems of government through parliaments or assemblies elected by universal manhood suffrage or something approaching it. The other countries were thought to be headed in the same direction. There were serious imperfections in these "democratic" systems, but at their best they provided a link between government and people that helped integrate the masses into the national community. Even more effective, perhaps, was the economic upgrading of the lower classes, which gave the majority of them some stake in the community, however modest it might be. At about the same time that British Prime Minister Benjamin Disraeli was writing on the two nations within his country, the rich and the poor, Karl Marx and Friedrich Engels were identifying class struggle as the key to modern history. While such class conflict had by no means vanished, it was considerably less stringent in 1900 than it had been in 1850.

A vital component of nationalism, of course, was language and the literature that had grown up in that language. Perhaps the real architects of national cultures were Schiller and Goethe, Dickens and Tennyson, Musset and Hugo, Pushkin and Lermontov, the beloved nineteenth-century poets and tale tellers. As a definer of nationalism, however, language no more than any other one component sufficed; the Swiss managed to be something of a nation with three languages, Belgium with two, though these were anomalous cases. A basically similar language did not unite Portugal and Spain, though they shared the same well-defined geographic area; nor did it prevent severe north-south strains in Italy or the separation of Austria from Germany. In many places the boundaries of European states did not coincide with ethnic divisions. Both nationalism itself, at times degenerating into a narrowly intolerant jingoism or xenophobia, and this failure of ethnic and political units to agree were dangerous forces in Europe, threatening conflict and war, as a country claimed some unredeemed region. After Germany annexed Alsace and Lorraine in 1871, some French zealots kept alive the sense of grievance and the demand for redemption of the lost provinces; a whole literature of "suffering Alsace" existed around 1900 (it was largely false; German rule did not inflict persecution on the inhabitants of Alsace and Lorraine). Italians dreamed of recapturing some Italians who lived under the flag of Austria-Hungary. The most flagrant of many offenses against national independence was that of Poland, which had been divided among Russia, Germany, and Austria since 1795 except for a brief interval during the Napoleonic years, 1806–1815.

The sovereign states of Europe had been shaped in the centuries before the rise of nationalism. They had not been formed by consulting the wishes of the people or ascertaining their languages and cultures. They had grown up at a time when the decisive political principle was the quasi-feudal and antinational one of monarchism, or loyalty to a person. Boundaries had been determined by war and diplomacy, not plebiscites. As late as 1815, following the wars of the French Revolution era, the peacemakers had at least partly employed the traditional principle of ruling-house legitimacy (ancestral right) in drawing up countries' borders. They had deliberately placed Italians under Austrian rule and Poles under Russian. They had kept Germany divided and put French and German-speaking people under one government in the Low Countries.

During the nineteenth century, the rise of democratic nationalism had impelled changes in these arrangements, and it was responsible for the chief interferences with peace. The revolutions of 1848 were in good part nationalistic. Italians rebelled against Austrian rule in search of national unity, as did Hungary, while the Germans awkwardly sought to unite under one federal republic. Under the guidance of Otto Bismarck, Prussia then succeeded in uniting many small German states to make a larger German Reich, at the cost of brief wars with Austria (1867) and France (1870–1871). Nationalistic discontent among subjects of the Ottoman Empire, or the Austro-Hungarian Dual Monarchy (as it was after 1867), produced intermittent crises from 1878 until the beginning of World War I in 1914.

The states of Europe differed greatly in political constitution, social structure, and economic level. One common cultural element contributing to a tenuous basic unity was nominal adherence to the Christian religion, although Russia subscribed to the Greek rather than the Latin branch of the Church; there were numerous Jews (as well as a few Muslims), especially in eastern Europe; and Western Christianity itself had long been sundered among Catholics and various Protestants. All European elites had inherited something from the rich Greek and Latin civilization of classical antiquity, though Russia had missed much of the revival of that civilization in early modern times. (That there had been virtually no Russian Renaissance or Enlightenment explains a great deal about twentieth-century Russia.) More basically, except for the Finns, the Hungarians, and the Basques, nearly all Europeans shared an Indo-European language structure. This did not prevent their languages being too different to be comprehensible to each other, however. Among numerous complexities of European cultural relations was the bond of unity possessed by the Latin countries (Italy, France, Spain, Portugal, and Rumania), as against a Germanic group (England and the Scandinavian peoples, Germany, and the Netherlands), and the Slavs of eastern Europe.

But the principal basis of distinction among the score or so of European states was undoubtedly power. The five great powers were Russia, Germany, Austria-Hungary, France, and Great Britain, which at this time included all of Ireland as well as England, Wales, and Scotland. The student is doubtless familiar with the names and locations of most of the smaller countries—Spain and Portugal on the Iberian peninsula; the Low Countries of Netherlands, Belgium, and tiny Luxemburg; the Scandinavian states of Denmark, Sweden, and Norway (a union between the latter two was peacefully dissolved in 1905); and so around to the east, where there were fewer independent nations than there are today, chiefly because of the multinational Dual Monarchy. Bulgaria, Rumania, Greece, and Serbia, together with her small sister Montenegro, did then exist, along with what remained of the Ottoman Empire in Europe; but Czechoslovakia was then part of the Dual Monarchy. Italy was a kind of intermediate or almost-great power; Switzerland was the classic neutral; for the rest, there were only the tiny states of Lichtenstein, Monaco, and Andorra, interesting primarily to collectors of postage stamps and gamblers.

Of the great powers, only France managed without a crowned head, and almost all the minor states had kings, too. If we think of Europe on the eve of 1914 as poised between past and future, the persistence of the 500-year-old Hapsburg dynasty in the form of the emperor of Austria and Hungary was a living link with the Middle Ages and even with the Roman Empire. The Romanovs had sat on the throne of Russia since 1613; the Hohenzollerns had ruled Prussia since the sixteenth century, though they added the throne of Imperial Germany only in 1871. No monarch was more popular than Britain's Queen Victoria, symbol of an age until her death in 1901; her son and successor Edward VII also became popular. But few of these royal personages any longer disposed of awesome power. The king of England was virtually a ceremonial symbol. Only the tsar of Russia claimed to be omnipotent.

Represented at each other's capitals by ambassadors, the governments of Europe conducted relations by making treaties or other formal agreements, worth only as much as their honor and interest allowed. It had long been considered essential to prevent any one power from becoming overmighty, thus threatening the independence of others, and so the chief formal goal of the art of diplomacy was a balance of power. Evidence that power prevailed over linguistic or cultural similarity, religion, or any other ideological affinity could be found abundantly in the history of European relations. The most recent surprise had come in 1894 when democratic France and autocratic Russia, polls apart in political outlook but drawn together by a common mistrust of powerful Germany, had formed a military alliance. The rather shaky Franco-Russian combination faced a *Mitteleuropa* bloc of Germany and Austria-Hungary. In a game of five, European diplomats sometimes said, the object was to line up three; but Great Britain preferred to stand clear, watch the balance, and practice "splendid isolation" except in severe emergency. As the 1900s were to show, the balance was precarious; imperialist rivalries, unsatisfied nationalism among the smaller countries, and internal insecurity within the Great Powers were destabilizers.

Despite jealously nationalistic sovereign states, Europe was in some ways a single society, more so then than later. Not only its goods but its ideas freely crossed national boundaries. In this pre-1914 era, the predominant economic ideology stressed free trade and an exchange of currencies in terms of gold, which provided in effect a single international money. International patents and copyrights, mail delivery among countries, canals and railroads, along with bigger and faster ocean-going ships and improved harbors, were knitting the countries of Europe together and bringing Europe closer to the rest of the world. It was common to hear talk of a global economy. War was thought to be obsolete because the economy was so interdependent that no country could possibly profit by war, which would disrupt commerce and wipe out investments. Barriers to trade among nations and to people travelling across frontiers were far weaker than they were to be later in the century. For example, except for a few backward and tyrannical lands in the East, there were no passport requirements for travel among countries. One index of the rising European economy was the growth of international trade. Between 1880 and 1914 international trade more than doubled, and Europe had the lion's share. Of this European trade, much the largest percentage was among the various countries of Europe, rather than with the other continents. Despite a certain trend toward protectionism in the later nineteenth century, tariffs were relatively low in 1900.

Economic Progress and Problems

The story of Europe at the end of the nineteenth century was in important ways a fabulous success story. Europe had refuted the long-held belief that population must always approach the limit of available resources, thus preventing any appreciable rise in the standard of living; for though population had greatly increased during the nineteenth century, wealth had grown even more rapidly. This was true, at least, of the more advanced industrial societies. Thus, between 1750 and 1900 the population of Great Britain increased sixfold, but national income rose at least fifteen times. In the last quarter of the nineteenth century, real wages rose 40 percent in Great Britain and nearly 25 percent in Germany.

This period was one of classic technological achievement; to it belongs the foundation of the modern industrial society. It was the age of steel, of railroads, of electricity, and of chemicals. The basic railroad grid of Europe was built between 1870 and 1900. Steel output in Germany, for example, climbed from one and a half million tons annually in 1880 to nearly seven and a half million in 1900. The recital of further technological advances is almost endless. The first practical automobile dates from the late 1880s. Hertz discovered radio waves in 1885, by which time the age of electricity was arriving in the form of electric lights, electric trolleys, and motion pictures (1889). Mass production of electricity had begun and so had the petroleum age, signalled by the first oil wells in 1869. Edison's first electric lamp twinkled in 1879. Berlin had an elevated electric railway by 1900. The great French doctor Louis Pasteur's discovery of immunization in 1881 was followed shortly by the Koch-Pasteur germ theory of disease. The American Wright brothers, whose epochal Kitty Hawk flight took place in 1903, were inspired to undertake it by reading of German attempts earlier. German industrial chemistry brought forth a succession of minor miracles in dyestuffs; Roentgen perfected x-rays.

If radio was already a reality by 1895, such later marvels as television, atomic energy, and space travel were theoretical possibilities familiar to science fiction writers by 1900. Of more interest at that time was the nearing of completion of the Trans-Siberian railway linking Europe and Asia. The Suez Canal had been finished in 1869; the Panama was being built by the United States in 1903. Among many other maritime improvements were the Kiel Canal linking the Baltic and the Atlantic, the Manchester ship canals, and the improvement of the great Rotterdam waterway and port.

Such items only begin to tell the story of the burgeoning technological society of Europe and her offshoots. It was greeted on the whole with delight and was, more than anything else, responsible for the optimism that marked European thought in the nineteenth century. With this revolution in production came drastic dislocations and social problems, always tempering that optimism. Yet the comment of the American, E. L. Godkin, in 1888 is typical: "There is not a poor man in England," the celebrated editor wrote, "who is not conscious that he is vastly better off . . . than his grandfather was." Hymns of praise and wonder to the marvels of technology came as often from scholars and writers as from average citizens. Walt Whitman, sufficiently aware of grave imperfections and monstrous injustices, nevertheless hailed the

> *Beautiful World of new, superber Birth, that rises to my eyes,*
> *Like a limitless golden cloud . . .*

Europe was the source of that enormous revolution that altered the face of the earth more drastically than anything had ever done in all history, for she had exported the Industrial Revolution to other peoples. And she has continued to be among its leaders.

As the twentieth century began, however, there was a strong feeling that the nineteenth century's impressive increase in power over nature, which some estimated in the neighborhood of a hundredfold and in which clearly it had far surpassed all preceding centuries, had not carried with it a comparable increase in human happiness. British critic Alfred R. Wallace asserted that "huge masses of people suffer untold misery and want in our great cities, and in country villages." Crime was increasing and so was insanity; poverty, as Henry George put it, was paradoxically growing along with progress. This in the most industrialized part of the Western World. Certainly discontent was growing. This is not surprising, upon reflection: when people were unaware of the possibility of change they were content with extreme privation, but once they began to see the possibility of improvement they quickly developed wants that far outstripped the ability to satisfy them.

Widespread impatience with traditional economic arrangements and answers was evident around 1900. Socialists asserted that "production is not carried on for the purpose of supplying the wants of the producers (workers), but solely with the object of creating wealth for a capitalist employer." They also asserted that governments, which had been content to resign the workings of the economic order to the natural process of accident and drift, must now take intelligent action to guide the course of production and distribution. From Great Britain, where the Labour party was born in the year 1900, to Russia, where student strikes and demonstrations in the leading Russian cities in 1899–1900 foreshadowed agrarian uprisings in 1902 and then the revolution of 1905, social protest seethed in one form or another—legally in the more democratic West, violently in the autocratic East. Strikes in the Ruhr coal mines and on the London docks in the late 1880s had begun this epoch of unrest.

Whatever the definition of poverty, it was beyond dispute that society was marked by great inequalities of wealth. In 1909, the British author Arnold Bennett thought that "the prosperous crowd," who stood out from the rest, numbered about one million out of the forty. Only 375,000 earners paid the new income tax (under protest!) in that year. In the country with the largest middle class, that class was smaller than 25 percent by any sort of reckoning: a contemporary British investigator estimated it at 23 percent, counting everything above the blue-collar level, which obviously included many clerical employees of modest income.[2] Statistics show that in 1913, 10 percent of the popula-

---

[2] Statistical information throughout this book is derived chiefly from B. R. Mitchell, *European Historical Statistics 1750–1970* (New York: Columbia University Press, 1975); B. R. Mitchell and Phyllis Deane, *Abstract of British Historical Statistics* (Cambridge: Cambridge University Press, 1962), and its sequel,

tion owned 92 percent of personal wealth in Britain; such students of poverty as Seebohm Rowntree calculated that almost 30 percent lived below a tolerable standard of existence.[3] Extremes of wealth and poverty, with corresponding attributions of cultural prestige and the lack of it, marked all the countries of Europe, even those most democratic in political form.

In the less modernized parts of Europe the social gulf was naturally greater. A vast, ignorant, and impoverished populace confronted a rich, proud ruling elite not only in eastern Europe but also in southern Italy and in the Iberian peninsula. In 1908, in a typical case of extreme polarization, assassination of Portugal's King Carlos was followed by fighting between an aristocracy backed by church and army and various types of revolutionary socialists and anarchists. Of greater importance was the 1905 revolution in Russia, where industrialism was just beginning and the greatest threat to the status quo came from a dissatisfied peasantry. This revolution, sporadic and uncoordinated, followed Russia's defeat in war at the hands of Japan. It petered out, leaving no major changes in the land of the tsar but the memory of "days of liberty" to be recalled in the future. The revolutionary urban workers had formed *soviets*, or committees, a term destined for much future importance. But the only tangible result of the 1905 disorder was an elected national legislature with extremely limited powers—the first Russia had had.

The protest was often against the economic and social order, which Karl Marx and others had called "capitalism," Henry Maine had described as based on "contract" rather than "status," and the liberal economists of the nineteenth century had discussed in terms of the "free market" or "free enterprise." Those who admired it pointed out that the free exchange of goods and services in the marketplace is both just and efficient. It rewards efficiency and penalizes ineptitude, awarding the prizes to those persons who produce the best products at the cheapest price and attracting capital investment to those areas where it is needed. It does all this by a natural process; the alternative is some monstrous bureaucracy making arbitrary decisions. The market economy, they held, was justified by its results, for it had presided over that vast increase in wealth that had set the nineteenth apart from all other centuries.

Those who condemned it sometimes lodged an esthetic objection against this regime of scrambled chance, which put a price on every-

---

Mitchell and H. G. Jones, *Second Abstract of British Historical Statistics* (Cambridge, 1971); and annual government publications such as *Annuaire statistique de la France, Statistisches Jahrbuch für die Bundesrepublik Deutschland*, and *Annual Abstract of Statistics*.
[3] *Poverty: A Study of Town Life* (London: Macmillan), 1901.

thing and joined people together only by the callous ties of what Thomas Carlyle had called the "cash nexus." More often they cried out against its injustice. The poor and the rich did not meet as equals in the marketplace. The competitive order was not really competitive, for monopoly still existed. Above all, it was cruel to dismiss all those who lost in the competitive rat race as deserving of poverty, humiliation, or even extinction. The system was not justified by its results, for it had enriched only a few and had left the many in dire want.

Moreover, periodic depressions or panics had marred the growth of the economy. International in scope, somewhat mysterious in origin, such severe downswings in the business cycle had occurred in the mid-1870s, the mid-1880s, and from 1893 to 1896. No major one marred the years just prior to 1914. But fear of unemployment or bankruptcy haunted people. A structural crisis in agriculture in Great Britain, Germany, and the United States contributed to the severity of such depressions.

In the economic debate, several kinds of socialists or anarchists argued against either liberal or conservative defenders of a free-enterprise society. The debate had been going on since fairly early in the century. The pioneer socialists appeared at about the same time as the liberal ideology, not long after the French Revolution. An old and a complex argument, sometimes hardening into bitter ideological passions, reached a climax about the turn of the century. Socialists agreed with capitalists about the huge potentialities of wealth unleashed by technological discovery; they simply disagreed on the best means of tapping this reservoir. The growth of technology, bringing with it skills to flood great cities with light and power, make machinery to produce goods far faster than unaided human labor, and transport goods quickly and cheaply across vast distances engendered a feeling that for the first time in history people might master their environment and shape for themselves a good life. But it also brought a bewildering complexity of problems far more difficult than those faced in the past.

Despite the socialist rhetoric, which emanated largely from the intellectual elite rather than the workers, most of Europe was not revolutionary in the 1900s. On the one hand, the discontents of modernization had not yet penetrated far into a society still largely dominated by traditional values. In a typical German town, men were content to stay in one's *Stand,* or appointed social station, except in unusual circumstances and to follow one's father's craft with all the security that it brought. The excess of population, younger sons perhaps, was likely to migrate to the United States or Brazil if not to German cities. Social mobility, in brief, was deplorably low; but not many missed it. On the other hand, the urban working class in western Europe had retreated from the revolutionary militancy it had felt in the time of Karl Marx and the British Chartists back in the hungry 1840s. It was both materially better off and more cautious in its claims.

Trade Unionism were the words of the day, a practical movement not questioning the existing institutional structure of capitalism but seeking a bigger share of the proceeds for labor. From 1900 to 1913, membership in unions grew from two to four million in Great Britain, from one to three million in Germany, and from one-half to one million in France, where huge industrial plants were less common. In Great Britain, a distinctive working-class culture was emerging in the industrial cities; it was marked less by red flags and revolutionary cries than by the pub, the music hall, the soccer game. The rise of professional football as a mass spectator sport dates from the 1880s; in 1910, 100,000 people watched a cup match at the new Wembley Stadium. If this was the opium of the proletariat, it seemed to work. But in fact the working class *was* increasingly better off in terms of real wages—almost spectacularly so.

European Society In an Age of Urbanization

In 1889 a British student of urbanization declared that "the concentration of population in cities" had been "the most remarkable social phenomenon" of the century just ending. The twentieth century has continued and extended this trend, but as in so many other matters, the nineteenth century pioneered the changes that the twentieth was forced to carry on. Between 1801 and 1891 the percentage of Britain's population living in cities over 20,000 grew from 17 to 54 percent. Since the total population had more than tripled, this meant that the absolute number of city dwellers multiplied tenfold. The percentage of those living in cities over 100,000 during the same period had increased from about 10 percent to 32 percent, as the number of cities in this category climbed from one (London) to sixteen. For Europe as a whole, the figure was close to 20 percent.

Overall, Great Britain was the most heavily urbanized of any major European country; certain regions in Germany were even more so. In 1871, less than 5 percent of the population had lived in German cities over 100,000. The rapid surge of German industrialization after 1871 brought this figure up to 21 percent, a trend particularly marked in the heavily industrialized Rhine provinces and Saxony, areas that increased greatly in both total and urban population. Lagging behind in heavy industry, France nevertheless had fifteen cities over 100,000 by 1914; as in Germany, about one in five French citizens lived in such cities. The urban wave had still not struck with full force in southern and eastern Europe. Although there were such great capital cities as Rome, St. Petersburg, Warsaw, and Budapest, the largish secondary cities, usually a byproduct of industrialization, had yet to increase in numbers. As late as 1920, 56 percent of Spaniards, 82 percent of Bulgarians, and 85 percent of Russians lived in rural areas, compared to less than 10 percent in England.

The nineteenth century had tackled massive problems accompanying urbanization. At its peak in the 1840s and 1850s, disease, in the form of typhus, cholera, and typhoid, had threatened the very existence of cities. Accustomed as we may be to thinking of the "crisis of the cities" as a recent phenomenon, we should realize that for the Edwardians the crisis had come earlier, and by the end of the century it had been surmounted, particularly in the areas of public health and sanitation. Death rates from contagious disease were down; streets and transportation facilities had improved (London had already built its underground rail system); and the worst conditions of dirt, squalor, overcrowding, crime, drunkenness, and general human degradation were no longer so common, even if much remained to be done. London had devised a new form of local government, the London County Council, to deal with the whole urban area. Beginning in the 1860s, Paris had submitted to a massive face-lifting process, which beautified the grand old city with boulevards and plazas at the cost of removing some of her narrow old streets. Berlin was the pride of Germany, and Vienna could claim to be the most civilized city in the world. This was in some ways the great age of large European cities, which were past their initial crisis and not yet fully into a new one.

A good deal of the significant literature and thought of Europe around the turn of the century reacted in one way or another to the presence of the large city. Novels were more likely to have an urban than a rural or small town setting. Of course there are exceptions to this generalization, for there was already a literary and intellectual rejection of the city, as illustrated in the early 1900s by the Georgian poets, who sought out the simplicities of an older England. The influential French novelist, Maurice Barrès, dwelt on the "deracination" of man—his uprooting from the soil. The pioneer German sociologist, Georg Simmel, noted that city dwellers had different mental processes, different values, a different life style from rural people.

Indeed it might be argued that sociology's status rose at this time primarily because of the impact of drastic social change, at the core of which lay urbanization. Emile Durkheim, the French sociologist, used the term *anomie* to describe the condition of people who have lost contact with a firm social structure and who therefore feel confused

Bank of England, about 1910, London. *Courtesy Library of Congress.*

and in need of values. For the city released people from the control of traditional tightly-knit communities, enabling them to be free. But sometimes this freedom was dangerous. Friedrich Tönnies distinguished between the *Gemeinschaft* ("community") found in the traditional rural society—tightly–knit, face-to-face, strongly authoritarian—and the *Gesellschaft* ("society") characteristic of the city—vast, impersonal, governing by bureaucratic rules.

Human nature itself seemed to change in the new environment of the city, the factory, the mass society. Culture further altered under the impact of new techniques in communication, new media. The radio was not yet a real factor in 1900, but the motion picture was beginning to be; within a few years, Bijous and Apollos appeared on urban streets. There are good movies of Queen Victoria's funeral, the great public event of 1901. Cheap newspapers had been around for some years; there were more of them from which to choose in 1900 than there are today. Sensitive people complained of the vulgar fare offered in some of them, then as now. And the automobile, of course, had not only begun its career but by 1910 was already eliciting complaints for polluting the environment, endangering life, and making an intolerable racket.

The age of professional spectator sports had also begun. This transformation from bear-baiting, cock-fighting, and public executions, the last of which had occurred in England in 1865, brought a certain refinement to post-Victorian culture. Life had tended to become less raw and brutal; John Stuart Mill attributed this to "a perfection of mechanical arrangements impracticable in any but a high state of civilization," keeping pain and death out of sight. Livestock as well as criminals were now dispatched efficiently out of public view; the surgeon, the butcher, and the executioner plied their specialized trades behind closed doors. Nevertheless the conditions of life of the lowest urban class, which Charles Booth described in 1895 as "almost savage" and which were still marked by riotous violence, belied this claim.

The city air sped up processes of change and bred a restless spirit. In St. Petersburg on January 9, 1905, a huge crowd, intoxicated by the rhetoric of a labor organizer priest, assembled before the Winter Palace to petition the tsar. The troops' firing upon them touched off the 1905 revolution, which spread to factory workers and students in the cities and later spilled over into the villages. The same year on November 29, an estimated 250,000 workers paraded through the streets of Vienna in an appeal for universal suffrage. The city was the scene of dramatic action and excitement. "From the village street into the railway station is a leap across five centuries from the brutalizing torpor of Nature's tyranny over Man into the order and alertness of Man's organized dominion over Nature," wrote George Bernard Shaw, echoing Marx's slap at "rural idiocy." Nostalgia for the countryside was rarer than it would later become, perhaps because people were too close to its realities. Shaw knew it as savage, malodorous, back-breaking and unsanitary. The Futurists, leading artistic revolutionaries of the 1900s, exulted in the spectacle of "great crowds excited by work, by pleasure, and by riot . . . the multicolored, polyphonic tides of revolution in the modern capitals." [4] The city was where, if one was fortunate, one could attend the theater or opera, watch a Russian ballet, visit the cinema. It was also where, at this time, one might attend a socialist rally, a political meeting, or a trade union picnic.

Possibly an even more exciting urban modernism was the feminist revolt. At their peak around 1910, mass rallies attracted 250,000 women in London. Over 100 were arrested at one demonstration in front of Parliament. Women refused to pay taxes, broke windows, slashed pictures, tied themselves to railroad tracks, threw themselves under horses, went on hunger strikes in prison. Primarily from the middle

[4] F. T. Marinetti, *Selected Writings*, ed. R. W. Flint (New York: Farrar, Straus and Giroux, 1971), pp. 39–44. Marinetti's Manifesto was first published in the Paris newspaper *Le Figaro* on February 20, 1909.

Suffragette being removed from a meeting, England, 1913.
The Press Association, Ltd.

and upper classes, the embattled women were not only demanding the right to vote but also discussing everything from trial marriage to payment for housework, as they combatted deeply ingrained Victorian prejudices. "The notion that women have minds as cultivable, and as well worth cultivating, as men's minds, is still regarded by the ordinary British parent as an offensive, not to say revolutionary paradox," James Bryce had reported in 1864.

The feminist movement was much weaker in France; as the *Frauenfrage*, it had some currency in Germany; but it was stormiest in England. All over Europe just before World War I, emancipated women were announcing their claim to be the equals of men in the honored professions. Although a small number, they were emblemized by the aristocratic spirit of Virginia Woolf, Beatrice Webb, and Lou Salome. They were the precursors of a crusade later to be taken up much more widely.

The astute American historian Henry Adams thought that at about 1900, humanity moved into a new phase of history in a change comparable to the scientific revolution that had occurred between 1400 and 1700. "Human character changed in 1910," Virginia Woolf remarked.

All of consciousness seemed to be changing, as a new art, a new literature, and a new philosophy arose, and revolutions were underway in fundamental human relationships. This was not entirely because Western society had accustomed itself to city lights and sounds, but that was part of it. The pace of change had been quickening all through the nineteenth century, and now it reached so rapid a rate that the sense of continuity was being lost. The new art, announced in scores of manifestos during the 1900s, labeled itself futurist, expressionist, abstractionist, cubist, vorticist, suprematist, and a dozen other names; the new schools rejected traditional ways of painting, sculpture, music, and poetry in favor of startling novelty.

The Politics of European Democracies

From about 1880 on, certain sophisticated currents of European political thought revealed signs of a severe disenchantment with democracy in the form of representative government with a mass electorate. Many argued that it only transferred power from one elite to another, perhaps less desirable, ruling class. Some socialists thought it a bourgeois fraud. Nevertheless, the feeling that democratization was an irresistible tendency of the times prevailed, and most people thought that the tide of progress would gradually remove the imperfections. Those who worried about a cheapening of thought and culture often placed their faith in the expansion of education, a process that had equipped most European countries with free, compulsory public educational systems by 1914 and reduced illiteracy in western Europe to almost zero. It was still a major problem not only in eastern but in southern Europe; in 1910 illiteracy in Italy was still 38 percent.

Democracy was relatively successful under conditions of a high standard of living, cultural homogeneity, and social equality or at least mobility. Where substantial numbers of impoverished peasants were dependent on rich landowners, or where deep ethnic hostilities divided the land, as in Hungary, it could hardly flourish. Great extremes of wealth and poverty provided a barren soil for democracy. Urbanization and a highly mobile social order seemed to favor it. Some of the smaller states of northern and western Europe did better with it than the larger countries. Switzerland, Sweden, Denmark, and the Low Countries provided object lessons in the successful functioning of democracy, even direct democracy: Switzerland held frequent popular referenda on significant issues.

With all its uneven application and flawed performance, democracy (in the sense of universal manhood suffrage and government by elected representative legislative bodies) was in more or less effective operation through most of Europe by 1913 and was expected to continue making progress. Although there was an undercurrent of grave concern about a political regime being dependent on the fickle mood of the masses, the great majority paid tribute to democracy as an ideal. Even the Marxian Social Democrats, or Socialists, substantially converted, after 1890, to the view that the great change from capitalism to socialism or communism would come via the ballot rather than violent revolution. To a degree their political parties took part in the democratic process. The end, Socialism; the means, the Republic. Writing in 1908, the astute British political scientist, Graham Wallas, noted that representative democracy was in operation everywhere in Europe. "Forty years ago it could still be argued that to base the sovereignty of a great modern nation upon a widely extended popular vote was, in Europe at least, an experiment which had never been successfully tried." [5] But Wallas, who noted a certain puzzled disenchantment with the results of democracy, thought that it was now an ongoing institution, even in Austria and Russia.

It was obvious that some if not all of these arrangements fell far short of a democratic ideal. The German Reichstag had no power to compel the German emperor to change his ministers; the Russian Duma turned out to have no power at all. Although government by popularly elected representatives worked best of all in Great Britain, even there the hereditary House of Lords held some power until 1911, and the reins of government remained by and large in the hands of a small aristocratic group. France, the most democratic, having no monarch and with a cabinet responsible to the democratically elected legislature, was often politically turbulent. Some said that France was governed by the permanent civil service, not the cabinet.

There were other countries of Europe where democracy was a farce, but even in these places its outward forms were likely to exist as a concession to the spirit of the age. Spain, Italy, and Bulgaria, for example, were all supposed to be governed by elected parliaments; Spain supposedly had universal suffrage after 1890, although in Italy suffrage was restricted by a literacy requirement until 1912. In all three cases elections were rigged, and voters were subject to manipulation or compulsion. Thus formal democracy was as fraudulent as it was in certain American cities where political bosses ruled behind a facade of election.

The issues that had to be decided via this machinery of government in the years just before 1914 were important ones. Standing out

---

[5] *Human Nature in Politics* (London: Constable, 1908), p. 1.

among them was the question of whether the state should assume some responsibility for the welfare of the workers in an urban, industrialized society in which the old personal and often informal means of looking out for human needs had seemingly become obsolete. In 1881, Germany's Bismarck announced that the state must either assume such responsibility for the well-being of its citizens or watch them join revolutionary movements to overthrow it. He threw his heavy weight behind a plan of social welfare that would provide health, old age, and unemployment insurance for industrial workers out of a fund to which employers, government, and workers all contributed. Little Denmark pioneered in a similar system at about the same time. These plans became models for other countries; on the eve of their war with Germany, ironically, the British were engaged in setting up a national insurance system inspired by the German example.

The passing of this National Insurance Act in 1911 signalled "the greatest scheme of social reconstruction ever attempted," a prominent British newspaper declared. The 1911 act provided for the government to contribute 2/9 of the sum set aside for unemployment insurance, the employer 3/9 and the employee 4/9. Modest enough by later standards, the government-administered welfare payments plan constituted a break with long tradition and encountered strenuous opposition. The nineteenth-century legacy included a powerful tradition of antistatist social and ecoomic policy. It was by allowing competition in the free market and keeping taxes low and private businesses immune from state regulation and control that British industry had flourished.

The great Liberal party, even more than its perennial rival, the Conservative, stood for maximum individual liberty in all respects against the state. In the words of the brilliant Fabian Socialist, Beatrice Webb, British liberalism "thought in individuals" and saw government as the foe of liberty. Not without great difficulty could it come around to a positive conception of government, the neoliberalism of the welfare state movement. But in their minority report to the massive investigations of the Poor Law Commission of 1905–1909, Beatrice and Sidney Webb argued that not relief of poverty but its prevention should be the goal and that privation is a social problem, not a matter of individual effort.

The Liberal government elected in 1906 was a talented one, including among its young members Winston Churchill and David Lloyd George, who was chancellor of the exchequeur in Prime Minister Herbert Asquith's cabinet. Confronted with expenses for the new welfare program and also rising defense costs in a naval race with Germany, the Lloyd George budget of 1909 proposed new taxes, including an income tax. Among the nicer things opponents said about it was that such a tax was inquisitorial, unfair, and socialistic; it raised basic issues of individual versus social justice. Sent to the House of Lords after being passed by the House of Commons, the budget was rejected by the peers in a breathtaking act of defiance, this being the first time in nearly 200 years that the hereditary house had refused to endorse an important bill passed by Commons. Dramatic scenes ensued. In 1911, when Asquith conveyed the news that the king had agreed to create enough new peers to assure a majority for the reform bills in the House of Lords, the normally sedate British Parliament became a screaming mob.

A Parliament bill deprived the upper house of the power to prevent legislation passed by Commons from becoming law, though it could still delay a nonrevenue bill. The country seemed mostly to agree with Churchill's assertion that the House of Lords, a voice from England's past, had become "an institution absolutely foreign to the spirit of the age." This act also authorized salaries for members of Parliament for the first time, a measure helpful in prying political power from the hands of the aristocratic elite that still largely controlled it.

A landmark in the development of both democracy and the social state, this 1909–1911 imbroglio about the welfare state, taxation, and the powers of the upper legislative house stood out in British politics in the prewar years, but it was not the only great issue nationally debated. Its chief rival was Ireland, a problem that came to a fever point just before the outbreak of World War I. On July 27, 1914, the London *Times* announced that "the country is now confronted with one of the greatest crises in the history of the British race." The editorial did not refer to the international crisis then looming in Europe, which would erupt in major war just a week later. It was talking about a rebellion in the British army in Ireland and the creation of a volunteer army in northern Ireland to resist the granting of "home rule" to all of that country. This resistance was encouraged by Conservative political leaders in the British parliament. Civil war in Ireland between Green and Orange, Catholic and Protestant, seemed likely to spread to England.

Postponed by World War I, armed conflict did indeed break out in 1920–1922. The issue was the refusal of the Protestant part of the Emerald Isle, Ulster, to join an autonomous Ireland, fearful of oppression at the hands of the Catholic majority; and the refusal of Irish Catholics to accept a partition of Ireland. Behind it lay seven centuries of English rule over the Irish, a long and mostly sorry record of cruelty and absentee domination, the repercussions of which still went on in the 1960s and 1970s. Dependent on Irish votes after receiving a diminished majority in the election of 1910, the Liberal party pushed a home rule bill only to encounter this bitter opposition verging on mutiny in the army. Small wonder the *Times* called the crisis grave.

These and other questions made the prewar decade an exciting if turbulent period in British politics. Author Herbert Read later recalled that in his Edwardian youth "the great issues of Free Trade and Protection, Home Rule for Ireland, the Disestablishment of the Church, and the Reform of the House of Lords, were being debated with fervour and energy in every newspaper and at every street corner," with the aid, it may be added, of such fervent spirits and talented pens as Lloyd George, Winston Churchill, George Bernard Shaw, H. G. Wells, Rudyard Kipling, Arnold Bennett, and the Webbs. Adding to the turbulence were the militant suffragettes, who were joined by crusaders for birth control, advocates of greater sexual knowledge, and believers in "free love" or release from Victorian moral conventions. The continuing thrust of trade unionism raised such issues as were dealt with in the Trade Disputes Act of 1906, which among other things largely exempted unions from damage liability resulting from strikes.

Politics: France and Germany

Issues in other European countries were not greatly dissimilar from those in the oldest industrial society, Great Britain. In some ways French politics differed from British quite markedly: numerous small political parties rather than two large ones; no monarch; a past colored by passions reaching back to the great 1789 revolution and its sequels in 1848 and 1871; an underlying social structure of small farms, small businesses, small factories. France had several million landowners, whereas in England 1,500 great families held half the land. There was no real French equivalent to the industrial Midlands of England or the Ruhr Valley of Germany. The combination of a freehold peasantry and numerous small traders and producers endowed French politics with a decided "petty bourgeois" flavor. Although trade unionism grew more slowly than it did in Britain and Germany, only one in six French industrial workers belonging to a union in 1914, it was often extremely militant.

Fragmented until 1905, the French Socialists (SFIO) succeeded in electing about a sixth of the delegates to the Chamber of Deputies in 1914; the party was stronger among intellectuals and professional people than among workers. This Socialist strength contrasted with the almost total lack of a socialist party in Britain [6] and with the much

---

[6] The Labour party, born in 1900, did not adopt a socialist platform until 1918 and was in any case a tiny party prior to World War I. An offshoot, the Independent Labour party, further to the Left, was smaller yet, as were the little groups of Marxist intellectuals headed by William Morris and H. M. Hyndman. The Fabian Socialists, quite influential, deliberately refrained from any attempt to create a mass party, preferring to feed ideas to the established political leaders.

larger German Social Democratic party, which gained more than a third of the votes in 1912.

As the century turned, France had just been torn apart by the Dreyfus case, which polarized Left and Right over the issues of national security versus individual rights, a kind of Gallic Watergate and Alger Hiss case rolled into one. The result of this protracted controversy, during which Captain Alfred Dreyfus submitted to two trials for treason, was sent to prison, touched off anti-Jewish riots, and was finally exonerated, was a qualified victory for the Left. Consequently, between 1899 and 1905 a coalition of Radicals (a democratic party of the petit bourgeoisie) and moderates governed with Socialist support. But in 1904, after a long argument, the Socialists decided against participation in "bourgeois" governments, regarding this as a collaboration with the class enemy that could only prolong capitalism—a position they held until 1936, except during the 1914–1918 war. Nevertheless under the leadership of the brilliant writer and orator Jean Jaurès, the SFIO was far from addicted to revolutionary violence.

The French Left was fragmented; but so was the French Right. French politics in general was fragmented. Aided by the practice of proportional representation, which allowed the smaller parties to gain representation in parliament roughly proportional to their popular vote (by abandoning the single-member electoral district in favor of one with a number of representatives), this division into numerous small parties forced the Third Republic into numerous changes of government. Dependent on coalitions of parties to command a majority in the Chamber of Deputies, governments could be overthrown on small issues. It was a system that prevented major political decisions, but this suited petty-bourgeois France, which was suspicious of the state. Born of political defeat in 1871, long hated by the socialist Left as much as the monarchist Right, the Third Republic survived because no one could suggest or implement anything better; it was, as Georges Clemenceau said, the least intolerable of the many frightful evils.

France lagged behind in industrialization and in social policy, a backwardness historians tend to think of as a scandal: the stalemated society. But most of the French liked it that way, and can we blame them for not wanting to move into the age of big business, big industry, big government? With all their often bitter family quarrels, the French were basically a happy people. Certainly in this era France's intellectual and artistic brilliance continued. Paris was the cultural capital of the world. The most interesting movements in literature and art—symbolism, cubism, art nouveau—originated or centered in the French capital. The French also did more in the 1890s to develop the automobile than anyone else, as names like *carburetor* and *chassis* still remind us; they had given the world photography, x-rays, pasteurization. Paris claims credit, if that is the right word, for the first cinema. As Charles de Gaulle later remarked, France was a greater land than her politics.

On the eve of 1914, a "national revival" mood swept over France, affecting prestigious writers and thinkers with the theme of a return to order, discipline, national tradition, the grandeur of *la belle France*. The rising menace of war with Germany deeply colored French politics. At the same time, there were working-class unrest and a wave of militant strikes. Labor strikes, often violent, also shook Italy in the 1900s, along with active socialist and anarchist agitation.

Basking in the highest growth rate in this period, Germany was less agitated; but there were massive strikes in 1905, and it was in Germany that the Marxist Social Democratic party became the strongest such group in the world, winning more seats in the Reichstag in 1912 than any other party. It dominated the world socialist organization, the Second International, founded in 1889 by the friends and disciples of Karl Marx and Friedrich Engels. In its own highly developed newspapers and magazines, the SPD radiated confidence that the coming victory of world socialism would begin in Germany. The party also entered into generally good relations with the powerful trade unions. Yet it faced the frustration of having little influence on the authoritarian government of the kaiser, who could appoint the chancellor and cabinet without the approval of the Reichstag. Wilhelm II strove to be a friend to the workingman in his·way, flattering himself that he was well abreast of the new age and its social issues. The German system of social insurance against sickness, old age, and unemployment, among the first to be established in Europe, was also the most advanced.

Germany was proud of its science, its musical culture, and its educational system, in all of which it could well claim to lead the world. The paradox of Germany was that although she was the greatest of industrial countries, her political structure was dangerously weak because it was lacking in liberalism and democracy. By 1900 she had passed Great Britain in both population and most of the indices of economic power, including production of coal, steel, chemicals, and electrical power. This economic strength allied to the potent military tradition of Prussia made the Wilhelmine Reich the leading power in Europe. This success not unnaturally induced a spirit many observers thought to be arrogant, or at least complacent. For centuries a divided Germany had been victimized because she was weak. The miracle of the 1860s brought her unity and strength beyond her wildest dreams, and it is small wonder that Germans became overly proud of themselves. Unfortunately, their political institutions had failed to advance as rapidly.

Underneath the formal unity, Germany was still a deeply divided country. Regional differences, especially those between the Catholic South and the Protestant North, were more marked than in France. Extremely rapid industrialization and urbanization after 1870 resulted in some social shock effects. If the political development of Germany was an oddity by the standards of France and Britain, probably the main reason was that the German national state had not grown up slowly over a long period of time but had been achieved suddenly in the 1860s. For the next two decades the more or less benevolent despotism of the great Bismarck impeded the growth of parliamentary government.

Germany was far from an illiberal country. Civil rights under the law were fairly well protected; there were a constitution, a reasonably free press, elections. But there was no strong parliamentary system, no vigorous political life. In place of parliamentary government stood the bureaucracy, an honest and able body committed to high standards of administration but not democratically controlled. Most people, someone has said, want not to govern themselves but to be well-governed. The Germans were not badly governed, but they did not govern themselves. The stubbornly individualistic English and the passionately democratic French accused the Germans of bending their knees too readily to authority. In compensation, the Germans had pioneered in welfare legislation. Bismarck had handed it down from above, allowing Germany to avoid these bitter political battles waged over this question in France and Britain. The German industrial middle class had been politically too weak to resist. Although a greater social principle informed the German society, it was at the cost, it seemed, of individualism.

The weakness of liberalism may be seen in the election results. In the 1912 election to the Reichstag, when the Social Democrats won their victory with about 35 percent of the total vote, the National Liberals and Progressives (*Fortschrittpartei*) together won only 26 percent. The rest went either to the conservative parties or to those representing local or particular interests. Of these, the Center party (*Zentrum*) was much the most important, with about a sixth of the electorate; traditionally dedicated to the interests of the Catholic church, the Center tended to ally with the conservatives. The National Liberal party could not collaborate with the Social Democrats because of profound disagreement on questions of national defense and military policy. If liberalism meant refusing strong support to army, navy, and colonies, nationalism came before liberalism to this party representing the German middle class. The support the National Liberals had given to Bismarck and the whole authoritarian structure of politics in the German Empire precluded this group from developing much of a reform impulse.

Reform of this political structure seemed to be needed for Germany to evolve in a democratic direction. Changes in the constitution were blocked, as in France and Britain, by the upper house of the legislature. Unlike the French and British second chambers, the German upper house (*Landtag*) was based on the various states of the national union. The German situation was peculiar in that one state, Prussia, was far larger and more powerful than the others, really than all the others combined. Prussia alone, with some of the tiny states of the North who were her satellites, could block an amendment to the constitution. And within Prussia the voting system, harking back to 1851, was profoundly archaic. Frankly weighted in the direction of wealth, her "three-class system" gave the wealthiest the most representation, the poorest the least. Reform tended, then, to focus on the Prussian voting system. The key to Germany was Prussia; so long as Prussia remained dominated by a conservative minority, no fundamental change was possible in Germany. In 1910 there were again extensive public demonstrations against the Prussian election system, but nothing came of it. Only a revolution, some said, could break the vicious circle of oligarchy.

But the Social Democrats in the great majority were far from revolutionary. They remained committed to peaceful and legal acquisition of power. Marxism itself had the effect of supporting this position. Marx had taught that there are inexorable laws of historical change that make the victory of socialism inevitable. Revolutionary agitation could be dismissed as left-wing infantilism or romantic adventurism. The wheels of fate rolled steadily toward the future, which would come in due time, Marxists believed; it could not be rushed, but it was certain. The working class was bound to increase in numbers and in proletarian consciousness, the believing Marxist was sure. Capitalism destroyed itself by its own operation; it did not have to be shot down from outside.

At the beginning of the decade the German Social Democratic party debated revisionism. Eduard Bernstein, one of the party's most talented writers, suggested giving up dogmatic Marxism altogether. Marx's prophecies had not proved correct. Capitalism was not steadily digging its own grave, the working class was not growing more miserable each day, society was not being polarized into two classes. The day of revolution was not inevitable, regardless of Marx's alleged laws of history and capitalist development. Socialists ought to work toward a more just society little by little and with a pragmatic attitude, like the English Fabians. After a rousing debate, the party rejected Bernstein's revisions and remained in principle committed to the Marxist dogmas. Like the French Socialists, they declared their unwillingness to accept power in any but a completely socialist government. Yet only a small left wing of the party took Marx to mean revolutionary activism. As Marx's collaborator, Friedrich Engels, had said before his death in the

1890s, the hour of revolutionary conspiracies led by elites had passed; the masses themselves, by democratic means, would bring about the great transformation to socialism.

For all its success, the Social Democratic party remained curiously impotent and isolated. With a million members and scores of publications, which were read by several million Germans, this huge organization had already developed its own hierarchy of bureaucrats and mandarins. It attracted highly educated bourgeois intellectuals as well as workers. In large German cities, it won almost half the vote in 1912, doing much worse (less than 20 percent) among the farms and villages. But its influence was at best intellectual and moral. A glowingly idealistic faith informed its adherents, but it was faith in tomorrow, after the revolution. Meanwhile, its critics on the Left thought, it tended silently to support the status quo.

It was widely believed that the Germans had made the best of all adjustments to the machine age. More so than the British and French, they ranked as an up-to-date, go-ahead people in technology, commerce, education, social services, and industrial relations. If the prestige of German science was high, her writers and artists such as novelist Thomas Mann and poets Stefan George and Rainer Maria Rilke won international acclaim, too. In Berlin, scientists Albert Einstein and Max Planck were at work revolutionizing humanity's conception of the cosmos. In Munich just before the war, a remarkable group of painters, including Paul Klee and the Russian-born Kandinsky, joined to create one of the leading movements of contemporary art. In philosophy such figures as Edmund Husserl and Max Scheler continued the German dominance of pure thought, challenged in this generation only by Henri Bergson of France and Bertrand Russell of England. Sigmund Freud, who worked in Vienna, and Carl Jung of Switzerland belonged to the German-speaking culture. The preeminence of Germans in the new science of sociology—Georg Simmel, Friedrich Tönnies, Max Weber, and others—has been mentioned. The German educational system, from *kindergarten* to graduate seminar, remained a model for the world, and in 1914 more Germans attended universities than was the case in any other country.

All in all, Germany was doing splendidly, except for the curious lag in political institutions. But the widely shared gospel of progress persuaded most people that her institutions would soon catch up. Germany was thought to be in the process of evolving toward parliamentary government. The autocracy of the kaiser and his bureaucracy would be democratized in one way or another. Indeed, perhaps this would have happened peacefully were it not for the great war. Yet the impossibility of a breakthrough to parliamentary supremacy by any normal means was increasingly felt on the eve of the war, too, and thus the revolution that came to Germany at the war's end may have been a necessity under any conditions.

The Eastern Powers

In 1910 Austria-Hungary was a land of fifty million people. It was the third most populous of the European powers, after Russia (165 million) and Germany (sixty-five million). Economically it was by no means undeveloped, although overall it ranked well behind the highly industrialized countries. Certain areas of the Dual Monarchy, including the great cities of Prague, Vienna, and Budapest and the industrial region of the Sudetenland, were as advanced in all respects as any in Europe. "The Austrian half of the Empire," a leading student writes, "enjoyed a very high level of freedom for the individual and a much higher level of social welfare than for example, England." [7] Vienna, with its great musical traditions, its gaiety and waltzes, its lovely baroque architecture, also possessed a distinguished scientific community; among the doctors it gave to the world in this period was Sigmund Freud. It was probably the most civilized city in Europe. Ambassadors and other foreign service employees thought so; they preferred Vienna to any other post. It was the ultimate diplomatic plum.

Budapest, the glamorous capital of the Hungarian part of the Dual Monarchy, was almost Vienna's equal. In Bohemia, as the Czechs' land had long been known, Prague boasted a great university where Kepler had once started the whole age of modern science.

The empire itself, of course, traced its ancestry back to the Holy Roman Empire, which had been at the center of the world in medieval times. The Hapsburg dynasty was the oldest and most distinguished ruling house in Europe, if not the world, and it formed Europe's most obvious link with its medieval past. The Hapsburgs could recall such past emperors as Charles V, who came close to uniting all Europe in a single state as late as the sixteenth century. Hapsburgs had once striven with France for the mastery of Europe; after the Napoleonic wars, the great peace settlement of 1815 took place at Vienna, and for many years thereafter Austria's leading statesman, Count Metternich, served as a kind of prime minister of all Europe. As late as 1851 Austria outranked Prussia as a central European power.

Then came Bismarck and the Prussian coup of 1867–1871. Prussia smashed Austria in the short war of 1867 and went on to create the

---

[7] Edward Crankshaw, *The Fall of the House of Hapsburg* (New York: Viking Press, 1963), p. 303.

powerful new German state, attracting to it the smaller principalities that had once made up the Holy Roman Empire (after 1815 the German Confederation). Nationalism and the unitary state were now all-powerful; the old empire was an anachronism. Its focus had always been in Germany, but at the peak of their influence the Hapsburgs had annexed many territories in the largely Slavic southeast. They had fought against the Turks when the Ottoman Empire seemed about to overrun all Europe in the sixteenth and again in the seventeenth centuries. At that time the Christian peoples of southeastern Europe were happy to receive such protection as the emperor could give them, much preferring his rule to that of the terrible Turk.

In 1867 the empire signalled its expulsion from the German world by granting the Hungarians (Magyars) a large measure of autonomy and renaming the country Austria-Hungary, or the Dual Monarchy. With a single monarch in Vienna shaping a common military and foreign policy, Budapest got a free hand in its portion of the empire on domestic matters. The Magyars, who occupied Hungary, were a proud people, neither Germanic nor Slavic but derived from an oriental people out of the plains of central Asia who had invaded Europe as conquerors in the ninth and tenth centuries. They had long been restive under Vienna's domination, and they now hoped to build a new state.

But the two master peoples were not the only inhabitants of the Dual Monarchy. Its twelve million Germans and ten million Magyars shared the multinational house with twenty-four million Slavs of various sorts, including Poles, Czechs, Slovaks, Croats, Slovenes, and a few "Ruthenians" (Ukrainians). In addition there were some four million Latins, mostly Rumanians but also some Italians in the Trentino area, and a considerable Jewish population. Many of these groups had old and proud national traditions. In an age of rising nationalism they increasingly demanded recognition of their rights to cultural or even political autonomy, to a role in the state equal to that of the Germans and Hungarians. By 1900 it had become the critical problem for Europe. The problem burgeoned in proportion as the Sick Man of Europe, the Ottoman Empire, weakened, for the waning of this threat made the small Balkan peoples less dependent on Austria. It also increased when after 1905 Russian policy retreated from its Asian mission and played up its role as protector of the Slavs.

As usual, scholars disagree about how badly treated the minorities were and whether it was possible to grant them all autonomy. To those who lodged complaints of intolerable arrogance against both German and Magyar—especially the latter, in whose zone of control lived numerous Croats, Slovenes, and Rumanians whom the Hungarians tended to regard as an inferior class—the reply was that the subject peoples were not badly treated and that it would be impossible to give them territorial autonomy. Since they were so numerous and so widely distributed, any such plan would amount to chaos. Suggestions were made for a triple monarchy. But the Slavs were not in a geographically contiguous area. Czechs and Slovaks lived in the north, Croats and Slovenes in the south. The Poles, occupying the northeast, were not anxious to blend with Slovaks or Croats. The Poles in Austria were, in fact, treated well, and they regarded their own lot as much better than that of their fellows who were ruled from St. Petersburg or Berlin.

To satisfy everyone, it would have had to be not a triple but a quintuple monarchy. The sequel to World War I and the dissolution of the Dual Monarchy showed this clearly; it dissolved into four or five small pieces, not all of which were very stable. Statesmen feared to open up this Pandora's box lest the state die in the ensuing pandemonium, and so the status quo basically continued. Some concessions short of self-government were granted to Czechs as well as Poles. The result was what has been described as "an intricate hieratic system." In the hierarchy of subject peoples the Poles and Czechs stood highest, the Slovaks and Rumanians lowest; the Croats had gained a small measure of autonomy. The Austrian part of the empire was not very repressive, the Hungarian part more so. Whether, in a nationalistic age, there was any possibility of evolving politically in a way that would satisfy all or most of the twenty-eight million majority made up of minorities is doubtful. Adding to the complexities, in Vienna the Social Democratic party, akin to the German Socialists and hostile to the monarchy, was growing stronger.

The troubles of the Dual Monarchy were not confined to its discontented minorities. The two "master races" also quarreled. The Magyars regarded the Compromise of 1867 as virtually an alliance between sovereign states, insisted on complete independence in their part of the dual state, and often refused to cooperate on matters of joint policy. Count Tisza's refusal in July 1914 to go along with the war policy of Vienna against Serbia (see p. 65) was typical. Franz Ferdinand, the heir to the throne, was violent in his dislike of the Magyars, a rather typical Austrian feeling; in private, among his kindest adjectives for them were "vile, perfidious, and unreliable." That the crown prince played with ideas of a triple monarchy, having a third capital at either Prague or Zagreb, probably reflected more his dislike of the Hungarians than his love for the Slavs.

Under such circumstances parliamentary government naturally could not work. There was a national parliament, elected by something near universal manhood suffrage after 1906, but it was normally a scene of wild disorder featuring obstructive practices and occasionally erupting into violence, as each of the ethnic groups used the Diet as a forum for the agitation of its own demands. These were sham battles, as the body had no real power. As in Germany, the real work of government was carried on by a fairly honest and efficient bureaucracy, which took its orders from the emperor. The aged Franz Joseph (he was eighty-four in 1914 but still quite vigorous) was one of the most beloved figures in Europe. He had reigned ever since 1848. Many wondered if his death would not prove to be the signal for a breakup of the ancient empire.

On the other hand, the perpetual political crisis did not destroy this state, which was needed geographically and economically. In Vienna, the lighthearted city, people said in jest, "The situation is desperate but not serious." So matters stood when after 1905 the rise of the small but ambitious neighboring state of Serbia intensified the difficulties, as we describe in the next chapter, and led to a frightful world war as the price of the dissolution of the Dual Monarchy. When this work of dissolution was done, many wished that the old empire would come back again.

Let us postpone any extensive discussion of Russia until we come to her great revolution of 1917. Between 1901 and 1914 this huge land of amazing contrasts, an enigma as much to its own small educated elite as to foreigners, experienced all the following: the first phase of industrialization, force-fed by the state, with all the dislocations that brought; defeat in war by Japan, followed by the revolution of 1905; the basic beginnings of constitutional government with an elected national assembly, the Duma; the continued activity of a revolutionary socialist and anarchist Left; an attempt to deal with the problem of a vast body of illiterate, backward, and discontented peasants by encouraging the creation of independent farmers, owning their own land and practicing capitalistic agriculture.

Struggling to Westernize, Russia yet contained many who thought she had a separate destiny, some kind of a third way between Europe and Asia. Yet her Asian mission was rebuffed, and Nicholas II, a man of limited abilities who was destined to be the last Russian tsar, tried to be the architect of industrial progress for his backward country. Russia had many troubles, including the gulf between classes, communication and transportation problems because of her vast spaces, and economic backwardness. To these was added the cultural disunity of a huge land embracing literally scores of national minorities, from Poles, Balts, and Finns to the primitive tribesmen of Russian Asia, Georgians and Armenians in the south, Tatars and other Turkish peoples—

Barricades in Moscow during the Revolution of 1905.

altogether constituting more than half the total population, though widely distributed around the Great Russian nucleus, and most more or less unhappy under Russian rule.

Strikes, peasant riots, and assassinations punctuated the Russian scene, continuing a fairly long tradition. Peter Stolypin, the enlightened statesman who tried for agricultural reform, was killed in a Kiev theater in 1911. The Bolshevik faction of the Russian Social Democratic party, breaking away from the mechanistic passivity of the majority Marxists, created a revolutionary underground. Too weak to contemplate war after her stunning defeat by the Japanese, Russia submitted to several diplomatic humiliations of her Pan-Slav ambitions in the Balkan arena between 1908 and 1914.

Despite such imposing problems, many thought Russia was on the way to ultimate success, that she would eventually join the rest of Europe. Her economic growth rate was among the highest in the world; she was building industrial plant and an infrastructure of railroads; the Duma, although nearly powerless, was learning the ways of parliamentary government. Most observers in this generally optimistic period thought that Russia had set her feet on the path of progress, European style, and would continue onward and upward. Historians argue about whether the great 1917 revolution would have come had there been no war; the best answer seems to be that it was chiefly the terrible war that caused the downfall of the Russian state in 1917.

Europe before the War, 1914

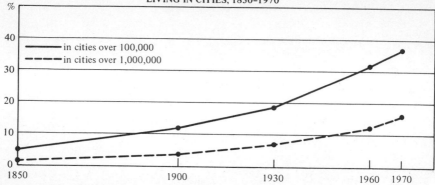

PERCENTAGE OF POPULATION OF EUROPE INCLUDING U.S.S.R.
LIVING IN CITIES, 1850-1970

in cities over 100,000
in cities over 1,000,000

The greater glories of the land of the tsars were undoubtedly cultural and intellectual. Until Leo Tolstoy's death in 1908, his home had been a shrine visited by people from all over the world; he was the nearest thing to a globally famous prophet, sage, and genius that this era afforded. A "silver age" of literature, art, and music arose in Russia just after the time of Tolstoy and Dostoevsky, destined to be blighted by the Revolution but testifying to the vitality of Russian artistic genius. In 1911, London lost its customary aplomb in a rage for the intoxicating Russian ballet, nothing like which had ever been seen there. In the international mixture of ideas and styles that Europe enjoyed, from Yeats' Ireland to Rachmaninoff's Russia, the Russians made not the least contribution.

It was—or it was not?—*la belle époque* of carefree happiness before the roof caved in, suddenly and unexpectedly, in late July of 1914.

The Coming of the Great War

2

Some General Causes of the War

I see the time approaching when the nations of the world, laying aside their political animosities, will be knitted together in the peaceful rivalry of trade; when the barriers of nationality which belong to the infancy of the race will melt and dissolve in the sunshine of science and art; when the roar of the cannon will yield to the soft murmur of the loom, and the apron of the artisan, the blouse of the peasant be more honorable than the scarlet of the soldier; when the cosmopolitan armies of trade will replace the militia of death; when that which God has joined together will no longer be sundered by the ignorance, the folly, the wickedness of man; when the labour and the invention of one will become the heritage of all; and the peoples of the earth meet no longer on the field of battle, but by their chosen delegates, as in the vision of our greatest poet, in "the Parliament of Man, the Federation of the World."

This effulgent prophecy appeared in a book written by an English socialist, G. Lowes Dickinson, in 1905;[1] it is quoted not because it was unusual but because the sentiment was so commonplace that only the adornments of rhetoric could give it any distinction. The nineteenth-

[1] *A Modern Symposium* (Garden City: Doubleday, Page & Co., 1905), pp. 26–27.

41

century ideologies of liberalism and socialism alike prophesied that war would become obsolete as the feudal warrior gave way to the industrial producer. Among popular statements on war in the 1900s Norman Angell's *The Great Illusion* stood out, its title self-explanatory. There could no longer be any glory or profit in war. The international economy was too complexly independent to stand for such archaic interruptions. As the American radical Randolph Bourne put it (in 1914!), "Our modern civilization with its international bonds of financial and economic dependence is a civilization organized for peace and for peace alone." In his article in *International Conciliation*, June 1914, Bourne declared that war is "definitely and for all time relegated to the dusty limbo of the past" and "almost unimaginable" today.

Only a few cantankerous outsiders thought otherwise. The widely read Englishman H.G. Wells, among whose incredibly versatile range of writings were science fiction novels, had imagined a "war for the world," predicting atomic weapons and aerial bombardments, eventualities reserved for the Second World War (*War in the Air*, 1908, and *The World Set Free*, 1914). But Wells later wrote that he didn't really believe his fantasies; "I will confess I was taken by surprise by the Great War." Almost everyone was. The learned international team of scholars who had just completed the impressive multivolumed *Cambridge Modern History* saw a rosy future in general for Europe, and they held that the rather high level of armaments was a force for peace, making it too risky for any nation to think of war (an argument heard long before the post-1954 "balance of terror"). They also stated that Germany was stabilizing central Europe and that Russia had turned toward peaceful domestic development after 1905. These opinions were held by the overwhelming majority, educated and uneducated, radicals and conservatives.

So much for the art of prophecy. Popular opinion in Europe during the two decades prior to 1914 was hostile to anything that did not suggest steady progress toward humanitarian goals. In addition, attention had been absorbed by domestic issues. Newspapers, journals of opinion, and parliamentary debates found little room for foreign affairs, compared to those questions of social welfare and political democratization that seemed so vital. Among overseas crises, first the Boer War and then the Irish question, neither of which had anything at all to do with the outbreak of war in 1914, alone had bulked large in British opinion. An exception might be made for the naval race with Germany, which had inflated the government budget and helped cause a tax crisis. At the other end of Europe Russia, too, paid far more attention to such issues as Stolypin's land reforms than to any matter of foreign policy, and after the embarrassing performance of 1905 against Japan most

Russians regarded few things less favorably than the prospects of another war. Experiencing an economic boom, the tsar's empire was in the process of modernizing its economy and its army with the aid of French capital, but the process was far from complete. In July of 1914 its chief attention was riveted on a series of industrial strikes.

No wonder the sudden outbreak of a major international war at the beginning of August caught everyone by surprise. The sobering lesson was that war could happen without anybody seeming to want it or to will it. All kinds of myths grew up later, as bewildered people attempted to explain the outbreak of war. As usual, conspiracy theories flourished. In particular it was alleged that the Germans plotted war; Wilhelm II, the unhappy German monarch, was depicted in the Allied countries as a monster with tentacles reaching out to ensnare small countries. That "Prussian militarism" was the canker in the olive branch became an article of faith in France and England and later, after she had joined the war, in the United States. For their part, the Germans believed that jealous neighbors plotted to encircle and destroy a country whose only crime was her economic success.

Then, too, the theory arose that the capitalistic economic system, far from being a force for peace, had engineered the war because war was profitable or because there was competition for markets and raw materials. Although they may contain germs of truth, all such simple-minded "devil theories" must be dismissed as inadequate to the serious study of events, more interesting as folklore than as history.

Though it is tempting to look for it, no single all-embracing cause can successfully explain the war or any other major historical event. We can, of course, say that the basic cause was something like the "system of sovereign states"; and this was in fact probably the most widespread diagnosis during the war. This diagnosis led to the many schemes that proliferated from 1914 on for a League of Nations or an association of nations or even a world state. However, people must be politically organized in one way or another; one might almost as well say that the "people system" caused the war. One could cite human nature, or more specifically humanity's relentless pursuit of power, as the cause. Such explanations are too general to take us far; human nature is the necessary condition for any human activity, but it does not explain why this particular war happened at this particular time. Were the sovereign states more sovereign, human nature more aggressive, power more sought after in 1914 than in 1890 or 1880? Evidently not.

We may get an idea of the differences of opinion among those who sought to account for the war by noting how contradictory the explanations were. Some blamed it on lack of democratic control over foreign policy, which was said to be the monopoly of a secret elite; but others said that an erratic and frequently bellicose public opinion had taken over the reins of power from the professionals. Some blamed it on military men, who were madly eager to try out their weapons; but others argue that the military was far from eager to go to war.

More realistically, scholars have frequently argued that nationalism was more pervasive and intense than at any previous time and that the balance of power had become upset. These two key factors, one subjective and one objective, are worth keeping in mind amid the vast concatenation of possible causes of the outbreak of war in 1914.

On anybody's analysis, the situation was a complex one. The five major powers—Great Britain, France, Germany, Austria-Hungary, and Russia—dominated the scene. Of the other states of Europe, neither the Scandinavian nor the Iberian countries (Spain and Portugal) played any significant part in the coming of the war. Neither did the neutrals, Switzerland and the Netherlands, although Belgium was to be dramatically if unwillingly involved. Italy ranked as almost a great power and was a part of the alliance system. The role played by Serbia and less directly by the other states of the turbulent Balkans (Bulgaria, Greece, Rumania, and what was left of Turkey in Europe) is well known. The United States of America was a powerful factor in the background. The European powers were engaged in colonial rivalries all over the globe, sometimes involving quasi-independent native governments. And each of the powers had a highly developed, extremely complex machinery of government and richly diverse societies, consisting of many different interests, ideologies, occupations, and organizations.

The states of Europe were like individuals living in a primeval state of nature marked by incessant strife between one and another. They acknowledged no higher authority that might have forced them to keep the peace. What was called "international law" was not in fact binding on them, being backed by no more than a moral or customary sanction. In the optimistic climate of the pre-1914 years, nearly everyone assumed that international law was making steady if slow progress. Attempts were made to secure agreement on laws of war providing for humane treatment of prisoners, sparing of civilians, and rights of neutral and belligerent ships to trade in nonmilitary materials. In the 1914–1918 war, as also in the 1939–1945 one, the worthlessness of such rules was revealed from the very first days of the war, as each side ignored them if there was an advantage in doing so. Two international conferences on world peace held at The Hague, Netherlands, in 1899 and 1907 tried to establish a world court for the settlement of disputes among states. But this court was no more than a panel of jurists available for the conciliation or the arbitration of a dispute if the quarreling states wished to use it; it had no power to compel them to use it or to hail them into court if they broke the peace. Nothing in the nature of a world state or a European state existed. Among themselves, the states had various agreements, which they could always find a reason for dishonoring were a vital interest involved.

Of course, they exchanged diplomatic representatives and negotiated treaties and other agreements with each other. The traditions surrounding this activity, reaching back to ancient times and particularly to the fifteenth century, were numerous and complex. But underneath the velvet glove of diplomacy one could see clearly enough the iron fist of national self-interest backed by armed force. Within this tradition, war, the ultimate court of appeal, had its recognized place. It was itself the formalization of violence.

No one doubted the right of nations to declare war under certain circumstances. Not until after 1918 did people seriously think of "outlawing" war. War in the long European tradition was not an outlaw, just a solemn member of the family whose visits, it was hoped, would be rare, but who might have to be summoned at any time. War had always been thought to be justifiable in self-defense; so was coming to the aid of an ally under attack. But even an aggressive war, it was generally conceded, might properly be undertaken under certain conditions: to forestall later disaster by "checking the overgrown power of some ambitious neighbor" (Jonathan Swift), to revenge an injury, or to pursue some other just cause. Rebels and radicals had stressed that fighting a war for liberty from a tyrant or for the freeing of an oppressed people was noble. They had also said it was a nation's duty to aid others fighting in such meritorious causes. Some anarchists preached the holiness of revolutionary violence. Hegel, Marx, and Nietzsche, leading nineteenth-century philosophers, all approved of war, which the first two saw as a "locomotive of history" and the latter as a means of redeeming the souls of men.

More and more people had acquired a larger stake in defending the state. This was the natural result of democratization and increase in wealth. However imperfectly or inequitably these had come about, the large majority of citizens had some interest in defending the political community of which they were a part. All over Europe, 1914 was to prove that the masses as well as the classes were militantly patriotic when they thought their country was being attacked.

In a situation of sovereign states unlimited by a higher law and backed by nationalistic public opinion, balance of power was one means of keeping peace. Power does check power; a state is less likely to attack another if it fears retaliation, and it is more likely to do so if it has no fear of encountering resistance. This principle had long operated in European affairs, often drawing many states together to check an overmighty power that constituted a threat to all. They had united against France, for example, both in the later seventeenth century and during Napoleon I's rampaging years at the beginning of the nineteenth century. The balance created by the Congress of Vienna in 1815 was not a bad one,[2] but it later broke down over the issue of nationalism. The upheaval of 1870–1871, which created a strong, united Germany, was dangerous to the balance. Although Bismarck's skill kept his rivals apart, after his departure the alliance between France and Russia was a natural reaction to the powerful German nation. This alliance, however, alarmed Germany with fear of encirclement and encouraged her to think of ways to prevent being caught in a squeeze. The famous Schlieffen plan, which formed the basis of German strategy in 1914, assumed the necessity of knocking out France with a massive and speedy attack before the slow-moving Russians could mount an offensive on Germany's eastern front.

The balance of power between the Franco-Russian bloc and the Austro-German one was also dangerous.[3] Germany was rendered dependent on Austria-Hungary, an unstable state, and France was dependent on an equally unstable Russia. Russian and Austrian interests clashed in the turbulent region of southeastern Europe. They dragged their allies into their quarrel, thus maximizing what might have remained a local conflict. The danger of alliances in a precarious balance of power is that any small war can escalate into a major one.

The Diplomacy of the Early 1900s

Against this background, significant events in the 1900s threatened to upset the delicate balance. A key to the unstable equilibrium was the role of the fifth and uncommitted power, Great Britain, who had refrained from alliances and sought to keep the scales even. Her movement in this decade was clearly toward commitment to the Franco-Russian

[2] Though deprived of her Napoleonic conquests the defeated nation, France, was treated leniently and remained an important power. Prussia was strengthened but the rest of Germany became a weak confederation of more than thirty small states. Hapsburg Austria was given control of northern Italy. Russia was prevented from annexing Poland outright, though she did so in 1830 when other provisions of the settlement began to break down.

[3] Italy was a nominal member of the Triple Alliance with Germany and the Dual Monarchy, but this connection, dating from 1882, no longer coincided with Italian interests, and no one expected Italy to be an active partner. Italy's territorial claims were chiefly against Austria-Hungary. The quarrel with France, which had led her into the German camp, was no longer a factor after 1904.

side. To bring this about, she had to overcome a good deal of past mistrust.

In 1900 Great Britain clearly regarded Russia as her first enemy and France as the second. Favorably disposed toward the Central Powers, she had no quarrel and a considerable tradition of friendship with Austria-Hungary. In 1900–1901, she almost concluded a formal treaty with Germany. The negotiations miscarried, leaving some mistrust on both sides. Subsequent kibitzers frequently decided that the Germans played too hard to get and overestimated their hand. Yet the British animosity toward Russia remained and led to a treaty with Japan in 1902. This was the first breach of a long-standing British refusal to enter into alliances. Because of the tsar's supposed designs upon India as well as a general detestation of his despotic government, British opinion had long looked upon Russia as the chief enemy, and the alliance was clearly made with Russia in mind. That celebrated music hall song that included the lines

> We don't want to fight, but by jingo if we do
> We've got the ships, we've got the men, we've got the money too

had been induced by a threat of war with Russia and ended with the line,

> The Russian shall not have Constantinople!

Though the German naval law of 1900, which provided for an accelerated battleship building program, had just introduced a sobering note, Great Britain had no real quarrel with Germany. (The anti-British implications of the German naval expansion do not seem to have dawned on the British cabinet until late 1902). One sensational book of 1895 predicted a war to the death for world markets between the two industrial powers, but it was an irresponsible potboiler. Queen Victoria, of German extraction and the grandmother of German Emperor Wilhelm II, had been notably pro-German and anti-Russian. In 1899 prominent British politician Joseph Chamberlain, a leading figure in the government, declared that, "the most natural alliance is that between us and the German Empire."

A significant change lay ahead: the celebrated *entente cordiale* with France in 1904. Traditional foes from Louis XIV's time, if not all the way back to the Hundred Years War, France and England had fought for supremacy between 1778 and 1815, but they had enjoyed moments of friendship in the nineteenth century. They astonished the world by fighting on the same side (against Russia) in the Crimean War of the 1850s. But this attack of congeniality scarcely lasted, and the British resumed acute colonial rivalries with their old foes in the late nineteenth-century outbreak of imperialism. The French believed the British squeezed them out of Egypt and wrested control of the Suez Canal from its builders in 1882. Then in the summer of 1898, the English under Kitchener and the French under Marchand arrived almost simultaneously at the upper Nile village of Fashoda and hoisted flags side by side. This was a kind of grand climax to the scramble for African territory, which resulted in the annexation of almost all of that continent in the last two decades of the nineteenth century, mostly by Britain and France. But war was avoided.

It often happens in diplomacy that after a grave crisis has been surmounted, the momentum of detente carries on to much better relations between the erstwhile protagonists. The reverse is also true: a missed chance for spectacular agreement can lead to a long slide downhill. It seemed to work this way with England's relations with France and Germany between 1900 and 1905. They reversed themselves dramatically. Between Westminster and the Wilhelmstrasse mistrust grew, while between Westminster and the Quai D'Orsay it lessened. Among forces affecting this development was the long ascendancy in the French foreign office of an able minister, Théophile Delcassé, whose goal was reconciliation with Britain in order to confront Germany. Delcassé pursued the politics of *revanche* dear to embittered French patriots who vowed never to forget the loss of the provinces of Alsace and Lorraine to Germany in 1871.

On the English side, the new monarch, Edward VII, was pro-French. The king took one of the earliest initiatives of reconciliation when in 1903 he invited the president of the French republic over for a visit. The popularity of Edward and the changed mood of Edwardian times induced one of those switches in the mercurial public's moods, and a wave of Francophilia swept over the normally "frog"-hating English. As for the French, although they jeered Edward in the beginning, he quickly captured their hearts.

The issue of Morocco happened to come up at this time. One way to pursue an anti-German diplomacy was to tug at the loose ropes binding Italy to the Triple Alliance, and Delcassé was not one to overlook this. Italy and France had been parted by colonial disagreement stemming from Italy's hurt pride at seeing France monopolize North African colonial acquisitions. The descendants of the Caesars had been humiliated in Ethiopia in one of the few defeats an African people pinned on Europeans in this era, and they watched the French take Tunisia, which lay just across from Italy. But in 1900 a treaty between France and Italy promised Tripoli (today Libya) to Italy; in return Italy recognized that the kingdom of Morocco lay within the French sphere of influence. This naturally led to discussions with both Spain and Great Britain, whose interest in Morocco centered on Gibraltar and control of the Mediterranean straits.

The French asked for British recognition of their Moroccan supremacy (as a protectorate), provided British and Spanish interests were protected and freedom of trade guaranteed. In return France agreed to give up her old objections to Britain's protectorate over Egypt, a sore point ever since 1882. Long negotiations went on in 1903–1904 on these points and a few minor ones, culminating in an agreement signed on April 8, 1904. It is a significant date in diplomatic history, to be placed alongside the 1894 Franco-Russian treaty of alliance. This agreement was not an alliance; but it settled outstanding differences between France and England and was greeted with enthusiasm in both countries as ushering in a new era of friendship. We would be inclined to say today that the exchange, in effect, of Morocco for Egypt was in the worst tradition of imperialist diplomacy, bartering non-European peoples about like pawns. Then, however, it was hardly viewed in such a light, since almost everyone accepted as both inevitable and right the African countries' political tutelage and economic aid from the more advanced Europeans. In 1903 even Jean Jaurès, the French Socialist leader, agreed that the French had a civilizing mission in North Africa. Few Frenchmen doubted it. Jaurès later attacked the Entente on the grounds that it caused a quarrel with Germany, not that it oppressed Morocco.

The entente between France and Britain was naturally a severe setback for German diplomacy. The Germans were the more aggrieved in that they were snubbed in the matter of Morocco. Everybody had been consulted about the fate of that kingdom, it seemed, except the Germans and of course the Moroccans. Italy and Spain, second-class powers, had been consulted, but not Germany. The answer was that Germany was not a Mediterranean power and had no particular interest in Morocco. This answer did not impress the Germans, needless to say. The German chancellor, Bernard von Bülow, later wrote that Britain and France had "disposed arrogantly of a great and most important field of colonial interests, without even deigning to take the German Empire into consideration."

While Kaiser Wilhelm and Bülow meditated responses, the Russo-Japanese war broke out. It tended temporarily to confuse the issues. Wilhelm, who was fond of expatiating on the "yellow peril,"pulled for the Russians. On the other hand, in a bizarre episode, some Russian battleships fired on English fishing boats off the coast of England, mistaking them for Japanese torpedo boats, and set off an anti-Russian uproar in Britain. The Russian fleet in the Baltic, dispatched to the Far

East after the Russian fleet there had been mauled by the Japanese, had to sail westward, halfway around the world, to get there. (Upon its arrival it was promptly wiped out.) But this Dogger Bank episode was smoothed over with the aid of the French, while the kaiser wrote to his cousin Nicholas, the tsar of Russia, vainly suggesting an alliance of Germany and Russia against England.

As the Russian cause worsened in Manchuria and revolution broke out at home, the Germans were strongly tempted to take advantage of the grave weakening in the rival alliance. Morocco lay at hand as a seemingly worthy case, and the Germans chose to make this their ground by openly challenging the Morocco arrangements and refusing to accept them as binding on Germany. In a melodramatic gesture, the German emperor himself landed on Moroccan soil in Tangiers on March 31, 1905, posing as the defender of Morocco against the Anglo-French vultures about to swoop down upon it.

Delcassé, facing an angry Germany without an ally, had indeed overplayed his hand. While the realistic Clemenceau accused the foreign minister of maneuvering France into dangerous waters, the idealistic Jaurès attacked him for favoring reactionary Russia and not believing in Franco-German reconciliation. Even on the far Right, which mistrusted "perfidious England," Delcassé found little support. He resigned on June 6. The Germans demanded a conference to take up the Morocco question, and this was granted.

This moment of German victory coincided with the depths of Russia's misfortunes. Germany did not threaten Russia but sought to cajole her. Wilhelm went off to meet the tsar at Bjorkoe, on the coast of Finland, where the two emperors emotionally agreed to a friendship pact. "A turning point in world history," Wilhelm called it; but the rather simpleminded Russian monarch had acted totally on his own without consulting his ministers, who managed to persuade him to withdraw it as inconsistent with the French alliance. And Bülow also threatened to resign over the issue of the kaiser's personal diplomacy. This experiment in monarchical summitry misfired badly.

Moreover, the Morocco conference held in 1906 at Algeciras in southern Spain proved disappointing to the Germans. Among the powers invited to the conference, including the United States and Italy as well as France, Great Britain, Russia, and the Dual Monarchy, only the latter proved a loyal supporter of Germany. England and France tended to draw closer together. The new Liberal government of England did not prove more pro-German than its predecessor, though Germany had hoped it would. On the key issue of placing the Moroccan police power in the hands of the French and Spanish, only Austria-Hungary—and Morocco—voted with Germany in opposition. The French case was strengthened by the proximity of France and Spain to Morocco, France long having had control of neighboring Algeria, where many French lived. Morocco was believed to be in a state of near anarchy. Police power is best exercised by a single state rather than a condominium.

Bülow collapsed on the floor of the Reichstag and had to be given a long rest. Almost everyone thought that German diplomacy had failed. It had managed to alarm the world with a war scare and given an impression of theatrical belligerence without achieving anything, except to solidify the other side and leave Germany almost isolated. Forcing the fall of Delcassé might be counted a minor victory, but neither England nor Russia had been pried loose from the French connection, and England was even closer to France than before.

In France and especially in Great Britain the Germans were seen, perhaps wrongly, as making a bid for world sea power. Already alarmed by Germany's building of a strong war fleet, the British noted that if Germany got control of Morocco she would have ports on the Atlantic, thus breaking out of her confinement in the Baltic and North Sea. The powerful French right-wing publicist, Charles Maurras, wrote a widely read book, *Kiel and Tangiers,* coupling the Morocco bid with the widening of the ship canal linking the great naval base at Kiel on the Baltic with the North Sea. From 1905 dates the firm belief of many in France and at least a few in England that the kaiser and his circle meditated ambitious plans of world conquest. This was undoubtedly 90 percent fantasy. But its acceptance indicates a clumsiness on the part of German policy, whose game of pressure by threat had backfired.

In 1908 the main problems of Europe shifted to southeastern Europe. It was in this area that the war of 1914 really began, of course. Postponing consideration of this powder keg for the moment, let us pursue the affairs of France, Britain, and Germany. Between the latter two the naval question, the *Flottenproblem,* became an increasingly painful one. The new British foreign secretary, Edward Grey, was by no means averse to some sort of improvement of relations with Germany. Unfortunately there appeared at this moment (1906) a new and superior type of battleship, the dreadnaught. This larger and stronger ship made all previous ones obsolete. Created first in England, its technology was quickly mastered by the Germans. This change in the mechanics of warfare tended to favor the Germans, in that more of the larger British fleet was outmoded. The previous British superiority no longer existed or was considerably reduced. The situation touched off a naval building race and put Germany and England in the sternest competition. The Germans could hardly be blamed for seeing a magnificent opportunity to steal a march on the proud monarch of the seas. For their part the

English regarded supremacy on the seas as their very life blood, and the entire nation instinctively reacted to any threat to this supremacy. The high cost of this naval competition certainly stimulated adverse British reactions to Germany. There were some converts to the idea of an inevitable showdown with the kaiser. In 1909, spurred by stories of an accelerated German production of dreadnaughts, the English were chanting, "We want eight and we won't wait." Prime Minister Asquith pledged that Britain would build two ships for every one the Germans laid down, which in fact Britain could do and did.

When, partly as a result of domestic battles, Bülow resigned the German chancellorship in 1909, opportunities for fresh attempts to diminish this unfortunate rivalry emerged. The new German chancellor, Theobald von Bethmann Hollweg, who was to remain in that office until 1917, was less dashing but inspired more trust than his predecessor. There were reasonably sincere efforts on both sides to find a formula for naval peace. Though the experts in the British foreign office tended to mistrust Germany, self-interest dictated a limitation of the costly building race. On the German side, even the personification of the big navy program, Admiral Alfred von Tirpitz, friend of the emperor and a powerful influence on German policy, was prepared to go along with an agreement. Germans thought the death of King Edward VII in May 1910, removed a powerful enemy, but British policy clearly did not depend on the will of the king.

Despite somewhat promising indications, agreement proved impossible. The English insisted on keeping their naval supremacy at a ratio of two to one over the German fleet. The Germans would accept this only in return for political concessions amounting to a British renunciation of the entente with France, most especially a guarantee of British neutrality in the event of war involving Germany. This Britain would not give. Lengthy negotiations failed to find any middle ground. The Germans thought Britain owed them a concession for permitting her to maintain her naval supremacy, but the British considered this supremacy nonnegotiable and wanted an agreement only on numbers of ships to keep down costs. The Germans thought the British more vulnerable than Germany to the financial pressure of such a race. In Berlin, the kaiser and Tirpitz were not willing to sell cheaply their fond dream of Germania, the queen of the ocean.

Evaluation of this important failure contributing to the collapse of peace in 1914 must take two factors into account. First, it was not unreasonable for the British to insist on naval supremacy and to refuse even to regard it as negotiable, when one remembers that the navy was their essential defense. England had no large standing army, manned by conscripted soldiers, as did the Continental powers; her navy was also her army. It had to defend not only the homeland but the far-flung overseas empire. The whole history of England was built around sea power, and she depended on imports of food and primary materials for her livelihood. The navy was not so essential to Germany for either national defense or economic welfare. It is a luxury to you, a necessity for us, Churchill told the Germans.

Second, to ask for English neutrality in the event of war, which could plausibly be a Franco-German war, was to ask too much of a country dependent on a Continental balance of power. Could England stand by and watch France be defeated? Could she pledge her neutrality in such an encounter? On the other hand, the Germans had a legitimate interest in trying to break up or defuse what must have appeared to them as a dangerous and hostile coalition. Sea power seemed a trump card to play against England, and there was no sense in throwing it away. Thus it is hard to blame either side, though historical partisans have blamed both for arrogance and vainglory. And some of Germany's own best political brains thought it a grave mistake to alienate England in this way for no sufficient reason.

The Balkans

A second Morocco crisis was further to muddy the waters of Anglo-French-German relations in 1911. Meanwhile, the center of attention shifted to the region that was to prove the cockpit of war in 1914. Not many in the Western capitals attached high importance to what occurred in the (to them) remote and rather miserable south-eastern part of Europe, as infamous for its tangled blood feuds as for its unpronounceable names. Bismarck had once made the notable statement that the Balkan region was not worth the life of a single German soldier. Bosnia, Novibazar, and Macedonia were hardly household names in London or Paris. But in such places fate was preparing the outbreak of the great war in 1914. (A British humorist once remarked that the Balkans produced more history than they could consume locally.)

In 1908 the ambitious minister of foreign affairs in Vienna, Lexa von Aehrenthal, believed the time had come for a bold initiative in foreign policy as one way to solve the domestic difficulties of his deeply divided multinational state. Traditionally Austria-Hungary was content to follow Berlin's lead, since she was the weaker partner and wholly dependent on Germany. But Aehrenthal thought the time had come to change this passive tradition. Helping him to this decision was the fact that the little South Slav state of Serbia was being actively wooed by

Russian diplomacy, and she was a source of propaganda aimed at stirring up discontent among the South Slav (chiefly Croatian) subjects of Emperor Franz Joseph. The mounting conflict in the Balkans must be attributed in good part to three factors: one, the reorientation of Russian policy towards Europe after the crushing rebuff in the Far East in 1905; second, a palace revolution in Belgrade in 1903 that brought to the throne of Serbia a pro-Russian dynasty; and third, the continuing decay of the Ottoman Empire, culminating in the "Young Turk" revolution of 1908. All might be tied to the larger general force of nationalism.

Russian nationalists stressed Russia's Slavic mission. Speaking the Slavic tongue and sharing, to some extent, a Slavic culture with the Great Russians were the Poles; the Czechs and Slovaks; the South Slav (Yugoslav) Serbs, Croats, and Slovenians; and a few others (the Ukrainians held themselves to be a separate branch of Slavdom, though incorporated mostly in Russia). This common Slavdom by no means always meant brotherly affection; the Poles, for example, partitioned since 1795 among the three states of Russia, Germany, and Austria-Hungary, hated the Russian oppressor more than they did the Austrian. The Serbs had not always been pro-Russian, but the new ruling house, more popular and nationalistic, tended to look to Moscow as the big brother protector. Serbia's goal now was to escape from her vassalage to Austria, attain economic independence, and gain access to the sea. A small economic war went on between Serbia and the Dual Monarchy from 1906 to 1908.

Aehrenthal proposed to break up the Serbo-Russian threat. In 1878, a previous outbreak of the "Eastern question" had plunged Europe into a crisis from which Bismarck and Disraeli had rescued it at the Congress of Berlin. Since then, Austria had been permitted to administer Bosnia and Herzogovina, which adjoined the Dual Monarchy. These areas still formally belonged to the decrepit Ottoman Empire, whose decay was an underlying cause of the entire Eastern question. Austria could also keep some troops in the adjoining Sanjak of Novibazar, separating Serbia and Montenegro. These areas were populated chiefly by Serbs and Croats. Aehrenthal proposed to build a railroad through the Sanjak. The Russians challenged this as illegal. They felt that the Austrian move represented an attempt to extend her influence further into the rather amorphous territory of the Balkans in order to forestall Russia and her client, Serbia. In this way, Austria could take steps against South Slav nationalist discontent within the Dual Monarchy, the potential danger from which, of course, was enormous.

The situation was soon complicated by the Young Turk revolution, which overthrew the despotic regime of old Sultan Abdul Hamid.

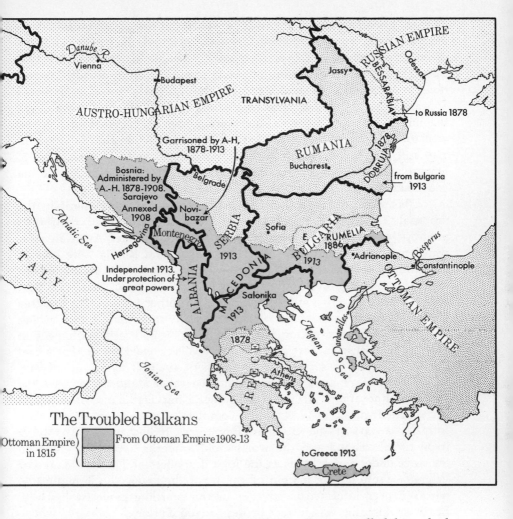

The Troubled Balkans

Ottoman Empire in 1815 | From Ottoman Empire 1908-13

The government of "Abdul the Damned," as Europe called him, had continued the low standards characteristic of the fading Ottoman Empire: cruelty, corruption, and almost every other possible mode of misgovernment. This government had scandalized the world for half a century and created most of the problems of the Balkans. In 1878 it had not been thrown out of Europe "bag and baggage," as British Prime Minister Gladstone demanded, but it had been considerably diminished. The sultanate still held some territory in Europe, including Thrace, which was coveted by Greece, and Macedonia, which was notorious for its anarchy. And, as we have noted, certain areas that still technically belonged to the Ottoman Empire were actually administered by others.

In Constantinople on July 24, 1908, a palace revolution was engineered by young army officers who deposed the sultan and announced a constitution. This revolution was stimulated by fears that the great powers would again intervene to put a stop to dreadful conditions in Macedonia, since all efforts to reform the sultan's government appeared to have failed. The immediate effects of the Young Turk revolution, however, were to sow more confusion and to cause statesmen to think that now was the time to strike, while the Balkan iron was still hot and malleable. Aehrenthal struck again: on October 5, Emperor Franz Joseph proclaimed the outright annexation of Bosnia and Herzogovina.

This was a bombshell. Intrinsically, there was some merit in the proposal. The anomalous status of the provinces impeded their own progress, and they would probably be better off under Austrian rule, which was fairly progressive. But both Serbia and Russia were sure to object to the annexation. Aehrenthal was ready to offer Russia compensation: the opening of the straits of the Dardanelles to Russian warships. He had discussed this with the Russians. But other powers had to agree to this change in the status of the strategically important straits, which involved old treaties dating back to the Crimean War's settlement in 1856. While Russian Foreign Minister Isvolsky went off to Paris and London seeking to secure their agreement (vainly, as it turned out, in the case of England), Aehrenthal went ahead and announced the Bosnian annexation! At the same time, King Ferdinand of Bulgaria declared that his country was now completely independent rather than formally a part of the Ottoman Empire, as it had been. "The lying hypocrite Ferdinand and the worthy old Emperor appear together on the stage under garish lights as the joint despoilers of Turkey!" Emperor Wilhelm wrote on the margin of the report he received. Germany had not even been informed in advance of this startling move by her ally. Berlin at this time was in fact trying to woo Turkey.

The rage of Isvolsky, who felt he had been tricked, knew no bounds, and he referred to Aehrenthal as "this dirty Jew." The anger of the Serbs, whose country was to play a key role in the coming of the great war, was equally intense. Inhabited by two and a half million people, mostly peasants, Serbia looked across the border to see some six million Serbs and Croats living under the rule of the Hapsburgs. It is true that between the Roman Catholic Croats and the Greek Orthodox Serbs some differences existed, which later hampered their efforts to live together (and still do). But at this time members of both communities declared they were a single people who should live together in an independent state. Serbia aspired to play the role that

THE BOILING POINT.

A 1912 cartoon view of the European powers and the Balkans.
Punch Publications.

Prussia had played in the unification of Germany and Piedmont in the unification of Italy. She, together with her tiny sister, Montenegro, had been the first of the Balkan peoples to win independence from Turkey, and she had developed a strong sense of mission to liberate all the South Slavs, from Austria as well as Turkey, and create a South Slav independent nation. This kind of mission was a noble one by all the standards of nineteenth-century ideology, summoning up the shades of Washington, Bolivar, Mazzini, and Garibaldi. Serbs believed in it with passion and courage. No account of the Balkan backgrounds of

World War I could leave out this moral fervor. It must also be said that the terroristic methods employed by some Serbs—the assassination of June 28, 1914, was not the first—cost their cause much sympathy.

Obviously, the annexation of Bosnia struck a blow at Serbia's hopes. In fact, the major goal of Austrian policy here was to "root out the Serbian nest of revolutionaries." The new Turkish regime also naturally opposed the loss of the provinces, and it had more claim on sympathy than the contemptible tyranny it had just overthrown. Aehrenthal clearly was in trouble. His German ally was prepared to give but lukewarm backing. Yet in the face of the Austrian *fait accompli,* Russia and Serbia proved powerless. France and England, while arguing in behalf of Russia, were not prepared to go to war for her in this cause. Grey was not even willing to give Russia her "compensation" in the form of a revision of the Straits convention. Still suffering from the military trauma of 1905, Russia was not prepared to go to war alone. Turkey was bought off with a payment of money. The angry Serbs then had no choice but to back down, though for a time in 1909 an Austro-Serb war threatened.

German opinion was thrown into an uproar when on October 28, 1908, the London *Daily Telegraph,* one of England's largest newspapers, published an interview with the kaiser. Contrary to popular belief, Wilhelm declared, he was a true friend of England, offering as proof of this that he had even offered to give them a plan for winning the Boer War! He also assured his English friends that the German navy was aimed not at them but at Japan. The interview struck almost everyone as fatuous and caused a confrontation between Wilhelm and Chancellor Bülow, who eventually resigned. During the resulting storm in Germany, the Kaiser was openly criticized from all directions, especially the Right, which was a novelty. Though well-intended, the *Daily Telegraph* interview was a typical blunder on the part of the impetuous German monarch.

Despite this distraction, Germany stood loyally by Austria-Hungary during the Bosnian crisis, grumbling only in private. It was largely through German diplomacy that the crisis was wound down. The Bosnian crisis, a most serious one, ended with Austria-Hungary annexing Bosnia, but at the price of having inflamed the Balkans, alienated Russia, and enraged Serbia. Omens were not good for the future; and the Balkans continued to simmer down to the fateful moment of June 28, 1914. Indeed, they did more than simmer; they erupted into war in 1912–1913. France had failed to help her ally, Russia, in 1908, and thus felt impelled to stand by Russia the next time. Russia now had to back Serbia, and she embarked on a diplomacy of revenge in the Balkans.

Although it is difficult to moralize about the complex affairs of nations and although Aehrenthal had excellent reasons for doing as he did, posterity has on the whole judged his 1908 initiative harshly. It stands out as a key moment in the drift toward war from 1904 to 1914.

From 1911 to 1913

Morocco popped up again in 1911 as a touchstone of French-German-British rivalries. The outcome of the first Morocco crisis had, of course, rankled in German hearts. As an aftermath of the Algeciras conference, Germany and France reached an agreement in 1909 by which, in return for French pledges to grant German economic interests equal rights with others in Morocco, Germany recognized the special French political position there, that is, her role as keeper of law and order. It did not work particularly well. In 1911 serious uprisings broke out in Morocco, making it necessary, for a time, for French troops to march into the capital city of Fez itself. The new German foreign secretary Alfred von Kiderlen-Wächter, declared that this action revoked the Algeciras agreement. To punctuate this claim, a German gunboat, the *Panther*, landed at the Moroccan port of Agadir, on the excuse that in a Morocco where the existing French-protected sultanate manifestly could not keep order, each state must defend its own citizens.

What the jovial, hard-boiled Kiderlen-Wächter wanted was compensation. If the French wanted to drop the pretense and assume sovereign power in Morocco, they might do so—but only if they gave Germany something in return. This was little short of blackmail, mitigated only by the fact that the victim was herself victimizing another. In the end Germany got a slice of the French Congo as her reward for recognizing French supremacy in Morocco. The territory itself was not worth much. Kiderlen eveidently became a little frightened at the storm he had aroused and backed down, content with a formal victory. If a victory, it was hardly worth the price, for again the British reacted with strong indications of support for France and anti-German feelings. The spectacle of a German warship in an Atlantic port galvanized all the old British suspicions of a Teutonic menace.

The second Morocco crisis was most notable for the public excitement it engendered, evidence of an inflamed nationalism. The more popular sections of the press in Germany hailed the *"Panther's* spring" with glee and rejoiced at the thought of Germany at last wresting Morocco from the greedy hands of France. The French press cried for German blood. German opinion was disappointed when not Morocco but only a piece of the Congo passed into German hands. French opinion denounced the cession as surrender to blackmail. British opinion was aroused too, as Lloyd George, once a staunch peace man, took the podium to issue solemn warnings that England would never submit to international blackmail. It was at this time that word of secret Anglo-French military cooperation, begun in 1906, was allowed to leak out. These discussions, some later alleged, constituted a de facto British alliance with France, committing Britain to France's side in any Franco-German war. The two governments had secretly agreed to remove most of the British fleet from the Mediterranean, which the French took over, leaving the Royal Navy free to guard the North Sea against Wilhelm's growing sea power.

The diplomatists themselves kept cool; Kiderlen and the veteran French ambassador, Jules Cambon, actually seemed to have enjoyed the game. Yet the general public was not playing the game at all in this spirit.

That this somewhat petty, if not sordid, squabble over colonial spoils, mixed with the politics of vindictiveness, could shake the structure of peace was not reassuring. Perhaps by this time nerves were raw from other rubbings. For the Balkans had entered the picture, first with the protracted Bosnian crisis of 1908, next with an Italian attack on Turkey, then by preparations for the two Balkan Wars of 1912–1913. Out of these grew the last fateful crisis of 1914.

The Italian attempt to seize Tripoli from the weakening hands of Turkey (as the Ottoman Empire was called after 1908) is a kind of link between the two zones of conflict, the French-British-German competition centering on Morocco and on sea power, and the Balkan rivalries of Russia, Austria, and Serbia. For in order to buy Italy's support for the Entente Cordiale and win her away from the Triple Alliance, France had promised to support Italian claims to Tripoli at an appropriate time. The Italians thought that time had come and, inflamed by a tide of nationalism, sought to make amends for former humiliations and garner a share of imperial glory.

Wounded though he was, the Turk proved a stubborn foe. This involvement of their enemy in turn encouraged the Balkan League, a union of Serbia, Bulgaria and Greece, which had been formed in 1912 with the encouragement of Russia, to attack Turkey and drive her entirely out of Europe, seizing Thrace and Macedonia as well as the Sanjak of Novibazar. The Turks hastily made peace with Italy on the latter's terms, thereby losing Tripoli. Rather surprisingly, however, they could not cope with the Balkan states in the First Balkan War of 1912. The Bulgarians overran eastern Macedonia and most of Thrace; the Serbs liberated part of Macedonia and the Sanjak; the Montenegrins seized the port of Scutari; and the Greeks were successful in southern

Macedonia and Epirus. The Serbs and Bulgars joined forces to take the important Thracian city of Adrianople. The Turk was now out of Europe "bag and baggage," except for a very small segment of Thrace. Crete also passed to Greece.

The results of the first Balkan War were a disaster for Austria-Hungary and even alarmed Russia somewhat, the tsar's government having no desire to see the Bulgarians take Constantinople. Trying to regain control of the bad children in the Balkans, the great powers held a conference at the end of 1912 to deal with the problems. The London meeting forced Serbia away from the sea by creating an independent Albania. At one point in November 1912, the powers seemed to stand on the brink of war, Germany backing Austria and Russia committed to Serbia. The Russians again backed away from war, feeling unprepared for it, and accepted a defeat for Serbia. What was ominous about this was the fear that Russia could not afford time and again to be humiliated and might next time desperately refuse to retreat.

The Balkan pot continued to boil. The victorious allies of the Balkan League proceeded to quarrel over the spoils. Never very happy together, possessing old scores of their own to settle, they fell into a renewal of the Balkan War. In July 1913, Bulgaria attacked Serbia and Greece, but she was soon defeated when Rumania, previously not involved, fell on Bulgaria from the north. In August, Bulgaria was forced to make peace, granting the lion's share of Macedonia to Serbia, surrendering the important Aegean port of Salonika to Greece, and ceding territory on her northeast border (the Dobruja) to Rumania. The Turks also regained some of Thrace. Again Austria-Hungary reacted with alarm, forcing Serbia to remove troops from Albania; but the outcome nevertheless was a considerably enlarged Serbia, almost double her former size.

In hindsight, one can see the two Balkan wars of 1912–1913 setting the stage for the explosion of 1914, heightening the tension between Serbia and Austria and applying mounting pressure on Serbia's and Austria's allies to support them. A final showdown between ambitious, rising Serbia and powerful but crumbling Austria-Hungary, fearful of her many minorities, was clearly indicated. The question was whether this conflict could be kept localized. From the vantage point of London or Paris these events seemed remote and somewhat bizarre; few there could believe they threatened a general European war. But what if a desperate Austria tried a double dose of Aehrenthalism—the destruction of Serbia as a solution for domestic problems? Would not Russia back Serbia, leading to a shoot-out between Hapsburg and Romanov for the whole southeastern theater? Could Russia let Serbia down again, and could France leave Russia in the lurch as she had in

1908? Did Germany have any other choice than to support her sole ally, Austria-Hungary? In 1914 statesmen found themselves prisoners of the past.

Acute observers in 1913 were already reading the future gloomily. In an article written for the Vienna *Neue Freie Presse*, on March 23, 1913, the distinguished German scholar Gustav Schmoller asked, "Will the Balkan flame leap over to the Great Powers?" He answered that while he believed this time the European diplomats would overcome the crisis, "the storm will sooner or later return." Later the same year, French diplomatist Paul Cambon wrote privately, "Despite my usual optimism . . . I begin to find the atmosphere a bit charged. A great deal of calm and discretion will be needed to reestablish the equilibrium which is now disquietingly unstable."

In March 1913, the Reichstag voted to increase the German Army by more than 130,000 men, added to its existing size of some 800,000. Simultaneously, the French government proposed to lengthen from two to three years the term of military service, which every able-bodied Frenchman was required to give. The measure was fiercely debated but finally approved. Russia and Austria-Hungary took similar steps, reflecting but also increasing international tension. Late in 1913, in Alsace, at Zabern, an incident that was trivial in itself took on international significance in the light of Franco-German abrasiveness. Conversations between Germany and England led to settlement of minor colonial matters but failed again to reach agreement on the big problem of naval limitations. Russia and Germany bickered over the presence of a German general as adviser to the Turkish army, which was being reorganized. Nobody would have remembered these affairs except that they later seemed like straws in the wind before the gale.

The Immediate Origins of the War

The war was evidently brought on by a conjunction of three basic clashes: the rivalry of Austria-Hungary and Russia in southeast Europe, the Franco-German hostility reaching back to 1871, and the naval competition between Germany and Great Britain. On the other hand, not all issues ranged Germany and Austria against the French-British-Russian combine. The British retained a considerable measure of mistrust of Russia. If it came to a simple choice between Russia and Austria in the Balkans, British opinion would have voted for Austria, with whom traditionally the English had no quarrel. There was little enthusiasm in London for seeing the Great Bear on the Straits, as 1908 had proved. Not long before 1914 the French tried to draw Russia into the joint military planning of the Entente, but after an initial expression of interest Grey turned away from this. As an experiment in cooperation with Russia, Persia was divided between Great Britain and Russia in 1907, but this arrangement turned out to leave something to be desired. Definitely committed to France against Germany, the British were by no means committed to Russia against Austria or anybody else. Their ambivalence in 1914, which may have been dangerous, reflected this fact.

Everything was ready for the spark that set off the explosion. Serbia had become more powerful and more ambitious as a result of the Balkan wars, and she redoubled her propaganda and her intrigues against the Dual Monarchy. In the latter's councils of state, there were powerful voices raised in favor of settling with Serbia once and for all. The assassination of Franz Ferdinand, nephew of the old emperor and heir to the throne of Austria-Hungary, on a visit to the storm center of Serb-Austrian rivalry, Bosnia, was so obviously provocative an event that all kinds of suspicions about it have naturally existed. Conspiracy theories flourished. Did the Serbian government or at least prominent Serbian circles contrive the murder? Or did Franz Joseph's high ministers deliberately sacrifice the crown prince to provide a good excuse for wiping out the troublesome Serbs? Or was it simply the action of one man who pulled the trigger on the greatest war yet in human history unknowingly? The assassination of June 28, 1914, gave rise to as many controversies and versions as did the assassination of John F. Kennedy

The Archduke Franz Ferdinand moments before his assassination, June 28, 1914 at Sarajevo. *United Press International.*

Gavrilo Princip is hustled into custody after shooting the Austrian prince. *United Press International.*

in 1963. Charges were made that prominent persons in Austria-Hungary and even Germany plotted it, if not to provide the excuse for a premeditated attack on Serbia, then to get rid of the archduke because of his views on reform within Austria-Hungary: Franz Ferdinand was thought to favor a devolution to grant the Slavs more autonomy. Many wondered why the archduke went to so dangerous a place on the very day the Serbs commemorated the loss of their independence to the Turks in 1389. Why were police precautions so lax? And on the other hand, Austria-Hungary labored to show that the terrorists who struck down the crown prince were helped by or encouraged by the Serbian government.

The murderer was a restless, idealistic, and alienated youth of a type all too familiar in the modern world. He had failed in school. His head was filled with an intoxicating cloud of the exciting ideas available at the end of the nineteenth century—socialist, anarchist, Nietzschean. Though a resident of Bosnia and technically a citizen of the Dual Monarchy, Gavrilo Princip was a passionate Serb patriot. He and his two nineteen-year old fellow conspirators were members of the Union

of Death, or Black Hand, a secret Serbian terrorist society that was
subsidized by the Russian government.

The Serbian government knew of its activities but feared to destroy
it because of public opinion. The Serbian prime minister even received
intimations of the plan to assassinate Franz Ferdinand and tried obliquely
to tip off the Vienna government, but he failed to get the message across.
The youths were smuggled to Belgrade, where they received training
and weapons, then smuggled back across the border with the aid of
Serb customs officials. The top man of the Black Hand was the chief
of intelligence of the Serbian General Staff, but the Serbian government
as such did not support him and did not want war with Austria at this
time, the Serb army having yet to recover from the Balkan Wars of
1912–1913. The assassin was thus not acting as an agent of the Serbian
government; yet it failed to take steps against the Black Hand and
against inflammatory anti-Austrian propaganda, which streamed from
the Belgrade press. Under international law, the Serbian government
could be held responsible for acts of violence emanating from its
borders against a foreign country.

Such were some of the details eventually disclosed about the
assassination, surely history's most fateful one. The emperor's government in Vienna scarcely needed most of these details to reach the
decision that the time had come to settle with Serbia once and for all.
The foreign minister, now Count Leopold Berchtold, believed it necessary "to make Serbia forever powerless to injure the Dual Monarchy."
The influential army chief of staff and practically everyone else in the
Austrian government agreed that "the very existence of Austria-
Hungary was at stake" and that the assassination, which turned world
opinion against the Serbs, was too good an opportunity to pass up. But
an immediate ultimatum to Serbia was delayed by the reluctance of the
old emperor and especially by the Hungarian prime minister, Count
Stefan Tisza, who did not want Serbia annexed to Austria-Hungary.
Berlin was consulted, too, and on July 5 Germany sent assurances of
support, the so-called "blank check" to Vienna to deal with the Serbs
as she saw fit. The delay may have been costly.

It is possible, even probable, that a quick strike at Serbia within
a few days after the assassination, while world opinion was still angry
at the Serbs, would have been allowed to pass. The effect of the German
approval was to doom all resistance to the Serbian war in Vienna, but
Tisza managed to delay matters a few days. Then for various reasons
there was a delay of several more days. One reason for the delay in
sending the ultimatum appeared to be a desire to wait until French
President Poincaré, who left for a visit to Russia with his foreign

minister on July 16, was on his way home again. For obvious reasons Vienna did not want the message received while the two allies were meeting together. Also, they waited for completion of the investigation providing evidence for Serbian complicity in the assassination plot. Not until July 23 did the ultimatum find its way from Vienna to Belgrade.

By that time the psychological moment had passed. Most people believed the crisis was over. Lloyd George in England made a speech declaring that conditions for peace were steadily improving in Europe! On July 9 British undersecretary Arthur Nicolson "expected the storm to blow over." When it blew up again, people were inclined to blame Austria. The ultimatum dispatched to Serbia was, Lord Grey claimed, the most formidable document ever sent by one state to another. It demanded not only rooting out all the terrorists in Serbia but also ending anti-Austrian propaganda in Serbia, thus implying the suppression of all newspapers engaging in this activity. To this end it demanded that Austrian officials be allowed into Serbia to oversee the work and to keep an eye on educational practices. The note was a severe ultimatum in that it demanded either a total acceptance by the the Serbs within forty-eight hours or else war. It was not expected or even desired in Vienna that the Serbs would accept these terms; they were the preliminary to a war against Serbia. But in deference to Hungarian wishes, Serbia was not to be destroyed, only forced into the role of accepting Austrian tutelage, much as minor Latin American countries had to allow the United States to police them.

If this crushing communication made a bad impression in Europe, the reply of the Serbs was a triumph. Within the stringent time limit they produced what a prominent Austrian diplomat himself called "the most brilliant specimen of diplomatic skill" he had ever known. It accepted almost all the Austrian demands, rejected some on clear constitutional grounds, and suggested arbitration of these by the Hague Court or a conference of the great powers. The note breathed a spirit of sweet reasonableness and seemed to remove all cause for war, despite its technical failure to meet all the sweeping Austrian demands. Even Wilhelm, the German emperor, believed that "every reason for war disappears," while explaining that the Austrian note had been composed without Berlin's knowledge.

But Austria had already set its war machinery in motion and was of no mind to stop it. The order to mobilize went out as soon as the forty-eight hours were up, on July 25. Eight army corps were ordered up; the other states did not know that they would not be ready until August 12. Mobilization was a process that played a critical part in the unfolding tragedy. Although the order to mobilize was thought to mean war, it took up to twenty days to bring the troops to a war footing. Germany could do it fastest; Austria-Hungary was relatively slow; and the Russians were slowest of all because of their great distances and relatively poor transportation facilities. When Austria mobilized eight corps, Russia felt impelled to begin mobilizing, too.

On July 28, Austria-Hungary declared war on Serbia. A few bombs were dropped on Belgrade the next day. Russia decreed a partial mobilization of four districts, including Kiev and Odessa near the Balkan front. They had evidently received assurance of French support from the hawkish French ambassador in St. Petersburg. By this move St. Petersburg intended to show that it was prepared for a possible war only against Austria, in defense of Serbia. This in turn stimulated the Austrians to escalate their mobilization to a total one. They were urged to this course by a telegram from the chief of the German General Staff, Helmuth von Moltke, leading to Berchtold's famous reaction: "Who then is giving the orders in Berlin?" Chancellor Bethmann was going the opposite route, trying to restrain the Austrians. And then Russia, on the 31st, changed its partial mobilization to a total one. Thus began the day that plunged Europe into the bloodiest of wars.

Volumes have been written about the Russian mobilization order, which was all-important in that it frightened Germany into taking measures designed to defend the Reich against a Russo-French squeeze. In a sense, however, the issue was a meaningless one. If Russia went to war with Austria, Germany would have to help Austria by waging war on Russia. There was no escape from the balance of power logic via partial mobilization. Almost everyone thought the tsar's government did not want war, certainly not war with Germany. Russia felt compelled to back up the Serbs and was gradually forced to the conclusion that a war with Austria-Hungary could not be avoided if Vienna insisted on assaulting the "little brother" in which Russia had invested so much political capital. But Russia had every reason to try to keep this war localized. The decision for total mobilization lies at the door of her military men, who were aware of Russia's backwardness and terrified of being caught napping. If it did come to general war, of which there undeniably was grave danger, Germany could attack Russia within a matter of a few days because of her much more efficient railway network and shorter distances to the frontier. The Russian regiments, summoned from all over the vast country so inadequately served by railways, would take weeks to assemble in military preparedness on the western borders.

The generals managed to convince the tsar and his foreign minister, Sergei Sazonov, that immediate total mobilization was essential. Nicholas took this decision with every indication of sadness and even a sense of doom. He did not want war with Germany, towards which he felt almost an affection (he had always gotten on well with his cousin the German emperor). Yet he saw no alternative.

The Russians sought to explain that their general mobilization did not necessarily mean war, that it was an essential precaution related to the peculiar circumstances of their country. But now there was no restraining the German generals from mobilization. Military imperatives were taking over. There is certainly a sense in which the Germans, too, did not want war. They (Bethmann-Hollweg and the kaiser) had come to regret the impulsively given blank check of July 5; they remembered Bismarck's advice not to be dragged into a war by Austria for Austrian purposes. Did Germany really have that much at stake in the Balkans? Plans for some compromise solution, by which Austria would get satisfaction and security from Serbia without war, emanated from the Wilhelmstrasse in the July 25–30 period. But Russian mobilization aroused the terror of encirclement. On July 31, a German ultimatum demanded that Russia cease mobilization; another addressed to France asked what course France intended to follow in the event of war between Russia and Germany. The ultimata had twelve- and eighteen-hour time limits, respectively, and the threat was of German mobilization. If the French did agree to neutrality, they were to be asked to pledge the frontier fortress cities Toul and Verdun as bond!

The Russians answered with a curt "Impossible!"; the French did not deign to answer at all. On August 1, Germany declared war against Russia, and France issued mobilization orders. At the same time the French urged the British to announce that they would fight to defend France in the event of a German attack. The British, with a divided cabinet, would not do so. Some have thought they should have, that this might have been the last hope for peace. Although this seems unlikely, the irresolution of the British government was hardly helpful. The Germans waited two days, until August 3, to declare war on France, out of a lingering hope that Britain might stay neutral if France could be induced to declare war first. A Russian-German war would certainly not draw her in; no Englishman would have fought for Russia in a war limited to the east of Europe. But in a German-French war, the likelihood of British intervention had to be rated high, whatever London might say—especially if the Germans took the initiative.

Unfortunately, as we know, the German war plans hinged on an early attack in the west, through Belgium into France, as the strategy to break the two-front nutcracker. France could thus be knocked out before the Russian army was ready. In 1870 Prussia had smashed France within a matter of weeks; in 1914 Germany was even stronger compared to France than she had been then. The strategy could hardly fail, believed the German officers, but it depended on speed of execution. Furthermore, the plan as modified since 1871 required an attack through neutral Belgium, the French having heavily fortified the Franco-German border. For the English this was certain to prove decisive. It would also put Germany generally in a bad light throughout the world, as a violator of a neutral state pledged by international agreements. Germany would begin the war and begin it as a treaty breaker. Such were the plan's grave political defects, which did not overcome its military advantages in the eyes of Germany's policy makers.

Some Final Considerations

Thus the war began, to the incredulity of most of the world, when the Germans marched into Belgium on August 4. All bluffs had been called. On the eve of the war a German diplomat (Ruedorffer) wrote a book in which he declared that diplomacy had become a game of bluff entirely, since no one wished to make war. Everyone bluffed with increasing recklessness, arguably, because each was sure the bluffs would never be called. Thus the widespread feeling that in the end no one would *really* go to war may have contributed to the coming of war. One gambles for high stakes if one is pretty sure one will never have to pay. But there had been too many uncalled bluffs for the game to continue this way. The moment of reckoning finally came.

Controversy about the origins of the war both during the war and after it, when more data became available, roared on and on. It became a major scholarly industry, as well as a continuing popular polemic; it is perhaps the classic historical debate. Such debates are in the end not entirely resolvable, since unprovable value judgments as well as factual evidence are involved. However, a good many things were eventually decided beyond reasonable cavil.

Only the least critical can believe in a deliberate plot of aggression. The nations were prisoners of their fears, and all acted as they thought they had to in self-defense. Austria-Hungary certainly willed the destruction of Serbia and was ready to go to war to achieve it; in this sense Vienna was guilty, and her policy from 1908 on was both aggressive and reckless. But public opinion throughout the Dual Monarchy was convinced that the very existence of the state was at stake. Not a German nor an Austrian but a British commentator, the fair-minded G. L. Dickinson, conceded that no state in existence "would not under similar circumstances have determined, as Austria did, to finish the menace, once for all, by war." Serbia had attacked her with words and deeds, with propaganda and murder when she was already mortally menaced by internal crisis. The old emperor, Francis Joseph, was not a warmonger but the most respected gentleman in Europe; yet in the end he saw no other solution (it is not correct to say that Berchtold and Conrad tricked him).

The whole conduct of the Austrians during the final crisis speaks against any preconceived plan to wage war. As we know, their long delay may even have been one cause of the war. Had they been prepared to swoop down on Serbia within hours or even days of the murder, they probably could have carried it off without reaction from the other powers. But they delayed, argued, and finally after nearly four weeks produced not an attack but an ultimatum—and they began mobilizing their troops, which took three more weeks, only after Serbia's reply to the ultimatum. This was the response of both a cumbersome bureaucracy and a divided council, reflecting less an iron will to war than a floundering about from which war was a kind of last resort.

It is equally vain to blame the Serbs, who were in the grip of nationalism, for wanting to unite the South Slavs. It is futile, too, to blame nationalism itself. A deeply human emotion, nationalism was backed by the force of powerful nineteenth-century ideologies, and it appealed especially to peoples who had lived in the shadows of history, backward and ill-treated, and who wanted to assert their dignity and worth. We would have to condemn Washington and Lincoln, Bolivar and Saint-Martin, Joan of Arc, Martin Luther, and Martin Luther King— indeed, condemn virtually the whole of modern history—if we were to reject nationalism.

One school tried hard to shift the blame from the Central Powers to Russia, noting how deviously the Russians intrigued in the Balkans after 1908. They helped organize the Balkan League and poured money into Serbian terrorism. By backing Serbia in 1914, they converted a local conflict into a general war. They were greedy for the Straits. But Russia could plead legitimate interest in the fate of fellow Slavs and in the need for access to the sea. The humiliation of 1908 damaged the tsar's prestige and made future diplomatic defeats intolerable. Many sins can be laid at the door of the tsar's government, no doubt, but it did not want war in 1914. It simply saw no honorable alternative to backing a client and ally against the threat of extermination that would ruin Russia's status forever throughout southeastern Europe. The prestige of great powers may strike us as unworthy, but it exists as a brute fact of political life and human nature. Russia's severe internal problems made the tsar's throne itself shaky, as 1905 proved; he felt unable to afford another international humiliation.

During the war and for a long time afterward most people in England and France assumed that Imperial Germany had plotted war and that the kaiser was a great criminal. But in fact Berlin did not call the shots in the Balkan crisis; she was as unconsulted by Berchtold in 1914 as she had been by Aehrenthal in 1908. On the eve of the war she was trying to restrain Austria as best she could. Erratic, impulsive, on the whole a misfortune for his people and for Europe, Wilhelm did not want war in 1914 in any deliberate sense. The Germans suffered severely from the fear of encirclement for understandable reasons. They were surrounded by the hostile Franco-Russian team, believed they had been deliberately snubbed in 1904, thought the English arrogantly denied them great-power status on the seas. When the German emperor told the American emissary Colonel E. M. House just before the war that "every nation in Europe has its bayonets pointed at Germany," he was doubtless sincere. Germany in 1914 simply could not afford to abandon her last ally, Austria-Hungary, in her hour of need. The plans that dictated Germany's aggression against Belgium, right or wrong, were the fruits of long consideration on how to avert disaster in a two-front war.

French diplomacy pulled off the most brilliant but the most dangerous coups of the preceding decade by winning first Russia and then Britain as allies, breaking out from the isolation that Bismarck had imposed on France. (She was helped in this feat, of course, by German ineptness.) French desires for a return to a position of pre-eminence in Europe were understandable in view of the shock and humiliation of 1871, feelings that were kept alive by the German annexation of Alsace-Lorraine. Equally natural was her fear of her much more powerful neighbor to the east, which possessed a mighty army, a greater population by far (some sixty-five as against forty million people), and an increasing industrial superiority. France needed allies to feel secure against the threat of Germany. France certainly did not want war in 1914, but she felt, like Germany, that she could not abandon an ally, the more so because she had previously let Russia down. If Germany could not see Austria crushed by Russia, France could not stand by while Germany and Austria smashed Russia.

British diplomacy has been blamed for irresolution, not only by others but by the English themselves; Lord Derby expressed a common view when he remarked in 1920, "I have always believed that if Germany had known we were going to range ourselves along side of France, she would never have unleashed the offensive." But this irresolution was inherent in the British position. Moreover, Derby's proposition is questionable, if only because the Germans counted on a quick victory over France, a victory that the British, who kept no large standing army, would be able to affect very little. The British cabinet was divided on going to war even after the German invasion of Belgium. Two cabinet members resigned over the issue. Most English citizens saw no advantage in supporting Russia. Britain was not committed to the defense of France by any formal alliance. In reality, it was impossible for Britain to allow Germany to overrun France, but British reluctance to be drawn into the maelstrom of the Continent's alliances was old and deep-rooted. Lord Morley, in his memorandum on resignation from the cabinet, said, "If Germany is beaten and Austria is beaten, it is not England and France who will emerge preeminent in Europe. It will be Russia. Will that be good for Western Civilization?"

A great majority of the English in 1914 finally disagreed; but since British opinion rested on such nebulous calculations about the balance of power, rather than on direct and obvious interests, it was necessarily somewhat uncertain. Eyre Crowe's key memorandum of July 24 asked, what if Germany crushed France and stood on the Channel, with her sea power as well as her military might? But Crowe, notably anti-German, also raised the question, what if France and Russia won without England? Or were defeated and then joined Germany in an attack on Britain? The only conclusion was that to defend her interests Britain had to enter the war, one way or another! It may be noted that Germany offered the British assurances that she would annex no French, Belgian, or Dutch territory as a result of the war if Britain would remain neutral.

If it is difficult to make any one state the villian, it is equally hard to blame any one class or economic interest group. It is an illusion to suppose that great capitalists or financiers had much direct influence; few of them were anywhere near the corridors of power. A fairly small body of professional diplomatists made policy. In the last analysis a handful of men committed Europe to the flames in 1914. Of all types represented in this ruling political elite, men of business were the least prominent. In Russia and very largely in Austria and Germany, the diplomatic corps was a last preserve of the aristocracy; it was filled with people who abhorred businessmen as vulgar. The Liberal government of Asquith and Grey in England, devoted to social reform in its domestic policies, was not known for its closeness to capitalistic economic interests. The news of the war caused stock markets to plunge all over Europe, and Lloyd George reported finding no man of finance or industry in the country who was not appalled by the war, which they thought would bring socialism or revolution.

The prime minister and the foreign minister of France were both (independent) socialists, and we must note that the socialists as well as the trade unionists, the working class, rallied enthusiastically in support of their countries, forgetting whatever vows they had made to socialist internationalism. This was also true of the intellectuals—the vast majority of writers, artists, historians, scientists, clergymen, all hailed, blessed, and delighted in the war at its beginning. The later attempt to find scapegoats for what was at its start "the most popular war in history" cannot conceal this fact. A war into which professional politicians had blundered could not have been waged for more than four years without the nearly total commitment of popular opinion.

The argument occasionally presented that Europe's leaders deliberately sought war as a way out of severe domestic difficulties is also preposterous. A superficial case for it, based on circumstantial evidence, can be made. There *were* serious problems at home. Asquith, just after the assassination and before the magnitude of the Serbian crisis became apparent, remarked to a friend that he welcomed it because it would take people's minds off Ireland! But it would be grotesque to argue that Britain helped rig up a war to escape from the Irish question. As we know, it is correct to say that Austria-Hungary regarded the elimination of Serbia as a solution for the minorities problem at home. But she did not want, and hoped somehow to avoid, general European war. There were serious strikes in Russia, serious constitutional issues in Germany on the eve of 1914. But these had existed many times before without bringing war. Social conditions generally in 1914 were not worse but better than they had been in 1878 or 1885 or 1898, and war had been averted in each of those years. Anyway, it was no answer to leap from internal fire into external frying pan. Nicholas of Russia was sadly aware that a war would bring down his regime. Regimes weakened by threat of revolution can seldom afford the risk of war. A threat of internal dissolution from the Slavic minorities did exist in Austria-Hungary and possibly in Russia, but not elsewhere in 1914. The workers who had struck with frequency during the 1905–1914 period sought not social revolution but tangible economic benefits within the going capitalistic system.

Imperialism was not a main cause of the war, either. Colonies or protectorates sometimes served as pawns in the game of power, but they were not an essential component. Morocco had no great economic value either to the French or the Germans; they quarreled over it because of prestige. France and Britain had been the chief colonial rivals from 1880 to 1904, but their rivalry did not lead them to war, and they used colonial concessions to cement their alliance. Great Britain and Germany were able to resolve such colonial issues as the Baghdad Railway in 1913–1914; they went to war for other reasons. Southeastern Europe was the chief arena of conflict leading to World War I. The rival interests of Russia and Austria were indeed deployed there, in a matter, however, of power and strategy more than economics, for this was the poorest part of Europe.

Military men, far more influential in decision making than were businessmen, did play too great a role. Historians have noted, probably correctly, the relative weakness of the civilian leadership. Bethmann-Hollweg, the kaiser, Grey, Viviani, Sazanov, Nicholas II, Berchtold were not an impressive lot, to say the least. They "glided, or rather staggered and stumbled" into a war they did not want was the verdict of Lloyd George. Rather irresponsible militarists, such as the kaiser's friend Tirpitz; Conrad Hoetzendorff, the Austrian chief of staff; the mad Russian Sukhomlinov found their judgments too readily accepted. It is hardly correct to argue, as used to be done, that "the enormous growth of armaments," in Grey's words, led to war. By today's standards military budgets were not large. More to the point, nations arm because they are afraid; thus the real cause is to be sought in the reasons for their insecurity. The naval race between Germany and England clearly takes rank as one of the several primary and unresolved antagonisms that lie in the background of the war; by itself, however, it would not have led to war. It had been going on for some years by 1914, was not any worse than it had been, and in fact seemed to be improving. Winston Churchill has described how just hours before the outbreak of war, German and British sailors fraternized during ceremonies at Kiel.

Virtually no one had expected war; it came with dramatic suddenness. When it did come, the typical reaction was not that of Edward Grey. Standing at his office window on the night of August 4 and watching the lamps flicker off as the British ultimatum to Germany to withdraw from Belgium expired, Grey said, "The lights are going out all over Europe, and no one now living will ever see them come back again." The historian must regretfully record that a sense of joy rather than of gloom prevailed. Huge cheering crowds surrounded the kaiser, stood outside Buckingham Palace, saluted departing French troops at the railroad stations, made love publicly in St. Petersburg. A Parisian observer on August 2 described a "human torrent, swelling at every corner" screaming, shouting singing the "Marseillaise." In Berlin, crowds passed through the streets incessantly for two days singing "Deutschland über alles" and "Wacht am Rhein." A mob attacked the German embassy in St. Petersburg. An "indescribable crowd" blocked the streets around government offices in London a few minutes after midnight August 4–5, and continued to fill the streets for days. It was with exultation, not sorrow, that the peoples of Europe greeted the war, a fact that in the last analysis may go farther to explain its coming than all the details of diplomacy.

The Great War
of 1914-1918

3

The First Year

In his memorable description of the battle of Borodino in *War and Peace*, Tolstoy argued that on the battlefield all is confusion, plans go awry, orders are not carried out, and in this "fog of war" chance determines the outcome. The German General Staff thought it had reduced war to an exact science, but the outcome of history's most famous gamble, the attack through Belgium that began on August 4, 1914, perhaps vindicated the Russian author. In the end, the German offensive failed by a margin small enough to have depended on accidents. Certainly some plans did go astray; some orders were disobeyed. One celebrated story attributes the German defeat to a disobeyed British command. At the battle of Le Cateau, Sir Horace Smith-Dorrien declined to follow his order to retreat, probably thereby saved the little British Expeditionary Force from annihilation, and may have saved the whole Allied cause. His stand checked the Germans and allowed time for Allied consolidation prior to the critical counterattack along the Marne River. This counterattack frustrated the German drive, which up to then, after four weeks of steady advance, was ahead of schedule in its plan to turn the left flank of the French armies in one mighty thrust.

(For his pains the British officer was implacably persecuted by the incompetent British commander in chief, Sir John French.)

Moltke, the German commander, was so sure of victory at that point that he took troops away from the western front to send to meet the Russians, who were advancing in the east more rapidly than most had thought possible. Joffre's improvised counterthrust between two German armies halted the German offensive. The German armies had outrun their supplies, stretched their endurance too far, and lost their communications on the very threshold of victory. The "miracle of the Marne" resuscitated French morale.

The biggest mistake about the war was the almost unanimous prediction that it would be a short one, lasting six months or, at the outside, a year. Previous experience as well as general principles argued for this. Since 1867 all European wars had been brief; the destructive force of modern armies seemed too great to be sustained very long. The whole German strategy was based on the premise that one great battle would probably settle it. In England, the brilliant young economist John Maynard Keynes explained to his friends that the war could not last much more than a year, because convertible capital would be exhausted. What happened confounded generals and economists alike. The defensive suddenly triumphed over the offensive, technology dictated long stalemates on the western front, and the people found ways to supply and endure the war for more than four agonizing years.

Once the massive German thrust had collapsed just short of its objective, with the guns of battle audible in Paris, the two armies tried to outflank each other. Reaching to the English Channel to the northwest and the mountains to the southeast, they dug in for the winter and thereafter found they could not move each other at whatever cost of lives. Armies did not have tanks, as they would have in 1940. Each side built deep fortifications of trenches, barbed wire, and concrete "pill boxes" that defied enemy attack. (No one had anticipated this essentially improvised defense.) When attacks were tried, they resulted in appalling losses for paltry gains of territory. The sweeping fire of machine guns mowed down the advancing foot soldiers even after hours or days of cannonading had prepared their way.

Though deep in French territory, the Germans had not destroyed the French armies. With a million troops tied down on the western front, they faced war in the east against Russia. As a million volunteers joined the British army, the Allied position strengthened, even though the Germans had a slight advantage of interior lines. Having failed in their great gamble and facing the dreaded encirclement, the Germans were in a grave situation. However, they succeeded brilliantly in the east.

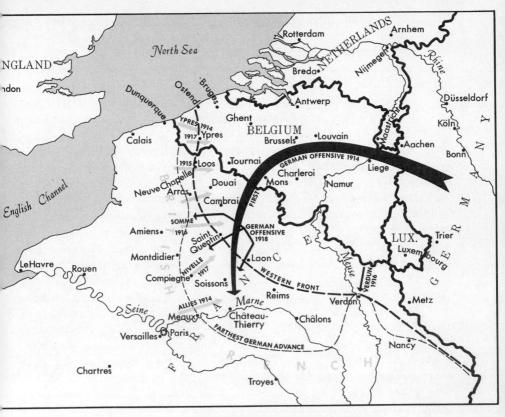

The Western Front, 1914–1918

At the beginning of the war, the total population and potential resources of the Entente or Allied powers, France, Russia, and Great Britain, considerably exceeded those of the Central Powers, Germany and Austria-Hungary. One must add Serbia to the Allied side, of course; and within a year Italy and Rumania joined the Allies, while Turkey and Bulgaria threw in their lot with the Germans. The population of the three main Allied countries outnumbered Germany and Austria-Hungary by about 245 million to 115 million, better than two to one. The British, controlling the international sea lanes, could draw additional strength from their dominions and colonies. But two-thirds of the Allied population was in ill-equipped Russia, which soon revealed its inadequacy for modern warfare. On the other hand, Germany's ally, Austria-Hungary, was severely handicapped by its many doubtfully loyal minorities. The acquisition of Italy was supposed to be a coup for the Allies; but Turkey aided the German cause even more by making it difficult to ship badly needed supplies to Russia through the Straits.

The German army was probably the best in the world, but the French army was excellent, too. Germany held about a tenth of France, including the most industrialized part, which contained 4/5 of French coal and 9/10 of her iron resources, plus an excellent rail network around Lille; the Germans also occupied almost all of Belgium, including the port of Ostend, which proved valuable as a submarine boat base.

In terms of military strength, then, one can find many reasons for the long stalemate that ensued, in which each side was to suffer cruel frustration. In the end, the New World tilted the balance.

The Russians had advanced quickly against eastern Germany, loyally carrying out their commitment to France, and perhaps they forced withdrawal of German troops from the west. At any rate, whether from overconfidence or anxiety, Moltke shifted a substantial number of men on August 25. But the results were dismaying to the tsar's forces. In February 1914, a Russian official named Durnovo had written a memo in which he argued that war with Germany would prove fatal to Russia, because of his country's "technical backwardness," her "insufficient network of strategic railroads," and her "embryonic" industries. He was right. The Russian troops were magnificently brave and capable at times of great élan, as well as incredible feats of endurance, but they lacked equipment, supplies, transport, medical care, and adequate military organization. They sent messages uncoded on the new radio equipment of which they had too little, and they forgot to tell each other where they were taking their armies. The Germans dealt them shattering and demoralizing blows in the early battles on the eastern front. Surrounded at Tannenberg at about the same time as the climax of the war in the west in late August, a Russian army lost 120,000 prisoners, and its commander committed suicide. The defeat was soon repeated at the Masurian Lakes. Here there was no trench-warfare stalemate, for the terrain was not suitable, and the Russians lacked the equipment and supplies.

On the other hand, the Russians defeated the armies of Austria-Hungary. (Even the Serbs were able to do that in early December; it took Bulgarian aid to overrun Serbia in 1915.) At the Carpathian frontier in southern Poland, the Austro-Hungarians lost 350,000 men. But the Russians were unable to exploit the victory, for as they plunged into the Dual Monarchy their supply lines became too long, and the Germans sent troops to stiffen the Austrian armies. This pattern was to be repeated.

By the beginning of 1915 Russia was already in bad shape. Of her six million soldiers no more than a third could even be supplied with rifles. Accepting their disastrous inferiority to the Germans, the Russians confined offensive operations thereafter to the south, where they again attacked the Dual Monarchy in March 1915, forcing their way through the Carpathian passes at great cost. At this time, Italy was moving toward entrance into the war on the Allied side. The goal of knocking out Austria seemed feasible, a feat that might persuade the small neutrals, Rumania and Greece, to "come to the rescue of the winning side." But the Germans rescued Austria again, and the Russians were drawn in too far. They suffered from a counteroffensive that caused them to flee in a near rout, losing practically all of Poland in the summer of 1915.

But the Germans could not win the war by mauling the Russians. Unlike Napoleon and, later, Hitler, the German generals refused to be tempted into an invasion of Russia. There was a great debate about this. Paul von Hindenburg, German commander of the eastern front, wanted to invade Russia, but he was overruled. Chief of Staff Falkenhayn argued that there was no way of annihilating a country with such immense reserves of space and manpower, whose transport problem would improve as her armies returned homeward. It would be preferable to hold the front with relatively small forces. But the Russians would not make a separate peace, although forces around the tsar, including Rasputin, wished to do so. With quixotic gallantry the tsar stayed in the war, even assuming personal command of the armies in September 1915—a step often seen as crucial on the road to revolution, for it laid Nicholas' personal prestige on the line.

Both Germany and the Western Allies, it appeared, were "fettered to a corpse." The most promising or at least imaginative idea on the Allied side in 1915 was to revive their corpse by injecting the lifeblood of supplies. Substantially cut off from the West, Russia could hope to receive such badly needed equipment only through the Straits of Constantinople, but Turkey blocked this route. To knock Turkey out of the war by a combined naval and land assault, thus opening communications between the Western allies and Russia, was an obvious strategic idea. Credit for it is usually awarded to the dynamic Winston Churchill, who was serving as first lord of the admiralty in the British cabinet. But both the British naval mission commander in Turkey and the Greek General Staff had thought of this earlier than Churchill, who did urge it as early as September 1914 and continued to back it. Unfortunately a divided Greece refused to enter the war on the Allied side, King Constantine, a brother-in-law of the kaiser, being pro-German. Had Greece followed the wishes of Prime Minister Venizelos, who later rebelled against the king to set up a separate, pro-Allied government at Salonika (1916), the Dardanelles campaign might have turned out differently.

As it happened, however, the failure of the Dardanelles campaign cost Churchill his job and almost his career. Aided by German advisers and two German warships that had slipped through the Mediterranean, the Turks possessed formidable defenses. From Whitehall came much debate and many delays in mounting the campaign. Unfortunately any plan to divert extensive forces, either naval or land, to the eastern theater (Lloyd George backed another plan to send troops through the Aegean to Serbia) ran into opposition from those who argued that it was dangerous to denude the western front or the North Sea, where the British navy stood guard against a possible eruption of the German fleet from its Heligoland lair. An Anglo-French fleet bombarded the Straits in February 1915, stopped, resumed again in March, and brought in an expeditionary force only in late April, by which time the Turks had had time to bolster defenses. Surprise was lost, and the initial expeditionary force was too small.

The Gallipoli peninsula, which extends out like an upper jaw over the narrow passageway that links Europe and Asia, proved a trap for the mainly British and Australian-New Zealand troops who fought there all through the long, hot summer of 1915. Reenforcements had to be sent, which intensified the dispute within the British government about priorities. To no avail over 200,000 men were lost (dead and wounded), along with some naval vessels, victims of German submarines. Though Turkish losses were at least equally heavy, the expedition was finally withdrawn. This episode damaged not only Churchill but the Asquith government itself and became a prize example of faulty planning in this war in which nothing seemed to go right. It was an appropriate end to the first frustrating year of war.

1916: The Year of Slaughter

The Central Powers might take comfort from Gallipoli and from the brilliant German performance against Russia, which was achieved with much smaller numbers of troops. The eastern front lay almost quiet from October 1915 to March 1916, as the Russian bear licked his deep wounds. During this period Bulgaria entered the war on the German side. Striking at Serbia from the southeast while Austro-German forces invaded her from the northwest, Bulgaria brought about Serbia's defeat. What remained of the gallant Serb army escaped in a wild flight into Albania, whence it was conveyed by British and Italian ships to the island of Corfu (technically a Greek possession). After this, Venizelos set up his pro-Allied Greek splinter regime in Salonika, which was occupied by Allied troops departing from Gallipoli.

All this, however, was not very decisive. The Allies were mildly

Trench warfare on the Western front, July, 1916. *Courtesy Imperial War Museum.*

heartened by Italy's adhesion to their cause in May 1915, by a growing war trade with the United States, and by Japan's entry on the Allied side in August. But 1916 was to be the year of the western front: the year of Verdun and the Somme.

During 1915, the western front was relatively quiet as the rival forces perfected their defenses by digging, stringing barbed wire, and cementing pill boxes. What action there was gave ominous warning of the difficulties of an offensive. The Allies were tempted to try one anyway to help Russia, the Germans because, landlocked and blockaded, they were more vulnerable to a war of attrition. Both sides wanted to mount an offensive because an impatient public saw little sense in a war that lasted forever. Armies were expected to win wars, not sit dejectedly in trenches. With the collapse of the Dardanelles campaign, Allied attention returned to the main theater; meanwhile, the Germans absorbed the fact that they could not win the war by mauling the Russians, no matter how badly. So 1916 was fated to be a year of sickening losses in France and Belgium.

Analyzing the situation, German General Staff Chief Falkenhayn convinced himself of the necessity for a German offensive in the west.

The impregnable fortress of Verdun was a symbol of France's will to resist. Falkenhayn seems to have reasoned like the football coach who says, "attack them at their strongest point," (though the defenses of the Verdun trench line had been left relatively thin by Joffre). The great battle of Verdun, the largest of the war, began in February and was not broken off until December, thus stretching over most of the year; it is estimated to have cost the unimaginable total of 700,000 casualties, of whom slightly more were French than German. Falkenhayn believed that the French would be bled white at Verdun and that they could afford the losses less than more populous Germany. If, as has been claimed, Verdun was the most terrible battle in all history, Falkenhayn's decision must surely stand as history's greatest folly, if not its greatest crime.

The German offensive began with a titanic artillery barrage from 850 big guns, including 420 of the huge "big Berthas." Advised to withdraw to the more easily defended west bank of the Meuse River, Premier Briand refused on the grounds of morale; he had taken the German bait in prizing Verdun as a symbol. In the swaying and bloody battles of the next months, the defense of Verdun did indeed raise French morale. It became a national expression of the will to resist: "They shall not pass." Verdun sealed the fate of General Falkenhayn, who became one of many high military leaders to fall in disgrace during this war. Among the French, however, a reputation was made, a rarity in this war: General Henri Petain emerged a hero.

Falkenhayn's example did not keep the Allies from a similar madness. The hell of Verdun was followed by the slaughter on the Somme. The Somme offensive was waged partly to get the British involved; the French being engaged in paying their sacrifice of life at Verdun, it seemed monstrous that the British should not bleed too. This chiefly British-held sector lay some 150 miles northwest of Verdun in the north of France (Flanders), within 50 miles of the English Channel. Here were to fall hundreds of thousands of British soldiers, nearly all of them volunteers. The attack was preceded by *seven days* of continuous bombardment, creating an unearthly noise that seemed to some like a strange music. The assault began on July 1, with 100,000 men advancing across "no man's land"; more than half of them were killed or wounded, setting the pattern for all that followed. The immense bombardment had not destroyed the deeply planted German machine gunners. For weeks the grisly battle went on. Although Douglas Haig, the British commander, had hoped for a breakthrough, it turned into a battle of attrition, like Verdun. The Germans suffered terribly, but the British could gain only slight ground, and any gain was subject to being wiped out by a well-timed counterattack before engineering could

Shelling to prepare for an attack: eight-inch howitzers at the Battle of the Somme. *Courtesy Imperial War Museum.*

consolidate it. The total losses in the vast Somme battle seem to have exceeded even those at Verdun.

At least two million men died in battle in Europe in 1916. In addition to the titanic struggles on the western front, the Austrians and Italians were busy fighting in the east. To take pressure off both the French at Verdun and the Italians in the Trentino, the Russians gallantly if inexplicably renewed the war on the eastern front in June. They had raised new armies and accumulated supplies since the 1915 disaster. After an ineffective tangle with the Germans in March, the Russians reverted to their favorite target, Austria, under fresh leadership from General Alexei Brusilov. Seeking this time the advantage of surprise, something that days of preliminary bombardment at Verdun and the Somme obviously failed to attain, Brusilov launched attacks on a broad front from eastern Poland south to the Rumanian border. These began successfully; an Austrian army was routed, gains up to fifty miles made, many prisoners taken. But the Russians could not exploit their gains. They ran out of supplies, and Germans were sent to stiffen the Austrian forces. To the north, Russian commanders feared to attack German armies with good reason. At the cost of much acrimony between the two Central Powers, substantially a single command under German management was now created over the whole eastern front.

"Brusilov is the only commander of the First World War after whom a great victory has been named," war historian Cyril Falls noted. The Brusilov offensive was a stellar one-man performance, but it was not enough. Curiously, so great an effort had the effect of sinking both sides, the Hapsburg and Romanov empires. For the Dual Monarchy it was a staggering blow, and, as we have just noted, Vienna lost independent control of its forces to Berlin. The death of the old Emperor Franz Joseph shortly thereafter sealed the fate of the polygot empire, and it began to dissolve. Its threatened dissolution had begun the war, and the war completed that dissolution.

For Russia, the Brusilov campaign was also the last straw. From here the road led steadily toward the 1917 revolutions and the breakup of her suffering armies. Another country also suffered: at the height of Brusilov's success, Rumania was finally persuaded to enter the war on the side of the Allies, having been promised both Transylvania and some Bulgarian territory. The Rumanian army proceeded to attack in both directions, only to encounter double trouble. One of its opponents was the recently deposed German commander in chief, Erich von Falkenhayn, who proved himself a capable field commander in a brilliant campaign in the Transylvanian Alps. As a Bulgarian-Turkish-German army invaded from the south while Falkenhayn crashed through from the north, most of Rumania was overrun and the capital, Bucharest, taken. Aided by rain and the onset of winter, the Rumanians were able to hang on to a piece of their country in the north, establishing an emergency capital at Jassy.

The bloody year of 1916, during which the storms of battle swirled from the English Channel to the plains of Rumania and the mountains of Italy, tested men's courage and endurance to the limit. Yet in the end victory again eluded both sides, and stalemate was the word at the year's end as much as at its beginning. In one further arena, the result was a draw. War at sea broke out for just about the only time in a major battle between the rival war fleets at the celebrated Battle of Jutland, fought May 31–June 1, 1916. The bulk of the British navy stood guard in the North Sea, maintaining the blockade of Germany but not willing to risk destruction by venturing into the Baltic. Had the British navy destroyed the German Fleet, it would have opened a lifeline to Russia. For its part, the German fleet did not dare go out to take on the larger Royal Navy, although it did conduct night raids on British ports. The Germans had a powerful naval fortress at Heligoland in the North Sea, from which the ships could slip back into the Baltic through the Kiel Canal should the British try sailing through the Skagerrak. The bulk of the British dreadnaught fleet stayed at Scapa Flow, off the north coast of Scotland.

The one great naval battle of the war was not exactly planned; it resulted from German Admiral Scheer's tactic of attempting to divide the British fleet by luring part of it out to pursue raiders and then hitting that part with the German main fleet. During this engagement, to speak of the "fog of war" is an understatement; it would require a volume to describe the confusion of ships all over the North Sea in an intricate naval chess game of which both commands lost track. The fog was more than a metaphor. At one point, Scheer's trick seemed to have backfired and the British had him trapped. The German ships escaped by sailing north, while Jellicoe, the British admiral, guessed south; the Germans made their way home the long way, through the Skagerrak and around Denmark—a fitting end to a confusing battle.

When it was all over, after a furious afternoon and night, both sides bore scars, and their mutual respect was intensified. The British losses were slightly greater than the German in terms of tonnage sunk and casualties; but the British dreadnaught fleet remained powerful, and the Germans had had a close call.[1] Neither side cared to repeat the performance. For the British the risk was too great, since to lose their fleet would bring down the whole blockade and the assurance of their world supply routes, including the growing trade with the United States. The Germans turned increasingly to submarine warfare; the High Seas fleet's idleness in port was a cause of the mutiny that later broke out at Kiel. Historian Arthur Marder, a leading student of the Royal Navy in this war, claimed that it actually won a great victory at Jutland, though this was not everywhere appreciated, especially by the French. The British fleet contained and rendered impotent the kaiser's proud navy. But by denying the Baltic (and the Straits) to Allied sea power, the German fleet guaranteed the collapse of Russia.

The Crises of 1917

In desperate straits, leaders searched for a way out of the terrible impasse. Tanks were used for the first time by the British late in the Somme campaign, but they were yet too few and too primitive to have much influence. It was not until 1918, in the last months of the war, that they made any significant contribution. Airplanes were, of course, available in World War I; the "dog fights" of individual aviators in one-seaters provided about the only exciting dimension of the war. But these tiny craft were used mainly for reconnaissance, in which

---

[1] The ships lost were entirely battle cruisers, light cruisers, and predreadnaught battleships; no dreadnaught was sunk. Submarines as well as surface ships were used in this battle.

Aerial dogfight. About the only romance of the 1914–1918 war was provided by the intrepid "aces" who duelled each other one-on-one in fragile aircraft.
The Granger Collection.

capacity they were helpful to ground forces but did not play an independent tactical role. Zeppelin raids, before these unwieldy monsters were abandoned in 1917 after numbers were shot down or blew away, killed or wounded about 1,800 in London, a few less than airplane raids; Paris suffered more from long-range cannon in 1918 than from air attack. The day of the bomber lay far ahead. Tanks and military aircraft, the two chief innovations that emerged from the war, were developed afterwards. Although they dominated World War II, they had nothing like that capacity yet in the first war.

More widely used was poison gas. It was also widely discussed as one of the more hideous ideas of World War I. Allied propaganda made much of the German inauguration of chlorine gas in 1915 on the western front, but both sides occasionally used chlorine, mustard, and tear gas thereafter. The trouble was that winds were too prone to shift, and gas masks could be used as counteragents.

As the carnage continued into 1917, military leaders' careers were ruined, the penalty for their failure to find a way to victory and to avoid the frightful casualties. It was a veritable slaughter of the top brass and some civilians, too. After Joffre had removed over a hundred French generals in the first few months, he himself had to go in 1916. Moltke, the first German commander in chief, gave way to Falkenhayn, who in turn left after Verdun. Douglas Haig succeeded John French as chief military commander on the British side, only to be tagged as the butcher of the Somme. Churchill was the victim of Gallipoli, and in 1916 Lord Kitchener, the British war secretary, was lost at sea when, starting on a visit to Russia, his ship hit a mine left over from the recent Battle of Jutland. He had been under strong attack, and the Russian visit was partly to get him out of the way. The Russian war minister, Sukhomlinov, was tried for high treason but convicted only of gross incompetence.

These are only some examples of the premature retirements that were forced in this war. They reached a scale hardly matched in history. Nor were the heads of government immune. France switched premiers twice before choosing the old "tiger," Georges Clemenceau in 1917. After one cabinet shakeup in May 1915, Herbert Asquith was deposed as British prime minister in late 1916, a major upheaval bringing in a coalition headed by David Lloyd George. The maneuver left permanent scars on the Liberal party. "War always destroys the government that waged it," John Bright had claimed This proved true in 1914–1918, for no government in power at the beginning was there at the end, and in three cases the fall encompassed the entire regime. German Chancellor Bethmann-Hollweg was to lose his office in 1917, preceding his emperor by only a little more than a year.

The vast, unprecedented demand for material was one problem for ministers. The habit of prefacing any attack by up to seventeen days of steady bombardment, with hundreds of heavy guns and thousands of smaller ones virtually wheel to wheel for miles, naturally required quite a bit of ammunition. It is estimated that at the 1917 battle of Messines alone, three and a half million shells were fired. Millions of tons of high explosives were also set off underground, planted by miners under the Messines ridge near Ypres, the Belgian town around which four mighty battles were fought during the war. Such war requirements forced a kind of "war socialism," in which the government had to ration goods, set priorities, impose price and wage controls, and requisition factories. In Britain, War Secretary Kitchener and Commander in Chief John French, both of whom were incapable of handling their demanding jobs, bickered constantly, French claiming he got insufficient supplies of ammunition and Kitchener implying that supplies were wasted. Asquith, the prime minister, shrank from measures of compulsion, even from conscription of manpower; until mid-1916, the British armies were filled by volunteers.

In 1917, Great Britain and France found leaders who were able, popular, and ruthlessly dedicated to victory at any price. Revolution came to Russia, and Austria-Hungary began to fall apart. In Germany, a political crisis forced the replacement of Bethmann-Hollweg; the actual rulers of Germany were the ablest generals, Hindenburg and Ludendorff. For the almost total collapse of Russia, the Allies found compensation in winning the biggest prize of all: the United States of America.

A year that began with the accession of a new British government and ended with the Bolshevik revolution, a year that included the first Russian revolution, mutiny in the French armies, Clemenceau's assumption of office, a political crisis in Germany, Italian disaster at Caporetto, and the entry of the United States into the war, was not lacking in action and indeed might well be called the critical year of this century.

The Russian Revolution and its ramifications is so important a subject that we will consider it in a separate chapter. It is enough to note here that the February Revolution (actually early March, on the calendar used in the West) brought to power a government pledged to democratize Russia and to continue the war with a more effective system. Perceptive observers were skeptical, but not until the next November did a group that was pledged to take Russia out of the war at any price manage to seize power. During the summer of 1917 the Russian armies were rapidly breaking up as attention turned to domestic revolution and a struggle for power following the abdication of the tsar. But an illusion existed in the West that the new Russian government, having thrown off the shackles of tsardom and proclaimed democratic principles, would actually strengthen the Allied cause. A delegation of European socialists brought words of encouragement in the spring.

At just that moment, however, socialist support of the war was beginning to waver in the West. A small fraction of the German Social Democrats, led by Rosa Luxemburg and Karl Liebknecht, son of a founding father of the party, opposed the war early. Liebknecht's was the only vote cast against war credits in the Reichstag late in 1914. A year later, nineteen others joined him. But socialist support for the war in all countries remained remarkably firm, with only slight signs of wavering. Called upon the initiative of Italian socialists, the Zimmerwald conference held in Switzerland in September 1915 witnessed the debut of Lenin's drive to turn the international war into a class war within each country. But few socialists from the warring countries even attended, and the Zimmerwald socialists did not entirely accept Lenin's platform. Three obscure French socialists voted against the war credits in May 1916 after attending another conference at Kienthal.

In frustration, Friedrich Adler, also the son of a famous socialist, assassinated the Austrian prime minister, Count Carl Stürgkh, at his midday meal in a Vienna restaurant on October 21, 1916. The following year in Berlin, a large and distinguished minority of the German socialists founded the Independent Social Democratic party. The Independents were not Leninists; they did not oppose the war as such, but they did oppose annexationist war aims, considering only a defensive war to be justifiable and alarmed at openly proclaimed goals of acquiring additional territory if the kaiser's government won the war. The collapse of Russia was beginning to raise this issue sharply. The socialists were joined by others, including the great sociologist Max Weber, in demanding democratization of Germany so that a truly popular basis for the war might be found. This was a position resembling that adopted in England by the Union of Democratic Control, a group of intellectuals and socialists who, without denying the need to wage a war of self-defense, campaigned for a compromise peace and asked for democratic control of foreign policy. They accused British policy of having helped cause the war by its secret commitments to France.

The German crisis of July 1917 was mostly the result, however, of disappointed submarine hopes. In May 1916 the Germans called their submarines off of commercial vessels after the sinking of the *Sussex* brought a sharp American warning. The previous year's sinking of the British ocean liner *Lusitania*, with considerable loss of American life, had blighted German-American relations, which had already been cooled by the American tendency to grant loans to the Allies for purchasing war supplies. But desperation nourished renewed hopes that using her large submarine force might win the war for Germany. Beginning the war with a fairly large submarine force, the Germans energetically added to it until they had more than 400 of these relatively new weapons. The blockade was beginning to tell on the Central Powers; actual hunger faced them. In January 1917, Berlin took the momentous decision to resort to unrestricted warfare around the British Isles, sinking everything in an effort to starve out the British. High naval leaders assured the kaiser that this strategy could win the war within five months. In March, the Germans made some withdrawals on the western front to a more heavily fortified line, the "Hindenburg line"—tacit admission that there no longer was any hope of winning the war in this area. Germany could afford no more Verduns.

The submarine campaign resulted in a declaration of war by the United States against Germany on April 6, for German defiance of previous American warnings against submarine warfare would inevitably mean the loss of American lives and property. After April, however, it became evident that the sub war could not deliver its promised results. U-boat victims were numerous, over 100 boats a month; but after rising between February and April, the toll of tonnage began to subside. Countermeasures in the form of destroyer-protected convoys were effective enough to assure the survival of Britain, now aided by her powerful American ally.

On July 6 in the Reichstag, Matthias Erzberger exposed the failure of the submarine war. Two weeks later, the Reichstag passed a resolution supported by Centrists as well as Socialists, calling for a peace without annexations. This followed by five days the resignation of Bethmann-Hollweg. He was replaced by the obscure George Michaelis, who in fact was subordinate to General Ludendorff's influence. The German government allowed delegates to attend the current Stockholm Socialist meeting, which was more than the British and French governments did. And a little earlier, the emperor had announced an end to the notorious Prussian three-class voting system in favor of a democratic suffrage. All this was a curious mixture of reform and reaction, indicative of faltering German will to carry on the terrible war. This summer of 1917 also brought the first revolt at the Kiel naval base, the harbinger of a much greater one in November.

The Germans would have felt better had they known about the mutiny that swept through the French army at this same time. This crisis of morale followed a disastrous offensive that bears the name of French general Nivelle, who had replaced Joffre as commander in chief. Radiating exuberant confidence, Nivelle concocted an ambitious plan of attack over a broad front. At Arras and in Champagne, British and French attacks in April failed so badly, again with ghastly casualties, that soldiers finally lost all confidence in the high command. They refused en masse to obey orders to attack. The extent of this mutiny is indicated by the official figures: 23,385 court martials and 432 death sentences. As many as 50,000 were actively involved. Nothing like that had occurred before; the war had been marked by high morale and an infinitesimally small desertion rate. It affected almost all the five French armies (fifty-four divisions) that had taken part in the offensive, perhaps a third of the total French forces. With the aid of General Petain, the hero of Verdun, control was regained at the cost of a promise of no more offensives. The French joined the Germans in wishing no more part in the long game of mass slaughter. It is remarkable that the Germans learned so little of the mutiny.

Nerves were stretched taut. A former president of the French Republic suggested a negotiated peace and was imprisoned for it. The British sent UDC (Union of Democratic Control) leader E. D. Morel to jail for the same heresy; and when Lord Lansdowne, a distinguished elder statesman, made a similar suggestion it was received with a shower of abuse. The grimness of the situation persuaded some that it was time to end the madness, but others reacted by asking for ever greater dedication and showing a savage intolerance of defeatism. After shedding so much blood, could one settle for less than victory?

Morale and Propaganda

The war began with wild celebrations in an ecstasy of general rejoicing. Such a mood later seemed incredible, was therefore almost forgotten, and, in many accounts of the war, ignored. It should not be, for the "August ideas" constituted an essential basis for the widespread support that held public morale high through several years of what one would have thought unendurable agony.

The war spirit embraced the articulate classes as well as the masses. Indeed, one of its principal ingredients was a joyous rediscovery of solidarity in the community of battle. Alienated European intellectuals— a term that had come into general usage only in the preceding generation—happily returned home to the bosom of the people. "Our petty social divisions and barriers have all been swept away," Kipling exulted. In every belligerent nation an exultation at being "again one people," feeling the "sacred union" of national brotherhood, afflicted the educated elite, it seems, even more than the average person.

At any rate a quite irrational, mystic sentiment of this sort found expression in many outbursts. "I discovered to my amazement," Bertrand Russell wrote—he was one of a small minority not sharing the mystique and appalled by it—"that average men and women were delighted at the prospect of war." A flood of manifestoes and declarations that blessed the war, damned the foe, and strove to put their side in the right before God and history testified to an equal delight among leading philosophers, poets, scientists, historians, sociologists. University youth were among the most eager to volunteer; there was a strong feeling that the war was a youth movement, and such young poets as Rupert Brooke and Alain-Fournier who marched off to die in the early battles became heroes.

A desire for adventure after the tameness of a bourgeois society marked by mediocrity—*wust und tand* ("trash and triviality") German poet Stefan George called it—was one obvious motive for young men to march off to a war that they initially expected to offer glorious excitement and a chance for heroism. It was a poet's war, although between 1914 and 1918 the poetry changed from celebration of honor and bravery to grim commentary on useless bloodshed. In the beginning, as Robert Graves recalled,

Never was such antiqueness of romance
Such tasty honey oozing from the heart.

But the war was more than adventure; serious thinkers hailed it as a chance for "moral regeneration," a cleansing fire burning away the corruptions of a decadent society or "washing away the ruins of a shattered world" (wrote Ernst Lotz, a young German poet, the Rupert Brooke of his land). People who later had trouble understanding how they could have behaved so foolishly were swept into the war craze in a rage of excitement. "When war is declared we all go mad," Shaw commented. The madness that accompanied the outbreak of this war was exaggerated by boredom with the long peace; the restless discontents with a shabby commercial culture; and the Nietzschean mood, which taught that through struggle and battle the spirit might redeem itself and the world.

Few indeed were the voices raised against the hysteria, and they were reduced to despair. "Among the elite of each country," Romain Rolland lamented, "there is not one who does not proclaim and is not convinced that the cause of his country is the cause of God, the cause of liberty and of human progress." Rolland's plea to the intellectuals to stand *au-dessus de la melée* ("above the battle") went largely unheeded and scorned for at least two years.

Though the feverish idealism of the first days naturally proved ephemeral, its results tended to last. The intelligentsia in each country manned the ministries of "information" if they did not actually fight, as many of them did even at quite advanced ages. There were numerous examples of enlistments by men of middle age, and old Anatole France—socialist and radical—even tried to shoulder a rifle at seventy. The "decadent" Italian novelist and poet Gabriele D'Annunzio, associated with eroticism earlier, compiled a heroic war record although he was in his fifties. Popular writers and entertainers visited the front to raise morale. Women proved as warlike as men; anxious to assert their equality, most sufragettes supported the war with deeds as well as words. Reversing the lesson of *Lysistrata*, girls cold-shouldered sweethearts who wouldn't sign up, chanting, "We don't want to lose you but we think you ought to go" at every able-bodied young male they sighted. With few exceptions, socialists and trade unionist were patriotic. In England, veteran independent socialist Keir Hardie found himself hissed from working-class platforms when he questioned the duty to subordinate everything else to winning the war.

This excess of belligerent ardor led to propaganda that extended even to the more or less deliberate manufacture of stories about the enemy. Allied propaganda soon developed a view of the Germans as barbarians, "Huns," who descended without warning on small nations, determined to extinguish their independence. Led by "Prussian militarists" to whom they were blindly obedient, encouraged to be ruthless by Nietzsche (actually a hater of German nationalism), they had not only deliberately contrived the war to impose their German culture on everybody, but they delighted in cruel treatment of their victims. Teutonic love of despotism, of course, was contrasted with the democracy of the Allies, a line to which Russia was something of an obstacle until March 1917.

Less successfully, German propaganda accused the British of sordid materialism, the French of decadence, the Russians of menacing Europe with a savage barbarism, all of jealousy of German cultural and economic superiority. Governments organized and subsidized the publication of such bizarre distortions, freely offered by the leading brains of each country. The extensive literature of this sort has to be seen to be believed.

The home front was more affected by propaganda than were the soldiers, who soon found themselves distanced from it. On the whole, soldiers in the trenches showed greater respect for a brave foe. Still, the famous "Christmas truce" of December 1914, when rival forces suspended hostilities to celebrate the holiday season with gifts and parties, was not repeated. Disenchanted with their leaders, the "scarlet Majors at the Base" who in Siegfried Sassoon's poem "speed glum heroes up the line to death" and toddle home to die in bed, as well as with those at home who could not grasp how it really was at the front, the men in battle developed a remarkable cameraderie based on their mutual dependence. Men at the front learned to hate the war but love each other and often found the experience with all its frightfulness humanly valuable.

Each side accused the other of atrocities. Most of these stories were made up. Ironically, these falsehoods contributed to a failure to believe in very real atrocities in World War II; so much skepticism had been engendered by learning of the deliberate lies of 1914–1918 that at first few would accept stories of mass murder in Nazi concentration camps. In any war terrible things happen, of which both sides are guilty—shooting prisoners, for example. There was vast Allied indignation at the German execution of a nurse named Edith Cavell, but the French also executed female as well as male spies in considerable numbers. In 1917 the London *Times* claimed that the Germans were converting human corpses into fertilizer and even food, a story later found to have been based on a mistranslation (horses, not people). Other mistakes were not so innocent, and after the war there was a wave of rueful confessions by people who had manufactured tales of enemy inhumanity. The Germans were more vulnerable, since they were the occupiers of Belgian, French, Serbian, Rumanian, and Russian territory, whereas no foreign soldier stood on German soil throughout the war—this was largely true, too, of the Dual Monarchy. (It is a curiosity of this war that the defeated were never invaded.) They also bore the onus of submarine warfare with its inevitable loss of civilian life. And one of the few authenticated cases of something like the genocides practiced during World War II implicated Germany's ally, Turkey, whose attempt to exterminate the Armenians was unfortunately not a new practice. The Germans made what capital they could of alleged bestialities inflicted by French African soldiers on their victims. In actuality, whenever conditions of battle made it possible the soldiers on both sides seem to have behaved honorably, and German administration of the occupied zones was far from barbarous.

The atrocity stories and the war propaganda did neither side credit. The war was atrocious enough in itself. It was mechanized slaughter, impersonal and unheroic. As Shaw put it, the soldier

> has no sight or knowledge of what he is doing; he only hands on a shell or pulls a string. And a Beethoven or a baby dies six miles off. . . . The notion that these heavily bored men were being heroic, or cruel, or anything in the least romantic or sensational, was laughable.[2]

World War II, with its tank battles and vast movements, was more interesting than World War I. Typically, men sat in idleness behind the front or in the trenches, waiting for those occasions when they went "over the top" into "no man's land" protected by nothing but a helmet and loaded down with equipment, probably to be mowed down by gunners who never came near them.

On the other hand, Shaw was wrong in supposing the guns would hit a baby; unlike the next war, civilians were reasonably safe in this one. The western front battle zone itself became what Edmund Blunden called "the most terrifying devastated area perhaps ever yet seen on our planet," but it was a narrow zone. In such savagely contested regions, year after year, as in the country around Verdun or Ypres, all life was wiped out; villages disappeared forever; shells and even bodies could be found for years afterwards. But towns just a few miles behind the lines were never shelled. There, in rest and recreation centers, soldiers might write or relax between spells of duty at the front.

---

[2] *The Wit and Wisdom of Bernard Shaw*, ed. Stephen Winsten (New York: Collier Books, 1962), pp. 311–312. Cf. the Viennese Shaw, Karl Kraus, "Mit der Uhr in der Hand," *Die Fackel*, May, 1917, pp. 457–461. Shaw's account of his visit to the Front first appeared in the London *Daily Chronicle*, March 5–8, 1917.

It is erroneous to suppose that they spent all their time being eaten by rats and lice in the trenches. A considerable number got venereal disease.

In the end the war was a test of the wills of whole peoples. The elder Moltke, genius of the German Army, was one of the few who had predicted the nature of this war long before. "It will become a war between peoples which will not be concluded with a single battle but which will be a long, weary struggle with a country that will not acknowledge defeat until the whole strength of its people is broken."

In such a contest, ideology and propaganda were all-important; and it is fair to say that the Germans lost this battle. Persuaded that their cause was just, the Germans had trouble explaining it, and they had less access to the outer world. Much of the neutral world, though not all of it, thought that democracy, progress, and freedom were on the side of the Allies. In the greatest neutral arena of all, the Allies won the moral struggle by persuading the United States of America to join them. Though critics alleged then and later the American motive was a material one (profitable war trade and saving those who owed them money), one cannot realistically leave out the ideological factor. Most Americans had become convinced that the kaiser and the Prussian war lords were waging a "warfare against mankind," in President Woodrow Wilson's words, and that "the principles of peace and justice in the life of the world as against selfish and autocratic power" would be upheld by opposing the Central Powers.

War Aims and War Diplomacy

Except for Austria's desire to eliminate Serbia, no warring power had any clearly formulated goals beyond self-preservation when the war started. Whatever propagandists alleged, neither side went to war in 1914 in conscious search of territorial or other aggrandizement. But the very fact that war had occurred caused demands to be raised. Each thought it had been attacked or forced to forestall attack because its security had been insufficient, and victory would have to bring changes. Besides, the large casualties cried out for compensation. Were such immense sacrifices to be made in vain? No government could survive that did not press for future gains and the reward of victory, so that the foe would be prevented from striking again and one's own necessary security would be provided.

Complicating the formulation of such war aims were more immediate and pressing goals: keeping allies happy, avoiding costly quarrels within the team of fighting powers; winning new allies by persuading or bribing neutrals to enter on one's own side; and stirring up trouble within the enemy camp if possible. These goals could clash painfully, forcing hard choices. If the British and French kept Russia happy by agreeing to her goal of acquiring the Straits of Constantinople, they could not expect to gain Turkey as an ally. They alienated an ally, Serbia, and sacrificed an opportunity to weaken the shaky allegiance of Austria-Hungary's Slavic subjects, if, to lure Italy into becoming an ally, they offered to give Slavic territory to Rome. The possibility of getting the Dual Monarchy to make a separate peace—a real coup, which the Allies in fact thought existed—contradicted a policy of weakening her by appealing to her minorities to rebel and set up separate governments.

All these dilemmas were actual ones, and there were others. The Germans had to make the memorable decision whether submarine warfare was worth the enmity of the United States; and they had to decide whether to woo Russia into a separate peace or assail her by offering aid to her discontented subjects.

There was the further possibility, if unhappily a rather remote one at most times, that terms between all the enemy powers short of absolute victory could end the dismal slaughter with some sort of compromise. The friendly offices of neutrals might perhaps facilitate this process. In January 1915, President Wilson sent Colonel E. M. House, his trusted aide, to visit London, Paris, and Berlin and sound out prospects for a settlement; House was forced to judge the situation hopeless. Each side had a shopping list. The Allies demanded, at the least, German withdrawal from all invaded territories with indemnification for damages, the return of Alsace and Lorraine to France, the Straits to Russia (Britain and France had already promised this to Russia by secret agreement, an issue growing out of the Dardanelles campaign). But German opinion would tolerate no drawing back from territory gained and demanded at a minimum keeping strategic areas in Belgium and France.

Nearly two years later, another American initiative failed. At this time, in response to a Wilson request for a statement of aims, the German government declared that in general it was ready to make peace, but it irritated the Allies by implying that it was, if not victorious, at least not defeated. It has been debated whether the Germans at this time were ready for a peace without annexations; the Allies did not think so.

From one point of view the huge human and material losses, the whole disruption of the fabric of international life, the hateful propaganda seemed to be destroying Western civilization, and reaching peace seemed to be in everyone's interest. From another point of view, however, the more blood and treasure spent, the less easy it was to accept an end to the war without commensurate gains. Could one confess that the whole thing had been a mistake and go back to where one had begun after losing a million lives? A grisly logic decreed that terms for peace rose and positions stiffened in proportion to the length and cost of the war. An initiative from Pope Benedict in 1917 made no more headway than American industrialist Henry Ford's Peace Ship. At any given moment in a war, if one is doing relatively well, why compromise? We may win tomorrow. Or if one is doing badly, why not wait until tomorrow to bargain? Today we are in too weak a position. The time is never ripe for peace until one side totally collapses.

Of such ingredients was wartime diplomacy made. The "secret treaties" in which territories were pledged to Italy, to Russia, to Rumania in order to gain their adherence to the Allies and their entry into the war later became a notorious issue. Russia and Rumania subsequently left the war and wiped out the agreements, but the Bolsheviks exposed the secret agreement of 1915 about the Straits soon after they seized power in late 1917. The secret Treaty of London with Italy (April 1915) caused trouble at the peace conference. In fact it caused trouble earlier than that, for the Serbs and other South Slavs resented it. Italy was promised part of Dalmatia, across the Gulf of Venice; the Istrian peninsula, inhabited mostly by Slovenes; territory from Austria-Hungary south of the Brenner Pass; and miscellaneous islands. This was largely inconsistent with the national self-determination principle sometimes proclaimed as an Allied war aim.

In 1917 secret negotiations went on between Austria-Hungary and the Allies. The new emperor was eager to get out of the war and perhaps save his throne. One obstacle was a strong South Slav lobby in London, where a Czech government in exile, headed by Thomas Masaryk, set up headquarters in 1916. The goal of liberating the various Slavic minorities—Czech, Slovak, South Slav, Polish—made effective propaganda: freedom for small peoples, national self-determination. Breaking up the Dual Monarchy would also unlock the back door to Germany and allow the Allied force based on Salonika to enter. Making terms with the emperor on the basis of Austro-Hungarian territorial integrity precluded such a strategy. On the other side, since late 1916 the Germans had been increasingly in effective military control of Austria-Hungary. Negotiations for a separate peace nevertheless went on between Vienna and London or Paris all through 1917. The gloomy prognosis for victory that many Allied leaders shared in 1917, after the Russian Revolution and the French mutinies, encouraged these talks. But the Italians complained, the South Slavs complained, and Vienna would not agree to the dismemberment of the empire. These talks dragged on into 1918, and in the end events overtook the diplomats.

The other theoretical possibility would seem to have been a separate peace between the Central Powers and war-weary Russia, but though there were sporadic contacts through Sweden and even through Japan, they never came to anything. The tsar's loyalty to the Allies is less astonishing when we reflect that the Germans were prevented by their alliances from offering anything the Russians wanted. Russia had gotten the Allies to pledge her the Straits, a long-coveted prize; Germany, of course, as an ally of the present owner, Turkey, could not match this offer. Perhaps the Russians would have liked more of Poland, but Germany and Austria possessed her themselves. The Russians stood to gain much from Allied victory, nothing tangible by a peace with the Central Powers. Defeat and dismemberment of the Dual Monarchy would presumably favor Russian policy in Southeast Europe, which had, of course, been the initial source of the war.

Realizing this impasse, German policy sought to sow dissension in Russia by subsidizing and encouraging revolutionary movements, whether among such dissident nationalities as Georgians and Ukrainians or among the antiwar socialists. Quite early in the war Germany began to make use of the talents of the remarkable Alexander Helphand ("Parvus"), a former Russian revolutionary socialist and one-time friend of Trotsky and Lenin, who now worked for the Germans. He used his knowledge of the Russian revolutionary underground to funnel financial aid to any group that would sabotage the Russian war effort. This policy culminated in the famous sealed train that brought Lenin back to Russia, through German territory, in April of 1917. Obviously this strategy played with fire, but the immediate goal of winning the war took precedence over all other motives.

Allied propaganda aimed at Austria-Hungary's discontented minorities was inhibited, as we have mentioned, by the hope of a separate peace with Vienna; but in the last year of the war Allied policy tended to look more and more in the direction of disrupting rather than seducing the Hapsburg state. Growing American participation in the war strengthened this trend, for Wilson, an enthusiast of "rights of small nations" and "self-determination," was much more inclined than the Europeans to stress broad, idealistic slogans as war aims. He was about to give to the world his Fourteen Points. The good Lord himself had only ten, Wilson must have fourteen commandments, grumbled the blunt old tiger, Clemenceau. But European "cynicism," expressed in secret deals and old-fashioned diplomacy, had seemingly failed. The Americans came preaching "open diplomacy," principles of justice, morality in politics.

Winning the United States as a powerful ally, which was destined to tilt the balance for victory in the end, was less a triumph for Allied diplomacy than an exposure of German ineptness. Miffed because the Americans sold goods to the Allies, the Germans early tried their policy of sabotage, to the great annoyance of Americans, and used their U-boats to sink merchant ships. This cost innocent lives, including American ones.

But American opinion was initially neutralist, and neither the president nor the public had any desire to enter an affray whose causes they only dimly understood. An important German community in the U.S. naturally pulled for its own land of origin. The Poles were at best divided, Russia being the most hated of the oppressors, and Jews were also inclined, if anything, to be pro-German because they were anti-Russian. The worst persecutor of Jews in the pre-1914 era had been Russia. Most Irish-Americans were more anti-English than anti-German. The broad hinterland of the American states simply believed that European wars were irrelevant to American life and interests. Sale of goods to the Allies did not reflect lack of neutrality but the opposite, since American policy traditionally stood for maximum rights of trade with both sides in a foreign war; it was only accident that the British, controlling the high seas, could take advantage of this and the Central Powers could not.

A series of blunders extending to the famous Zimmerman note, which solicited Mexico as an ally in a German-American war, marked a suicidal German policy of losing friends in the United States. The decision to renew all-out submarine warfare, taken early in 1917, was a military-based blunder that exposed the basic weakness of German political leadership—so thought so great a German as Max Weber.

Finally entering the war in 1917, in part because of the failure of efforts to arrange a negotiated peace, the United States did not formally join the Allies but was an "associated power," pursuing something of an independent course, desirous of marking off her position from those of all European states. Unprepared for war, the U.S. was not able to make much of an impact until 1918; she then exerted a decisive influence in the final months of the war.

The Last Months of the War

Both sides approached despair at the end of 1917, a year that, we may recall, witnessed Russia's agony and ultimate departure from the war, mutinies in the French armies, signs of war weariness even in England after another bloody failure around Ypres, and, as a final disaster, the Italian rout at Caporetto. Here in the mountain war the Italian troops, demoralized and confused in a battle fought in a snowstorm, simply threw away their guns and ran. The Italian losses included 10,000 killed, 300,000 prisoners, 400,000 deserters! This was the only Austrian victory of the war and a near catastrophe for Italy. With Allied help, the Italians finally stabilized the front along the Piave River. Italian morale was low; in August the Vatican had called for an end to "this useless slaughter," and workers had gone on strike in Turin.

But while the Allies were buoyed by American troops just beginning to arrive, the Central Powers had their own share of gloom, not least from hunger and declining morale. Everybody was near exhaustion. The Germans had one final ray of hope, however. Lenin's revolutionary government, committed to peace at any price, paid a terrible price in the settlement of Brest-Litovsk early in 1918. Russia had to give up Poland, the Baltic states, Finland, and even the Ukraine, which became nominally an independent state with its capital at Kiev.

This annexationist peace further alienated the German socialists at home, but it freed some divisions for use in the west. There was a chance to finish off the Allies in France before American troops came in large numbers. One last titanic effort might do it. It was widely understood that this was the last bid for victory; if it failed, German victory was hopeless. There were food riots in Vienna in January, and a strike in Berlin had to be crushed by the military.

But the team of Ludendorff and Hindenburg was now firmly in command. The former was probably the most talented military leader the war produced, the latter a respected symbol. Ludendorff showed immense skill in planning the "last act" German offensive of 1918, taking incredible pains to conceal troop movements (wagon wheels wrapped in feathers!) and inventing a new type of warfare. This was based not on mass frontal assault, the recipe for lethal failure all through the western war, but on initial infiltration by elite "storm troop" units. To preserve the element of surprise, the artillery barrage, though very intense, was short. The Germans hit the British in the north on March 21 with some success, gaining forty miles at one point and capturing nearly 100,000 prisoners. But the attack fell short of real breakthrough, as did another offensive in the Ypres-Armentières area in April.

On April 12, the war trembling in the balance, the Germans stood close to a major victory. For the first time, the Allies achieved a united command, with French General Foch commander in chief over all the Allied armies. These German offensives won more territory than any previous offensive by either side. But they failed to gain victory. The Allied armies remained capable of counterattacks. April 24 was notable for the first significant tank battle, in which metal mastadons capable of the immense speed of seven miles per hour fell into holes or scorched the men inside of them—a forecast of the warfare of the future but hardly an auspicious debut.

The Germans tried again in May, choosing an area further to the south, and on May 27 they advanced a record twelve miles in a day. Shells were heard again in Paris. The front was at last becoming more fluid. But the gaunt German soldiers stopped to loot, feast, and drink the wines of Champagne (perhaps their famous national drink saved the French). At this time American troops, green at first but young and eager, received their baptism of fire. German morale began to collapse with the failure of this final offensive to force a decision. Within two months the Allies launched a counteroffensive with increasing numbers of tanks as well as Americans, and they began slowly but steadily to push the Germans back. August 8 would be the black day of the German Army. The final gamble, like the first, had failed.

On September 14, Austria-Hungary unilaterally published a peace statement, in effect announcing its departure from the war. Bulgaria asked out of the war on September 29. Rumania, which had been forced to accept harsh terms from the Central Powers after the collapse of Russia, managed to come out on the winning side by declaring war again a few hours before the Armistice! Greece also belatedly leaped in the direction of the victors. As the Germans desperately sought for terms short of total surrender, mutiny and revolution finally broke out at home.

Facing defeat, the Germans sought to make peace on the most favorable terms possible. They appealed to the principles Wilson had expounded as his idea of a just and lasting peace, the Fourteen Points. It appeared that under the Fourteen Points, Germany would have to return the provinces Alsace and Lorraine to France and would probably lose some territory on her eastern border to a restored Poland, but she would incur no further penalties. But the Allies were scarcely prepared to be so forgiving, and Wilson himself was by no means prepared to grant lenient armistice terms, although he was suspected of wishing to do so. The American commander, General Pershing, was against anything short of an unconditional surrender. Handling of the armistice was left to the Allied commander in chief, the French Marshal Foch. When the Germans tried to appeal directly to Wilson, he refused to deal with the kaiser's government at all. This aided the revolution, which broke out in Germany early in November. A war-weary people, now without faith in their government, overthrew authority in the navy and in city after city; the kaiser was forced to abdicate and flee to Holland.

Although the Germans who faced Marshal Foch in the forest of Compiègne on the morning of November 11 represented the new Socialist-led government, the armistice terms were severe. They were not quite as severe, however, as some Allied leaders had wished. Later it seemed an incredible blunder, a climax of a bungled war, that the onus of signing the surrender and later the humiliating peace treaty fell upon the new government rather than the old, on liberal rather than reactionary Germany. Hitler was to declare with superficial plausibility that the socialists and republicans had betrayed Germany. The Germans had to agree to withdraw their army behind the Rhine; surrender all their submarines and heavy artillery and the major part of their navy; and allow the establishment of Allied garrisons east of the Rhine at Mainz, Coblenz, and Cologne. With their country in chaos, the German delegates could do nothing else. The war was over, and Germany lay helpless.

But Allied armies did not invade and occupy Germany, as they did after World War II. There seemed no need for it, and the Allies themselves were heartily weary of the war. The German Army retired into Germany in good array, clearly beaten but not really shattered in the field. In the Second World War, Hitler defiantly refused all terms, and the Allies refused to grant him any, so that the only possible outcome was the invasion of Germany and the capture of its capital. Things did not proceed so far in 1919. The armistice terms; the abdication of the kaiser; the chaos in Germany; and the naval blockade, which continued until the signing of the peace treaty, gave the Allies abundant security that the Central Powers could not hope to renew the war. It remains a curious fact that the armies of the defeated power were still on enemy soil at the war's end.

Austria-Hungary had collapsed, too, never to be reconstructed; the Czechs, Slovaks, Croats, and Poles were busy making arrangements to create several new states where the Hapsburg empire had lain for half a millennium. The war had destroyed the three great dynastic empires of Eastern Europe: Russia, Austria-Hungary, and Germany. The democracies had proved stronger, it was said. But Germany had actually put up a magnificent resistance against heavy odds, enduring hunger and severe shortages of nearly everything. In his history of the Great War, Winston Churchill, with that gallantry toward a brave foe that was always one of his traits, graciously acknowledged the magnitude of the German achievement; though succumbing in the end to insurmountable odds, they had held out longer than anyone could have believed. The Germans undoubtedly felt they had earned the right to honorable terms. But the fact remained that their inadequate political structure had collapsed; they were helpless; and public opinion in the democracies, aroused by war propaganda, did not follow Churchill's line but was almost hysterically vindictive, calling for appropriate punishment to be inflicted on the guilty aggressor. *Vae victis.*

Europe Transformed:
The Revolutions and
Restorations of 1917-1921

From the February to the October Revolution
in Russia

Strikes and bread riots in early March 1917 signalled the last gasp of battered Russia's discredited government; it simply crumbled. The tsar abdicated on March 15 (March 2 by the old calendar then in use in Russia), as this almost bloodless revolution deposited power in the hands of a provisional government until elections to a constitutional assembly could be held. The new government was dominated by a prince, the liberal George Lvov, and a professor, the equally liberal Paul Milyukov, a founder of the moderate Constitutional Democratic party. This leadership reflected the views of those who thought that Russia would now establish a liberal and democratic form of government like that of her Western allies, France and Britain. Some of those who believed this were socialists, for the Menshevik faction of the Marxian Social Democrats—actually a majority of the party—had long held that Russia must pass through bourgeois democracy and capitalism before she could advance to the higher stages of socialism and communism.

As we noted in the previous chapter, the new leadership did not contemplate taking Russia out of the war but even thought in terms of a more effective prosecution of it and closer relations with the now ideologically compatible Western Allies. London, Paris, and Washington were equally optimistic; the latter, trembling on the brink of entrance into the war, saw Russia's conversion to democracy as an additional reason for taking the plunge. Many thought that the revolution would unleash new military strength, much as the French Revolution of 1789–1793 had done. We have referred to the powerful incentives for Russia not to make a separate peace: the secret treaties pledging her Constantinople, the Dardanelles, and an additional slice of Poland and the Central Powers' inability to offer these inducements.

Yet from the beginning the authority of the provisional government lay in doubt. There was a gulf between those who had organized the revolution and those who had inherited political office from it. This "duality of power" has characterized other revolutions. Extralegislative bodies arose spontaneously out of the first 1917 Russian revolution, in the form of soviets, or committees (councils), of workers or soldiers. Among the peasantry, they scarcely appeared at all.

The soviets, which had first appeared in the 1905 revolution, took on many of the real functions of government, while the nominally sovereign provisional government, based on the quite unrepresentative Duma, became more or less impotent. In institutional terms, there are three keys to what happened between the February and the October revolutions: (a) the provisional government steadily lost what little prestige it had and failed to win respect as the legitimate authority; (b) the soviets exercised more and more real power through their central elected body and their central executive committee, which began to speak for them; (c) the Bolshevik party (later called the Communist party), which was the radical, antiwar wing of the Social Democrats, gained control of the soviets. After April, the Bolshevik party was dominated by Lenin.

Why did these things happen? Certainly the most damaging thing the provisional government did was to try to carry on the war. In trying to reform the armed forces, the government succeeded only in demoralizing them further. In May, the provisional government moved somewhat to the left with the resignation of Milyukov as minister of foreign affairs and the emergence of Alexander Kerensky, a socialist (though not a Social Democrat) as the strongest figure in the cabinet. A persuasive orator, Kerensky tried to galvanize the troops by passionate appeals to their patriotism. In July he succeeded Lvov as prime minister, but the summer offensive soon collapsed, just as it had before, with costly reverses. As the army began to break up in disorder, the commander in chief whom Kerensky himself had appointed, General L. G. Kornilov, decided to use his troops to march on Petrograd and overthrow the Kerensky government, which he blamed for the breakdown of military discipline. Kerensky turned to the Bolsheviks for support against this counterrevolutionary movement. Like the emigré nobles in the French Revolution or the Presbyterians in the Puritan Revolution, Kerensky might have deserted the revolution and returned to the arms of the old regime, but he did not do so; he was to be devoured by the revolution anyway, from the Left rather than the Right.

Why was the Bolshevik party able to eat up Kerensky and emerge as the ruler of Russia by the end of the year? That outcome was unprecedented in the history of major revolutions, for the extreme Left had gained power in none of the classic modern revolutions, including the English, the French of 1789, the American, and the 1848 revolutions. Historians are nearly unanimous in attributing this success primarily to the genius of Lenin. Surely if ever one man swayed the course of history it was he, beginning with his dramatic return to Russia in April.

When the revolution broke out, the forty-four year old Lenin was living rather obscurely in Zurich, having been exiled from Russia for most of the time since 1900. The son of a relatively prosperous Volga-area bureaucrat, young Ulyanov was expelled from Kazan University in 1887. He was allowed, however, to study for the examination leading to a law degree and passed it easily at Moscow University in 1891. In 1887 his brother, Alexander, had been involved in a plot to assassinate the emperor, Alexander III, and was put to death for this along with several others. Perhaps it was this that turned Vladimir Ulyanov into a revolutionary; but he had had from the beginning a violent, powerful nature and a vigorous, polemical mind.

He was a revolutionary before he became a Marxist. The district school supervisor's son read Nikolai Chernyshevsky's *What Is To Be Done?* at the age of sixteen or seventeen, and this oddly influential book, written in prison in 1863 by one of the revolutionary nihilists, converted him to the life of a professional revolutionary, prepared to sacrifice everything to the cause. Lenin seems never seriously to have contemplated any other career. From Chernyshevsky and others of this generation, he got the idea of a revolutionary elite, totally dedicated and fanatical, the "salt of the salt," which would seize power and hold it in the name of the people—a very un-Marxian idea, for Marx and Engels had almost invariably opposed such romantic conceptions of revolution.

Marxism was becoming popular in Russia in the 1890s, and Lenin adopted it in 1891 or 1892. Until 1900, he was on the whole an orthodox Marxist engaged in the scientific study of social development rather than spontaneous acts of heroic will; he authored a legally published scholarly work, *The Development of Capitalism in Russia,* in 1899. This did not prevent him from being arrested in 1895, exiled to Siberia in 1897, and expelled from the country in 1900. He returned to Russia late in the 1905 revolution and stayed until 1907, when he was again threatened with arrest. Abroad, mostly in Switzerland and France, Lenin participated in the politics and publications of the Russian Social Democratic party. His imperious will and potent personality soon pushed him to break with its leadership and mark out for himself a new position.

The trouble with orthodox Marxism as applied to Russia, from Lenin's point of view, was that it counseled waiting a long time for the socialist revolution. To Plekhanov, the founding father of Russian Marxism, this seemed to follow from the rather mechanical sort of Marxian determinism then current. Society has to pass through the capitalist phase, drawing from it all that it has to offer, before the time is ripe for the more advanced stage of socialism. One must crawl before one can walk. Russia had barely begun the capitalist crawl. A Marxist should work with the existing currents of history to push Russia through bourgeois ascendancy, political democracy, and private capitalism. To attempt socialism prematurely would be foolish. To dream of violent revolutions led by heroic elites was to fall back into anarchism or romantic adventurism. The science of society teaches that social development is a complex and organic process.

As a Marxist, Lenin (the revolutionary name he adopted) accepted some of this, but his subtle mind searched for ways to accommodate his impatient spirit. He split the party in 1903 on the issue of the party: should it be a mass, democratic one or, as Lenin argued, a small, tightly organized, highly disciplined vanguard, boldly guiding a working class unable to lead itself? "Independently and by its own intellect," Lenin argued, the working class can never develop a "socialist consciousness"; it can rise no higher than a "trade union consciousness."

This frank elitism shocked the majority of pre-1914 Marxists, who were committed to the slow development of democratic socialism. It appealed to the adventurous. But Lenin was regarded as an inveterate troublemaker, and his Bolshevik faction remained small, a minority of a very small group to begin with. He studied, wrote, and dominated a small number of doting disciples. To his idea of an elite, vanguard party he added theories to justify in Marxist terms a revolutionary seizure of power. Russia was only a part of world capitalism, in fact its "weakest link." So the Russian Communist party might seize power, touching off revolution throughout the world. Or it might guide the country through the capitalist phase, greatly speeding up this unpleasant growth period if not bypassing it. The latter theory of "permanent revolution" Lenin shared with his brilliant colleague, Leon Trotsky. He did not, however, adhere altogther consistently to such views.

Fairly early in the war Lenin began to preach that it should be transformed somehow into a civil war, a class war within each country, leading to an international proletarian revolution. But a majority of the Russian leftists were "defensist," thinking like the socialists of other countries that their country had to be defended; would it, or they, be better off under the heel of German imperialism? At the Zimmerwald international socialist conference of September 1915, Lenin and Trotsky (whose real name was Lev Bronstein) got some of their antiwar ideas adopted, but few socialists from the main warring countries attended. Busying himself with philosophical studies, Lenin seemed destined to remain a lonely rebel until the first Russian revolution of 1917 and the German decision to ship him back to Russia changed the course of history.

Arriving at the Finland station in Petrograd on April 16 after an eight-day journey from Zurich across Germany and Sweden, the famous Trojan iron horse carried Lenin; other leading Bolsheviks, including Karl Radek and Gregory Zinoviev; Lenin's wife; and his sometime mistress, Inessa Armand. But the one that counted was Lenin himself. He soon changed Bolshevik policy, which had been supporting the provisional government, to ferocious denunciation of these imperialists and lackeys of British capitalism. Peace should be made immediately, and there should be social revolution and liberation of oppressed peoples in Russia. International revolution would then begin in Germany: "the German proletariat is the most loyal and reliable ally of the Russian and international proletarian revolution." The magnetism of Lenin's personality and the power of his oratory gained supporters, but they also aroused foes. Many were angered and astonished at such a plan, which involved apparent surrender to the Germans, whose agent they thought Lenin to be. Kerensky defeated Lenin by a five to one margin during the first All-Russian Congress of Soviets on June 17.

Events were on Lenin's side. "Peace, Bread, and Land," the Bolshevik slogan, grew in appeal as the July offensive crumpled and the Kerensky government faltered. In three years of war the Russians had mobilized an astonishing total of some fifteen million men and had lost half of them as prisoners and casualties. Oddly, the troops not fighting, those on garrison duty behind the front, were the most susceptible to subversion (this was true also in the French mutinies of 1917 and later the German revolution). The Petrograd and Moscow garrisons, the Kronstadt fortress near Petrograd, the Baltic fleet—these were the sources of insurrection.

The Russian Revolution of 1917: Storming the Winter Palace, St. Petersburg, during the October Revolution. *Tass from Sovfoto.*

In July the Bolsheviks were tempted to try a coup against the government, but it proved premature, and Lenin and Zinoviev fled to Finland. In general, however, the Kerensky government tolerated its opponents. And the Kornilov rebellion, as we have noted, forced Kerensky to seek support on the Left. The Petrograd soviet brought about the collapse of Kornilov's coup, as his soldiers deserted him.

From here events moved rapidly toward November. But, again, it was Lenin almost alone who guided the Bolsheviks toward the seizure of power on November 6–7. They were still very much a minority in Russia. An illegal revolutionary coup might succeed, but what would they do then? They would inherit a ruined country, defenseless against the Germans, committed to a disastrous peace, and probably faced with civil war. The prospect dismayed all except Ulyanov, alias Lenin, who was more than ready for it.

The so-called October Revolution, like the February one, was achieved rather easily. With Lenin issuing orders from Bolshevik headquarters at a former seminary for aristocratic ladies, soldiers and workers of the Petrograd soviets seized communications, transportation, and utilities. No one rallied to defend Kerensky, who fled after vainly trying to raise loyal troops. In Moscow there was only a little resistance. Government ministers were arrested; a soviet congress voted power to a Council of People's Commissars, Lenin its president. It remained to be seen whether the largely peasant masses of Russia would obey this regime and whether amid defeat and disorder the Lenin regime could last. Most observers thought it would not.

The Bolsheviks had won partly because they had a leader of genius and partly because they were both disciplined and ruthless. "The dictatorship of the proletariat is power based on force and not constrained by any laws," Lenin had written. Mostly, though, they won because no one else in Russia was able and willing to govern in a hopeless situation. Amid suffering, starvation, economic chaos, the dissolution of the army, and outbursts of long suppressed popular desires for drastic social change, the established order had simply ceased to exist.

Civil War in Russia

Lenin's appeal for an international revolution was not heeded, at least not for more than a year after the October Revolution. Meanwhile the Germans were at the gate. The battle line ran from Riga on the Baltic southeast to not far west of Minsk; in the south, troops of the Central Powers, holding most of Rumania, stood close to the Ukraine. With the Russian Army virtually gone (troops were flocking home to get in on the expected redistribution of land), Russia was at the mercy of the Germans. In early December the Bolshevik government began negotiations for an armistice with the German military command at the latter's headquarters in the Polish town of Brest-Litovsk; the armistice announced on December 16 was followed by peace negotiations that opened in the same place on December 22.

Lenin's government had already published and denounced the secret treaties made with the Allies. Since practically all the diplomatists of the foreign ministry had walked out or been arrested, it was a rather unkempt bunch of erstwhile revolutionary conspirators who met with clean-skulled and monocled German aristocrats at Brest—one of the strangest peace conferences in history. The Germans had no interest in doing more to Russia than would enable them to withdraw troops to the western front, where they had long since known the war must be decided. The Bolsheviks hoped to use the conference as a sounding board for world revolutionary propaganda. They demanded that Paris, London, and Washington join the talks, threatening these governments with working-class revolution. They also tried to appeal over the heads of the Central Powers diplomats to the people. Trotsky irritated the Germans by behaving much less like the representative of a defeated power than of a victorious one. His illusions soon vanished. The Allies were not going to make peace, the people were not going to rise up, and the Germans were in a hurry.

Further complicating the situation was a decree issued by Lenin's government in the first flush of revolutionary enthusiasm, granting any nationality within the Russian empire the right to withdraw from it if they chose. The Ukrainians took advantage of this to proclaim autonomy and then independence, as Finland had already done. A veritable orgy of self-determination broke out, stimulated by the Bolsheviks' publication of the secret treaties. Lloyd George and Wilson, who at this time (January 8, 1918) unfurled his Fourteen Points, competed with the new Russian regime in maintaining a right of peoples to independence on the basis of nationality. If applied to Russia, such a principle meant wholesale disruptions. Thinking in terms of a future world socialist state, Lenin was initially prepared to accept the breakup of the Russian empire.

Faced with the demands of the military-dominated German emissaries that Russia surrender huge amounts of territory, Trotsky played for time, suggested not signing any treaty—"neither peace nor war"— and opposed Lenin in the Central Committee of the party. Lenin's amazing flexibility manifested itself here as a determination to sign the humiliating treaty immediately. With the German Army set to march into Russia, any other policy was sheer illusion. A majority of the Bolshevik leaders finally came around to Lenin's view, and the treaty of Brest-Litovsk was signed on March 3. The territory under Soviet control shrank by some 26 percent of the population, 27 percent of cultivated soil, and 75 percent of iron and steel production. Poland, the Baltic provinces, the Ukraine, and some Caucasian areas ceded to the Turks were either annexed by the Central Powers or became independent, which meant that they were in actuality subject to German domination. Wiped out later by German defeat in the west, the Brest peace was truly draconian; but Russia was powerless to resist it. It further divided Russia and weakened Lenin's popularity. Cries of "Traitor!" rang from the Congress of Soviets' executive committee as this body approved the treaty by a narrow margin. The great revolutionary had seemingly presided over the total liquidation of the Russian state, gambling for the stakes of world power via social revolution and losing.

Bolshevik ideology did suggest the dissolution of the state. Lenin's essay, "The State and Revolution," written during the very year 1917, affirmed the utopian element in Marx's thought: after the proletarian revolution inaugurating a classless society, the last turn of history's wheel, the state would (in Engels' phrase) wither away, at least as a coercive authority. Affairs would be administered by plain men in their everyday activities; workers and peasants would replace ministers and judges. Everything would be handled spontaneously and informally by those freed from exploitation and oppression. Neither law nor government in their objectified forms would be needed. Workers would manage the factories; comrades gathered together in friendly conclave would deal with what antisocial behavior lingered on as a vestige of the past. Of course, crime and corruption could be expected to vanish, along with the poverty and injustice that bred these social evils.

The state, which was defined as the ruling class's foundation for economic exploitation, would naturally melt away in a classless and nonexploitative society. Authority, no doubt, there would have to be, since a complex urban, industrial society such as Marxist theory envisaged for the future could hardly function without managers and planners. But this authority would require no force to back it up; it would emerge as natural leadership in an ideally organic society.

Of such dreams is utopia made; but the realities of postrevolutionary Russia were far different. It was a nightmare world of brutalized masses driven mad by the sufferings of war and now released from social controls. Having seized power by insurrection, using a fairly small number of urban workers and soldiers, the Bolsheviks did not have the support of a majority of Russians; or if they did at one moment have it, that moment did not last long. Even among the revolutionaries, the Bolsheviks were a minority. In elections held soon after the revolution to a constitutional assembly, the Bolsheviks won only about one-fourth of the delegates. The largest party was that to which the peasants were most loyal, the Social Revolutionary party.

But the Red Guards were loyal to Lenin, and on his orders they dispersed the Constituent (left over, as it were, from the first 1917 revolution) when it attempted to meet on January 18, 1918. All other parties, except a few left-wing SRs who lasted until the summer of 1918, had left the government, which was rapidly becoming synonymous with the Bolshevik party. The liberal Constitutional Democrats were suppressed first, along with the "bourgeois" press: "We cannot give the bourgeoisie the opportunity to slander us," Lenin declared. The SRs and the Mensheviks continued in existence for some time, but their publications were censored and they were subject to harassment. "The Terror and the Cheka [Bolshevik political police] are indispensable," Lenin said. He was quite prepared to "carry out merciless mass terror." Only sentimentalists believed you could create the new society without smashing the old ruling class; to create the new society, you seized state power and used it ruthlessly. Later, the utopia; now, the final great battle of the class war. And in war, whoever is not with us is against us; a Menshevik who shrinks from revolutionary terror is "objectively" an imperialist reactionary.

"White" rebellions against Lenin's government began in May of 1918. White Guards and Red Guards had begun fighting in Finland in January, the Germans supporting General Mannerheim's "White" (anti-socialist) forces. With the country rapidly falling toward anarchy, local regimes sprang up, usually under the leadership of some military commander who rallied former tsarist army elements and capitalized on growing disenchantment with the Bolshevik regime.

Although Lenin had tried to win their favor, the peasants mistrusted the Bolsheviks. Lenin realized that any successful revolution in Russia must include peasants as well as urban workers. The immediate issue was food for the primary source of Bolshevik power, the urban workers. The government fixed prices at a low level, and when the peasants refused to sell at these prices it sent troops to seize farm produce. The White leaders often represented the old landlord class. Thus they alienated the peasants, who were engaged in seizing the land formerly owned by landed nobility and the state. The peasants seem to have hated both sides; at any rate they did not feel any love for the Bolsheviks. (Involved in the fighting in some areas, the Cossacks were a third force, neither reactionary nor Bolshevik.)

Of course, until November the war was still going on in Europe, and White regimes could pose as friends of the Allies against the Bolshevik defectors, whose separate peace with Germany made them highly unpopular in France, Britain, and the United States. To compound the confusion, 30,000 Czech prisoners of war got loose in Russia and fought the Bolsheviks all the way to Siberia; the minorities in the Dual Monarchy were making their own nationalist revolutions, which depended upon Allied victory. Chiefly to protect military supplies in such areas as Archangel, the Crimea, and the Baltic states, the Allies adopted a policy of limited intervention and sent some aid to the White leaders.

The Japanese entered Siberia by way of Vladivostok. They were followed by the Americans, some of whom were as concerned with watching the Japanese as with combating communism. At one time various White regimes held a good part of Russia, receiving some aid from the Allies and capitalizing on disillusionment with the Bolsheviks. But the White groups could not cooperate with each other, and some of them were viciously reactionary. Finns, Poles, and Balts, fighting for their national independence, were not compatible with such Russian chauvinists as Generals Wrangel and Denikin, White warlords of the South.

It is false to assert, as the Russian Communists have always done, that the Western capitalist powers intervened to try to overthrow Lenin's government primarily because their reactionary capitalist hearts hated socialism. The Allies had no clear understanding of what was going on in Russia for some time and no desire to get involved in the massive and hopeless task of governing Russia or reshaping its society. They did dislike the Bolsheviks intensely, less because they were Communists than because they were helping Germany. Lenin was regarded, for understandable if erroneous reasons, as simply a German agent. The British feared that a German-Russian combine might threaten India and the Middle East. There was a widespread belief, some of it justified, that the Bolsheviks were cruelly persecuting people who had befriended the Allies during the war. There were military supplies in Russia, which the White generals promised either to keep away from or to use against the Germans. German troops were being transferred to the west in 1918 to mount the last great offensive, and anything that promised to delay this was attractive. Had Lenin been willing to fight the Germans, the Allies would have clasped him to their bosom no matter what his politics, just as they embraced Stalin in 1941. Lenin incurred their displeasure by leaving the war, not by being a Bolshevik. It is true that the new regime's repudiation of all Russia's foreign financial obligations went down hard, particularly with the French, who held large amounts of Russian debt. The White generals and admirals earned support by holding out some promise of returning Russia to the war.

The amount of support given them was not very great. President Wilson, in particular, insisted on limiting intervention to a few thousand troops; he was interested only in protecting military supplies and helping the Czech legion get out of Russia. After the war ended, the Allies lost most of their enthusiasm for aiding the Whites, and by early 1920 the last of them had surrendered or been evacuated. The French took General Wrangel and some 135,000 of his followers from the Crimea. At the Washington Conference of 1921–1922, the Western statesmen persuaded Japan to abandon her intervention in Siberia.

Though the Russian Reds failed to win back Finland, the Baltic states, and Poland, by 1921 they had the rest of the former Russian empire under control. The Poles, aided by France, finally defeated the Red Army after a wildly fluctuating war. In the 1921 Treaty of Riga, they made favorable terms securing eastern boundaries that took in some territory that was ethnically more nearly Russian than Polish. But within Russia the Red Army, forged chiefly by Leon Trotsky, was generally victorious over the White forces. Against a disunited foe on the peripheries, the Red government held the solid center of Russia, moving the capital to Moscow. By forcing former Imperial officers to serve by holding their families hostage, instituting a compulsory draft, and enforcing strict discipline, the Red Army became a prime example of how the Bolsheviks created a tyrannical state even more stringent than the one they had overthrown.

It was a grim and nasty war, as all civil wars tend to be. This one was charged with the authoritarian fanaticism of the Bolsheviks, class hatred of them by their old-regime enemies, and the hopeless rage of much of the peasantry against both. Unspeakable cruelties were committed by both sides; the Red Terror opposed the White. The civil war left Russia even more ruined, a prey to famine in 1921. Lenin's regime had proved that his iron will and the stern discipline of his elite Communist party could hold on to Russia, but it looked like they had won a lifeless body.

The crowning event of this ghastly interlude was a futile revolt in 1921 by the soldiers and sailors of Kronstadt, the island base in the Gulf of Finland. Originators of the revolution, in the name of freedom and of the soviets they now accused Lenin's government of betraying the revolution. Their ideology of left-wing communism tinged with anarchism, they claimed, spoke for the real revolution—the one the soviets had envisioned as a free, decentralized, democratic, nonauthoritarian society. Lenin himself had described such a society in "State and Revolution." But the new Lenin, as he himself freely confessed, had been forced by conditions into "bureaucratic deformations" in a "war communism" marked by centralization of power, suspension of democracy, and the use of terror, secret police, and concentration camps. It was unclear in 1921 how long this paradoxical situation could endure. The bloody suppression of the Kronstadt revolt, in which the army of the workers' revolution shot down the workers, symbolized the first great moral crisis of the Soviet Communist state.

Abortive Revolutions in Central Europe

Lenin had expected, indeed demanded, the spread of revolution throughout Europe, and he had placed most hope in Germany. The German Social Democratic party was much the largest and most prestigious in Europe before 1914. Its Marxism was not revolutionary for the most part, but the SPD had its left wing, and its members—Rosa Luxemburg, Clara Zetkin, Karl Liebknecht, and Franz Mehring–had shown more courage in opposing the war than any other European socialists save Lenin and Trotsky. Luxemburg and Liebknecht suffered imprisonment. In 1916, eighteen socialist Reichstag members had been expelled from the party for voting against the war credits.

Only a tiny minority, the Spartacists who followed Luxemburg and Liebknecht, directly resisted the war; but a larger minority, including distinguished elder statesmen Karl Kautsky and Edward Bernstein, founded the Independent Social Democratic party in 1917 to oppose annexationist war aims. The peace of Brest-Litovsk severely disillusioned them. In January 1918, a half-million German workers went on strike in Berlin, defying their trade union leaders; the strike was broken, ironically, by troops released from the eastern front after the Bolshevik revolution. Under the virtual military dictatorship of Ludendorff, there was little overt unrest in the ensuing months, which were dominated by the final German offensive.

The failure of that campaign set the stage for Germany's dramatic collapse. The German war leaders were ready to negotiate an armistice, which they hoped would lead to a compromise peace, in September. In October a change of government in Berlin, engineered from above, was designed to clear the way for peace. Prince Max of Baden, who had long favored a compromise settlement, was appointed as chancellor. Facing the news that victory was not possible, German morale suddenly fell apart. On November 3 a naval mutiny broke out at Kiel and became the signal for a series of uprisings all over Germany. The discredited Wilhelm, whose presence had become an obstacle to an armistice, abdicated, and socialist leaders proclaimed a republic.

Subsequent investigations of the Kiel mutiny—a German parliamentary committee conducted elaborate inquiries in 1925—determined that socialist propaganda had not been a significant factor. Much more important were deterioration of morale from long inactivity, poor food, the arrogance of officers, and excessively strict discipline. In general, the German "revolution" was not a revolution like the Russian one. If Lenin expected it to be, he grossly misunderstood the situation. Many on the Left believed the Spartacist revolt of January 1919 was about to succeed when it was betrayed by the treachery of the majority Socialists, who allied with the Right to crush it. It is true that a cleavage existed between the majority socialists, who had supported the war, and a minority that was partly revolutionary and partly pacifist. But even the latter were rarely revolutionary in Lenin's sense. Rosa Luxemburg did not approve of the Bolshevik philosophy. She repudiated a minority revolution; the socialist revolution must "secure victory for and through the great majority of the workers themselves." The Spartacists were not Bolsheviks; they would not take power without a mandate from a majority of the workers. This they never came close to having. They never seriously contemplated a coup like Lenin's.

Rosa agreed with the Lenin of "State and Revolution," who dreamed of a republic of soviets, or workers' councils, abolishing the military-bureaucratic state. The Spartacus Union, she said, "is no party wanting to climb into power on the shoulders of the mass of workers" but rather "the conscious party of the proletariat." She severely criticized the Bolshevik dictatorship, though somewhat moderating her rebukes near the end of her life. At the same time, the Spartacists denounced the majority Socialists who headed the new German government as "lackeys of the capitalist class" and called for a true socialist revolution to come from "the great mass of the socialist working class." But the great mass of the German people, confused by the trauma of defeat, suffering from severe food shortages and disease (the terrible flu epidemic began at this time), did not want a socialist revolution.

The alleged Spartacist putsch attempt of January 1919 emerged from a situation in which some radical trade unionists, the "revolutionary shop stewards," joined the new German Communist party, which was made up mostly of Spartacists, for a mass demonstration. Together they called for the overthrow of the government. This demonstration was a chaotic and rather leaderless outburst, which the KPD (Kommunist Partei Deutschlands) leadership supported only hesitantly, Rosa Luxemburg being decidedly ambivalent. The government suppressed the disorders that marked the second week of January; and on January 15, Rosa Luxemburg and Karl Liebknecht were arrested, released, and then murdered by Berlin soldiers in what amounted to a lynching. Although the crime further embittered the radical Left, the whole episode revealed the weakness and the indecisiveness of the German Communists. They had produced no Lenin. Even if they had, Germany was simply not Russia, and a revolutionary dictatorship was scarcely conceivable.

Disorders spread throughout Germany as the new government, saddled with the onus of defeat, struggled with the returning army and a host of economic problems. It lacked legitimacy in the eyes of many Germans. Bands of ex-soldiers (the Free Corps) often took the law into their own hands. In Bavaria, an unlikely place for a revolution, dislike of Prussia combined with particularist sentiment for the local Wittelsbach dynasty, which still survived from the 1871 amalgamation of German states. These emotions helped trigger a revolution that temporarily deposited a socialist government in power. Munich seemed on the brink of becoming a communist city. On January 12, an aristocratic monarchist assassinated left-wing socialist Kurt Eisner. Further turmoil ensued, and on April 7 a group of writers and intellectuals proclaimed a Soviet Republic in Munich. No more interesting group ever appeared than these poets, playwrights, and philosophers—Ernst Toller, Gustav Landauer, and Karl Korsch among them—but the Communist party denounced them as romantic amateurs, a "coffee-house clique." Free Corps troops commanded by a Prussian general soon invaded the city and began a White terror.

Although there were somewhat similar episodes in other German cities, what may have seemed to Moscow like the beginning of the world socialist revolution was in reality more nearly the reverse. Amid the confusion, a strong right-wing reaction was evident. Bewildered by Germany's loss of the war after so much heroic dedication, returning soldiers more often than not blamed the socialists and communists— not much distinguishing between them—for betraying the nation at a critical moment. Socialists and communists were accused of delivering a *dolchstoss*, a stab in the back, to the valiant troops who, they alleged, had not been defeated in the field. The soldiers resented the upstart regime that had replaced the kaiser, to whom they had pledged loyalty. In Russia, a completely demoralized army came home to help a revolution of the Left; but although it had been forced to end the war, the German army was not completely demoralized. Regrouping as the Free Corps, the more brutalized and adventurous elements of the army terrorized the Left and once even attempted to seize power (the Kapp putsch, 1920).

Partly to control them, the republic made terms with the Free Corps. Some were diverted to fight Poles and Lithuanians in the east. They were not brought under control until 1921 or 1922, by which time they had been absorbed into the reorganized army or had joined such nationalist, right-wing political clubs as the one Adolf Hitler led. They specialized in assassination, and among their victims were not only "reds" but such political leaders of the democratic center as Walter Rathenau and Matthias Erzberger. These men were guilty only of accepting the new republic and the peace treaty that emerged from Paris in 1919—the *diktat* of Versailles.

These terrorists of the Right out-Lenined Germany's would-be Lenins. From the ashes of defeat, in both Germany and Italy, a new political phenomenon was rising. In Italy, it bore the name of fascism. Its genesis was clearly evident in the immediate aftermath of the war. The Marxists could not fit fascism into their somewhat simple framework. It was popular but antisocialist, not internationalist, but nationalist, not revolutionary but counterrevolutionary; Fascists hated socialists, intellectuals, and Jews, as well as the old aristocracy and plutocracy. The right-wing terrorists' predominant impulse was the restoration of order; and the revolutionary socialists, who fomented disorder but lacked the will to a new order, became the victims of their authoritarian instinct.

Outside Russia, other postwar revolutions of the Left proved equally ephemeral. Caught in the shambles of the Dual Monarchy's disintegration, Hungary was ruled for four months in the spring and summer of 1919 by a Hungarian Communist. Bela Kun had been a prisoner of war in Russia at the time of the Bolshevik revolution, and he knew Lenin personally. The first government of the Hungarian Republic, which lasted from November 1918 to March 1919, was shattered by the loss of territory to Rumania and the new states of Czechoslovakia and Yugoslavia. Bela Kun then formed a somewhat incongruous alliance with the Hungarian Social Democrats and proceeded to try to carry out an ambitious program of agricultural and industrial nationalization. But there, as in Germany, the result was confusion rather than reconstruction. The hostility of its neighbors, who had the Allied peacemakers on their side, doomed the Hungarian Soviet Republic. Bella Kun fell in early August, and counterrevolutionary terror followed. Russian-inspired revolutionary experiments like the one in Budapest and similar ones in Munich and Vienna filled a temporary vacuum of power left by the collapse of the old order. But they had no sufficient social basis to last.

It is hardly surprising that such confusion existed. "The spectre of unrest haunts the whole world, from the Western United States to China, from the Black to the Baltic seas," the London *Times* commented on July 19, 1919. "The symptoms are everywhere present that the elementary bonds of society are torn and decayed as a result of the long exertion." In Great Britain, the Labour party adopted a socialist program for the first time in 1918. The Liberal party was dealt a deathblow. War is the locomotive of history, Karl Marx had understood. The exigencies of war had uprooted people and flung them into new and trying circumstances, not only on the battlefield but on the home front. For the first time, millions of women left the home to take over jobs left vacant by men departing for military service. "Soldiers from the war returning" found it hard to take up the threads of life as before. The cake of custom had been broken. But in the West, the shape of the new social order could not be as stark and as simple as it was in backward, semi-Asiatic Russia.

The Paris Peace Conference and the Versailles Treaty

It was this sense of a world in crisis that lent urgency to the convening of a peace conference at Paris. It began with almost unseemly haste, within a few weeks of the armistice, and produced a peace treaty with

Germany by June 1919. Lenin, someone said, was the invisible partner at the Paris conclaves. One of the many postmortem criticisms of this peace was that it would have been better to wait until passions cooled; but at the time, the very turbulence of these passions seemed reason for cooling them by the clear mandate of an authoritative settlement. Boundaries lay in obscurity; three great empires had collapsed; revolution was rife; and the world demanded a definitive end to the war so that it might begin the process of reconstruction.

To Paris, then, in January, came President Woodrow Wilson, the first American president ever to leave his native shores while in office and a symbol of hope to many in the Old World; David Lloyd George representing Britain; Georges Clemenceau from France; Italy's Vittorio Orlando; and hosts of their ministers and advisers. Subsequently, a great array of "suitors and suppliants" came from all over the world, each seeking something from the all-powerful statesmen who had assembled to end the terrible war with a peace of justice and stability. The notable absentees were Russia and the defeated power, Germany.

Unfortunately the statesmen proved neither omnipotent nor omniscient. The world was not altogether consoled, and many of the suppliants went away empty-handed. The Paris peace conference of

At the Paris Peace Conference: The "Big Four" of Orlando (Italy), Lloyd George (Great Britain), Clemenceau (France), and Wilson (United States).
National Archives, Washington, D.C.

1919 remains one of history's most dramatic scenarios, around which a furious controversy has raged. Wilson, the hope of the world, was said to have failed in his mission, perhaps, though he was the most intellectual of statesmen, from want of knowledge. Clemenceau and Lloyd George were said to have imposed harsh and vindictive terms on Germany, guaranteeing that feelings of revenge would flourish east of the Rhine. On the other hand, some critics thought Germany was too leniently handled, that she got off with slight loss of territory and indemnities that never were actually paid. Although one rationale of the settlement was national self-determination, unsatisfied nationalisms remained to plague the future. Strategically, the peace was glaringly weak: too few had a stake in maintaining it, too many in overthrowing it.

Judged by its results, the settlement obviously left something to be desired, for another world war broke out within twenty years—this peace turned out to be nothing but a long armistice. Whether this can be blamed on the participants in the Paris conference is another question. Many forces were beyond their control. They could hardly put the Dual Monarchy back together again, even if they wanted to. Neither could they cause Lenin's Bolsheviks to cooperate with the capitalists; revolutions had broken out before they met. Nor could the bitter hatred aroused by a war that had cost so many millions of casualties be diminished. Two of every three able-bodied Frenchmen in the prime of life had been killed, wounded, or captured. The war had bitten deeply into everyone's consciousness.

The victorious Allies were not united in their approach to the peace settlement. Though two of Wilson's Fourteen Points were specifically withdrawn at the time of the armistice, they constituted a quasi-official basis for the peace. Wilson was the man of the hour; millions of cheering people crowded to greet him as he made a brief triumphal tour of the Continent prior to the convening of the conference on January 18, 1919. The Fourteen Points were often vague, but they indicated disarmament on all sides; "a free, open-minded, and absolutely impartial adjustment of all colonial claims"; return of Alsace-Lorraine to France; "a readjustment of the frontier of Italy . . . along clearly recognizable lines of nationality"; "autonomous development" for the peoples of Austria-Hungary; and an independent Poland with access to the sea. They spoke of "historically established lines of allegiance and nationality" as guides to a Balkan settlement. The Fourteen Points were against secret diplomacy and for "open covenants openly arrived at." They recommended "a general association of nations . . . under specific covenants," [*covenant* was one of Wilson's favorite words] "for the purpose of affording mutual guarantees of political independence and territorial integrity to great and small States alike"—the famous League of Nations so extensively discussed during the war.

From these and other Wilsonian pronouncements, people perhaps inaccurately associated the American president with a nonpunitive peace. He advocated settling boundaries on the basis of ethnicity, a general disarmament, and a completely new deal in international relations. Wilson had powerfully advocated the democratic principle of self-determination of peoples. Although the Fourteen Points as modified did mention indemnities, Wilson was associated with a moderate position, one that would not leave too many scars on the defeated powers or breed a spirit of revenge. But in discussions with the Allies about what the Fourteen Points meant, Wilson withdrew point 2, relating to "freedom of the seas," on British protest. A statement was inserted that Germany must pay compensation "for all damage done to the civilian population of the Allies and their property by the forces of Germany." It became evident at this time, just before the armistice, that the French and the Italians objected to nearly all the points. The United States threatened to withdraw from the war if they were repudiated, however.

Against the Wilson peace outlook, with which they almost entirely disagreed, the French had drawn up a shopping list. It included (a) French military control of the Rhine, (b) a crushing indemnity levied against Germany, (c) German disarmament, (d) German territorial reduction, (e) "crippling the German political organization," and (f) depriving her of economic resources. Though they wanted the great powers to form a permanent alliance, Marshal Foch and his military adviser cared little about anything except the destruction of German power and her territorial dismemberment. To the French, determined to prevent a repetition of 1914, some such program was almost a sine qua non; and Clemenceau fought hard for it, although he did not personally believe in the partition of Germany. A League of Nations appealed to the French less as an idealistic new way in diplomacy than as an alliance to stand guard against Germany.

The British government stood somewhere in the middle, but Lloyd George had tied his hands by promising the British people that Germany would be made to pay for the war. Britain's best interests might dictate keeping Germany intact. Whereas the French believed that their security depended on destruction of German power per se, the British were much more inclined to settle for a payment to ease the British taxpayer's burden.

There were also secret treaties—particularly, now that Russia and Rumania had cancelled out, the one with Italy, which promised German and Slavic territory to the Italians. Others dealt with Asia. There was a series of evidently contradictory dispositions about the Middle East. Palestine was the much-promised land. In the famous Balfour Declaration, which was designed largely to win Jewish support for the war, it had been promised to the Jews as a homeland. But it had also been promised to King Hussein of the Arabs as a reward for joining in the fight against Turkey. Meanwhile, the Sykes-Picot agreement of 1916 seemed to have partitioned the region between France and Britain. The Americans cared little about the Middle East, but they turned out to care a great deal about China. Japan's acquisition of Shantung, formerly in the German zone of influence, struck American opinion as a sordid "imperialist" deal.

Of such jarring counsels was the hectic peace conference made. The Allies (France, Britain, Italy, and the United States) did not argue with the defeated powers; they argued with each other. They excluded Russia, boycotting the Communist regime completely and at one moment coming close to recognizing the Siberian White warlord, Admiral Kolchak, as the legal Russian government. Lloyd George initially wanted to invite the Bolsheviks, but he stood alone in this position and, criticized even within his own government, soon gave in. It is doubtful that Lenin's government would have come anyway, or come in any spirit of cooperation. Allied policy was rapidly retreating from giving any great amounts of aid to the Whites, though Winston Churchill advocated it. The compromise solution was neither to recognize nor to intervene against the Russian Reds, which added up to total negativism. Such positive policy as there was took the form of hoping for a "sanitary" zone of new states to serve as a buffer against Bolshevism and to be potential allies for France.

The loss of Russia as a powerful ally was a key to French policy at Paris. France felt it was necessary to weaken Germany and to build up a strong Poland as a potential substitute alliance partner. Thus many of the features of the settlement with Germany may be traced to the silent factor of Russia's defection.

The Allies seem to have intended to negotiate with the Germans after they had resolved their own differences. In the end, exhausted by the preliminary task, they simply called in the Germans and told them to sign. Unlike past peace conferences, the defeated side did not even have a chance to state its case. No wonder German opinion rejected the Versailles treaty as a *diktat*.

The adjustment of Big Four disagreements was not accomplished without much friction. At one point, Wilson summoned his ship to take him home. Orlando did walk out, after furious exchanges with the American president, although he subsequently returned. Clemenceau regarded the moralistic Wilson as a self-righteous and narrow-minded hypocrite; Wilson considered all the Europeans to be touched with evil. Lloyd George, aided by the more supple Wilsonian chief adviser, Colonel House, worked to secure compromises. In the end these prevailed. Wilson's attempts to teach virtue to the soiled Europeans were hampered by his relative ignorance of complex European questions. Furthermore, the

United States, powerful though her role had been, had simply not expended nearly as much blood and treasure in the war as had France and Britain. Wilson was something of a disappointment to those European liberals who had expected much from his leadership; he was "unable to clothe with the flesh of life the commandments which he had thundered from the White House," John Maynard Keynes wrote. Yet Wilson withstood terrific pressure for a truly "Carthaginian" peace, including the partition of Germany.

The most acute clash of wills at Paris occurred when the British and the Americans joined in refusing the French demand for territorial dismemberment of Germany. The French wanted the western, Rhineland portion of Germany to be made into a separate state. Wilson stood firm on the principle of self-determination; the British had more in mind the balance of power, fearing that any drastic weakening of Germany might open the dikes to Bolshevism. Germany did lose some territory. She had to return Alsace and Lorraine to France and a small portion of land to Belgium. The Saarland was given over to French economic use, under international administration, for fifteen years, after which there would be a plebiscite. Most galling to the Germans were significant cessions to the restored Poland in the east. The German city of Danzig was internationalized, Memel given to Lithuania. The "Polish Corridor" now awkwardly separated part of Prussia from the rest of Germany. But Germany was neither partitioned nor deprived of the great bulk of her population, resources, and territory.

In few cases were the territorial cessions really unjust; not even the Germans complained about returning Alsace-Lorraine to France, and the population in the east was ethnically mixed and a minority one way or the other inescapable. Since Poland had to be given an outlet to the sea she was ceded Danzig and the Corridor. Poland was awarded less territory than she and the French had wanted. East Prussia remained German only at the insistence of Wilson. All told, Germany lost about 10 percent of her 1914 population, mostly from Prussia's provinces of Posen, Silesia, Brandenburg, and West Prussia. Within a few years, natural population increase made up her losses, so that Germany's 1933 population exceeded that of 1910. Her most serious resource losses were the iron ore of Lorraine and coal from the Saar. Yet after the war French iron still had to come to the German steel mills in the Ruhr.

By way of compensation to the French for a sacrifice they regarded as tremendous, Germany was subjected to immense reparations claims. Here the British supported France over the U.S., and Wilson had to give in. Some British economic advisers were skeptical about the reparations bill, fearing that it would disrupt the world economy. Some French hoped to use it as a basis for future German dismemberment.

The total figure was left open, to be finally calculated by May 1921. But the inclusion of indirect damages (for example, payment for pensions to widows and orphans of dead soldiers) as well as direct damages meant that the bill would be astronomical by current standards; many billions of dollars.

Additionally, Germany lost all her colonies, which Germans thought a clear violation of one of the Fourteen Points. Although German colonies were put under League of Nations "mandate," the Allies did not so surrender their own colonies to supposed international control. Germany was unilaterally disarmed; she had to reduce her army to 100,000 men and give up large guns, submarines, military aircraft, and all but six warships. The Heligoland fortifications were to be demolished. Any army so deprived of the tools of modern war would be impotent. The Allies were to occupy strategic points on the Rhine for at least fifteen years, and Germany was forbidden to keep troops in a demilitarized zone extending thirty miles east of that river. This gave France strategic security so long as it was maintained, but the area remained German.

While severe, the terms were hardly savage. Perhaps, as some argued, they were either too harsh or too lenient. Machiavelli had long ago pointed out that you can either crush a foe or make friends with him; what is most dangerous is to insult him and let him go free. The compromise of Versailles treated Germany as if she were guilty and hurt her in small ways, but it by no means destroyed her as a potentially powerful state. It offended her pride without greatly impairing her strength. Could one enforce the disarmament provisions or collect the indemnities against a Germany determined to resist them? Much depended on the shape of events to come.

Given a chance to make a statement before signing the Versailles treaty, the Germans protested that it was "a peace of violence and not of justice." The reply of the Allies was that justice was being done for Germany's "crime against humanity." Germany won a few minor concessions as the result of her appeal. This has led to speculation about what Germany might have achieved had she been able to worm her way into the conference as Talleyrand had done in 1815. No such diplomatic talent emerged from the German side on this occasion.

Both sides thus accepted the view that this was a punitive peace, the Allies alleging German war guilt (which was specifically affirmed in article 231 of the treaty), the Germans denying it. This led to an intellectual battle of historical interpretation in the ensuing years, leading on the whole to a qualified German victory: in the 1920s, most scholars who studied the records with care concluded that either everybody was guilty, or nobody was. Versailles left an uneasy sense of guilt in the West, and the whole peace conference was said to have been poisoned by irrational hatreds. "Paris was a nightmare, and everyone there was morbid," Keynes thought. "The Treaty is a crime born of blind revenge and insatiable greed," U.S. Senator William Borah declared as he prepared to lead a senatorial rejection of Versailles, chiefly because of the League of Nations. Colonel House himself, one of the treaty's leading architects, wrote gloomily in his diary just after the treaty's signature on June 28 that

> To those who are saying that the Treaty is bad and should never have been made and that it will involve Europe in infinite difficulties in its enforcement, I feel like admitting it.[1]

But, House added, "I would also say in reply that empires cannot be shattered and new states raised upon their ruins without disturbance." "Sad peace! Laughable interlude between the massacres of peoples!" exclaimed Romain Rolland, ending thus his long wartime journal on June 23, 1919. Rolland was one of the very few European writers who had opposed the war from the start. To him, the peace was as bad as the war.

Other Peace Treaties and Settlements

The treaty with Germany, which also contained the Covenant of the League of Nations, was only one of several made in various parts of Paris in 1919 and 1920. Some of the negotiations dragged on long after the signing of the Treaty of Versailles, which took place with a great flourish in the Hall of Mirrors on June 28, 1919. Wilson sailed home to encounter a hostile Senate and suffer a stroke later in the year. Europe continued in disorder as the Russian civil war went on, Bolshevism appeared in Hungary, and near anarchy reigned in both Germany and Italy. The signing of the Versailles treaty permitted an end to the Allied blockade of Germany, which had continued through the first six months of 1919. Soviet Russia was also subject to the blockade, which was a factor in the terrible Russian famine of 1921.

The treaties of St. Germain and Trianon treated Austria and Hungary, the two remnants of the now dismembered Dual Monarchy, as defeated powers, limiting the size of their armies, compelling them to pay reparations, depriving them of territory, and forbidding Austria to unite with Germany, even though this was undoubtedly the wish

[1] *The Intimate Papers of Colonel House,* ed. Charles Seymour (Boston: Houghton Mifflin Co., 1928), vol. IV, 488–489.

of an overwhelming majority of the Austrian people. They were required to recognize the independence of Poland, Yugoslavia, and Czechoslovakia, the other successor states. Austria ceded territory to Poland, Italy, and Yugoslavia. The Italian demand for what had been promised them in the secret Treaty of London had occasioned one of the sharpest clashes at Paris when Wilson refused to be bound by it. The Italians declared that having lost his virtue to France and Great Britain, the American president sought to regain it at Italy's expense. They demanded even more than had been promised them, adding the city of Fiume to the list. In the end, a compromise only partially appeased the angry Italians, among whom talk of the "mutilated peace" helped the Fascist cause.

Hungary was handled even more savagely than Austria. Having sacrificed any lingering claim on Allied sympathy by going communist in the middle of the Paris conference, the Magyars found themselves invaded and pillaged by the Rumanians (August–December 1919). They were forced to sign a treaty that gave away most of the old Hungary to Czechoslovakia, Rumania, Yugoslavia, and even to Austria—and required to pay reparations on top of this. Of all the victims of the war, Hungary could perhaps claim the most injustice, for although it was Vienna, not Budapest, that had wanted war in the first place, Budapest's losses were the greatest of all the countries. But Slovaks, Croatians, and Rumanians who had suffered second-class citizenship under Hungarian rule in the past could muster little sympathy for their former oppressors, and they were on the winning side.

The boundaries of these more fortunate successor states were not determined without a struggle. Yugoslavia and Italy quarreled over territory along the northeastern shores of the Adriatic, previously a part of the Dual Monarchy. The two countries set the boundary late in 1920 by a treaty at Rapallo, although there was still more trouble until Fiume was given to Italy in 1924. Yugoslavia, the new kingdom of the Serbs, Croats, and Slovenes, also had to settle its boundaries with Rumania and Austria. Two other of the new states, Poland and Czechoslovakia, clashed over Teschen, which Lloyd George confessed he had never heard of before coming to Paris. The battling Poles also fought Russia for two years, as we know, to settle their eastern borders, and they struggled with Lithuanians for possession of the city of Vilna, an issue at length decided by a plebiscite in favor of Poland. The restored state of Poland, by winning rather generous settlements from all her neighbors, thereby incurred their ill will, which haunted the Poles down to 1939.

The device of a plebiscite did not always persuade the losing party that justice had been done, for much depended on how the voting unit was defined. For example, while Fiume and Trieste, both Adriatic cities, were themselves mainly Italian, the surrounding rural regions were Slavic. In the important industrial region of Silesia, which was inhabited by both Poles and Germans, voting results depended on the size of the district polled, and the Germans complained of gerrymandering.

Bulgaria's fate was settled in the treaty of Neuilly in November 1919; she also lost territory, agreed to pay damages, and had to reduce her army to a handful. But in attempting to treat Turkey as a defeated power, the Allied peacemakers caught a tartar. A nationalist revival under Mustapha Kemal, hero of the Dardanelles victory, brought the former Ottoman Empire out of the war with high morale. The 1920 treaty of Sèvres dismembered the Turkish empire, depriving it of its Arab provinces, delivering territory in Thrace to the Greeks, and declaring the Straits (once promised to Russia) an international zone. But Kemal's nationalist movement repudiated the government of the sultan that signed this treaty; turned on the Greeks, who had marched in to enforce the treaty; and eventually defeated them. This dragged on until 1922, by which time the Allies had almost ceased to exist. In 1923 a new treaty, signed at Lausanne, secured more favorable terms for Turkey, where Kemal now headed a new government. Turkey recovered some territory from Greece and regained control of the Straits, which she agreed to demilitarize and open to ships of all nations. This was the only defeated country, or even victorious one, that came out of the war with better morale than it started with.

All of this confused even the experts at Paris in 1919, and if the student finds it confusing, small wonder. Empires had been shattered and new states raised. Let us try to summarize. Austria-Hungary had ceased to exist. Russia had come close to dissolution. Imperial Germany remained but was forced to disgorge territory. The three great empires of the Hapsburgs, the Romanovs, and the Hohenzollerns had fallen. Many peoples had gained their independence; no fewer than nine new states appeared in Europe (and several others in the Middle East). Finland, Estonia, Latvia, and Lithuania, formerly subject to Russia, were now lined up along the east shore of the Baltic Sea, a kind of *cordon sanitaire*, as the French said, between the Union of Soviet Socialist Republics (Communist Russia) and the West. Poland, a large country, was restored to national existence for the first time since 1795. She received land from each of her former partitioners, Russia, Austria-Hungary, and Germany, and profited from the defeat of all three. Czechoslovakia and Yugoslavia came from the old Dual Monarchy, Czechoslovakia entirely and Yugoslavia partially. Yugoslavia, of course, contained prewar Serbia as its nucleus but also added large chunks of pre-1914 Hungary and Austria and a little of Bulgaria. The other two new states (new as such) were Austria and Hungary. Now disjointed relics of the old empire, each was left derelict by the detachment of its former possessions. Rumania emerged as a much larger state—luckiest of all, considering her war record.

But these new countries in the east and center of Europe were untested, dubious, fluctuating. Those who looked into the future with trepidation stressed the instability of boundaries and the strategic weakness of a "Balkanized" continent. The losers of the war, especially Germany and Russia, would surely try to regain what they had lost. The winners, including Poland, Yugoslavia, Czechoslovakia, and Rumania, were not only new and weak but divided. Several of them had never existed in all previous history.

It was frequently remarked that to create new boundaries is to create new problems. The attempt to organize Europe along principles of nationality resulted in political instability, not only because it created many small and unstable countries but because it had proved impossible both to honor the principle of nationality and to divide up Europe in a way that gave each linguistic or cultural unit its own independent government. Minorities of nationalities were left over even in the new Europe. Czechoslovakia was an amalgamation of Czechs and Slovaks, with some Germans thrown in; and the two Slavic peoples were not always perfectly harmonious. The Croats, Slovenes, and Serbs who were to try living together might all be Yugoslavs, but they had very different traditions and characteristics; they were divided by culture and religion. Poland contained German, White Russian, and Lithuanian minorities. Rumania had absorbed many Magyars. There were disputes between Yugoslavia and Italy, Poland and Czechoslovakia, Greece and Turkey in areas where peoples were hopelessly intermixed. There was no way to satisfy every ethnic claim and still retain viable states that were large enough to be prosperous and to have defensible borders. The new Europe was a kind of desperate compromise among the conflicting and incompatible demands of languages, culture, economics, and defense.

The League of Nations

Its creators knew better than anyone else the serious defects of the peace settlement. We have not named all these defects. In general, the non-European peoples, who were victims of colonialism and many of whom had expected that the war and the new Wilsonian diplomacy would bring them relief, went away disappointed. It scarcely lay within the province of the peace conference to tell the British to grant inde-

Europe after the War, 1919

pendence to India and Ireland, or Japan to Korea, or France to Indochina. Among the disappointed suppliants at Paris in 1919 was one later known as Ho Chi Minh, who thereafter turned to communism. The war had led to demands from these and others for their freedom. All over the colonial world, the war deflated the white man's image and encouraged movements of liberation from Western domination.

The Arabs, who had fought with the British against their Turkish overlords, now bitterly reproached the Allies for not giving them their liberty; and in the Far East both China and Japan, for different reasons, lacked confidence in their wartime partners. Japan had entered the war with a promise that she would receive the former German island possessions in the Pacific and the German leasehold in the Chinese province of Shantung. China had entered the war in its later stages chiefly to be able to make an appeal against imperialism at the peace conference. At Paris Japan got her rewards, imperialism received no rebuke, and the Chinese were bitter. In the United States especially, a strong reaction against this seemingly cynical "deal" caused angry denunciations of both Japan and the Paris peace. Shantung as much as anything was the reason many Americans decided to repudiate the Treaty of Versailles, refuse to enter the League of Nations, and write off the European world as morally lost. At Paris the Japanese requested and were refused a statement affirming the equality of races; also rejected was a Chinese demand for an end of the "unequal treaties" by which the Europeans in their country had obtained a privileged position.

The months following the "peace" of 1919 witnessed violence in Ireland, India, Egypt, and Korea, as well as in Russia, Turkey, Hungary, and Dalmatia; there seemed to be less peace than there had been even during the war. In 1920, Lord James Bryce, one of the leading architects of the League of Nations, saw "lunacy everywhere. . . . We all say to one another that the war was bad, but this sort of peace is worse." "No one believes that the inequalities temporarily established by the Treaty of Versailles can be made the basis of a real peace," added Swiss professor William E. Rappard. Faced with a world in such volcanic eruption after the mighty upheaval of 1914–1918, Wilson and others hoped that new machinery of international relations could work as a stabilizer. The new League of Nations might serve as adjudicator of disputes, administrator of world justice, and, in the last resort, maintainer of the peace. As the world cooled down, this agency of world government, replacing the old "international anarchy," should preside over its readjustments.

At Paris, President Wilson devoted a great deal of his personal attention to the drafting of the "covenant" of the League—his own word, one intending to convey the solemnity of a biblical rite. The League was indeed the object of an almost religious faith. It was widely believed that the "old regime" in foreign affairs was now as obsolete as the pre-1789 internal political order; it was to be swept aside by a revolution in the conduct of international relations. This discredited old way employed such dubious means as secret treaties, rival alliances, and devious diplomacy; it represented national selfishness dependent on armed might, and it tried to keep the peace only through the balance of power. Had it not failed so badly in 1914 that an entirely new way must be found? The world must replace power blocs and national militarism with international cooperation.

In a general way, almost everybody approved the popular idea of a League of Nations during the war. And a number of groups had attempted to work out the specific plans of such a league. When one got down to details, though, agreement often broke down in the face of practical difficulties. Would the greater nations really relinquish control of their armed forces to an international institution—which would then be a world government or superstate? Would they agree in advance to abide by the decision of such an international body in any dispute? If not, could the League be anything more than a place to exchange views? On the one hand, utopian expectations surrounded the notion of a League of Nations—it was expected somehow to abolish war and usher in the international millennium. On the other hand, when the moment of truth arrived nations were simply not prepared to hand over to the League any real power, for this would mean surrendering the jealously guarded sovereign power to choose war or peace, to defend the nation, to provide for national security.

Wrestling with such contradictions at Paris, Wilson and the other Allied statesmen hammered out the Covenant and wrote it into the Treaty of Versailles. Some people thought it a mistake to tie it so closely to the peace settlement. Some thought it too weak; others feared it might be too strong. It was attacked as a "Holy Alliance" of the big powers rather than true international democracy, because it gave somewhat more power to the larger nations, who were to hold permanent seats on the council, or upper chamber. Briefly, the member nations who joined the League (initially it excluded Germany and the other Central Powers, a feature often criticized) agreed to submit their disputes to conciliation or adjudication before going to war; that is, they had first to try to settle conflicts by peaceful means through the machinery of international organization. If after trying this procedure they still could not agree, presumably they might go to war with the League's blessing—another point that was criticized by those who hoped to do away with war altogether. If member nations went to war before going through this procedure, they were liable to such punishment as the breaking off of normal relations, economic boycotts, or even war.

Another article of the Convenant, one put in at the insistence of President Wilson, declared that all members guaranteed the political independence and territorial integrity of each member state. In case of a violation, however, the League might only recommend action; it could not demand it. The meaning of this article 10 was somewhat obscure and probably not by accident. It represented an ambiguous compromise between those who, like the French, wanted a strong League and others who wished to avoid ironclad commitments. Article 10 was destined to cause the most controversy when the United States Senate debated the League and finally refused to approve it, after proposing a number of "reservations" that Wilson refused to accept. Its foes claimed that article 10 violated the U.S. Constitution and endangered the nation by constituting an obligation to go to war automatically at the behest of a foreign body. In fact it obviously did not mean that; yet its lack of clarity helped discredit the League.

While all members sat in the League's assembly, only twelve held seats on the council, where the important decisions, such as whether a violation of the Covenant had occurred were made. The major powers held permanent seats on the council, and the unanimous vote of this body was required on important matters. But the parties to a dispute could not vote when it came up for decision.

There were other important features of the League. To deal with the thorny issue of imperialism, the League provided for a mandate system; countries held colonies as trustees of the League and were supposed to report to the League on their progress. Also established were various agencies for international cooperation in such fields as health, conditions of labor, and collection of information. A permanent secretariat was to administer the League's activities from headquarters in Geneva, Switzerland. An affiliated World Court was expected to develop into a real instrument of international law.

What did all this mean? Those who had dreamed of a world state were obviously disappointed, for the League had no real power except as the separate member nations chose to grant it on any particular occasion. The League did not possess its own armed force, for example; it would have to request forces from the various member states in case of an emergency. That the Covenant ventured as far as it did in article 10 was sufficient to frighten off the United States, which dealt the young institution a serious blow when it refused to join. The appeal of nationalism and the system of sovereign national states were far from dead. The war, in fact, had everywhere strengthened nationalism. No major power would accept in advance an obligation to uphold the status quo; boundaries were too insecure, their moral value too unclear.

What the League might amount to only time would tell. Those who were skeptical about its ability to install a whole new peace system hoped that it might at least serve a useful purpose in bringing nations together on a regular basis, teaching them habits of cooperation, and providing a forum for the solution of disputes. But with the refusal of the United States to take part in the League, the French felt that a blow was dealt to their hope for security in Europe. Her allies politely declined to take any appreciable part in upholding a peace settlement they had helped to write. In addition to the ambiguous pledges of the League, France had obtained from Wilson and Lloyd George promises of a guaranty treaty pledging the United States and Great Britain to defend the Versailles treaty frontiers. This, too, the United States refused to approve; in fact, it was never even brought to a Senate vote, the situation being hopeless.

Thus the Allies were breaking up, another ominous sign for the future. In his memoirs of the war, one of many literary masterpieces the war produced (its only saving grace), British poet Robert Graves remarked that just after the war "Anti-French feeling among most ex-soldiers amounted almost to an obsession. . . . Pro-German feeling was increasing." His buddies said they would never fight another war, unless it was against the French! American-French relations cooled rapidly, too, after an initial euphoria. And American opinion turned sharply on England because of the rebellion in Ireland. This popular sentiment would be mirrored on the diplomatic front; familiarity had bred contempt, and the Allies were tired of each other. The Americans retreated to their isolation from foreign entanglements as suddenly as any great people has ever changed. The British and their dominions (Canada, Australia, South Africa, New Zealand), who had played such a stalwart part in the war, were only a step behind. The great era of disenchantment with the war and with the peace was about to begin. In such soil the League of Nations could hardly take root and grow.

Aftermath of War:
Europe's Turmoil
in the Twenties

5

Damages of War and Problems of Recovery

Census statistics dramatically reveal the loss of life in the countries that had borne the major brunt of the war. In France the 1921 count disclosed a shortage of about two million males, more than a million of them from twenty to forty years old. What French statesman Edouard Herriot called "the sinister balance sheet of slaughter" also showed a million British dead, two million Germans, a half-million Italians, and how many Russians no one knew. Herriot's estimate of eight and a half million total battle deaths for Europe was surely conservative; other guesses ran from ten to thirteen million. The war itself slid into the postwar revolutions, anarchies, civil wars, famines, epidemics. To battle deaths were added the tolls from influenza and other diseases, which struck most severely at the aged and infirm. Overlooked in some of the citations of statistics, little Serbia, the original crux of the conflict, had suffered most of all in terms of percentage of population lost—some 12 percent. Authorities put the Russian toll altogether, counting the civil war and the famine, at twenty million.

For every battlefield death there were probably two soldiers permanently wounded, so that the Frenchman who could not show his wooden leg or at least his lost ear was almost an oddity. Such grievous casualties, hitting at the youngest and most robust, "a loss even more serious in quality than in quantity," was, needless to say, a fantastic disaster; it silently weakened Europe for many years and may have accounted for her slippage in economic strength after the war.

On the other hand, the physical disaster can be exaggerated. The resiliency of populations is amazing; the cynicism of Napoleon, who remarked after a military defeat that "Paris can make it up in one night," seems justified. Germany, despite war casualties and ceded territories, had by 1933 regained her 1914 population of some sixty-five million. Even the French losses amounted to no more than 4 percent of total population. In none of the Western countries save perhaps Italy was there a real breakdown of the social fabric and the administrative order. Even the situation in postwar Germany did not at most times and in most places amount to anarchy. As for war damages, they were confined to a fairly narrow zone. Although everything along the western front was totally destroyed, outside this battle region losses were slight by World War II standards, when whole cities were destroyed from the air. Nothing like that happened in the 1914 war.

Familiar with the spectacular economic boom that followed the much more destructive World War II, we may wonder why Europe did not recover rapidly after 1920. In fact she did not, on the whole. The situation varied, but in few places was there genuine recovery.

In Great Britain, the immediate postwar economic adjustment was heartening; in 1919, demobilization went smoothly, and unemployment was low (less than 3 percent). Women went back to the home or to domestic service, men took their places in industry, consumer goods shortages caused a brisk demand. But within two years unemployment soared, and it remained high all through the 1920s—about 16 or 17 percent on the average. It fell to 9 percent in the "prosperous" year of 1929, but after that the Great Depression shot it up to 20–23 percent. The effects were somewhat mitigated by an extension of unemployment insurance in 1916 and 1920 and by a general reduction of the hours of work. A normal 54-hour work week changed to 46 to 48 hours right after the war.

The war had brought a movement toward economic equalization. Everyone agreed that the working classes' courage and loyalty had earned them the right to a greater stake in the national wealth. The war produced feelings of solidarity. In a famous slogan of the day, the returning soldiers must have "homes fit for heroes." But this note turned sour amid the postwar slump. Strikes, leading up to the great general strike of 1926, reflected the restless disappointment of workers, as did the rising strength of the Labour party, now considerably more radical than it had been.

So far as Britain was concerned, there seemed to be a basic structural flaw in the economy. Unemployment was most severe in traditional export industries, including coal, textiles, and shipbuilding. The war had caused England to lose markets, which had passed primarily to the United States and Japan during the years in which the British had turned their resources to war production. Britain had also lost income because she had liquidated overseas investments to raise war funds. She still owed billions in war debts to the United States.

"Europe has lost its role as banker to the world. The financial power of the United States is increasing. The power of Japan is growing. Our North American friends have seized domination of the great routes which lead from the Atlantic to the Pacific." This complaint came from a Frenchman, Edouard Herriot. Great Britain was more dependent on overseas markets than was France, having built the structure of her economy during the nineteenth century, when she was "workshop of the world." But all of Europe felt this migration of basic economic power to other continents.

In France and Germany, the question of war reparations payments clouded the economic scene for several years. As you may recall, the Versailles treaty fixed no exact sum for Germany to pay; the amount was to be calculated by a reparations commission. The French figured the liability as high as 200 billion dollars; the Germans thought it unfair that they should pay anything. Unenthusiastically, they offered about seven billion dollars. More detached analysts thought Germany could not afford to pay anything like the total potential bill without ruining her economy and disrupting the international monetary system. But the French government floated large reconstruction loans based on the expectation that the Germans would pay for them.

In the immediate postwar years, Germany was expected to deliver large amounts of coal as payments on her reparations bill. Although they sent some, the Germans partly could not and mostly would not fulfill the Allied quotas. A conference at Spa in July 1920 resulted in agreements that led only to new arguments. The Germans, who were allowed to deliver less than previously required, demanded further reductions. The French bitterly charged betrayal and, with the British, wondered whether they should send troops into the Ruhr. Germans and some British argued that Germany could not recover until she was free of the burden of reparations and that German recovery was essential to general European recovery. On this view, the sum Germany owed ought to be clearly established and much pared down.

Muddle was the word for the reparations question; it was complicated even further by the American attitude toward Allied debts, which was almost as unfeeling as the French view of what Germany owed her. American insistence on repayment of war loans forced France and Britain to maintain their hard line on German reparations payments. But the two Allies had trouble keeping a united front, the British being more prone to compromise on reparations than the French. In 1921 and 1922 opinion in both France and Germany hardened, the Germans defiantly unwilling to continue shipping their surplus off to the West, the French determined to make the "Boches" pay for French reconstruction. The 1921 economic slump intensified this standoff and put the two countries on another collision course. For advocating "fulfillment," the brilliant Walther Rathenau, who had steered the German economy through the war and was now in charge of reconstruction, suffered death at the hands of right-wing terrorists.

Suffering from inflation, strikes, and economic stagnation, the German government in 1922 adopted the slogan, "First bread, then reparations." The Germans offered to settle the reparations bill for fifteen billion marks, a figure insulting to the French. Though the British refused to go along, French Premier Poincaré resolved to employ sanctions by sending troops and engineers into the Ruhr early in 1923.

This was virtually a renewal of war, and the episode did not end until it had dealt grave damage to the European economy. Germany resorted to passive resistance; workers struck in the Ruhr; and German inflation shot up to fantastic heights, the greatest inflation of all times, as the economy ground to a virtual halt while money continued to be printed in massive quantities. The 1923 crisis threatened to finish what World War I had begun, the ruin of Europe.

Postwar Politics in the West

Behind this mismanagement lay the muddled politics of the postwar years in all the belligerent countries. The new, precarious German Republic, struggling to establish its credibility against Spartacists and Communists on the Left and disgruntled nationalists and monarchists on the Right, had to unite moderate socialists with liberal, Catholic, and moderate conservative parties. Such a coalition was necessarily vacillating and vulnerable.

The German "revolution" of 1919 had not led to a Bolshevik-style dictatorship but to a parliamentary democracy. The majority Social Democrats had not forged a Red Army to destroy the old regime. They had not dismissed the constituent assembly but had summoned it to write a liberal constitution, and they leaned on the old army to put down a mildly threatening revolt from the Left. Moderate conservatives applauded this relative defense of order, but they retained a suspicion of the potential for socialism lurking in a republic whose first president was a Socialist, Friedrich Ebert.

A new Democratic party arose to rally nonsocialist liberals to support the republic and collaborate with the Ebert Socialists. Somewhat to its right but still willing to accept democracy was the People's party, led by a man destined to become the leading German politician of the 1920s, Gustav Stresemann. Both DDP and DVP (*Deutsche Demokratische Partei, Deutsche Volkspartei*) were remnants of the prewar Liberals, who had been destroyed by the war (as, in effect, had been the British Liberal party). These successor parties never succeeded in getting a mass following. The socialists, themselves split, could not command

NOTHING BUT MONEY AND MONEY BUT NOTHING.

THE GARRET-DWELLER—" I now have a million. Three-quarters of it goes for rent and heating, and I may be able to get some bread and cheese with the remainder."
—*Lustige Blätter* (Berlin).

The great German inflation of 1922–1923: When a billion marks would not buy a loaf of bread. *Historical Pictures Service, Chicago.*

a majority in parliament without seeking allies among the bourgois democrats. The Weimar majority consisted of a rather incongruous amalgamation of industrialists, trade unionists, Social Democrats, army officers, and Roman Catholics, all struggling for stability against the forces of disintegration.

The Weimar Republic of 1919–1933 was so called because its constitution was framed in this Thuringian town famous for its associations with German culture (Cranach, Bach, Liszt, and especially Goethe). This occurred less because of any conscious desire to invoke "the other Germany" than because in early 1919 Berlin was too disorderly. The seat of government soon returned to Berlin, the traditional capital.

The first "Weimar coalition" of Social Democrats, Democrats, and Catholic Centrists resigned in June 1919 over the peace terms. In the troubled year 1920, the Kapp putsch attempted by Free Corps elements was defeated by a strike, which briefly increased trade unionist strength. But in the elections of June 1920, the Weimar parties' strength fell from over 75 percent of the popular vote to less than half, beginning Weimar's strange career as a "republic without republicans." The rightwing Nationalist party (DNVP) gained, as did the dissident left wing of the SPD, the Independents (USPD), and the Communists (KPD), though the latter was a small minority. This made finding a ruling coalition all the more difficult. A precarious government was finally assembled under a Centrist premier, the SPD not in it but agreeing to support it in the parliament. In 1921 this ministry stumbled over reparations troubles, and another Centrist, Joseph Wirth, formed another shaky government, which was fated to watch the mark sink to 1/50 of its 1914 value by the end of the year. Wirth resigned in October 1921, when the League of Nations ruled against Germany in plebiscite disputes involving Upper Silesia, much of which passed to Poland. But he came back again with a shuffled cabinet when no alternative emerged.

Quarrels between wage earners and employers simmered during the reparations and economic crisis; who should bear the burden? Employers said that lengthened workweeks and suspension of strikes were essential to stabilization; the socialists and trade unionists naturally found these prospects less than enchanting. In 1922–1923, the director of the Hamburg-America ship line, Wilhelm Cuno, replaced Wirth and proceeded to precipitate the reparations crisis. He was thus destined to preside over the liquidation of middle-class savings and incomes.

In France, too, the elections of 1919 brought in a rightward-leaning *bloc national*. Dissatisfaction with the outcome of the peace settlement, which the French thought yielded too little security and too little recompense for the vast damages she had suffered, dominated the public mind. When Georges Clemenceau sought the presidency of France, an honor he coveted and seemed obviously to have earned by his war leadership, he was defeated because of French anger over the peace settlement. The "battle of the Ruhr" in 1923-1924 hurt France almost as much as Germany and did not solve the reparations problem. This unhappy outcome caused a turn to the left in 1924, when a coalition of Socialists and Radicals took office. Their election set the stage for the politics of accommodation, which replaced the politics of resentment from 1924 to 1930.

The most significant development in postwar British politics was "the strange death of Liberal England"—the almost complete collapse of the once dominant Liberal party. It is ironic that the party of John Bright and William Gladstone and David Lloyd George, the party associated with peace, antiimperialism, and domestic reform, had led England into the war and then endured all the crises of that dismal experience. In 1914, a few Liberals angrily resigned. Lloyd George's 1916 replacement of Asquith as prime minister began another feud, for a minority of Asquithians never forgave him. More significant, perhaps, was the fact that the war and the postwar depression pushed the working class and others toward the Labour party, which had adopted a Socialist platform in 1918 and whose leader, Ramsay MacDonald, was one of the few who had opposed the decision for war in 1914. In a basically two-party system, Labour moved up rapidly as the alternative to the Conservatives. It won more parliamentary seats in the elections of 1922, 1923, and 1924 than did the Liberals.

In 1922 the Conservatives won a comfortable majority after they had precipitated an election by leaving Lloyd George's wartime coalition government. The next year, Prime Minister Bonar Law retired because of illness, being replaced, to the infinite chagrin of the abler but incurably aristocratic Lord Curzon, by the rather obscure Stanley Baldwin. Baldwin decided to appeal to the country in late 1923 on the issue of protective tariffs versus free trade, a venerable British political battleground.

He was defeated, and a Liberal-Labour partnership took office with Ramsay MacDonald as the first Labour prime minister. This coalition soon broke up, though MacDonald's year was a memorable one in foreign policy, coinciding with the French withdrawal from the Ruhr and the Dawes Plan dealing with reparations. The 1924 election again firmly installed the Conservatives in power; it was remarkable for nearly wiping out the Liberals, who have never since regained their status as a major force in Parliament.

So the dismal years immediately after the war were marked by an unmistakable drift to the right, which moderated a little as the decade of the 1920s wore on. This was true in the main countries of Europe except for Communist Russia, and even there there was a similar trend, in a sense, during the "retreat to capitalism" that began in 1921. One of the reasons for this conservative trend in the West was the fact of the Communist regime's existence. Fear and hatred of Bolshevism dominated the European middle classes and even some of the trade unionists. It is true that the French seemed to fear and hate the Germans even more, but their desperate search for security can be traced back to the loss of their Russian ally. In the 1924 British election, an alleged letter from a high Russian Communist (Zinoviev) advising the LP on how to seize dictatorial power cost the Labour party many votes. (MacDonald had negotiated a trade treaty with Russia.)

The election of a Conservative government had something to do with the general strike of 1926, Britain's closest approach to a social revolution. Though Winston Churchill drew up plans for the disposition of troops in the event of class war, the general strike turned out to be something less than that. It began where much of postwar British working-class discontent had been concentrated, in the Welsh coal mines. One of Britain's major industries before 1914, coal became a declining industry after the war, partly because oil was replacing coal as a source of power and partly because British mines suffered from technological obsolescence and fell behind foreign competitors. Ironically, by restoring a large source of coal to efficient production, settlement of the Franco-German struggle over reparations in the Ruhr war of 1923 hurt the British. The coal miners called for nationalization as a means of overcoming stagnation; the mine owners resisted this, needless to say, and a Conservative government sympathized with them. Their answer was cutting wages and increasing hours of work, which scarcely pleased the miners. A strike began in 1926, and the Trades Union Congress, the national British labor organization, called for a general strike in sympathy with the miners.

The general strike was never intended to be the social revolution in the way anarchist theory postulated; it was merely an expression of solidarity with the miners. British good humor was more in evidence than were the passions of a class war. "I think everybody enjoyed the strike, on both sides," Lord Beaverbrook wrote. "It was treated in a holiday spirit. . . . I am almost inclined to favour the idea of having a general strike once every year by law." Volunteers from the middle classes manned the various public services; Churchill got out a government newspaper that had a circulation of three million copies. The genial disposition of Stanley Baldwin, who made up in good will what many thought he lacked in intelligence, helped smooth the way to an early end of the general strike. Nevertheless, the coal strike dragged on for months and ended in defeat for the miners, who were forced to accept a reduction in wages. The miners' defeat set the pattern for a period of trade union decline, with membership far down from wartime highs and strikes infrequent.

The fiasco of the general strike typified the generally conservative mood of the times, underneath which lurked a pervasive fear of the Reds. Dislike of communism was not entirely based on myth and exaggeration. The Bolshevik regime displayed the worst possible international manners, inflicting outrages on citizens of other countries within Russia, seizing property, and conducting propaganda marked by vituperative denunciations of Western leaders. Its government had turned into a brutal dictatorship, which lost most of the support it initially had received among liberals in the West. Yet a part of the hysteria against communism reflected a fear that the contagion might spread and private property might be abolished, wiping out profits and deposing the dominant economic classes in the West.

Other and subtler reasons for the rightward swing in the twenties have to do with the whole movement of thought and culture, which is discussed in the next chapter. Disenchantment with all political causes accompanied the reaction against the "great crusade" of 1914–1918, with its high-sounding phrases. The "best people" in the 1920s cultivated a cynical disdain for politics, along with a distaste for democratic culture. They sought relief in art and literature, laughed at mass culture and the common man, contemplated the wasteland of a dying civilization with sophisticated despair. There was a return to religion because of the loss of faith in worldly progress, secular utopias, and the benevolence of human nature. Science, too, was interesting though apparently baffling in the age of Einstein and Planck. The "lost generation" felt that all gods were dead and all causes exhausted. This attitude helped the Right more than the Left, which thrives on secular hope. The apolitical attitude is quasi-conservative.

Along with the conservative trend went a tendency toward polarization. It was the liberal center that suffered the most. But this politics of extremism was more notable from 1919 to 1924 than it was in the ensuing five or six years, the all too brief period of economic recovery and international agreement.

The Rise of Italian Fascism

These generalizations hold true with a vengeance for Italy, which between 1919 and 1924 gave birth to a new political phenomenon, fascism, an extremism of the Right that arose in response to disorders on the Left.

The year 1919 was as wild in Italy as in any country in Europe. Her citizens never as firmly united in support of the war as the other belligerents', Italy was split even by the decision to fight; the rout at Caporetto then shattered national confidence, and finally at the peace conference Italians thought they were treated with contempt. When Wilson tried to deny them all the promised annexations, Orlando and his foreign minister, Sonnino, strode out of the Paris meeting, but they finally came back.

Meanwhile the Russian Revolution aroused great excitement in Italy. There were socialist riots and strikes, the latter stimulated by inflation and wartime shortages. Threats of a Lenin-type revolution brought a strong reaction, however. In March, the prowar ex-socialist Benito Mussolini organized *fasci di combattimento* ("combat groups") to fight the subversive elements. With Parliament deeply divided, Orlando's government fell on June 14, a victim of the "mutilated peace"; his succesor, Francesco Nitti, soon also found himself attacked from both Left and Right. He called for new elections in September, soon after the celebrated author and war hero Gabriele D'Annunzio marched at the head of a small private army into Fiume, the city on the Adriatic that was a symbol of frustrated Italian war demands. The government did not dare dislodge D'Annunzio.

Further to confuse the political scene, a new Popular Catholic party rose. Left, Right, and center were all divided within themselves. The results of the November election showed the PSI, the Italian Socialist party, winning the largest number of representatives with about 32 percent of the popular vote; the Catholic party came next with 20 percent, and the liberals suffered a sharp decline. More strikes and clashes between Socialists and Fascists followed the election. Inflation continued. Peasants in the south of Italy began to invade and confiscate state, church, and privately owned estates, while northern farm workers joined in a wave of often violent strikes.

The disorders continued into 1920 with factory takeovers and a showdown between the socialist unions and the great Turin industrialists, Fiat and Olivetti. Postal, railroad, and other government employees joined in the strikes. Italy looked to be in the process of a socialist revolution, which a confused and divided government was powerless to stop. On June 9 Nitti, who had held onto the premiership, was forced to resign. He was replaced by the old prewar political boss, Giolitti. At about this time the initiative swung away from the Left.

On analysis, it would appear that the Socialists had disrupted Italy without seizing power. It was, no doubt, a tribute to their democratic principles that they produced no Lenin. But constant strikes and disorders infuriated large sections of the populace and turned the

Italian bourgeoisie toward the Right. Workers controlled local factories in accordance with the syndicalist, or "soviet," philosophy of the Italian Socialists. But this system was unable to cope with economic problems on a national scale. Never a majority in the parliament, the Socialists did not try to seize the state. The government, perpetually divided, was too weak to institute effective reforms. In this vacuum arose the private armies of the right, the Fascist *squadristi*, who battled with the Socialists in city and country. At the end of 1920 the brilliant Italian Communist, Antonio Gramsci, wrote that the bourgeois state was decomposing and splitting into two components: "The capitalists are forming their own private state just like the proletariat." The impotence of parliamentary democracy, others might say, was forcing Italy toward civil war.

The strongest personal leadership this time came from an ex-leftist now on the Right. Editor of the Socialist party newspaper, *Avanti!*, Benito Mussolini had long been identified with the left wing of the much divided pre-1914 Italian socialists. In the debate about whether to enter the war that had animated Italy between September 1914 and May 1915, this son of an anarchist blacksmith, a man of much humbler birth than Lenin, had thrown his literary and oratorical talents on the side of intervention, whereas a majority of the traditional socialists had held back. Money to support his pro-Allied activities evidently came from French socialists, some Italian industrialists, perhaps from the Italian foreign office. His erstwhile comrades accused him of betrayal, and he broke with them. He did indeed do a complete turnabout from his "Abasso la guerra!" at the beginning; but Mussolini's switch resembled that of many Italians who had swung to the side of the democracies, the "fellow Latins" against "Prussian militarism." Syndicalists, anarchists, republicans, some socialists all found reasons for entering the war; many felt that the best reason was given by labor leader Corridoni: "Neutrality is for eunuchs!" Mussolini, disciple of Nietzsche as well as Marx, was neither a eunuch nor perhaps one to resist the tide of popular opinion.

A man with some intellectual interests, Mussolini helped provide fascism with an ideology. The fascist ideology was constructed of various fashionable pre-1914 ideas borrowed from Friedrich Nietzsche, Georges Sorel, Henri Bergson, and others. Mussolini's credo stressed action, elite leadership, and a new set of values to organize the masses. Fascism was a quasi religion, frankly accepting the need for symbol, ritual, and myth. D'Annunzio had already pioneered in organizing the private uniformed army with parades and mass meetings, the leader addressing crowds of massed followers from a balcony and they roaring slogans back at him. Adolf Hitler was to embroider on this pattern, but in 1921 Hitler was a most obscure person, an odd little ex-corporal addressing a handful of disciples in Munich beer halls. In 1921 Mussolini and his Black Shirts rose like a comet. The Pope, Pius XI, called him "a man sent by God," and the king of Italy was converted to fascism.

Eloquently proclaimed by Mussolini, fascism asked for national revival and blamed the parliamentary system and "the lie of universal suffrage" for Italy's weakness. It was thus antidemocratic as well as anti-Marxist. It was also antimodernist, preaching the natural inequality of man and exuding a Nietzschean neobarbarism moved by the ideal of purging corruption and decadence from society.

Not many Italians could be found to defend the corrupt and ineffective parliamentary system, though after it was gone they regretted not having done so. Mussolini was a dynamic and colorful personality. He now proclaimed the need for a new order, postliberal, post-Marxist and postdemocratic, a kind of national socialism. Although he found support from industrialists and landowners anxious to destroy socialism and communism, fascism could scarcely have triumphed had it been only a conspiracy of the rich. It possessed a mass appeal. Peasants, shopkeepers, white- and even some blue-collar workers accepted at face value this great man who promised to solve Italy's problems. They were tired of chaos and thought socialism had missed its chance. The Fascist program was vague, but it suggested that the state should be an instrument of bringing the "corporations" of capital and labor together in fruitful cooperation rather than in class strife.

Those who regarded fascism as the morbid excrescence of a dying world may have been more nearly right than those who hailed it as a new principle of social reconstruction. What mattered most in 1921 and 1922 was that chaos reigned, parliament was impotent, and Mussolini alone seemed a forceful personality. Between May 1921, when the Fascists won only a handful of seats in the elections, and the march on Rome in October 1922, fascism rapidly gained converts. Philosophers, as well as the king, responded to its dynamism. The old system of government, never very successful since the *risorgimento* (unification) of Italy in 1860–1870, had broken down under the strain of the war and the postwar crisis.

Named prime minister after the march, Mussolini moved to strengthen the executive power and weaken Parliament while building the Fascist party into the one great national political organization. Not until 1925 did he begin to crush opposition, arrest and imprison enemies, bring the press and education under fascist control, and create a one-party state. Prior to this reversion to simple tyranny, Mussolini received much praise from all over the world for restoring order in Italy and creating a new sense of national purpose.

Mussolini, October, 1922: *Il Duce* with other Fascist leaders during the "March on Rome." Mussolini promised to end Italy's civil strife. *Historical Pictures Service, Chicago.*

He turned out to have no plan capable of transforming the Italian society and economy, but at least he managed for a time to restore national morale and "make the trains run on time." Puzzled by fascism, Marxists were inclined to tag it as petty bourgeois. But its appeal lay in a claim to abolish class warfare and regain that sense of all pulling together, that organic unity people had felt at the beginning of World War I. And its heroic, pseudoaristocratic mystique was anything but bourgeois; indeed, it affected to despise the merely calculating and commercial spirit. Fascism borrowed Lenin's idea of a dynamic elite and turned it toward a different goal, that of national solidarity and greatness. Unlike German nazism, Italian fascism did not place much stress on race, rather, it talked of Italy's ancient glories reaching back to the Roman Empire, which it dreamed of restoring. War, Mussolini announced, "brings all human energies to their highest state of tension, and stamps with the seal of nobility the nations that dare to face it."

146

While indulging in such chest-thumping rhetoric, *il duce* in practice struggled with deep divisions within his Fascist party, some elements of which soon predictably denounced him for betraying its goals. He stayed out of war for a dozen years. When at length he turned in that direction it was to prove disastrous. In 1923 Mussolini discharged his belligerence on the relatively safe target of Greece. Following the assassination of an Italian member of the commission to establish the frontier between Albania and Greece, Italy sent an ultimatum to the Greek government and bombarded the Greek island of Corfu. Greece appealed to the League of Nations, whose failure to take any significant action against an act of aggression was the first demonstration of its impotence.

The Soviet Union until the Death of Lenin

If Germany was a republic without republicans and Italy a great man state without real leadership, the Union of Soviet Socialist Republics [1] might perhaps be said to have been a proletarian Communist regime without proletarians or Communists. Certainly the most startling paradox was that the 75 percent of Russia that was peasant did not want socialism or communism at all. The peasants were for the Bolsheviks when they threw out the landlords and redistributed the land, but they were against the Bolsheviks when they nationalized the land. The peasants wanted individual land holdings. They had not created soviets, and they did not like communism. During the revolution, they had reverted to their traditional peasant village, the *mir*, even more strongly than before. The mir was an institution with profoundly cooperative features, but it presented a united front against the urban-oriented and urban-based Communist regime. Leninist attempts to stress a class division within the peasantry between rich capitalists and poor proletarians did not have much basis in peasants' mentality.

This was but one facet of the main Bolshevist dilemma. Lenin's party contemplated the failure of world revolution, leaving only one Communist regime holding a backward, almost precapitalist country, if a vast and potentially powerful one. In many of his pre-1914 writings, Lenin had conceded that a revolution in Russia alone would make no sense. Seizure of power by a small vanguard elite in a land

---

[1] This name was not formally adopted until 1924, when previously independent Ukrainian, White Russian, and Transcaucasian SSR's were merged with the Russian, and others created to form a "union" of what were supposed to be "culturally autonomous" SSR's, but were in fact increasingly under centralized control through the Party.

of backward peasants with very little industry could only by itself mean a reversion to "Asiatic despotism." One cannot, on Marxist principles, escape the need for revolution to be a part of an entire social process.

As we know, Lenin believed that the Russian Revolution would touch off revolution in the West. Russia was a part of world capitalism, not a separate society. As the weakest link of world capitalism, it would crack first, and the whole world capitalist order would follow. The vanguard party was justified only insofar as it could perform this initial function in the global class struggle, capturing, as it were, one vulnerable salient on the long capitalist front, enabling other forces then to move in for the main battle.

When the revolution did not occur elsewhere, Lenin's party was left with a problem, and it is no wonder it engaged in strenuous arguments. Should one continue to expect world revolution? Meanwhile, what should be done with Russia? How could the Bolsheviks avoid betraying the basic values of Marxism if they ruled in Russia alone? Would not the dictatorship, based on a primitive social structure, revert to a traditional despotism? On the other hand, to industrialize Russia must entail either intensifying the dictatorship or allowing capitalism to return, perhaps under the general control of the party, in accordance with the theory of "permanent revolution." This latter was in fact what Lenin decided to do in 1921.

"War communism," which between 1918 and 1920 had nationalized all industry and seized food from the peasants by force, was justifiable only as long as the emergency lasted, Lenin thought. It had been a temporary measure necessitated by civil war. In deciding that it would never do as the basis of Russia's peacetime society, Lenin again startled most of his Communist colleagues. Lenin thought that like the Brest peace, another drastic if temporary concession to reality would be necessary. One could not, in Russia, proceed immediately to a communistic economy. Such an economy did not exist and could not exist for some time in the social conditions of Russia. It was "necessary for a time to live within the bosom of capitalism"! Lenin's capacity for daring paradox seemed revealed in this proposal that the Communists preside over capitalism, but it was in fact a reasonably obvious conclusion from Marxian theory applied to Russian conditions. Early on, Trotsky as well as Lenin had suggested something of the sort. Continuing to hold political power via the machinery of the state, the disciplined vanguard party would permit a kind of controlled capitalism to function. Unless and until the revolution spread to other countries— and hope for this could not entirely vanish—the party must engage in a holding action in Russia.

In his late years Lenin seemed sometimes, like some of the Western Marxists to believe that a democratic cultural revolution had to accompany or precede socialism. If so, he was not well understood by most of the Bolsheviks. In May 1922, the unquestioned leader of the party suffered a paralytic stroke. (This may have stemmed from the wound Lenin received in August of 1918, when a bullet fired by a Socialist Revolutionary woman, Fanny Kaplan, creased his skull. This shooting was the signal for an outburst of Bolshevist terror aimed indiscriminately at "bourgeois" elements.) He partly recovered from the stroke, but clearly his political career had ended. Though the secret was guarded, from that time on Lenin was a dying king around whom the possible heirs gathered to watch both him and each other.

The Communist party was already hardening into an organized and arrogant power elite. Although the party adopted the New Economic Policy, permitting private trade by small businessmen and farmers, it did not, of course, surrender any political power. It kept the reins firmly in its hands. Its hierarchical structure was growing, with a small group of men on the Politburo, a steering committee of the Central Committee, determining policy; "democratic centralism," more centralist than democratic, meant that once a decision had been taken by the party, its members must accept and obey the decision unquestioningly. Leadership, however, was supposed to be impersonal and collective; Lenin was an uncrowned king, not a self-proclaimed *duce* or *führer* like the Fascists. The party's legitimacy came not from any personal charisma but from its alleged mastery of the secrets of scientific Marxism. The party's infallibility was openly proclaimed, but this was because, rather like the medieval Catholic church, it collectively held the keys to the Marxian kingdom.

So, if Lenin in his last year had doubts about what had become of the Revolution, he was powerless to change his own creation. There can be no myth of a gentle or humane Lenin; he had consistently called for ruthless terror, and in 1922 was still calling for it. In that year the trial and condemnation to death of twelve Socialist Revolutionary leaders marked an extension of the repression to fellow revolutionaries of a different hue, who could by no means be called reactionaries or bourgeoisie. (The trial caused a bad reaction among socialists abroad, and the death sentences were commuted to life imprisonment—a mere stay of execution, as it turned out.) What can be alleged is that Lenin did not intend to perpetuate the terror, and he became dismayed when it looked as if a harsh despotism was settling in for good. To him the terror was a brief interlude between the old order and the new, not a permanent way of life. He grumbled about illegality, a low level of culture, "bureaucratic misrule and wilfullness," abuse of authority, "lack of civilization." His last testament warned against Stalin's "rudeness." But his comrades probably thought him a victim of brain softening. He had another stroke on March 9, 1923, just short of his 53rd birthday, and was pathetic after that. He died on January 21, 1924.

Had he lived as long as Mao Tse-tung, Tito, or even Stalin, who knows how drastically the history of the world might have been changed? Careful students of Lenin think he may have intended the New Economic Policy (NEP) to be quasi-permanent. Russia would have to go through a prolonged bourgeois phase before it developed sufficient civilization for socialism. But most of the Bolshevik leadership thought of NEP as only a breathing space. It would buy a few years of time while they regrouped, considered the situation, and hammered out a policy. The stage was set for a momentous and memorable debate, along with a struggle for power, in the three years after Lenin's death. Meanwhile NEP semicapitalism brought a modest degree of recovery; by 1926 the economy was almost back to its 1913 level! [2]

Illusions of "Normalcy": The 1924 Restoration of Order

The year 1924 was a turning point. The death of Lenin, following his second stroke in 1923, may be set alongside the settlement of the Ruhr-reparations crisis, after its devastating eruption in 1923. In 1923 Hitler attempted a putsch in Bavaria; 1924 saw the Nazi leader in jail and his party almost destroyed. For the Soviets, this period meant the collapse of the last hopes for world Communist revolution. Such hopes had remained alive, particularly in Germany in 1923, and while they were, Soviet leaders could live with the NEP, their eyes still fixed on the impending world revolution. The last failure was to come in China in 1927, when the slaughter of the Moscow-directed Communists by Chiang Kai-shek's Nationalists led to acrimonious disputes in Russia about where to fix the blame.

French and Belgian troops marched into the Ruhr in January 1923, following the breakdown of the last of many reparations conferences. The German managers of the Ruhr coal syndicate left, the local people adopted passive resistance, and the German government declared that it would subsidize the striking Ruhr workmen out of

---

[2] This was not achieved without some capitalist help. Responding to an appeal from the great writer Maxim Gorki during the terrible 1921 famine, an American Relief Administration headed by Herbert Hoover provided much food to Russia between 1921 and 1923. A confirmed anti-Bolshevist, Hoover ironically helped Lenin's regime to surmount the crisis.

public funds and suspend all reparations deliveries to France. The British member of the Rhineland High Commission (the American one had just gone home) did not support the Franco-Belgian action and somewhat handicapped the occupation effort, thereby engendering no little Franco-British friction. By seizing the Ruhr industries, French Premier Poincaré hoped to force the Germans to make good on reparations payments. The Ruhr basin contained 80 percent of Germany's coal and 80 percent of her iron and steel production. It could well claim to be the industrial heart of the continent.

German defiance and British opposition did much to frustrate Poincaré's plans. British diplomacy sought to bring the United States back into the picture and, with American aid, to negotiate a reasonable reparations settlement. And world opinion tended to side with the Germans against the French.

The most extraordinary consequence of this virtual renewal of war was the collapse of the mark. This was history's most stupendous inflation. Incredible as it may seem, by the end of 1923 the German lucky enough to have 10,000 marks in the bank found that that sum, which had once been worth $2,500, now equalled about a millionth of a penny. In January the value of 10,000 marks had already fallen to about half a dollar, but during the spring and summer of 1923 it grew more and more valueless each day and each hour. Life savings were wiped out, and money lost all value. A 100 billion mark note, which would have bought the whole Rhineland a few years before, would now hardly be enough for a loaf of bread.

One historian characterized the French action as the cause of Hitler's triumph and therefore the cause of World War II. This analysis rests on an alleged destruction of the middle class; the loss of faith in all values prepared the German mind for Hitler's nihilism. But in fact some German industrialists profited from the inflation.

The Cuno government resigned and was replaced temporarily by the ablest of German statesmen of this era, Stresemann. Curzon, the British foreign secretary, was convinced that ruin awaited everyone if the madness persisted. Desperate, the Germans finally capitulated; but Poincaré tried to go further and separate the Rhineland from Germany, thus achieving the old 1919 goal of French policy. He proclaimed a "Rhineland Republic" in October, and he enlisted a few Germans who thought Germany was breaking up to head it. Even Konrad Adenauer, then mayor of Cologne, almost played the French game. A British report condemned the "revolver republic" forced upon the local population against its will by French military force. Poincaré gave up, the separatist movement evaporated, and a number of the quislings were assassinated. The franc showed signs of following the mark into oblivion. Poincaré's government fell. A leftist bloc won the elections in the spring of 1924 and brought a different attitude to the French government.

Meanwhile, the old mark having gone on its flight into the stratosphere (a *trillion* old marks for one new mark was the exchange rate), the Germans created a new currency, the *rentenmark*. The new currency was based on a mortgage taken against the national wealth held by bankers, merchants, industrialists, and farmers. Stabilization succeeded but at the cost of massive temporary dislocations resulting in huge unemployment. Nevertheless, Germany came through this grave crisis without a revolution. The German Communist party (KPD) increased its percentage of the popular vote to 12.6 percent in the May 1924 elections, but it sank to 9 percent in another election held in December. The leading right-wing party, the nationalist DNVP, gained 20 percent, and a right radical National Socialist Freedom party got some support. The extreme Right outgained the Left.

Although at times in 1923 communism threatened in the Rhineland and Saxony, the KPD suffered from internal disputes. Formed from elements of the Spartakus Bund and other extreme leftists, the KPD resisted Russian attempts to control it. Paul Levi, its first leader, was expelled after denouncing Kremlin intervention in 1921, but it remained for the party to be "Stalinized," that is, subjected to strict Moscow discipline, and in 1923 it was hesitant and confused. It isn't likely that even the best leadership could have brought a Lenin-like revolution to Germany. An attempted Red uprising in Hamburg was suppressed.

Small wonder, though, that Lenin, brooding over the troubles of the Soviet socialist state in his last months, took heart from the fact that, after all, the capitalists were even more stupid: "Because of greed they hate each other." Capitalist France seemed bent on ruining capitalist Germany and wrecking the very heart of European industry in order to meet short-range obligations. Great Britain and France were at odds, divided by Poincaré's Rhineland policy, which was generally popular with the French public; nothing was more likely to win approval than squeezing the hated Germans to pay for the devastation they had wrought on France.

It was the capitalists who rallied to save the situation, finally. American bankers, headed by the formidable J. P. Morgan, were persuaded by the British that they had a stake in international stabilization. Was not repayment of Allied war debts conditional upon a reasonable reparations settlement? Furthermore, the whole circuit of international trade was at stake. The United States was slowly recovering from the shock of revulsion it had felt against Europe in 1919 and 1920, when the Senate had rejected membership in the League of Nations amid a wave of isolationism. Though it refused to muddy itself with European politics, the American colossus was prepared to make a modest economic contribution. The committee of economic experts that worked on a solution to the reparations muddle in 1923 and 1924 was chaired by an American, the distinguished banker and government financier, and later vice-president of the United States, Charles G. Dawes. The time was ripe for a settlement, for the Franco-German silent war was about a stand-off: Germany was in utter economic chaos. France had advanced little if at all toward her objective of extracting wealth from Germany, her Rhineland policy had failed, and much of world opinion criticized her for recklessly fomenting trouble.

The Dawes Plan, agreed upon by all parties in 1924, was a complex instrument. Its most significant elements were (a) a scaling down of reparations obligations, together with an annual schedule of payments supposed to start at one billion marks (in kind) and rise to two and a half billion marks by 1928; (b) a plan to finance the payments in Germany by various bonds and special taxes; and (c) to sweeten the package for Germany a $200 million foreign loan. French troops were to be withdrawn from the Ruhr, and in the future no creditor nation could unilaterally apply sanctions, as France and Belgium had done in 1923. Though extreme German nationalists denounced it for retaining reparations payments, most Germans greeted the plan with relief. It represented a fairly major French defeat. But for the French, too, Morgan money made the bitter dose go down more easily.

France suffered a period of cabinet instability while grappling with the financial issue. So did the Weimar Republic. For both parliamentary systems, there was little relief from the problem of juggling a half dozen political minorities to create a workable coalition. In 1926, German unemployment stood at 18 percent, and her industrial production was about 92 percent of 1913 production. In the next two years it rose to 118 percent of 1913 production. In France in 1923, industrial production was 87 percent of the 1913 rate; by 1927 it had risen to 126 percent. The prosperity of the later twenties, spectacular in the United States prior to the great collapse of 1929, was never as great for Europe as a whole.

Nevertheless the Dawes Plan marked the beginning of a new if brief era for western Europe. It was to be followed by a major diplomatic agreement, the Locarno pacts; by German admission to the League of Nations; and by an experiment in Franco-German reconciliation. This brief period gave rise to the illusion that after five years of postwar disturbances, things at last were getting back to normal.

The Locarno Spirit

It was during 1923, while inflation raged and Germany seemed to be breaking up, that military hero Marshall von Ludendorff and the ex-Army messenger Adolf Hitler, an incongruous pair of conspirators, tried to seize the Bavarian government. This Munich "beer hall putsch" failed ignominiously, and for the next five years Hitler's extremist National Socialist Workers' party was all but forgotten. The nightmare experiences of the first five postwar years gave way to a much more stable period between 1924 and 1930, both in Germany and through most of the rest of Europe. The stabilization of the mark, the Dawes Plan, and loans from abroad cleared the way for a considerable economic recovery. Separatist movements, whether in Rhineland or Bavaria, faded away; and the troublesome Free Corps bandits were brought under control. Responsible conservatives gave support to the republic, and though its political life was never easy, it seemed to be making progress in these years. The election of old Marshall Hindenburg as president in 1925 strengthened the republic. (Largely honorary and ceremonial, but with some important emergency powers in case normal government broke down, the presidency was held by Hindenburg for nine years; Ebert, the Social Democrat, had held it first.)

In France, Premier Edouard Herriot and after him Aristide Briand, who remained as foreign minister through a series of French governments, were willing to move cautiously toward reconciliation with Germany as an alternative to the failed policy of disruption and dismemberment. On the German side the able Gustav Stresemann, an architect of the 1924 stabilization, had a long tenure as foreign minister under Chancellors Hans Luther, Wilhelm Marx, and, after the elections of 1928, Hermann Mueller. Stresemann and Briand worked well together. Both colorful and able, they caught the imagination of a world barren of political heroes in the 1920s. They were a symbol of Franco-German reconciliation and a new era of peace.

While extremists of both Left and Right denounced him for surrendering to the enemies of World War I and to the Allied capitalists, Stresemann preached that cooperation with Germany's former foes was her only possible route back to national strength. An ardent nationalist and a man of the Right, Stresemann protected the Reichswehr, which was engaged in some practices that would hardly bear inspection, from the eyes of the Allied Control Commission. He did not accept a weakened Germany. He simply thought that a Western orientation offered the best chances for recovery. There were Germans who thought otherwise, and in 1922 they had secured a treaty with Soviet Russia (the Treaty of Rapallo). Secret and mutually profitable military arrangements between the two countries continued. But Stresemann wooed the West with much success.

In 1926 Germany entered the League of Nations, from which she had previously been excluded, and after some controversy received a great-power position on the League Council. A year before, the Locarno treaties had signalled the new orientation, and the "spirit of Locarno" symbolized a new era. In these agreements Germany, France, Italy, and Britain joined in guaranteeing the existing frontier between Germany and France-Belgium. This meant that Germany accepted as final the cession of Alsace and Lorraine to France and Malmedy to Belgium. She also repeated her acceptance of the Rhineland demilitarization provisions. In these ways Locarno was a curious reiteration of the Treaty of Versailles and the League of Nations, as if the powers were saying, "We really mean it this time." The powers also agreed to submit their disputes to arbitration.

Although representatives from Czechoslovakia and Poland also came to Locarno, no such German guarantees were given in the east. Nevertheless, arbitration treaties were signed, and France pledged help to Czechoslovakia and Poland if they were attacked by Germany. In later years people spoke of the *equivoque*, the ambiguity, of the Locarno pacts: each side understood them in a different way. To the Western powers, the agreements that were concluded in October 1925 in the little Swiss town meant that Germany totally accepted the post-World War I peace settlement. To the Germans, Locarno meant that they accepted the settlement *in the west* but left open and hoped for a future revision in the east. We are familiar enough, from many later examples, of pseudoagreements constructed of ambivalent words that each side interprets in its own way. (Compare Yalta, 1945, or Geneva, 1967.)

The bait held out to Germany for renouncing any attempt to revise Versailles boundaries included early withdrawal of the Allied troops that had been occupying the Rhineland since 1919. Originally, this occupation had been set for fifteen years, with the possibility of renewal, but after a series of reductions all forces were removed by 1930. The Military Control Commission, appointed to see that Germany complied with the disarmament provisions of the treaty, went home in 1927. Germany continued to ignore some of these provisions, in particular, she reorganized the equivalent of a general staff, and she used Russia as a place of military training. The Allies certainly knew about and chose to ignore these noncompliances. So the effective pledges that France held against German renewal of the war were gone. The Germans had pledged themselves to respect the demilitarized zone, and Locarno provided for Franco-British-Italian cooperation in the event they breached this commitment, but there was no longer any concrete obstacle to their sending troops into the region.

Finally, a disarmament conference began in 1927 at Geneva, Switzerland, site of the League of Nations, which (though it never achieved its goal) was based on a kind of commitment to equalize armaments by disarming the Allies to Germany's level. All in all, the Locarno agreements and their sequels constituted a considerable German victory. Later, the French thought that "the seeds of Munich were in Locarno"; that is, the policy of appeasement of Germany had begun. But of course from 1925 to 1930 Germany was not ruled by Hitler. Extremist movements of both Right and Left had subsided. In the election of 1928, the Communists received 10 percent of the popular vote, whereas Hitler's NSDAP got only 2.6 percent. The "Weimar parties" now had a sizeable majority of the Reichstag, and even the DNVP, with 73 seats, was no longer a completely implacable foe of the system. The republic seemed to have succeeded and to be dominated by the "other Germany" of philosophy, music, art, religion, humanism. The peaceful Social Democrats and Catholic Centrists were the strongest political parties.

Weimar suggested a brilliant renewal of German culture, symbolized in the Bauhaus school art and architecture located there. Great German writers like Thomas Mann renounced their World War I attitudes and changed into advocates of peace and internationalism. Berlin, Frankfurt, and Munich resumed their positions as international centers of the arts. Berlin was wickedly decadent, but this suited the mood of the hour. The Wilhelmine Germany of pointed helmets and goose-stepping soldiers belonged to a now-remote past, given the fast pace of change in the postwar world. No one foresaw the Germany of brown-uniformed storm troopers and screaming mass political rallies.

The Locarno spirit merged with the Geneva spirit, for the League of Nations, damaged at its birth by American refusal to enter and soon confronted with the hopelessness of its ambitious plans for a new sort of "collective security," began to take on some prestige as an international meeting place. Attempts in 1924–1925 to clarify and strengthen the commitments of members to the security provisions of the Covenant, that is, to participate actively in putting down any "aggression," revealed that Great Britain and the dominions were as opposed to this as the United States had been. No longer dreaming of becoming a world government, the League was content to be a vehicle of communication and an instrument of social service. Its specialized agencies encouraged international cooperation in dealing with problems of working conditions, health, transportation, and crime. Statesmen came to Geneva to consult and hold conferences.

The great disarmament conference began in 1927 with high hopes.

An impressive physical establishment in the Swiss city took the form of a stately neo-classical edifice, not the modernist design submitted by the great Swiss architect Le Corbusier. An organization began to take shape. A somewhat tattered symbol of "the peace that passed understanding," the League looked a little brighter in the late 1920s than it had at the end of the war. And so did nearly everything else in that short moment of hope before the economic roof caved in, crushing the frail plant of international understanding.

A further emblem of the times was the Kellogg-Briand Peace Pact, which was named after an American secretary of state and a French statesman. It was signed amid great fanfare in 1928 by nearly all the governments of the world (sixty-three of sixty-seven) after it was ceremonially initialed in Paris. The fact that the United States cosponsored it was significant. A vague encomium to peace entailing no concrete commitments, the pact had only a moral value; but world opinion thought it highly important that war had been outlawed by this solemn declaration. Its signers "condemned recourse to war" and "renounced war as an instrument of national policy." Future events, unhappily, revealed how little this might mean. A clash between China and Russia managed to coincide with the final promulgation of the pact in 1929! But that its creation was something of an international sensation in 1928 testifies to the hopefulness of that year, if also to its pathetic illusions.

The Soviet Debate and the Rise of Stalin

"Comrade Stalin, having become General Secretary, has accumulated enormous power in his hands, and I am not quite sure whether he will always be able to use that power carefully enough." Thus wrote Lenin in December 1922 when, increasingly ill, he penned the letter that became known as his "Last Testament." (The document was known only to a few insiders until 1956.) A year later, when Lenin was a hopeless invalid nearing the end of his life, a group of prominent party members complained that "free discussion in the party has all but disappeared," and the Central Committee is no longer elected by the general party membership but determined by "the secretarial hierarchy."

Thus Stalin's famous seizure of power began while Lenin was still alive, and indeed Lenin's later strokes may have resulted from his agitated anti-Stalin campaign in late 1922 and early 1923. The doctors had prohibited all but the smallest amount of work, but Lenin ignored the orders. Yet the Georgian, born Joseph Djugashvili, with his rude manners and his Caucasian accent, was still not considered to be at the top

Lenin and Stalin, 1923: The past and the future of Communist Russia. At this time Lenin was gravely ill and soon to die. *The Granger Collection.*

of the party heap, though a city (the old Tsaritsyn) was named after him in 1922. After Lenin, the usual ceremonial hierarchy was Lev Kamenev, Gregory Zinoviev, and of course Trotsky. Intellectually more distinguished than Stalin, certainly more cultured, these men were unfortunately no match for the practical general secretary, whose talents were both administrative and political.

The story of how Stalin outmaneuvered his rivals and became the all-powerful boss of an increasingly dictatorial Communist party is a classic one, and it has stimulated many attempts at explanation. The least mysterious is Stalin's obvious ability, which, of course, is not the same thing as virtue. Many people, not least the Trotskys, Kamenevs, and Zinovievs whom he defeated and eventually murdered (along with literally millions of others), have thought that Stalin betrayed the Revolution, that he was a moral monster without equal in all the bloody annals of history. And among Stalin's qualities a certain gangster-like cruelty and amorality is evident. He did not lack knowledge of Marxism, though it was a crude Marxism, nor the ability to write and think cogently, though his theoretical manner was simplistic. He added to these abilities an immense capacity for work, a vast talent for intrigue, and an utter ruthlessness that frightened even Lenin.

Additionally, he had something of a popular touch, unlike the

Jewish intellectuals who were his rivals in the struggle for power that followed Lenin's departure. Not that he favored democracy; he stood for absolute authority at the top, because, he declared, "we are surrounded by enemies" and must be able to move quickly, maneuver rapidly, and "strike a sudden blow." It was his mission to eliminate whatever remnants of grass-roots influence remained in the party, converting it into an instrument of power completely under the control of its singleminded master. But Stalin could at least talk the language of the average Russian.

Rather short, not very handsome (the later portraits were touched up), and for long an indifferent public speaker, Stalin did not gain power through his charismatic appeal, like Hitler and Mussolini, but by his skill at manipulating the machinery of power. He found that machinery already in existence, waiting to be set in motion toward a goal. Lenin's elite party of dedicated, disciplined, devout revolutionaries had already been forged. It had been tempered in the fires of long revolutionary activity before, during, and after the October Revolution. It had eliminated all its organized enemies, who had been killed or imprisoned or had fled Russia during the Civil War. Gone was a high percentage of the old ruling and educated class. Lenin and Trotsky had established instruments of terror, including the secret police (Cheka, GPU, NKVD). This power structure had laid hold of the state.

In theory, power belonged to the soviets, or people's councils, but the All-Russian Congress of Soviets delegated its power to an executive committee, which in turn delegated it to a council of commissars made up solely of Communists. The Congress under Stalin was to turn into a farce. It met for a few days each year to approve, by unanimous vote, everything that had been done. The Communist party, the only political party allowed, had a parallel hierarchy. It culminated in the Central Committee and its various bureaus, especially the Politburo. A small group of fifteen or twenty men, sitting on both the Politburo and the Sovnarkom, ruled Russia.

Lenin made the critical break with democratic Marxism that finally led to Stalinism. Trotsky, before he became a Leninist, once made the acute remark that when you have substituted the party for the proletariat, it follows inevitably that you will substitute the Central Committee for the party and finally one man's will for the Central Committee. This was an accurate prophecy of what happened, the irony being that Trotsky allowed himself to accept the first two steps and became the victim of the last. Yet under Lenin the Bolshevik oligarchy functioned as a team. If they followed Lenin's leadership, it was because they willingly deferred to his superior intellectual powers. There was much debate within the Politburo, and Lenin did not always have his way.

Trotsky, Bukharin, and others did not hesitate to argue with him. "Democratic centralism" decreed iron discipline once a decision was reached, but it allowed open debate within the party in reaching that decision.

Stalin was to end all this and rule by a combination of manipulation and terror. But he did not much change the basic pattern developed in the first years of Bolshevist rule; he only extended it in directions already begun.

The wily Georgian used his seemingly secondary post as general secretary of the Central Committee to influence selection of members to the Central Committee, to the "purge" machinery, and to administrative and executive positions at all levels of the growing political apparatus. Thousands upon thousands of local Communist party leaders, the *apparatchiks*, owed their careers to Stalin's sponsorship and watchful eye, and they were as attached to him as any feudal knight to his lord. Trotsky and the other high Communists, Kamenev, Bukharin, and Zinoviev, woke up too late and found that while they had been making the speeches, Stalin had been working quietly behind the scenes to put his men in key party positions.

He also exploited jealousies among them. There is evidence of a personal feud between Trotsky and Stalin reaching back much earlier; it was based on a natural antipathy between the intellectual, esthetic, essentially aristocratic Trotsky, whose favorite sport was hunting in the manner of a country gentleman, and the plain, boorish, tough-minded Stalin.

This power struggle underlay the great discussions of policy, which, in Marxian terms, were a kind of superstructure. But real issues, as we know, confronted the Communists—major questions of what path to take, assuming one could not long remain in the NEP stage of lapsing into capitalism. One of the issues was the relative stress on world revolution and the possibility of building socialism in Russia alone. Should the USSR continue to work toward world revolution, or should it resign itself for the time being to the necessity of going it alone? Hopes for the spread of revolution to Germany, to Italy, or to China faded between 1921 and 1927. There was a Communist disaster in Bulgaria in 1923, too. Using Russia as the headquarters for an international revolutionary movement dictated different policies than did placing primary stress on Russian development. The most obvious difference was that under the latter policy, Communists would have to cultivate good relations with foreign capitalist states, a goal inconsistent with attempts to stir up revolutions inside them. The Zinoviev letter of 1924, which we mentioned previously, is an example; this invitation (perhaps forged) to a British proletarian revolution not only cost the

Labour party the election but caused Great Britain to retract its recognition of the Communist government of Russia, which interfered with economic relations. Such episodes raised the additional question of whether attempts to intrude Russian influence on national revolutionary movements was not counterproductive to the success of these movements.

Other difficult decisions had to be made about domestic policy. Marx had said remarkably little about how to organize socialism, and even Lenin had seemed confused. Should the peasants be conciliated by allowing them to hold farms and sell produce to the cities, or should they be forced into collective farms? Marxian socialism was evidently a proletarian and industrial program that aimed at wiping out "rural idiocy" and bringing the factory to the farm, or vice versa. But could such a program be realized in Russia at this time? Should industrialization and urbanization be pushed forward rapidly or slowly? Should there be a totally centralized economic system, with everything nationalized and the state planning the whole economy, or was this too drastic and too un-Marxian, given the Marxist and occasional Leninist stress on the state's disappearance under socialism?

This discussion was reasonably open. Stalin had not yet closed off all debate. During the 1920s, Russia's great generation of poets and thinkers dropped gradually by the wayside, eliminated in one way or another—some were suicides—by the stresses of the new era. But many who were later arrested and shot still spoke freely in the debate of the mid-twenties, and a variety of views were expressed.

Stalin distinguished himself more by "dialectical" skill (elsewhere known as "slipperiness") than by intellectual consistency. As far as possible, he stood in the center, avoiding commitment to any position. He first supported the Right's opposition against Trotsky, isolating that moody and haughty personality whom many envied and disliked. The Right generally thought that collectivization of the peasants and too rapid industrialization were dangerous and unwise. Economic experts generally took this line.

Stalinism was later to stand for (a) rapid, forced industrialization; (b) open war against the peasants, forcing them into the *kolkhozes*; (c) "socialism in one country," making international revolution subordinate to this goal; and (d) centralized planning, with total control of economic activities by the central bureaucracy. To carry out this draconian program, Stalin advocated absolute dictatorship, the use of terror on a gigantic scale, and repression of all freedom to criticize. But these were not what Stalin had always advocated. Earlier, he doubted that rapid industrialization was possible. In 1925, he warned against pushing the peasants too hard. In 1927, he tried (and failed) to mastermind the Chinese Communist revolution.

Stalin profited by being underestimated. He was considered a good clerk but, in Trotsky's contemptuous words, "a third-rate, provincial mind." It was Trotsky who was vulnerable and who made mistakes. Stalin kept reminding the party cohorts that Trotsky was not an Old Bolshevik but had joined the party only in 1917. In failing to attend Lenin's funeral, though he had the excuse of being a long distance away and ill, Trotsky put a trump into his enemies' hand. Initially, Trotsky perceived Stalin as an instrument in the hands of the Zinoviev-Kamenev team, whom he was trying to outmaneuver; only belatedly did he and they realize that in the Georgian they had caught a tartar. A series of blunders delivered the war commissar into Stalin's hands.

Basically, however, it was Stalin's control of the Central Committee and eventually, through it, the Politburo, which he packed with three additional members in 1925, that made the difference. Trotsky, and then Zinoviev and Kamenev, could not win. They sent in Lenin's widow, Krupskaya, at the crucial Fourteenth Party Congress in 1925, but even she failed to impress the pro-Stalin majority. One is left wondering whether Stalin's victory rested most on his political machine, the ineptness of his foes, his own obvious abilities, or the antiintellectual and antisemitic nativism that swept the party—a sort of counterpart of the Ku Klux Klan in the United States or of fascism.

Or one might—it was frequently done at the time, for the Russian Revolution saw itself in the image of the French—consider Stalin's victory a "Thermidorian reaction" (so-called because of the peaceful period following Robespierre's execution on Thermidor [July 27, 1794], when France began to return to normal after her revolution). Every revolution comes to a point when it must organize the new society. The revolutionary ecstasy of exciting oratory, insurrection, and battle cannot last; the revolution ends, the hour of reconstruction begins, and a new sort of leadership is required. The orators and the improvisers will not normally serve for the next task, for it demands very different talents. According to this view, those, like Trotsky, who had made their reputation as revolutionary leaders could not adjust to the era of "building socialism." Trotsky had been the Robespierre of the Revolution, and Stalin was to be its Napoleon. Whether the genius of Lenin could have straddled the gap we will never know; his premature death, like his appearance on the stage of history in 1917–1918, must be accounted one of the greatest of historical accidents.

In any case, by 1926 Stalin was strong enough to get Zinoviev, Kamenev, and Trotsky removed from the Politburo and other high posts, making their opposition to him seem like disloyalty to the party. In 1927 Trotsky's group was expelled from the party Congress, and Trotsky himself was shipped out of the capital. When the former hero continued to try to oppose Stalin, he was finally forced to leave the country. Trotsky subsequently lived in Turkey, Norway, and Mexico, always hounded by Stalin's agents and finally murdered in Mexico. Zinoviev and Kamenev were tried and convicted, along with thousands of lesser officials, in the sensational political trials of 1936–1938; by that time, those Old Bolsheviks like Bukharin and Radek, who had cast their lot with Stalin in 1925–1926, were in the dock with them, headed for the same firing squad. Stalin wanted no rivals, no equals. He intended to be the absolute boss of the Communist country, and he achieved that goal by a skillful campaign of utterly unscrupulous politics. The Revolution devours its own children.

This set the stage for the great struggle to build "socialism in one country," a slogan Stalin used in the ideological battle with Trotsky. Trotsky felt that attempting such a campaign in backward Russia was bound to fail or to lead to drastic distortions of the socialist ideal. As we have noted, that was probably Lenin's view, too. It seemed like irreproachable Marxism. But it suffered from the practical disadvantage of negativism. Given the realities of no world revolution, was one to sit and do nothing in Russia while capitalism crept back? The powerful machinery of the party stood ready to act. Such machinery cannot remain idle, or it will destroy itself. "With the party as his army and the Secretariat as his general staff, Stalin launched his war in 1929," writes historian Adam Ulam. The aim of the war was to develop Russia into an industrial state surpassing even the largest capitalist ones, but in some ways it turned out to be a war against the Russian people.

Other Democratic Failures

As the supposed "victory of the democracies" in World War I slipped away into a swamp of disillusionment, other dictatorships arose in postwar Europe. Most were not as novel as those of communism and fascism. In Rumania, Yugoslavia, and Bulgaria, unsatisfactory experiences with parliamentary government gave way to old-fashioned personal monarchical rule. King Carol of Rumania and King Alexander of Yugoslavia were exercising royal dictatorships by the end of the decade. In Yugoslavia, the union of the Serbs, Croats, and Slovenes born of World War 1 failed to work, and in 1928 a breakdown of parliamentary government followed the assassination of the Croatian peasant leader, Radich, *on the floor of the Assembly*. The Croats quickly came to resent Serb domination of the multiethnic state, which was made up almost entirely of Slavs, true, but Slavs with varying traditions and experiences. Croat nationalism was treated harshly by Belgrade; the assassination of the king in 1934, in Marseille, France, was a later and most significant outcome of this ferment in South Slavdom.

Political murder was an old Balkan custom, and in 1923 Macedonians and army conservatives brutally killed the Bulgarian peasant leader, Stambolisky, who was an ardent advocate of a union of the Balkan peoples on the basis of a common peasanthood (the "Green International"). Peasant strength, along with land reform, made southeastern Europe remarkably resistant to Bolshevism. The Green International was the best antidote to the Red; as in Russia, where they did not get their way, Balkan peasants wanted land of their own, not socialized agriculture. But political democracy could not survive the turbulence of this area, where too many peoples were mixed and where experience in democratic practices was lacking. In Poland, which had no king, the popular military leader Marshal Pilsudski exercised nearly absolute power.

In Spain, a power emerged from behind the throne. Miguel Primo de Rivera, a general who became dictator from 1923 to 1930, was a picturesque personality who was somewhat similar to Mussolini but who lacked anything so lowbrow as an ideology. An enemy of the corrupt old regime, Primo made some attempt to modernize Spain economically and spent money on public works, but he lost the support of the liberals and the intellectuals. (His son later founded the Falange, the organization of Spanish fascism, and was executed by the Loyalists at the beginning of the Spanish Civil War in 1936.) Primo de Rivera the elder's resignation and exile in 1930, followed soon by the abdication of the king, inaugurated the Spanish Republic. After five turbulent years, civil war broke out, and Spain was the unhappy fulcrum of European politics from 1936 to 1939. The great gulf between the classes, bitter class hatreds, and Catalan separatism doomed Spanish democracy as did much the same kind of combination in other countries of the south and east of Europe.

Premodernized societies do not generally accommodate patterns of democracy, in the sense of a pluralism of interests and outlooks adjusted by compromise. Compromise depends on a relativism and skepticism about absolute values that has to be acquired gradually. "The Spanish temperament" (one can substitute Hungarian, Polish, Greek, and many other temperaments) was said to be hostile to habits of moderation; but moderation is not natural to humanity. The growth of democratic institutions of government, like the growth of the nation-state to which they correspond, was a process that took centuries.

Several kinds of socialism and anarchism had more appeal to Spanish workers than did either democracy or communism. Peasant-based "populist" ideologies, rather like the old Social Revolutionary party in Russia sought the breakup of big estates, land redistribution, and aid to the small independent landowner. Such ideologies flourished in the southeastern part of Europe, the real home, as Stambolisky claimed, of the peasant interest.

The remnants of the Hapsburg empire had special problems because of their newness, their smallness, their disruption from old patterns. Austria and Hungary were left stranded; the great cities of Vienna and Budapest were deprived of their hinterlands by new boundaries and barriers to trade. Austria was destined to endure a cruel civil war as well as national bankruptcy. Vienna itself was dominated by the Social Democrats, but the countryside was Catholic and conservative. Until they were all swallowed by Hitler in 1938, the Austrians fought among themselves, occasionally in open civil war. The little republic had wanted to join Germany, but the Paris peace prohibited this; again in 1931, a close and controversial decision of the World Court, a body coordinate with the League of Nations, denied the *Anschluss* of Austria to Germany.

The Austrian socialists were too civilized to attempt a ruthless dictatorship. In opposition to them, an Austrian version of fascism, the *Heimwehr*, formed a secret militia and plotted against the republic. There was street fighting in Vienna in 1927 between Left and Right; Austrian students, in these days, were generally on the latter side. The able Jesuit priest Ignaz Seipel was chancellor through much of the 1920s and served Austria well, arranging for international loans to keep her afloat, but he was strongly antisocialist and, his foes charged, secretly sympathetic to the fascist *Heimwehr*. He feuded with the Viennese socialists. Mussolini's intrigues and, later, those of the Nazis complicated the harried life of the little country that had been created by a process of elimination.

In the aftermath of the White Terror that followed the overthrow of Bela Kun's short-lived Communist dictatorship, Hungary was ruled by a strongly conservative aristocrat regime that frustrated even the peasant smallholders. The batterings Hungary took from the peace settlement, leaving her shorn of territory to everybody else's gain, made foreign policy dominant in Hungary; every effort had to be bent toward revising the treaties. But for Hungary this was a forlorn quest. Elections were rigged, and there was no real democracy; a fascist element looked to Italy and later to Nazi Germany for leadership.

Among the new states, only Czechoslovakia adapted reasonably well to a liberal and democratic order. The republic fathered by Thomas Masaryk produced other able leaders committed to a free society. The new Czech republic abolished the old semifeudal system of land ownership and created small holdings. The Agrarian party consistently dominated Czech governments. This process was made easier by the fact that the large estate owners had mostly been German, while the Slovaks and Czechs were peasants. Yet not only did three and a half million Germans remain a more or less disaffected minority within the Czechoslovak state, but the Slovaks and the Czechs were only slightly less incompatible than Serbs and Croats. Culturally more backward because of conditions within the old empire, in which the Czechs had received favored treatment, the Slovaks were Roman Catholics (like the Croats), whereas the Czechs had a significant Protestant (Hussite) tradition. Slovak separatism, fed by resentment of Prague's domination and to some extent by a Czech habit of looking down on these country cousins, was not a serious threat, but it did lurk in the background. The German minority, inhabiting the more highly industrialized part of the country, considered itself mistreated by those it regarded as its cultural inferiors.

Despite these problems, Czechoslovakia seemed to be both an economic and a political success, a keystone of relative stability in disturbed central Europe. Wiser leadership and greater prosperity softened the impact of the frictions. Unfortunately, Czechoslovakia quarreled with Poland over boundaries. The two chief partisans of the Paris peace, enemies of territorial revisionism and allies of France in upholding the existing boundaries of Europe, Czechoslovakia and Poland were themselves not on the best of terms.

Political instability was not a monopoly of backward southern and eastern Europe. Civil war broke out in Ireland after the war. The war had interrupted a parlous situation. The Protestants of the North, with the British Tories backing them, violently objected to home rule for Ireland. During the war, most of the Irish loyally supported the Allied side, and their members sitting in the British Parliament backed the war. Conscription, however, which was introduced in 1916, was far less popular. The Easter Week rebellion in Dublin in 1916, though the action of a tiny minority, left behind a romantic legend: "a terrible beauty was born." The British blundered by court-martialling and shooting fifteen of the little group of nationalists who had, in typically Irish fashion, launched an impossible uprising. But widespread Irish anger awaited the end of the war, when the Irish expected home rule if not full independence. Fighting broke out in 1920 between the Irish independence party (the Sinn Fein) and the British "black and tans," or constabulary police. Savagely fought by both sides, the civil war aroused world opinion against the British, who were cast in the role of oppressors; Irish-Americans helped defeat the League of Nations on the grounds that it underwrote British imperialism.

The British offered home rule (dominion status) within the empire to the southern and northern parts of Ireland separately. A narrow majority of the Sinn Fein accepted this solution, but the Irish Republican Army continued the insurrection. Its members were not content with partition of the emerald isle, and they demanded full independence. The Irish problem did not entirely quiet down until 1927, when an assassination caused a reaction against the extremist Republicans. The Irish did not get full independence at this time, and, although the Protestant majority wanted separation of the northern counties (Ulster), the Catholic minority definitely did not. The Irish Free State, as it was known, accepted the oath of allegiance to the Crown, but it had a large measure of self-government. In 1926 the Ottawa Declaration announced the dominions to be "autonomous communities within the British Empire, equal in status, in no way subordinate one to another in any aspect of their domestic or external affairs." Thus to all intents and purposes, the Irish Free State was really free of British rule at long last, though the moral bond of Commonwealth unity remained until after World War II. The most galling thing was partition. The Irish Republican Army carried on a tradition of illegal violence that had begun in the civil war of 1920–1921.

The self-governing dominions of the British Commonwealth were Canada, Australia, New Zealand, South Africa and the Irish Free State. This was spelled out in the 1931 Statute of Westminster. Northern Ireland preferred to become a division of the United Kingdom of Great Britain and Northern Ireland, sending members to the British Parliament though also having its own government. Other portions of the empire were still crown colonies with a British governor advised by native consultative bodies that he appointed. In India, there were major riots, strikes, and campaigns of "civil disobedience" led by the great Indian nationalist leader, Mohandas Gandhi, in 1920–1921 and through the 1920s.

Such was the rather mixed record of the European countries in the 1920s. Looking at the scene in 1927 or 1928, one might have felt justified in concluding that Europe was gradually recovering from the tremendous shock of a war that had destroyed empires, caused revolutions, formed wholly new states, and stirred up further claims for freedom. That such a trauma produced enormous problems of reconstruction was hardly surprising. In time, these might have been solved. Unfortunately, time was not to be allowed.

The Dissolution
of the Ancestral Order:
Culture and Thought
in the 1920s

6

The Alienation of the Intellectuals

Einstein, Freud, Picasso, Le Corbusier, Virginia Woolf, James Joyce and many another spokesperson of the mind or spirit brilliantly lit up the 1920s, contrasting with the rather depressing spectacle of public affairs. There were also exciting political ideas, but these were revolutionary and iconoclastic, and, in general, politics was not in favor. In these years, there was a strong reaction against the overheated political idealism of the Great Crusade. "No intelligent man can afford to be caught holding the illusion that any public event matters very much," American political commentator Walter Lippmann complained, and internationally renowned American novelist Ernest Hemingway put these words into the mouth of the hero of his great war novel, *A Farewell to Arms*:

> I was always embarrassed by the words sacred, glorious and sacrifice and the expression in vain. . . . There were many words that you could not stand to hear and finally only the names of places had dignity.[1]

[1] New York: Charles Scribner's Sons, 1929, p. 191.

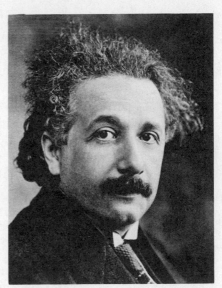

Two of the intellectual masters of the postwar years: (l) Sigmund Freud, founder of Psychoanalysis, (r) Albert Einstein, father of Relativity. *Wide World Photos and Yerkes Observatory.*

"The holy war to save humanity," as the *Manchester Guardian* put it, preached by the politicians in exalted rhetoric, had not only bloodied the soil of Europe but had left the world worse off than before.

The lusterless politicians of the postwar decade, the age of Baldwin and Coolidge, could not rally political hopes. "I do not remember whether I voted in those years, certainly not for whom," German writer Ludwig Marcuse recalled. The Russian Revolution had supplied a ray of hope, but slowly it seemed to fade. Although the liberal intelligentsia might defend Russia against its foes and march in sympathy with those alleged martyrs of intolerant antiradicalism, Sacco and Vanzetti (the Massachusetts case was an international *cause célèbre*), their heart was hardly in it. Intellectuals had bad experiences with the increasingly Stalinized Communist party in the 1920s. Ironically, it was not until the full Stalinization of the Soviet Union in the 1930s that a major movement of Western intellectuals toward communism took place. Alienated and disenchanted, the 1920s avant garde could not get really interested in any political crusade.

The term *intellectual* itself was of fairly recent origin. It first became current during the Dreyfus case in France around the turn of the century, when a "manifesto of the intellectuals" appeared. The word came to mean not merely someone who, as writer or artist, makes his living and lives his life as a "toiler of the brain" and who, being neither businessperson, farmer, or factory worker, seems peculiarly without a class, but also one whose exceptional sensitivity sets him apart from the "kindly race of men." In works of literature from 1900 on, the artist-intellectual appears as a spirit crippled by detachment from real life, or in some way rendered abnormal by it: he is Thomas Mann's *Tonio Kröger*, André Gide's *Immoralist*, or perhaps T. S. Eliot's impotent Prufrock, who has "measured out his life in coffee spoons." He was the outsider Stephen Dedalus (the Greek mythological Daedalus tried to fly and fell to earth) in Joyce's postwar sensation, *Ulysses*. This critical view came from the writers themselves; no one was more scornful of "les intellectuels" than intellectuals like Maurice Barrès or Georges Sorel in France. During the war Rudyard Kipling wrote scornfully of "brittle intellectuals who crack beneath a strain."

The war in some ways represented an attempt by the intellectuals to join the national community in a worthy cause; it was capable of curing their scorn for a bourgeois, money-grubbing, "philistine" society that drove them mad with its stupid triviality. The vast majority of them rallied enthusiastically to the war in 1914, characteristically viewing it as a chance for solidarity as well as splendid adventure. But for most of them the experience failed. They spat out their distaste in a host of war novels that adorned the 1920s. The was was certainly a literary success, but its literature deflated it. In many of the war books there is a strong feeling for the war as a memorable experience and for the comradeship of the trenches. But the ultimate verdict was one of powerful disillusionment. The bravery of the soldiers had been betrayed by homefront hypocrisy or profiteering or blundering.

And the heroes who returned, leaving many a comrade under the soil, found it hard to adjust. The war was over, but their spiritual hunger remained. One could never again believe in the romance of the battlefield. The war literature was poignant with memories of those

> . . . *who went*
> *Ungrudgingly, and spent*
> *Their all for us* [2]

and it told of the restlessness of the ex-heroes who tried to return to humdrum postwar life.

Gradually, the most popular theme became that of simple disgust, feeding the *nie wieder krieg* (no more war) sentiment that waxed in the thirties. A list of books written about the war, either as novels,

---

[2] From Wilfrid Wilson Gibson's poem "A Lament," in his *Collected Poems 1905–1925* (London: Macmillan, 1926).

plays, poetry, or as straight autobiography or personal narrative, would be a long one; among the best known were Henri Barbusse's *Le Feu*, by one who became an uncritical Communist; Erich Maria Remarque's *All Quiet on the Western Front (Im Westen Nichts Neues)*, which was made into a memorable movie; Hemingway's *Farewell to Arms*; poet Robert Graves' classic personal narrative *Goodbye to All That*; the trilogy of Ford Madox Ford; Sacheverell Sitwell's war memoirs. This list is no more than a sampling. The war made the literary reputation of dead poet Wilfrid Owen and enhanced that of novelist Romain Rolland, who had been its leading opponent from the start. *Heartbreak House* was Shaw's play about the war, and such it was—a breaking of hearts over heroism wasted, great deeds come to naught.

The war now seemed not a means of salvation but a seal of the ultimate damnation of the West. Postwar thought lamented the defeat of Western civilization. A retired German schoolteacher named Oswald Spengler had started work on his *Der Untergang des Abendlandes* before the war and had it finished in time to catch the crest of postwar gloom; as *The Decline of the West*, the book had an international success. So deeply implanted in the popular mind was the theme of slow but certain progress, from the benighted Middle Ages onward through the age of kings to the era of science and democracy (and/or socialism) that to be told that Western civilization peaked in the later Middle Ages and had been falling apart ever since was startling, as much so to the Left as to the Right. A need for total reexamination of the past impelled another amateur excursion into world history to fabulous sales: famed British writer H. G. Wells' *Outline of History*, by no means as pessimistic as Spengler's, catered to this anxious reassessment of Europe's traditions.

The shock of war started Arnold J. Toynbee on an even vaster chronicle of comparative civilization. He attempted to discover why civilizations fail, though the first volumes of his monumental *A Study of History* did not come from the press until 1934. A Russian emigré historian who had settled in the United States, M. I. Rostovtzeff, addressed himself to the question of Rome's fall, with many signs of intruding contemporary perspectives; Rome fell from an excess of democracy, a decline of public spirit. "Things fall apart, the center will not hold," as Yeats memorably put it.

Decline and Fall was the title of Evelyn Waugh's first novel (1928), a brilliant satire by the English writer who converted to Roman Catholicism as a sign of his rejection of the whole modern age. A similar kind of wittiness with a sting in its tail came from Aldous Huxley, in a series of 1920s novels that held the Victorian idols up to ridicule, as did Lytton Strachey of London's Bloomsbury Circle in *Eminent Victorians*. And a similar if more serious gesture of rejection arose on the Continent, especially in the German-speaking world. Soon recognized as the greatest of modern theologians, Karl Barth began a sharp attack on liberal theology, which had adopted the idea that human progress is the realization of God's purposes. The Lutheran Barth, the Swiss Calvinist Emil Brunner, and others reminded a generation of optimistic vipers that Christ's kingdom is not of this world. There is a barrier between man and God in this life, and that barrier condemns earthly existence to tragic imperfection. The old Lutheran and Calvinist message of original sin, the depravity of man's fallen nature, never received stronger stress than it did then. The obvious motivation of these works was a refusal to accept the idea that present-day human society is in any way a realization of God's purposes. Much more is it the Devil's work.

Influenced by Hegel, pre-1914 German theological thought visualized history mediating between God and man; it is the Holy Spirit working to realize God's purposes by translating His goodness into tangible things. This is not accomplished without travail and suffering; but through a constant interaction of the divine *geist* with the physical and human world, progress toward a perfect society does take place, on this view. Now, Barth postulated a dialectical gap: God and human society are not in continuous contact.

Karl Barth's 1919 *Epistle to the Romans* was a theological bombshell. At the same time, the works of the nineteenth-century Danish seer Kierkegaard were revived; Russian Orthodox refugee from communism, Nicolas Berdyaev, and Jewish theologian Martin Buber brought much the same message. "The belief in Progress," said England's Dean William Inge, "has been the working faith of the West for about a hundred and fifty years." But "if we turn to history . . . we find . . . that civilization is a disease which is almost invariably fatal, unless its course is checked in time." Berdyaev thought that "Man's historical experience has been one of steady failure, and there are no grounds for supposing it will ever be anything else."

All the idols of the nineteenth century, associated as they were with this crumbled idea of progress, came under attack. The scientist's dream of perfecting knowledge and leading humanity to a glorious conquest of nature had turned sour; scientists had spent the war making poison gas, and in any case their formulae offer nothing for the real human needs, those of the spirit. Lord Tantamount, in Huxley's *Point Counter Point*, eyes glued to the microscope, does not understand human relations at all. The Einsteinian revolution attracted wide attention precisely because it seemed to explode all the assumptions of nineteenth-century materialistic science.

Sigmund Freud, a hero of the intellectuals, turned increasingly in the 1920s to moral and philosophical speculation, represented by one of his most popular books, *Civilization and Its Discontents.* The aging founder of psychoanalysis, shocked by the war into believing in a death wish as well as a life force, presented the pessimistic view that humanity can never solve its problems; people will always be torn asunder between the conflicting demands of psychic individuality and of society, the id and the superego—the more civilized we become, the more society must repress the individual. "The price of civilization is neurosis," said Freud. It was a vision strangely congenial to that of the neo-orthodox theologians; the tough-minded scientific atheism of Freud was in the same camp with the return to religion. The human subconscious is a snakepit filled with all the demonic forces Christians had always called sin.

Democracy was another fallen idol. Not likely to go all the way with either Lenin or Mussolini, intellectuals of the 1920s were inclined, like George Bernard Shaw or Georges Sorel, to admire both. This was simply because they abhorred what they considered to be a flaccid bourgeois democracy, the tyranny of the hopelessly philistine average person. Many Italian intellectuals were half implicated in fascism, since they believed in elite rule, not democracy—in those qualitatively a majority if quantitatively a minority, as Benedetto Croce put it. Repelled by the vulgar mass civilization abundantly visible in the 1920s, the intellectuals typically sneered at the common man, hoped for some sort of guardian or "clerisy" class to rule, lamented with Yeats that

> Base drove out the better blood
> And mind and body shrank.

In Spengler's scheme of decline, democracy is a product of the decay of natural, organic culture and of positive values, a kind of detritus left by skepticism, nihilism, and social disintegration. Weimar Germany produced whole schools of neoconservatives who lamented "The Rule of the Inferiors" (the title of a 1927 book by the Lutheran romantic reactionary Edgar Jung) and dreamed of a mandarin elite. Although they helped prepare the way for Hitler's Brown Shirts, most of them saw the Nazis as upstarts from the vulgar masses. Later they were Nazi victims. Antidemocratic strains were by no means confined to Germany. The Spaniard José Ortega y Gasset's widely read essay, *The Revolt of the Masses,* articulated the sense of dismay at the collapse of civilized traditions. Even in the United States, Henry L. Mencken's sophisticated set laughed at the "gaping primates" of rural and small-town America. James Joyce's remarkable *Finnegans Wake,* in progress during these years, is in part a story of the passage of Western civilization into its last, democratic stage.

Marxists could agree that bourgeois culture was dying in the West while having faith that a new and better one, based on the proletariat, was coming to rough birth in the East. Most Western intellectuals in the 1920s were skeptical of this innocent faith. Beatrice and Sidney Webb, the deans of British socialism, wrote in 1923 about *The Decay of Capitalist Civilization,* but they were not yet prepared, as they would be a decade later, to find a worthy successor in Soviet civilization. John Maynard Keynes lectured in 1926 on *The End of Laissez Faire,* but what would take the place of old-fashioned competitive capitalism? The great economist was not sure.

In the main, the writers of the 1920s found their consolation in making brilliant art of their vision of social decay. T. S. Eliot's celebrated poem, *The Waste Land,* begins with a quotation from Petronius: we yearn to die. "April is the cruellest month" because it can no longer bring forth new life; the world has lost its creativity. Filled with all the subtle devices of modernist technique, Eliot found images to express the futility of religion, love, everything once productive of life:

> *Here is no water but only rock.*

The energizing springs of culture that fertilized Western society in the past had dried up, leaving people fearful and timid. The great tradition ends not with a bang but a whimper.

The Artistic Renaissance

Such visions of ruin stand in strange opposition to an actual revival of the arts that marked one of the most esthetically exciting of Western decades. There was a feast for the eye, the ear, and the mind during the postwar years. As even Yeats admitted,

> *Though the great song return no more*
> *There's keen delight in what we have:*
> *The rattle of pebbles on the shore*
> *Under the receding wave.*

The literature, architecture, and art of the 1920s were more than the rattle of pebbles. The modernist movement had begun before the war, as we know. But now it burst on the world with full force, charged with the special tone of revolutionary defiance that the war had induced. "Before and after 1914 differed absolutely, only nominally on the same earth," Franz Kafka's friend Max Brod declared, and we should not forget this complete change in mood even when we observe continuities between pre-1914 and post-1914 techniques in the arts. Form might be carried over, but content was new.

Writers Kafka, Joyce, Yeats, Eliot, D. H. Lawrence, Marcel Proust, and Thomas Mann; painters Klee, Picasso, and Kandinsky; architects Walter Gropius and Le Corbusier; and many other ornaments of literature and the arts had begun their careers before the war. But it was after the war that they attained their greatest fame and, in most cases, their fullest development. By breaking the authority of tradition, the war prepared the public mind for the startlingly novel qualities of the new art. This art still shocked people, but it did make an impact. Joyce's *Ulysses*, which began its life in one of the numerous "little magazines" devoted to experimental literature and art, was first banned, then published in Paris. The first, limited edition of 1921 quickly escalated to $300 a copy. It immediately became controversial. Called "morbid and sickening," "an immense mass of clotted nonsense," and "the foulest book that ever found its way into print," it was also hailed as a work of supreme genius. T. S. Eliot, the angular American from St. Louis who was working as a bank clerk in London while readying his *Waste Land* and other poems, was among those who acclaimed it. On one level a vivid, realistic, comic, often hilariously ribald story of one day in the life of present-day Dubliners, *Ulysses* was also an allegory of the human situation and a commentary on the decay of man since Homeric times. It quickly gained and kept its place as the century's greatest work of literature.

Technically, Joyce made breathtaking use of "stream of consciousness" to show us the unedited thoughts of people in all their illogical complexity. This intense subjectivism, along with the eroticism that sometimes accompanied it (people's secret thoughts presumably not excluding sexual fantasies) suggested Freudianism, but may also be viewed as the consequence of a flight from public themes and from the whole social order. Virginia Woolf's *Mrs. Dalloway*, the heroine of another novel exploring one day in the inner life of a person, cannot get interested in the life of her politician husband and retreats to an inner world of fantasy; it is this world that Mrs. Woolf tried to recreate.

"I will not serve that in which I no longer believe, whether it call itself my home, my fatherland, or my church," Joyce had declared (through Stephen Dedalus in *Portrait of the Artist*). It was a time of exiles. Americans Ernest Hemingway, Gertrude Stein, T. S. Eliot, and Ezra Pound fled to Europe; Europeans fled sometimes to America (D. H. Lawrence to New Mexico, Malcolm Lowry to Mexico and British Columbia) or elsewhere. "In Europe he had made up his mind that everything was done for, played out, finished, he must go to a new country" said Lawrence of one of his protagonists. Writers sought out primitive peoples or exotic cultures; Lorca, the Spanish poet, turned to the gypsies, Lawrence to the Indians. Herman Hesse was among the first to discover Buddhism. One's own society was a waste land; anywhere else was better.

To express one's own esthetic consciousness and make art out of an inner chaos were the achievements of the modernist painters and sculptors. Whether they called themselves expressionists, abstractionists, cubists, surrealists, or something else, they agreed in the program "Away from the Thing, away from Matter"; "abolish the sovereignty of appearances." In brief, they chose not to represent the everyday world realistically (something that anyone with a camera could now do anyway), but to depict something else, perhaps an inner vision such as might appear in dreams or perhaps a purely formal design, the imagination working in mathematical dimensions. Surrealism sought to tap the unconscious mind; symbolism looked for something deeper than the external phenomena of nature. The new "depth" psychology of Sigmund Freud and Carl Jung fertilized this strain of modern art, Jung in particular suggesting the importance of archetypal images manufactured in the collective unconscious of the human mind—images of religious as well as esthetic significance, as old as humanity, redolent of primeval myth and symbol.

Clearly this nonrepresentational art flowed from the desire to evade existing reality, too; the escape was to an inner world of the pure imagination, an abstract world of geometrical patterns, an ideal world or a metaphysical one. Klee, Kandinsky, Mondrian, Picasso—a Swiss, a Russian, a Dutchman, a Spaniard, working chiefly in Germany or Paris —were among dozens of great artists creating a fresh vision of life. Strange as their work seemed to eyes unaccustomed to it, they now received a degree of acceptance, no longer the targets of vegetable throwers or the police as had been the case just before 1914.

Futurist acceptance of the machine age continued somewhat into the twenties, spurred by the new inventions of technology and by interest in Einsteinian science. The *Neue Sachlickeit* reacted against expressionist subjectivism in the direction of a severely mathematical esthetic.

Architecture, too, experienced a revolutionary transformation. In revulsion against the old styles—classical, gothic, and baroque—designers tried to create a completely different building style, breaking altogether with tradition. Sometimes they tried to relate architecture to the machine age, but elements of a new esthetic were also present. Among the greater names in the architectural revolution were the Swiss-French who called himself Le Corbusier and in Germany the master of the Bauhaus, Walter Gropius. The Bauhaus was the leading expression of the "Weimar renaissance," which gave Germany a few brief years of renown before Hitler moved in to repress modernism as Jewish-internationalist decadence. Klee and Kandinsky joined Gropius in this institution, which was at once a community, a school, and a place for creative work design of all sorts. The goal was a style uniquely suited to twentieth-century civilization—urban, industrial, technologically modern, yet beautiful. It would owe little or nothing to the ancient modes.

Le Corbusier's defeat in the League of Nations competition clearly indicated the resistance that still remained to such startling novelties. But Le Corbusier, Gropius, and the American master Frank Lloyd Wright began to be known. The Bauhaus settled in Dessau in 1925 in buildings designed by Gropius. The advent of Hitler forced Gropius out of Germany; he joined numerous other German luminaries in Britain, France, the United States, and elsewhere. Gropius was later to work at Harvard and design many American structures, as Mies van der Rohe did in Chicago. Insofar as there has been an authentic twentieth-century style in architecture, it clearly made its public debut in the 1920s after being born just prior to the war.

Other manifestations of the creative German spirit appeared in the new art of cinema, where German expressionist films (*The Cabinet of Dr. Caligari, Blue Angel*) came as close as any to giving this popular

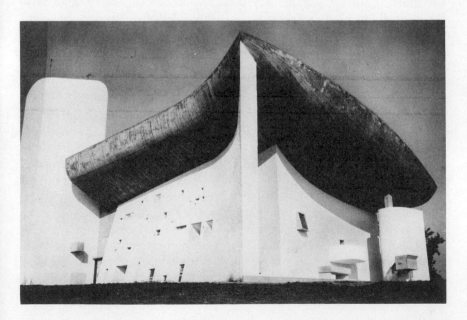

Charles-Edouard Jeanneret, the Swiss architect who called himself Le Corbusier, was an acknowledged master of the artistic avant-garde. This building, a product of his later years, is his Chapel of Notre Dame de Haut in Ronchamp, France. *Wide World Photos.*

genre significant esthetic expression. Bertolt Brecht's strikingly innovative theater also flourished in this period, when Berlin was wicked,
decadent, exciting, its cabarets where every adventurous spirit wanted
to be. In this post-Kaiser and pre-Hitler interlude, Germany seethed
with new ideas. The philosopher Martin Heidegger was writing his *Sein
und Zeit*. Critical Marxists of the Frankfurt school began to try to
rescue Marx from Stalin.

One of the decade's literary masterpieces was Thomas Mann's
Magic Mountain (*Zauberberg*, 1924). Like *Ulysses* and like Marcel
Proust's mammoth chronicle of the decay of French society,[3] *Magic
Mountain* sought a total revaluation of the tradition. A teacher looking
for documents of the twenties that best exemplify that rich, teeming
epoch might well choose this one. Set in a Swiss sanitarium among the
sick and dying—a symbol comparable to Eliot's waste land—the novel
contains figures representative of the modern mind: a scientific rational-
ist, a Dostoyevskyan irrationalist, a pagan sensualist, a soldier, and
others. The device resembles Huxley's gallery of types, including Communist, Fascist, nihilist, scientist, esthete, in *Point Counter Point*. There
is an exotic Russian girl with whom the protagonist, Castrop, has a
brief but intense affair—perhaps the ephemeral appeal of communism?
The quest is for some value Western civilization can seize hold of to
rescue itself. In Mann's masterpiece, Hans Castorp (whose name may
suggest catastrophe, castration, chaos, Castor and Pollux, caste or
casting about) nearly dies in a snowstorm but rouses himself by sheer
effort of will.

The ultimate reliance on an elemental will to live, accepting life in
all its terrible irrationality and building values by human affirmation,
is Nietzschean, existentialist, and Lorenzian. It was the creed of D. H.
Lawrence, the most creative writer England produced in this era, whose
Sons and Lovers, Women in Love, The Rainbow, and *Lady Chatterley's
Lover* from 1913 to 1928 proposed salvation via the miracle of physical
love. Lawrence's great talent was for taking us into real human situations
and making us feel intensely the actual anguish of the living searcher.

This attempt at total revaluation was a feature of the new art and
philosophy, along with formal experimentalism and revolutionary novelty. It was a natural outcome of the rejection of traditions. Sometimes,
in reaction against the modern world, the quest led back to old religions,
as happened with the neo-Lutherans, the neo-Catholics, the primitivists,
and the Western disciples of the Buddha. Lawrence found solace in the

---

[3] The frail invalid Proust died in 1922; the concluding volumes of the series that
comprised *A la recherche du temps perdu*, begun in 1909, were published after
his death. Translated as *Remembrance of Things Past*, their impact was scarcely
less than Joyce's.

ancient Etruscans, who represented a path not taken by Graeco-Christian culture. Eliot, most daring of poetic experimenters, soon announced himself an Anglo-Catholic, a royalist, and a classicist! "Revolutionary traditionalists," someone tagged these people. By and large they were reactionaries, for they found in older societies, more ordered and more esthetic, an antidote to the whole ugly face of modern, industrial, mass-democratic civilization.

Yet the restless quest went on. The French surrealists flirted with left-wing politics in the 1920s, only to reject the Communist party's inhuman discipline and especially its turn toward "socialist realism" under Stalin, which made the party of political revolution artistically reactionary.

Writers under Dictatorships

A special and tragic chapter in the saga of the postwar writers unfolded in the Soviet Union as it passed from revolutionary euphoria to the grim stage of totalitarian organization. In one way or another, the process took its toll of poets and intellectuals. Alexander Blok, poet of the October Revolution (*The Twelve*) died of starvation during the 1921 famine. In the same year Nikolai Gumilyov was shot (without trial) as a counterrevolutionary. Yessenin, after the breakup of his stormy marriage with the fabulous American dancer, Isadora Duncan, who went to Russia after the war, committed suicide in 1925. Four years later, so did the great Vladimir Mayakovsky, who like all these poets had greeted the Revolution with enthusiasm, only to find he could not adjust to its demands for conformity and propaganda.

The Silver Age of Russian art and literature—some think it should be called the Golden Age—blossomed just before the war, producing genius seldom matched anywhere. The composer Alexander Scriabin died during the war; Rachmaninoff left Russia to spend the rest of his life abroad, as many other Russians did, in a massive migration of the White Russians especially to Paris. In exile many were condemned to waste their talents.[4] Of those who stayed, unable to leave their beloved country, the greatest ones could not make their peace with an increasingly tyrannical regime. Some survived until Stalin's time, but tension between these nonconformist esthetes and the regime was evident early. They had joined the Revolution out of high spirits and a hatred of the old society. They soon found that they disliked the new one quite as much. Doubtless they would have hated any established order. Lenin

---

[4] In exile they might yearn to come back. One of the saddest cases was that of Marina Tsvetaeva, brilliant poetess who returned in time to be a victim of Stalin's purge, committing suicide on the way to a prison camp in 1940.

called them "hooligan Communists" because of their highly irregular artists' lives, and thus began that warfare between the Soviet state and independent minds that has continued into the present. Mayakovsky, a poet of rare genius, wrote a long ode to Lenin but soon was satirizing the new breed of bureaucrats.

There was a kind of philistinism about the Communists, expressed in Lenin's often quoted remark that he could not let himself be seduced by the beauty of Beethoven's music while there was revolutionary work to be done. One cannot readily combine the business of extinguishing the ruling class with tender nights watching the ballet or opera. Moreover, Marxian dogma readily lent itself to the view that the old bourgeois culture was tainted all the way through. "Bourgeois decadence" was the epithet applied to those artists too subtle, too individualized, too preoccupied with formal novelties. Art should serve the "people," which meant the Communist party; in other words it must be propaganda, filled with simple ideas attuned to the mass consciousness. But this dreadful tyranny of the commonplace was exactly what the intellectual-artist wanted to escape.

As the Revolution passed into its Stalinist phase, the philistines and the bureaucrats more and more forced writers and artists either to join the party and serve its interests or to perish. Rewards were held out for those who joined and served, but the nonconformist increasingly found life difficult. The freedom to experiment that the Revolution had initially offered changed into a demand to conform at the price of extinction. The state monopoly of publication, the censorship, and the punishment visited on "enemies of the Revolution" crushed individuality.

The situation worsened in the 1930s, when the party adopted the esthetic principle of "socialist realism" and the dictatorship tightened. Writers who had managed to survive the 1920s perished a decade later. For writing a poem against Stalin that was never published but read only to a small group, Osip Mandelstam died in a prison camp. Vsevelod Meyerhold, the famous theatrical producer, also died in a camp, though the movie director, Sergei Eisenstein, whose films about the Revolution were among the most prestigious productions of Soviet art, lasted until 1948. Stalin himself seems to have longed for great Soviet artists, realizing that most of those who served him were hacks; an Eisenstein was a rarity. But he demanded total obedience, and his own taste in the arts was appalling.

Of the great Silver Age writers, Boris Pasternak survived but largely ceased to write, except privately; many years later, he would publish Dr. Zhivago and become a belated martyr. Anna Akhmatova also lived on, though subject to some mistreatment, writing insincere poems in praise of Stalin and, in World War II, sincere ones in behalf of Russian patriotism. In the 1920s, all the writers had hoped for a renewal of culture. Party politicians agreed with intellectuals and artists that Soviet arts, like the Soviet people, must surpass those of previous times. But the politicians demanded that art become the servant of politics, praising those policies the party promulgated. "A negative depiction of contemporary life" was the worst fault; the writer mustn't speak critically of Soviet realities, for this was to serve the class enemy. And the Stalinized party was soon condemning, as "formalism," practically all of what writers and artists regarded as progressive, exciting, and interesting, all that had been happening since about the turn of the century. They were supposed to go back to the realistic or naturalistic style of the nineteenth century, but they were not even allowed to use it critically. They were asked to be Balzacs, Dickenses, and Tolstoys without exposing corruption and hypocrisy.

Those who refused to bend the knee to Mussolini faced a similar predicament. It is true that by the standards Stalin and Hitler set, Italian fascism was a mild thing. In her classic study of twentieth-century totalitarianism (the century's one original contribution to the art of government, someone has disquietingly remarked), Hannah Arendt refused to classify Mussolini's regime as truly totalitarian, though it invented the idea. Hitler and his German Nazi comrades agreed with this, acknowledging an intellectual debt to Mussolini but holding that he had failed to carry the thing through. "Fascism has nothing in common with National Socialism," Joseph Goebbels noted in his journal. "The latter goes to the roots, the former is only superficial." The Nazis thought that Soviet communism *was* totalitarian, the true rival and enemy of their own, and they accorded it a certain respect for its total fanaticism and ruthlessness.

Whereas the Nazi and Communist dictatorships were to slay millions, Italian Fascist terrorism, by comparison, took scarcely any life at all. Special tribunals to deal with political "crimes" were indeed set up, but not only did they condemn relatively few; they adhered to a certain semblance of legality. This was enough to brand fascism as utterly flabby in the eyes of true totalitarians. Ms. Arendt counted only seven condemnations to death between 1926 and 1932, which were the most active years; there were about 1,600 prison sentences and many more exiles, but no fewer than 12,000 were acquitted, "a procedure inconceivable under the Nazi or Bolshevik terror." The great Italian Communist leader, Antonio Gramsci, was jailed, but while in prison he wrote essays and books that were subsequently published and became landmarks of Marxian theory. This is equally hard to imagine happening in a Soviet prison camp or a Nazi concentration camp.

Nevertheless, one should not overlook the antiliberal and dictatorial features of Fascist rule. Mussolini's rhetoric had proclaimed not only "the lie of universal suffrage" but, in 1923, fascism's willingness "to trample on the more or less decomposed body of the Goddess Liberty." The Fascists turned the elections of April 1924 into a farce, as their "squadrists" terrorized opponents, though Mussolini's undeniable success in restoring order probably earned him an honest majority at the polls. There soon followed the famous episode of Giacomo Matteotti's murder by Fascist thugs. This action shocked the whole country, and the martyred Socialist member of Parliament seemed destined to bring down Mussolini's government. Mussolini was repentant (again, it is hard to imagine Hitler or Stalin publicly apologizing for the liquidation of a political enemy) and thought of resigning. "Supported by king and pope, by Senate and industry," Ernst Nolte puts it, he did not fall, but turned to the Right, breaking his last ties with the socialists among whom he had spent so many years.

There were several attempts on *Il Duce's* life in the next few years. Some of these may have stemmed from extremists in his own party, who alleged betrayal of fascism's true goals in Mussolini's tendencies to come to terms with the old established order. Not without some evident regret, in 1927 Mussolini turned to such totalitarian measures as suppressing hostile newspapers, arresting political foes, banning opposition parties, and constituting the "corporative state," which deprived Parliament of power and deposited it in the Fascist Grand Council dominated by Mussolini.

If this power was used less ruthlessly by Mussolini than by Hitler or Stalin, it nevertheless laid claim to totality: every Italian was supposed to serve the state, making it a "monolith" of one national will expressed through the leader. There was no place for opposition or dissent. Yet, somewhat inconsistently, Mussolini proceeded to negotiate a treaty with the papacy in 1929, leaving the "care of souls" to the church.

The most distinctive element in the somewhat erratic Fascist "ideology" was the idea of a "corporative" economy, which was held to be the natural successor to capitalism. In opposition to capitalism, Marxism had proclaimed the sterile program of class conflict, Mussolini explained; fascism proposed the constructive plan of collaboration between capital and labor through the mediation of the state. Italy, a poor country struggling to catch up with more industrialized ones, could not afford strikes and lockouts. The state, representing the public interest, would bring big capital and big labor together, as equals, but with itself as the third and presumably strongest party. Agreements on wages and working conditions would then be reached in a manner equitable to all parties. Opponents claimed that in practice, by undermining independent trade union leadership, Mussolini's corporative state played into the hands of the capitalists, who were almost ecstatically happy to find themselves in a world without strikes. There is, however, little reason to doubt Mussolini's sincerity in proposing a new and more progessive way toward industrial peace and growth.

The idea was reasonable enough to appeal to the American reformist President Franklin D. Roosevelt early in his "New Deal" regime (the National Recovery Act, 1934). So the Fascist regime was by no means universally abhorred in the world. Mussolini had a fairly good press in Western countries; many Italian-Americans were exuberantly enthusiastic about his supposed restoration of Italian strength. His worst days lay ahead. Yet a number of courageous Italians opposed his illiberal regime. Some were his own early followers, like Cesare Rossi, who broke with Mussolini at the time of the Matteotti affair, dared to write a hostile exposé, and was sentenced to imprisonment. (He survived to write post-1945 books, unlike Trotsky or Ernst Röhm.) Gaetano Salvemini, one-time socialist colleague of Mussolini, joined the distinguished G. A. Borgese among those in exile who wrote eloquently from the United States against the Fascist regime, exposing its corruption. The Italian emigration was indeed extensive, including leaders of anti-Fascist political parties, such as Francesco Nitti, Filippo Turati, and Dom Sturzo. The Communist Togliatti found his way to Moscow, while the engaging writer, Ignazio Silone, at length left Italy to publish his widely read political novels of the 1930s, the best known of which is *Bread and Wine*.

Inside Italy there was some underground resistance; but the major impact came from Italians of the emigration like Salvemini, Borgese, and Silone, whose books became favorites of the anti-Fascist, anti-Nazi, usually pro-Communist intelligentsia of the 1930s. Silone first joined, then left the Communist party, a story he told in the series of essays later published by disillusioned ex-Communists, *The God That Failed*. The experience of being driven underground helped the Italian Communist Party to develop habits of cooperating with non-Communist anti-Fascists. In later times this distinguished it from other Communist parties.

Frontiers of Scientific Thought

If intellectual life in the 1920s generally turned away from politics, this was due not only to the dismal quality of political leadership but to the attraction of other areas. In addition to the exciting experiments in art and literature, there were general ideas, philosophical in nature, that provided rich fare for inquisitive minds.

Though the school of psychoanalysis had emerged before the war, as in other cases we have noted, it now became more widely known. Sigmund Freud, having developed the germs of his system as early as 1892, had, together with Carl Jung, founded the International Psychoanalytical Association in 1910, when the Austrian and Swiss psychiatrists, still in fruitful collaboration, carried news of their revolutionary ideas as far as the United States. The psychoanalytical movement was mature enough to produce its first major schism in 1913, when Jung and Freud parted company. Yet it is safe to say that only the intellectually precocious were more than dimly aware of psychoanalysis before the war. Now the Freudian doctrines burgeoned in the atmosphere of the 1920s, when the founding father was aging and ill but still creative. Freud lived and worked in his native Vienna until Hitler took Austria in 1938, upon which he fled to London, where he died the following year.

He was a universally acclaimed master of the interwar generation, and there were attempts, not always successful, to synthesize Freudianism with Marxism, with Christianity or Judaism, with nearly everything else. Stream of consciousness novelists as well as surrealist poets and painters acknowledged his influence. Freud coincided with many cultural trends in the 1920s, some of them contradictory. To many, his bold emphasis on physical sexuality as the prime mover of human behavior stamped him as leader of the revolution against Victorian morality and prudery that marked the postwar years.[5] This association rather overlooked the fact that Freud, who was apparently one of the few major intellectual figures of his generation who stayed faithful to his wife, thought that the wild urges of the primal unconscious had to be kept under tight social control or they would destroy civilization. Again, attempts to marry him to Marxism or other left-wing social ideologies ran aground on Freud's views about human nature, which, he thought, contains ineradicable traits that no social engineering can alter. We have already mentioned the modish pessimism of *Civilization and Its Discontents*. While this pessimism agreed with the Neo-orthodox stress on man's imperfect nature, Freud was a determined atheist.

His genius conformed to no other mold, and its unique vision of

[5] The American writer and world traveller Vincent Sheean wrote in his autobiographical *Personal History* that
> It was very swift, this decay. When I left the University [Chicago] in 1920 it had scarcely begun. Five years later it was, so far as I could determine, common among people of my age in the bourgeoisie. . . . The gulf between generations had suddenly become immense. . . . To our grandparents the ordinary manners, conversation, conduct and morals of educated and "respectable" people would have seemed suitable to the underworld. (New York: The Literary Guild, 1934, pp. 310–312.)

man imposed itself ineluctably on an age eager for new formulations of human nature and destiny. To some it was utterly subversive, for it completed that relentless unmasking of human ideals begun by Darwin and Marx. Those ideals, including all religion and art and philosophy, might be traced back to the wolf lair of some secret sexual encounter, some traumatic event of childhood, some anal or oral fantasy. People are not the masters of their own motives, which are the product of unconscious forces.

On the other hand, Freud held out the hope that by scientific understanding such heretofore unguided forces could be brought under control, though in his later years at least he does not seem to have believed this possible. Professional psychoanalysts supplied, for a goodly fee, the modern equivalent of the confessional. Although Freud's own fascinating case histories suggest that the curing of neurosis is scarcely an exact science, it was now purveyed as such. Beset by the stresses of modern life, people went to the psychiatrist in lieu of the priest. Americans, especially prone to this, were said to think you could have your psyche taken care of once a year like your automobile or your teeth. Such a facile view was not Freud's, needless to say, but it did testify to modern people's need for messages of salvation and consolation.

The Viennese doctor's influence extended not only to the psychiatric profession, and to literature and art, but also to education. In general, the Freudian vocabulary grew to be a part of the language of knowledgeable people, a tool of understanding and of interpretation; *id* and *superego*, *dream analysis* as *wish fulfillment*, *Oedipus complex*, *libido*, and other Freudian terms became almost household words. Not far behind him in this role was his erstwhile colleague, Carl Jung of Zurich, popularizing *introvert*, *extravert*, and *archetypes of the collective unconscious*. With such terms did harried twentieth-century people arm themselves against their troubles.

The other great name of the twenties was Albert Einstein. Here again the roots of the "revolution in physics" go back well before 1919, but only then did they become literally front page news. One of history's more interesting coincidences is that an observation confirming Einstein's relativity theory, the second, generalized version of which was announced in 1915, took place on the same June day in 1919 as the signing of the Treaty of Versailles. Conscientious intellects, anxious to keep up and aware that the Jewish genius was on to something immensely important, struggled to understand him, a task far from easy; many books appeared attempting to explain relativity and other elements of the new physics to laymen, for example, Bertrand Russell's *ABC of Relativity*.

It seemed clear in a general way that the foundations of the physical sciences, which had been thought certain since the seventeenth century, had been overthrown—proof, to some, of ultimate skepticism or intellectual anarchy. "The last certitude," science, had fallen. Newton's laws of motion and gravitation no longer stood as universally valid. Space and time were no longer separate, nor mass and velocity. Absolute space and time did not exist. Light was not wave but particles. The unity of physics was broken, for the behavior of subatomic particles followed radically different rules. Determinacy no longer reigned at the level of the smallest particles, which indeed might be only ideas; or if they existed they exhibited qualities impossible to comprehend.

The nineteenth-century picture of the world was rapidly disappearing with the discoveries of Einstein, Max Planck, Niels Bohr, Werner Heisenberg, and other brilliant students of a "mysterious universe." The return to religion or metaphysics as well as the pessimism of the twenties often took sustenance from this apparent revelation of chaos where there had been Newtonian order. The witty response to Alexander Pope's famous eighteenth-century couplet

> *Nature and nature's laws lay hid in night*
> *God said "Let Newton be!" and all was light*

was

> *This did not last. The Devil, crying "Ho!*
> *Let Einstein be!" restored the status quo.*

The world of Dr. Einstein was as curious as was Dr. Freud's dream world or the visions of Picasso. Bertrand Russell, thinking of the odd unpredictability of individual electrons, called it an anarchist universe.

The paradoxes resulting from Einstein's exposition of the necessary absence of any absolute measurement of time and space (the ether having been exposed as a nonentity) defied common sense: time is longer to the observer of a moving body than to one on it, so that if you were able to go off on a trip around the cosmos at high speeds, on your return you would be younger than you were in comparison to those who stayed behind. The jingle that ran

> *There was a young lady named Bright*
> *Whose speed was much faster than light.*
> *She went off one day in a relative way*
> *And returned on the previous night*

got a good many things wrong, including her speed; she would return on the following day, since a longer period of time would have elapsed for those who stayed home than for her. The confusion was perhaps understandable. You would also become squatter and heavier at extreme speeds, reaching a stage of virtually no mass but extreme weight as you approached the speed of light.

Another incredible feature of Einstein's world became all too true with the atomic bomb: energy and mass are interchangeable, $E = Mc^2$, c being the speed of light. By another curious coincidence, the work on neutrons and the fission of heavy nuclei ripened in 1939, just as World War II began. Heisenberg said that in the summer of 1939 this knowledge was known to only about twelve people in the world, who might by coming to an agreement have prevented the construction of atom bombs. This indicates how extremely difficult these frontiers of thought were. Theoretical physics was of course an international collaboration. Einstein and Planck worked in Berlin in the 1920s; Bohr was a Dane; Mr. and Mrs. Joliot-Curie made vital contributions from France, Ernest Rutherford at the Cavendish Laboratory in Cambridge. James Chadwick discovered neutrons at Cavendish in 1932; the Curies were pioneers of radioactivity; while the Comte de Broglie, scion of an old aristocratic French family, worked on the puzzling problem of subatomic wave mechanics, which found electrons acting like particles at times and like waves at others. Italian, Hungarian, Austrian, American, and other scientists made various important contributions to the new field of nuclear physics.

All this added up to a radically different vision of the universe, as well as to new and sometimes awesome power over nature. Television, x-rays, radiation, and other electronic miracles eventually joined nuclear energy as the practical byproducts of this theoretical speculation. Real as these powers were, their foundations were mysterious. Max Planck's quantum theory found a constant number relating energy to frequency of radiation, and the number bobbed up again in wave mechanics, in subatomic indeterminacy. Like the speed of light, it provided a clue to the workings of physical nature. But what it meant could not be discerned.

Mathematical formulae are obviously not reality itself. "The world as seen by science is not the world as it really is," Joseph Needham noted. One could no longer visualize a common-sense universe. Nineteenth- and early twentieth-century scientists had had the goal of making science clear enough to be understood by everyone. "The laws of physics should be simple enough that a barmaid can grasp them," declared C. T. R. Wilson, the inventor in 1911 of the cloud chamber. It now became evident that science could not get to the bottom of reality. This conclusion would not have surprised Immanuel Kant, but it upset the whole mechanical-materialistic model that had dominated progressive European minds for a century.

One result was that scientists became comparatively humble. "We are no longer taught that the scientific method is the only valid method of acquiring knowledge about reality," J. W. N. Sullivan observed in a 1933 book titled *The Limitations of Science.* Scientists themselves talked of "the mysterious universe" or speculated on the possible truth of philosophical idealism: mind determines what we know about the world; what is "out there" is in itself formless and meaningless. Reality is, in brief, a set of mental constructs. Wave mechanics suggested that the world might be inherently ambivalent or dialectical.

It was at this time, too, that the universe grew, in our understanding, to even vaster dimensions. There are countless other galaxies like that one of which our own solar system is an infinitesimally small part. Ancient and medieval thinkers had in effect supposed that our own planetary system, of which the earth is the solid center, comprised the whole cosmos. Galileo's proof that the sun is the center and that the other planets are qualitatively like earth began the demotion of human being from central figure in the cosmic drama to insignificant speck of dust; but now layer on layer of immensity was piled on, until the size of the universe became unimaginable. Indeed, in Einstein's terms, the universe is infinite, space being not a "something." It is evidently expanding constantly and with extreme rapidity. The theory that it will eventually contract into a body as small as a baseball, to explode again in 80-billion-year cycles, bore a startling resemblance to ancient Indic metaphysics or to Nietzsche's vision of eternal recurrence. The scientists produced ideas more bizarre than those of poets or prophets.

Ever since the eighteenth century, science had stood for reason, order, and progress. In the popular mind, the "myth of the Enlightenment" portrayed the scientist as a hero-savior leading mankind at last to a fair haven of material and intellectual success, after eons of error, by casting out metaphysics, mysticism, and pessimism. That belief was now, in the twentieth century, to a large extent impaired. Fascinating perhaps, the new frontiers of science offered no final victories and no simple answers. Science joined literature and art in a violent iconoclasm that tore down the comforting traditions of thought and culture to create weird visions of a cockeyed world.

One of Thomas Hardy's later poems ("Drinking Song"), written in the 1920s, calls the role of the ideas that beginning with Copernicus and ending with Einstein, have disabused people from the notion that "everything was made for" them. Each stanza ends with the ironic refrain

> *Fill full your cups, feel no distress*
> *'Tis only one great thought the less!*

Deists, sceptics, evolutionists, higher critics of the Bible all made the old Victorian poet's list of detractors from human centrality—"and now comes Einstein." Admittedly "not yet quite clear," Einstein seemed to annihilate time, space, and motion, assailing the last remaining certainties and leaving us "in piteous case." Such a gloomy perspective was not far from the intellectual average in the 1920s.

Popular Culture

Though Einstein and Freud did become familiar names, it is doubtful that many ordinary people in the 1920s concerned themselves much with such dazzling perspectives. Most would not have read more than fragments of *Ulysses*—perhaps those with the groundbreaking four-letter words—or of Lawrence, Proust, Mann, or Kafka.

The "common man" or woman was capable (then as now), however, of taking an extraordinary interest in the ancient Egyptian monarch, King Tut, whose tomb British archaeologists opened in 1922; or in the American aviator, Charles Lindbergh, who flew alone from New York to Paris in 1927, though his was far from the first transatlantic flight.

If popular culture seemed silly and stupid to the intellectuals of the 1920s, its "shop-girl mentality" a leading feature of the *Waste Land* landscape, its popular music inane and its reading material beneath contempt, this was perhaps mainly because of the many new toys technology had provided, which were more interesting than books or paintings. The automobile, the airplane, the cinema (movies), and radio were of course the foremost of these. Already before 1914 Bijous or Apollos were appearing in every neighborhood, and there were complaints that motor cars were killing people and creating an intolerable racket. And radio was far enough advanced to have created a scandal in government. In 1912, David Lloyd George got into trouble with regard to the contract for supplying His Majesty's government with "wireless telegraphy." Nevertheless, mass consumption awaited the postwar years, and it was in some ways a product of the war; large-scale production of motorized vehicles and radios for military use led to the need to find other markets when the war ended.

The three inventions (along with radio's electronic spinoff, television) that have most affected social and cultural life in this century followed a rather similar time schedule of development. The first practical automobile dates from the 1880s. Hertz discovered radio waves in 1885, and Marconi made radio transmission and reception a reality by 1895. The first motion pictures jerked dimly across the screen in 1889. They all underwent significant development in the 1890s, became commercially feasible by the 1900s, and then took off into the growth stratosphere after the war. Autos were only for the rich before 1914,

Actress Marlene Dietrich in a scene from *The Blue Angel*, famous German film of the 1920s. *Wide World Photos.*

and roads were still inadequate. In Great Britain in 1913, a total of 34,000 motor vehicles were built; they came in 198 different models. After the war, annual output rose to 95,000 in 1923 and 511,000 in 1937. Meanwhile, the price fell from an average of about £300 ($1,500) to £130 ($650), and the market was dominated by six manufacturers. The first "mass car" builders, analogous to Henry Ford in the USA, were Austin and Morris, who dominated the market in the 1920s but ran into competition from more luxurious models in the 1930s.

"Wireless" broadcasting, as distinct from telegraph-like communications, was entirely a postwar development. Use of radio for public entertainment and information is said to have arisen as the unexpected outcome of an advertising campaign by the Westinghouse Company in Pittsburgh, where the first radio station was established. In Britain, unlike the United States, where private broadcasters soon covered the country, broadcasting became a public monopoly under the British Broadcasting Company (later Corporation). Before long, receiving sets, much less expensive than automobiles, multiplied until there were more than two million of them in 1926, a number that had increased to nine million by 1939. Whereas prior to World War II by no means every

British household possessed a motor car—the ratio was more like one in four—almost every home was equipped with a radio receiver of some sort. Television was undergoing development, and there were a few broadcasts just before 1939, when about 20,000 TV receivers existed in the British Isles. The BBC operated more than a score of radio stations and broadcast several kinds of programs, both regional and national. (The Third Programme was serious and intellectual, the First light and frivolous.)

The economic and social effect of these new contrivances was enormous. The manufacture of automobiles not only became a great industry in itself, employing tens of thousands, but it created or expanded many related industries: rubber, oil refining, metals, glass, road building, service, and repair. Living habits—all the way from how one spent one's holidays and weekends to where one lived—were profoundly changed. All things considered, the automobile clearly has claims to priority as the leading technological influence on the life of mankind in this century. But if we think of things more specifically cultural, relating to interests, ideas, taste, leisure activities, then the movies and radio/television can challenge for the first spot. Transportation affects people physically, helping determine both their work and their leisure in geographic terms; to be sure, it does more than that, for what one is physically able to do impinges on the quality of one's activities. Changing habits of courtship, of visiting friends, of travel to distant areas for cultural purposes entailed psychic alterations of all sorts. Some detected a relationship between changes in sexual morality and the culture of parking in dark places. But to provide new objects of consciousness, visual and auditory, for millions of people in most of their nonworking hours was the destiny of the new media of entertainment and communication.

Little that happened in this decade was unaffected by the new media. Critics of popular culture noted, among other manifestations, a tendency toward crazes, fads, sensations, novelties, a nine days' wonder each fortnight destined probably to quick oblivion. Popular songs flitted in and out, one being heard incessantly for a few weeks, after which some equally inane ditty replaced the former "hit," now happily sunk without trace. Sports heroes were glamorized; records were broken every month or so to ecstatic applause: first woman to fly the Atlantic, fastest flight over Atlantic, first person to swim the English Channel, first woman to swim the Channel, and so on.

Such phenomena stemmed primarily from the new ease of mass communications. Radio—and also the newspapers and magazines, old media but now distributed more widely and more quickly via automobile and airplane—spread the "news" to an insatiable audience. The need to supply this immense demand impelled the exploitation if not the manufacture of sensational items. It cannot be claimed that the sort of newspaper that specialized in scandal, crime, and sex was new, for such organs were familiar in Victorian times. But they now had infinitely larger circulations. Radio enabled a vastly enlarged audience to sit in on athletic events, thus swelling the craze for sports. And popular movie actors and actresses became the best-known of personalities, much more famous than mere politicians or writers.

Popular culture tended to be international. American movies went everywhere. Long disparaged as culturally backward, if mechanically progressive, compared with Europeans, the Americans now showed their genius for democracy by excelling in low culture. While high culture spokesmen, including some Americans of the "civilized minority," indignantly rejected this brash product and retreated to even higher pinnacles, American technological and entrepreneurial skills created a new kind of popular art.

Such cultural products were not art as it had been understood for centuries in Western and other civilizations, in the sense of being the inspired creation of individual genius. They were triumphs of organization. They manufactured an art-product with skills analogous to the factory assembly line, which was now becoming the chief method of commodity production. To make a movie was to synchronize a large team of builders, painters, actors, photographers, electricians, special effects experts, and later, with the introduction of "talkies" in 1928, sound men. The mass market for films enabled huge investments to be made in such elaborate organizations, creating on some "set" a whole world of fantasy. The key figures were producers. Gathered in Hollywood, California, these people manufactured dreams for the masses. For prestige they might gather in authors as distinguished as Aldous Huxley or F. Scott Fitzgerald, but for the most part no such literary genius was needed or wanted. Plots could be made to formula, dialogue turned out in standardized format. Even people might be replaced by animated cartoon figures.

In the process of being manufactured on the assembly line, such cultural products were purged of all complexity, subtlety, sophistication, irony; they lacked any aura of "style." They became primitive statements of the least common denominators of mass consciousness, rendered palatable by dazzling techniques and the sheer giganticism of screen effects, simulating huge battles or stampedes or giant apes toppling city skyscrapers. Occasional works of art did make an exception to the rule, and from the early days of filmmaking emerged the genius of a Charlie Chaplin. But as they became organized and Hollywoodized, elements of personal artistic creation vanished from the great bulk of movies. In some ways they were a kind of modern communal rite, celebrating the same simple myths of love, heroism, adventure over and over. As such they played an enormously important part in mass consciousness. And they irritated the artist-intellectual beyond all measure, standing for everything he or she detested.

"Mass culture" thus seemed a new phenomenon. In the past there had been elite cultures, shared by that relatively small number who had the leisure and the wealth to absorb the complex inheritance of Western civilization stretching back to the ancient Greeks. The size of such elites may be suggested by the number who attended universities—only a few thousand before 1914, less than one person in a thousand in most countries.

The rest of the populace had scarcely any literary culture, subsisting on the remnants of old folkways. Something midway between the literate culture of a civilized elite and the folk lore of a traditional peasant society emerged fairly early in the career of modern nation-states. There were subcultures in urban underworlds, in the urban working class, in the Victorian lower middle class, but these were too fragmentary and tentative to provide more than curious footnotes to cultural history. Research into the less lighted corridors of literary history has uncovered "trash literature" reaching back to the beginnings of book production—an abundance of it existed in the eighteenth as well as the nineteenth century. It is thus not possible to claim that "cheap" literature, printed in detective novels, movie magazines, household journals, *True Confessions,* or in pornography ("girlie" magazines, in the argot of the twenties) and the like, was something new, extruded from the unhappy consciousness of twentieth-century mass man. It only appeared in greater quantities and perhaps in even worse taste. The British *Annual Register* for 1926 noted with some dismay that " 'Detective stories' came from the publishers in a positive torrent to meet an eager public demand." The vogue for whodunits, coinciding with one for crossword puzzles, bridge, and other games, suggests a need for something challenging but innocuous to occupy the mind and can thus be related to withdrawal of interest in public affairs as well as to the tedium of jobs in the assembly-line age; or to more leisure provided by shorter working hours and improved transportation. More people now had a secondary school education.

There had always been a gulf between those who read Shakespeare or listened to Beethoven and those whose taste ran to the evening tabloid and the latest tune from Tin Pan Alley. But it was disconcerting that this gulf, far from diminishing with the passing of the years and the advance of public education, had even increased.

The inexorable advance of social democracy had been going on ever since the early nineteenth century, more frequently deplored than welcomed by European intellectuals. Traditional society was organic and hierarchical, marked by very intense group feelings but inequality of status. As European society developed in medieval and early modern times, it preserved these features while gradually dissolving the local communities into the larger nation-state, which possessed much less natural unity. With the bourgeois revolution of the nineteenth century, aristocratic claims of social superiority on the basis of birth suffered fatal blows. Contractual relations between legally equal individuals replaced status as members of an "order" or corporate group as the basis of social relations, the source of rights and obligations. This dissolution of social community into an assemblage of atomistic individuals, a "society of strangers," the ideal of some bourgeois social and political theorists, gradually penetrated into wider and wider circles. Largely an urban phenomenon, it spread with the triumph of city over country, the erosion of rural conservative communities.

Democracy was one consequence of this process, for people were increasingly perceived as social and political equals. That a formal equality was not a real one was as evident to impoverished unskilled workmen as it was, a little later, to women; economic dependency might subvert any real independence. But the process of melting away privileges on the part of any hereditary privileged order went steadily on. From the vantage point of those who cherished Europe's civilized traditions, this could seem like a disaster. The artist, as French poet Stephane Mallarmé declared, has to be an aristocrat, inasmuch as he does not believe in the equality of values. The "plebification" of knowledge, thought, and culture degraded them. High art, along with all difficult, advanced thought, is only for the few, and this precious commodity has to be protected. In Nietzsche, Ibsen, and other end-of-the-century haters of a society that seemed stupid, tasteless, and vulgar, the outcry against the mass-men, the noisy dwarves, the newspaper-reading "last men" who represent the dregs of a dying culture reached a stage of near hysteria. "What the majority of people think is stupid" became their motto. And by and large the disciples of the Nietzschean generation dominated European literature in the 1920s. Freud's "aristocratic distaste for the rabble" was matched by that of Yeats, Eliot, Lawrence, Gide, and many others. They feared that in this "tragedy of mediocrity," mankind would lose "everything of genius, beauty, grandeur" (Edmond Scherer).

The masses themselves certainly viewed the matter otherwise. Esthetically uncertain as their new culture might be, for most of them it was better than their parents' lives of poverty and unremitting toil. An expansion of consciousness was going on. Appalling degradation of taste as measured by a former aristocratic standard might look like a decided elevation if the comparison was made with the Victorian lower class, which had dwelt in foul slums often without manners or morals. A large gulf existed between the people of letters, art, and science on the one hand and the shopgirl or tabloid-newspaper reader on the other. But the shopgirl of the 1920s probably had more cultural awareness than her mother.

Despite the many complaints about a radical gulf between low and high culture—weeds and wildflowers, the American literary critic Van Wyck Brooks put it—examination of the literary market reveals a lively middle-brow segment. While Joyce and most of Virginia Woolf was too much for them, a middle-class reading public in England supported a vigorous literary industry, showing a taste for biography, auto-biography, history, as well as fiction of a less formidable variety than *Ulysses* or *To the Lighthouse*. They made bestsellers of H. G. Wells' outlines of knowledge, Bertrand Russell's history of philosophy, Winston Churchill's history of the war, and other serious works. Their taste in novels ran to such now-forgotten amusements as Michael Arlen's *The Green Hat* (sophisticated adultery, a popular line) and Margaret Kennedy's *The Constant Nymph*.[6] American writers were read in England as never before, especially Sinclair Lewis, perhaps because he showed his countrymen in such a bad light. More sentimentally, American hits including Thornton Wilder's *Bridge of San Luis Rey* and Edna Ferber's *The Show Boat* appealed to an earnest if not very critical British audience. As for American movies, of course, the complaint was that the British film industry was so totally unable to compete with them that it had trouble surviving.

This ingestion of Americana was true in somewhat smaller measure in France and Germany. To the high-culture intellectuals, of course, the United States symbolized all that they hated; visions of a regimented ant-world, a "cosmic man" without culture, total dehumanization came to their minds. The French writer Georges Duhamel's *Scenes of Life in the Future* (1930; *Scènes de la vie future*) was once printed with the subtitle *America, the Menace*. Yet the American writers Ernest Hemingway and William Faulkner deeply influenced French literature in the 1930s.

In this connection Adolf Hitler's tastes are revealing and not atypical. His political success was based in no small measure on a kind

---

6 Books often have strangely unexpected effects. Stalin blamed his wife's suicide in 1932 on *The Green Hat*, which she had been reading. And some analysts of the Communist dictator's mind blame his subsequent cruelty in part on this event. It is astonishing to think that millions may have died because of Arlen's literary trifle.

of intuitive understanding of the mind of the "little man." Devotee of Nietzsche and Wagner, Hitler felt and conveyed a Spenglerian sense of "cultural pessimism" associated with stinging verdicts on the corruption of modern mass-man by commercialism and democracy. Yet his favorite author was really Karl May, a German equivalent of Zane Grey or Sax Rohmer, the author of scores of trite adventure stories. He enjoyed Wagnerian opera but also movies and sentimental operettas. And he despised twentieth century modernist art, music, and architecture, branding it Jewish and decadent.

The war had accelerated the democratic revolution in various ways. In Britain women, as a reward for shouldering men's work, got the vote they had vainly agitated for in the 1900s. The democracy of the trenches had challenged class lines. Labor leaders entered into governments; politicians promised that soldiers on their return should be rewarded without regard to pedigree. As Lord Curzon discovered, aristocratic traits of dress and temperament were now fatal handicaps to high elective political office. The era of Coolidge, Baldwin, Herriot, and Mussolini was in one of its various manifestations an era of the "common man." The new modes of transportation and communication broke down old provincialisms, opening visions of a richer world to the view of countless people. Mass taste was shocking to a refined few, and the whole mixture of values, accompanied by the intellectual revolution of the 1920s in so many different areas, gave rise to a feeling of acute crisis. At the end of the decade American commentator Walter Lippmann summed it up as "the dissolution of the ancestral order."

The Years of the
Great Depression

The Economic Crisis

It was appropriate that the terrible economic slump of the 1930s started in the United States, to which Europe seemed to have surrendered economic leadership during the great war and on which she had been dependent ever since. The stock market crash that began on a black Friday in October 1929 and deepened in the ensuing months had immediate repercussions in Europe. Indeed, even before this, the superheated boom in stock prices that marked the bull market of 1928 syphoned money from Europe. The pricking of the bubble sent shock waves throughout the world. Large exports of American capital had helped sustain Europe, besides providing an outlet for American surpluses of capital, during the 1920s. Investment in European bonds now contracted sharply and swiftly, as banks that were "caught short" with too many of their assets invested in securities desperately tried to raise money. By June 1930, the price of securities on Wall Street was about 20 percent, on average, of what it had been prior to the crash; between 1929 and 1932 the Dow-Jones average of industrial stock prices fell from a high of 381 to a low of 41!

The American market for European imports also dropped sharply as the whole American economy went into shock; and, to compound trouble, Congress insisted on passing a high tariff law in 1930 against the advice of almost all economists. The Americans, additionally, continued to insist upon repayment of war debts, until finally in 1931 a general moratorium was declared. Well might Europeans complain of American blindness, but these events only exposed Europe's vulnerability.

An economic depression was by no means a novelty. Severe and prolonged ones had afflicted the world in 1873–1878 and 1893–1897. Others had been shorter. They were usually preceded by a speculative and inflationary boom. A typical boom had immediately followed the war, in 1918–1919, giving way to a short and sharp slump in 1921–1922, which had in turn led to the general prosperity of the years up to late 1929. The exceptions to this we already know: Great Britain remained in a kind of chronic slump, which was the result of her loss of overseas markets and which was intensified by her refusal to devalue the pound in the 1920s. Germany had experienced the strange agony of the massive inflation, climaxing in 1923, because of the continuing struggle with France over war reparations. The Communist revolution had largely cut Russia off from the world economy, despite its limited toleration of capitalism from 1921 to 1928. Carving up the Hapsburg monarchy left Austria a charity case, and in 1931 a fresh wave of economic disasters started with the failure of the Austrian central bank.

These exceptions may seem more numerous than the rule, but the United States and most parts of Europe did enjoy relatively favorable economic conditions between 1924 and 1930. But it turned out that this prosperity rested on American loans and American markets, which now

THE GREAT DEPRESSION

Indices of Industrial Production, 1929–1938,
in Major European Countries
(1937 = 100)

	1929	1930	1931	1932	1933	1934	1935	1936	1937	1938
France	123	123	105	91	94	92	88	95	100	92
Germany	79	69	56	48	54	67	79	90	100	92
Italy	90	85	77	77	82	80	86	86	100	100
Great Britain	77	74	69	69	73	80	82	94	100	101

Unemployment (in thousands)

	1929	1930	1931	1932	1933	1934	1935	1936	1937	1938
France	neglig.	13	64	301	305	368	464	470	380	402
Germany	1,899	3,070	4,520	5,575	4,804	2,718	2,151	1,593	912	429
Italy	301	425	734	1,006	1,019	964	–	–	874	810
Great Britain	1,216	1,917	2,630	2,745	2,521	2,159	2,036	1,755	1,484	1,791

almost vanished. A European economy still recovering from the trauma of the war and its aftermath was too frail to weather this storm.

The business cycle had long had its ups and downs. If this downswing turned out to be worse than any previous one, the reason must be sought in the profound structural changes heaped on top of a normal cycle. Fulcrum of the world economy, the United States had not yet learned how to play that part, as its erratic financial policies and high protective tariffs indicated. Deeper changes were going on in the world. Policies of "autarchy" had developed after the war and were to be perpetuated during the depression: that is, countries that were no longer prepared to trust the international order tried to insulate their economies by tariffs, import quotas, or a managed currency. During the 1920s, while sometimes readjusting the rate at which their currencies exchanged for gold, most nations clung to the gold standard, which facilitated international trade by permitting currencies to be freely exchanged in terms of gold. But beginning in 1931, when Great Britain was driven off the gold standard, country after country left it in order to protect themselves against a flight of gold leading to deflation and unemployment. The flight from gold was followed by all kinds of nationalist economic policies—exchange controls, import quotas, tariffs. International trade was thus further impaired.

According to the economic theory dominant throughout the nineteenth century and still uppermost in the minds of public leaders, these periods of depression represented a temporary disequilibrium that would soon right itself. The traditional wisdom did not see any role for government in an economic crisis further than to provide "financial stability," which meant balancing the budget and avoiding inflation. The idea of having the government borrow and spend in order to counterbalance deflation in time of depression ran counter to orthodox economic theory in 1929–1932. Unpleasant no doubt in the short run, the orthodox policies were supposed to restore economic health, like a nasty medicine needed to cure a disease. Thus, at the cost of unemployment, deflation would lower prices and lead to the recovery of markets. Interest rates would fall, again attracting capital investment. The needle of the business cycle meter was supposed to hover around full employment, and there would be maximum use of resources under "normal" conditions. The natural operation of forces would soon draw the economy back upward, unless a ham-fisted government in its ignorance tampered with the delicate machinery. This machinery was supposed to function under conditions of a stable currency, political stability, international free trade, a competitive economy.

This model was based on impressive theoretical work reaching back to the later eighteenth century; it had had the imprimatur of most of the great economists of the "classical" nineteenth-century era, with only a few outcasts dissenting. In the light of later analysis, based on sad experience, this theory came to seem disastrously naive in assuming all kinds of ideal conditions that did not exist in the real world. Perfect competition was obviously lacking in an era increasingly prone to both corporate business monopolies or semimonopolies and trade union influence on wages. The model made no allowance for wars, revolutions, dictatorships, the dismemberment of countries, and all kinds of political factors. Of course, unconverted advocates of the traditional economics might argue that their remedy did not work because it was not tried; governments did not adhere long enough to the spartan measures necessary to make it work. But facing massive unemployment, bankruptcies, and bank failures, governments now could not resist demands to do something other than wait patiently for the storm to run its course. Not knowing quite what to do, they floundered, and their flounderings perhaps made the situation worse. The depression of the thirties found the old economic world dying and the new one still struggling to be born. The result seemed to be the worst of both worlds.

Whatever the causes, panic soon spread through Europe. In 1931, after the World Court refused to allow Austria to enter a customs union with Germany, that economically distressed country collapsed. Its central bank failed, touching off a panic that threatened Great Britain next. President Herbert Hoover of the United States proposed a moratorium on all war debts and reparations, but French opposition delayed its acceptance.

In Britain, a Labour government faced a flight of gold, which threatened the pound. Elected in 1929, Labour had taken office with Liberal support.[1] As unemployment soared, payments to the jobless under the national insurance program strained the budget. A special committee recommended cutting unemployment benefits, and bankers in New York and Paris refused to lend money to the beleaguered British unless this was done. The Labour cabinet split. On August 24, 1931, Prime Minister Ramsay MacDonald, Chancellor of the Exchequer Philip Snowden, and some other Labour ministers joined Conservative and Liberal politicians to create a "national" government; elections in October gave this coalition an overwhelming victory. But the action divided the Labour party and left scars that were long in healing. The party expelled MacDonald and his friends as traitors.

---

[1] Labour gained 289 seats to 260 for the Conservatives and 58 for the Liberals; thus it was dependent on Liberal votes for a parliamentary majority. This pronounced swing away from the Conservative victory of 1924 reflected the economic difficulties of Britain, with continuing high unemployment and a failure to share much in the general world prosperity.

Bowing to the edict of the international banks did not save Great Britain from being driven off gold, which happened on September 20. The whole episode reflected the confusions of policy. Labourites and, in Italy, Fascists were as uncertain what to do about the economic blizzard as anyone else. The only thing that was indisputable was the continuing catastrophic collapse. Unemployment rose to 22 percent in Britain, and industrial production sagged to 84 by 1932 (1929 = 100). This was much better than other countries did, but Britain started from a lower base. In 1932, French production stood at 72 percent of 1929, German and American at barely more than half (53). In July 1932, world industrial production was 38 percent less than it had been in June 1929. Few parts of the globe escaped, and there were an estimated thirty million men in the world seeking vainly for work.

Historian Arnold Toynbee called 1931 the *annus terribilis*, the terrible year. This year of descent into the economic depths of mass unemployment, hunger, breakdown of international exchange, failure of great financial institutions was also a year of floundering governments, the rise of the National Socialist party in Germany, and Japan's absorption of Manchuria. Japan's move, at least partly inspired by economic desperation, later looked like the beginning of the decay of international order leading to World War II. From the vantage point of a despairing West, caught in what looked like the last capitalist crisis, Stalin's first five-year plan appeared as a beacon of hope. In fact, however, Soviet Russia went through the awful experience of the Communist government's forcible extermination of peasant landed property, a veritable war that cost millions of lives.

In the ensuing years things got a little better in some places. Apparently saved by what the experts regarded as a disaster, the British economy improved after Britain's departure from the gold standard resulted in a substantial devaluation. The recovery that took place between 1932 and 1937 reached a sort of boom in 1937, when unemployment fell to a mere 9 percent, low for the interwar years. But it rose to 13 percent in 1938–1939. Worldwide, by 1937 the indices of economic activity had returned to the 1929 level. France had not climbed back quite this far; Germany just about had.

One of the most punishing features of the depression had been the drastic fall in agricultural prices, together with other primary products. The years from 1925 to 1928 brought good harvests all over the world, the latter a record in wheat. The price of grain tumbled just as the industrial and financial slump hit, compounding the crisis. Loss of urban and international markets afflicted farmers already in trouble from overproduction and, frequently, from a burden of debt incurred in expanding production and buying agricultural machinery. With unemployed workers suffering from hunger, the sight of farmers refusing to harvest crops because the price was too low to make it worthwhile drove home the bitter lesson of poverty in the midst of plenty, the curse of Midas fallen on man. But by 1936 agricultural prices had risen somewhat.

Depression Politics

For understandable reasons, the economic disaster was usually fatal to the party or parties unlucky enough to be in office when it struck. The fall of the British Labour government has been mentioned. In the national coalition that succeeded it, the same prime minister, Ramsay MacDonald, presided over a mixture of renegade Labourites, Conservatives, and Liberals. It continued to govern England and became even more conservative in 1935.

Around the 1931 change, legends clustered, especially on the Left— MacDonald had conspired to betray the cause, he was the lost leader who had sold out to the upper classes ("Fame is the Spur," one novel based on these events alleged.) Defenses of the Scotsman, who had been

The Depression caused a panic-stricken outbreak of economic warfare among nations. International trade collapsed and banks faced disaster. July, 1931, brought acute crisis to banks in Germany and Austria. Here a huge crowd in Berlin waits to withdraw savings, just as Americans were to do in their banking crisis early in 1933. *Wide World Photos.*

one of the Labour party's founding fathers and who had shown outstanding courage in World War I when he opposed the tide of martial
spirit, claimed that he had the courage in 1931 to put country above
party. It seems likely that MacDonald had gradually lost his early faith
in socialism as he confronted the sobering responsibilities of power. In
this sense he was a "traitor" to socialism. But the bankruptcy of the
Labour party program as a means of dealing with the depression was
underscored by its shattering defeat in the October election. Brandish-
ing worthless German marks during that campaign, MacDonald indicated how strongly the shadow of 1923 lay over these years: to avoid
inflation at almost any cost was the goal, and he accused his former
Labour colleagues who had voted against reducing unemployment benefits of "fiscal irresponsibility."

The remaining four years of his prime ministership were not happy
ones for MacDonald, a man without a party. He struggled with the
reparations problem only to see that whole house of cards fall to the
ground, as everybody simply reneged. Banking on partnership with the
United States, he received a rebuff when, at the London economic conference of 1933, new American President Franklin D. Roosevelt
rejected international monetary stabilization in favor of unilateral American devaluation of the dollar. Nor was this long-time advocate of disarmament any man to confront Adolf Hitler. MacDonald became
increasingly an anomaly in a Conservative-dominated cabinet, and he
resigned in 1935 in ill health. Stanley Baldwin took over the prime
minister's post, and in the elections that followed, the national coalition
won another overwhelming victory; but with Baldwin at its head and a
Conservative also at the foreign office, it looked much less like a coalition than a Tory government spiced with a few mavericks from the
other parties. The fading Liberals were in as much disarray as Labour,
for in 1935 they split three ways, one of which became a kind of branch
of the Conservative party.

Thus in Britain a basically Conservative government faced the
depression, and it did comparatively well. Under provisions of the Housing Acts of 1936 and 1938, slums were cleared and new housing constructed, in perhaps the most notable social program of a regime headed
by a far from reactionary Tory. Housing was recognized as a public
service, along with education and health; Baldwin's government added
millions of people to health insurance coverage and built hundreds of
thousands of homes as public housing. In the end it was most condemned for its "appeasement" of Hitler's Germany, but in the mid-
thirties British public opinion wanted nothing less than a bold program
of rearmament and confrontation.

Britain's relative success in rising from the ashes of 1932 did not
prevent depression-bred bitterness; the literature of the thirties turned

to social realism, describing poverty, unemployment, the humiliation of being on the "dole" (unemployment benefits), the class struggle. But the energetic leftism of the intellectuals was scarcely reflected in popular opinion. Of the 615 members of the House of Commons elected in 1935, only one was a Communist. Nor was there a single Fascist, though one of Labour's most brilliant members, Oswald Mosley, deserted the party to organize the British Union of Fascists in 1932, in imitation of Mussolini and Hitler, and Fascists fought with Communists in the streets of London. The British adhered to their traditional moderation, their suspicion of intellectual novelties, even in hard times. Not Stalin or Mussolini, those violent and flamboyant types, but Mr. Average Middle-class Englishman, Stanley Baldwin, presided over their depression politics.

The depression affected French political life by quickening the already rapid ebb and flow of governments. There were six of them between late 1932 and early 1934, barely over a year. This performance more than matched that of the German republic, whose downfall at the hands of Hitler's Brown Shirts resulted from disgust at the impotence of parliamentary government in the teeth of adversity. The issues were similar to those of Great Britain in that attempts to balance the budget, under conditions of declining revenues and increased demands for government aids, were prominent among the causes of strife. Strikes increased as employers tried to cut wages.

A deep sense of malaise culminated in the Stavisky scandal that surfaced late in 1933 and threatened to become another Dreyfus case or Panama scandal, joining earlier episodes of this sort that crystallized French national controversy around a single dramatic "affair." Serge Stavisky was a flamboyant and talented swindler, originally a small-time crook (he began by stealing gold from his dentist father) who worked his way up to an empire of high living and high finance based on manipulation of municipal lending institutions. Neither the first nor the last shady financial speculator to profit by political corruption, Stavisky was one of the most outlandish. He found friends in the Chamber of Deputies, and when, his crimes about to catch up with him, he was reported to have committed suicide under somewhat bizarre circumstances, there was suspicion that he had been done away with. Charges of extensive parliamentary corruption and a conspiracy to suppress the truth were wildly exaggerated. (In the 1970s an excellent movie was made about the Stavisky affair.)

The Stavisky affair on top of the dismal showing of Parliament set off an antigovernment campaign organized by the French Fascist leagues. On February 6, 1934, 200,000 demonstrators attempting to storm the Chamber of Deputies fought police in an all-night battle. A number of people were killed, and thousands of demonstrators and more than a thousand police were wounded. It was an affray to match any in the bloody annals of Paris uprisings, a ceremony performed at least once every generation (more violent if less prolonged than the student revolt of May 1968, of more recent memory). Most notable of the several Fascist leagues was the Croix de Feu, headed by Colonel de la Rocque, and veterans of the war were prominent in the riots. But some French intellectuals worked for fascism. Hitler had just conquered Germany, and the Austrian demagogue still had the mystique of sudden and dramatic success. Fascism seemed to be spreading over Europe. Three-quarters of a million Frenchmen joined fascist organizations.

That fascism did not prevail in France, which might have proved a key to its international success, was owing in good part to a rallying of the nation around its elder statesmen, a French habit in time of self-induced internal crisis. There was no one führer in France to play Hitler's part—the French Fascists predictably fought among themselves—nor was there any mass rallying to the fascist party as happened in Germany. The Daladier government, which had just replaced the Chautemps government, resigned on January 30, 1934, a year to the day after Hitler became the German chancellor; but a solution to the crisis was found in a government of national union, somewhat comparable to the British 1931 move. Elderly figures, including Marshal Pétain of World War I fame, rival party leaders Edouard Herriot (a Radical Socialist), and André Tardieu, the long-time spokesman of conservative nationalism, [2] joined under the premiership of former President Gaston Doumergue.

Tardieu had retired from politics in 1931 to pen some severe criticisms of the whole French parliamentary system, which he thought incapable of governing in the national interest. Had he lived long enough, he would have joined Charles de Gaulle. He was condemned to die watching his beloved France defeated and occupied by the Germans. He was no fascist. Tardieu's rallying to the Republic in 1934 typifies a French dedication to liberty in the last ditch, which saved France from fascism.

The national union government of Doumergue, however, proved little more enduring than any other, lasting less than a year. French politics continued its turbulent course. By 1935, the Left had succeeded in temporarily suppressing some of its violent divisions, chiefly that between Communists and Socialists, and a Popular Front government prevailed for a time, amid sit-in strikes and fears on the Right of

---

[2] Though, to be sure, the old curmudgeon had as little regard for most of the Right as he did for the Left: "Clemenceau used to wonder whether they are stupider than they are mean or meaner than they are stupid," Tardieu said of "the gentlemen on the right." "They are both very mean and very stupid." Tardieu was a type of conservative who despised party spirit.

socialism. Having bungled badly in helping Hitler destroy the German republic, only to find that he had used them rather than vice versa, the Communists, under orders as usual from Moscow, switched strategies and began to advocate a "popular front" of all antifascist groups. Previously they had stood aloof, condemning the democratic Socialists as "social fascists" and refusing any cooperation with such bourgeois parties. More or less uneasily working with the other left-wing parties, they backed a government headed by the distinguished socialist intellectual-politician Leon Blum, which sponsored a French "new deal" including prolabor legislation and the nationalization of a few industries, to the accompaniment of bitter criticism from business circles.

By providing a model of vigorous leadership addressed to problems of economic reform and economic recovery, the American presidency of Franklin Roosevelt helped ease the painful choice between fascism and communism or socialism as the desperate answer to desperate conditions. And from John Maynard Keynes as well as some Scandinavian economists came a general economic theory promising an attack on the roots of depression.

Unfortunately for the French New Deal, it had to deal with a deteriorating international situation and the threat of war; the Popular Front broke up at the time of the Munich Pact of 1938. Disunity over foreign policy was added to controversy about social policy. On the eve of World War II, France still presented a picture of internal disunity and weak government that did much to encourage Hitler on his path of aggression. It had surmounted the threat of fascism and achieved some economic recovery (slightly less than in England or Germany), probably from natural processes—the record suggests that governments did not make much difference to the process of recovery. A Conservative government in Britain, a New Deal progressive one in the United States, a Fascist one in Italy, and a Nazi regime in Germany achieved about the same results as the French anarchy, to judge by the charts of economic activity from 1929 to 1939. But the Third Republic's politics remained a scandal, and the depression further envenomed the ideological divisions that fueled these political quarrels.

Germany: The Rise of Nazism

A messenger in the German army during World War I who was considered a rather ludicrous figure although a good soldier, [3] the ob-

---

[3] "He was neither popular nor the reverse with his fellows; they just smiled at him and his vague rambling speeches on everything in the world and out of it. . . . He interested himself particularly in the important question of seeing

scure Austrian-born Adolf Hitler settled in Munich after the war to join and rise to the leadership of an equally obscure political group, the National Socialist German Workers party (NSDAP). It was only one of a number of such right-wing groups grumbling about the betrayal of the country by Jews, profiteers, politicians, or Communists and demanding a return to discipline and ancestral values. Hitler came into his own as a public speaker, transformed from a private nonentity to a hypnotic orator possessed by certain simple ideas that he blazed forth with obvious sincerity.

The man who, along with Stalin, was most to dominate, fascinate, and horrify the world in the troubled era of the two world wars seemed to have vanished from the pages of history after a brief and inglorious appearance in 1923. With some support from war hero General Ludendorff, Hitler had tried to seize the government of Bavaria in that year of wild confusion and the threatened breakup of the Reich. But he had failed ignominiously and had been imprisoned for a time. People laughed at this "beer-hall putsch," and Hitler seemed dead as a political figure. The coming of better times after 1924 caused his party to decline to almost nothing. A reputable history of Germany published in England in 1930 mentioned Hitler only in a footnote, remarking that he fell into obscurity after 1923. In the elections of 1928, the National Socialist (Nazi) party got 2.8 percent of the vote, winning 2.5 percent of the Reichtag seats.

In that election the Social Democrats won about 30 percent, the Communists received 10½ percent, and, on the Right, the respectable conservatism of the German Nationalist party got 14 percent, easily outdistancing Hitler's bunch of hardly reputable roughnecks. The Nazis were an unusual political phenomenon, which one might describe as a conservatism of the disinherited. Most of them were outcasts or failures, as Hitler himself was. He had failed to win admission to art school and had resorted to a dubious career as postcard painter before the war. (Along with the Tsar's execution of Alexander Ulyanov, the decision of the Vienna Academy of Fine Arts to turn down Adolf Hitler's application for admission in 1907–1908 must be accounted one of the major blunders of modern times!) In some desperation, theorists on the Left tried to construe the Nazis as puppets of the great capitalists, but

---

the officers' washing done or doing it himself. This secured for him the good graces of the colonel who removed him from the more constant dangers of the trenches and appointed him a runner between regimental headquarters and the front line." This was an account of Hitler as soldier published in the *New Statesman*, July 29, 1933. Hitler spent most of the war as a private because, his adjutant later said, "we could discover no leadership qualities in him"! But by most accounts Hitler was a brave soldier; at the war's end he was in hospital recovering from a blinding gas attack incurred at Ypres.

nothing could be farther from the truth. They were very much "little men," restless misfits usually from a lower middle-class or declassed background, with some intellectual pretensions. It is wrong to underestimate the extent to which Hitler, a brooding loner, read omnivorously if erratically in his dropout years between 1908 and 1914. He acquired a large store of general ideas from which he would build his *Weltanschauung*, his world view.

It is true that Hitler fascinated (and exploited) some rich ladies of the bored *bon ton*, whose "radical chic" led them to lionize this charismatic political curiosity. Though a few mavericks from the upper classes supported the movement early, the great bulk of respectable wealth came to his rescue only after he was obviously a winner. A Hermann Göring of aristocratic connections or a Fritz Thyssen from the capitalist class were exceptions. It was difficult for the people of money to find much attraction in a party whose speechmakers exhorted their listeners to "Storm the commercial banks! Set the money on fire! String up the white and black Jews!"

The finances of the NSDAP are shrouded in mystery because it kept few records, of which even fewer were preserved. At first it was very short of funds, but by 1923 it clearly began to dispose of larger sums. Most of this probably came from the enthusiastic support of many small contributors, but there may well have been money from wealthier people who, in the desperate conditions of 1923, were willing to bet on any anti-Communist. Nevertheless, all evidence indicates that Hitler made no deals with big business.

Konrad Heiden called the Nazis "the armed intellectuals"; Thomas Mann dubbed them "truants from school." Among the would-be intellectuals in the early Nazi party were the civil engineer and amateur economist, Gottfried Feder; the antisemitic Wagnerian folklorist and poet, Dietrich Eckhart; the aspiring founder of a pagan Nordic religion, Alfred Rosenberg; frustrated artist and writer Joseph Goebbels; small pharmacist Gregor Strasser; and industrial chemist Robert Ley. There were, of course, the ex-soldiers who could not adjust to peace, among whom the airplane pilot ace Hermann Göring was one. Founder in early 1919 of the German Workers party, from which the NSDAP evolved, Anton Drexler was a machinist angry about trade-union tyranny as much as "price-gouging" profiteers.

Skilled workmen and small shopkeepers gave the Nazi faithful a decided petty-bourgeois character. Hitler himself, down-and-outer as he had allowed himself to become at one point in his misspent youth, was the son of a moderately elevated bureaucrat. But what really tied the Nazis together was their susceptibility to seizure by ideas—simple yet strong ones, ideas of a conspiracy by the rich and the Jews to ruin the German people, of criminal Marxists who had betrayed the country into defeat, of corrupt politicians and swindling businessmen, of "interest slavery" and "speculation" as the enemies. Nazism has been called a revolt of the losers, and many have found the leading psychological traits of the Nazi activists to be a rebellion against the norms of their particular group: emotional nonconformism. For this reason the movement made a considerable appeal to disturbed youth.

In his study of 581 early Nazis (*Political Violence under the Swastika*), Peter Merkl found "a childhood of poverty and frustrated upward mobility in the city" to be prominent in the social background of the most militant Nazi activists. The portrait is of people with intelligence and energy who found their careers frustrated, perhaps by their own orneriness, perhaps by circumstances. A strong element in the Nazi ideology was a levelling, anti-aristocratic, quasi-democratic spirit among the *Volksgenossen*, the racial comrades, who were all held to be equal. Hitler himself, the PFC who rose to lord it over haughty Prussian generals, was a symbol of the little man climbing to the top. Many of his followers harbored a desire to climb with him, winning recognition and success by their participation in a revolt of the outsiders.

The Triumph of Nazism

Ruined petty bourgeoisie, souls damaged by the war and postwar insecurity, the "fatherless generation" resulting from the war, those whose confidence in all government had been shattered by the loss of savings in the inflation—such people were more numerous in Germany than in most societies. Still, one must explain why a party that amounted to little in 1928 suddenly, within four years, swelled to become the largest party in Germany, with a third of the electorate.

The obvious answer is the depression, which brought fresh distress, mass unemployment, the ruin of farmers and small businessmen. As in France, government fell into impotence when the economic crisis shattered the coalition on which a workable parliamentary majority depended. The coalition split on the familiar issue of the budget for unemployment insurance.

The German republic, of course, had shallower roots by far than did the British and French systems. Only in Britain, it was frequently said, did Parliament really command any respect. France's scandalously mercurial Third Republic aroused popular scorn and contempt; but France had a long tradition of individual liberty and regard for popular democracy in a general sense, if not for political parties. "Liberty, equality, fraternity" were slogans for which generations of Frenchmen since 1789 had shed their blood; *la patrie* meant the whole people, not an authoritarian monarchy or state. First of European peoples to do away with monarchy and aristocracy, first to establish universal manhood suffrage (though one of the last to enfranchise women), the French had succumbed to a "democratic despotism" under two Napoleons, but those experiences had inoculated them against a repetition.

Born of defeat and nurtured in civil strife, the Weimar Republic had a precarious claim on the loyalties of too many Germans. One answer to the question of why so bizarre a concoction as National Socialism triumphed in Germany is simply that there were no viable alternatives. Winston Churchill thought it had been a mistake to destroy the monarchy; but that had been done, and indeed by the German people themselves, who clearly had had enough of the kaiser. One option that was contemplated in the crisis of parliamentary government that began in 1930 was a military dictatorship, but the Versailles army was not up to such a task and shrank from it. President Hindenburg, a father figure to the Germans, who was reelected in 1932 by a resounding majority with Hitler running against him, was too old to do more than help in some plan of political reconstruction. Communism, redolent of Russian tyranny as well as war defeatism, chipped away somewhat at Social Democratic strength among the working class but commanded the support of only a small percentage of Germans, its percentage of the vote rising from about 10 percent to 15 percent between 1928 and 1932. There was no outstanding German Communist leader; the party had fallen into the hands of obedient clerks carrying out orders from Moscow. The Right was split between monarchists and supporters of the republic, the Left between Communists and Social Democrats, the center between Catholics and liberals. The death of Gustav Stresemann in 1929 deprived the parliamentary republic of its one outstanding leader.

The depression broke up the coalition between Socialists and middle-class parties and turned the wrath of the people on all the parties associated with the government, thus turning protest votes toward the extremists. A two-party system enables the voters to vent their rage on the incumbents by voting for the opposition party, as American voters did in 1932. More than six million American voters changed their minds between 1928 and 1932, not because they knew much about Democratic presidential candidate Franklin D. Roosevelt but because they wished to register a resounding protest against the Republican administration that had failed to cope with the economic disaster. In so doing they did not need to vote for a radical party. When all the moderate parties, as a coalition, are the "ins," popular frustration protest can express itself only by voting for the extremes.

The Mueller government of 1928–1930 broke up on economic differences between Social Democrats and the bourgeois parties over the familiar issues of the government budget and wages. The elections of September 1930 registered a slight Communist rise, to 13 percent, and a large Nazi gain, all the way up to 18 percent. No combination could find a majority in the Reichstag. The KPD (Communists), NSDAP (Nazis) and, much of the time, the DNP (Nationalists) voted against every government, and the potential partners in a governing coalition (mainly SDP, Center, People's, Democratic), together possessed only a little over a half of the seats and could not agree. Under these conditions parliamentary government had become impossible.

The Constitution through its article 48 provided for a way out; though hardly intended to apply to this situation, it did allow government by decree if a public emergency existed. President Hindenburg put the 1930 budget into effect by decree after the Reichstag rejected it, and thereafter for nearly two years a government headed by Centrist Heinrich Brüning governed by such decrees, as the depression worsened. Brüning pursued policies of the orthodox sort, keeping government expenditures down, seeking to reduce salaries, hoping by deflation to regain export markets, and through low interest rates to stimulate reinvestment. Such were the policies followed by Herbert Hoover in the United States, by the MacDonald government in Britain, and by most other governments, adopting the prescriptions of traditional economic theory. As we have said, this program might have worked in the long run, but in the long run unemployed men and their families can die of starvation, and this bitter economic medicine was scarcely digestible.

Government by presidential decree could not go on forever. Brüning resigned in May 1932 when Hindenburg refused to authorize a decree that would have broken up bankrupt East Prussian estates into holdings for small farmers. The president was himself a "Junker," a member of this East Prussian landholding aristocracy. Franz von Papen then formed a cabinet that included General Kurt von Schleicher as minister of defense. In July 1932, the path of a general election was tried again, with even more disastrous results. (See Table 7–1.) This time over 37 percent of the Germans voted Nazi, the maximum that the party reached under free conditions. It fell to 33 percent in another election held in November. The Communist vote again rose slightly, reaching nearly 17 percent in November; with the SPD losing heavily and the People's party nearly wiped out, prospects for a workable coalition now totally vanished.

What was the answer? Historians have severely criticized the maneuvers that preceded Hitler's coming to power early in 1933, but

TABLE 7–1   Reichstag Election Results, 1928–1933

Party	May 20, 1928	Sept. 14, 1930	July 31, 1932	Nov. 6, 1932	March 5, 1933
	% of eligible voters voting				
	75.6%	82.0%	84.0%	80.6%	88.7%
Communist (KPD)	10.6%	13.1%	14.6%	16.8%	12.3%
Social Democratic (SPD)	29.8	24.5	21.6	20.4	18.3
German Democratic (DDP)	4.9	3.8	1.0	0.9	0.9
German People's (DVP)	8.7	4.5	1.2	1.8	1.1
Center (Catholic)	12.1	11.8	12.5	11.7	11.2
German National (DNP)	14.2	7.0	5.9	8.8	8.0
National Socialist (NSDAP)	2.6	18.3	37.4	33.1	43.9
Misc. others	17.1	17.0	5.8	6.5	4.3

unless the army established a military regime, which it was unwilling to do, there seemed no answer other than an attempt to draw Hitler's party into the government. People allowed themselves to hope that the experience of holding office would tame the Nazis, or that as part of a coalition, they would have to compromise.

General Schleicher also hoped to detach the more responsible wing of the Nazis, if such a thing existed, from Hitler. Gregor Strasser was his hope, but this plan did not work, and the party stayed loyal to Hitler. For their pains Schleicher and Strasser were to be among Hitler's victims on the "night of the long knives," June 30, 1934.

Hitler was not about to settle for half a loaf after the electoral successes of 1932. The brown-shirted Nazi storm troopers stepped up their lawless violence, as street wars between Nazis and Communists became a nightly occurrence. When the November elections again failed to break the political deadlock, the Nazis' slight loss being compensated by a Communist gain, Papen resigned. Hitler was offered the chancellorship under limiting conditions, which he rejected. Hindenburg, no friend of the Austrian guttersnipe, refused his demand for emergency powers. Schleicher formed a new cabinet but could not gain sufficient support in the Reichstag. His resignation paved the way for Hitler's assumption of the chancellorship on January 30, 1933, bringing Göring and Wilhelm Frick into a cabinet but also accepting other ministers who were not Nazis.

Papen thought he had caught Hitler and would now tame him. But the Nazi leader was able to work his way into complete control. He soon forced fresh elections, which took place under intimidation by the now uncontrolled storm troops. It was during this election campaign, on February 27, that the Reichstag fire took place; branding it a Communist plot, Hitler persuaded President Hindenburg to issue emergency decrees suspending basic liberties of free speech and press. Many thought the Nazis themselves had set the fire, and evidence strongly suggests that they did manipulate a demented Dutchman by the name of Van der Lubbe. When the elections gave the Nazis 44 percent of the vote, they found allies among the Nationalists and Centrists who agreed to outlaw the Communist party and pass an Enabling Act, which granted dictatorial powers to the government for four years. Only ninety-four votes, all by Social Democrats, were cast against the Enabling Act in the end. Germany had surrendered to Hitler.

The extent to which his was a legal accession to power may be debated; Nazi violence and intimidation, along with abuse of the emergency decree power, provided a decidedly illegal atmosphere. Nevertheless, all was done by technically legal actions, and it is evident that Hitler had an overwhelming mandate from the German people. It is often pointed out that at most 44 percent of the German people, and probably fewer, approved of the Austrian fanatic; but this was far and away the largest percentage to vote for a party in all the years of the republic. No other party in 1932 came within 13 percent of this total, and in the March 1933 election the nearest competitor was 25 percent behind. Given the circumstances, a party that could win 35 to 40 percent of the vote was a marvel and could hardly be excluded from power according to the normal rules of democracy. Moreover Hitler's party got out voters that normally stayed at home; the 1932 and 1933 elections attracted a significantly larger number of voters than usual (more than 80 percent of those eligible), and most of these seem to have voted National Socialist. It is difficult to deny that Hitler was backed by a mandate from the German people.

In view of the extraordinary nature of the National Socialist party, this support obviously calls for explanation. There was grave need to combat the terrible depression, of course, which hit Germany harder than any other major country. But Hitler's party offered no economic program worthy of the name. *Der Führer* had an aversion to economics, and it was not even clear whether his party stood for socialism or capitalism, since it fulminated against both Marxism and "international capitalism." The Nazis alleged that the Jews dominated both and were part of a secret conspiracy to conquer the world, apparently after thoroughly confusing it. Claiming to stand for a kind of socialism, the Nazis in rejecting the Strasser brothers seemed to turn away from any specific socialist doctrine. They exuded an anticapitalist spirit, often in association with archetypes of rural rootedness and folk culture. "Among his phobias," Joachim Fest writes of Hitler, "were American technology, the birth rate of the Slavs, big cities, 'industrialization as unrestricted as it is harmful,' the 'economization of the nation,' corporations, the 'morass of metropolitan amusement culture,' and modern art. . . ." Like more recently alienated people who would not want to be associated with fascism, Hitler disliked modern urban industrial society and harbored images of a pastoral utopia where nature reigned and people lived in premodern simplicity. Walther Barré, Hitler's agricultural expert, developed an ideology that pictured the German farmer as the quintessence both of racial Nordicism and the German national soul; Nazi propaganda consistently glorified the *Bauer.*

It is sometimes said that the Nazis won because they were superb propagandists, putting on a good show with their parades, uniforms, and songs and knowing how to appeal to the mass mind. But this does not explain why before 1930 most of Germany laughed at Hitler, with his rustic accent, and paid little attention to his antics. Did the propaganda suddenly become more effective? This seems unlikely.

One comes back to the point that Germans were not really voting *for* the Nazis so much as they were expressing their dislike of the reigning establishment in the only way possible. Of course, they could have voted for the Communists, who certainly expected to profit by the breakdown of capitalism and democracy. It is wrong, incidentally, to accuse Hitler of waving the flag of war and imperialism to distract the minds of the workers at this time (a frequent Marxist interpretation), for he said little or nothing about this during his climb to power. These themes were not popular in Germany, a country most of whose people are (contrary to legend) neither very nationalistic nor very militaristic. Hitler tried to mount a campaign in 1929 against the Young Plan, which further revised reparations payments downward while still retaining them. This was an extension of the Briand-Stresemann-Wall Street compromise by which the Germans were expected to "fulfill" their payments for war damages while having these considerably reduced and getting American loans. But this campaign fizzled, and the Social Democrats in 1928 won electoral victory on a "food, not armaments" platform. Thereafter the Nazis played down talk of rearmament and defiance of treaties. In opposing "the fetters of Versailles" in principle, they joined nearly all the other Germans; this was not a distinctive Nazi slogan.

We are left with the Hitler charisma, which undoubtedly existed. Many who came to laugh stayed to succumb to the hypnotic spell that emanated from this erstwhile clown. On paper his ideas seem a weird amalgamation of enthusiasms, but he could cast a spell when he addressed an audience. He had worked hard to make National Socialism mean Adolf Hitler's genius. He had demanded, as the price of his leadership, absolute and unquestioning obedience from all party members. He spoke of the party as an analogue to the Catholic church, with himself as the infallible pope. He refused to manufacture a party program because, he solemnly assured Germans, they should trust his genius to improvise the right policies at the right time. This strange image of a superman hero-leader was built up with the aid of parades and banners, searchlights playing on the swastika symbol, howling crowds shreiking "Heil!" to the uniformed figure with his right hand rigid in a raised salute. The spectacle reached deeply into the unconscious minds of simple people and touched chords of unreason.

Familiarity with subsequent phenomena at "rock" music concerts and festivals or the hysterical crowds which even in the 1920s wept at the funeral of movie star Rudolf Valentino takes us closer to the Hitler effect than does anything previously known in European politics. This was "pop" politics. Not without reason the fascist leaders of this era, including the Louisiana populist "kingfish" Huey Long, claimed that they understood the mentality of the "little people" better than any of their opponents.

This demagoguery was not entirely a triumph of unlettered instinct. Hitler borrowed from many movements and ideologies, past and present. He learned from Lenin the value of the disciplined elite party and outdid the Russian in fanaticizing such a gathering of the militant faithful. He borrowed from Mussolini the idea of a totalitarian society, completely molded into one shape, but he went far beyond Mussolini in seeking to carry this out. He read about mob psychology in Gustave Le Bon's study of *The Crowd*, a French book that Sigmund Freud also admired. Hitler in fact read omnivorously in his earlier years, soaking up ideas in a highly selective way to fit into his patchwork philosophy.

Like Spengler and Freud he saw the world in slow decay, falling apart from an excess of civilization. He had read Nietzsche and was to make him the Third Reich's official philosopher, though sadly misunderstanding that great tragic seer. Many of the pre-1914 ideas find somewhat crude echoes in Hitler's thought. But he rejected modernism in art as decadence, one of the few points on which he agreed with the Marxists. The infinite pains he took with the staging of the great Nazi spectacles reflected Hitler the would-be artist and architect; he choreographed politics like a Hollywood director.

Hitler's pathological hatred of the Jews was born in Vienna, where he went in 1908 at the age of nineteen, after a childhood spent chiefly in the smallish city of Linz. Hitler's violent racialism was more characteristic of Austrian Germans than those in Germany. It was germinated in the pre-1914 multinational Hapsburg empire, filled with Slavs and other minorities, where the Germans themselves were a rather small minority compared with the non-Germanic peoples. (Baltic Germans were also prominent in the Nazi party.) There, in the thought of such Pan-Germans as Hitler's youthful idol, Georg Ritter von Schoenerer, who used the swastika symbol, the myth of the *Herrenvolk* ("master race" is the usual translation) threatened by inferior blood strains was born. There, stories circulated from the east of a great Jewish conspiracy, such as that contained in the fraudulent *Protocols of the Elders of Zion.*

It is a curious fact that in Germany itself, where the biggest antisemite of all times was to win power and attempt to exterminate the Jewish race, virtually no Jewish "problem" existed. A Jewish population of just over a half million, less than 1 percent of the total population, had become assimilated into German culture; there were no ghettoes as there were in east Europe and perhaps even less social resentment of Jews than in France or England. It is especially curious that the Nazi vote in Germany was strongest in those regions where there were the fewest Jews, East Prussia, Pomerania, Schleswig-Holstein, Hannover, Lower Saxony, that is, the agricultural North. Dispersed all over Germany, the Jews were an insignificant minority everywhere, and they were growing less and less significant all the time. Hitler's antisemitism was entirely mythological, and it is therefore oddly logical that it should have been most effective where no real Jews existed.

One part of the myth was the allegation that Jewish capitalists owned everything and ruled Weimar Germany; in fact, Jewish influence was confined to a few cases, such as large department stores, some of the (better) big newspapers, and entertainment. The great industrial corporations were no more Jewish-dominated than were the professions, literature, or, despite significant Jewish contributions, intellectual life. Those Jews who did rise to intellectual prominence did not exhibit any peculiarly Jewish qualities. Zionism was weak. Though Hitler outrageously alleged the opposite, Einstein's physics was no more peculiarly Jewish than was Stefan Zweig's widely popular fiction. It is probably true that both Marxism and Freudianism attracted a higher than average Jewish component; but both rejected Judaic traditions—it is singular that these allegedly Jewish ideologies repudiated Jewish religion, Jewish culture, and Jewish nationalism. They were in fact a way station for Jews engaged in losing their Jewishness.

In brief, Hitler's antisemitism was a triumph of fantasy over reason; yet as a scapegoat symbol the International Jew was effective, for the symbol brought together all those otherwise illogically linked things that Hitler hated and that millions joined him in hating. Exploitative capitalism, financial speculation, political corruption, disloyalty to and betrayal of the German state, Marxist subversion, the decay of traditional society, vulgar mass culture—all these could be blamed on a mythical Jew. This Jew ruined small businessmen, corrupted German girls, organized revolutions, and spoiled German culture. He overcharged the worker, made bad movies, created an ugly commercialism, spied for Russia, and sold out Germany in diplomatic negotiations with Wall Street capitalists and conniving Frenchmen. He was indeed a versatile villain.

Only a people morbidly ill could believe such legends, it will be said; but indeed the German mind was shell-shocked from war, defeat, inflation, unemployment, and depression.

Depression Literature and Thought

The terrible economic and political crisis of the early thirties hit European writers and intellectuals just when they were ready for a change anyway. Withdrawal to the ivory tower of aristocratic estheticism is a pleasing gesture; one casts scornful glances at the disgraceful scenes below and meditates on the collapse of civilization. But it soon becomes tiresome, and one yearns to rejoin the human race. Ever since the earlier nineteenth century, the Western literati had vascillated between revolution and revulsion. The revolution of 1848, a "revolution of the intellectuals," failed so badly that the next generation found solace in science and "art for art's sake." Ecstatic participation in World War I was followed by the profound disillusionment of the 1920s. The mood changed again about 1930.

Events in the real world became exciting, a fact that helps explain the shift. Apart from the rise of Nazism and Stalin's five-year plan in the Soviet Union, there were dramas closer to home for British and French writers. The depression-bred growth of trade unions among the less skilled led to new excitement on the labor front. The CIO story in the United States was paralleled in France, where union membership grew from three-fourths of a million to four million between 1934 and 1937, climaxed by great "sit-in" strikes in 1937 when workers occupied factories. The London streets were filled with marches of the unemployed and with occasional physical conflict between Fascists and Communists. With the American New Deal and the French Popular Front, politics became more exciting. The grand climax was the Spanish Civil War, which the intellectuals of the 1930s made into their Great Crusade. Such events provided themes for a literature of "social realism," the sort being recommended by the Soviets.

The general rush of the intellectuals toward the Left was a typically extreme swing of the pendulum, leading many of them into or at least close to the Communist party. The whole amazing sequence of events in the 1930s suggested a final apocalyptic struggle between good and evil. Nazism and fascism were ranged against communism, with little left in between. Hitler's phantasmagoria of embattled anti-communism faced Stalin's cohorts in a last struggle for the world. People must choose.

The Spanish Civil War was wrongly forced into such a framework. Prior to outside intervention, neither fascism nor communism had much strength in Spain. But the grim strife that began in Spain in 1936 with the rebellion against the republic (discussed in the next chapter) grew into a symbol of the war between Left and Right, socialism and fascism.

> *And private stars fade in the blood-red dawn*
> *Where two worlds strive,*

wrote C. Day Lewis, one of the young British poets who turned toward communism. Artists must descend into the arena, "drop those priggish ways forever," and join the struggle. Suddenly, refined esthetes and intellectual snobs were out; proletarian poets on the barricades were in. It is true that not many of the poets managed to make this conversion in actuality, but many tried, and at least in spirit they were all for commitment and participation.

When we find Virginia Woolf writing for the *Daily Worker* and Harriet Weaver ("Dear Miss Weaver"), the eccentric rich woman who had backed James Joyce in the twenties, now selling copies of the Communist paper on street corners, we realize what a change there was. Romain Rolland, the hero of the antiwar movement, a resolute nonconformist who had almost alone held out against the tide in 1914, criticized the Communists in the twenties for repressing individual consciences; but now he became one of the least critical of "fellow travellers." He joined a band that included German novelist Lion Feuchtwanger, French writer Henri Barbusse, and the "Red Dean" of Canterbury, English churchman Hewlett Johnson, in glorifying Stalin and defending every action of the Soviet Union. Barbusse's 1935 biography of Stalin, an example of hagiography scarcely equalled since the Middle Ages, was hardly unique in this respect.[3] And these writers were major figures, not hacks or time-servers. Among the conversions,

---

[3] A representative passage: "If Stalin has faith in the masses, this is reciprocated. The new Russia worships Stalin, but it is a worship created by confidence, which has risen wholly from the bottom. The man, whose silhouette on the gigantic posters appears superimposed on those of Karl Marx and of Lenin, is the man who looks after everything and everybody, who has done what has been done and who will do what is to be done. He has saved Russia in the past, and he will save it in the future." *Stalin, A New World Seen Through One Man* (tr., New York: Macmillan, 1935), p. 281.

none was more startling or more famous than that of Sidney and Beatrice Webb, venerable intellectual leaders of British socialism, whose Fabian Society pedigree had heretofore guaranteed their respect for democratic, gradualist methods. But the Webbs lost their faith in gradualism during the Great Depression and, after visiting the USSR in the early thirties, published a massive treatise on *Soviet Civilization* that hailed the birth of a new humanity in Stalin's Russia. Hewlett Johnson's *Soviet Sixth of the World*, a far less critical paean of praise, sold millions of copies.

These Western intellectuals had totally lost faith in their own civilization, which they now saw on its deathbed—a dying culture that, being only one phase of human evolution, would give way in the era of revolutionary turmoil to a higher one. Such clichés of popular Marxism they had heretofore rejected as much too simplistic; but now they thought they saw the new society coming to historic realization. "I have seen the future and it works," American writer Lincoln Steffens declared upon his return from a visit to the USSR. Through a haze of preconceptions they idealized what they imagined to be the brave new world of Communist Russia. Their guided tours of the USSR were carefully managed by the Communists.

At any rate, they were now certain about the collapse of their own society. A spate of books announced the news that capitalism was now at last, as Marx had foreseen, strangling on its own insoluble problems of social relations. Only an end to private ownership of the means of production and the socialization of industry could realize the productive potential of modern technology, leading to plenty for all rather than poverty and unemployment amid idle plants and unused resources.

Well might Karl Radek (soon to be a victim of Stalin) boast in 1934 that, "In the heart of bourgeois England, in Oxford, where the sons of the bourgeoisie receive their final polish, we observe the crystallization of a group which sees salvation only with the proletariat." The Left Book Club flourished; so did *Left News*, the *Left Review*, and others. Left was right. And Left meant, by and large, the most militant and confident of the radical groups, the Communists, radiant with the message that salvation was coming through Soviet Russia's great experiment in remaking humanity.

The new Marxists' crystal ball was occasionally clouded. A widely read 1932 book, John Strachey's *The Coming Struggle for Power*, foresaw a war between Great Britain and the United States, in which the desperate capitalists fought over receding markets. It predicted a Communist victory in Germany. Strachey also thought that John Maynard Keynes was about to become a Fascist. Keynes' *General Theory Of Employment, Interest, and Money*, published in 1936, actually became the most important answer to Marxism published in this decade, offering a middle way between the apparently sterile formulae of the traditional economics, which counseled in effect doing nothing, and the doomsdayism of the extreme socialists.

Against the orthodox policy of balancing the government budget to lower costs, Keynes proposed that the government borrow and spend to counterbalance what he saw as the chief problem: a tendency to underinvest because interest rates failed to draw savings into investment. A temporarily unbalanced government budget, "deficit spending," should stimulate the private sector in crucial ways. Keynesianism departed from traditional dislike of government intervention without advocating total government control of the economy. Using its fiscal powers as a balance wheel, the government should expand or cut spending, lower or raise interest rates as the economic situation dictated. The economy would not "go of itself," as economic science had basically assumed ever since Adam Smith; but neither should one scrap private capitalism and the free market for an entirely different and probably unworkable system of state ownership. The Keynesian model resembled that of some Swedish economists and was tried out in Sweden as well as, partially, in the American New Deal. It visualized a managed or directed capitalistic economy, something of a halfway house between pure capitalism and pure socialism. It was to become the leading plan of theoretical macroeconomics for the next generation outside the Communist world.

As Keynesianism mollified the harsh alternative of starvation or communism, the attractions of Russian-style communism weakened in the later 1930s. Ironically, the Western intellectuals discovered Soviet communism just as it was hardening into a grim tyranny. They sought to make an idol of a cruel dictator. The dynamism of the first Soviet five-year plan, which many in the West contrasted with the passivity of their own governments, accompanied a war to collectivize the peasants that cost millions of lives. (See the next chapter for a discussion of Soviet affairs in the 1930s.) There was no unemployment in Russia, but there was virtual slavery.

The purge trials of the mid-1930s, when Stalin destroyed all the old Bolsheviks and hundreds of thousands more, confronted Western intellectuals of the Left with a painful dilemma. Just then at the peak of their enthusiasm for Soviet Russia, with Popular Front Communist-Socialist collaboration growing, they often tried to explain away the evidence of faked confessions extracted by torture, of the arrest and execution or imprisonment of huge numbers of obviously innocent people without trial or with a travesty of one. The British scholar-socialist, Harold Laski, thought that Stalin's prosecutor, Andrei

Vishinsky, would make "an ideal Minister of Justice" for Great Britain; Lion Feuchtwanger's doubts "dissolved like salt in water" when he attended a Moscow trial and listened to Lenin's friend, Karl Radek, confess to all manner of crimes against the Soviet state. But the doubts of others grew. The immensity of Stalin's crimes could be more than guessed at in the 1930s: the American philosopher John Dewey headed a committee of investigation that exposed most of them, for which he was reviled as a "Trotskyist" by leftist pundits.

The Spanish Civil War itself brought doubts about the Communists to some of those who fought for or sympathized with the Spanish Republic, for the Communists under Russian domination used their power to terrorize other socialists and non-Stalinist Communists in the Republican coalition. Chief victim of Communist repression among the leftist parties in Spain was the POUM (Partido Obrero de Unificacion Marxista, i.e., Workers' Party of Marxist Unification), which the Communists branded "Trotskyite," but which was in fact simply anti-Stalinist. The Nazi-Soviet Pact of August 1939 was the final lesson in Soviet duplicity for most of the left-leaning writers of the 1930s. Whatever its sins or excesses, the Soviet Union, they thought, at least fought fascism at a time when the Western democracies were abjectly yielding to Hitler's demands. When Stalin, for whatever reason, made a deal with Hitler, who called him "a hell of a fellow," it was the signal for a mass exodus of those Western intellectuals remaining in the party; they later filled volumes with repentant explanations of "the god that failed."

This love-hate relationship with the USSR and its terrible but effective leader did not prevent a swing to the Left and to social realism. The literature of the thirties was perhaps not as brilliant as that of the previous decade. Attempts at proletarian realism by basically bourgeois writers were marred by insincerity; ideology rather than reality dictated character and plot and, at its worst, produced caricature. Writers who completely committed themselves to communism almost invariably found the experience creatively frustrating, because they had to write a formula. The Stalinist line required rejection of such modernists as Kafka, Joyce, Eliot, and Proust; rejection of nonrealistic art; and, along with this stylistic conservatism, the necessity for literature to serve politics, that is, the Communist cause. It was very good to project a picture of capitalism in decay, and here Western intellectual and Soviet commissar could see eye to eye. But the only approved plots were those in which the bourgeois intellectual sank happily at last into the arms of the party or some other version of redemption by Stalinism. To simplify human experience in this way was impossible for modern European minds, heirs to a sophisticated and subtle tradition of thought and expression. With Graham Greene they looked for paradox and irony, on "the dangerous edge of things."

In flight from "a hideous and decomposing world" in which they felt "an anguished sense of alienation," writers might join the party seeking a faith to live by and write about, but once in they were far from happy and seldom stayed long. Those who did stay, like Bertolt Brecht, had to learn to suppress all individuality and obey the Party blindly—difficult indeed for artists and intellectuals. Brecht's adherence to communism did not save his plays from being banned in Moscow as "formalist" and "decadent."

Nevertheless the decade produced an exciting literature. Some centered on depression-bred themes: George Orwell's *Road to Wigan Pier* and his other novels of down-and-outers and John Steinbeck's *Grapes of Wrath* about American dustbowl migrants, for example. Others focused on the great political issues: another American, Ernest Hemingway, wrote now about the Spanish Civil War in *For Whom the Bell Tolls*, and André Malraux also devoted one of his greatest works, *Man's Hope*, to the same struggle. Vast Balzacian chronicles of fictionalized social history appeared. Jules Romains produced no fewer than twenty-seven volumes in his *Les hommes de bonne volonté* cycle, carrying his "men of good will" through the twentieth century's memorable events from then to now. Other French novelists who specialized in the *roman fleuve* were Georges Duhamel and Roger Martin du Gard. Communist luminary Louis Aragon, once a surrealist, authored a political trilogy after his conversion. Such works generally focused on the congenial theme of social decay, chronicling the collapse of a civilization through meticulous analysis of individual psychology. Its decadents were more convincing than its socialist or proletarian heroes. George Orwell finally came to see that in fact all the socialists were bourgeois intellectuals: "The first thing that must strike any outside observer is that Socialism in its developed form is a theory entirely confined to the middle class."

Even as they attempted social realism, French writers could not escape the subjectivist influences of those subtle psychologists, Marcel Proust and André Gide. Gide himself flirted briefly with Stalin but was a notable defector at the time of the Moscow trials. Romains was a socialist, not a communist. Orwell, after being very close to the party in the early thirties, finally became its most persistent critic. Another was Arthur Koestler, a versatile German writer whose novel, *Darkness at Noon*, explored the nightmare psychology of the purge trials and whose autobiographical writings, *Arrow in the Blue* and *The Invisible Writing*, give a matchless picture of life in the party.

A few conformed to the spirit of the 1930s in committing themselves to a cause but defied that spirit by going right rather than left. The neo-Christian revival started by Karl Barth and Jacques Maritain continued in the thirties. T. S. Eliot, the famous poetic critic and the most thrilling of modernists, now announced himself a High Anglican, a royalist, and a classicist. As the editor of *Criterion*, he rallied religious humanists around a defense of traditional Western values against both fascism and communism. He saw both of them as rival religions, debased ones, that filled the vacuum in the Western soul left by its apostasy from the ancestral faith. A similar point may be found in Arnold J. Toynbee's inquiry into the decline of the West, *A Study of History* (1934–1939). Evelyn Waugh, C. S. Lewis, and others made their way back to traditional religion, "mere Christianity." French novelist François Mauriac continued his long literary exploration of the roots of human nature's profound corruption. After having written in 1926 about *Nôtre Inquietude*—modern humanity's restless distress of spirit—Henri Daniel-Rops worked on a long multivolumed history of Christianity that was as popular as any work of historical scholarship these years produced, not only in France but elsewhere.

This very distinguished body of traditionalists sheds doubt on the generalization about the 1930s belonging entirely to the Marxists. But even traditionalists, in their apparent conservatism, reflected a radical alienation. In some ways their position embodied a more basic critique of all modern civilization than the Marxists'. Marxists accepted industrialism, science, democracy, and most other characteristics of modern Europe, claiming only to be able to manage them better than the bourgeoisie. But to actually believe in "mere Christianity"—what position could be more at odds with all the dominant forces of the twentieth century?

> The world is trying the experiment of attempting to form a civilized but non-Christian mentality. The experiment will fail. . . . (T. S. Eliot, 1930)

A third group of writers of the thirties might be identified: those whose bitter despair found no solace either in Marxism or in Christianity or Judaism. One of these was Louis-Ferdinand Celine, author of *Le Voyage au bout de la nuit*, a book one critic described as "a terrible satire on the human race." Celine's voyage to the end of the night led him personally to become a Nazi collaborator with the German conquerors of his native France in World War II. In the same year that Celine's scatological masterpiece was published, 1932, Aldous Huxley turned to savage satire in his *Brave New World*. One of the first of the "dystopias," or reverse utopias, this novel showed what the triumph of technology and science and socialism and "progress" could bring. An earlier but then less well-known example of this genre was Yevgeny Zamyatin's *We*, by an early critic of Soviet communism. *Animal Farm* and *1984* were George Orwell's best-known sequels.

A final case is Jean-Paul Sartre's first novel published in 1938 and titled simply *Nausea*. *Nausea* was the beginning of a quest that led the most famous of the existentialists to a courage beyond despair, but this first novel affirmed only the terrible absurdity of existence.

Even Sartre was always a man of the left, dominated by his hatred for the class from which he sprang. The bourgeoisie had always lacked culture; now they could not even produce material goods. Their "system" of universal selfishness stood convicted not only on moral but on practical grounds. Capitalism was in deep trouble; fascism, the Marxists claimed, was its death agony; only socialism was sailing along toward a bright future under Stalin's benevolent guidance. So things seemed to an alienated intelligentsia in the era of the Great Depression. "In communism I see hope," said the British novelist E. M. Forster in 1936. "It does many things which I think evil, but I know that it intends good." Such faith—in a "working class" they did not understand and a dictatorship they did not even know—was typical of the mid-thirties intellectual. He turned to it as solace from human suffering in his own land and the spectre of Hitlerism abroad, as the last remaining hope.

Although they were aware of some of the harsh features of Stalin's rule, which they accepted as "the necessary price of forging a new humanity"—no omelets without some broken eggs—most people in the West who were pro-Soviet had no notion of the magnitude of the suffering and killing, nor of Stalin's sadistic megalomania. Nor did most people in the USSR. Stalin's effective public relations team presented him as the kindly leader, stern only with traitors and wreckers, leading the USSR steadily upward toward a more humane and bountiful society. With such illusions did some Westerners steady themselves in the doleful depression years.

The Totalitarian Regimes

8

National Socialism in Power

People often complain that politicians do not keep their promises; in Hitler's case, the trouble was that he did. He had promised a complete change in the system, a "revolution comparable to the Russian Revolution," to "get rid of a world of opinions and install another in its place." The frightening thing about Hitler was that he really meant everything he had said in his campaign. In the end, this meant war against the Slavs for German living space, and it meant the slaughter of the Jews.

Initially, however, Hitler moved cautiously in foreign affairs. He did create a sensation by taking Germany out of the Geneva Disarmament Conference, where for many years Germany had pleaded for arms equality without much success. Now, in 1932, Germany won the concession of a statement favoring equality of armaments in principle. But faced with French stalling in implementing this principle, Hitler suddenly withdrew from the conference, and also from the League of Nations, in October 1933. It was a bold defiance of the Versailles system, which in retrospect may be seen as the first crucial step on the road to World War II. There was talk of sanctions and war against

Germany but, just as he did five years later, Hitler felt sure the Allies were bluffing; their peoples were in no mood for military adventures. An immense propaganda campaign preceded a plebiscite in Germany on November 12, 1933, one day after the fifteenth anniversary of the armistice, to approve this action. A huge majority endorsed the withdrawal from the League. It was becoming increasingly dangerous to oppose Hitler, but most Germans undoubtedly did like this nose-thumbing at the arrogant victors who had humiliated Germany for so long.

But Hitler followed this withdrawal with a surprising nonaggression pact with Poland in 1934 and presented to the world an apparent picture of moderation and restraint. "Germans and Poles will have to learn to accept the fact of each other's existence," he said. In other speeches he insisted that Germany asked only equal rights and desired peace. Privately, Hitler reserved his future actions; the immediate need was to restore Germany's strength.

Once in power, Hitler was able to expand and intensify his pageantry. The organization of parades, spectacles, and rituals dazzled Germany and astonished the whole world. It was a good show. "Germany now enjoyed a splendor of ceremonies such as it had never previously known," the French ambassador, François-Poncet, wrote in semiadmiration. Wagnerian opera came to politics in a massive way. These quasi-religious rites were tuned to the theme not only of Hitler as the supreme leader but of a new national unity. There was a surge of community feeling reminiscent of August 1914.

This honeymoon phase of the Nazi revolution brought almost everyone temporarily over to Hitler's side. With what later seemed to have been surprisingly little resistance, the intellectuals, the universities, the churches followed the masses in joining the all-German team that, according to der Führer, was to bring a renaissance of the German spirit as well as recovery from the Great Depression. Something of this lyrical optimism is caught in Leni Riefenstahl's extraordinary movie, Triumph of the Will, made in 1934.

There were a few notable exceptions. The ugly side of Nazism manifested itself quickly also. A book-burning symbolically purged the country of writings not amenable to the "racial community" as National Socialism visualized it. Jewish businesses were boycotted, and government pressure forced newspapers to conform or be squeezed out of business. A distinguished body of intellectual leaders, not all of them Jewish, led by Albert Einstein and Thomas Mann, chose to migrate rather than face harassment. But the loss of hundreds of eminent writers, scholars, scientists, and artists was countered by the support given to the Nazi regime by a coterie of eminent figures, ranging from musicians Richard Strauss and Wilhelm Fürtwangler to philosophers Martin Heidegger and Max Scheler.

Triumph of the will: so Hitler conceived the goal. A single national will, organized by the "leadership principle," should direct the nation, which should be a "racial community," a *Volksgemeinschaft*. Such a focusing of national energy would make anything possible, he thought. The revolution that would bring this about had to keep the masses keyed up by constant propaganda, it had to destroy pitilessly anything that stood in the way of unanimity, and it had to get rid of all remnants of the selfish individualism of the past. This included such matters as political parties and freedom to criticize the government. The price paid for a *Volksgemeinschaft* was persecution and intolerance. Hitler set about the task of *Gleichschaltend* ("coordinating") German institutions, that is, bringing them into line with the Nazi spirit. The task was never completed, and in fact as an administrator Hitler turned out to be a good artist. But much was done in a rather unsystematic way to Nazify education, the press, the arts, the law, labor, and every other facet of the national life.

Under Hitler Germany achieved a good deal of economic recovery, which of course it might well have achieved anyway. Rather like American President Franklin D. Roosevelt, whose New Deal came into being about the same time as Hitler's New Reich and tried similarly, though by less illiberal means, to restore national confidence, Hitler put into effect large public works projects, of which the "autobahn" superhighway network was the best known. He ignored the bankers' orthodoxy by loosening credit and spending government money; he organized a Labor Service, which may be compared with the New Deal's Civilian Conservation Corps, to put idle youth to work. Rearmament contributed to a dramatic reduction in unemployment.

Hitler went much beyond Roosevelt in merging all trade unions into a single state-sponsored Labor Front. This action wiped out strikes, to the joy of employers, but it compensated somewhat by providing vacations, travel, and various cultural activities for workers. The Volkswagen, the "people's automobile," was an eventual product of this "Strength through Joy" workers' recreation program, which was lavishly subsidized by the government. This was a variation of "welfare capitalism." Real wages fell, but workers were thankful they at least had jobs.

Hitler also employed the banking wizard Hjalmar Schacht to manage foreign trade successfully. Schacht's methods included exchange controls, which allowed currency rates to vary from country to country, and bilateral trading agreements, which were successful in winning markets in southeastern Europe. Agricultural prices were artificially raised, as they were in other countries. Until 1935 at least, Nazi economic policies by the standards of the day were far from unenlightened.

This achievement earned Hitler rather widespread respect. In 1935 Winston Churchill praised Hitler's "courage and vital strength" and as late as 1938 repeated that, "If we had been defeated in war, I would hope we might find a Hitler to lead us back to our rightful position among the nations." Regaining international prestige at the risk of war did not come until after 1937; until then, by and large, the German dictator concentrated on internal problems. His success came at a heavy cost. Constitutional safeguards of all sorts were swept away. The totalitarian state allowed no limitations on its authority. The seventeen German states, or "lands," lost their powers, at least on paper, the Reich becoming a unitary state, no longer a federal one. In principle individuals had no rights and liberties per se, since the rights of the national community took precedence (and Hitler decided them). There was not supposed to be any separation of powers; an independent judiciary was subverted by the existence of a secret police system outside it—the dreaded Gestapo (*Geheime Staatspolizei*)—as well as by Hitler's appointments to the judiciary. *Ein Reich, Ein Volk, Ein Führer*—as Stalin spoke for the Communist party, so Hitler spoke for the German people.

The most ominous event of the Third Reich's early years was the massacre that took place on the night of June 30, 1934. In large part, this was Hitler's settlement with powerful rivals within his own party. A violent and lawless movement, the NSDAP had attracted violent and lawless men, especially those *condottiere* from the Free Corps who had joined the party. One of them, Captain Ernst Röhm, was commander of the SA, the storm troopers. This brawling wing of the Nazis had grown to a very large number. Röhm's disreputable life style symbolizes this group's hostility to any established order. Hitler was right in thinking they had become a danger to his rule.

For his part Röhm thought Hitler had sold out to the establishment. Mussolini faced the same problem with the "old fighters" of the party after his accession to power; and one may perhaps draw a comparison with Stalin's position vis-a-vis Trotsky. The revolution devours its own children; and Röhm was a threat to Hitler. The SA began to talk of the need for a "second revolution," viewing Hitler as a Kerensky or a Mirabeau: one who had failed to carry the revolution to its completion. The SA crowd was a community of tough old soldiers with strong *esprit* if little subtlety of thought. They harbored a grudge against the "Prussian generals" of the regular army, with whom Röhm accused Hitler of now associating. The SA leader wanted to absorb the army into his organization.

Röhm burst into open and outspoken criticism of Hitler, thus violating the leadership principle: "Only one man can be the Leader." The SA captain evidently lacked the clarity of thought or the resolution to do more than bluster, and thus, by being "willing to wound and yet afraid to strike," he sealed his doom. Other high Nazis, including Goebbels and Göring, envied him. And a rival source of armed power arose in the form of the SS (*Schutzstaffel*), an elite guard originally a subdivision of the SA, headed by Heinrich Himmler, who was soon to control the Gestapo also.

With President Hindenburg now on his death bed, Hitler felt released from what restraints the old chief had placed on him. On the night of June 30 and the following day, a series of raids arrested and summarily executed Röhm and other SA leaders, throwing in for good measure a number of Hitler's other foes of past and present: Gregor Strasser, General Schleicher and an associate, Catholic oppositionists Erich Klausener and Father Stempfle, conservative intellectual Edgar Jung. Jung was a close friend of von Papen, who had just made an anti-Nazi speech. Papen, long close to Hindenburg, just barely escaped with his life and was shipped off to Turkey.

This lawless slaughter, which took hundreds of lives, could not be kept secret. Hitler waited two weeks before attempting to justify it in a rambling speech to the Reichstag, pleading the need to save the nation from those who had "lost sympathy with any ordered human society." If this was so, the menace had come from his own organization, and Germany seemed to be at the mercy of rival gangsters, one of whom had gotten the draw on the others. The terroristic basis of the Nazi state stood unmasked. But President Hindenburg thanked Hitler for "saving the German people from a grave peril," and the army sighed in relief. Their turn would come. With the death of Hindenburg, Hitler assumed the presidency as well as the chancellorship, getting this move ratified by a plebiscite on August 19, 1934, in which 84.6 percent voted "Ja."

Despite the lawlessness of the "night of the long knives," Hitler's first years in power were more constructive than his later ones, and indeed the slaughter of the Röhm gang could be viewed as an attempt to control the more violent and fanatical wing of the Nazis. A change began about 1937. In that year, relatively moderate influences within the government left. Hjalmar Schacht resigned in late 1937, his economic functions passing to Hermann Göring. Early in 1938 Joachim Ribbentrop, a Nazi, replaced traditional diplomatist Neurath at the foreign office. It was in this year that Hitler evidently made his decision for war, which we shall discuss in the next chapter. He moved to secure control over the army, a campaign climaxed in 1938 by the Fritsch

Brown Shirts

affair, in which the leading general of the German Army was deposed after being accused (falsely) of homosexuality and general immorality. The proud German *Wehrmacht*, allowing this to happen, here yielded its honor and its independence. Also getting rid of Minister of Defense Werner von Blomberg, Hitler personally assumed command of the armed forces.

The campaign to enlarge Germany's frontiers by aggressive war, securing "living space" in the East at the expense of the Slavic "inferior men," dominated Hitler's mind. He talked of building a Reich so strong it would last a thousand years. Always the architect, he dreamed of a rebuilt Berlin able to hold 10 million people—the capital of the world!

As Hitler moved down the road to war, through the Austrian and Czechoslovakian crises of 1938, persecution of the Jews intensified. Pogroms, or violent attacks on Jews and destruction of their property by SA thugs, grew more numerous in 1938. They reached a dreadful climax on the night of November 9–10, the excuse being the assassination in Paris of a German diplomatic official by a young man whose parents had been mistreated in Germany. Egged on now by Goebbels, who declared that all German Jews could be held accountable for the crime, Nazi storm troopers burned hundreds of synagogues, plundered Jewish shops, arrested and mistreated Jews.

The clumsiness of this method of "solving the Jewish problem," involving damage to the economy and adverse publicity abroad, caused a reaction against Goebbels, who, though protected by Hitler, was generally despised in high Nazi circles. Göring, Himmler, and Heydrich thought there were tidier ways of making Germany "free of Jews." Wild rioting of this sort against Jews was not repeated, but the infinitely more sinister plan of a "final solution" by systematically exterminating all the Jews began to take shape.

The *Gleichgestaltung* or hammering of Germany into a National Socialist society did not proceed very tidily. While the outer world received through Nazi propaganda an image of a totalitarian society, in which everybody was forced into one mold by a master plan, the truth was later discovered that in many ways Hitler failed to accomplish his goal of restoring a pure "folk community." He did next to nothing for that *Mittelstand*, or petty bourgeois, sector that had been the main source of his strength, or for the farmers. The urbanization of Germany continued; big business, if willing to bow to Nazi desires, prospered at the expense of small. Agriculture diminished in importance. And the National Socialist government, far from being perfectly organized, was a chaos of private administrative empires. Göring, Himmler, Goebbels, the SA, the SS, the local party officials, and others formed a mixture of factions struggling for power, held together only by the brooding

Hitler's unquestioned command over them all. This was a structure for which feudalism seems the best model, rather than the totalitarian state.

Hitler was capable of imposing his will at any given moment through his charisma and forcefulness. But he was better at grandiose visions than day-to-day administration. His turn toward imperialism and war reflected the failures and contradictions of his regime. The economic problem, he came to feel, was solvable only by conquering new domains for Germany to exploit. So was the Jewish problem, for the great bulk of world Jewry dwelt outside the Reich, chiefly in eastern Europe. Above all, the Nazi movement had to be dynamic, a trait it shared with Stalin's Communist party. The restless forces Hitler controlled had to be given a goal capable of channeling their energies. War alone provided such a focus.

It should be added that in many ways Hitler's movement did accomplish a kind of democratic revolution in German society. The "little man," provided he was not contaminated by Jewish blood (and the number of Jews in Germany was even by the most generous reckoning hardly more than 1 percent of the population) could use the Nazi

The Party Days in Nuremberg were occasions for Hitler's extravagant pageantry. This picture is of the 1936 rally. *Wide World Photos.*

party as a ladder to climb up the social scale. Nazi doctrine taught the equality of all the *Volksgenossen* ("racial comrades"); in brief, one German was as good as another. The spectacle of the erstwhile gutter-snipe and army private Hitler giving orders to aristocratic Prussian generals or to haughty barons of business delighted the hearts of all who had once kowtowed to these mighty people. Never again would the latter dominate a class-conscious society as they had done in the past. Social mobility increased during the Nazi years.

Many new men made their way to positions of power, usually in the swelling bureaucracy, or perhaps in a state-owned enterprise like the Herman Göring Steel Works. (Born of a need to keep the old steel barons under control, this enterprise bore the name of the famed corpulent Nazi lover of the good life, who also stole a great art collection for himself.) Many others who aspired to similar success had to be given opportunities. Hitler had unleashed forces of envy that threatened the stability of German society. It was a kind of socialism of greed. In the end, only by ever new conquests of territory could National Socialism satisfy its built-in appetites for power. It was an old story, for the classic student of power politics, Machiavelli, had long ago pointed out that despots must look to war to keep their power.

Rival Totalitarians

Stalin's revolution aimed at a vast and sweeping transformation of "backward" Russia under very different conditions from those in Germany. Soviet communism and German nazism, the latter paired with Italian fascism, were often designated "totalitarian" regimes, but the differences should be noted. Nazism was a postdemocratic and post-liberal phenomenon that grew in a well-developed industrial society. Hitler appealed to a lower middle-class mentality scarcely present in Russia. In contrast, communism in Russia sought the forcible urbanization and industrialization of a huge undeveloped land. Nazism in Germany tried to preside over a *retreat* from the industrialized technological society, returning to a simpler society and traditional virtues that had been lost. Russia had never really known either democracy or liberalism. It was still overwhelmingly rural and largely illiterate. Stalin's mission was to whip and drive his people up a mountain that Hitler's people had already climbed and, finding the top not all that enticing, sought to descend. If the two totalitarianisms met, they came from opposite directions.

The regimes of Hitler and Stalin agreed in their rejection of the liberal-democratic principles. They were totalitarian in putting the group above the individual, regarding individuals as having no rights against the community. They were similar in creating a quasi-religious ideology, which was declared to be the sole Truth and deviation from which invited harsh punishment or banishment. Hitler's "One Reich, one People, one Leader" matches Stalin's creed of one party in possession of the scientific truths of Marxism, to be interpreted by a small number of party leaders. Both regimes were, of course, prepared to use extreme force in suppressing heresy and enforcing conformity. Concentration camps and prison camps were their chief social inventions, Auschwitz and the Gulag Archipelago their symbols.

The group that held priority over the individual and that possessed and enforced the monolithic faith, was class for the Communists, race for the Nazis. The mythology that each built around these concepts was structurally similar. To Communists, the theme of all history is class struggle or class war. Suppressed and exploited throughout history, the masses finally rise up (led, of course, by their Marxist mandarins) and make the last great revolution, which is followed by a perfect, classless society. The archetype closely resembled the Christian vision of the apocalypse, when the Great Beast (or Whore) of Babylon will be slain in a bloody battle, and Christ's kingdom will then be extended preparatory to the end of the world.

The Nazis, for their part, propagated the myth of a struggle of races as the master motif of all history. Only a few races are creative, and only one, the Aryan, is supremely so (so ran the commonest version of the racial myth). The villain, which corresponds to Marxist ruling classes or capitalists, is the polluter of racial purity, especially the Jew, "poisoner of all peoples." In the end, after a terrible conflict, the master race uncovers and destroys its foes and takes over the world.

Bizarre in their credulous simplicity, these myths were modern religions filling the place of a dying Christianity, reflecting no doubt the need most people feel for a faith to live by. For intellectuals, those skeptical types who criticize everything and argue endlessly, both Fascists and Communists entertained much contempt. "Bourgeois intellectuals" had to purge themselves of their individualism by many an exercise in self-abasement before they were allowed to enter the service of the Kremlin's church. Goebbels said he reached for his revolver when he heard that word *intellectual;* they belonged with Jews (being almost the same, in fact) as corrupters of a sound racial spirit.

The fanaticism that goes with absolute faith and absolute power marked both movements. A dreadful slaughter of the class enemy or the racial enemy was necessary; so was constant vigilance lest the enemy return—necessitating censorship, secret police, concentration camps. National Socialist "eugenics," supposed to breed a pure race, can be compared with Soviet Russia's periodic purges of the party to weed out the wreckers and spies. Incessant propaganda drummed home the simple messages: the leader, or the party, is omniscient; the people must stand unanimously together under this leadership. No effort was made to report the news objectively or impartially. Education was mobilized to produce unthinkingly loyal devotees of the National Socialist Reich or the Soviet Communist party.

Centered in Russia and Germany, the rival totalitarian systems and ideologies of communism and nazism/fascism both staked out international claims and attracted followers in other countries. Fascism, which triumphed in Italy and Germany, existed in every other European country. Belgian Rexists, Rumanian Iron Guards, Austrian Home Guards (*Heimwehr*), French members of the Fascist leagues whose violent activity in 1934 we have already mentioned, Spanish Falangists—these were some of the other fascisms. Since "integral nationalism" was a basic theoretical ingredient in fascism, it was hard for them to form an international movement; and the contradiction became apparent when Hitler destroyed the native Austrian Fascists after he took over that country in 1938. Nevertheless the movement and the ideology were European-wide, indeed worldwide.

As for communism, it claimed in theory to be internationalist. The Comintern, the organization of the Communist International, although headquartered in Moscow was technically separate from the Soviet government. Communist parties existed in every country, although they were illegal in some. With the outlawing of the German Communists by Hitler, the French Communist party became the most important one in Europe outside of Russia, rising in the 1930s to considerable importance; but like all the others, it suffered from the stigma of being Russia's tool. Communist internationalism was thus handicapped, too, by Russia's de facto domination of it, forcing other Communist parties to sacrifice themselves to the interests of the Soviet Union.

Stalin's Terrible Revolution

In the 1930s, Western intellectuals typically found Stalin's regime to be more defensible than Hitler's, not only because Russia had the excuse of her "backwardness" (they often pointed out in apology for Stalinism that Russia had never known human rights and the rule of law as these existed in the West), but even more because they thought the goal at which Stalin aimed was a worthy one. Not just another industrialized country was being created, but a new kind of person, freed from all the old corruptions. This aspiration would affect not just the Russians but all the workers of the world. Soviet communism appropriated the symbols of the old European socialist faith, itself pretty obviously a secularized version of the Christian Gospels. The toilers of the world were on the march toward the promised land, these symbols proclaimed.

In the atmosphere of the Great Depression when capitalism's failure seemed self-evident, the Soviet experiment, glimpsed from afar, looked like a beacon of hope. And if Russian communism was the only possible alternative to German nazism, which seemed to be the case, then people of good will could not hesitate. That Josef Stalin, son of a Georgian cobbler, expellee from divinity school, professional revolutionary, and now heir of the October Revolution, was no country gentleman or refined intellectual could be granted. But he was headed in the right direction.

Contemporary observers were not unaware of the cost of the Great Socialist Offensive, which began in 1928. An American engineer, John Scott, who had worked at the industrial center of Magnitorsk that the Soviet planners tried to create beyond the Urals, wrote that "Men froze, hungered and suffered, but the construction work went on with a disregard for the individual and a mass heroism seldom paralleled in history." The Czech observer, Maurice Hindus, published in English a widely read account of The Great Offensive, describing Stalin's terrible war on the peasants with much awareness of its dimensions.

Stalin later told Winston Churchill that this was a worse war than World War II, this drive to collectivize the peasants. It raged between 1929 and 1932 as the leading campaign of the first Five Year Plan. By 1928 Stalin had completely triumphed over his rivals for leadership within the Communist Party of the Soviet Union (CPSU). Unquestioned master of the powerful party apparatus, Stalin decided to use it in a great offensive to build socialism in Russia alone.

Did this mean putting world revolution on the shelf for the time being? Good relations with the capitalist countries would be necessary should their aid be needed for technologically backward Russia to achieve the goal of "overtaking and leaving them behind." Yet, because capitalism seemed to fall into grave crisis just as the Five Year Plan was launched, the Communist parties abroad were ordered not to play down their subversive effort but to step it up, spurning cooperation with other parties and denouncing all forms of moderate socialism or liberal idealism as "social fascism." Until 1933, German Communists helped the Nazis destroy the republic by adopting a policy of disruption. Hitler's crew, they were sure, would soon collapse and prepare the way for a Communist takeover. Stalin was playing for all the marbles. Not *either* world revolution or socialism in one country, as Lenin and Trotsky had imagined; *both* were possible. Success in Russia would encourage communism abroad and discourage the capitalists. The downfall of capitalism would then force its technology into the Soviet world. Such was the grandiloquent dream.

Collectivization of the peasants was the primary task. That individual peasant ownership of small plots of land was less efficient than large units, which could be run like factories, was probably a less compelling argument to the Communist leadership than was a noneconomic one: peasant Russia was the bastion of private property. After all, at least 75 percent of Russia was living in what Karl Marx had once genially called "rural idiocy." In the minds of the urban-oriented Marxists of the Communist party, rural Russia was the kingdom of darkness and superstition, holding Russia back from an advance into the modern industrial age like a huge ball and chain. A powerful offensive had to break this chain, or the goal of achieving socialism would be hopeless.

What was in fact a war against virtually the whole peasantry was disguised as a class war between poor and rich peasants. The enemy was declared to be the "kulak," the rich capitalistic peasant. According to Communist propaganda, the mass of the peasantry was willing and eager to join the collective farms, the *kolkhozes*, where they would jointly own and jointly work the land.[1] In fact, there was little class feeling in the countryside, where poorer and richer peasants generally stood together against the threat of losing their property. So the war against the kulaks was really a war against a majority of the peasants, waged by party enthusiasts who were backed by the Secret Police (GPU).

"Accession to the collective farms must be voluntary," it was solemnly proclaimed; but in actuality zealous party officials, prodded from the top, forced peasants into the collective farms by confiscation and, if there was resistance, by arrest and imprisonment. Peasants fought back as best they could with terror; arson; sometimes with sabotage, killing farm animals rather than surrendering them to collectivization; and sometimes even with suicide. This terrible human tragedy in the end cost several million lives and dealt Russian agriculture, particularly livestock production, blows from which it took many years to recover.

Yet at first collectivization seemed to succeed. Figures showed rising numbers of collective farms together with an increase in grain production. In 1930 the drive was stepped up. The goal was nothing

---

[1] State-owned farms, the *sovkhozes*, also existed but were much less numerous than the *kolkhozes* in which, theoretically, peasants cooperatively and jointly owned the land. In practice there was not much difference.

less than total extinction of peasant proprietorship, immediately. Being a kulak or a member of a kulak's family was like being a Jew in Nazi Germany: they were "vampires and bloodsuckers" who must be exterminated, purged from society. And Stalin decided who a kulak was as Goebbels said he decided who was Jewish in Germany. The collectivization campaign swelled to a peak of hysterical extravagance, driven by the party's massive zeal.

On March 2, 1930, Stalin signalled a retreat in a *Pravda* article titled "Dizzy with Success." It had come to his attention that some peasants were being *forced* to join the collectives! Comrades, let us not be too rash, the general secretary cautioned. The truth is that his own rashness and ruthlessness had brought Russia to the verge of national disaster. Peasants were burning their crops and killing their farm animals in desperate protest against forced collectivization, which was Stalin's own policy. A new famine threatened.

With his brazen political cunning, Stalin, as he did on so many other occasions, put the blame on the "wreckers," who were trying to discredit collectivization by their excesses. Reasonable Stalinist policies had been unwisely distorted. A new set of scapegoats was found. Meanwhile the campaign momentarily subsided. Peasants were allowed to keep small plots of their own, on which they might raise vegetables and dairy products for the market in their spare time after their work days on the kolkhoz—a concession that has remained ever since in the USSR, fluctuating in amount but never entirely abandoned. The goal of collectivization was by no means given up, however. Slightly subtler means were used—crushing taxation levied on the individual proprietor, tax concessions to the collective farms. By 1937 almost all of agriculture was organized in collective farms. A virtual famine in 1932–1933, marked by a drop in meat consumption of almost two-thirds since 1929, had not deterred the regime from this dreadful progress.

The goal was to convert farms into factories, to wipe out the gulf between city and country, destroy the peasants' petty bourgeois mentality, and create a homogeneous totalitarian society. This conversion accompanied rapid industrialization. Surplus population driven from the country by consolidating small farms into large collective ones was forced into new industrial areas. In order to control this sudden influx of millions into cities where housing was deplorable, the government required them to carry identity papers and to move only with permission—a kind of compulsory labor system: compulsion exercised against the proletariat as well as the peasants and the capitalists.

Russia did industrialize under Stalin. The cost was appalling, leading to charges that even the horrors of capitalism could not have been as bad. It was not, however, an egalitarian society. Communism, the ultimate goal, lay far in the future. The formula for the interim stage of preparation for communism was "from each according to his abilities, to each according to his work." There were wide differences in wages. A managerial class received special privileges and higher salaries than did common workers. Managers were given the power to discipline the workers, who were no longer protected by trade unions—for the unions, a relic of capitalism, were said to be no longer necessary in the "workers' state." Soviet communism resembled German National Socialism in serving as the vehicle for ambitious new men who rose to power over the bodies of the old ruling class. And those workers who performed heroic feats of exceeding their quotas and working overtime—without pay—were rewarded with citations and decorations!

Stalin's principle was to build heavy industry's basic plant first and postpone consumer industries. Thus the Russian citizen was forced to postpone the fruits of industrialization. Great steel works and hydroelectric plants were built. The totally planned economy, in which decisions were made at the center for the entire country, could successfully divert resources toward particular targets. The Five Year Plans (first, 1928–1932; second, 1933–1937) set targets and tried to surpass them, sometimes successfully. The cost, critics alleged, was not only human freedom but gross inefficiency in the consumer and distribution sectors of the economy. But Soviet propaganda, enthusiastically disseminated by the party faithful all over the world and believed by sometimes naive "fellow travellers," declared that Stalin's way was the only rational way for a backward and exploited people to raise itself to the level of the capitalist economies. Surpassing the capitalists and ushering in a new era of plenty for the ordinary citizen would come later.

Students generally agree that the Soviet "command economy," which was able to ignore the sovereignty of the consumer, sacrifice consumption to investment, and discipline and exploit labor, forced a more rapid rate of industrialization than had ever been achieved before. (After 1945, Japan's growth and perhaps western Europe's went even faster for a period.) The USSR also made considerable progress in reducing illiteracy. The appalling cost of this success was not fully realized at the time. Economic near-miracles were performed, or so it seemed. Whole new industrial cities arose in the Ural region—not so surprising, in view of the fact that such urban centers are always an accompaniment of industrial revolutions, but presented by Soviet propaganda as a miracle of human energy. Such stir and bustle in the heretofore stagnant Russian society did contrast with unemployment and demoralization in the depression-ridden capitalist world.

The crash program of collectivization and industrialization demanded the sacrifice not only of personal freedom but of many of the revolution's original social goals and ideals. Free love, the emancipation of women, easy divorce and abortion, liquidation of the bourgeois family—such modernisms were eagerly proclaimed just after 1917 by Communist intelligentsia, but faded under Stalin, who reinstalled the values of motherhood and the family, as well as patriotism and other "bourgeois" standards.

The Great Terror

Research indicates that at a conservative estimate some twenty million people perished as victims of Stalin's police state between 1930 and 1950. First there were about seven million casualties of collectivization. Later, during the time of the great party purge of 1936–1938, between seven and nine million people were arrested, of whom roughly a million were executed and the rest sent to labor camps in distant places where life expectancy was short (about a third of the prisoners died in their first year).[2] In all the bloody annals of man's inhumanity to man, it is hard to match this record.

The Bolsheviks had always practiced ruthless terror against their class enemies, but until the 1930s they had rarely terrorized members of their own party. Even the Mensheviks, erstwhile comrades in the Marxist Social Democratic party, were allowed to leave Russia in the 1920s if they wished. In 1931, Mensheviks who had chosen to stay in the USSR were placed on trial, scapegoats for the failure of forced collectivization. Both native and foreign engineers who were so unfortunate as to have worked on projects that did not progress speedily enough found themselves accused of sabotage. Shooting some of them to encourage the others was a favorite Stalin incentive system. But all this was a mere warm-up for what astonished the world in 1936 and 1937, the spectacle of well-known Old Bolsheviks, comrades of Lenin and Stalin in the Revolution, placed in the dock where they confessed to enormous crimes of treason, sabotage, spying.

In mid-1934 the OGPU was reorganized to become the NKVD. This change in the Secret Police accompanied creation of a central Purge Commission under Nikolai Yezhov, who succeeded Genrik Yagoda as NKVD chief in 1936. Yagoda was tried along with others in 1938 and

---

[2] For a sifting of the evidence see Appendix A of Robert Conquest's *The Great Terror*. Part of the evidence is the census of 1959, which showed, for the age group 55–59 (people in their late twenties or thirties during the 1930s) a 66.6 to 33.4 percent surplus of females over males.

executed, an example of Stalin's habit of getting rid of his own tools. Several thousand Yagoda men in the NKVD were killed, the terrorists themselves being terrorized. Yagoda was associated with the Bukharin-Rykov "opposition," destroyed in the last great trial of the 1930s. The names of Yagoda, Yeshov, and of the head of the Central Committee's "special sector," Stalin's own private secretary A. N. Poskrebyshev, were to become the most sinister ones in Russia.

This renovation of the security machinery signalled Stalin's drive to purge the party, which he did with both savagery and thoroughness during the next few years, until hardly more than a handful of the Old Bolsheviks remained alive. And before being led away to the firing squad they were made to abase themselves, confessing to crimes it is clear they never committed and abjectly apologizing for nonexistent errors and sins. In these public "trials," opened to foreign observers and much discussed throughout the world, it was evident that the guilt of the accused had already been settled; the purpose of the trials was to inflict public humiliation on them or to expose the depth of their degradation. As Stalin's loyal henchman Vyacheslav Molotov once put it inadvertently, "the guilty will be brought to trial."

Meanwhile, hundreds of thousands of lesser party members, involved with these higher-ups—with Zinoviev and Kamenev, the old "opposition," or with Bukharin, Radek, Rykov, or high military men now accused of spying for the Germans—suffered the fate of their friends and employers, in a widening circle of victims that seemed to expand endlessly. Each arrested person, subject to NKVD torture, implicated others in order to end his ordeal.

Why did Stalin do this? Students of this strange and powerful man, no less fascinating than his counterpart, Adolf Hitler, find it difficult to agree. The diminutive Georgian was paranoid, vindictive, stubborn, and cruel. He fully shared the Bolshevik view of morality (Lenin had held it) that "whatever helps the Revolution (the party) is right," that individuals do not matter, that the drive toward utopia justifies any immediate sacrifice. Horrified by the collectivization campaign, Stalin's second wife, Nadezhda, committed suicide in 1932, and this loss (he seems genuinely to have cared for both his wives, the first of whom died in 1910 not long after their marriage) left Stalin more alone and stony hearted.

More objectively, Nazism was abroad in these years, and German generals had in the past cooperated with their Russian counterparts. The exiled Trotsky, whom Stalin's agents finally succeeded in murdering in Mexico only in 1940, had a large world following who argued that Stalin was a false leader. Countless Russians had reason to hate Stalin, who could feel safe only by terrorizing the opposition. It is doubtful that Stalin himself knew the extent of the terror, which, as we noted, got out of hand and spread of its own momentum like a wildfire.

Victims of their own illusions, Stalin and his staff projected grandiose goals in the Five Year Plans and then, when these goals were not met, assumed that the reason was sabotage. When all this has been said, and there is some truth in each of the explanations, one must feel that on the bottom line of the terror is written Lord Acton's edict, "absolute power corrupts absolutely." Stalin had obtained absolute command of the immensly powerful party machinery and could use it as he wished. Not a single voice was raised in the Central Committee or its Politburo to protest any of this ghastly business. Not until three years after Stalin's death, twenty years later, did people dare to speak out.

The Popular Front

The purge was intended to strike terror into the hearts of all enemies of the Soviet state and thus strengthen that state. But from the evidence of the millions arrested, one had to assume either that the USSR was filled with treason from one end to the other, or else that a madman was at its helm. In particular, the vast army purge, wiping out the entire leadership of the Red Army including its most able and vigorous figures, such as Marshal Tukhachevsky, threatened incalculable damage to Soviet military capability. Thus the result of the purge, which subsided somewhat only in late 1938, was to increase distrust between the USSR and the outer, capitalist world. Paradoxically, though, even at this same time Stalin was engaged in trying to woo the outside world. Though a rationale of the purge was the need to stand guard against assumed attempts by the agents of capitalism constantly to spy on, to wreck, to subvert the workers' state, yet Stalin had now decided, with another part of his mind, for detente with France and Great Britain, against the greater menace of Germany.

From 1935 on, the strategy of the popular front dominated Russian policy abroad; it was associated with the attempt to make alliances with the democracies against fascism. By 1936 Stalin was granting interviews with foreign journalists and writers (Roy Howard and H. G. Wells) in which he assured them that Russia did not seek to export Communist revolution. "Socialism in one country" required peaceful relations with the outer world, trade with capitalist nations, and normalization of diplomatic relations with their governments.

Communist party policy changed abruptly in 1935, doing the

first of two about-faces in the 1930s that embarrassed those party members who had qualms about being intellectually inconsistent. Hitler's triumph caused a basic rethinking in Moscow. Underestimating and misunderstanding the Nazi movement, Communists had actually helped Hitler gain power. National Socialism's evident solidity and German rearmament forced the Kremlin to adopt an entirely different line, with stress now on what was known as the Popular Front strategy of seeking allies against fascism among other parties of the Left. Having spent much of their time since 1927 calling the socialists "social fascists" and hired agents of reaction, the Communists now suddenly began to hail them as comrades. The main object was to influence foreign policy, especially in France, a potential ally against Germany. To strengthen French military power, secure an alliance with the Soviet Union, and prepare to defend against Hitler's expected attack became the goal of the French Communist party.

The Socialists (SFIO) were the larger of the two left-wing parties. In 1934 it was the second largest French political party, with 131 of the 618 deputies. But the previously quite small Communist party increased its strength after 1931, and the two parties were bitter rivals for the leftist vote. The SFIO was itself split, with a left wing close to communism and a right wing closer to the bourgeois liberals. Bad feeling between the two parties stemmed from the war and the secession of minority Socialists to join the Third International just after the war. French Socialists resented Moscow's persecution of Menshevik Social Democrats, their comrades in the Second International. Communists sneered at the Socialists as "traitors to the working class." Socialists replied that the French Communists were kept by Moscow gold and unworthy of trust, and insults were freely exchanged until the reconciliation of 1935–1939.

Communists who had yesterday jeered at "social chauvinism" now became ardent patriots, as well as proponents of class collaboration. This strategy was followed until September 1939, when another startling *volte face* accompanied the Nazi-Soviet pact. Stalin had by then decided, for all too evident reasons, that the Popular Front had failed to swing French foreign policy to resist Germany. But between 1935 and 1938, until the Munich Pact, Communists in all countries outside the USSR were willing and eager to work with other parties to form coalitions. The other parties were understandably wary of this sudden change of heart, coming as it did from those who had long assailed them with bitter denunciations. That the new line was manufactured in Moscow was too apparent. On the other hand, the logic of a united front against fascism, both within the country and without, did appeal to Western socialists and liberals.

The Popular Front posed severe problems for the Communists. Opinion on the Left in France, Britain, and the United States was generally hostile to rearmament and to risks of war. Domestic issues took precedence over foreign ones; the action was on the picket line or in agitation for measures to lessen unemployment. Yet Moscow wanted rearmament and a strong anti-German foreign policy. Strikes weakened national defense. The Communists faced a losing battle in their attempts to convert the Left to war in the atmosphere of the Great Depression. In France they supported Leon Blum's government in alliance with Socialists and Radical Socialists, then supported even the Radical Socialist Edouard Daladier. But when Daladier's government initialed the Munich settlement of October 1938, appeasing Hitler at the price of Czechoslovakia, the Communists tried to organize strikes in protest against this policy. They met with little success. Communists did not really believe in the reformist policies of the Popular Front government, which could only prolong capitalism's life, but they had to pretend to do so.

If the Popular Front in France was a failure from the Communist point of view, it was equally a disappointment in Spain, the other main arena where it was tried out. With the outbreak of the Civil War in 1936, Spain became a main focus of European politics and provided one of the decade's most dramatic contests between communism and fascism/nazism.

The Spanish Civil War

Established in 1931, the Spanish Republic stumbled over the same obstacle that troubled other parliamentary democracies: the rivalry of numerous disagreeing parties, who were unable to form the basis for a stable government. One of Spain's leading philosophers and historians categorized her as "invertebrate," that is, lacking unifying elements. When the dictator Primo de Rivera fell in 1930, followed soon by the monarchy itself,[3] a wave of republican sentiment swept over Spain, and a peaceful revolution seemed to have the support of almost everybody. This proved to be an illusion. The republic's history was to be short and tragic.

The revolution aroused hopes of widely varying sorts, which the new regime was too weak to fulfill, and bitter hostilities reappeared. The Cortes elected in June 1931 contained a majority of Socialists and

---

[3] Alfonso XIII did not abdicate but withdrew, expressing the hope that eventually he would regain the love of his people. The Cortes soon voted him guilty of high treason.

leftist liberals; with the Right temporarily discredited and the Anarchists on the extreme Left abstaining from politics, there appeared to be a comfortable parliamentary basis for a moderate leftist coalition. But the more extreme Socialists, headed by Francisco Largo Caballero, demanded proletarian revolution—seizure of power and property by soviets of workers and peasants. They were also violently anticlerical, in a country where many associated the church with aristocracy and monarchy. The first republican government alienated the army by drastically reducing the number of officers and embarked upon the confiscation of estates to give land to the rural poor. Divided between moderates and revolutionaries, the republic thus earned the bitter hatred of three powerful elements on the Right: army, church, and aristocracy.

A split between the president, Alcala Zamora, and the prime minister, Manual Azaña, provoked the fall of Azaña and new elections in 1933. The Left now suffered a reverse; the antisocialist Catholic Popular Action party emerged as the strongest party. Meanwhile the son of a former dictator, José Antonio Primo de Rivera, created a Spanish Fascist movement, the Falange, to join the more traditional, monarchist Right. In 1934 the Asturian miners rebelled against the government and were put down with the aid of Moorish troops at the cost of several thousand casualties. The socialists cried that the revolution was being betrayed; the army conspired; the Catalans of the northeast insisted on autonomy. A general strike was called. The events of October 1934, were a rehearsal for the bloody civil war that began two years later. Governments became feebler and shorter in duration. Invertebrate Spain reverted to its disunity.

Elections held in early 1936 brought a lurch back to the Left. Proclaiming a crusade against fascism, the new government now found itself confronted by an open rebellion led by army elements under the command of Generals Francisco Franco and Emilio Mola.

World public opinion was to dramatize the Spanish Civil War as a showdown conflict between communism and fascism. With the intervention of Mussolini and, to a lesser degree, Hitler on the side of Franco's "Nationalists," and of Soviet Russia on the side of the Republican "Loyalists," it did take on some such quality. But it should be noted that neither communism nor fascism had much strength when the civil war began. A small Spanish Communist party existed, but communism of whatever sort usually made little appeal to the Spanish radicals, who gave their allegiance either to a democratic, gradualist socialism or else to the Anarchists. In largely premodernized Spain, the strength of the revolutionary movement lay in the country, not the city. Anarchism, with its romantic cult of direct action, its suspicion of the state and all centralized power, its intense moral idealism and "cult of courage," appealed to the Spanish temperament.

The temperamental and philosophical clash between anarchism and communism goes back to Karl Marx's stormy debates with the Russian Michael Bakunin. Bakunin's chief concern about Marx, whom in many ways he admired, was that in seizing the state and exercising a centralized dictatorship, the Communists would become corrupted by power and end by establishing another oppressive tyranny. Anarchist doctrine always preached economic rather than political action, total destruction of the state rather than seizure of it, and a decentralized society after the revolution. As anarcho-syndicalism, such ideas found their way into the labor movement; the revolution would come via the general strike, after which the unions would manage industry locally and democratically. French anarcho-syndicalist ideas, strong at the end of the nineteenth century, made a powerful impression in Spain.

As for Spanish fascism, represented by the Falange, it was unim-

The Spanish Civil War: Nationalist leader General Francisco Franco salutes his followers at Salamanca, 1936. *United Press International.*

portant prior to the civil war, and, contrary to a persistent legend, never struck roots in Spain. Only military dependence on Italy and on Russia caused the Spanish Fascists and Communists to exercise influence out of all proportion to their numbers once the civil war began in earnest. The execution of Primo de Rivera early in the civil war gave the Falange a martyr, but Franco always distanced himself from this rather revolutionary Spanish fascism, which was anticlerical and populist and which never had a very large following. Communism attained some popularity in 1936–1937, aided by the charisma of Dolores Ibarruri, "La Pasionaria."

No military genius, Franco was forced to depend on German and Italian military advice as well as aid. The same thing happened to the Republican Loyalists in the later part of the civil war. Sustained by Soviet aid, the Loyalists had to allow the Spanish Communist party power as the price of this aid. The anti-Communist Socialist, Indalecio Prieto, resigned as minister of defense in April 1938, on the issue of Communist influence. Juan Negrin, the professor of physiology who became prime minister in May 1937, was not a Communist, but he worked closely with them, feeling that this was the only way the war could be won.

If the failure of the republican regime was in part the fault of too many divisions among its supporters, so too was their defeat in the civil war of 1936–1939. The Left was badly split; its own divisions as much as the strength of its foes brought on its defeat. Basically, the split was among the elements: (a) moderate socialists, along with some liberals or republicans (Prieto and Azaña being among the leaders of

Guernica: Spanish-born artist Pablo Picasso's commentary on the horrors of war was inspired by German destruction of a defenseless Basque town during the Spanish Civil War. *United Press International.*

this group); (b) the left-wing Socialists, aligned loosely with Anarchists and the anti-Moscow POUM Communists (often called "Trotskyists"); and (c) the official Communists and those who, for practical reasons, allied with them. But such a model scarcely does justice to the volatility of the Iberian temperament. Largo Caballero, most formidable of the Republican leaders, was an emotional revolutionary socialist whose rhetoric alarmed middle-class elements but who also resisted Communist police-state methods, which he said smacked of the fascism they were fighting.

The Western democracies failed to support the Loyalists. While until mid-1938 France went so far as to permit supplies from the Soviet Union to enter via the Spanish-French border, neither France nor Great Britain sent aid to the republic after the first few weeks. They organized a nonintervention committee among the powers, which Hitler and Mussolini joined even as they were openly aiding Franco's Nationalist side. Refusing to distinguish between the legitimate government and its rebel foes, they declared an arms embargo, and the United States followed suit in voting a ban on the sale of weapons to either side. Britain

Hitler and Mussolini meet, June 6, 1936. The Spanish Civil War helped draw the two Fascist dictators together after early suspicions of each other. *Radio Times Hulton Picture Library.*

under Neville Chamberlain was well launched on its policy of appeasing Hitler.

From the beginning of the civil war Spain became a pawn in the games of the great powers. Hitler sent the Condor Legion to practice modern warfare; Mussolini wished prestige; the Russians were playing for a Popular Front alliance with the Western democracies against Nazi Germany. None really cared much about Spain, and that was a part of the tragedy. In November 1937, discussing plans for German expansion at a secret conference, Hitler argued that a complete Franco victory in Spain was not immediately desirable; to have the war continue would best serve German interests, by keeping alive tensions between Russia and the democracies and diverting attention from other areas.

The Spanish Civil War became a symbol of the age chiefly because, in this ideology-intoxicated era, the intellectuals of the world adopted it as one. They sent volunteers to fight fascism in a crusade reminiscent of 1914, only this time it was seen as an international civil war ranging the sons of light against the sons of darkness. Forty thousand volunteers served in the International Brigade, where many anti-Hitler refugees from Germany joined British, French, and American idealists. The Abraham Lincoln battalion came from the United States. Among British writers who served in Spain were W. H. Auden and George Orwell. André Malraux, who volunteered and hired twenty pilots, wrote a great novel about the war (*Man's Hope*), as did the American Ernest Hemingway (*For Whom the Bell Tolls*). "Spain was the first and the last crusade of the British leftwing intellectual," Neal Wood writes, with only a slight exaggeration. "Never again was such enthusiasm mobilized."

The war was a dramatic one, colored by the somber tones of the Spanish countryside and the Spanish temperament. It was bloody. Of some 2,500 British volunteers, nearly 550 were killed. The whole war, marked by massacres and cruel reprisals against civilians by both sides, cost at least half a million lives (popular lore said a million), in a land with a total population of twenty-five million. The apparently pointless extinction of the defenseless Basque town of Guernica by German bombers inspired Pablo Picasso's immortal painting. The heroism of the armed workers was celebrated in liberal circles all over the world. But from the start the rebel Nationalists, with most of the regular army, held the military advantage.

Germany supplied only a few thousand men but several hundred planes and military supplies and weapons. Mussolini kept about 30,000 Italians in the field. In the decisive battle of Bilbao, in June 1937, Italian troops played an important part; it is not true that the Italians generally fought badly. On the other side, though Stalin gave substantial military supplies (over a thousand aircraft), he committed only a handful of men, chiefly military advisers. In return, he insisted on controlling the republic's policies, which led to fierce in-fighting between Communists and other Loyalist factions.

The fall of the French Popular Front government in June 1938 led to the closing of the route through which Russian aid had passed. Even before that, Stalin had begun to withdraw Soviet support from Spain. His intervention was largely dictated by the desire to forge an alliance with the Western democracies; giving up on that, he lost interest in Spain. Franco soon launched his final offensive in northeast Spain against the last Loyalist stronghold, and the greatly outnumbered Loyalists could not hold him back. Hundreds of thousands of people fled from Catalonia across the border into France. The end came on April 1, 1939, with the unconditional surrender of the last Loyalist forces. France and Great Britain, capping their basically pro-Franco "neutrality," had already recognized the Nationalist government on February 27.

It took Spain a generation to recover from the trauma. For her, World War II had started early. (She stayed out of the 1939–1945 war.) For the rest of the world, Spain was a battle in the war for the minds of men between fascism and communism, with democracy a bewildered onlooker. In the context of 1930s diplomacy, the civil war was a chapter in the history of appeasement, for Britain and France (along with the United States), hoping to avoid war, let Hitler and Mussolini have their way.

The Background of the Second World War

9

"No More War!"

By the time Franco had conquered Spain, Europe was on the brink of its second nightmare of general destruction, this one to spread across the whole globe.

The approach to World War II differed markedly from the beginnings of World War I. For one thing, World War I had come unexpectedly, a bolt from the blue, while the second war was all too predictable. As soon as they read the 1919 peace treaties, shrewd observers knew that another round was coming. The 1919–1939 period was a "long armistice" with only brief moments of stability. After Hitler solidified his control over Germany, it hardly required gifts of clairvoyance to perceive the dire threat to peace. And from 1935 on, the world lived with almost constant international tension. Statesmen put off the inevitable with desperate expedients until they ran out of them in 1939.

There was far less enthusiasm for war this time. Not wildly cheering crowds but quiet, almost sullen ones greeted Hitler's announcement of war against Poland at the end of August 1939—quite a contrast with that other August a quarter of a century earlier. From a British perspective, T. S. Eliot noted the paradox in September 1939: "It is strange that in 1914 we did not expect a war and were not confused when it came. Now we have been expecting this for some time but are confused when it has come." What confused the approach to World War II, of course, was the deep revulsion against war, scarcely present at all in 1914 but very much so in the 1930s. Hitler was incomparably more evil than Wilhelm, Germany much more arrantly the aggressor in 1939 than in 1914—in this regard, the choice should have been easier for Germany's foes in 1939 than in 1914. But the feeling against war as such was infinitely stronger on the eve of 1939 than it was before 1914. This feeling operated to inhibit preparations for war and thus inadvertently played into the Nazi dictator's hands. He profited from the weakness of the democracies.

"The distinguishing feature of the 1930s in England was that it was a time of resolute non-heroism," writes L. C. B. Seaman. While dictators in Italy, Russia, and Germany advertised dynamic ideologies, and even in the United States a charismatic president exhorted his people toward a "rendezvous with destiny," while Spain experienced a civil war and France had furious ideological battles, Great Britain celebrated the Silver Jubilee of King George V and reelected Stanley Baldwin in 1935. The earnest entreaties of Britain's Left Book Club could not much disturb the complacency of a people who often seemed able to enjoy even the depression. George V himself, who warned in 1934 that "Germany is the peril of the world," could not persuade his people and ministers to take alarm. Later revealed as the scandal of the 1935 election was Baldwin's characteristically frank admission that he did not dare tell the truth about German rearmament to the British public, for raising such disturbing prospects would have guaranteed his defeat. Instead, there was a great "peace ballot," which demonstrated that the people would like the League of Nations to do something about the dictators, while Great Britain disarmed!

Franklin D. Roosevelt's rendezvous with destiny was, prior to 1940, conceived in purely American, domestic terms. The United States was so profoundly isolationist that it passed measures severely restricting trade with both sides in any future war. In 1934, also, the Congress passed a bill denying loans to European countries that had defaulted on their war debts. This bill was aimed primarily at France and Britain. (The United States Army and Navy in the 1920s devoted most of their planning to an anticipated war with the United Kingdom!) This "storm cellar" idea, which sought to insulate the United States from future wars by cutting off all contact with the belligerents, was a policy obviously based on the supposition that there could be no American interest in any war. It was based also on an interpretation that American entry into World War I had been totally and tragically mistaken. This wave of antiwar sentiment, marked by pacifist plays, novels, organizations, and demonstrations on college campuses, was at its peak about 1935. It was found most strongly among exactly those people who cheered for Roosevelt's programs of domestic reform—people on the Left, the naturally antifascist. In this instance, they were objectively profascist, in that their emotional hostility to war impeded any resistance to Hitler.

Young men in England took the "Oxford Oath," a popular vow among university students never again to march to war "for king and country." The motto of the French Socialists was "not a man, not a cent" for any military appropriation. Some even declared, "better servitude than war"—so deeply had the hatred of war penetrated. As we have already mentioned, during the Popular Front, 1936–1938, the Communists were unable to persuade the French Left that there should be preparations for a war against Germany.

France, in fact, suffered from defeatism almost from the start. She simply was not prepared to face the prospect of another war with Germany, unless it was a war in which she could stay on the defensive and rely on her allies, Britain and the U.S., to carry the brunt of battle. Again helplessly watching the rise of a powerful Germany, much more populous now than France—for French population was stationary at about forty million, while Germany's had risen to sixty-five—the great majority of French people could not bring themselves to think about another conflict. World War I had drained them of the will.

Another factor preventing a firm front against Hitler was ideological conflict within the democracies. In conservative circles, the greater fear was of Stalin's state. "Better Hitler than Stalin!" (or even Blum!)

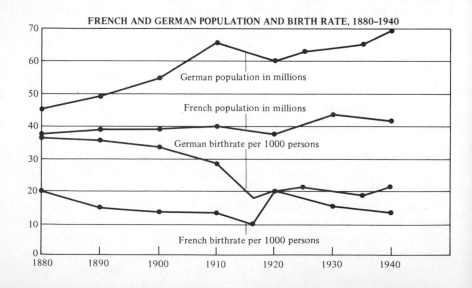

FRENCH AND GERMAN POPULATION AND BIRTH RATE, 1880–1940

German population in millions

French population in millions

German birthrate per 1000 persons

French birthrate per 1000 persons

was alleged to be the motto of the French Right, and this was not far from the truth. While the Left opposed fascism in principle but rendered this position useless by its pacifism, the Right found fascism preferable to communism. The Left, one English commentator remarked, wants to intervene everywhere and disarm; the Right wants to rearm but intervene nowhere. In France, ideologists of the Right as well as the Left fully accepted the drastic view that democracy was dead, and it only remained to choose between fascism and communism. Leaders of business and finance felt that fascism maintained order and upheld private property; bad as it was, one could live with it (Mussolini was admittedly a better model than Hitler). Communism was far worse, they thought.

The third sentiment that made it difficult for the victors of World War I to resist the resurgence of Germany was their sense of guilt about the Treaty of Versailles. This, too, was true on the Left as well as the Right. Historical investigations into the origins of World War I in the 1920s tended to be "revisionist"; they found that the Central Powers had not been solely guilty of bringing on the war. Perhaps the Allies had been equally to blame, or perhaps the culprit was that convenient abstraction, "the system"—political or economic. The peace settlement had been an act of unjustified hatred and revenge, in which the Allies had betrayed their own principles of democracy and self-determination of peoples.

Between 1935 and early 1939, Germany's aggressive actions could be interpreted as no more than her claim to rights that other countries held. In 1935, Germany demanded equality of armaments, in 1936, the right to send troops into her own territory (the Rhineland). The Austrian *Anschluss* and the annexation of the Sudetenland, granted to Hitler in 1938, were justified by the fact that Germans of similar culture and language lived in these regions. Neville Chamberlain, prime architect of the much-criticized policy of "appeasing" Germany, reflected such an outlook in March of 1939. He declared that, up until then, all of Germany's gains—the Rhineland, Austria, the Sudetenland—"however much we might take exception to the methods," might be defended, "whether on account of racial affinity or of just claims too long resisted." The British prime minister may have been looking for excuses, but Hitler had been able to make a case, attractive to large sections of British opinion, for righting the wrongs of an unjust peace and restoring equality of rights to Germany. The West's uneasy conscience assisted him.

The appeasers of Germany, as they were later called, at this time plausibly argued that in the long run a stable world required Germany's readmission to the comity of nations. One could not forever hope to exclude a great and powerful people from equal rights in the international community. Given these rights, Germans would perhaps lose their resentments, even reject Hitler, and resume a constructive role. Denied them, the Germans would support Hitler, brood on their wrongs, and plan for a war of revenge.

Faced with the unpleasant alternatives of war against Hitler, alliance with Stalin, or coming to terms with the German dictator, politicians in Great Britain and France opted for the last. If the self-proclaimed crusader against Bolshevism would only discharge his aggressions in that direction, one might kill off both birds, they thought. Or Germany might be content with an empire in the East, where the Nazis declared their ambitions to lie.

These Western politicians, architects of appeasement, later looked like fools and received an appropriate verdict from critics and historians. But in truth they were in an uncomfortable position as leaders of peoples who made no secret of their refusal to countenance military measures. They were the victims of their publics. Preoccupation with the great economic depression mingled with ideological strife and, in France, the usual weakness of coalition governments to frustrate any strong foreign policy. But the most important factor was the hatred of war that World War I had left behind. "Never again!" "No more war!"

Germany Regains Her Strength

Such views had been prevalent in Germany, too, prior to the Nazi revolution. One of the most famous of all antiwar novels, read all over the world and made into a poignant movie in 1931, was Erich Maria Remarques' *All Quiet on the Western Front*. Weimar wits made fun of Prussian militarists. Thomas Mann led a parade of repentant intellectuals, now crying "Nie wieder krieg!" But German opinion was always strongly colored by resentment at the unjust Treaty of Versailles and by feelings of revenge.

Even before 1933, Germany was not so helpless as she has usually been depicted. The respectably democratic Weimar Republic secretly evaded some of the disarmament provisions of the Treaty of Versailles. The 1922 Treaty of Rapallo between Germany and the Soviet Union, a marriage of outcasts, paved the way for significant military cooperation between the two governments. Germany provided Russia with war materials and established factories on Russian territory, and in return *Reichswehr* units were trained in the USSR.[1] If the Weimar

---

[1] There is no evidence that military collaboration persisted between Germany and Russia to any significant extent after 1933. Indeed, it diminished after 1927 when withdrawal of Allied inspection removed much of the need for conducting mili-

Republic spent little on the military, the same was true in France and England, as public opinion turned against the fighting forces. While technically complying with the Versailles limit on the size of her army (100,000), Germany made it an "army of captains" capable of rapid expansion into a much larger force. After repudiation of the Versailles military clauses in 1935, the German military expanded rapidly to 800,000 by 1939 with a million more in reserve; during World War II, ten million were to be mobilized.

It is also clear that the attempted breakup of the German General Staff did not succeed in ending German military planning. The Germans proved more inventive in the arts of war than did the World War I victors during this period. Colonel Charles de Gaulle tried in vain to interest the French in mobile tank warfare, which the Germans were to use with such devastating effect in 1940. The French thought in terms of the defensive, building great lines of fortification and, for the rest, playing with theories of victory by strategic air power. The Germans developed military aviation as a tactical arm that could cooperate closely with ground forces in offensive operations. They used Spain as a practice grounds for these tactics, garnering field experience that was denied to the nonintervening French and British. Hitler restored two-year compulsory military service in 1935 and raised the morale of the previously neglected armed forces by praising the *Wehrmacht* (the armed forces) as the incarnation of German character and will. Proud Prussian generals succumbed to the ex-corporal because of the favors he lavished on the fighting forces and his obvious interest in building them up.

The 1919 safeguards against German military revival broke down, one by one. Allied occupation of the Rhine bridgeheads came to an end in 1930. In 1935, as provided for in the Versailles Treaty, a plebiscite was held in the coal-mining and industrial area of the Saar, on the Franco-German border, a region the French had been allowed to administer since 1920. The result was an overwhelming majority for reattachment to Germany. When later in this same year Hitler openly denounced the military provisions of the peace treaty, he met no resistance. The British, at least, had already conceded Germany's right to arms equality; and they proceeded to negotiate a naval treaty with Hitler that in effect acknowledged their own discarding of the Versailles disarmament terms.

---

tary exercises outside of Germany. German-Soviet collaboration came to a halt with the arrival of the rabidly anti-Bolshevik Hitler to power in 1933. Stalin accused his generals of continuing to work with the Germans, as a pretext for his massive purge of the Red Army in 1937. The German Security Service forged and planted documents, seeking in this way to disrupt Russian military organization. It is not clear whether Stalin was deceived by this German trickery or simply wanted to destroy all potential rivals in the military as he did in the civilian government.

By this treaty the Germans were to have a fleet no more than 35 percent of Britain's, thus more than maintaining the historic two to one ratio.

Given the disarray of his foes, Hitler moved with considerable circumspection at first. His provocative actions included taking Germany out of the Geneva arms conference and out of the League of Nations, denouncing the Treaty of Versailles, and proceeding to rearm Germany. Having gotten away with these, in 1936 he sent German troops into the demilitarized zone of the Rhineland, defying not only Versailles but the Locarno Pact. It was a bold move, for such plans as the French had for security against Germany relied on keeping allies in the East—Poland and Czechoslovakia—by occupying a position of menace against Germany. They held such a position so long as the rich and populous Rhine regions of Germany lay undefended and thus open to attack. Once the Germans had reoccupied this region, they could and did build powerful fortifications which rendered a French attack extremely difficult. So the 1936 move was crucial, and many historians have placed the decisive surrender at this point. For when Hitler turned next to the annexation of Austria and the Sudetenland, there was not much the French and the British could do about it.

Hitler used rearmament as a weapon against the depression from 1934 on, but stepped it up as he moved toward war from 1937 on. *Wide World Photos.*

Nevertheless, they did not react in 1936. The Germans were, after all, only occupying their own territory, something every other sovereign state had a right to do. We have already discussed the reasons for diplomatic passivity in the democracies. They were subsequently to regret their missed opportunity of 1936, when German rearmament had not yet proceeded very far. Neither, however, had British or French rearmament, both of which had been neglected for many years. France was undergoing a characteristic cabinet crisis. Moreover, both countries were distracted at this time by a quarrel with Italy. And again, what would be the result of marching into Germany? The French had memories of 1923. Chaos would result, perhaps Hitler would gain rather than lose German support, and the problem of restoring Germany to her normal status would remain.

Hitler Prepares for War

There were those in the West who thought that Hitler's goals were simply those of a German nationalist who wanted to restore Germany to her 1914 borders or reclaim only those peoples who were ethnically German. These people failed to judge the true dimensions of Hitler's "world view." He intended to conquer and enslave the Slavic East, whose "sub-men" were destined, he thought, to be ruled by the superior Aryans. This *Weltanschauung* was so bizarre that the aristocratic gentlemen at Whitehall and the rational bureaucrats at the Quai d'Orsay may perhaps not be blamed for refusing to believe it, even if Hitler had set it down in his autobiography, *Mein Kampf*, some years before. But in fact he was serious.

The National Socialist *Weltanschauung* was constructed of various bits and pieces of modern thought, each in itself far from unfamiliar. One was a crude "social Darwinism." "Nature is cruel, therefore we too may be cruel. . . . I have a right to remove millions of an inferior race that breeds like vermin." Thus spake *Der Führer* in 1934. He was to practice euthanasia on sick and old people in Germany, until public opinion forced a halt, and later he would try to exterminate the Jews of eastern Europe. It may be noted that this viewpoint cut right across German nationalism, for Hitler was as prepared to sacrifice the weak to the strong in Germany as anywhere else, and indeed he was prepared to see the whole German nation perish if it could not meet the challenge of struggle. When Germany was losing the war in 1944–1945, Hitler thought the German people should rightly perish, for it "has proved itself weak." Those who remain after battle are of little value, he reflected, for "the good have fallen." This frighteningly literal and utterly consistent application of the law of the jungle to human affairs is probably the closest idea of any to the heart of Adolf Hitler's philosophy.

The German frontiers of 1914 had obviously not been good enough, for had not Germany lost that war despite valiant efforts? She must expand or die. "Every people strives for world domination," said Hitler. The key to success in diplomacy and war is "an iron will," an ability to be "fanatical," to stop at nothing. His foes, Hitler thought, did not have this quality. France was degenerate, the United States Judaized (Hitler seems to have thought Roosevelt was a semitic name), Britain decadent, Russia racially inferior and led by Jewish Marxists. Antisemitism was with Hitler "so intensive a mania that it completely shattered the faculty of reason," as one who knew him testified and as is obvious from all he did. Purged of the Jewish poison that infected other states, Germany was bound to be stronger than they. Strength relies basically on the will, on moral factors; Hitler scorned economics and even technology in favor of racial purity, strength of will, "fanaticism" as the most important survival qualities.

The national will-to-power must be expressed through its one leader, a principle the Nazis had insisted on from the beginning: *Führerprinzip*, the leadership principle. The democracies' clumsy system of divided counsels and fluctuating government prevented them from acting with firmness and dispatch, as Germany could under Hitler. With this great advantage, Hitler thought he was certain to be an easy winner in any game of power with the democracies.

The Nazi dictator was capable of skillful acting. At times a raging madman, he could be charming, gay, relaxed, or totally calm and composed as the situation demanded. He accompanied each of his daring thrusts with soothing words, promising that this would be Germany's final demand. In this regard he was a disciple of Machiavelli: "In politics there are no sentiments, only toughness." Like Stalin, he was totally unscrupulous. The end justifies any means. The end, for Hitler, was the power of the German nation and state, driving for world power in an international jungle where the rule was eat or be eaten; do unto others before they do it unto you.

In particular, Hitler believed, Germany must have land and food for her growing population. This could be found in Russia, where the Slavs would be conquered and enslaved or exterminated to make way for the Aryans. Since the Jewish Bolsheviks were unable to organize and govern a state, Russia was ripe for the taking. (Hitler seemed unaware that Stalin represented, in part, a Great Russian antisemitic rejection of the Jewish element in the Marxist party.) Reenforcing Hitler's instinctive anticommunism and anti-Slavism, which he had acquired in Austria in his youth, was his attachment to the geopolitical ideas of Professor Karl Haushofer, whose pupil Rudolf Hess was an early Nazi and close friend of Hitler. Haushofer, building on theories of Sir Halford Mackinder, taught that the key to world power lay in control of the Eurasian heartland. "At long last we break off the colonial and commercial policy of the pre-War period and shift to the soil policy of the future," Hitler put it in *Mein Kampf*. Such a formula had the advantage of being consistent with the Nazi yearning for a rural folk community.

Whether Hitler in power would stick to these earlier theorizings was not certain. He had also talked of the need to deal with the implacable enemy, France. Toward the English he was usually more favorably disposed. A tough and tenacious people, racially akin to the Germans, they had much to teach him; he admired their imperialism and seemed willing to let them keep the seas if he could have the land! Hitler's susceptibility to *mal de mer* has been suggested as a reason for his lack of interest in sea-power, a trait he shared with Napoleon; in any case the *Weltanschauung* led him toward a kind of agrarian imperialism. The drive to the East stayed with him, and in 1941, apparently against all reason, he returned to it, feeling then "spiritually free." Meanwhile the ever-growing might of his Germany, and the weakness of any force that could oppose it, tempted the Nazi dictator to push whatever gates offered themselves for the opening.

November 5, 1937, has been selected by some as the day Hitler definitely opted for war. At least it brought a rather sensational revelation of his grand designs, which he presented to his foreign minister, war minister, and commanders of the army, navy and air force at a secret conference. Germany must secure space, and this *Lebensraum* would have to be obtained by "the way of force." The time was ripe, for all Germany's rivals were in trouble. It is hard not to agree with Hitler here. The Soviet Union, remember, was in the middle of the purge; a new recession had hit the West. A few more years and it might be too late. Austria and Czechoslovakia would be the first victims; England and France would not defend them.

Stunned by the shameless belligerence of Hitler's speech, Neurath, Blomberg, and Fritsch warned of the risks involved. Within a few months, they were all out of office. Not only was Fritsch framed on charges of homosexuality, but the obliging Heinrich Himmler was also able to discover that Werner von Blomberg had recently taken as his second wife an ex-prostitute. With himself as head of the war office and the subservient Joachim von Ribbertrop, former champagne salesman, as his foreign minister, Hitler was ready to unleash the dogs of war with little to restrain him. Schacht's resignation and the cessation of cabinet meetings mark this as the moment Hitler became absolute master of the Third Reich and embarked on a policy of territorial expansion.

The Diplomacy of Alliances

What was to stop him from becoming master of all Europe? "For every Frenchman between the ages of twenty and thirty there are two Germans," a French army officer named Charles de Gaulle wrote in 1934. Germany produced twice as much steel as France, and greater quantities of most of the other industrial products that are the sinews of war. Ardent patriot that he was, de Gaulle was forced to concede that alone, France had no chance against Germany. The French at this time overestimated German military strength. They probably held an edge in 1936, we now know, but they did not think so. The French generals were depressed at the low state of French military power, which General Weygand lamented in 1934 had "sunk to the lowest level that the security of France can allow."

The only answer lay in finding allies. Great Britain was a highly unreliable one. She had shrunk back into her old isolation and was not committed to the Continent. The Anglo-German Naval Treaty of 1935 showed that she would make her own terms with Germany without so much as consulting France. France's habit of looking to London for a lead was fatal in 1935, 1936, and 1937, for the British had no intention of "pulling French chestnuts out of the fire." Acceptance of German rearmament and a friendly policy toward Germany were the deliberate policies of the British government, approved in 1935 by Tories and Labourites alike. Britain's strength was simply not great enough to police both Europe and the now unstable Far East.

Given the weakness and the divisions of the smaller countries of eastern Europe, there remained only Italy—and Russia. France tried each in 1935, with little success. The Franco-Italian detente was nourished on hopes that Mussolini did not want Germany to take over Austria, and in 1934 this seemed true. Civil war broke out in Vienna in February 1934, after the failure of a socialist general strike. The army shelled a working-class housing project, the Karl Marx Hof, that was defended by socialist militia. Torn by civil strife, Austria then experienced an attempted Nazi coup that same year, when the Christian Socialist head of government, Engelbert Dollfuss, was assassinated. Mussolini sent Italian troops to the Brenner Pass in a show of force that caused Hitler to back away from the Austrian Nazis at this time. At this time there was scarcely any love lost between the two Fascist dictators; *Il Duce*, at least, both feared and disliked Hitler. Not only was the little Austrian a rival in the field of international fascism, stealing Mussolini's thunder in an uncouth way, but he opposed Italian interests in Austria. We must remember that Italy had fought against Germany in World War I.

In April of 1935 British Prime Minister Ramsay MacDonald, nearing the end of his career, journeyed with his foreign secretary, John Simon, to join France's Pierre Flandin and Pierre Laval in meeting with Benito Mussolini at Stresa in northern Italy. Hitler had just torn up the Treaty of Versailles. The British were even then engaged in negotiating the naval treaty with him that so enraged the French. In retrospect the "Stresa front" was an abortion, but for the moment hopes were raised of a Franco-Italian-British union, which might deal firmly with the German threat. But not only did it quickly become evident that the British wanted no part of any continental involvement carrying the risk of war, it also became clear that the Italian leader was now on a course that would bring him into collision with the British. The French were caught hopelessly in the middle between their two dubious would-be allies. The Ethiopian crisis was about to distract everybody's attention, allowing Hitler to pick up the Rhineland.

Africa had not just recently caught the Italian eye. Italians had long smarted from the defeat they had suffered at the hands of Ethiopian warriors in 1896, and Italy had long harbored African ambitions. In a 1934 speech Mussolini proclaimed that Italy's "historical objectives" lay in Asia and Africa: "Of all the large Western powers of Europe, Italy is the nearest to Africa and Asia." This was the focus of the ancient Roman Empire, which Mussolini had promised to revive.

The Italians had been trying to penetrate Ethiopia for some time. Laval, the French foreign minister, had led Mussolini to believe that France would approve his Ethiopian project in return for opposing Hitler in Europe. But the British did not approve. They had their own interests in this part of the world, so near the Suez Canal, and they reacted by attempting to keep Italy out of all but an insignificant portion of this area.

An incident at Wal Wal led to fighting; Ethiopian Emperor Haile Selassie eloquently appealed to the League of Nations for help against Italian aggression; and the British took up the cause of Ethiopia at Geneva. Rome's reaction was an angry one: perfidious Albion sought selfishly to hog colonial spoils while sanctimoniously condemning anyone else who played the imperialist game. In the autumn of 1935 the issue caught the attention of the world as a test case of "collective security." A general election was impending in Britain, and the League was a popular symbol. Somehow, it was expected to stop the dictators.

As the small states rallied to the cause of collective security, the

League branded Italy an aggressor and voted economic sanctions against her. The British mounted a show of naval strength in the Mediterranean. Italy was almost isolated, and *Il Duce's* political career seemed threatened. Laval, however, still trying to keep Italy as an ally against Germany, desperately sought a compromise. Hitler offered to help the British against Italy. In return, he wanted British support for his annexation of Austria.

The outcome of this almost classic muddle was about as bad as it could be. Economic sanctions, never applied more than half-heartedly, did not prevent Italy from conquering Ethiopia, in an unexpected display of military efficiency. Ill and suffering from exhaustion, the inexperienced Samuel Hoare replaced John Simon as British foreign secretary in June of 1935. Adding to the confusion in British affairs was the death of King George V followed by the dramatic crisis of Edward VIII's abdication, the result of his proposed marriage to an American divorcee. This absorbed British attention throughout the year 1936. Half way into the Ethiopian crisis, the British retreated and joined with France in a compromise, the Hoare-Laval plan, which managed to undercut the idealism of the collective security crusade. Having condemned Italy in righteous terms as a criminal, the policemen now offered to give her half of the loot. A public outcry forced withdrawal of this "deal," but the Italians pressed on to capture the Ethiopian capital in May 1936.

Perhaps more important, Mussolini was bitterly estranged from Britain and turned toward Hitler, soon cementing the start of the "brutal friendship" by collaboration in Spain. Hitler, who took advantage of the confusion to occupy the Rhineland (March 1936) was the only clear winner in this comedy of errors, which reenforced his contempt for the democratic leaders.

Laval, an able politician with a reputation for slipperiness that followed him to his tragic end a decade later, also explored the Soviet alliance. Pushed by Louis Barthou during his foreign ministry in 1934, the project suffered a setback when Barthou was assassinated along with King Alexander of Yugoslavia in October 1934 at Marseille. Alexander had been working to form a Balkan alliance aimed at Germany, so that the assassination, the work of Croatian and Macedonian terrorists headquartered in Hungary, perhaps with Italian connivance, was a double blow at the policy of shaping an alliance against Hitler. Laval continued the approach to Russia, and in 1935 a treaty was concluded, in which France and the USSR promised each other aid in the event of "unprovoked aggression."

The treaty was anathema to the French Right and not very appealing to much of the Left either. Events in Russia soon intensified skepticism about the value or the morality of having Stalin's regime as an ally. London was cool to the Franco-Soviet treaty, which clashed also with the concurrent attempt to woo Italy. Despite the valiant efforts of Soviet Minister Maxim Litvinov, a real "collective security" front against Germany never got off the ground—the main diplomatic tragedy of these years, many think. If leading French and British circles were hysterically anti-Soviet, Stalin was remote and suspicious. He decided early that the rulers of the Western democracies were plotting to appease Hitler at Russia's expense. Their actions in 1937 and 1938 gave all too much support to this paranoid view.

The Diplomacy of Appeasement

A huge majority of Austrians wanted to join their fellow nationals in Germany after the breakup of the Hapsburg monarchy in 1919, but the World War I victors would not let them. The World Court frustrated an attempt at peaceful *Anschluss,* or union, with Germany in 1931. It is not surprising that Austrian-born Hitler, who had mentioned the matter on the first page of *Mein Kampf,* raised the *Anschluss* issue early in his career of expansion. He found the way open after he made friends with Mussolini.

Early in February 1938, Hitler invited Kurt von Schuschnigg to his "Eagle's Nest" at Berchtesgaden and there browbeat the unfortunate Austrian chancellor into appointing a Nazi as minister of interior and legalizing the Austrian Nazi party. Returning to Vienna, Schuschnigg recovered his courage and proposed a plebiscite on the issue of *Anschluss.* A majority of Austrians were prepared to reject it now that it meant Nazism. Hitler hastily mounted an invasion of Austria; Schuschnigg called off the plebiscite, but the German troops continued on, unopposed, and Hitler proclaimed the outright annexation of Austria, not just a federal union. Scenes of terror occurred as the Nazis took revenge on political enemies, Jews, leftists. The flight of old Sigmund Freud to London symbolized the end of Austrian freedom March 11–13.

All this drew no response from the world except perfunctory protests. Hitler was most worried by Italy, in view of the 1934 action, and when Mussolini smiled this time Hitler effusively thanked him. France, as so often, was without a government on this weekend. Neville Chamberlain thought it "an unpleasant affair" but looked past it to better relations with a happier Germany. It is true that serious British rearmament dates from this revelation of Hitler's brutality. But a plebiscite, arranged by the Nazis, soon produced a predictably overwhelming mandate for them in Austria, endowing the seizure with a facade of legitimacy.

The next victim on Hitler's schedule was Czechoslovakia. This was a very different situation. True, a minority of Germans lived in the land of the Czechs and the Slovaks, along the northern fringe. They had been left there, perhaps unwisely, in 1919. Toward this minority (some three and a quarter million of fifteen million) Hitler directed his propaganda, aided by a vociferous Sudetenland Nazi party. But they were not capable of threatening the Czech state. Czechoslovakia had a substantial and efficient army, a well fortified frontier, a notable arms industry (the Skoda works at Pilsen and Brno were world-famous), and a generally loyal public opinion. She also had an alliance with France. Whether all this could defend her against Nazi Germany remained to be seen. There was hardly any way of "blitzing" Czechoslovakia or of intimidating Prague, as Vienna had been.

"Who is master of Bohemia is master of Europe," Bismarck once said in words that keen student of history, Adolf Hitler, doubtless remembered. After the annexation of Austria, the more populous and prosperous end of Czechoslovakia intruded itself into Germany like a large thumb pressed against her midsection, an obvious target for engulfment. More to the point, Prague was closer to Berlin than was Paris or London; Czechoslovakia was an "aircraft carrier" in the heart of Europe, Hitler said.

Still more to the point, Czechoslovakia was vulnerable. Her alliance with France was useless unless France attacked Germany, for neither the French nor the British could get troops to Czechoslovakia by any feasible land route. Having constructed his Siegfried Line of fortifications on the French border, Hitler could be sure the French would hesitate to attack. In any case, the French seemed politically in chaos and quite demoralized. For the future, Russia might be a threat, but hardly now, just after the shattering purges of military and party. Reason enough not to delay; Hitler did not think time was on his side.

He asked for the return of ethnic Germans, oppressed, he claimed, by Prague. The Sudetenlanders, occupying the northern tier of Czechoslovakia, had some legitimate grievances but were far from an oppressed people. Yet the German case was plausible enough to win over the British ambassador at Berlin, Neville Henderson, who asserted that, "It is morally unjust to compel this solid Teuton minority to remain subjected to a Slav central government at Prague." The British, unlike the French, had no treaty commitment to defend the Czechs and made it clear from the start that they did not intend to go to war for them. It is often supposed that Prime Minister Neville Chamberlain gave in at the Munich conference only after long pressure from Germany, but in fact he had never intended to resist. The series of conferences at Berchtesgaden, Godesberg, and Munich in September of 1938, in which

Chamberlain and Hitler at Munich, October, 1938. *Wide World Photos.*

Chamberlain and French Premier Edouard Daladier dealt with Hitler, concerned the *means* by which Czechoslovakia was to be dismembered; the principle was never in doubt.

The disgraceful part, as it later seemed, was that Britain and France actually joined in browbeating the little country into giving up territory without a fight. Their object was to avoid war by granting to the Nazi dictator what he was threatening to seize by force. At Berchtesgaden Chamberlain agreed to "self-determination" for the Sudeten Germans, and he got Prague to accept this. But when he brought this agreement back to Hitler at Godesberg on September 22, the Germans made new demands: the transfer must take place within eight days, a haste that ensured disorder and humiliation for the Czechs. Angered, Chamberlain returned to London; but on September 29 he came back to Germany and, at Munich, secured only small modifications of this timetable. It was a case of offering to pay $1,000 blackmail, being asked then to pay $2,000, and settling for $1,500.

Had the Czechs chosen to fight, their excellent defenses and strong army could surely have put up much more than token resistance. The

Wehrmacht was hardly yet the formidable machine it subsequently became; some of Hitler's generals were restive, and a center of opposition to him appeared in the army at this time. Perhaps this was one of history's great missed opportunities. Such was the legend that later grew: but for cowardice and narrow vision, Hitler might have been stopped in his tracks and the ghastliness of World War II avoided.

But it is necessary to record that public opinion in the democracies overwhelmingly supported Chamberlain and Daladier. Cheering crowds greeted them on their return. ("The fools, why are they cheering?" the French premier wondered; Chamberlain seems to have had no such doubts.) Poet laureate John Masefield hailed Chamberlain as a modern hero, going into the night

> *To ask that young men's bodies, not yet dead,*
> *Be given from the battle not begun.*

He had snatched safety from danger, saved the world from a horrible war. Very few wanted it otherwise. War was too terrible to contemplate. Simone Weil's view that the Munich *amoindrissement* (or "calming of tensions") was "a thousand times right" was typical of the intellectuals, the Communists apart. President Roosevelt sent Chamberlain a telegram of congratulations.

More realistically, Chamberlain knew that British rearmament was just getting under way and that both Britain and France would be stronger later. No fool, Chamberlain was buying time, aware that the gamble of appeasing Hitler's appetite with Austria and part of Czechoslovakia might fail. "They had to choose between war and dishonor. They chose dishonor; they will have war." Churchill's thrust struck home. But war later may have been preferable to war earlier. By 1940 Great Britain was to have Spitfire fighters and radar, plus something far more valuable, a will to fight that was simply not there in 1938. The gamble of appeasement probably had to be made. Of course, Germany grew stronger too. And Czechoslovakia was far more defensible than Poland was to be.

In the Munich calculus, so often discussed and reassessed, one problematical factor was the USSR. She too had a commitment to defend Czechoslovakia, but only if France did so first. This mutual assistance pact had been negotiated at the same time as the Franco-Soviet pact of 1935, which had proved abortive. No military agreements or consultations ever followed it up. Preoccupied with his own grisly business at home, Stalin watched in sullen silence as Hitler took Austria without consulting him; he was now to see the Czechoslovakian matter also carried out with the deliberate exclusion of the USSR. Stalin was not invited to the Munich party, though even Mussolini was. Eduard Benes, the Czech leader, seemed not to wish for Soviet help, despite his desperate straits. On September 20 he asked the Soviet ambassador if Russia would carry out her commitment to help Czechoslovakia and received an affirmative reply. We do not know whether Stalin was bluffing here or not, but in later times the Soviet leaders made much of the West's betrayal of Czechoslovakia when the Soviet Union stood ready to do her duty.

In order to aid the Czechs, Stalin would have had to march troops through Poland or Rumania, both of which at this time would have refused this request and fought to prevent it. (Czechoslovakia then had no border with the USSR.) These Eastern European countries feared and mistrusted the Soviet Union even more than they did Nazi Germany; "better Hitler than Stalin" was the motto of their rulers, too. Poland and Hungary were indeed to take their pound of flesh from Czechoslovakia after Munich, acquiring small amounts of territory in disputed frontier areas. In the end, Benes chose not to ask for unilateral Soviet aid; he preferred the dismemberment of his country to a war in which the Soviet Union would be his only ally, with the West neutral or even hostile.

All that he got by way of consolation was a guarantee of the independence of the remainder of his country, in which Britain now joined France. This proved to be worthless. And there was, of course, peace. "We would not be understood by Europe and the world if we provoked the war now," Benes told his generals, who wanted to fight. "The nation must endure. Do not give way, whatever happens, and wait for the right moment. Then we shall enter the struggle again, as we did in 1914. And we shall win again."

It did not quite happen that way.

The Approach of War, 1939

For all the joy with which it was received, Munich left a nasty taste in the West, which grew ever more uncomfortable in the next months. For Neville Chamberlain and British public opinion, the turning point came in March 1939, when Hitler ignored his promise to respect the independence of the remainder of Czechoslovakia. At that time Germany completed the destruction of Czechoslovakia, conferring nominal independence on a now separate state of Slovakia and incorporating the Czech area into the Reich as the "Protectorate of Bohemia and Moravia." Hitler fomented discontent among the Slovaks as he had the Sudetenland Germans, as a weapon to break up Czechoslovakia. He had certainly not intended to stop with annexation merely of the Sudetenland, and he waited only a few months before fulfilling his vow to smash the hated symbol of the World War I peace settlement. This cannot have surprised Chamberlain, one would think; and yet it seems clear that for him and for British opinion in general, the occupation of Prague was the straw that broke the back of appeasement.

Hitler had thrown off all pretense of seeking only self-determination and the restoration of German rights. "Is this not, in fact, a step in the direction of an attempt to dominate the world by force?" Chamberlain asked. When Hiter followed with annexation of the city of Memel, extorted from Lithuania, and began to make demands on Poland regarding Danzig [2] and the Polish Corridor, the British government (March 31) joined France in a guarantee of Poland's independence, extending this two weeks later to Rumania and Greece. Whether this meant a firm intention to draw the line was not yet clear.

Hitler did not intend to let up while he had the opposition on the run and proceeded full steam ahead with his expansionist campaign. Some Germans worried about his recklessness, but no internal force was capable of overthrowing him. Munich was a blow to the anti-Hitler plotters who had begun to appear in Germany. "Bring me certain proof that England will fight if Czechoslovakia is attacked, and I will put an end to this regime," Chief of Staff Ludwig Beck told General Ewald von Kleist on the latter's visit to London in the summer of 1938. Such approaches to the British got nowhere. Beck then tried to organize a kind of strike of the generals against Hitler's war plans but soon resigned in disgust. Beck's successor, General Franz Halder, also disliked Hitler, as did many of the old Prussian officer caste. Halder, together with Schacht, Dr. Karl Bonhoeffer, and others planned a coup d'etat to coincide with the outbreak of war against Czechoslovakia. The Munich capitulation cut the ground from under them, and they sank back in despair. It is possible that they could have succeeded in overthrowing Hitler had England and France stood up to him at the time of Munich. German resistance to Hitler did not seriously revive again until 1944.

Hitler's popularity had never been greater, by all signs; his fiftieth birthday, April 20, 1939, was the occasion for enormous pageantry and effulgent idolatry, with pictures of *der Führer* in every window. Goebbels' propaganda machine hammered in the image of Germany miraculously reborn under the leadership of the simple soldier who had brought salvation to a troubled people.

---

[2] Since 1919 Danzig had been a free city under League of Nations supervision. In this chiefly German city, Nazis had won control of the administration and demanded annexation to the Reich. This Baltic Sea port was vital to Poland as an outlet to the sea.

Poland was a more popular target within Germany than Czechoslovakia was. Few Germans failed to resent the Versailles boundaries in the east, which forced several million former German citizens to live under Polish rule. Hitler spoke of "frightful mistreatment" of Germans under Polish rule, and the newspapers blazed with such stories, which in the main were manufactured or grossly exaggerated. But most Germans, with Munich in mind, believed that the Polish "problem" would be "solved" without war. They did not want or expect war, and they were shocked when it came. The same, probably, can be said for Adolf Hitler.

There is, at least, much evidence that Hitler thought the British and French would back down again. Why should they fight for Poland when they had almost fallen over themselves to give him Czechoslovakia? The former country was far less defensible and far more susceptible to the arguments about self-determination for Germans. "I have seen these little worms at Munich," he told his officers on August 22.

Public opinion in the West does seem to have behaved irrationally and thus must bear some responsibility for World War II, the main cause of which was Nazi Germany's brutal campaign of expansion. The United States, like Great Britain, began to rouse herself from her isolationist slumbers after Munich. There too the Munich agreement had been hailed for saving the peace, but its delivery of Europe into the hands of Hitler almost immediately produced second thoughts. Moving with glacial slowness, but at times capable of a massive landslide, Western public opinion switched from emotional pacifism to intense indignation at Hitler and his shrill propaganda, bad manners, and constant aggression.

The Poles, bolstered by the British guarantee and perhaps by a national temperament less cautious than the Czechs', now refused to be intimidated as Benes had been. "You have only to show a Pole a precipice and he will throw himself over it," Balzac said in the nineteenth century. Perhaps the romantic Polish temperament was less relevant now than the fact that military officers, headed by Colonel Josef Beck, governed Poland. The military would have fought in Czechoslovakia; it was the vast influence of the civilian chief, Eduard Benes, that restrained them. The Polish Army did not propose to repeat the disastrous Czech surrender.

And thus the stage was set for World War II. The other ingredient was Russia. Stung by his exclusion from Munich, when Mussolini had joined Hitler, Chamberlain, and Daladier in a pact that seemed based on Fascist dominance of Eastern Europe, Stalin soon came to feel certain that there was a conspiracy to turn Germany against the Soviet Union. Both Hitler and Stalin, those ideological zealots, prided themselves on

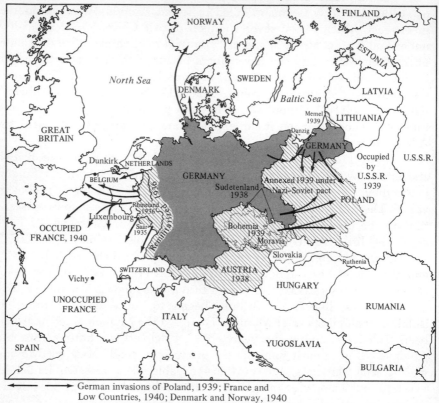

German invasions of Poland, 1939; France and
Low Countries, 1940; Denmark and Norway, 1940

an ice cold realism in regard to tactics. This was an aspect, in fact, of their fanaticism: absolutely sure of their goals, they were prepared to violate any code of ethics to achieve these ends. Neither would hesitate at a marriage of convenience. Sentiments, as Hitler was fond of proclaiming, have nothing to do with the hardboiled realm of foreign policy. Stalin inherited from Lenin the belief that "morality is what serves to advance the Revolution." There is therefore no real reason to be surprised by the Nazi-Soviet pact that astonished the world in August 1939 and set the stage for the war.

The victim of this strange alliance was Poland. This was the fourth partition of that unhappy people situated between powerful and expansionist neighbors. In three bites, between 1772 and 1795, the ancient Polish kingdom had been swallowed up by Prussia, Russia, and Austria. Partially restored by Napoleon, it again fell under the dominance of others after 1815. (Congress Poland survived for fifteen years as a ward of Russia, being annexed outright by Russia after the revolution of 1830.) World War I restored the Polish state, which profited from the temporary ruin of all three of her oppressors in that war. Poland went too far in her intoxication of victory after long defeat; she took land in abundance from Russia and Germany, pushing her frontiers out in both directions. Thus she was the target of territorial claims from both her neighbors as soon as they regained their strength.

Thus the two totalitarian states could make a deal in which each satisfied its greed for expansion, at the expense of the smaller states of eastern Europe. Each reserved its action for the future. For the moment the Nazi-Soviet Pact was an astonishing coup. Hitler and Stalin were soon hailing each other as "good fellows," while mystified Communists in the Western world, who had been denouncing fascism and pleading for a popular front, had to tear down the type and substitute stories that attacked the democracies and were silent on the topic of fascism. Excessive antifascism could now land you in a prison camp in the Soviet Union. Western Communism never quite recovered from this blow to its credibility. Hitler's old ideological associates were equally dismayed at this sudden friendship with the archenemy and could only take comfort in the reflection that politics makes strange bedfellows.

Qualms on each side were eased by the solid territorial gains and by the discomfiture of the democracies, which had again missed the boat. In the spring and summer of 1939, half-hearted approaches to Stalin from France and Britain failed to achieve anything. One reason was the attitude of the states to which Britain had given guarantees— Poland and Rumania. They would still not consent to the passage of Russian troops across their territory, which was essential in any military alliance aimed at Germany. In all good faith the British and French could not compel their allies to do so. Poland and Rumania feared the USSR at least as much as Nazi Germany and could not see jumping into the fire to escape the frying pan.

What could the western European democracies offer Stalin? Not annexations of territory, as Hitler did. They could only offer to help defend eastern Europe against Germany. But in the first place, they had already given their guarantees to Poland and Rumania and thus did not have this as a bargaining counter; beyond this, the Communist dictator did not thrust them; further, what effective aid could they bring to this region? Buying time for the restoration of his military machine, which had been badly disorganized by the purge of a high percentage of its senior officers,[3] Stalin evidently saw no alternative to a deal with Hitler. The Nazi-Soviet Pact was pushed hard from the German side; Hitler was burning for his campaign against Poland. He gave orders to prepare

[3] Estimates given by Robert Conquest in his *Great Terror* include 14 of the 16 army commanders purged, all 8 admirals, 60 of 67 corps commanders, 136 of 199 divisional commanders, 221 of 397 brigade commanders, and 75 of 80 members of the Supreme Military Soviet.

for the campaign on the same day that the pact was signed, August 23. The secret articles of this nonaggression pact divided Poland into Russian and German spheres of influence, and within a month the country had been partitioned. While Germany got the lion's share of Poland, the Baltic states, including Lithuania, fell to Russia.

Though Mussolini attempted to mediate, there was to be no salvation from war via a Munich agreement this time. Other last-minute peace efforts through the mediation of a Swede, Birger Dahlerus, which began on the 23rd, led to pleas from London that the Poles negotiate, that is, give up territory to Germany. The Poles refused, or at any rate they delayed too long for Hitler, who ordered German troops to cross the Polish frontier on September 1. When a still hesitant Neville Chamberlain reported to a restive British House of Commons on that day, a member of his own party rose to ask the Labour spokesman, Arthur Greenwood, to "speak for England," and the Tories as well as the Labourites cheered when Greenwood pressed for war. The British ultimatum came on September 3, ordering Hitler to call back his troops or stand in a state of war with Britain. France followed suit later the same day. Save for Russia, the major states of Europe were at war. Stalin momentarily rejoiced.

In 1914, Germany had faced war on two fronts against the powerful encirclement of Russia, France, and Great Britain. In 1939, she had divided her foes—or they had divided themselves—and Russia was neutralized. In 1914, Germany struck first at France. She was to attack France again this time, eight months later, but the war began in 1939 with an attack on a country that had not existed in 1914. It is also interesting that at the beginning of both World War I and World War II, Germany misjudged the British. On each occasion the Germans were confident that England would stay neutral. Both times, after some hesitation England decided that she could not resign the Continent to a powerful Germany. The balance of power again was decisive; but in 1939, the ideological currents were stronger. German Nazism and its leader had become a hateful symbol to the British, more so than the kaiser and the Prussian militarists had been at the start of World War I. In 1939, Germany was more clearly the brazen aggressor; but Hitler had not intended to start a *general* war. Germany was not prepared for that.

These are some of the comparisons that may be made between the origins of the two world wars of the twentieth century. The astute student will think of others; but the fact of war was the same. This one would last even longer, prove even more destructive, spread even farther throughout the world. It would end once again in the ruin of Germany, but the path to that destination would not be the same. It would again lead through the intervention, somewhat belatedly, of the United States of America. It would include a smashing Germany victory in France, unlike 1914; but it would also involve what the German leaders of 1914–1918 steadily refused to undertake, a massive invasion of Russia.

The Second World War, 1939-1940

10

The Wehrmacht Triumphant, 1939–1940

World War II was a gigantic tidal wave of conflict that engulfed the entire globe, affecting the lives of nearly every one of its more than two billion inhabitants. It took a ghastly toll of lives and caused suffering too immense to be told. When he began it with what appeared to be a short and simple annihilation of hapless Poland, Hitler cannot have had any idea of how the war would spread. Out of this titanic upheaval came incalculable changes in governments, economies, societies, ideas. The imagination can hardly encircle it, and the documents of history can only suggest its magnitude, even though it has become the most written-about historical subject of all time.

The war began with Germany quickly overrunning Poland in September 1939. A curiously unreal optimism prevailed among the Western allies at the beginning of the war. The French commander-in-chief, General Gamelin, believed that "Hitler will collapse the day we declare war on Germany." The British thought a bloodless application of economic warfare would soon bring Germany to her knees. But the armored *panzer* divisions knifed through Poland's plain, which provided excellent terrain for tanks. The weather smiled on Germany—no rain.

The Poles had an army not much inferior to Germany's in number but far less well equipped, with scarcely any tanks and a much smaller air force. It was all over in a few weeks, and the Russians moved into the eastern portion in accordance with the secret agreement. France and Britain honored their commitment to Poland by declaring war on Germany, but they did nothing else except drop propaganda leaflets. Gamelin promised a French land offensive within sixteen days, but by that time it was too late. The Chamberlain government in London was firmly opposed to any military action. Hitler had not misread his adversaries.

It has been argued that any sort of attack on the western front, where the French and British much outnumbered the Germans, would have done Hitler in. The military opposition, centered on Generals Beck and Halder, might have moved against him. But the democracies were still morally if not physically unprepared for an offensive war. And so the travail of Poland began. The first victim of the war was the worst; some 20 percent of the Polish people were to be killed, the large majority simply murdered in one way or another. In this the Germans were assisted by the Russians, who shipped several hundred thousand Poles to prison camps and shot thousands of Polish officers at Katyn. The Nazis, of course, saw the Poles as a subrace to be eliminated in favor of German settlers. The Polish government escaped to London.

Hitler, who always thought in terms of a *Blitzkreig*—a war won in a lightning thrust—paused after the conquest of Poland. He put out some feelers to the Allies, who refused to listen. Western opinion had completely hardened against the Nazi. The winter of 1939–1940 witnessed what the French called the *drôle de guerre* and the Americans called the "phony war." The war was said to be a joke or a fraud. The British opposed any plans for opening an offensive, at least for the moment; they had convinced themselves that an economic blockade and boycott could win the war, and if any British statesman had the will to send troops back to another continental holocaust, his name was not Neville Chamberlain. The British did use this time to good advantage, however, in building planes. The French government and probably the French people were also without a will to war. Observers reported soldiers' morale low in many of the Maginot Line forts. The Communists in France now devoted their talents to ridiculing the war and fomenting strikes in munition factories.

At the same time, in this strange interlude of deceptive calm before the storm, the note of Allied overconfidence continued, too. In late November early events in the war that the Soviet Union had suddenly launched against Finland enhanced Allied illusions. This brazenly aggressive assault by a large power on its tiny neighbor strained Soviet-

Western relations even more, blighting whatever chance remained for friendship after the Nazi-Soviet pact. A wave of sympathy for Finland swept the democracies; Hitler was almost forgotten for the moment in anger at Stalin. Both totalitarian regimes seemed alike. The defeats that the Finns at first inflicted on the Russians in this winter war convinced Western leaders that Russia was "a colossus with feet of clay." Perhaps both dictatorial states were. Would not the German as well as Russian regime, lacking popular support, collapse at the first serious test? Hitler hesitated to attack because he was afraid, people convinced themselves. There was talk in France and Britain of going to war against *both* Germany and Russia—inconceivable later, but possible in the garish light of the *drôle de guerre* months. Some military men and politicians in Paris and London half-seriously discussed striking at the Baku oil fields in the Caucusus from Syria and Turkey. Moscow, picking up the scent of such stories, confirmed its already deep suspicions of the British and French. Never was illusion more rampant, policymakers more at sea.

As Russia finally overcame valiant Finnish resistance to win the winter war and annex strategically valuable territory near Leningrad, Germany was preparing for the classic *Blitzkrieg* against France and Belgium in the spring of 1940. In fact, Hitler cancelled orders to attack or prepare to attack no fewer than eleven times between November and April, either because of the weather or because of foot-dragging by the generals, who argued Germany was not ready. During a confrontation on November 5 Hitler shouted at General von Brauchitsch to shut up. There was an assassination attempt on Hitler on November 8 in Munich, but the generals did not act. Hitler continued during this period to build a separate high command (the OKW) with his own men in control, over the head of the OKH—an armed forces high command over the army high command.

The first major clash between Germany and Britain took place at sea, far from Europe. After being chased into the River Plate in South America by British cruisers, the German small battleship *Graf Spee* finally destroyed itself (December 13–17). In February, a British destroyer attacked a German ship in Norwegian waters, and the British and French soon mined the Skagerrak area. German sea and airborne forces then invaded Norway, also occupying Denmark. Norwegian resistance, although aided by British naval power, could not prevent a rapid German conquest during the month of April. The seizure of Norway was cleverly planned and showed the superiority of German air power to British sea power in such narrow waters.

This was but the warm-up for the next month's spectacular campaign, when the western front burst into flames. But this time, unlike

1914, the campaign exploded in a fantastic war of movement. It is said that the French and British thought in terms of defensive war, mesmerized by a Maginot Line psychology that went back to the lessons of the last war. But in fact the French did attack, and by doing so they committed a fatal error. While the Maginot defenses would surely hold in the south, Belgium was not fortified, and it was here that the Germans were expected to strike. When on May 10 they did attack Belgium, along with Luxemburg and the Netherlands, French and British forces went into Belgium to aid King Leopold III's army. Unfortunately in doing so they left their right flank exposed. The hilly, forested area of the Ardennes, in southeastern Belgium, was terrain not thought suitable for tanks and motorized vehicles. It was here that the Germans showed their mastery of a new art of warfare.

The fall of France and Belgium within six weeks was one of the most stunning events in all history. In the bitter post mortems among the French, all kinds of allegations were made. Paul Reynaud said that the French had neither allied themselves nor fortified themselves nor armed themselves. But the French, who had spent vast sums on the Maginot fortifications, actually had more tanks than the Germans and probably even had better ones. It was neither in the quantity nor the quality of their armored vehicles that the Germans excelled, but in knowing how to use them. Rather than dispersing them among infantry divisions as auxiliary forces, young German officers massed the tanks in divisions and used them in combination with motorized infantry, tactical air power, and parachute troops. They were able to knife through in a "scythe cut," as Winston Churchill termed it, and then fan out in a war of mobility, spreading confusion among the defenders. The irony was that a French officer, Charles de Gaulle, early had developed such ideas in 1934.

The success of these tactics astonished even Hitler. From the Ardennes breakthrough the *panzer* forces fanned out to attack the rear of both the Maginot defenses and the Allied troops advancing into Belgium. At the same time, another scythe cut to the south, in Alsace, slashed down the northwest slopes of the Jura Mountains and then turned northeast to take the French in the rear. Through these apertures opened by the *panzer* divisions sped motor-borne troops to cut communications, disrupt supply lines, and generally spread confusion deep behind the enemy lines. They raced to the English Channel at Abbeville, thus cutting the Allied armies in two. Rotterdam and Brussels fell; the Germans were soon at Boulogne, and after much debate, King Leopold III's government decided to surrender. This was on May 28, only eighteen days after the start of the offensive. The British forces, some 250,000 strong, which had rushed to the defense of their allies, were forced back against the sea at Ostend and Dunkerque, along with many French troops.

By June 5, the British had managed to evacuate over 300,000 soldiers across the English Channel from Dunkerque, a miracle that lifted British spirits. The German high command does not seem to have understood the extent of the victory, and they were not prepared to exploit it fully. One of the numerous might-have-beens of World War II about which amateur strategists argue is whether the Dunkerque evacuation might have been prevented by bolder German action. But the Germans were in pursuit of other prey, and they now turned southward to complete the conquest of France. On June 10, Italy declared war on France and tried to invade southern France. On June 13, Germans entered Paris. On June 15, the World War I fortress of Verdun fell. On June 16–17, World War I hero Pétain became head of the French government and immediately asked for an armistice!

This *Blitzkrieg* was at least relatively humane, in terms of casualties. Total lives lost were no more than 30,000 Germans and 100,000 Allied. The French and the Belgians had preferred surrender to hopeless struggle. In later years the French engaged in lengthy self-scrutiny about the shattering defeat. The Right blamed the Left, the Left blamed the Right, and everybody blamed the politicians, who blamed the generals. More objectively, many felt it was inhuman to expect France to fight a second war twenty years after she had lost the prime of an entire generation in the first one. More analytically, some claimed that the French stuck to their strategy of 1914–1918, which had stressed the defensive, while, in an example of what Arnold J. Toynbee named creative "challenge-and-response," the Germans had been stimulated to a fresh consideration of military operations.

It was not a pretty scene; defeat seldom is. The British almost all thought that the French refused to fight. "F---ing French scamper as soon as they see a jerry tank or plane," was a typical British comment, "officers first." But the French believed that the "dirty English" arrived too late and then saved themselves by evacuation, leaving the French and Belgians behind. According to the armistice that was signed on June 22, France was to be disarmed and three-fifths of her land given to Germany. In early July, the British sank or captured a portion of the French fleet at Oran in Algeria and seized other French ships in British ports, because they regarded Marshal Pétain's government as a German satellite.

The Germans soon opened a bombing campaign against England. The only bright spots were the Dunkerque evacuation; the arrival of new British Prime Minister Churchill, who said, "We shall go on to the end. . . . We shall never surrender"; and the hope of help from the United States, which was jolted out of her complacency by the fall of France. General Charles de Gaulle set up a Free French government in London, rallying a few Frenchmen to continue somehow the resistance against Germany.[1]

The Widening War, 1940–1941

The whirlwind of battle swirled into Africa, Asia, and Russia within the next year. In the summer and fall of 1940, chief attention focused on "the battle of Britain." With Russia still an ally of Germany and the United States just beginning to think about getting involved, only Great Britain stood against Germany and her allies. These now included Japan as well as Italy, the three countries having signed a pact on September 27, 1940. Hitler's spectacular success withered the faint traces of opposition to him in Germany and made him seem even more of a superman. He had in fact overridden caution among the establishment generals to back the *panzer* advocates, Manstein and Guderian, whose ideas had proved so successful.

The man who now assumed leadership of the meager forces standing in Hitler's path was no ordinary mortal, either. At sixty-five, Winston Churchill could look back, though he never did, on a remarkable career as writer, soldier, politician, historian—he also painted. He was the British prodigy of the century and had been recognized as such from his early years, when he bulldozed his way to prominence by sheer exuberance. He had fought in wars and written about them later, from his early accounts of expeditions in India and *The River War* in the Sudan (Kitchener's 1898 campaign) through World War I, where we recall his misfortunes with the Dardanelles plan. Churchill had always inspired mistrust in direct proportion to his genius, audacity, and gargantuan energy. He had been in and out of both major political parties until neither one was sure of him. He was often out of step with party and with public. (An example is the abdication crisis of 1936, when he sided passionately with Edward VIII.) He was the bad boy of politics, thought to have, amid all his scintillating gifts, one fatal flaw: lack of judgment. But he possessed one gift that, above all others, guaranteed his political fame, the gift of a matchless eloquence. And he was thoroughly at home in war. "His high and turbulent spirit

---

[1] "Why have you brought me this gloomy brigadier?" Churchill asked Major-General Louis Spears when the latter returned from France with de Gaulle. "Because no one else would come," was the reply.

is entirely happy only when politics and war are merged in one theme," A. G. Gardiner wrote.

Many weaknesses, in fact, Churchill had. His record of having steadfastly opposed nazism since the beginning was not perfect. He had praised Hitler's restoration of the German people's spirit in 1936— a generous appreciation of other nations' achievements was one of Churchill's many attractive qualities—and in 1937 he had said that if forced to choose between nazism and communism he would take the former. A Liberal in his youth, Churchill was now a *bête-noire* to the Left because of his fierce anticommunism and imperialism. But Austria opened his eyes to the danger of Hitler's domination, and he fought the Munich appeasement, with very few allies. Now his hour came, and he was to make the most of it. He immediately transformed both the spirit and the tempo of the government. Whitehall would never again be the same. Sleeping only a few hours a night, Churchill seemed to be everywhere, bombarding everyone with memos ("Action This Day," the famous stamp demanded). He cut through red tape and galvanized Britons into action by the sheer force of his will, spreading a spirit of confidence throughout the government even as his eloquent speeches heartened the people.

By his own admission, Churchill had not foreseen the new developments in warfare that the Germans exploded on the world. He had not "comprehended the violence of the revolution effected since the last war by the incursion of a mass of fast-moving armour," he said in the history of the Second World War that he lived to write, as he had written the history of the first. Only a few had. (Churchill might have learned from two British military writers, Generals J. F. C. Fuller and Basil Liddell Hart, who were among the first to argue, totally without effect, that armored and motorized vehicles could revolutionize warfare.) But in 1938 the British had foreseen the importance of building "fighter" airplanes for the defense of their island, a decision for which the chief credit seems best given to Thomas Inskip. And the British were leaders in operational applications of radar, the recently discovered system of detecting the position and motion of objects in the sky by means of radio waves. The English physicist Henry Tizard was most prominent in this application of radar to air defense. The Spitfires and radar were to save Britain and the world from Hitler's power in the fall of 1940.

Control of the air was preliminary, perhaps, to an invasion of Britain or to uncontested bombings of British cities by the *Luftwaffe*, which would surely force England to sue for peace. It was up to Fighter Command to make the Germans pay an unacceptable price for their bombing of Britain. We know now that the British had another weapon in this battle: knowledge of the German secret code used to transmit *Luftwaffe* messages. Early German raids, in August, were aimed primarily at British air fields; they were designed to weaken the enemy's air power. On September 7, raids on London began, continuing to a climax on September 15, when 1,000 planes came at London. Each night brought more terror from the skies. Hitler had been infuriated by a British raid on Berlin and vowed to "wipe their cities off the map." While the *Luftwaffe* suffered heavy losses, so did the British Fighter Command, which was losing both planes and pilots faster than it could replace them. "Never was so much owed by so many to so few," Churchill said in his tribute to the fighter pilots.

Hitler set September 22 as the date for the invasion of England, then on September 17 called it off, because British bombers struck hard at the invasion ports on the French and Belgian side of the Channel. Temporarily at least, Britain was saved. The world watched her heroic resistance, and American opinion was deeply affected. Following the shock of France's fall, the U.S. moved rapidly away from the stringent neutrality she had heretofore adopted in favor of aid to the foes of Nazi Germany; but noninterventionists had argued that it was futile to enter a war Hitler had already won. Now it seemed that Britain was going to hold out. "Give us the tools and we will finish the job," the unquenchable Churchill declared. His inspiring speeches struck the American imagination, and he formed a close relationship with President Franklin Roosevelt, once a foe of American involvement in overseas quarrels. American aid now began to flow into Britain. But Atlantic shipping absorbed punishing blows from German U-boats.

Although German air attacks did not end after September, they tailed off sharply. Both winter weather and losses reduced them; and the Germans largely abandoned mass bombing of cities in favor of again concentrating on ports and shipping. Antiaircraft guns and balloon cables helped cause the loss of ninety German bombers in the first three months of 1941. By April, Hitler was looking to the East. He had forgotten operation "Sea Lion" the invasion of England, in favor of "Barbarossa," the Russian campaign. It is remarkable that the British, having shown that terror bombings could not break a people's will to fight, soon adopted the same "Victory through air power" formula themselves. They sought to destroy Germany with their own bombers, supplemented by American ones from 1942 on.

In March 1941, the United States Congress passed the Lend-Lease Act, granting all possible aid to Britain without counting the cost, after having earlier granted credits. German submarines could not prevent the shipment of millions of tons of convoyed supplies across the Atlantic. Though the United States hesitated to enter the war as a belligerent, "all aid short of war" was the American policy.

War in North Africa began to attract attention in 1940. In September the Italians left Libya in an offensive against Egypt. But British forces under General Wavell counterattacked in December and routed the Italians, whose military ineptness now became the subject of bitter jokes among the Germans. (In 1939, Churchill is supposed to have responded to a German who was boasting of having Italy as an ally by saying, "It's only fair, we had them last time.") It was in the wake of Wavell's successes that the German commander, Erwin Rommel, landed in Tripoli on February 12 to begin one of the war's legendary stories. The "desert fox" was to bring *panzer* tactics to the sands of North Africa with brilliant success in 1941, spreading panic among Germany's foes.

Hitler also won 1941 victories in Greece and Crete. Italian ineptitude helped precipiate these victories; in October 1940, Mussolini attacked Greece from Albania, which he had managed to conquer in 1939. He was defeated, however; the British helped Greece by bombing the Italian fleet. German troops entered Greece after the Yugoslavian campaign of April 1941, capturing British supplies. Then Germany invaded Crete with air power and parachute troops and brilliantly defeated the British navy there, forcing evacuation of a small British army to Cyprus and Egypt. The Greek king fled as the Germans took command of Greece.

But Hitler did not pursue a Mediterranean strategy. Had he done so, theorists speculate, he might have cut the British "lifeline" of Suez and Gibraltar (though in fact traffic was successfully taking the long route around South Africa). He might even have been able to link up with the Japanese after their entry into war in late 1941. But Hitler was not in search of colonies and preferred partnership with the British Empire to war with it. He had already decided on war against Russia to win a "heartland" empire for Germany.

Franco helped frustrate Hitler's Mediterranean plans by stubbornly refusing to be drawn into the war. After a meeting with the Spanish dictator on the Spanish border in the autumn of 1940, Hitler said he would rather have several teeth extracted than go through another one. Franco formally acceded to the Axis pact but refused to permit German troops to cross the Pyrenees and march on Gibraltar. Hitler, as Franco probably knew, "was not in a position to force his hand, having already become a prisoner of his own timetable of aggression in the East," according to historian Donald Detwiler.

After the French debacle, Churchill tried to restore contacts with

Moscow, but he had no luck. Stalin was seemingly committed to his pact with Hitler. The latter's victory in the West, however, encouraged the Russians to a bold policy in eastern Europe. Stalin seized the Baltic states and annexed territory from Rumania; in Rumania he went beyond what the Nazi-Soviet Pact had assigned to the Russian sphere of influence, trying to get Bukovinia as well as Besserabia. Stalin must have thought that Nazi Germany had the feet of clay, not his Soviet Russia. These were tough tactics, and they deeply annoyed Hitler.

Soviet Foreign Minister Molotov's visit to Berlin in November 1940 was the last straw. The Russians staked out claims to dominance in eastern Europe, which Hitler had long marked for his own. Despite the agreement, he never intended to allow Russia a place in Europe. Stalin might have found a place in Hitler's world had he looked eastward rather than westward—to India or the Middle East. Hitler encouraged this, but when the Soviets stubbornly insisted on a role in Europe, he determined to make war on them. A directive to seek a military showdown with the USSR by May 15 was issued on December 18.

The greatest mystery about the German attack on Russia, which began on June 22, 1941, is why the Russians were caught by surprise. German policies in southeast Europe from early 1941 on should have alarmed Stalin. Most of the small states in this area jumped onto the Berlin-Rome-Tokyo bandwagon—Hungary on November 20, Rumania three days later, Bulgaria on March 1. Only Yugoslavia balked; the leaders who signed the Tripartite Pact on March 25 were overthrown in a coup at Belgrade the next day, and the ensuing government, while it was careful not to appear anti-German, angered Hitler by seeking Russian support. German troops, already massing in the east, overran Yugoslavia in the first weeks of April. They went on to finish off the Greeks and tangle with the Royal Navy in Grecian waters. This Balkan excursion, caused by Yugoslavia's reluctance to join Hitler's New Order and by Italian problems in Greece, delayed the beginning of Operation Barbarossa by a month.

Everybody except Stalin seems to have known about the coming attack on Russia. The British, of course, were reading the German code. In May, Hitler's old comrade Rudolf Hess parachuted into England, without Hitler's permission, to tell the British of the impending Russian campaign and seek to bring about a negotiated peace between Germany and Britain. But Churchill already knew about Barbarossa and had decided he would continue the war against Germany even with the Soviet Union as an ally. Both Churchill and Roosevelt tried to warn Stalin. But the overly suspicious Russian leader thought they were trying to trick him. Watching the Germans move into Yugoslavia, Bulgaria, Rumania, and even Finland, Stalin unaccountably refused to believe they would attack Russia, and he was caught totally unprepared on June 22. Russian troops guarding the border fell into confusion because they received no coherent orders; Stalin did not credit news of the massive attack for hours and then sank into bewildered inaction for more than a week.

Three million German invaders had achieved virtually total surprise. Hundreds of Soviet planes were destroyed on the ground; hundreds of thousands of Soviet troops were surrounded and killed or captured as the now-familiar *panzer* scythe strokes cut deeply into the Russian plains. The Russians had learned nothing from the western campaign of a year ago; the purged army was commanded by incompetents. Among Hitler's reasons for taking the enormous risk of waging war against Russia, a major one was his conviction that victory would be easy—another *Blitzkrieg* would repeat the lightning successes in Poland and France. In the first few months of the war, nothing seemed to contradict this view.

High Tide of the Axis, 1941–1942

"No battle in history compares to it," exclaimed Alan Clark, an historian of the German-Russian war. This was "the head-on crash of the two greatest armies, the two most absolute systems in the world." Not even the first days of August 1914 could rival this onslaught. More than three million Germans, with 3,500 tanks and thousands of planes opposed an even huger Russian army, not badly equipped—its tanks again, in quality as well as quantity, probably superior to the Germans'. But the open plain was made for the German tactics, and as the Russian giant stood stunned and bewildered, the Germans drove forward on three fronts to wheel around and encircle vast numbers of Russian troops. In the south, the incompetence of Marshal Budyenny, an old political Communist, lost a great army at Kiev. At the peak of his genius, Heinz Guderian led a breakthrough in the center, annihilating Timoshenko's army. By July 3, General Halder was saying "the war has virtually been won," and in October Goebbels announced "the war is over." No wonder: by then, it is estimated, Russia had lost 2½ million soldiers, 18,000 tanks, 14,000 aircraft, and more than 300,000 square miles of land, including the richest part of that immense country.

Even as Goebbels spoke, however, there were signs that things were going to get difficult for the Germans. The vast distances; supply and communications problems, which worsened as the German armies got further and further from home; the scarce roads; the fall rains; and Russia's rally after the first shock were beginning to have an effect.

By this time, too, material was flowing into Russia from the United States. Gradually the Russians found able commanders, learned how to fight this kind of war, and brought new armies in from the east. The gaping wounds Germany administered with the first terrible blow would undoubtedly have destroyed a more advanced society. Perhaps Russia was saved by her backwardness; it is often said that the Germans were defeated by their successes. These were the paradoxes of a war unlike any other ever fought.

Among the many factors that joined to determine success or failure in history's greatest battle, two stand out: the question of German military grand strategy and German policy toward the conquered Russian people. In the German High Command, a great debate pitted Hitler against his chief generals to some extent. Those who were not his creatures—men like Halder and Brauchitsch—basically favored a single-pronged drive on Moscow. Hitler, who had learned to scorn the professional military mind during his experience with the French campaign, stuck to a three-pronged plan. Under Hitler's strategy, a northern finger would reach for the second largest Russian city, Leningrad, and a southern one would push deep into the Ukraine and beyond, toward the Black Sea, the Donetz basin, and then the oil-rich Caucasus. This was to risk straining German resources beyond the breaking point. The southern front, particularly, became too large to be manageable.

What was to be done with all this captured land and all these captured people? Here the Nazis' racial arrogance proved to be their own worst enemy. Millions of Russians felt little or no loyalty to the Communists; the Ukraine was a potential mass of unrest. A German policy based on treating the conquered people sympathetically could certainly have offered prospects of success. Instead, brutal German treatment aimed at enslaving or exterminating the Slavs brought bitter hatred of the invader, and partisan bands arose to harass him.

If the German goal had been to destroy Russia's armed strength, she had failed to reach it. Despite the enormous losses inflicted, a land with three times the population of Germany could raise fresh armies and, with Allied aid, equip them. If the goal was to seize and exploit the Ukraine and other western Russian lands, the task was rendered all but impossible by German failure to win the cooperation of the inhabitants. The Nazis had a bear by the tail, a terribly wounded but nevertheless formidable giant. Their woes were to be compounded by the weather, which now compensated for having smiled on them earlier. The worst winter in 140 years was about to bring unbelievable suffering to soldiers who had not even been equipped with winter clothing.

On December 10, the thermometer plunged to an unbelievable $-60°$, and men froze to death in their tracks. In early December, just as the Japanese were steaming towards Pearl Harbor on the assumption that Germany had won the war, Marshal Zhukov launched a counter-offensive that drove the freezing Germans back a few miles—enough to save Moscow. The Russian offensive soon petered out, but the German force was spent for the time being; the *Blitzkrieg* had failed. After relieving Brauchitsch and assuming personal command of the armies as well as the combined *Wehrmacht*, Hitler ordered a new offensive in the spring of 1942 and again achieved temporary successes. But he was headed for the fateful rendezvous at Stalingrad.

Meanwhile the United States had entered the war, or rather her entrance had been assured by the actions of others. Japan had taken advantage of the collapse of France in 1940 and occupied Indochina (Vietnam, Laos, Cambodia). She had evident designs on the oil-rich Dutch East Indies (today Indonesia). In September, she signed the Tripartite Pact with Italy and Germany. The United States protested these Japanese advances in Asia and began to impose economic embargoes on the shipment of products to Japan. In the summer of 1941,

Pearl Harbor, December 7, 1941: The USS *California* sinking. The Japanese surprise air attack on the American naval base at Pearl Harbor in Hawaii brought the United States into the European as well as the Asiatic war.
United Press International.

Churchill and Roosevelt met and agreed to put pressure on Japan to call off her expansionist ambitions, which might threaten the British possessions of Malaya, Burma, and India, as well as the American-held Philippine Islands. The United States then froze all Japanese credits and assets and added oil to the embargo list. Negotiations between the U.S. and Japan went on for several months in the late summer and fall of 1941, but they got nowhere. On December 7, the Japanese astonished the world by striking boldly in a surprise attack from the air on the Pearl Harbor naval base in Hawaii. It was startlingly successful, but it aroused the angry Americans to an all-out war effort. When Hitler declared war against the U.S. in accordance with his role as Japan's ally, the U.S. war effort was also directed against Germany.

The United States had been a de facto economic ally of Great Britain against Nazi Germany and Italy at least since the Lend-Lease Act. She had even been a military ally insofar as she convoyed supply ships and fought German submarines in the Atlantic. She had promptly extended the benefits of Lend-Lease to the Soviet Union on June 22, 1941. Hitler doubtless thought that the war against Japan would divert American strength away from him to the Far East. Some American critics of the Roosevelt foreign policy could not understand the president's hostility toward Japan, which formed the background of the Pearl Harbor attack, and a few charged him with conniving to achieve American entrance into the war by provoking an attack, his real goal being the defeat of Hitler.

But whatever the explanation, once aroused to fighting fury by the Japanese "crime," the United States, with its tremendous industrial power, proved able to sustain both wars, unloosing an awesome flow of tanks, planes, ships, and other materials of war while mobilizing millions of men and women in the armed forces. In the American wartime mind, the European Fascist dictators merged with the Japanese warlords in an image of a single plot to conquer and enslave the world. In actuality, Japan and Germany fought separate wars for separate purposes and engaged in no joint military planning. But Japan's ambitions to create an East Asian "coprosperity sphere" under her control was somewhat analogous to Hitlerite Germany's drive for a National Socialist Europe headquartered at Berlin. The USA now stood fully committed to all-out war against both German and Japanese imperialism, with the almost unanimous backing of a thoroughly bellicose public opinion. It was hardly a good omen for the Germans, who were rapidly becoming bogged down in the vast spaces of Russia.

The Japanese followed up their stunning strike against the American Pacific fleet in Pearl Harbor with a series of additional victories, soon taking the Philippines and the great British base at

Singapore, which fell swiftly to the determined Nipponese in a defeat that shocked England. Within a few months Japan ruled all of East Asia and the Pacific, including Indochina, Thailand, Burma, Hong Kong, Malaya, the Dutch East Indies, and the Philippines. The Chinese government retreated to Chungking, deep in the interior, as Japan took control of the coastal regions and major cities of China. The Japanese mastery of a new mode of warfare combining land and sea operations paralleled the German leadership in mechanized land warfare. About midway of 1942. with the Germans again smashing deep into Russia and the Japanese on the borders of India, the so-called Axis came closest to winning the battle for the world. But the tide was about to ebb.

This was also Rommel's year in Africa. The glamorous and capable commander of the Afrika Korps used concentrated armored divisions, joined to artillery and motorized infantry, with spectacular success in the desert war. Initially handicapped by lack of support from Berlin, since all forces had been thrown into the Russian campaign, Rommel received reenforcements in 1942 and drove on Egypt, capturing the port of Tobruk before finally being checked at El Alamein, only seventy miles from Alexandria.

It was in October that the tide really turned in Africa. A British counteroffensive was now led by another of the great World War II commanders, Bernard Montgomery, who abandoned the old tactics to imitate Rommel's massed tanks and artillery. The North African war became an epic of World War II, curiously beloved to all who fought in it and marked by a kind of chivalric grandeur that contrasts with its real importance. It certainly produced two of the most fascinating military mystiques, those of Rommel and Montgomery. But it was less the main arena of world struggle than a colorful sideshow.

El Alamein stands with Stalingrad and, in the Pacific, the naval battles of Midway and Coral Sea as the moment when the Axis was checked at its zenith, thereafter to sink. But of these crucial battles, the mammoth encounter on the Volga was the greatest.

German Defeats

A surprising feature of the war was Germany's lack of preparation for it. Committed to a lightning war intended to last only a few weeks, Hitler was as cool to a protracted bloodletting of the World War I sort as was Winston Churchill. Conversion to "total war," with the whole economy geared to war production under emergency government dictatorship, came to Germany later than it did to the Allies. Only in 1942, with the dismaying fact of his failure to blitz Russia staring at him, did Hitler move toward a war economy. Fritz Todt and then Albert Speer became powerful national economic administrators. A 55 percent increase in arms production took place in Germany in the first half of 1942.

As in other warring countries, women assumed a greatly increased role in both industrial employment and in the nonfighting part of the *Wehrmacht*. Foreign workers and prisoners of war provided a slave-labor force numbering as many as six or seven million. Germany exploited France and other occupied countries effectively by levying vast sums for "occupation costs" and by unequal bilateral trade agreements. In fairness, it should be noted that the Allies also used prisoners of war as a labor supply; at the end of the war some 225,000 prisoners were working in Britain, most of them Italians.

In Poland and Russia, "the savagery of the German administration produced an economic chaos which both prevented any rational economic exploitation of these territories for war purposes and any rational planning for the economic future there," says historian Alan Milward. And the National Socialist administration in general continued to be chaotic, mixing bureaucratic expertise with party fanaticism and the private empires of various high Nazis. Göring, one of those in charge of economic policy in occupied lands, declared, "I intend to plunder and plunder heavily." "We will take everything we can use," Hitler affirmed. Plunder in Russia was simple and direct. In France, Norway, and the Low Countries it was indirect but almost equally exploitative. To replace expelled natives, nearly a million Germans were recruited to settle in western Poland. This was the beginning of a projected long-term policy, managed by Himmler, of colonizing the Slavic East with Nordic "pioneers." But in the main any orderly planning was postponed until after the war.

In 1942, the Allies began pounding German cities from the air. Nevertheless, that same year Hitler was able to mount another great offensive in Russia with even more tanks, planes, and guns than he had the previous year.

Hitler again debated with his generals whether or not to resume the offensive, for the always conservative military establishment feared disaster. But Hitler was now totally in charge, and he was not a man to refuse a gamble. With the United States now in the war, Germany faced a growingly powerful world coalition and needed a quick victory. Russia had surely received mortal wounds and needed only to be finished off. The drive toward Stalingrad was a compromise between the old one-pronged versus many-pronged strategies, for from this center of industry and communications on the Volga (today it is called Volgograd), armies might wheel north to take Moscow from the rear or south toward the Caucasus. But Stalingrad was more than a thousand miles from Berlin. Exposure to a Russian counteroffensive increased as the front lengthened.

One premature Soviet counterattack came to grief because the Russian central command continued to show incompetence.[2] Beginning on June 28, almost exactly one year after the start of the war, the German offensive broke through on either side of Kursk and below Kharkov, crossed the Don, and swept through the plains toward its goal. Again the Panzers seemed irresistible, again the Germans were jubilant; "the Russian is finished," Hitler exulted. But at the city of Stalingrad, named after the Communist chieftain, the most terrible battle in history was shaping up. It was the Verdun of World War II: first a magnet, it became a symbol. The Russians pulled troops from the Moscow area to defend it; the Germans insisted on taking it. A million men struggled for possession of a few square miles. They fought street to street and literally room to room until the city was rubble; then they went on fighting in the rubble. The battle dragged on for months, beginning in late August.

In November, a Russian offensive from behind Stalingrad began to encircle and trap the exhausted German army. Finally, on February 2, what remained of a German army of half a million, now reduced to some 80,000, surrendered despite Hitler's orders to hold out to the last man, and their general was soon fronting a pro-Soviet movement. It was the first real German defeat, apart from El Alamein, and others were to follow. In Russia, a general Russian winter offensive recaptured Kursk, Rostov, and Kharkov, and in the north it broke the long siege of Leningrad, which had reduced that great city to a state of starvation. By this time Montgomery had driven Rommel out of Egypt, toward a final doom in Tunis, where 150,000 survivors of the Afrika Korps surrendered in April 1943. An Anglo-American force commanded by General Dwight D. Eisenhower had landed in French North Africa (Morocco and Algiers), overcome some token resistance from Vichyite French, and advanced on the German forces from the west to spring the trap on Rommel. Like Russia but in a smaller way, North Africa had proved to be a drain down which the Germans poured men and supplies, in the end to no avail. The destruction of German power there opened the way for an Allied invasion of first Sicily and then Italy in the summer of 1943. Meanwhile, however, it was from the air that

---

[2] It was on this occasion that General Vlasov became so disgusted that he let himself be captured by the Germans and later led an anti-Soviet "Free Russian" army. Vlasov was turned over to the Russians by the Allies after the war and executed. His position was, of course, weakened by the bestiality of Nazi rule in occupied Russia.

the Allies chiefly attacked Germany itself, and it was on the air that they pinned their chief hopes for victory.

Terror from the skies on a far larger scale than in the earlier war was a ghastly feature of the Second World War. The Germans, who had wiped out the center of Rotterdam during the 1940 assault on France and the Low Countries, plastered England in 1940 and 1941 in an attempt to break the will of the British. Then it was Germany's turn to suffer from incessant aerial pounding. Huge bombs were carried in planes larger than any known before. The First World War spared most civilians outside the immediate zone of battle; the second made them its chief victims. It was entirely appropriate that the war's end came when the invention of the atomic bomb forced the surrender of Japan after two cities had been virtually wiped out, each by a single awful explosion. Yet the war in the air also revealed surprising limitations of this horrible form of warfare. If the Germans failed to break the will of Britain and finally had to call off their attacks because of heavy losses, the Allies subsequently failed to break Germany, even thought they rained hundreds of times more bombs on her cities.

In 1942 the British, joined now by the Americans, thought that aerial bombardment could win the war by paralyzing German communications and destroying key industries. But this "strategic bombing" failed for lack of precision. Radar and fast fighter planes rendered daytime bombing too costly until quite late in the war, when better navigational systems and long-range fighter escort planes were developed. At night, it proved impossible to pinpoint targets as small as a particular factory. And so "stragteic bombing" evolved into "area bombing," the idea being to saturate highly industrialized areas on the assumption that something valuable was pretty certain to be hit; or, if not, at least the enemy would have to divert resources of labor and machinery to cleaning up. Quite often this strategy seemed to degenerate into rather indiscriminate bombing of cities without much attempt to distinguish between industrial and residential sections—often not far apart, in any case.

Since few believed that bombing could destroy a people's will to fight, after the first experiences, it is probably erroneous to speak of "terror bombing." Yet this appallingly inhumane policy eventually reduced most German cities nearly to rubble, killing or maiming hundreds of thousands of civilians as well as wiping out priceless historic buildings. Particularly infamous was the raid on refugee-crowded Dresden in February 1945, which killed as many as 50,000 helpless people.

Some of the bombs weighed as much as ten tons. Totals rose to a peak of 60,000 to 65,000 tons a month in 1944–1945, when round-the-clock bombing became the rule. German losses from the bombings can only be estimated, but a fair guess is 300,000 killed and 750,000 seriously injured. The amazing fact is that the many hundreds of thousands of tons of high explosives and incendiary bombs dropped on Germany (estimates of the total range from 2 to 2½ million tons for Germany and German-occupied countries, most of it on Germany proper) did not seem seriously to impair German war production. At least, it did not prevent a steady increase in the manufacture of tanks, planes, guns, ammunition, and other war supplies, which more than doubled in 1942 and continued to climb until about the middle of 1944. After that, the decline could plausibly be attributed to the defeats and invasion on land. By mid-1944 German armaments production as a whole was about 3¼ times as much as it had been in 1941. In return for what damage was done, the Allies paid a high price. No fewer than 57,000 British airmen died in these attacks. Much very expensive material was lost, too. The British were losing 170 big Lancaster bombers every month in 1943–1944. They once lost more than 100 bombers in a single raid (March 30, 1944, on Nuremberg). Altogether 18,000 U.S. and 22,000 British planes were lost or damaged beyond repair. The total cost of the bombing has been estimated at $85 billion.

In the end, the Allies had to do what the "victory through air power" school claimed they wouldn't, that is, mount a huge invasion of the Continent to defeat Germany. Those who called the bombing strategy a crime against civilization were less numerous than those who argued that it was a mistake simply in terms of efficiency: application of the same resources in other directions would have finished the war sooner.

Nevertheless many Germans were forced to undergo what Hamburg experienced in July of 1943, when fires started by days of intensive bombing raged out of control over most of the great city. The Allies were able to afford this expenditure of planes for incessant bombing because of the immense productivity of the American war industry. Nearly 100,000 bombers and 200,000 other planes came off assembly lines in the United States during the war, along with 86,000 tanks, 60,000,000 tons of shipping, and vast quantities of other miscellaneous materials of war. No other country came close to matching this record as a whole, though the Russians made more tanks and the Germans built 30,000 bombers, mostly smaller ones. British aircraft production also did extremely well, alone outproducing Germany.

The United States was able to supply the Soviet Union with motorized vehicles, tanks, and planes; with great amounts of food and other supplies, in quantities that certainly played a crucial role in keeping the Soviets afloat, however reluctant they were to admit this.

Already underway in significant amounts by 1942, total aid to Russia during the war amounted to around 17,500 aircraft, mostly pursuit planes or light bombers, 20,000 tanks, 140,000 jeeps, more than a million trucks, 400,000 submachine guns, over 4 million tons of food, and other supplies to a total value of at least $10 billion and a total weight of 16½ million tons. This stream of supplies travelled via three routes: to eastern Siberia from Alaska, over the oceans to Abadan on the Persian Gulf and thence across Iran, and—the shortest but most dangerous—the Arctic route to the northern Russian ports of Murmansk and Archangel. Nazi subs, planes, and battleships often made the last route a nightmare, but overall losses at sea were no more than 6 percent, or a million tons out of 17½ million shipped.

Courageous as they were, the Russians probably could not have prevailed against the Nazis without this freely given American aid, which was conveyed in American and British ships protected by American and British naval and air power. The Communist state owed its survival to capitalist America. All this the Americans contrived to do while also fighting the war against Japan; but grand strategy decided that the defeat of Germany was the first priority.

Bombing Germany and sending material aid did not suffice to please Stalin, who pressured the Allies to invade Europe, even to the point of threatening to make a separate peace with Hitler in 1943. The Stalingrad victory did not quite end the German threat. Indeed, Hitler, against the advice of his generals, managed another offensive in the summer of 1943. If they could shorten the front, hold key points, and build an elastic defense, the German generals thought, they could hold the Russians off indefinitely. At this point Hitler began to lose his grip on reality, seemingly preparing already for that *Götterdammerung* of destruction he arrived at two years later in the Berlin bunker. Refusing to retreat and forcing new offensives, he gave the Russians a chance to mount devastating counterassaults. Another mighty battle around Kursk staggered the Germans in July, after which the Russians pushed them steadily back, retaking Kharkov and then Kiev by the end of the year.

The Assault on "Fortress Europe"

The British were much more reluctant to launch an invasion of the Continent across the Channel from England than were the Americans, to whom it seemed obvious from the start that this was the shortest, most direct, most effective way of defeating Germany. "The fearful price we had to pay in human life and blood for the great offensives of the First World War was graven in my mind," Churchill conceded. In 1942 the Americans were forced to admit that the difficulties of such an operation were greater than they had thought, though American military leaders did not much like the decision made by President Roosevelt to appease Stalin (and their own itch for action) with the North African operation. Operation "Torch" (Africa) took the place of "Overlord" (invasion of Europe) for the time being, along with a stepping up of the bombing attacks on Germany. North Africa then led to the Italian invasion in the summer of 1943. This did not placate Stalin, and in the end it proved something of a sideshow.

The invasion did knock Italy out of the war, only to expose her to the horror of a Nazi occupation. The war had been a series of disasters for the Italians. They had no military victory to compensate for their steadily falling incomes, and Mussolini had lost all support. A wave of strikes crested in March 1943, even before the Allied invasion of Sicily from North Africa on July 10 and the bombing of Rome a few days later. Fortunately, the Allied bombers managed enough precision to avoid hitting St. Peter's or the Forum. There was a popular movement against fascism among not only the Communists and the Socialists but the more moderate parties, including the newly born Christian Democrats, as well. But the almost bloodless revolution that overthrew Mussolini on July 25 was a revolution from above, managed by army, clergy, and crown. The Fascist Grand Council, rescued from oblivion, voted against the now thoroughly deflated *Duce*, and King Victor Emmanuel III told him he was through. Too dispirited to resist, Mussolini allowed himself to be arrested, amid public rejoicing. The notables who overthrew Mussolini settled on old Marshal Pietro Badoglio, hero of the Ethiopian war, as his successor.

While publicly declaring that "the war continues," Badoglio looked despairingly for a way out of it, hoping for terms from the Allies. But the Americans and British, planning to invade the Italian mainland from Sicily on September 9, refused to grant any terms except those recently agreed upon among the Big Three (Roosevelt, Stalin, and, Churchill): unconditional surrender. This formula was destined for much controversy. While the Italian government hesitated before capitulating in so abject a manner, the Germans were able to move additional troops into Italy. Amid a fog of confusion and misunderstanding that has generated debate to this day, the Italians finally signed an armistice on September 2, just as Anglo-American troops landed in the south of Italy. There they discovered that German forces had seized control of Italy and were prepared to offer fierce resistance. To make matters worse, an Italian resistance movement, born at this time, was exposed to German revenge.

Some have thought that better timing might have forestalled the

German takeover, and they have blamed either the Badoglio government or the Allies or both. It is certain that the delay of six weeks between July 25 and September 2 helped the Germans. Mussolini, rescued or kidnapped by German paratroopers, again headed a pro-Nazi regime with headquarters in northern Italy near Verona. Enduring a bitter ten-day battle at Salerno before establishing a beachhead, Allied troops encountered further hard fighting in the rough country and narrow defiles of Italy. An attempt to outflank the German line by landing from the sea at Anzio, near Rome, early in 1944 incurred heavy casualties and failed to achieve its goal.

The Italian campaign came in for much criticism later. After invading Italy, the Allies lost some of their interest in this front, as they decided to make their major effort in the cross-Channel invasion—a decision, indeed, they had really made long since. Always something of a stopgap, the Mediterranean campaign suffered from the defect that one could not really get at Germany from this direction. The Alps lie between Italy and Germany, and no one thought an invasion through them possible. The justification for the Italian campaign was that it pinned down sizeable numbers of German troops, but this rationale was obviously something of an afterthought. The Allies were content to advance slowly or not at all in Italy. The Italian campaign diverted strength from a possible invasion of France from the south that was to be coordinated with the cross-Channel attack. All in all, the Italian front was frustrating and may have been wasted effort, except for two things: it satisfied the demand for action while preparations for the main event were going on, and it was a training ground.[3]

Meanwhile, D-Day, the much-postponed "Overlord," crept closer through the vast preparations of 1942 and 1943. A costly raid at Dieppe in 1942, carried out by Canadian troops, showed how formidable the task would be against heavy German coastal fortifications. That the invasion was delayed until June 1944 was not, as many Americans believed, the result of British foot-dragging. Churchill did indeed stoutly contend for a strong secondary effort in southeastern Europe, crossing swords with the Americans on this question; he did not question the need of a cross-Channel attack. It is now generally agreed that any earlier date was not feasible. By 1944, air superiority against the fading *Luftwaffe* was secure. Stalin, of course, believed that his Western allies procrastinated until his armies had bled the Germans white; and it must be admitted that the Allies showed little disposition to risk a major assault until it was clear that the Germans could not win in Russia.

---

[3] Another unpleasant aspect of the Italian campaign, revealed by Norman Lewis in his book, *The Honored Society*, was that the Allied Command had dealings in Sicily with the corrupt and vicious Mafia.

The huge operation was finally launched on June 6, 1944. The first assault wave on the Normandy beaches used 5,000 ships, artificial harbors ("mulberries"), artificial breakwaters made up of sunken ships ("gooseberries"), an air cover of 10,000 planes, airborne paratroopers, 20,000 vehicles, and more than 100,000 men. In planning "Overlord," the Allies also made good use of their secret intelligence weapons, for the Germans were deceived into thinking the attack would come at Calais, just as they had been tricked into expecting a Sicilian invasion in Greece. Even Stalin was impressed: "My colleagues and I cannot but admit that the history of warfare knows no other similar undertaking from the point of view of its scale, its vast conception, and its masterly execution," he wrote to Churchill.

Chilled, cramped, and seasick from crossing the Channel in tightly-packed craft in bad weather, the first to land encountered deadly machine gun fire. One of the two American landings almost failed; but the British succeeded in putting three divisions ashore, and the Normandy beachhead was finally secured. Then the American, British, Canadian, and Free French troops fought to break out from the beaches to begin the sweep through France. They were aided by Frenchmen organized in the Resistance, who supplied them with information and help. German troops under able commanders stoutly resisted, but they could not prevent the troops' landing and subsequent breakout into the plains of France.

Resisting bitterly, the Germans clung to the Channel ports and then wrecked them before surrendering, making the Allied logistics problem formidable. The advance was slow. A bold plan to drop airborne divisions behind the German lines was conceived by General Montgomery, now the top British commander under the general command of General Eisenhower; but it failed at Arnhem. In another long-debated decision, Eisenhower decided against Montgomery's idea of a rapid but risky single-pronged thrust toward Berlin in favor of a slower but methodical advance on a broad front. American General George Patton, commanding the southern wing, agreed with "Monty" in favoring a single thrust, except that he wanted to be the one to make it. On August 15, there was a landing in southern France. It was delayed because of Allied arguments, Churchill having clung to the idea of a Balkan front to link with the Yugoslav partisans under Tito. Almost a year of hard fighting remained after D-Day, and as late as the last weeks of 1944 the Germans were capable of a dangerous counterattack at Ardennes, the scene of their first great success four and a half years earlier. (On this occasion Hitler beat "Ultra" by ordering radio silence. "Ultra" was the code name for British interception of German radio communications.)

Wesel, Germany, devastated by bombing attacks to clear the way for Allied crossing of the Rhine, early 1945. *United States Air Force.*

But with the success of the cross-Channel invasion, combined with steady German retreat on the eastern front, the Reich's cause became hopeless. On July 15, 1944, General Rommel wrote as much to Hitler: Germany should seek peace. On July 17, Rommel was seriously wounded by a British plane that strafed his car as he was returning from a trip to the front. He had been prepared to act on his own, as German commander in the West, to negotiate a surrender, a part that he alone perhaps was equipped to play.

Three days later, Colonel Claus von Stauffenberg brought a bomb in his briefcase into Hitler's headquarters at Wolfschanze in East Prussia. The bomb exploded, killing several people but doing little damage to the Führer.[4] Having learned from Stauffenberg that Hitler

[4] In March 1943, a bomb placed on Hitler's plane by Fabian von Schlabrendorff failed to explode. Another bomb plot fizzled when the dictator suddenly cut short a tour of the Berlin arsenal. Another bomb exploded prematurely. Hitler's enemies got the feeling he really was destiny's favorite. A factor in the July 20 miscarriage was the last-minute shifting of the conference to a building with walls too thin to contain the force of the explosion.

was dead (as the courageous colonel thought), the German army in Paris arrested the whole of the local SS and SD, preparatory to contacting the Allies for the purpose of ending the war. But news of Hitler's miraculous survival unnerved most of the conspirators. General Karl Stülpnagel, who wanted to continue the coup, shot himself; and Kluge, caught hopelessly in a conflict of loyalties, took poison. Rommel was to be forced to commit suicide later, in the course of a terrible vengeance Hitler took on the military rebels.

Hitler himself was prepared, of course, to say *Weltmacht oder Niedergang:* rule or ruin. Having proved unworthy of the world role he had marked for her, Germany could perish along with him, in a Wagnerian twilight of the gods.

Thus Germany was not able to do what Italy had done, depose its dictator to shorten a hopeless war. She and the rest of the world were condemned to months more of horror, as the bombs rained on defenseless cities; European Jews were fed into Nazi gas ovens; and the Russians advanced into Poland, Rumania, Hungary, Czechoslovakia, finally into Berlin itself. Why was this so? Hitler's more demonic will and his more total control of Germany were clearly factors. There was no king or other head of state to appeal to; Hitler had taken over all offices. More important, leading Germans in the army, the government, and industry failed to act with sufficient boldness. True, there was a dedicated band of oppositionists, but they were relatively few. Even those Germans who bore no love for Hitler hesitated to turn traitor with the Russian on the doorstep. As for the Allies, they continued to demand unconditional surrender and to refuse to bargain with any German.

The fiasco of the July 20 attempt exposed Hitler's enemies, and his revenge was savage. The leading conspirators were killed by slow strangulation, of which pleasant scene Hitler had movies taken and shown. The Nazis borrowed from the Bolsheviks the practice of visiting revenge on relatives of the "criminals"; "the family of Count Stauffenberg will be wiped out down to the last member," Heinrich Himmler declared. All the circles of the secret opposition, from Carl Goederler's to von Moltke's Kreisau Circle, were broken. After this, no opposition was possible; links slowly forged over a matter of years had been destroyed. Germany could only suffer under the rule of a dying madman.

The Diplomacy of Coalition Warfare

By the time Hitler and Himmler vented their rage on the men who had tried to kill them on July 20, not only were the Anglo-American forces bearing down on Paris, but the Russians, having expelled the Germans from Russia, were pushing toward Warsaw. On August 10, anticipating Russian victory, the Polish underground in Warsaw rose up and seized control of portions of the city from the Nazis. The underground looked to the government-in-exile in London for leadership. But Stalin had created his own Polish National Liberation committee and had begun to denounce the London Poles as fascists. The Russians halted their advance toward the Polish capital and waited while the exposed Polish freedom fighters were slaughtered by the Germans. Three hundred thousand Poles were killed in one of the war's most appalling tragedies.

This was hardly an isolated example. Italian partisans failed to receive enough Allied help, as we know; and in the battle for France some premature rebellions were bloodily suppressed when the Germans were able to hold on for a while. The SS wiped out the French village of Oradour-sur-Glane and killed all 600 of its inhabitants. Earlier, in 1942, the Czech village of Lidice had been exterminated in retaliation for the assassination of Reinhard Heydrich, Himmler's sinister SS aide. During the drive on Germany through France (November 1944) de Gaulle once flatly defied an order from Eisenhower to pull back out of the city of Strasbourg, which had just been taken, to lend aid in the other crucial sector. He feared Nazi reprisals against French patriots if the Germans returned.

In the Warsaw case, the Poles charged that Stalin deliberately held back his forces, so that the non-Communist Poles could be killed off. From what we know of Stalin, such brutal realism was well within his capacity. But the Russians claimed they lacked the strength for a further advance at that moment, and the relatively neutral testimony of German General Guderian—stuck with the thankless task of staving off disaster —tends to support them. What the tragic episode does indicate is the increasing intrusion of politics among the Allies as the war neared its end. Nations were looking ahead to the postwar disposition of power.

The often acrimonious disputes between Americans and British about military strategy reflected the same motive. Churchill's insistence on diverting some Allied forces to a Balkan front failed to impress American leaders and was finally shelved, with Stalin's warm approval. Churchill warned about Russian dominance of the Balkans and wished to link up with the Yugoslavian guerrilla movement or movements. This possiblity was complicated by the rivalry between Colonel Mikhailovich's more conservative anti-German resistance group and the partisans, who were led by the more colorful, abler, more successful, and also more radical Tito (Josip Broz). Churchill was willing to back Tito and to support a "stab in the Adriatic armpit" of Fortress Europe by Allied forces.

In the end this was not done. Of all the resistance movements of occupied Europe, Tito's was by far the most successful. From late 1941, Mikhailovich seemed more interested in fighting Tito than the Germans. Stalin, who had first supported Mikhailovich, switched to Tito, who became for the time being ardently pro-Soviet. (This did not prevent the Partisan leader from dickering with the Germans on at least one occasion during the war.)

Montgomery's battles with Eisenhower have been mentioned. His chief objection to the slow-paced Anglo-American advance was that it permitted the Russians time to move into, with no likelihood of soon moving out of, all the countries of eastern Europe and a good part of Germany. Such matters were settled at the top level, in conferences between the Allied heads of state.

The diplomacy of coalition warfare and the planning for postwar politics is crucial in the history of World War II. Dramatically, the high leaders of state met in summit conferences to try to resolve the great issues. Roosevelt and Churchill's meeting at sea off the coast of Newfoundland in August 1941 had produced the Atlantic Charter, a rhetorical proclamation setting forth ideal peace aims. The Allied goal was a world without want or fear, armaments or conflicts. They wanted no annexations of territory contrary to the wishes of the inhabitants, a principle hard to square with Soviet actions in the Baltic states. In his "Four Freedoms" and other pronouncements, President Roosevelt sought to play a Wilsonian role in this war. Once again, high ideals and grim reality clashed. In practice the Allies had to arrive at a division of power. They agreed that the Axis enemy must be totally defeated and disarmed. It proved harder to agree on the disposition of vast areas of the globe that would be left as a vacuum of power once Germany and Japan fell.

Stalin having refused to come, Roosevelt and Churchill met in January 1943 at Casablanca in Morocco. This meeting took place in the immediate aftermath of the North African invasion, which had raised the problem of the Free French. Roosevelt did not like de Gaulle and tried to bypass him in Africa. The United States recognized the Vichy government. Angered by a Free French effort to seize some French islands off the Newfoundland coast from their Vichy governors, American leaders believed that de Gaulle had little support in France, and while the State Department pursued a pro-Vichy and an anti-Free French policy with strange tenacity, Roosevelt found the Free French leader a prima donna and a nuisance. He tried to build up another Frenchman, General Giraud, as the Free French head but found Giraud unable to compete with de Gaulle, whom the Allied chiefs finally reluctantly accepted.

At Casablanca the American and British military chiefs also con-

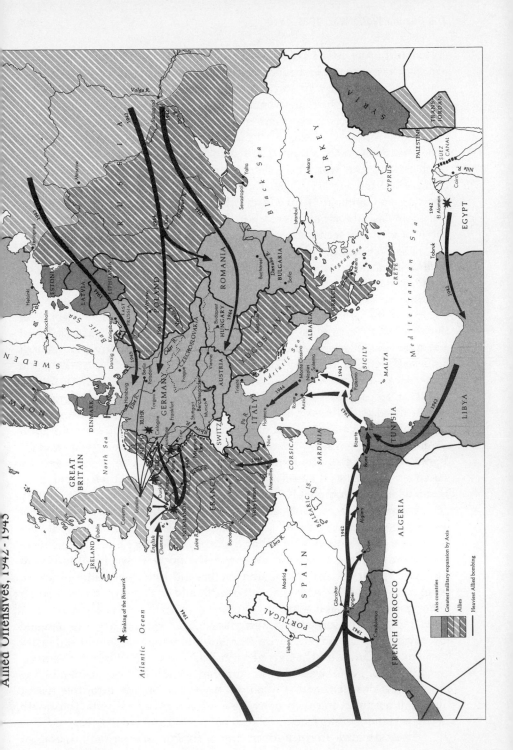

Allied Offensives, 1942-1943

tinued to bicker about the cross-Channel invasion. Their discussion of peace terms produced the controversial dictate of unconditional surrender. No terms of any sort would be made with any enemy governments; they must surrender completely.

In thus proclaiming total victory as the war's goal, the Allied leaders meant to reassure Stalin and everyone else that they would make no deals with Hitler. They also expressed the unique ideology of this war: total war, total victory, total reconstruction of the enemy countries after victory. The formula ensured war to the end, the invasion and occupation of Germany, and the complete destruction of the enemy's state apparatus, rather than some sort of negotiated peace. Modern war had seemingly become total and "ideological."

The first meeting between the Big Three—Churchill, Roosevelt, and Stalin—took place late in 1943. The Soviet leader played hard to get, pleading the urgent pressures of the war, and finally forced the others to come to Tehran (Teheran), Iran, near the borders of the Soviet Union. At the conference, Churchill and Roosevelt sparred warily with the legendary Communist dictator. They found him blunt but intelligent and even likeable, and they seemed to reach certain agreements with him. Assured that the long-awaited invasion of western Europe would take place the following spring, Stalin promised to launch a Soviet offensive to coordinate with it. Roosevelt told Stalin that he privately sympathized with Russian plans for Poland's borders but could not say so because there were many Polish-American voters—an ominous foreshadowing of the Yalta "betrayal" of eastern Europe to Russia, according to one school of thought. The three leaders issued a very general statement pledging themselves to remain united in their resolve to smash Germany completely—by land, sea, and air—and then to build "an enduring peace" through the United Nations, an international organization that would replace the defunct League of Nations. It was at Tehran that Roosevelt introduced the conception of the "four policemen" who would each patrol a beat in the postwar world—the USSR, the USA, Great Britain, and China. Stalin and Roosevelt, and Churchill more reluctantly, agreed that France should *not* play the role of a major power after the war.

In regard to Germany, Stalin was inclined to question the demand for unconditional surrender on the grounds that it would intensify German resistance. But he agreed with Roosevelt, who was enthusiastic, and Churchill, who was less so, on the desirability of dismembering Germany. Roosevelt had a plan to divide Germany into five parts. Churchill assumed that Germany would be partitioned, with the South German states perhaps being placed in a federation with Austria. The Big Three decided to turn over the planning of the occupation of

Germany to a European Advisory Committee on which the three powers would be represented. When it met in London, it encountered considerable frustration but finally worked out the zones of occupation; Roosevelt and Churchill confirmed them at the Quebec Conference of September 1944.

Many people throughout the world optimistically interpreted Tehran to mean that the Soviet Union and the Western democracies had learned to work together in war and in peace, overcoming their past hostilities and drawing closer together in their ideologies. A year later, with victory approaching, public opinion remained optimistic; but with the entrance of Soviet troops into Europe, critical questions arose.

As the Americans somewhat sanctimoniously washed their hands of such sordid politics, the harried Churchill had to deal with the Polish government-in-exile in London, whose leaders watched Stalin set up his own pro-Russian, Communist-dominated Polish government. In October, Churchill went to Moscow and initialed a territorial deal with Stalin. The Americans were kept informed of this agreement, which outlined a curious mathematical distribution. The Russians were to have 90 percent influence in Rumania, 75 percent in Bulgaria, and 50 percent in Yugoslavia and Hungary. The Western powers were to have 90 percent influence in Greece. The omission of Poland and Czechoslovakia implied that the Russians would have complete sway there, as had been intimated at Tehran. Churchill brushed off the outraged cries of the pro-Allied Poles: "If you want to conquer Russia we shall leave you to do it. . . . You are absolutely incapable of facing facts." The fact the Poles were being asked to face was the loss of their national liberty to Russian communism. The Russians were there with the Red Army, and nothing could be done about it.

Against this ominous background, the Yalta Conference of February 1945 marked the climax of wartime consultation among the Big Three, but it was also the beginning of the subsequent quarrels between Russia and the West. The ambiguous agreements reached on this occasion were to be bitterly controversial in later years. Had the Anglo-American leaders, in their eagerness to win the war against the Axis as quickly and fully as possible, failed to consider the postwar balance of power and allowed Soviet Russia to control all of eastern Europe? Could they, even if they had wanted to, have done anything at all to prevent Russia from dominating postwar eastern Europe?

Key decisions reached in the Yalta protocols and agreements concerned such important matters as the organization of the United Nations; policies toward Germany; the fate of liberated Europe, especially Poland; the trial of war criminals; and Russian entrance into the Far Eastern war against Japan. Of these Poland and the Far East were the most critical and controversial. In regard to Poland, the Western leaders formally gave in and agreed that the pro-Soviet Polish government, organized by the Russians and regarded in some circles as their puppet, should form the basis of the postwar Polish government. The Polish government-in-exile in London, which had been the legitimate 1939 government and had fled to London after the Nazi conquest, was thus rejected; it was the government on whose behalf the British had declared war against Germany in 1939. These Poles considered themselves betrayed and the war itself a mockery, since Poland had been rescued from Hitler only to be given to Stalin. Stalin did agree to bring a few of the London Poles into his Communist Polish regime and also to hold democratic elections in the near future, but he never did so; he seems to have regarded this agreement as a sop to American opinion and never felt the need to take it seriously. Poland's frontiers were also changed; Russia received territory from 1939 Poland, and in return Poland was allowed to occupy former German soil up to the Oder-Niesse rivers. Britain and the U.S. did not formally accept this boundary, although they accepted it in effect.

The Yalta decision in fact was a surrender to the Russians in eastern Europe, allowing them to install puppet Communist governments in Poland and subsequently in Rumania, Bulgaria, Czechoslovakia, and Hungary without opposition from Britain and the United States.[5] Since Soviet troops were already there, the Western powers could scarcely have done anything differently anyway without breaking the alliance and starting a war among the Allies. Perhaps by extracting some concessions toward democracy from Stalin they did the best they could, even though the Soviet leader chose to dishonor these pledges later.

In regard to the Far East, the Allies agreed that the Soviet Union would enter the war against Japan within three months after the surrender of Germany. In return she would receive "the former rights of Russia violated by the treacherous attack of Japan in 1904," that is, the southern half of Sakhalin, the lease of Port Arthur as a naval base, "preeminent interests" in an internationalized commercial port of Dairen, the Kurile Islands, and a share (along with China) in operating the Manchurian railroads. This meant that the Soviet Union would be powerfully established in the Far East. It was also an imperialistic agreement at the expense of China, made without consulting the Chinese

---

[5] Nicholas Kallay, the Hungarian premier, tried to arrange a surrender to the Western Allies, but the latter refused to deal with him. The Allies also delivered hundreds of thousands of refugees, against their will, back to Stalin to be imprisoned or shot.

government. Some argued later that this decision made possible the victory of the Chinese Communists over Chiang Kai-shek's government in the years after the war. They asked why such concessions had to be made to bring Russia into the war against Japan when Japan was already tottering and would soon be finished off by the atomic bomb. But at this time the bomb had not been completed, and American military intelligence believed (wrongly) that Japan was strongly entrenched in Manchuria and might be able to hold out there a long time unless Soviet forces helped attack them. General Douglas MacArthur believed that it would be necessary to bring Russia into the Asiatic war. Here, again, the Western leaders evidently wanted to secure Russian goodwill by giving them a share in an area that had long been of great interest to the Russians. They hoped for postwar partnership.

At Yalta, also, the zones of occupation for Germany were confirmed, and agreement was reached in principle on German reparations. The sum of $20 billion, of which half would go to the USSR, was mentioned "as a basis for discussion." Russia later claimed that she had received a firm pledge of $10 billion worth of booty from Germany. The United Nations, which Roosevelt regarded as a vital part of the new international order, obviously interested Stalin only insofar as it might further the interests of the USSR. Details of the U.N. were to be worked out at the San Francisco conference a few months later.

The Last Act

Hitler was never the same after Stalingrad. Increasingly an ill and shattered man, he was kept going by the bizarre ministrations of the quack he kept as a physician and was rapidly approaching the certifiably insane—had there been anyone in Germany with the power so to certify. Yet the horrible progress of the holocaust, or what Nazi jargon had named the "final solution"—the extermination of European Jewry— can hardly be blamed on Hitler's late insanity. In 1939, he had publicly threatened that if the war came it would bring "the annihilation of the Jewish race in Europe," and he continued to harp on this theme at every opportunity. Of course, since his adolescence this had been Hitler's *idée fixe*, the heart of his *Weltanschauung:* the Jews must be totally eliminated from Europe. But there were some moments, at least, when he wavered from the terrible goal of annihilation. German and Austrian Jews were allowed to emigrate, at a price; and Hitler played with the idea of settling all Europe's Jews in Madagascar.

Yet the concept of the final solution was well developed even before the war. The decision to carry it out coincided with the drive to the East, for here, in Poland and Russia, was the dwelling place of the great mass of European Jewry. A directive from Göring to SD head Heydrich on July 31, 1941, is the evident origin of the project that led to the organization of human murder as a mass production industry and the killing of at least four-and-a-half million Jews. A conference on January 20, 1942, began the planning; in the summer of 1942 the Warsaw ghetto was cruelly cleared out. The SS was put in charge. It has even been argued that Himmler and Heydrich planned the final solution without Hitler's knowledge, since no such order from Hitler has survived and since he apparently never discussed the extermination plan in his conversations, table talk, documents, and so on, of which a very substantial amount was preserved.

Strange though this is—for Hitler was addicted to interminable monologues in which he bored his involuntary auditors with every last detail of his thoughts—it is incredible to suppose that the faithful Heinrich would have mounted such an immense operation without his *Führer's* knowledge. The project is something Hitler was certainly capable of undertaking. We are left with the hypothesis that Hitler could not psychologically face the concrete results of his theories, and this we know to be true: he shrank from scenes of death on many occasions. So, indeed, did Himmler, who suffered an hysterical attack after once attending a mass execution. But at all times the terrible plan was kept in deepest secrecy.

Mechanized human slaughter via poison gas took place at Auschwitz, Maidanek, Treblinka, Belzec, and lesser centers. Official records and eye witness accounts eventually convinced the world that this hideous process had really gone on; during most of the war, the Allies refused to believe such stories. The SS officer Kurt Gerstein, who had witnessed mass murders and accumulated hard evidence of them, tried in 1942 to convince the Catholic church and the Swedish government of these stories' accuracy, but they refused to believe him. (The final irony was that he was selected for prosecution by the Nuremberg Tribunal after the war; he committed suicide on July 25, 1945.) Those who claim that most Germans must have known about the extermination camps have to contend with the facts that secrecy was total and that non-Germans refused to credit these stories at first.

Although Auschwitz was efficiently cremating 140,000 bodies a month, only the testimony of scattered escapees led Allied sources to suspect the dread truth by the summer of 1944. When the Hungarian head of state, Admiral Horthy, resisted the exportation of Hungarian Jews, the world was alerted to the situation. But the Western allies were largely helpless to stop the slaughter, and the Russians were not interested. An underground movement in the Auschwitz camps failed as badly as had the Warsaw underground to establish liaison with the approaching Red Army. It must be granted that the Poles were often antisemitic too.

The British and the Americans crossed the Rhine in March 1945, as a powerful Russian army was nearing Berlin. Long-range rockets were German's last hope in the last year of the war. The V-1s and V-2s on which Hitler had counted to rescue his fading cause fell far short of this goal. From September 1944, the V-2s were a menace; these "first long-range military rockets ever used in warfare" harassed southeast England and the important Allied invasion port of Antwerp. But by February the Germans had been driven back out of range of vital Allied targets; the V-2s were capable of only a little more than a hundred miles. It is possible that they might have affected the course of the war had there been more time to develop them. Here again British manipulation of German intelligence, causing rockets to be mistargeted, was effective in frustrating the Nazis.

But in applying advanced science to warfare, the Germans were strangely inferior to the Americans and British in this war. In view of the earlier history of the scientific knowledge necessary for the atomic bomb, one would have expected Germany to be in the lead. German and German-Jewish scientists—Albert Einstein, Max Planck, Werner Heisenberg—had pioneered the new physics on which atomic energy rested. The Hungarian-born Leo Szilard and the Dane Niels Bohr had worked in Germany. Berlin and Göttingen were leading world centers of scientific research. Germany had long excelled in the close connection between theoretical and applied science. It was an Austrian physicist, Lise Meitner, who first produced the theory of uranium fission in 1939.

But it was exactly these great scientists whom Nazi intolerance drove away. In August 1939, famed scientist Albert Einstein, who had fled from Germany and finally settled in the United States, wrote a letter to President Roosevelt urging the necessity to begin work on the super-weapon, lest Germany win the race to this mighty source of energy. The scientists whose brains made possible the bomb, among them the Italian Enrico Fermi in addition to Szilard, Frau Meitner, and others, were largely exiles from Hitler and Mussolini. Thus did Nazi racism accomplish its own doom, for these scientists might have provided the dictators with the atom bomb.

British, French, and Americans contributed to the vast scientific enterprise. The Cavendish Laboratory in Cambridge, England, where Ernest Rutherford had first achieved atomic disintegration in 1919, was an important research center; but the multibillion dollar project for building the bomb was headquartered in the United States. In 1943 the British were forced to accept a junior partnership in the project. Such brilliant Americans as Arthur Compton and Harold Urey contributed along with the Europeans. The first chain reaction uranium fission was achieved at the University of Chicago in 1942. A huge plant established at Oak Ridge, Tennessee, produced fissionable material in large quantity. Under the direction of American physicist J. Robert Oppenheimer, the actual weapon development took place at Los Alamos, New Mexico. Before Yalta, Roosevelt had known that a bomb of vastly greater destructive power might be available within six months, but no one knew for sure that this amazing device would actually work until July 16, 1945, when it was successfully tested.

By that time, Germany was already finished, and it was on Japan that the terrible weapon was to be used. It forced her speedy surrender on August 15. In Germany, the "absolute weapon" that might have rescued her from defeat was not in sight of attainment. By 1945 Cherwell thought Germany was three years behind the West. The Germans lagged less in pure theory, about which German scientists knew as much as did Western scientists, than in uranium reactor technology. The failure may be laid at the door of Hitler's ramshackle administrative system. Hitler took little interest in and hardly seemed to know about the fission bomb prospects. It has been suggested that such key German scientists as Heisenberg and Weizsäcker subtly sabotaged the German atomic project. Certainly they did not come forward to advocate it, as Einstein did in the U.S. In October 1943, Niels Bohr escaped from Denmark to Sweden and thence to London concealed in the bomb compartment of a Mosquito airplane.

Hitler could only hope for a miracle such as had saved Frederick the Great in 1762. That miracle had come about because Prussia's enemies, the Russians and the French, had a falling out. As we know, a similar disagreement was far from an impossibility this time; but at Yalta the Allies managed to pull together their threatened unity and work out an arrangement for the partition of Europe. After the February conference, Stalin furiously complained that the Americans and British made peace with Italy "behind the back of the Soviet government." The surrender of the German armies in Italy in April 1945 was worked out between American diplomats and the SS commander in northern Italy, Kurt Wolff. But the Western Allies allowed the Red Army to liberate Prague, Vienna, and Berlin, to the dismay of Churchill and subsequent critics of American policy.

Mussolini met his end on April 28, murdered by Italian partisans as he sought to escape. His body was hung up by the heels for public display in Milan. President Roosevelt had died of a massive cerebral

Nr. 366, Dienstag, 17. April 1945

NACHRICHTEN FÜR DIE TRUPPE

USA-Panzer stürmen Nürnberg

VS räumt Strassensperren

Der Endkampf um Berlin beginnt—Leipzig fast eingeschlossen—Halle fällt

NÜRNBERG, die Stadt der Reichsparteitage, ist gestern abend durch einen überraschenden Vorstoss der Amerikaner überrumpelt worden und bereits zur Hälfte in amerikanischer Hand.

Nach den letzten Meldungen dringen die Amerikaner mit Flammenwerfer-Panzern und Sturmgeschützen in den Stadtkern von Nürnberg vor, wo nur noch vereinzelt Widerstand geleistet wird.

Das Tempo des Vorstosses ist so schnell, dass der Stadt voraussichtlich die totale Zerstörung erspart bleiben wird, die in anderen Städten jedesmal durch schwere Strassenkämpfe verursacht wurde.

Der Volksturm hat die meisten Strassensperren und Panzergräben geräumt, um Nürnberg eine sinnlose Verwüstung zu ersparen.

Die Eizmarsch der USA-Panzer kam zuerst von Nordosten der Stadt, nachdem sie bereits von allen Seiten eingeschlossen war.

Die Nachricht, dass die Amerikaner in Nürnberg eingebrochen sind, folgt auf einen Tag, an dem Schlag auf Schlag Berichte über neue tiefe Einbrüche der Alliierten in Richtung Berlin, Dresden und Hamburg eintrafen.

Generalfeldmarschall ERNST BUSCH. Seine Aufgabe ist Berlin zu halten.

Gross-Offensive an Oder- und Neisse-Front bricht los

Mit einem Trommelfeuer, das alle Bewohner bis nach Berlin kurz nach drei Uhr morgens aus dem Schlaf in die Luftschutzkeller scheuchte, begannen die Sowjets gestern die Grossoffensive, mit der sie das noch unbesetzte Rest-Reich zwischen Oder und Elbe überrennen und die Reichshauptstadt in ihre Hand bringen wollen.

Tausende von Panzern, riesige Artilleriezusammenballungen und zahllose Flugzeugverbände wurden eingesetzt, denen von deutscher Seite noch nicht annähernd gleich starkes Material entgegengestellt werden kann. Allein am Neissabschnitt werden die russischen Sturmdivisionen auf über eine Million Mann geschätzt.

Stützpunkt Gironde-Nord vor dem Fall

Nur Stunden nach Beginn des Grossangriffs auf den abgeschnittenen Atlantikstützpunkt Gironde-Nord und Gironde-Süd kämpfen Zgruppen im Kessel den Kampf.

Letzter Führer-Appell an die Ost-Divisionen

Der Führer hat gestern einen letzten Durchhaltebefehl an die Divisionen der Ostfront erlassen, in dem er ein auffordert, der Sowjetoffensive der Sowjets Stand zu halten und den bolschewistischen Ansturm vor der Reichshauptstadt in einem Blutbad zu ersticken.

In alter Siegeszuversicht

Der Führer zeigte im Tagesbefehl bekannt, dass sämtliche deutsche Offiziere und Soldaten in deutscher Uniform gemeinsam mit den Sowjets gegen die Verteidiger Berlins kämpfen und fordern die Truppe auf, überall, auch im engsten Reihen, nach Verrätern Ausschau zu halten.

"Wer Befehl zum Rückzug gibt," so befiehlt der Führer, "ist schon festzunehmen und nötigenfalls augenblicklich umzulegen, ganz gleich, welchen Rang er besitzt."

Der Führer gibt dann seiner unerschütterlichen Zuversicht in den deutschen Endsieg Ausdruck und erklärt:

Altenburg rettet sich—Leipzig muss sterben

Zwei Städte haben gestern Entscheidungen über ihr eigenes Schicksal erlebt. Die Bürgermeister von Altenburg in Thüringen erklärten seine Stadt zur offenen Stadt; und die Amerikaner im kampflos besetzten.

In Leipzig wollte die Kampfkommandantur gleichfalls die Stadt zur offenen Stadt machen und sie kampflos übergeben. Aber die Oberbürgermeister von Leipzig, SS-Gruppenführer Freyberg, der mit der kriegsverbrecherischen und zu alien stimmungen finisch nicht wegdrängen.

Zwei Fronten treffen sich

Stützpunkt

Brillanten für Mauss

100 RM sind nur noch 25 Schweiz. Rappen wert

Bologna wird von Süden und Osten bedroht

Dönitz besucht Dönitzdivision

A German-language newspaper reports the bad news as the war nears its end in April, 1945: U.S. tanks storm Nuremberg, last battle for Berlin begins, Russian-Anglo-American conquest of the Reich almost completed. *Lothar Leser, Flugblattsammlung, D 75, Karlsruhe 21, Wiesbadenerstr. 59.*

hemorrhage two weeks before. Three days after Mussolini's death, with the Russians already in Berlin and the Americans and British smashing through to the south, Hitler and some of his cohorts (Eva Braun, Goebbels, and Goebbels' entire family) committed suicide in the underground bunker beneath the Reich Chancellery in Berlin. There the führer had spent the last weeks of the war, as Albert Speer was trying to save something from the wreckage Hitler intended to make of Germany ("If the war is to be lost, the nation also will perish") and even the faithful Himmler was contemplating treason. On May 7, 1945, German General Jodl surrendered the German armies in the West to General Eisenhower at Rheims, and the next day the Russians received a similar submission. With a ruined, governmentless Germany in their hands, the victorious powers assumed charge of separate zones of occupation, as previously agreed upon by the Allied Control Commission in London.

The War in Retrospect

Hysterically exultant crowds cheered the victorious end of the war in London and Paris; the most exuberant American scenes were reserved for three months later when Japan surrendered. The war, with all its horrors and immense loss of life, had not been a totally bad experience for some of the victor powers. In the United States, which was spared military damage to its own land, the depression had vanished as the government had ordered billions of dollars' worth of planes, tanks, ships, guns, construction of military bases, supplies for the armed forces, and supplies for Britain and Russia. In place of the unemployment that had blighted the 1930s, during the war there was overemployment. War industry required millions of new workers, while at the same time the armed forces were expanding from virtually nothing (a few hundred thousand) to twelve million men and women at the war's end. Women took jobs in unprecedented numbers. Although inflation obviously threatened under such conditions, consumer prices rose only 30 percent during the war, and national income more than doubled. Wages increased 76 percent. Home-front Americans were better off in material terms by some 25 percent during the war, though with shortages of consumer goods they mostly saved this money, responding to patriotic appeals to invest in war bonds.

Europe was, of course, less fortunate than America, but Great Britain also paid for military production in some measure out of a 64 percent rise in national income. Only in the last period of the war did the economy fail in Germany; and the USSR performed miracles by moving industries from the war areas to the Urals and western Siberia, managing to keep war production up even though consumer goods fell drastically from an already low level. Italy's economy was a disaster. France, first ruthlessly exploited and then a battleground in 1944, also touched bottom. In general, though, the war's experiences contributed to a consciousness of power in dealing actively with economic problems. If such miracles of production had been possible in war, why not in peace? Such documents as the wartime report issued in Britain by Sir William Beveridge's commission, *Full Employment in a Free Society*, were much discussed; they reflected a belief that poverty and want could be eliminated after the war by government regulation of the economy. President Roosevelt's wartime utterances stressed practical economic goals—freedom from hunger, ignorance, inadequate housing, poor health.

Much technological innovation had emerged from the war. This included not only atomic energy, which everyone hoped would find a more constructive use than the terrible destruction it brought to Hiroshima and Nagasaki; but also great advances in aircraft design, for example, huge cargo transports with long-range capability; radar; penicillin; and other inventions that, if not born of the war, had been powerfully stimulated by its urgent needs. Quite beyond the bounds of calculation were the experiences of millions upon millions of men and women whom the war dislodged from their routine to send to far places, often to their death but sometimes to the expansion of their consciousness and intellect. While World War II's crop of novels and poetry and memoirs did not come close to matching World War I's, it had value. For decades, both professional and amateur historians would research the war's amazing events as none other in world history had ever been explored.

The war drastically interrupted the affairs of nations in ways that might lead to creative new responses; at least the cake of custom was broken. Shattered industries would be rebuilt and modernized. The bombs had levelled slums as well as palaces, and new city planning was necessary in much of the world. Politically, a battered and enslaved France would have to reevaluate its whole system, its loyalties, its values; the trauma of defeat and Vichyism brought about a renewal of French political life in the guise of Gaullism or Christian Democracy or the Socialist-Communist Resistance. Obviously, for most of Europe 1940–1945 was an absolute boundary after which almost everything had to be different—maybe worse, but perhaps better.

After Hitler and Mussolini, the affairs of the defeated peoples had nowhere to go but up. Plainly, heroic anti-Fascist resistance movements, especially in Yugoslavia, regenerated national spirit. In all the warring countries, war had brought a feeling of national solidarity that at least temporarily broke through class barriers and aided minorities: women, the lower classes, blacks in the United States. People unanimously testified to the surge of human brotherhood in London under the 1940–1941 air attacks, and in the French Resistance.

Despite these possible uses of adversity, the war might be seen in review as a steady flow of unparalleled blunders. These offered twentieth-century humanity small grounds for its characteristic pride in human achievements. The Western democracies had allowed the swaggering Hitler to take what they had denied the peace-loving Weimar Republic. They had surrendered control of central Europe to Hitler out of weakness, cravenly sacrificing Czechoslovakia and Austria before drawing the line at Poland, which they neither could nor did defend either. They stood inactive while he overran Poland, and then in 1940 they proved they had learned nothing of the new arts of warfare the Germans had almost perfected.

For his part, Hitler, having won his war, could not stop. He attacked Russia without any real provocation and without adequate preparations. He compounded this mistake, which cost millions of lives, by refusing to fall back. He ordered new offensives and mistreated the Russian peoples in so brutal a manner that he could not gain their support. He allowed the British to outwit him on the intelligence front. Having been beaten in war, Hitler refused to make peace. He preferred to sacrifice his country, which had done little to try to overthrow the mad tyrant.

Stalin refused to believe a thousand warnings and allowed the Germans to catch him by surprise, thus losing masses of supplies, soldiers, and territory. His mistreated subjects rallied to the support of his regime only because the Nazis gave them no choice. The immense suffering that Russia endured during the war would not have been necessary had the USSR and the Western democracies cooperated against Hitler in 1939–1941 when Stalin joined Hitler in his greed for Polish territory.

For their part, the Allies left no loophole for negotiations, insisting on unconditional surrender while they plastered Europe's cities with high explosives and permitted the Nazis to exterminate the Jews. Advancing slowly across France in 1944 and 1945, after a belated invasion, they let the Russians take Berlin, Prague, Budapest, and Vienna and establish themselves throughout eastern Europe.

This catalogue of ghastly errors might be extended. Manifestly there is something unfair in so much wisdom after the event. Yet arguably all these mistakes were foreseeable and indeed foreseen. The erratic if imaginative Churchill, the naive and sloganizing Roosevelt were not much wiser than the narrow-minded bigots who ruled over Germany, Italy, and Russia. Hitler's occasional lapses into shrieking rages are well-known. Churchill was capable of lachrymose sentimentality. The Allied commander-in-chief, Eisenhower, was not a strong figure. Citizens in every country were blinded by hysterical hatreds. The horrible crimes of the Nazis, in both the extermination of the Jews and the savage mistreatment of Poles and Russians, could be rivalled— if not matched—by the Allies. Indiscriminate bombing of European cities; the extinction of Hiroshima by an atomic bomb (used despite the pleas of the scientists who had created it, and not really necessary for the defeat of Japan); the killing of 100,000 Japanese survivors of torpedoed ships; the imprisonment in camps of innocent Japanese-Americans—to mention only a few notable cases—were shameful. The continued inhumanity of Stalin's government, which uprooted whole nations and sent returning war prisoners and refugees to prison camps, was equally despicable.

From this incredible farrago of achievement and stupidity, destruction and construction, the world had somehow to recover after the summer of 1945.

Europe and the Cold War, 1945-1956

11

Europe at the End of the War

"An outraged and quivering world," as Winston Churchill called it, had suffered a total loss of life estimated as high as 75 million as a result of global war from 1936 to 1945. Such figures, together with estimates of property damage, loss of wealth, and all the rest, can only be guesses. For Europe, a war death toll of 38 million seems a fairly accurate estimate, of which 20 million were military casualties. Russian losses alone may have reached 20 million, at least half of whom were civilians. A million starved to death in Leningrad; 2 million Russians died in German prisoner camps. A vast area of Russia, of course, had been ravaged by the Germans, so much so that years after the war people were still living in caves or dugouts in White Russia and the Ukraine.

In revenge, German cities had been pulverized by air bombardment into "landscapes of the moon," their main districts reduced to rubble in percentages ranging up to 95 percent for Berlin; 60–70 percent for the cities of Hamburg, Dresden, Munich, and Frankfurt. Seven and a half million Germans were homeless. But these wagers of the War for the World did not suffer so much, proportionately, as one of their

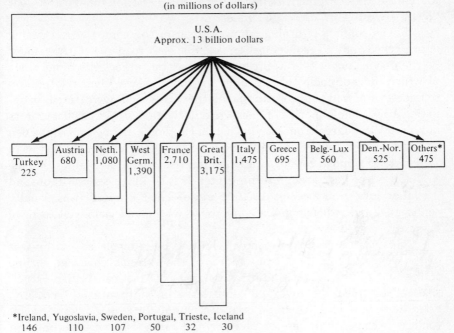

MARSHALL PLAN AID FROM THE UNITED STATES TO EUROPE, 1948-1952
(in millions of dollars)

U.S.A.
Approx. 13 billion dollars

| Turkey 225 | Austria 680 | Neth. 1,080 | West Germ. 1,390 | France 2,710 | Great Brit. 3,175 | Italy 1,475 | Greece 695 | Belg.-Lux 560 | Den.-Nor. 525 | Others* 475 |

*Ireland, Yugoslavia, Sweden, Portugal, Trieste, Iceland
146 110 107 50 32 30

innocent victims, Poland, whose population fell from 23.2 to 18.8 million. The city of Warsaw lost more people in World War II than the combined casualties of Great Britain and the United States. Sixty percent of Europe's 9,600,000 Jews had been killed. Yugoslavia, with 1½ million dead, sustained heavier losses proportionate to her population than did Germany, with her 4½ million casualties.

In addition to those who died—in battle, perhaps frozen to death in Russia, under a hail of bombs rained on their homes, in the Nazi death factories at such places of infamy as Auschwitz and Maidenek, worked to death as slave labor—there was immense suffering and social dislocation through the forced displacement of peoples. The Germans had brought in at least six and a half million forced laborers, mostly Slavic but some French and Dutch. As the war ended, many of these former prisoners rioted, creating havoc in some German cities. The Soviet Union uprooted whole peoples whose loyalty was suspect, including the Tartars of the Crimea. Just after the war, with the sanction of Allied agreements at the Potsdam Conference, some fourteen million Germans were driven away from eastern Germany, Czechoslovakia, Poland, and other eastern European countries under conditions that caused the death of perhaps 15 percent of them. Poles were also moved out of territory now assigned to Russia and into East Prussia or Silesia to replace the uprooted Germans; the entire nation of Poland was "pushed westward" about 100 miles.

Soviet soldiers returning from German prison camps were arrested and packed off to concentration camps, as readers of Alexander Solzhenitsyn know. A grim process was put in motion, the dimensions of which did not come fully to light for many years. Over two million refugees who were outside Russia at the war's end were forcibly deported back. The majority of these people were not Nazi collaborators but simply expellees from war-devastated regions; many were not even Russian citizens but Poles, Balts, South Slavs, or Germans. They were delivered to almost certain death or imprisonment at Stalin's hands.

On a less vast scale, returning Free French killed several thousand "collaborators" and arrested 100,000 more. Their property was usually confiscated and redistributed among those who could claim not to have flagrantly served the Nazis.

This vast migration of people who had been displaced by the war or the vengeance of the victors added to the extreme chaos in Europe at the end of the war. Invading Russian and American-British-French soldiers occupied the defeated countries and, not only in Germany, often took the liberties traditional for conquering marauders. Soviet soldiers became notorious for plunder and rape; Tito was to complain about it on behalf of the Yugoslavs, allegedly receiving the reply from Stalin that soldiers deserved a little fun. But in Germany the French were almost as guilty as the Russians.

Germany, enduring the hatred naturally felt by those who had suffered at her hands, felt hunger and cruel degradation. For nearly two years the object of the occupying powers was to seize her wealth as reparations while deliberately keeping Germans at a bare sustenance level. The death rate in Berlin in 1945 is said to have been unmatched in that country since the Thirty Years War; about half the babies born in August died, chiefly of malnutrition. This was true also in Holland, Poland, and elsewhere. The Hoover Report, in 1947, found German nourishment still at the lowest level of any Western nation in modern history. At the end of 1946, German production stood at a level one-third that of 1936. Every newspaper had ceased publication, there was no government save the military fiat of the occupying conquerors, and even the church had trouble delivering a message of consolation. A mission from the Vatican seeking contact with German Catholicism was rejected by the Russians and treated with extreme suspicion by the Americans and British.

But except for those few places that had escaped the war—Sweden, Switzerland, and Spain—the rest of Europe was not materially much better off than Germany (large areas of Russia were certainly even worse off). Europe still looked like a vast slum in 1947, when Americans began to give serious thought to assisting in its revival. For the first year or two after the war's end, the Allies' energies were spent largely in trying to regain their bearings and cope with the moral damages of the war. The victorious Allies, whose armies had met in the middle of Germany, tried to decide what to do with that country besides pillage and humiliate it; they struggled with their own problems of transition from war to peace; and they engaged in exercises designed to purge the world's burden of guilt and sin. Such an exercise was the Nuremberg Trials, which were held in the German city the Nazis had made their moral capital. The object was to discredit nazism forever by exposing its hideous crimes.

Begun early in 1946 after months of planning, the trials lasted 216 days, led to the printing of ten million words, and accumulated tons of invaluable documents. Four judges from each of the four victor powers, the United States, Great Britain, France, and the Soviet Union, sat in judgment on twenty-one of the leading Nazis who were still alive. The group included Göring, Rosenberg, Streicher, and Rippentrop, as well as men of industry and prominent generals; the entire General Staff and all the members of the SS and the Gestapo were named in a kind of blanket indictment. Evidence presented at Nuremberg documented the crimes of Hitler's state and made them known to the world in a dramatic way. The death factories of Auschwitz and Maidenek, the extermination of nearly six million Jews, the enslavement of more than six million forced laborers, the barbarities committed against the Russians and the Poles—all this and more emerged from the records. Other books published just after the war, such as Eugen Kogon's *Der SS Staat*, which became a best seller in Germany, revealed the horrors of the concentration camps.

Called a unique landmark in world jurisprudence, freely compared to the Bill of Rights and the Magna Carta by enthusiastic publicists, the trials nevertheless partly failed in their role as mythic regenerator of the Western soul. The Germans were allowed one lawyer each, against a battery of some 2,500 attorneys assembled by the prosecuting nations. They did not have access to the documents, and for the most part they were not allowed to raise questions about such Allied crimes as Stalin's mass murders, British and American terror bombing, and plundering of Germany then going on. While no one doubted Hitler's bestiality, there were nagging questions about how far collective guilt extended; and the attempt to couple the crime of waging "aggressive war" with the Nazi crimes against humanity did not altogether succeed. In the last analysis, the Nuremberg Trials were unfortunately tainted by more than a faint odor of "victor's justice"; those who won the war wreaked vengeance on the defeated under a thin disguise of legality, while refusing to countenance any discussion of their own crimes. Churchill observed that had Germany won the war, a similar trial would have hung both FDR and himself.

In the end, perhaps to their credit, although to the great indignation of the American and Russian prosecutors, the International Military Tribunal acquitted three of the twenty-one defendants outright, awarded death sentences to only ten, and let the General Staff as such off with a tonguelashing. Hermann Göring cheated Nuremberg justice by committing suicide, as scores of high Nazis had done previously—more than a hundred generals died by their own hand in the last weeks of the war. In the ensuing years the Allies, as well as the German courts, carried out thousands of de-Nazification trials. The Americans, in particular, enthusiastically brought suspected Nazis to trial, amid controversies about who the real Nazis were and how far one should or could go in attempting to punish every German who had signed up as a party member. Gradually, the belief that nazism lurked just beneath the surface of virtually every German faded, as the climate of opinion changed and Germany moved toward becoming a valued ally as well as a democratic state (in the western half) or a socialist one (in the east). But this process took several years.

The Occupation of Germany

The whole German question, embedded in the larger issue of a postwar peace settlement among the former Allies, scarred the immediate postwar scene. The Cold War, which began even before the war was over and had firmly settled in by early 1946, cast a pall of gloom over Europe, inhibiting efforts at recovery as the Russians and the Western Allies squabbled rather than cooperated.

So far as Germany was concerned, its division was determined at the end of the war, though few then realized it. "This war is different from all earlier ones; the conqueror of a region imposes his own social system on it," Stalin said in 1945, privately. Those parts of Germany and of eastern Europe lying within the zone of Soviet domination were marked for communization. Military occupation, expected to be temporary, turned out to be the basis for the division of Europe into two camps, a division destined to last.

But the goal of Russian policy in the immediate postwar period seemed to be to extract as much from Germany as possible, to meet the desperate material needs of a Russia exhausted by war. In brief, the Russians were after plunder, as much of it as possible, of any sort, as quickly as possible, to feed their own starving people and get back into production their own battered industries. At Yalta, the United States and Great Britain had agreed to let the Russians take reparations in kind, both manufactured products and industrial equipment. The Russians had suggested ten billion dollars' worth, a figure Roosevelt, though not Churchill, had accepted "as a basis for discussion"; Stalin simply assumed the matter settled. At Potsdam, in addition to a license for unlimited confiscation in their own zone of occupation, the Russians won a promise to receive industrial equipment and manufactured goods from the more industrialized American, British, and French zones. Ten percent of industrial plant was to be dismantled and removed to Russia, along with 15 percent of the German surplus of production (beyond what they needed to survive at a low level of existence). The total sum of Russian confiscations has been the subject of various wild estimates; it certainly amounted to many billions of dollars. The value of German industrial plant shipped to Russia between 1945 and 1950 amounted to perhaps three billion dollars.

This was a weird process, in which the cost of dismantling and shipping the heavy machinery often exceeded its value, and in which the machinery as often as not could not be used in Russia and ended up rusting on railway sidings. Partly, its aim was simply to punish Germany and to prevent her from rising again. Fear that Germany might somehow again use her fabled industrial prowess to dominate the world combined with hatred of her to produce a veritable anti-German psychosis. The Americans shared this quite as much, initially, as the Russians. Secretary of the Treasury Henry Morgenthau, who represented one wing of American German policy and at times had the ear of President Roosevelt, had wished to "wreck every mine, every mill and every factory" in the land that had produced Hitler; if his views did not prevail, they were at least partly represented in 1945 American policy. A people filled with "endemic barbarism," every one a potential Hitler (as the U.S. Army newspaper warned), Germans were not to be talked to, treated kindly, or allowed to convene in public; even children were wicked, and that apparently lovely fraulein smiling at you might be part of a plot for the revival of nazism. At first, Germans were not even supposed to leave their homes. Anton Webern, one of the century's greatest musical composers, was shot and killed by an American sentry when he went out for a bottle of wine.

Such absurdities soon broke down, of course, to be replaced, ironically, by a kind of love affair between American soldiers and the southern Germans who populated the American zone of occupation.[1]

---

[1] During wartime planning of zones, the Americans (FDR) had initially wanted the more populous and industrialized northwest as their zone, but the British

The children, the frauleins, and the wine and beer had the last word. But any thought that the United States ought to help German economic recovery scarcely arose until 1946.

Meanwhile the millions of refugees streaming in from the east added to the woe, and the French exploited their zone in the southwest almost as ruthlessly as did the Russians in the east. In theory, while the four powers each governed its own zone, they were supposed to formulate policies for all of Germany through a Central Control Commission meeting in Berlin and consisting of the four commanders in chief. But this never functioned effectively, the French proving even more an obstacle than the Russians. Whereas the three major allies had not accepted the goal of a partitioned Germany, the French believed in it fervently. Giving the French an occupation zone, which the British had insisted upon at the Yalta conference and which Stalin had opposed, thus played some part in the ultimate partition of Germany.

So economic cooperation tended to break down. But what finally led the United States to break with the policy of ruthless exploitation of Germany was a matter of self-interest, combined with some small measure of humanitarianism. Unwilling to see the Germans starve, the United States began to send them food. The western zones of Germany (British, American, French) had to import food, since they were far from self-sufficient agriculturally. The less industrialized Soviet zone was more self-sufficient in foodstuffs. Stripping West Germany of machinery and manufactures for the benefit of the Russians deprived her of any means of paying for her food needs by exporting other goods. The Americans ended up footing the bill, since neither the economically struggling French nor British could; the bill amounted to some three-quarters of a billion dollars a year.

If it was monstrous to saddle the American taxpayer with the cost of feeding Germany, it was hardly possible to allow mass starvation in Germany, either; wartime hatreds, by 1946, did not reach this far. Another thought began slowly to dawn, too: total European recovery was linked to German recovery. You could not make a desert between the Rhine and the Elbe and expect the rest of the continent to bloom. It was partly to alleviate the financial burden on the United States, Secretary of State James F. Byrnes declared in mid-1946, and partly to pave the way for a general European recovery that the United States decided she must restore the German economy.

This was to entail a break with the Potsdam policy and with the Soviet Union. But by this time, other issues had begun to poison

---

finally talked them out of it. The US did secure an enclave at Bremerhaven for supply purposes.

Russian-Western relations. The German problem cannot be seen in isolation and was not the only factor in the emerging Cold War. That war had broken out on a number of fronts by 1946.

Origins of the Cold War

That there were to be serious differences between the allies who had defeated the Axis powers, once that job was finished and the war ended, can hardly be regarded as much of a surprise. All previous experience testified to the ease with which friendship can turn to hostility when a common enemy is destroyed and problems of dividing up his inheritance arise. The many old suspicions as well as the obvious ideological gulf between Soviet Russia and the Western capitalist democracies made this rupture of harmony even more likely. A further factor contributing to the breakdown of friendship was the troubled state of the world, with area after area politically vulnerable. Meeting over the body of a nearly lifeless Germany, the recent allies also were inevitable rivals in many other areas, indeed almost all over the "outraged and quivering" world. Power was sharply polarized, and power vacuums existed in Europe and Asia, where the German and Japanese empires had so suddenly and totally collapsed.

Yet this collapse of cooperation between the USSR and the USA dismayed many people. It seemed so necessary to world survival after the brutal war. And during the war hopes had arisen. It later seemed astonishing how much Soviet-American good will burgeoned in 1941–1945; genial, courageous "Uncle Joe" Stalin became almost an American folk hero, and such respectable figures as Ambassador Joseph Davies (a Wisconsin corporation lawyer) and Republican presidential candidate Wendell Willkie assured Americans they had much in common with the peace-loving Russian people. FDR radiated optimism about the postwar future, at least until the very last weeks of his life, and a public opinion poll revealed that Americans expected more problems with Great Britain than with the Soviet Union after the war. Surely, if they had accomplished the titanic job of demolishing the German and Japanese war machines, Russia and the United States, aided by Great Britain, France, and perhaps China, could join together, under the flag of the United Nations, jointly to police and restore to health a world purged of fascism.

What went wrong? The Cold War itself eventually became a battleground among historians and pseudo-historians anxious to condemn one side or the other for an avoidable disaster. Still others held

to inevitability theories or stressed impersonal forces. Only a few ventured to note that a cold war, after all, is not hot, and that the real disaster of a war between Communist and capitalist worlds was mainly avoided. A noted British political analyst shocked an audience in the seventies by saying he preferred the simple confrontation of the 1947–1956 period to the more complex international rivalries of today; to deplore the Cold War seems *de rigueur* whether one chooses to blame it on Stalinists or McCarthyites. It certainly did seem deplorable at the time, holding as it did the threat of war even more terrible than the one of 1939–1945.

Eastern Europe more than Germany was a breeding ground for controversy between East and West. The Red Army drove the Wehrmacht from Poland, Rumania, Hungary, Bulgaria, Czechoslovakia, and Yugoslavia, getting significant help from national forces only in Yugoslavia. The Russians thought they had earned a right to exercise dominant power in these places both by the blood they had shed and by the need to prevent a recurrence of the deadly attack launched against them from this area, sometimes with the aid of these countries. Hungary and Rumania had joined the war against the USSR; prewar Poland had been anti-Soviet; prewar Czechoslovakia had been a tool of the Western appeasers of Hitler. In the wartime conferences Stalin had made it clear that he intended to have "friendly" governments in these countries after the war, and the Western allies had agreed. Roosevelt and Churchill had told the Poles they had better accept the need to come to terms with Russia. And they had given Stalin to believe he had a free hand in Poland. At the same time, Roosevelt deluded himself into believing that the Polish government could be democratic as well as friendly to the USSR. Stalin knew better. He established his own Polish government, in rivalry with the 1939 government that resided in London during the war.

At the Yalta conference, Roosevelt and Churchill got Stalin to agree to accept some of the London Poles into a coalition and to hold elections, as will be recalled. He never honored these promises. Sixteen Polish leaders from the London government were arrested after they had been invited to Poland; they were subjected to the usual mental torture and brought to trial in June 1945. Twelve of the sixteen were convicted and imprisoned. The Soviet security police terrorized anti-Communists and censored the press. After protests, the Peasant party leader Mikolaiczyk was allowed in the government where, surrounded by Communists, he was condemned to futility; in 1947 he fled to the West bearing stories of Communist duplicity. Meanwhile the American ambassador at Warsaw, Arthur Bliss Lane, resigned in disgust and wrote a book called *I Saw Poland Betrayed*, published in 1948. He had tried in vain to insist on democratic processes.

Stalin thought that the West had conceded him Poland, just as he let Britain and the United States have a free hand in Italy and Japan. He was impatient with their meddling in his backyard. The West was shocked at Russia's evident refusal to set up democratic regimes. Stalin thought he had made concessions by allowing a facade of coalition government. (And at Tehran, indeed, Roosevelt had as much as told him, "Only make it look good.") Government in the "People's Democracies" was normally in the hands of a bloc, or "front," which included members of some other left-wing political parties but which Communists dominated. It is perhaps an open question whether Stalin saw this as cynical manipulation or as a genuine concession to the West, but it was bound to look like the former to anyone accustomed to the processes of Western-style democracy.

There is no doubt that American and British opinion was deeply disillusioned with Soviet conduct and resented Stalin's actions as a breach of faith. Public opinion in favor of Russia dropped in late 1945 and into 1946 like the thermometer in a Siberian winter, from 55 percent who thought "we can trust the Russians" in the summer of 1945 to 7 percent in a poll a year later. President Harry Truman honestly endeavored to carry out what he regarded as Franklin Roosevelt's policy of cooperation with Russia but came reluctantly to an angry belief that the Soviet government was insatiably aggressive and respected only force. The same was true of the British Labour government, a party of the moderate Left initially inclined to see itself a bridge between capitalist America and Communist Russia. Possessed of enormous goodwill among the British people at the end of the war, Stalin's regime dissipated it by such apparently gratuitous cruelty as forbidding Russian wives to leave the USSR with their American or British husbands. In 1950, British Foreign Secretary Ernest Bevin, a veteran trade unionist who became one of the staunchest of the cold warriors, told the Labour Party Conference that he and the government had tried to be friends with the Russians but had got nothing in return except "aggression or threats of aggression."

Eastern Europe was not the only place where Russian actions seemed menacing. In northern Iran, Soviet troops failed to withdraw as they were supposed to after the war, obviously hoping to detach the Persian province of Azerbaijan. The Kremlin harassed Turkey about naval bases near the Straits and continued to emit a stream of anti-Western propaganda, accusing the U.S. of wishing to unleash a new war. All this, however, stopped much short of warlike action, for which the USSR was obviously unready.

Those "revisionist" American historians who later wished to show that the Cold War was really the West's fault pointed to certain provocations or unfriendly acts emanating from Washington. The American government ignored Russian requests for a large loan at low interest in 1945 and cut off lend-lease aid precipitously at the end of the war. It also tried to use its atomic monopoly as a bargaining point, though it is absurd to talk of "atomic blackmail." If the West failed to understand how badly the USSR had been hurt by the war and how badly it needed help, this was because of the ingrained Stalinist habit of secrecy and refusal to allow observers in devastated areas. But the West applied a double standard, not wishing the Russians to have any part in peace settlements with Italy and Japan but demanding a voice itself in Poland and Czechoslovakia. (The Allies never seriously questioned Soviet monopoly of arrangements in Rumania, Bulgaria, and Hungary, though Russian high-handedness annoyed them.)

Tempers flared, and rhetoric heated up the cold war. Truman decided at the beginning of 1946 that he was "tired of babying the Soviets," who understood only "an iron fist and strong language." Stalin responded in February with a speech stressing the incompatibility of communism and capitalism, inaugurating a new hard line.

Frustrated, Washington turned for advice at this time to the brilliant *chargé* in Moscow, George F. Kennan, who explained the Communist mentality: their hostility to the West is rooted in the need to legitimize their blood-stained dictatorship; they *must* believe in the inevitable triumph of communism after a final apocalyptic struggle with the beast (capitalism). So they will exploit every opportunity to extend their system and cannot be converted to doctrines of harmony and cooperation. But since they think history is on their side, Communists are in no hurry and will not risk major war; met with firmness, they tend to back off. Therefore, the right strategy is to "contain" them by pushing back. Resist, contain, be firm, negotiate from strength: the Kennan message was eagerly received all over the American diplomatic and military establishment. Kennan was no "cold warrior," in that he believed not in ideological crusades but rather in the realism of power; his authority was perhaps misused by those who welcomed a knockdown fight with the Communists. But it shored up the doctrine of military resistance.

One problem had been that the Americans, innocently convinced that the war was over, had dismissed their vast World War II armies with appalling speed. "In a wide-spread emotional crisis of the American people," General George C. Marshall complained in October 1945, "demobilization has become, in effect, disintegration, not only of the armed forces but apparently of all conception of world responsibility and what it demands of us." It was only gradually that the American people adjusted to the unexpected and dismaying fact that they would have to keep their armaments and armies, play a continuing role in the hard game of world politics, and offer persistent opposition, backed by military power, to the Soviet Communist challenge.

Kennan's analysis (reprinted in the July 1947 issue of *Foreign Affairs*) was not addressed to the masses. In March 1946, Winston Churchill mounted the rostrum in Harry Truman's home state of Missouri to deliver a memorable address:

From Stettin in the Baltic to Trieste in the Adriatic an iron curtain has descended across the continent. Behind that line lie all the capitals of the ancient states of central and eastern Europe. Warsaw, Berlin, Prague, Vienna, Budapest, Belgrade, Bucharest, and Sofia. . . .

Churchill's message agreed with Kennan's: the Russians despise weakness and will take advantage of it. The Anglo-American alliance of World War II must be restored to counteract this new threat to the freedom of Europe and the world. The embattled orator threw a gauntlet squarely in Stalin's face, as he had done to Hitler eighteen years earlier.

Escalation of the Cold War, 1947–1949

The result of Churchill's speech was not to tear down the iron curtain (a term not of Churchill's invention) but to strengthen it. Anglo-American policy moved to take the initiative. The United Nations was used to mobilize world opinion against Soviet actions in Iran, forcing them to withdraw their troops. Reparations shipments from the American zone of Germany were terminated in May 1946, an act Soviet Foreign Minister Molotov condemned as unlawful. (It was aimed at the French as well as the Russians.) Washington sent units of the fleet to the eastern Mediterranean in support of the Turks. Secretary of State Byrnes made a significant speech in Germany in September, suggesting that the economic recovery of Europe depended on German recovery. Truman's Secretary of Commerce, former Vice-President Henry A. Wallace, resigned from the cabinet at Truman's request after criticizing the new direction of policy for being unkind to the Russians.

Early in 1947 General Marshall replaced Byrnes as secretary of state, and in February came a push from the British, orchestrated in advance: England could no longer afford to send military and economic aid to Greece and Turkey, as she had been doing. An effective memo from "Ernie" Bevin and an eloquent appeal from Undersecretary of State Dean Acheson convinced American congressional leaders of both political parties that the United States must take up this burden, lest the world begin slipping into the swamps of despair and communism.

Most western European Communist parties were at a peak of their strength just after the war. The French Communist party won 28.6 percent of the vote in November 1946, an all-time high. Even in West Germany, the KPD, which later diminished to almost nothing, could gain close to 6 percent in 1949.

Those who like to stress the role of accident in history might well argue that the weather took a hand in the affairs of man during the terrible winter of 1946–1947, setting in motion a train of events that perpetuated the truly Cold War. Running out of fuel, the beleaguered British found themselves forced to cut their commitments all over the world; they terminated their Palestine mandate at this time, setting off Middle Eastern war between Israel and her angry Arab neighbors, as they also threw the Greek civil war hastily into Uncle Sam's surprised hands.

In Greece, Communist-led guerrillas, supplied from Yugoslavia,

Albania, and Bulgaria, were a serious threat to the unimpressive government at Athens that was recognized by the West. Civil war broke out there in 1946 amid economic chaos and distress. The whole area was strategically crucial. The Truman Doctrine, which announced aid to Greece and Turkey in the context of a general struggle against communism ("At the present moment in world history nearly every nation must choose between alternative ways of life") was followed in May by a decision to "reconstruct the two great workshops," Germany and Japan, and in June by Secretary Marshall's Harvard speech in which he proposed the plan of large-scale American economic aid to all of Europe, in return for their acting in cooperation with each other. The year 1947 was crucial for a rallying of "free world" forces to (a) resist Soviet aggressions, (b) shore up the military defenses of the non-Communist world, (c) tackle the problem of European and world economic recovery with massive American assistance, and (d) end the policy of repression of the defeated World War II powers and attempt to secure their recovery. Those who allege American guilt in intensifying the Cold War accuse Truman of an excess of rhetorical anti-communism.

If this was a declaration of cold war to some, it was a bracing revival of morale to others. Later it seemed like the greatest of times. Truman's spunk was rewarded by an unexpected electoral victory in 1948, as he overcame isolationist opposition and the secession of the pro-Russian Wallaceites. As the Marshall Plan pumped American money into Europe, West German economic recovery began to trigger a general European recovery. The cost was a deeper division of Europe. Offered a share in the Marshall Plan aid, the Russians turned down the bait and ordered their satellites to do the same. They denounced it as an American capitalist plot. The division of Germany deepened as the three western zones, soon to be merged, went their own way and indeed began to prepare for the creation of a German government by 1949. When the Russians replied in kind, there would be two Germanies. Moreover, the Russian reply was to intensify control over the eastern European countries, bringing them even more tightly under the grip of regimes loyal to the Kremlin.

The most dramatic example of this process was in Czechoslovakia. There, until early in 1948, the Russians had tolerated a coalition government in which several other political parties were represented. They had not proceeded toward full sovietization of the society even though Czech Communists held the dominant position. Outraged by their betrayal at Munich by the West and historically rather pro-Russian, the Czechs greeted the Russian liberators with some enthusiasm. Ejecting more than two million Germans had involved a vast transfer of wealth. In the relatively free elections of May 1946, the Communist party won 38 percent of the vote, far better than it ever did anywhere else.

But the popularity of the Communists was evidently waning in 1948. Orders came from Moscow to tighten control and prepare for intensified nationalization and collectivization of property. In February, twelve non-Communist members of the government resigned in protest over communization of the police and tried to force elections. But on February 25, Prime Minister Klement Gottwald, a faithful pro-Russian Communist, chose a virtually all-Communist government by decree and denied elections. In effect this was a coup d'etat ending the last vestiges of democracy. On March 10, the body of Jan Masaryk, son of the founding father and symbol of Czech democracy, was found lying on the street under his apartment window, an apparent suicide. Whether he was dead by his own hand or others', Masaryk's demise shocked the world; it was followed a few weeks later by that of Edward Benes, the other symbol of a free Czech republic, who had reluctantly and under pressure given his consent to the coup of February 25.

The Czech government, which had tried to join the Marshall Plan in July 1947, might have served as a bridge between East and West, some thought, but instead Stalin had defiantly forced it to cut all ties to the West. At this same time, Russia began a general tightening of control over the "satellite" countries. Previously designated "people's democracies" and allowed some measure of exemption from total Stalinization, they were now to be integrated much more closely into the Soviet system. But in Yugoslavia this policy backfired. All in all, 1948, the year of the Marshall Plan, the birth of NATO, and the Prague coup, was not a good year for the Russians. The worst disaster was the secession of Marshall Tito's government from the Kremlin orbit.

A loyal Stalinist, Tito had never previously wavered in his faith in Moscow. During the war, as we know, he had built his own organization and had gained popularity by his courageous resistance to the Nazis, which won him reluctant backing even from the Western allies. After the war he imitated Soviet policies and backed Moscow in its arguments with the West. Quarreling violently with the West over the city of Trieste, which he wished to wrest from Italy, Tito shot down two American planes in 1946 and was the chief supporter of the Greek Communist guerrillas, *against* the advice of Stalin. So it is strange and rather ironic that the Yugoslav Communists should have administered to Stalin his most staggering Cold War defeat.

The immediate cause of the Russian-Yugoslav break was Tito's attempts to organize, without Moscow's approval, a Balkan federation with Bulgaria and Albania. This demonstrated an independence to which

Stalin was far from accustomed. The creation of the Cominform in October 1947, a sort of successor to the old Comintern, was supposed to herald close cooperation among the communist countries. But Tito was not disposed to take orders. He complained of Russian economic exploitation. Yugoslavia was asking for equality of nations within the Red bloc, not subordination of the others to Russia.

Stalin handled this whole episode badly, his extreme arrogance showing through. Surrounded by adulation, treated as a god, the aging dictator simply had ceased to be able to work with people; he could only issue orders. One of the most damning documents to come out of the affair was written by Tito's lieutenant, Milovan Djilas, after he had been summoned to Moscow for talks. In *Conversations with Stalin*, Djilas revealed the abysmal degradation of late Stalinism, including its terrible drunkenness and vulgarity. Tito published the resulting exchange of letters with Stalin, in which the Russians looked bad—bullying, insulting, and threatening.

Yet despite much provocation from the Yugoslavs, Stalin did not unleash the Red Army. He did withdraw Soviet officials and organized an economic boycott of Yugoslavia. He could surely have crushed Tito, but the courageous Yugoslavs would have fought him, and they had fought against Hitler very well. One view of Stalin is that he always respected strength. He took his revenge on other potential Titos; heads rolled among the Communist elite in Poland, Hungary, Bulgaria, and Czechoslovakia, in a series of public purge trials reminiscent of the thirties. Bulgaria's Kostov, Hungary's Rajk, Czechoslovakia's Slansky were executed and Poland's Gomulka imprisoned. But though conducting a war of nerves Stalin held his fire in Yugoslavia.

Stalin's chief lieutenant, Andrei Zhdanov, a brilliant ideologist who specialized in demanding total thought control within the USSR, died in 1948. Some think he was a victim of Stalin; rumors spread that Zhdanov had opposed Stalin's handling of Tito. Perhaps there was too much disunity within the normally compliant Politboro on this question, even for Stalin.

Economic pressures forced Yugoslavia into desperate circumstances, but she did not yield. Eventually she got some help from the West. While retaining her own brand of communism—which eventually developed into a model significantly different from Moscow's, less centralized and bureaucratic—she never really returned to the Soviet camp. In 1948, however, every other Communist party joined Moscow in excommunicating Tito, evidence of the hold that discipline still had over the International. Even the Chinese, who were later to quarrel even more spectacularly with Russia, did so. Yugoslavia was a lone rebel, and Stalin could take comfort in the unity of the rest of the communist world under his leadership, which was enormously prestigious in these years. The French and Italian Communists, who had been ordered to refrain from rocking the boat too much in 1945–1946, were now unleashed to oppose their governments. This Cold War weapon did not prove very effective, though in 1948 there was lively fear of a Communist victory in the Italian elections.

Stalin's largest Cold War thunderbolt also proved something of a dud. This was the Berlin Blockade of 1948–1949. Surrounded by the Soviet zone of occupation, the city of Berlin was itself divided into four zones. When the Western powers merged their zones into one and began its economic development in 1947–1948, they technically violated the Potsdam agreement. Therefore, the Russians might well have claimed an end to Berlin's special status. Currency reform, in the form of a new German mark, was a key to the economic revival that now began in West Germany; but it widened the gulf between the two Germanies and added to the Berlin complications. Moreover, the Western allies had no written treaty guaranteeing them access to Berlin. In this city lived 6,500 of their troops, half of whom were Americans, and some two million West Berliners, who were fiercely anti-Communist and subject to much Russian harassment.

The Russians gradually tightened a blockade on West Berlin, first by delaying shipments, then by a full stoppage (June 24, 1948) of trains, trucks, and barges. Electric power to West Berlin was turned off, the main plant lying in the largely industrial eastern section controlled by the Russians.

The West had three options: to let themselves be forced out of Berlin, to challenge the Soviet blockade with force, or to find some alternate means of supplying West Berlin. The American military governor in Germany, General Lucius Clay, was determined to resist the Russians and wanted to try to force deliveries through. When he was overruled in Washington, he ordered air supplies, at first merely temporizing. Although the Russians sometimes harassed the planes, they did not try to shoot them down. The air lift program grew, and by the end of September a plane was landing every three minutes. The winter lay ahead, with the need to supply not only food but coal for home heating to the two million Berliners. Fortunately the winter was mild. With great fortitude, the citizens of West Berlin stuck it out and cheered as new records were set; by April, a plane was arriving every sixty-one seconds. The world saluted the West Berliners' courage and spirit as well as the American achievements in the airplanes. Finally, in May, Stalin agreed to call off the blockade, though reserving a right to renew it. The airlift had lasted more than a year and had cost a lot of money but very few lives; it had flown in over one-and-a-half million tons of fuel and food. General Clay declared that the people of Berlin had re-

West Berliners protest against the division of their city and harassment by Soviet authorities in the eastern sector. *Dorsey Press.*

stored Germany's honor and that their courage signalled the rebirth of a democratic people.

In this test of wills, perhaps the most remarkable, if somewhat overlooked factor, was the relative restraint shown by both sides. It was as if rules for the Cold War were being laid down. The Russians allowed the planes to land and eventually accepted defeat. The Americans did not try to shoot their way through Russian-held territory but resorted to the expensive alternative of the air lift. Although at one time President Truman had considered using the atomic bomb, he had second thoughts: the Soviet Union was about to explode its first A-bomb, on September 24, 1949.

World Conflict, 1949–1953

The 1947–1949 period was a hectic one, as lines in the Cold War were drawn: the Truman Doctrine, the Marshall Plan, the Prague coup, Tito's break with Moscow, and the Berlin blockade were only some of its events. Among others was the creation of the North Atlantic Treaty

Organization (NATO). The Prague coup and the Berlin blockade hastened this Western military alliance. In 1948, British Foreign Secretary Bevin initiated the organization of a "Western Union" alliance among Britain, France, and the Benelux countries (Belgium, the Netherlands, and Luxemburg), which was signed at Brussels. The departure of General de Gaulle and the exclusion of Communists from the government had put France in hands much more agreeable to participation in an alliance of this sort. Twelve countries then signed the NATO pact in April 1949; the United States, Canada, Iceland, Italy, Portugal, Norway, and Denmark joined the Western Union five in an alliance professedly aimed at defense against Soviet aggression: "To safeguard the freedom, common heritage and civilization of their peoples founded on the principles of democracy, individual liberty, and the rule of law." Russians declared NATO to be an "expression of the aggressive strivings of the ruling circles of the United States and Great Britain . . . for effecting the policy of unleashing a new war . . . to establish by force Anglo-American dominion over the world."

In fact, NATO was an outgrowth of Kennan's theory of "containment" and of a new semirealism in the United States. Americans no longer believed that world security could come through the United Nations (subject, alas, to Russian vetoes), but they still clung to the idea of some sort of collective security with an ideological base. The "Atlantic" nations were said to be bound together by both common interests and a common democratic commitment.

For western Europe, NATO provided a shield of security behind which economic recovery could take place; it was the political counterpart of the Marshall Plan, which channeled economic aid through the Organization of European Economic Cooperation (OEEC). The United States agreed to consider an attack on its European allies an attack on itself. For the United States, it was a memorable leap out of the traditional politics of "no entangling alliances," an acceptance of the fact that its own security was bound up with Europe's. Struck by NATO's spectacular success in sending western Europe into economic orbit, the United States tried to repeat the formula in other parts of the globe in the ensuing years, creating METO for the Middle East, CENTO for Western Asia, and SEATO for Southeast Asia with much less luck.

Despite its recognized advantages, NATO was subject to problems from the beginning. Neither Great Britain nor France proved capable of providing much military strength for a number of years, partly because each was heavily involved overseas; Indochina and then Algeria preoccupied the French army for the next decade. To raise the question of a Germany military presence was premature. The United States alone gave NATO its muscle. It was an unequal partnership, and, as such, it was sometimes galling to the Europeans and sometimes annoying to the United States. Increasingly, what counted was not the ground forces under NATO command in western Europe but the American "nuclear umbrella" acting as a deterrent against any Soviet temptation to attack.

Nevertheless, General Eisenhower returned to Europe as NATO commander along with tens of thousands of American GIs for the second time in a decade, this time to guard the enemy of World War II against one of the former Allies. While this buildup went on, NATO forces were still outnumbered many times by the Russian ground forces. What sustained Europe's spirit and perhaps deterred the Russians (who probably had very little intention of armed attack on Europe) was the assurance that such an attack would bring the United States, with all its great resources, into the war.

In 1949 the Russians exploded an atomic bomb—the fission bomb, created by the disintegration of Uranium-235. But advances in nuclear technology were about to make this sort of bomb, the one that had

Nuclear test explosion, 1946. The "A bomb" or fission bomb was far less powerful than the fusion H-bomb developed a few years later; nevertheless the Bikini test was a symbol of the new destructiveness. *Official United States Navy Photograph.*

horrified the world when it levelled the city of Hiroshima, as obsolete as a sixshooter. The first U.S. explosion of an "H-bomb," as it was popularly known, took place in 1952. The Soviets announced a similar success in August 1953. This fusion bomb, the product of the fusion at extreme temperatures of heavy isotopes of hydrogen, is many times more powerful than the A-bomb. In fact, since it operates by a self-perpetuating chain reaction, there is no limit to the size of an H-bomb except the capacity of the missile or bomber carrying it. A bomber can carry a 100-megaton bomb. The Hiroshima bomb, which killed 80,000 people, was 14 kilotons, that is about 1/700th as large as a 100-megaton H-bomb. Manufactured from one of the commonest of all elements, the H-bomb could readily be proliferated to a point sufficient to destroy the entire planet. Work then began on the development of rocket-powered missiles capable of carrying nuclear warheads long distances.

This was possibly the most dangerous period for nuclear war. Today, the vast growth in the numbers and kinds of long-range nuclear weapons (on submarines, in underground silos, on moving trains, and so on) means that neither the U.S. nor the USSR could hope to escape deadly retaliation, no matter how large its first strike; the deterrent now is much more effective than it was when nuclear weapons were few. The world shuddered at the thought of these horrendous weapons deployed by the two great powers who were shouting insults and threats at each other. Yet the logic of the "balance of terror" worked from the beginning: total war was now too dangerous; it would destroy everybody; there could be no victor in a nuclear war.

But already, before the appearance of H-bombs and missiles in 1954, war had erupted, not in Europe but in Asia. From one end to the other, that continent had been left as shattered and unstable as had Europe. During their season of power in the Orient, the Japanese had thoroughly upset the old order, and it could not be restored in its earlier form. India had demanded and won independence from Britain, but the subcontinent had had to be divided between Hindus and Muslims in 1947. The Dutch in the East Indies and the French in Indochina tried to reassert their authority, only to meet armed opposition. Each waged a losing battle, but the French did not give up until 1954, when a good part of their available armed strength was tied down in futile struggle against Ho Chi Minh's determined guerrilla warriors. All of Asia seemed in revolt against Western domination. The Soviet Union was quick to develop theories that these rebels against imperialism were really on the road to socialism, or they were at any rate allies in the struggle against capitalism and should be treated as such.

Led by Mao Tse-tung, the Chinese Communists were victorious in their struggle against Chiang Kai-shek's government in 1948–1949.

This seemed to the West like a staggering defeat and to the Russians like a glorious victory. Time was to cast much doubt on this verdict; but in the atmosphere of the Cold War the West, and particularly the Americans, usually did not distinguish among Communists, regarding them as all part of one gigantic conspiracy. The collapse of China into the arms of the Communists caused much criticism of Truman's government in the United States; had it done enough to help the tottering Nationalist regime? Should it have done more? Were the new Red leaders of China really Communists, or were they nationalist liberators and reformers essentially different from the Kremlin variety? Such unanswered questions introduced a degree of confusion into American thinking about Asia even before the Korean crisis of 1950.

Her limited ground forces already stretched thin, the United States had seemingly written off the mainland of Far Eastern Asia. Dean Acheson, now secretary of state, made a speech early in 1950 in which he said that the U.S. would defend Japan and the Philippines, but this seemed by implication to exclude South Korea. Like Germany, Korea had been divided at the end of the war into Russian and American zones of occupation, supposedly later to be reunited but now becoming a permanent division. The Russians had given much more military aid to the North Koreans than the Americans had given to the South. Cashing this chip in the Cold War game, and thereby providing some compensation for losses elsewhere, must have seemed to Stalin a relatively simple matter.

On June 25, 1950, some 70,000 North Korean troops attacked across the 38th parallel boundary and quickly drove the South Koreans southward. Faced with this situation, Truman decided to act to prevent another bastion from falling to communism. He was assisted by a United Nations Security Council decision that this was an act of aggression (the USSR was boycotting the Security Council at this time and thus could not cast a veto). Stationed in Japan since 1945, General Douglas MacArthur's Eighth Army entered South Korea, and in September it launched a counteroffensive that routed the North Koreans.

This was technically a United Nations army, though in fact it was overwhelmingly American. MacArthur, hearing no clear negative from Washington, decided to pursue the North Koreans beyond the 38th parallel. He drove them back to the Chinese border at the Yalu River, whereupon Chinese Communist armies struck into Korea, took the U.N. forces by surprise, and almost routed them. By February 1951, the Americans and their allies found themselves again far south of the 38th parallel, but they rallied and after bloody fighting restored the battle line not far from the original border. After a year of intense warfare, the result was a draw.

Students of American history will be familiar with this episode, which brought angry controversy, a dramatic conflict between President Truman and General MacArthur, and much trouble for American policy makers who had felt so euphoric after NATO. Here we need only look at it from a European perspective. Western Europe was ambivalent: it rejoiced that the Americans were willing to fight to resist communist aggression, but it feared the diversion of American strength to Asia, which might leave Europe exposed. In general, the European allies, especially Great Britain, tried to dampen the conflict and thought the Americans a bit unstable in their tendency to embark on ideological crusades. The Chinese Communists conducted a world propaganda campaign against the Americans, whom they accused of using germ warfare and other horrible methods. Some left-wing European intellectuals, led by Jean-Paul Sartre, accepted these charges (which were not in fact true). Their stand was indicative of a significant anti-American wing of West European opinion, which would increase in subsequent years. The Korean War sharpened the split within the British Labour party and thus may have contributed to its defeat in 1951.

The Korean War caused some economic dislocations in Europe, but it did not seriously blight the economic boom just then getting up a head of steam. It shocked the world with evidences of the destructiveness of modern warfare, even though it stopped short of nuclear weapons. But it also illustrated, like Berlin, a sense of limitations. Despite the wrath of General MacArthur, the Americans refrained from bombing Chinese territory. The fighting largely stopped after June 1951, when the countries began negotiations for a truce. These did not succeed until 1953, after Stalin's death and the election of a new American president provided fresh leadership. But the fighting halted with neither side a victor. Korea remained divided into hostile halves, as it has been ever since, but the great powers restrained their clients from renewing a war that threatened too many dangers. And the entrance of China into the equation as a third force (not really in coordination with the Soviet Union) introduced a new element into world politics.

Semi-thaw in the Cold War, 1954–1956

If from 1945 to 1951 lines were drawn and forces consolidated in the two-bloc polarization of world power, the next few years produced tendencies both to intensify and to diminish the Cold War, often simultaneously. The Korean War and the "McCarthyite" anticommunist hysteria that followed it in the United States certainly intensified Cold

War passions. The drive to create an effective NATO continued; Greece and Turkey were added to its membership, at whatever cost to "North Atlantic" logic; and the issue of German military contribution to NATO was raised. This caused a commotion. The French, in particular, though wishing a strong defense against the Soviets, flinched at the thought of any sort of revived German army. (Someone said that the French wanted a German army that was stronger than the Russian but weaker than the French.) But German opinion itself was, on the whole, opposed to a new *Wehrmacht*. The Americans pushed it hardest.

Faced with the need for some German divisions to give NATO credibility, the French countered with a plan for a European, internationalized army. But the British refused to join, and the French Assembly ended by rejecting this European Defence Community (EDC) in 1954, after much debate. German rearmament soon took place under a different formula. The West German government, in existence since 1949 but not yet fully sovereign (being subject to restrictions of the Allied High Commission), entered the Western Union group. In 1955 West Germany joined NATO and the Federal Republic was given full sovereignty, at the same time renouncing atomic weapons and long-range bombers and missiles. The French Assembly was barely persuaded to approve this. The British now promised to keep some troops on the Continent. The Communists bitterly charged the "imperialists" with plotting to use the West German *revanchistes* in aggressive war against the Soviet Union. It should be stressed that West Germany had no independent military command; her forces were placed under the integrated NATO command.

This brought a Soviet reaction in the form of creation of the Warsaw Pact, a counter-NATO made up of the eight East European communist-bloc countries: Albania, Bulgaria, Czechoslovakia, Hungary, Poland, Rumania, the USSR, and the newly established East German state, the German Democratic Republic (DDR). The division of Germany was made more permanent by this creation of separate sovereign East and West German states. As we have noted, 1954–1955 also brought the H-bomb and the first long-range missiles, hardly encouraging signs for peace.

Nevertheless, there were signs of a thaw. The death of Stalin early in 1953 unquestionably had something to do with this. A Korean truce was achieved. Soviet rhetoric cooled as both Malenkov and Khrushchev, candidates for the post-Stalin leadership, talked of the dangers of nuclear war and the need for a Cold War thaw. At this time the West did not seem to understand the significance of Stalin's death and the new Russian leadership, which marked an epochal change in the USSR. A 1955 peace treaty ended the occupation of little Austria, which ever since the war had had the great powers as "guests"—"four elephants in a canoe," the Socialist prime minister of Austria once called it. Austria pledged never to unite with Germany or to join a military alliance; in return for this pledge of neutrality and some economic payments, the Russians went home and left the little country its freedom.

Prior to this, the Geneva Conference of 1954 had achieved a settlement in Indochina, ending France's long agony of involvement there. As the French surrendered in the north, the Viet Minh followers of National Communist Ho Chi Minh were supposed to withdraw from the south, thus splitting Vietnam in two and neutralizing Cambodia and Laos. While time proved that this division only set the stage for a new and larger struggle, it seemed a relief at the time.

Early in 1955 the Communists suggested a settlement with Germany similar to Austria's, that is, unification, neutralization, and withdrawal. After Malenkov's fall, no more was heard of this suggestion. British Foreign Secretary Anthony Eden also proposed unification, but both sides soon decided that two Germanies were more convenient. However, German Chancellor Konrad Adenauer visited Moscow in September 1955, a sign of Soviet desire for normalization of relations. The new Soviet leadership paid a visit to Belgrade in May 1955 to offer apologies to Tito, and in general the Soviets seemed to wish to relax Stalinist harshness, both at home and in the bloc countries. This was difficult, however. The whole problem of de-Stalinization (which we discuss later) was involved. The most obvious danger was that a sudden relaxation of authority would lead to revolt and dissolve the whole Soviet system.

Soon after Stalin's death in 1953 there were riots in both Czechoslovakia and East Germany, the latter, beginning in East Berlin, the more serious. A combination of Soviet tanks and some reforms ended this June 17 *Aufstand*, but stirrings continued in the satellites. There were changes of leadership. Klement Gottwald of Czechoslovakia mysteriously failed to survive his attendance at Stalin's funeral. Then came the spectacular "secret speech" delivered by Nikita Khrushchev to the 20th Party Congress in February 1956, denouncing Stalin's crimes. This set the stage for further disturbances. A Polish uprising, centered at Poznan, caused the withdrawal of a Russian general and the appointment of a new Polish Communist leader, Wladyslaw Gomulka, who had been imprisoned. Then in October, Hungary exploded in revolution.

Forced into World War II on Hitler's side, Hungary lost most of her army in Russia, became a battleground at the war's end, and then, failing in an attempt to surrender to the Americans, suffered Russian occupation with severe reparation losses. The only resistance Hungarians could offer to a tough Communist dictatorship was to rally around Roman Catholic Cardinal Mindszenty, who was arrested and condemned to life imprisonment in 1948. Between 1949 and 1953, Matyas Rakosi was nearly all-powerful, and he pushed a program of sovietization, including collectivization of agriculture. In July 1953, during the thaw after Stalin's death, Imre Nagy replaced Rakosi and brought with him more tolerant policies. But in the spring of 1955, after Malenkov's fall from power in Moscow, Nagy was dismissed from office and expelled from the party. Rakosi was briefly restored, but in July 1956, he was replaced by Erno Gero, evidently to appease Tito. But Gero did not please a Hungarian people anxious to bring back the popular Communist professor, Nagy. Nagy stood for what twelve years later would be called "socialism with a human face." A convinced Communist, he believed that real communism was not Stalinism; it should be democratic and free. He had released political prisoners, offered freedom of expression and religion, and slowed down the pace of collectivization and industrialization.

On October 23, 1956, a meeting of students and writers was brutally broken up by the Hungarian secret police. This led to a spontaneous revolution, during which the Hungarian army and much of its police went over to the young revolutionaries, who destroyed Russian tanks and drove out the Soviet troops in Budapest. Even some of the Russians fraternized with the revolutionaries. Nagy was called back, prisoners were released, and Mindszenty was freed and treated as a hero. It was an intoxicating moment, a truly remarkable example of revolutionary ecstasy. Deeply embarrassed and perplexed, the Kremlin at first hesitated but then sent in reinforcements. They crushed the revolution and arrested and shot Nagy. Two hundred thousand Hungarians fled the country, escaping via the Austrian frontier; thousands of others were killed or deported to Russia. No one who participated in this remarkable event ever forgot its moment of glory. But though they appealed for help to the West and to the United Nations, the valiant Hungarians got none, and they could not cope with the might of Russia alone.

In late October and early November of 1956 there was a remarkable coincidence of two major crisis. One reason the Hungarians appealed in vain was the West's preoccupation at this moment with the Suez crisis. It is quite likely that the Kremlin's decision to intervene with strong military force in Hungary was affected by Suez, which provided them with assurance that there would be no Western reaction. The Russian decision to send in troops and crush the rebellion was taken on October 30, after several days of uncertainty. The Israeli attack on Egypt, which began the Suez crisis, occurred on October 29.

The Russians could still have called the troops back before November 3. By November 1, the British-French operation had been mounted and dissension within the Western alliance was apparent.

What happened in Budapest was of less moment to statesmen in Washington, London, and Paris than what was happening in Egypt. The background of the war, the intervention, and the international crisis that erupted there went back several years. The Arab-Israel feud dated from the creation of the Jewish state and its expulsion of a large population of Arabs after the 1948 war.[2] In 1952, humiliated by the weakness of their country and the corruption of its government, a group of young Egyptian army officers overthrew King Farouk and inaugurated a revolutionary regime. They were radical and anti-Western, blaming the establishment of Israel on Europeans. (In fact, in 1948 Stalin had supported the Jews, whose chief enemies then were the British. As the mandate power, the British had tried to hold back Jewish nationalism until they gave up the task in 1947.) The Egyptian revolutionaries were not Communists, but in 1955 they began to buy arms from the Soviet bloc.

Rising Arab nationalism focused on the Suez Canal. Though lying within Egyptian territory, the Suez Canal had long been controlled by an international company and protected by British troops. In 1954 the British agreed to withdraw their troops over the next twenty months if freedom of navigation through the canal were maintained. In July of 1956, Colonel Abdul Nasser, head of the Egyptian government, announced the seizure of the canal zone and the confiscation of the Suez Company's properties, alleging a sovereign national right to do so. The British and the French viewed this as a violation of the Suez treaty and, more to the point, a threat to their vital interests. Anthony Eden, who became obsessed with hatred for Nasser, said that the Egyptian dictator, whom he compared to Hitler, had "his thumb on our windpipe."

Nasser decided to seize the canal because the Egyptians wanted to build a huge dam on the upper Nile to bring economic improvement to their impoverished land. Nasser had hoped for American aid, but after long negotiations, during which the Soviets entered the bidding and Nasser raised his price, the United States refused to finance it. Inept Western diplomacy and Egyptian truculence had led to the worst possible Arab-Western relations.

---

[2] A small number of European Jews, influenced by the ideals of the Zionist movement founded in 1897, had made their way to Palestine after World War I. Committed by the Balfour Declaration of 1917 to help establish a Jewish "homeland" there, the British protected the Jews against frequent Arab hostility. But the trickle of migrants became a flood as the result of Nazi persecution.

The United States was unsympathetic to European traditions of imperialism. "We agree in Europe but not in Asia and Africa," American Secretary of State John Foster Dulles noted. He and Eden simply did not get along, and communications between them broke down. Eden had succeeded the aged Winston Churchill as prime minister, after long service as foreign secretary (1935–1938, 1940–1945, 1951–1955). Suez was to terminate his distinguished career and sow doubts about his capability as a leader. Impatient with Dulles and Eisenhower, enraged at Nasser, and convinced that Britain must rise to meet her challenges or sink into second-rate status, Eden entered into secret agreements with France and Israel for an attack on Egypt. The Israelis needed little urging; Egypt and Syria, still technically at war with Israel, had mounted border raids, or permitted the Palestinian refugees to mount them, and had closed the Canal to Israeli shipping. The Jews wished to gain more secure frontiers and destroy guerrilla bases. For them the Arab purchase of Soviet arms, threatening to upset the military balance, was the last straw. (Only France was then selling arms to the Israelis.)

As for France, her premier, Guy Mollet, not only joined Eden in fearing economic disaster from Egypt's control of the Canal but resented Egyptian aid to Algerian rebels, who began to be a problem for France in 1954. Mollet also participated in the "Munich reflex," seeing in Nasser another aggressor-dictator who must be stopped in his tracks. France was indeed the driving force behind the plan, eagerly seconded by the Israelis with the British evidently more reluctant.

It was all a bit confusing to the Americans; three of her best friends, good democratic countries, had conspired to commit aggression, which was what only Communists were supposed to do. The French, Israelis and British did indeed plan it in advance at a conference in France October 22–23, though they long denied this.[3] On October 29 the Israelis struck into the Sinai peninsula and quickly overran it. Two days later France and Britain delivered an ultimatum to stop the war (designed to freeze the Israeli gains). They then began bombing Egypt and, a short time later, moving troops in by air and sea to occupy Port Said, which lies at the head of the Canal. Their goal was to regain control of the Canal and cause the fall of Nasser. They had not reckoned on hostile reactions throughout the world, including their own citizens and the United States. President Eisenhower was morally outraged, and the world was treated to a rare case of American-Russian cooperation, as the United Nations condemned the aggression. The United States threatened economic sanctions against the aggressors if they did not withdraw, while the USSR, seeing how badly the West was in disarray,

[3] The most detailed and interesting account is by Moyshe Dayan in his *Story of My Life* (New York, 1976), pp. 218–234.

issued veiled threats of trying out "rocket techniques." Egypt blocked the Canal, and oil supplies began to dry up. There was an outcry in Parliament against the government, an outcry that extended to some members of Eden's own Conservative party as well as the Labour party.

Faced with such formidable pressures, it is not surprising that the French and British crumbled. Asked about this performance by his erstwhile protégé, Winston Churchill said, "I am not sure I would have dared to start it, but if I had, I'm sure I would not have dared not to finish it." Eden did not dare to finish it. The two countries called off their assault and in early December withdrew their forces, under cover of a United Nations peacekeeping force, that replaced the British and French troops in the Canal zone. The Israelis also had to give up their territorial gains, although they had gained military prestige. But Nasser did not fall, and the Western alliance had seemingly cracked open. It was just as well for the West that the Russians were preoccupied with Hungary, though it was a disaster for Hungary that the West was concentrating on Suez.

The first week of November 1956 stands as a kind of climax of the Cold War, the closing scene of its second act. In retrospect Suez marked the end of the independent world power of Britain and France, who had to accept the fact that they could not make major political moves without the support of the United States. It confirmed the long retreat of the British from their imperial role and opened the era of decolonization. On the other side, it showed that the Soviet sphere in eastern Europe was safe; countries in the Russian zone could not win their freedom by rebellion, for they would get no help from the West. Hungary and Suez underscored the giant role of the two superpowers. It was the apex of bipolarization.

The Recovery
of Western Europe,
1948-1963

12

Economic Recovery

In the previous chapter we discussed post-1945 international relations, primarily, and these may seem to have consisted of constant crises, threats of war, divisions of the continent of Europe into hostile blocs, and other near disasters. Nevertheless war in Europe was avoided, and during this period of Cold War, both eastern and western Europe made rather spectacular economic progress.

Western Europe's progress may seem the more surprising. Stalin's advisers had told him that the capitalist West was finished; uncritical leftists in the West parroted this slogan, claiming (to paraphrase the veteran British socialist G. D. H. Cole) that there were now only two choices for humanity, fascism (nazism) or communism. Even if he did not think that capitalism was on its death bed, having fallen fatally ill of the Great Depression and been nearly finished off by the great war, an empirical observer surveying the physical and moral ruins of 1945 must have thought that recovery was out of the question, at least for many decades. The two years after the war appeared to confirm this diagnosis.

Yet the forces of recovery were present and, boosted by American aid, Europe took off about 1948 on a boom that with only short pauses lasted until well into the 1960s, bringing a higher standard of living than Europeans had ever known. It was an economic miracle. Writing in 1963, French political and social analyst Raymond Aron marvelled, "In 1945, western Europe was a mass of ruins; today it is one of the most prosperous regions of the world." Western Europe's economic growth rate in the postwar years surpassed that of both the United States and the Soviet Union. (See Table 12–1.) In this period the leading nations of western Europe created instruments of economic cooperation that aided recovery, especially the European Economic Community started in 1957; yet the separate countries retained elements of a special national style in a social, political, and economic matters. What they shared, at least until the 1960s, was a pattern of steady success.

Germany's economic resurgence was the most amazing of all, a true *Wirtschaftswunder*. Having absorbed at least 12 million refugees, West Germany's population reached 60 million, or about 630 people per square mile (the United States has about 55 people per square mile). With this population, she achieved more than full employment: in 1961, unemployment stood at less than ½ of 1 percent, and West Germany began to import labor. By 1969 she had more than a million and a half Italian, Greek, Turkish and other non-German workers. Real wages rose 139 percent between 1950 and 1966, with a 10 percent shorter work week; although the growth rate was running about 6 percent, inflation was moderate prior to 1970. Unlike Great Britain,

TABLE 12–1

Gross National Product, in billions of dollars (rounded)			
Year	*USA*	*USSR*	*EEC (Six)* EEC (Nine)***
1952	350	115	85
1962	560	230	230
1972	1,150	440	660	825
Population, in millions of people (rounded)			
1952	160	185	155
1962	185	220	175
1972	200	250	190	250
Per capita GNP			
1972	$5,750	$1,760	$3,475	$3,300

* Belgium, France, Germany, Italy, Luxembourg, and the Netherlands; the EEC was created in 1957.
** With the addition of Denmark, Great Britain, and Ireland.

who had an unfavorable balance of trade, Germany's was favorable, so that the mark was twice evaluated *upward*. In 1946 the occupying powers had set an annual limit of 7½ million tons of steel for all Germany; in 1969, West Germany alone was producing 44 million tons. She became the economic giant of the continent, with a standard of living surpassed in Europe only by the small states, Switzerland and Sweden, and rivaling that of the United States. All this occurred in a land that had seemed so shattered, so hated, and so demoralized in 1945 that observers thought it could never rise again.

French recovery was equally spectacular, for France started from very nearly as low a point as had Germany in 1945. She had been occupied and drained during the war by the Germans and then had been a battlefield in 1944. Aided by the material they seized from their zone of occupation in Germany and from the whole Saarland for some years, the French made a fairly rapid economic recovery. After reaching prewar levels between 1947 and 1950, the French economy more than doubled in gross national product in the 1950s and almost tripled again in the next decade, an advance that just about parallels Germany's.

Since their railroads had been ruined, the French were forced to rebuild them on a modern basis, thus getting perhaps the best transportation system in the world—an example of some of the compensations of disaster. They were aided by Jean Monnet's genius for planning; French *planification* was more flexible and subtle than was the centralized nationalization model adopted by the USSR and to some extent by British Labour. There was some nationalization (the Bank of France, railroads, the Renault auto works, airlines, mines, gas, and electricity) but basic reliance was placed on private enterprise; what the state did was use its financial powers to guide investment so that modernization of basic industries occurred first and in the right order. Marshall Plan money was used wisely for such primary investment.

Though as a victor she did not receive all the advantages of defeat, Great Britain also experienced a very satisfactory rate of economic growth after the war, averaging about 3 percent between 1950 and 1970. Suffering far less war destruction, Britain did not have to modernize industrial plant as Germany and France did, and she paid a price for this in a less efficient economy. Although her advance was slower than that on the Continent, it was not until the 1960s that the English, watching the Common Market countries pulling away from them, were condemned to look a bit threadbare compared to French, Germans, Swedes, and Swiss. Except for this comparison, the British might have congratulated themselves on raising their average standard of living as no other era had ever done. The wage-earner was more than two and a half times as well off in terms of real wages in 1969 as he had been in 1939, not counting benefits from the famous "cradle to grave" social welfare system, which included free medical care. Unemployment was very low, 2 percent or even less.

The chief obstacle to even better economic performance was Britain's troublesome balance of international trade, which tended to blight every budding boom by raising imports to an unacceptable degree. Britain was more dependent on imported foodstuffs and raw materials than was any other major European country. Balance of payments problems caused devaluation of the pound in 1949 (from $4.03 to $2.80) and again by another 15 percent in 1967. At least initially, devaluation provided an export boost by making British goods cheaper in terms of foreign currencies. It also made foreign products dearer for the British buyer, thus discouraging imports. The British hoped devaluation would not raise the prices of raw materials and foods, which often came from the underdeveloped countries. It should be noted that international exchange worked reasonably well from 1945 to 1971 under the agreements reached in July 1944 at Bretton Woods, which created the International Monetary Fund and the World Bank.

But balance of payments problems led to a "stop-go" pattern of economic growth that brought headaches to many a British government. Inflation was the other, and related, aspirin-inducer. Between the end of the war and 1969, prior to the great inflation of the 1970s, prices more than tripled. Not until the 1970s, however, did these problems seriously threaten a basically hopeful economic situation. In 1954 an American magazine reported, "The British people today enjoy a prosperity unknown in their history," and the Conservative party won easy electoral victories in 1955 and 1959 on the strength of this prosperity.

Economic growth was hardly less startling in Italy. After quite impressive rates of annual growth in the 1950s, averaging around 5½ percent between 1951 and 1955, Italy took off into a real boom following the establishment of the European Economic Community in 1957. By 1963 Italian production had risen 70 percent over 1958 levels, a rate of growth exceeding that of any other country in the EEC, from which Italy appeared to profit most. Italy, of course, especially southern Italy, had a longer way to go to join the ranks of the modernized industrial societies. The boom originally even widened the gulf between the "two Italies," and plans to break up the pattern of stagnancy in the landlord-ridden south confronted formidable difficulties. But hundreds of thousands of poor people did leave the land to flock to northern Italian cities, where rapid growth created a demand for labor; other Italians went to work in Germany or Switzerland or France.

These years of her most spectacular economic breakthrough in modern history brought Italy such unwelcome accompaniments of affluence as the most spectacular traffic jams in Europe; moneyed Italians rushed to consummate their love affair with the automobile just as tourism reached a peak. (The tourists would migrate to Greece and Spain later, when Italy grew too expensive.) Italy struck back at the traffic problem with great superhighway projects, pulling together the once romantically divided peninsula, breaking down ancient regionalisms, helping to modernize a country long steeped in ancient habits. Modernization most definitely came to the land of artists, poets, peasants and long-robed clerics in these years of the fifties and sixties, bringing with it the usual array of problems, some more severe in Italy than elsewhere. A little later, modernization came also to Spain, which had long been considered hopelessly stagnant.

All these economic miracles were not accomplished without some difficulties. Development was uneven. The broad masses did not really begin to reap the fruits of technological modernization and innovation until the 1960s, for investment in basic plant had to come first. Inflation was a recurring problem almost everywhere, bringing special hardship to certain groups, such as pensioners, retirees, and those on relatively fixed incomes. To overtake the rising cost of living, workers frequently went on strike. Complaints that the vaunted national health system actually brought serious deterioration in the quality of medical service enlivened the British political scene. Housing was a critical area for many years, since it was both inadequate and too expensive.

It remains a paradox, though, that these years of struggle from 1945 to 1960 were happier ones than the later more opulent times. The spirit was generally optimistic. England, crowning a new queen in 1953, talked of a New Elizabethan Age, later an object of mockery among disillusioned youth. Germans and Italians set to work to rebuild their shattered countries and restore their standing in the world by exemplary behavior. Charles de Gaulle symbolized a resurgence of French national pride. A whole set of new French attitudes, toward modernization and technology, arose out of the war's trauma.

The "work ethic" of this postwar generation—later to get it into trouble with its own children—must be accounted the leading cause of the economic miracle. In the last analysis, whatever the theories of economists or ideologists, what seems to count so far as growth is concerned is a willingness to work hard, to save, to make sacrifices. Writing in 1949, the Spanish philosopher José Ortega y Gasset thought that the voluntary sacrifices Englishmen made in the years just after the war constituted "one of the most extraordinary examples in history" of "spontaneous and resolute national solidarity." In Germany, the millions of refugees who had lost all when they were ejected from their homelands were willing to work to make a new life; they had no choice.

In reaction to the fact of having touched rock-bottom, a crisis or disaster psychology led people to dig in and work hard. It was one of the paradoxical advantages of destruction.

In taking advantage of an opportunity to start almost all over again and create new institutions, western Europeans responded creatively, combining the best features of traditional free-enterprise capitalism with state-directed planning plus state-administered social welfare. Less rigid and authoritarian than the Russian Communist kind, "planning" was a part of the Western model, most notably in France but in some degree throughout the West. The British adopted both a comprehensive social welfare system and a commitment to maintain full employment by using fiscal budgetary devices, reflecting the Keynesian influence. The French plans were designed to direct investment into certain areas and to modernize basic equipment by controlling bond issues and providing tax incentives or disincentives. Even in West Germany, where, amid a reaction against both Nazi and Communist statism, the rhetoric of the dominant Christian Democratic leaders stressed free private enterprise, the slogan was "*social* market economy," and in fact a good deal of direction did come from Bonn in subtle ways.

The French word *dirigisme* perhaps best summed it up: a basically free enterprise, market economy but one *directed* by a state planning apparatus, thus combining the dynamism of the profit motive with enough central control to keep the engine of private capitalism from running off the track. In all these countries there was a great deal more outright socialism than there was in the United States. Basic industries were nationalized in France as well as in Britain right after the war. In Germany, with less state ownership, experiments in comanagement took place: worker participation in both ownership and management of industrial corporations. But in all countries the basic reliance was on old-fashioned profit incentives.[1]

French economist Jacques Rueff, a great favorite of de Gaulle's, joined the German Wilhelm Röpke, who taught in Geneva but advised Adenauer's government, and the Italian Luigi Einaudi in forming an international coterie of economic experts firmly committed to the virtues of the free market. Such a group, including Austria's Von Hayek, Britain's Lionel Robbins, and America's embattled Milton Friedman, met at Pilgrim Mountain in Switzerland in 1947 to foment a kind of conspiracy to revive that much-maligned entity, capitalism. Perhaps, like Christianity, it ought to be given a real try! At a time when the

[1] Faced with a (to them) puzzling mixture of capitalism and state planning, the European Communists decided to classify this as a variety of "state monopoly capitalism," thus linking it to Lenin's categories.

jargon of the welfare state and planned production was on nearly everyone's lips and Adam Smith was a dirty word, this international elite dared to argue that the private entrepreneur in a competitive society is the best bet to increase wealth and distribute it equitably. To a considerable extent, the war had wiped out the old possessors and set up a new competition. Thus, the 1948 currency reform in Germany tended to liquidate fortunes and start everyone off anew in a somewhat equal race. "The economic recovery of France," one authority concluded, was "due to the restaffing of the economy with new men and to new French attitudes."

In brief, the post-1945 generation was serious and hard-working. In 1968 its children would rebel against the vulgarity of this preoccupation with work and money. For those who had endured the tragedy of the war, there could be little question of esthetic niceties; they set to work to rebuild their lives because they had no other choice. In so doing they rebuilt Europe, no doubt at the cost of a certain philistinism. With affluence came complacency and the conspicuous consumption of a generation of the newly rich. The amazing thing is that the transition from poverty to affluence took only a couple of decades.

Postwar Politics in the Western Democracies: France

There was also encouraging progress in politics, if by "progress" one means stability, less extreme polarization of parties, and a reasonable compromise between democracy and authority. The commitment to a basically free, pluralistic society, with freedom to dissent and competition among rival political groups, was intensified in western Europe. There was a strong reaction against both Soviet Russian totalitarianism and the defeated, rejected but still sometimes feared nazism and fascism of World War II. In the 1950s there was a revulsion against political "ideologies," which were considered to be shrill and shallow invitations to hatred. There was little positive attachment either to democracy as an ideology or to any other "system"; people were disgusted with all total political systems that sought to regiment the human spirit in the name of some utopia, and which turned out in practice to mean the terroristic tyranny of a narrow-minded elite.

Democracy, as Winston Churchill put it, is the worst form of government except for all the others. Two cheers for it, if not three, British novelist E. M. Forster suggested. There was a declining interest in politics; up to 51 percent of the people in Fourth Republic France

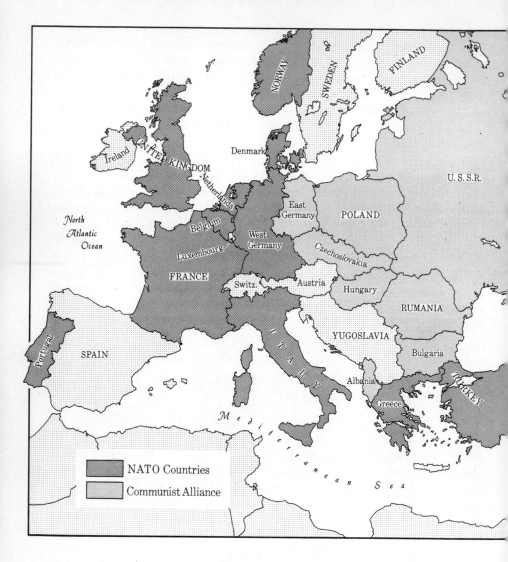

NATO Countries
Communist Alliance

indicated total disinterest. The work-ethic generation was "too busy with their materially-based freedoms to get excited about politics," a letter to a British magazine noted.

This end-of-ideology, apolitical, quasi-conservative mood of the 1950s, against which the young people of the late sixties reacted so sharply, will be discussed later, when we talk about intellectual trends. Here, let us briefly dicuss the main western European countries, which, for all their apathy, seemed lively and eventful enough.

Between 1945 and 1958 France created a new regime, the Fourth Republic, watched it fail, and changed regimes to the Fifth Republic— all without civil violence of any significant sort. The Fourth Republic, established in 1946 after an interval during which General de Gaulle served as head of a caretaker government, lived a precarious life. De Gaulle himself disliked the excessively parliamentary nature of this constitution, which he thought would weaken France. It was approved in October 1946 by a very indecisive margin, actually by a minority (31 percent voted against it and 31 percent abstained). The general then "went into the desert," boycotting all politics for the next twelve years.

As the Cold War heated up, the French Communist party, which consistently attracted more than 20 percent of the electorate, switched to opposition tactics and by 1947 was voting against every government. With total noncooperation on both left and right, the Fourth Republic repeated the weakness of the Third (and of the Weimar Republic): it was difficult to get a majority in the Assembly and impossible without a coalition of several parties. This weakness was intensified by a system of proportional representation, which magnified the parliamentary representation of the smaller political parties.

In 1951, for example, the Communist party gained 21 percent of the vote; the Socialists (SFIO) 11 percent; and the Popular Republican Movement (MRP), a Christian democratic-socialist party of the sort that had emerged during World War II, was down to 10 percent. Gaullists of two sorts, some boycotting the whole system, gained 17 percent, the old Radical Socialists 8 percent, various minor Rightists 11 percent; and those who did not care to vote at all made up 20 percent, "the largest party of all," someone called it. In Parliament, any government had to muster the support of a miscellany of groups and could expect a short life. There were in fact to be twenty-seven governments in the thirteen years between 1945 and 1958, their life span ranging from one day to sixteen months. (Guy Mollet, who managed, unlike Anthony Eden, to survive Suez, lasted the longest.)

By 1958 observers were saying that the Fourth Republic could be pushed over by the first hard wind. The weakness of its government had not prevented France from being administered well by the permanent bureaucracy, and as we know much had been accomplished in the way of economic recovery. But the government was incapable of resolving major problems that called for bold decisions. This was why the Indochina war dragged on for many years and why the Algerian war threatened to do the same.

It was Algeria that brought down the Fourth and led to a new constitution and the elevation of Charles de Gaulle to the presidency. By 1958, 400,000 French soldiers were trying to put down the revolt of some of the native Algerians against French rule, a struggle marked by atrocities on both sides. It was a second Indochina, the more unsolvable because a million French citizens lived in Algeria and many of the French regarded it as an integral part of their country, lying as it did just across the Mediterranean, where French settlers had lived ever since 1830. They could not consider the activities of the FLN, the National Liberation Front of the Algerian rebels, to be anything other than a mixture of criminal banditry and imported communist subversion, a Soviet weapon in the Cold War. But in fact the movement established deep roots in Algeria, touching the consciousness of an Islamic populace that had been long despised and discriminated against. The war that grew in Algeria resembled the Spanish Civil War in its fierce and cruel bravery.

The French military's use of torture as a weapon against a terroristic insurrection became a scandal in the eyes of many French people themselves. The issue threatened to pull France apart, much as the Vietnam War did in the United States a decade later. Some blamed the government for not giving up and some for not winning the war, as was also true in the Korean War and later the Vietnam War. On May 13, 1958, the French Army in Algiers revolted, and the Fourth Republic collapsed without defenders; it had ceased to command the allegiance of the French people.

General Charles de Gaulle being cheered in Rennes, France, September 20, 1958. At this time the war hero had been named Premier for a six-month period, while the constitution of the Fifth Republic, of which he would become President, was drafted. *Wide World Photos.*

In this rather desperate moment, almost everybody turned to the sixty-seven-year old de Gaulle as the only hope. The army favored him, but he also had strong Socialist support; he was a unique symbol of the France he so passionately loved and had so long served. After negotiations with the general, the Assembly passed its own death sentence, granting de Gaulle a six-month emergency rule during which a new constitution was to be written.

When written, this constitution of the Fifth Republic bore the unmistakable stamp of Gaullism. It was strongly presidential: a kind of uncrowned constitutional monarch, the president (indirectly elected in 1958, then elected by universal suffrage, every seven years) appointed the prime minister, proposed legislation to Parliament (which had limited powers to change it), could appeal to the people against Parliament via a referendum, could dissolve Parliament when he wished, and in other ways had powers enabling him to dominate the elected Parliament. Also, proportional representation was ended in favor of single-member districts, with one runoff by the two top candidates. Minority parties, including the Communists, lost representation under this plan.

Although it was criticized as excessively authoritarian, this long constitution was in some ways democratic, particularly in the provision for referenda. Weary of weak and divided governments, the French people approved the Fifth's constitution by a resounding 79 percent of the popular vote and elected de Gaulle president by 77 percent. Further signs of disgust with the old system appeared in a tendency to sweep the old leaders out in the parliamentary elections.

Thus given a powerful mandate, the powerful personality of de Gaulle was to dominate the French and try to dominate the international scene for the next eleven years, generally amid a swirl of controversy. So far as concerns Algeria, contrary to the hopes of the military who had backed him, he moved slowly but irresistibly toward granting full independence to the Arab state, overcoming enormous obstacles, in what was indisputably his finest achievement. He had decided as early as 1955 that the era of colonialism was over. His own conception of nationalism as the basis of human dignity forced him to this conclusion, he said; how could he deny to other peoples that same right of belonging to a free community that he claimed for his beloved France? At any rate, despite threats of assassination and acts of terror by French Algerians he granted Algeria independence. The agreements were approved in France by an overwhelming majority in 1962. It had taken four years, much courage, and much patience, but de Gaulle had extricated France from her most tragic postwar dilemma. He followed this by decolonializing the rest of France's old empire in Africa.

He had already shown his independence, and some thought his

remarkable stubbornness, when he had renewed his quarrel with the British and the Americans that had begun during World War II. He began his term of office by asking for equality within the NATO alliance with the United States and Great Britain—including access to nuclear secrets. He was rebuffed in an episode strangely similar to one going on at about the same time between the USSR and China. (This famous and unexpected quarrel flared when the Russians refused to share nuclear weapons know-how with their supposed ally in 1959.) In the aftermath of Suez the new British prime minister, Harold Macmillan, had decided to cultivate with the United States a "special relationship," which involved virtually giving up any attempt at an independent role—the evident lesson of Suez, but one that de Gaulle saw as insultingly servile. De Gaulle proceeded to order the removal of NATO fighter bombers from French soil and then to withdraw France from all military collaboration with NATO, though not from the alliance itself, as he proceeded at great expense to develop France's own *force de frappe* of nuclear weapons. A tiny one it might be, but a nation must have its pride, the general held; and there can be no pride without independence. He became a thorn in the side of the Americans and was, to Harold Macmillan, "as obstinate as ever." He was to try for good relations with Russia, then with China, then Rumania, and then, surprisingly, with Germany, with which he was to heal the ancient quarrel and cement friendly relations in an historic treaty of 1963. Anybody but the Anglo-Saxons!, who seemed heartily to reciprocate his dislike.

Charles de Gaulle perceived the movement he led primarily in terms of French nationalism; he aimed at a revival of the country's spirit: "rediscovered *élan*." He brought France back from the low point of frustration and humiliation she had reached in 1940–1944 to something like the dignity befitting the oldest and proudest of Europe's historic states. Others among the Gaullists stressed the tasks of modernization, breaking through the "stalemate society," and leading France into the twentieth century—"getting ready for the twenty-first." Or they talked about restoring the community, bringing the working classes out of their profound alienation from the nation, and healing the wounds that anomie had inflicted on the people. This latter aim impinged upon a Gaullist critique of the democracy of parties and parliaments, which he considered now obsolete. It needed to be replaced, he felt, by a democracy that was direct and participatory.

To a great writer like André Malraux, who became the most enthusiastic and the most articulate of Gaullists, the chief appeal was heroism and the grandeur of an authentic historic personality. Onetime Communist and Spanish Civil War fighter, later participant in the Resistance, Malraux asserted the betrayal of revolutionary ideals by

Stalin's totalitarian industrial state, and he said that if Trotsky were alive he would join him. De Gaulle offered a cause with character and dignity after the death of the Communist god. One might, of course, recall the ex-Communists who went over to Mussolini or Hitler or joined the Croix de Feu.

At times the mystique of Gaullism became embarrassingly reminiscent of fascism, with vast rallies, searchlights playing on the Cross of Lorraine, and similar displays. As with fascism, there was a left and a right wing of Gaullism, one traditionalist and conservative, the other restlessly oriented toward change. Anticommunism, nationalism, organic community, antiparliamentarianism, stress on heroism and grandeur—these all remind us of Mussolini and Hitler. Yet some Gaullists were modernizers and technocrats. The general preserved freedom of expression, tolerating even the Communists. In his memoirs, Khrushchev records his happy encounter with de Gaulle, with whom he got on famously in the 1960 visit despite the differences over Berlin.

De Gaulle was saved from nazism or fascism not only by the fact that he had spent the best years of his life fighting Hitler, but by the quality of his character. He had a saving component of irony and a sense of tragedy. Too civilized to be a fanatic, he did not hope to rescue mankind or set up a utopia. He knew the inevitable limitations of power, and he shared the disabused, disillusioned spirit of the fifties. "I am like Hemingway's Old Man of the Sea, I have brought back a skeleton," he said. He did not wish to destroy freedom, persecute minorities, or rule without a clear mandate from the people. He did not wish to wage aggressive war but to preserve a balance of power. He was not Hitler but de Gaulle. He was one of the century's greatest men.

Postwar Politics
in Other European Countries

No other western European political figure rivalled de Gaulle in stature, but Germany's Konrad Adenauer, who became the general's good friend, came closest. He presided over an adjustment to parliamentary democracy that those who remembered the Weimar failure, with its disastrous consequences, found as surprising as it was heartening. While there were to be some criticisms of an authoritarian streak in Adenauer and in the German people, of his commitment to democratic processes there was no real doubt. He had defied Hitler and spent his time in jail during the Nazi period. He did not threaten another such dictatorship.

Germany's achievement of political stability under a representative parliamentary system can be compared to France's unhappier experience with the Fourth Republic. First, the antiparliamentary or antigovernment groups were much less extreme in Germany; nazism had discredited the radical Right, and communism was equally unpopular because of the hatred of Russia. With André Malraux, the Germans might have cried, "Marxism is not something to the left of us but something to the east of us." Neither extreme gained more than infinitesimal support under the Federal Republic, which began in 1949.

Secondly, the 1949 German constitution did not adopt proportional representation. This, together with the fact that government funds were given to parties on the basis of their numerical strength, with a party getting less than 5 percent of the vote entitled to no subsidy at all, discouraged wasting votes on small parties. Thirdly, the Germans found in Konrad Adenauer a father figure who did not reject the parliamentary system. Chancellor from 1949 to 1963 (an office roughly similar to that of prime minister but carrying a bit more authority), Adenauer was much beloved. The old man, who was seventy-three when he took office and eighty-seven when he quit, was a salty character, a sort of Teutonic Harry Truman whose folk qualities appealed to the Germans and whose political guile kept his foes at bay.

"Der Alte," the Old One, was a member of the Christian Democratic Union, and under his leadership it dominated German elections until 1969. The smaller parties lost strength, and a three-party system emerged. The Social Democrats were a strong second, and the smaller Free Democrats, a bourgeois liberal group, held the balance of power and normally supported Adenauer. In 1969 the FDP finally swung over to the Social Democrats, by which time the Social Democratic party had abandoned its one-time Marxian stance entirely. Elections down to 1969 are shown in Table 12–2 (percentage of the vote in round figures).

The leading theme in German political life was what might be called wiping out the Nazi past. A certain reluctance to think about the terrible interlude of 1933–1945 and indeed about the whole dreadful

TABLE 12–2

	1949	1953	1957	1961	1965	1969
CDU/CSU (Christian Democratic/Social)	31	45	50	45	48	46
SPD (Social Democratic)	29	29	32	36	38	43
FDP (Free Democratic)	12	10	8	13	10	6
Others	18	16	10	6	4	5

experience since 1914 was noticeable in Germany after the war, and it lasted for many years. Albert Grosser tells of a writer who in 1966 addressed a memorial service by saying, "We were the barbarians in the last war, let's face it," and being reprimanded: "We came here to remember our dead sons and not to be told about the Nazis." The average German had much sympathy for the ordinary people who had obeyed orders and who had turned a blind eye to abuses during the Nazi period—"which of us would have done otherwise?" One might compare this feeling with the "I don't want to get involved" attitude of witnesses to crime so often noted in recent years.

This unwillingness to face up to the past was frequently criticized, but it should not be confused with real pro-Nazi views. The only neo-Nazi party of any consequence, the Socialist Reich Party, won only 1.8 percent of the votes in 1951, and it was soon declared illegal by the High Court of the Federal Republic. Books revealing Nazi crimes became best sellers in West Germany, the leading example being *The Diary of Anne Frank*. So, to be sure, did some memoirs of such ex-Nazis as Albert Speer.

Early on, Konrad Adenauer took steps to offer amends to the Jews. He pledged a payment of an indemnity of three billion marks to Israel from 1953 to 1966. "In the German people's name unspeakable crimes have been committed, which demand moral and material reparation," he told the *Bundestag* in 1951. A German office set up in Ludwigsburg in 1958 sought to track down Nazi criminals who had not yet been caught. Victims of the Nazis received compensation, though there were complaints about the slowness of the procedures and inadequate amounts of money. In 1969, a poll showed that only 44 percent of the German people thought that Nazi criminals should still be prosecuted. Germans were tolerant about ex-Nazis holding public office, and indeed in 1966 a man who had once been a member of the Nazi party became chancellor. Kurt Kiesinger's election elicited strenuous protest from Germany's leading writers, Günter Grass and Heinrich Böll, who by this time were joining a movement of revolt that accused German society of philistinism and decadence. But German opinion was more decidedly pro-Israel in the 1967 Mid-East war than was either French or British.

Adenauer's adroit foreign policy regained a respectable place in the community of nations for the Federal Republic. It became a staunch NATO partner, a member of the EEC, and a friend of France; the signing of a treaty of friendship in 1963 between these old enemies, France and Germany, must surely be accounted one of the leading achievements of the era. Adenauer was even able to keep a line open to Moscow, though in general the Russians always attacked the Federal

Republic as a nest of ex-Nazis plotting a war of revenge. (This did not prevent the East German Communist state, the DDR, from using many ex-Nazis in its government and party.) For its part, the Bonn government not only would not recognize the DDR but, in the so-called Hallstein Doctrine, said it would refuse diplomatic relations with any country that did recognize the East German regime. Diplomatic relations with the USSR, which were established in 1955, was the only exception to this policy. For many years Bonn did not deal with the other countries of eastern Europe.

Locating the capital in the little city on the Rhine, which was hardly large enough comfortably to house the growing federal bureaucracy, was intended in 1949 to be a signal that this was a temporary headquarters, to be used until the day when the government returned to Berlin as the capital of a united country. The Berlin Wall was yet to go up; but bitter relations between the two Germanies existed at all times until 1969, when the first Social Democratic chancellor inaugurated a new policy.

Germany's well-known administrative efficiency continued. The staggering task of handling a number of refugees as high as fifteen million (counting those who fled from the DDR) was done with such efficiency that the French used the German model for their resettlement of the three-quarters of a million French Algerians after 1962. The fabulous economic boom guaranteed Adenauer's electoral success, but his party never received more than 50 percent of the vote, and the Social Democrats steadily increased their vote after ineffective leadership early in the Federal Republic's existence. Perhaps West Germany suffered from the lack of an outlet for extreme views. The Communist party, a tiny minority in any case, was outlawed in 1955; the SPD steadily shed the last remnants of socialism. Political consensus has advantages, but it has the disadvantage of not representing the nonconformists, who may in their frustration turn to other methods. The radical student protest movement of the late sixties began in Germany. In the year before Adenauer's retirement, 1962, the government raided the offices of the prominent German weekly *Der Spiegel*, hard-hitting, brilliantly edited newsmagazine. It was a kind of German Watergate, which foreshadowed the scandals and troubles that were to plague the West in this decade. It marked the beginning of a new era, shook the government, and perhaps hastened Adenauer's retirement in 1963 (he was only eighty-seven).

Italian politics stood somewhere between the French and German models. As in Germany, the Christian Democratic party took the lead and held it long, gaining between 35 and 48 percent of the seats in Parliament in the elections between 1946 and 1963. But unlike Germany, and like France, the Italian Communist party attracted 20 to 25 percent of the voters (under a proportional representation system). The Socialists, at times bitterly at odds with the Communists, at other times exploring a common front for the two Marxist parties, were also strong. A neo-Fascist party gained 5 percent of the vote, and Monarchists, who were anxious to restore the House of Savoy (voted out of its long reign by Italian voters just after the war) won from 3 to 7 percent before fading in the 1960s. And there were a number of other small parties. The results of the first five elections are shown in Table 12–3 (percent of vote in round figures).

Italian politics was thus not as stable as German but not as volatile as Fourth Republic French. The Christian Democrats governed regularly, as in Germany, but they had more trouble putting together a majority in Parliament; they were never close to a majority by themselves except in the Cold War year of 1948, which was dominated by fears of a Red takeover. And they tended to lose rather than gain support. As they finally came to be outnumbered by Communists and Socialists, they were driven to explore the "opening to the Left" by luring at least some Socialists to their side, a strategy encouraged by the liberal papacy of Pope John XXIII during the early sixties. But this caused rifts in their own camp. The Italian CDs showed something of the same lack of enduring solidity as did the French MRP.

Moreover, the Italian Communist party (PCI) was the most flexible and in many ways the most moderate of all Communist parties. Forced underground throughout the long Mussolini era, they had to seek collaboration with other antifascists; and they developed habits, quite unusual for Communists, of cooperating with or at least tolerating non-Communists. From their early leaders, especially the remarkable Antonio Gramsci, they inherited a more subtle and flexible Marxism than Stalin's. Palmiro Togliatti, Italian Communist boss in this period, was among the most democratic and nationalist of all Communist leaders; that is, he argued for an "Italian way to socialism" that

TABLE 12–3

	1946	1948	1953	1958	1963
Christian Democratic	35	48	40	42	38
Communist	19	} 31	23	23	25
Socialist	21		13	14	14
Neo-Fascist	—	5	6	5	5
Monarchist	—	3	7	5	2
Others (Liberal, Republican, Social Democratic)	25	13	11	11	16

had to be different from Russia's. Following Gramsci's lead, he construed Marx as teaching not so much the dictatorship of an elite as a general cultural development as the necessary prerequisite for Communist political power and economic change. The PCI set out in 1945 to build a mass party, not a Leninist elite. The PCI was to enter into a dialogue with the Catholics in the 1960s, and in the next decade it would virtually accept the democratic, pluralistic social order.

During the Cold War years it stopped well short of that; but Togliatti was among the first and strongest Communist voices to welcome Khrushchev's 1956 denunciation of Stalinism and to call for a new Communist path, more humane and democratic. He responded eagerly to Imre Nagy's search for a more popular communism, and relations between the Italian and Russian parties grew strained after the suppression of the Hungarian revolution. On this path of compromise and adaptation the Italian Communist party led all others. Therefore it grew more popular in Italy and gradually ceased to be regarded as either a threat of violent revolution or a tool of Moscow's.

Elected in 1945 in a surprise triumph over Winston Churchill, the Labour party government of Clement Attlee—a moderate, humble, unassuming man—presided over the establishment of Europe's most famous welfare state, the nationalization of basic industries, and the beginning of economic recovery. As foreign secretary, sturdy Ernest Bevin was a key factor in the organization of the alliances that shored up western Europe in the face of threatening decay: the Truman Doctrine, the Marshall Plan, NATO. On the other hand, there were disappointments. Expecting to preside over the millennium of plenty, Attlee's cabinet had to face inevitable postwar shortages. It imposed such unpopular measures as rationing, price regulation, and high taxation. The ambitious cradle-to-grave social security system was expensive.

At this stage, the Labourites put their trust almost wholly in nationalization and state controls. But statism is not in itself an answer, as critics were to point out and events in some measure showed. Private, public, or mixed, the important thing is to make the economy go. Productivity must be increased, export markets won, excessive inflation avoided by wise management. Merely transferring ownership from a private to a public corporation does not automatically ensure this. Such were some of the lessons a Labour party that had never before held sole power, and which lacked experienced and capable leaders, had to learn.

The party's left wing was uncomfortable with the Cold War; the fiery Welshman, Aneurin Bevan, resigned from the cabinet in 1951 over rearmament and NATO, taking with him a young man named Harold Wilson. Bevan was supposed to have cost Labour many votes by referring to the opposing Tories as "vermin." The Korean War raised raw material prices and touched off a "stop-go" crisis. Also in 1951, an unhappy year for Labour, two left-wing undersecretaries in the foreign office defected to Russia, presumably taking with them state secrets, and there were allegations of loose security. Perhaps some of the English were angry with the Attlee government because it had presided over the beginning of the liquidation of the British Empire by relinquishing India, jewel of the empire. If so, they were destined to some further disillusionment when in the late fifties a Conservative government responded to the "changing wind" and began to decolonialize all over the map.

After having won so narrow a victory that another election was necessary in 1950, Labour lost the 1951 election. They would not return to power for thirteen years. The Conservatives increased their majority in the House of Commons from seventeen to forty-six seats in 1955 and won even more comfortably in 1959. They came to their own time of troubles only in 1963. They were fortunate in reaping the rewards of economic recovery. But they had learned something, too. Between 1945 and 1952 the Conservative party had profited from defeat by developing a whole new outlook, organization, and image. According to the historian of the Conservative Party, Robert Blake, the party "made a major effort to rethink its political programme, reorganize its internal constitution, and recover its parliamentary morale." It accepted the managed economy and the welfare state but contrasted its own flexible model, which was borrowed in some part from the French, with the straitjacket of Labour statism. The Conservatives worked to present themselves not as hidebound reactionaries but as a more modern, more efficient, and more knowledgeable party than the socialists.

Suez was a blow; but it brought to the prime ministership Harold Macmillan, a man of much culture and charm. Scion of the Anglo-American publishing company, Macmillan was a progressive Tory who favored economic planning, liberating the colonies, and thawing the Cold War. In the end, he was the victim of a rather bizarre scandal in his government. By then, the Conservatives had been in power for an exceptionally long time, and the country was ready for change.

During its long period of exile, Labour did its own soul-searching and underwent an internal struggle between pragmatists and ideologists. The man elected as party leader following Attlee's retirement, Hugh Gaitskell, was a moderate who urged his party to turn away from doctrinaire socialism, seek middle class support, and stop stressing the obviously unpopular nostrum of nationalization of industry. Gaitskell declared in his speech to the 58th annual Labour Party Conference in 1959, that "Our object must be to broaden our base, to be in touch always with ordinary people, to avoid becoming small cliques of isolated doctrine-ridden fanatics, out of touch with the main stream of social life in our time." To which a leftist, Michael Foot, replied, "In order to win an election we have to change the mood of the people in this country, to open their eyes to what an evil and disgraceful and rotten society it is."

Even more bitter was the continuing debate about foreign and military policies. "Unilateralists" demanded that Britain give up its attempt to be a nuclear power, but the moderate wing rejected this approach as unrealistic. The quarrel was more one of temperaments than of issues.

Gaitskell died prematurely in 1963, on the eve of the long-awaited change of fortune that would have made him prime minister. Harold Wilson, who had moved from the left wing of the party to somewhere near center, inherited the job. He was to encounter grave difficulties during his term, as economic conditions turned downward—bad luck, once more, for Labour. One socialist publicist invented the theory that with diabolical cunning, the Tories managed to arrange things so that they were out of office when economic downswings came, thus contriving to put the onus of bad times on Labour! Oxford political scientists, though, held that the longterm political swing was toward Labour, the more democratic party in an increasingly egalitarian society, and predicted that the Conservatives would never win another election. It took only six years to prove them wrong. It should be added that the Liberal party often received a significant percentage of the vote in these years, but it never won more than an insignificant representation in Parliament, because there was no proportional representation and the Liberals were almost everywhere a minority. (See Table 12–4.)

We can sum up the politics of western Europe in the generation

TABLE 12–4   British Elections, 1945–1966

	1945	1950	1951	1955	1959	1964	1966
Seats in Commons							
Labour	393	315	295	277	258	318	363
Conservative	210	298	321	344	365	303	253
Liberal	12	9	6	6	6	9	12
Other	25	3	3	3	1	0	2
Percent of popular vote							
Labour	48.0	46.1	48.8	46.4	43.8	44.1	48.0
Conservative	39.6	43.4	48.0	49.7	49.4	43.4	41.9
Liberal	9.0	9.2	2.6	2.7	5.9	11.2	8.5

after 1945 by calling it a politics of growing consensus, corresponding to the economic progress generally characteristic of this era. The extremes tended to become less extreme: even the Communists mellowed a bit, and the British Labourites and German Social Democrats dropped much of their socialism. On the other hand, conservative parties, accepting the welfare state and some degree of economic planning, heeded the changing winds and adapted to the needs of a new day. The distance between German CDU and SPD, between British Labour and Conservative, narrowed to the point where some observers thought them indistinguishable except for a lingering veneer of rhetoric. Charles de Gaulle's new republic sought to suppress the parties entirely in favor of a politics of national consensus. But partisan politics may be an index of alienation; there was in fact an "integration of the workers into the economic and political life of the nation." Political apathy was the result more of contentment than of disgust.

If we seek novelty and excitement, that, for the Europe of the fifties, was more nearly provided by its experiments in internationalism.

The European Community:
The Europe of the Six

The origins of the European Economic Community lay chiefly in efforts to resolve the role of Germany in Western Europe. Ravaged by Germany in World War II, her neighbors hated and despised her yet could not do without her economically. One answer to this dilemma was to contain German strength within an embrace of all western Europe. Just as the EDC and NATO tried to bring German military strength into the Western alliance without setting up a revived *Wehrmacht*, so the various forms of economic integration, beginning with the creation of the Coal and Steel Community, were intended to secure the advantages of Germany's great economic strength without allowing her to regain the ascendancy of Europe.

The Marshall Plan gave another boost to the idea of a transnational European economy, for the Americans persistently stressed the formation of a large single market, which should eliminate tariffs and even allow a common currency. The virtues of this became especially evident to such small countries as the Netherlands and Belgium. Then, too, the manifest failure of the old order caused many to look with favor on some wholly new one that would abolish the narrow nationalisms of the past and push Europe toward a fresh frontier.

The Organization of European Economic Cooperation sought to

organize economic cooperation among Marshall aid recipients, but it encountered obstacles. The British in particular were unwilling to abolish tariffs. Had Great Britain been willing to take the lead, western Europe would surely have followed her just after the war. But the British, while reluctantly agreeing to join in military defense through the West European Union and then NATO, hung back when it came to closer integration. Churchill had described the position of England as being at the intersection of three circles, only one of which was Europe. She looked across the Atlantic to her English-speaking brethren in the United States and Canada, and she looked to the other members of the British Commonwealth all over the globe, from Australia to Africa and the Mediterranean. If the traditional British imperial dream was to disintegrate in the next two decades, it was still very much alive in 1945; Winston Churchill had bristled with indignation when he thought Roosevelt was trying to get him to "preside over the liquidation of the British Empire." There were special economic ties between the home country and the Commonwealth lands that interfered with efforts at Britain's economic integration into Europe. Geography and history dictated that the island kingdom would not be quite at one with the Continent.

The lead came instead from two far-sighted Frenchmen, Robert Schuman and Jean Monnet. Schuman was a native of Lorraine, that province that had been shuttled back and forth between France and Germany since 1870. It was a region rich in iron ore, which travelled to the steel mills of the Ruhr Valley in Germany. In the Ruhr Valley, site of great coal fields, more steel was produced than anywhere else in the world between 1900 and 1945. When Lorraine returned to France in 1919, a Franco-German cartel was organized by the leading industrialists; it was a sort of preliminary to the Coal and Steel Community. This international economic cooperation, forced by necessity, transcended the political rivalry of France and Germany between 1933 and 1945.

In the trauma of the immediate postwar years, the French attempted both to seize and to limit German production, while detaching the Saar region (rich in coal also) from Germany. When the economic and political reconstruction of Germany became a necessity, this policy was of course discarded.

The phenomenal technocrat Jean Monnet was the genius of French *planification*. He also believed that national sovereignty was an obstacle to economic progress, an anachronism that Europe would have to get rid of if it hoped to keep pace with twentieth-century technology. (If his memoirs [1976] manage to leave the impression that he single-handedly saved European civilization, one readily forgives this remarkable man—he very nearly did.) Robert Schuman, leader of the MRP party and twice French prime minister in the 1948–1950 period, backed a report from Monnet proposing a start on European economic integration via creation of a European Coal and Steel Community. The French proposal was favorably received by Adenauer's government and by Italy, Belgium, Luxemburg, and the Netherlands; negotiations began in June 1950, and what became known as the Schuman Plan soon grew into an organization headquartered in the tiny country of Luxemburg and headed by Monnet. The Coal and Steel Community became a reality in 1952. It proved to be a success. Along with this internationalization of one important segment of the economy, other European institutions were established, too. These included a Council of Ministers, which represented the governments of each of the six countries involved, a Court of Justice, and a European Parliament.

As we already know, the next step toward Europeanization, a European Defense Community, stumbled and fell over the obstacles of French uncertainty, British reluctance to get involved, and fear of German rearmament on any terms. But the indefatigable Monnet continued to enlist support for European programs, and in 1955 the foreign ministers of France, Italy, Germany, and the Benelux countries met at Messina to plan both a full Common Market and joint atomic energy development. The Benelux three were strong supporters at all times, Belgium's Paul-Henri Spaak emerging as another dynamic leader of Europeanization. Still aloof, Britain declined to attend the Messina conference. A groundswell of popular support for the movement pushed reluctant French and German politicians along.

The Suez crisis, coming at this moment, provided an additional impetus, at least as far as France was concerned. Her estrangement from the United States pushed France toward finding friends in Europe; the threat of losing Middle Eastern oil focused attention on atomic energy as a source of power, which helped lead to the pooling of nuclear energy resources ("Euratom"). An additional attraction for the French was the hope of finding an expanded market in Germany for their agricultural products.

For about the fourth time, Great Britain now missed the Euro boat. In the aftermath of Suez and Eden's resignation, Macmillan chose to cultivate the "special relationship" with the United States rather than join the Continental states. The treaties of Rome, completed in that city in March 1957, were quickly approved with resounding majorities by the French, German, Italian, and Benelux parliaments. They created the European Economic Community, or the Common Market of the Six.

There ensued a period of spectacular economic success—expanding

European Economic Community: Leaders of nine European Economic Community countries assemble in Saint Patrick's Hall inside Dublin Castle in 1975, to start their summit talks. *Wide World Photos.*

trade, strengthening of the best industries within each country, economies of scale. It was never entirely clear whether the Common Market was responsible for this boom or whether it would have come anyway; it does appear that the Rome treaties gave a lift to confidence everywhere. The Brussels-headquartered EEC quickly became an important adjunct to the European scene. Its staff was small but intensely able and dedicated. The Council of Ministers, which made decisions for it, had to agree unanimously—in other words each of the member states had a veto—but it developed something of its own momentum and spirit.

De Gaulle's accession to power did not seriously interfere with this pattern. Although the general's nationalism caused him to throw some roadblocks in the way of political unification, he was by no means averse to an economic arrangement that benefited France as much as any country and that coincided with his plans for modernizing the economy. Moreover, his international strategy aimed at improving relations with Germany. Meanwhile, Great Britain had awakened from her insular slumbers and proposed a broader European Free Trade Area (EFTA), to include additional countries—Scandinavia, Austria, Switzerland, Portugal, Spain—whose purposes would be limited to trade; in brief, a customs union. What England feared was not so much the economic as the political implications of the Common Market; though she was perhaps willing to contemplate a business partnership with Europe, she did not wish to commit herself to a marriage. But the vision of Monnet and Spaak aimed at this ultimate pooling of sovereignties in a full political union, creating a United States of Europe.

It was here that de Gaulle became a problem, for his vision was different. Nationalism was not dead, he felt, and no superstate should be attempted. Rather, he wanted a "Europe of the Fatherlands," cooperating with each other but not losing their separate identities, which were so fundamental (he thought) to culture and human dignity. "Europe is no nation," the general said. His most shocking action was the French veto of Britain's belated application for membership in the EEC in 1963. The European Community—the merger of the Coal and Steel Community, Euratom, and the EEC—was to face a succession of crises on its road to unity. Some of them it surmounted, some it did not; but it remained alive, and interests with a stake in its survival began to grow.

The immediate project was the abolition of all duties on goods among the member countries. There was a timetable of twelve years, running through three four-year periods. In 1962 and 1965 the Common Market passed crucial milestones when it achieved agreements on agricultural policy. Movement of peoples between countries increased, though complete elimination of migration restrictions was a remoter goal, as was a common currency. Still further down the road lay (members hoped) an all-European parliament with real powers and a Council of Ministers not forced to obey the wishes of the individual governments. The hope was that momentum would carry the movement forward from strength to strength, each successive plateau engendering the force to climb to yet a higher one. Pessimists feared that each upward leap would be harder and that the initial impulse might weaken with time. Some argued that political unification would inevitably follow economic, while others said that the task was primarily a matter of building a European spirit or patriotism, something that the most sanguine had to admit was hardly yet much in evidence. Economic integration made more progress than did political.

De Gaulle's veto of British membership in 1963 (and again in 1967) was widely interpreted as an example of that inscrutable genius's remarkable obstinacy. In fairness to *le grand Charles*, it must be said that many in Europe shared his irritation about Britain's role in the past and his skepticism about whether she really yet accepted all the implications of membership. The Labour party, soon to replace the Conservatives in office, seemed hostile to the whole idea. The British still insisted that exceptions had to be made to allow for their special economic arrangements with commonwealth countries.

Nevertheless, most Europeanists were still deeply distressed by de Gaulle's veto and thought he had violated the spirit of the European Community. In January 1963, he instructed the French delegation in Brussels to break off negotiations, thus putting an end to an agreement that then seemed in sight after long negotiations between Britain and the Six. The general's decision to torpedo Britain's entry, which would have been followed by that of Norway, Denmark, and Ireland, was a reaction to Macmillan's continuing nuclear companionship with the United States, as reflected in American Polaris missiles being supplied to British submarines. De Gaulle saw the EEC as a pawn in the diplomacy of power, rather than an end in itself.

Despite the 1965 crisis, when France boycotted EEC meetings for seven months, the Common Market reached its goal of abolishing customs duties in 1968, two years ahead of schedule. A complicated Community agricultural plan set uniform prices, protected farmers against cheaper foreign produce by a system of variable subsidies, and financed modernization of equipment. By 1970, General de Gaulle having passed from the scene, negotiations were again underway for British entry, along with other EFTA members. A single currency was scheduled for 1980. Economically the European Community looked like a success, though it remained to be seen how it would weather an economic depression should one occur.

But the political side of unification did not keep pace. The separate nations still held a veto power over all major decisions of the Council of Ministers. A directly elected European Parliament, supposed to have come into being according to the Rome treaty of 1957, was delayed time and again until finally the first elections were held in 1979. Europe's national states hesitated to take the final steps that would convert an instrument of close economic cooperation into a sovereign superstate. Whether they ever would do so was anyone's guess in the 1960s and 1970s. De Gaulle's thrust, "Europe is no nation," still struck home. Italians, Germans, the French and the English might feel friendship for each other, but they did not appear to want to lose their separate identities.

Should the European Community become a single entity, it would constitute a power equal in population to the United States and even the Soviet Union (depending on how many countries joined it; in 1977 Greece, Spain, and Portugal were applying, after the entry of Great Britain, Ireland, and Denmark) and equal to or greater than the superpowers in wealth, technological skills, and human resources—in brief, a third superpower. But the historic nations of Europe, very old and very deeply rooted, seemed unlikely to merge into a Nation of Europe except over a long period of time. Nevertheless their attempts to do so, supported by people of genius, was one of the more exciting political ventures of the post-1945 generation.

The Mood of Postwar Thought

Few hopes or illusions remained after a war that had been marked by total inhumanity as well as nearly total destruction. Standing amid the ruins of European cities or contemplating the death factories of Auschwitz, one could only feel, with French philosopher Gabriel Marcel, "a more than physical horror and anxiety." Almost before this horror could be absorbed, it seemed that another war was impending. This one would be waged with even more terrible weapons, and Europe would this time be a helpless victim. If mankind had any future, it surely lay outside Europe, in the hands of peoples whom civilized Europeans were much inclined to regard as barbarous. A British historian wrote of *The Passing of the European Age;* a German sociologist—brother of the great Max Weber—bade *Farewell to European History;* and at the end of his long life H. G. Wells, that eternal optimist, for the first time found *Mind at the End of Its Tether.*

While a few clung to hope in communism, that hope vanished rapidly in the flood of disenchantment with Soviet Russia. "What have you done with our hopes?" André Malraux cried on behalf of a majority of the European intellectual community, addressing Stalin. It is true that the Communists in France and Italy, even for a moment in Germany, came out of the war with considerable prestige, because of their valiant resistance to nazism. But their slavish adherence to the Moscow line, along with Moscow's behavior in opposing the Marshall Plan and crushing freedom in eastern Europe, isolated them and diminished their standing. Zhdanovism, decreeing hostility to any kind of literature, art, or philosophy except one incredibly naive and obsolete by European standards, was an invincible obstacle for most European intellectuals. Marxism still meant Stalinist "diamat" crudity, literature and art confined to propaganda, and the arts dictated by a narrow-minded set of party officials. European intellectuals had been through that in the thirties and wanted no more of it.

The prevailing mood was a deep mistrust of all ideologies, which—whether Nazi or Communist—had betrayed men into slaughtering each other for abstractions. Both the Algerian-born Frenchman Albert Camus and the British writer George Orwell expressed the feeling that one must destroy the tyranny of concepts and get back to real human beings. Though socialists, they had a strong suspicion of Marxist intellectuals and faceless *apparatchiki;* they were more personalist and more tinged with the tragic view of life than traditional socialism had ever been. That

> The troubles of our proud and angry dust
> Are from eternity and will not fail

needed no demonstrating for those who had seen nazism and the war.

European intellectuals were inclined to reject the popular notion that fascism and nazism were caused by the iniquity of Italians or Germans. The handsome, athletic Camus, literary idol of the postwar years, told his audiences that we were all responsible for the war, the gas chambers, the concentration camps, the bombings. Humanity was guilty. Even if one side was somewhat more guilty than the other, "revenge is sour," Orwell said. This neo-Christian sense of original sin and the need for universal forgiveness was an authentic product of the war. The leading political movements to emerge from the war and the Resistance were the Christian parties in Italy, Germany, France, and the Low Countries. They were built on the courage of such martyrs as Martin Niemöller and Dietrich Bonhoeffer and on the reduction of life to the ultimate and simplest values by the "boundary situations" of the war.

"Never were we more free than when enslaved" under the Nazis, Jean-Paul Sartre wrote. Humiliated, without rights, people were faced with basic choices and, in the presence of death, made them. The postwar cycle of despair, reduction to human essentials, and revival of hope "on the far side of despair" was identified more with Sartre's radical and atheist existentialism than it was with old-fashioned Christianity, though the latter was strong and was sometimes existentialized. No theologian was more fashionable than Rudolf Bultmann, who brought the post-1919 "crisis theology" of Karl Barth up to date. But no theologian could compete with the glamorous Sartre. The author of novels and plays as well as philosophical tracts, hero of the Resistance, he was a mordant critic of bourgeois values. In plays like *The Flies* and *No Exit* he dramatized and popularized the existential analysis of the human condition. He had found this analysis chiefly in the works of German philosopher Martin Heidegger.

The roots of the existentialist philosophy, which was popularized from about 1940 on, lie in the nineteenth century, chiefly in Nietzsche, Kierkegaard, Dostoyevsky, and Hegel. It was not unlike the "life philosophy" popular before 1914, and it also had affinities with the subjectivism and pessimism of the 1920s. It was new only in the peculiar

quality of its mixture and mood. This mood embraced not only the sense of a powerful crisis, reaching to the very roots of modern humanity's relationship to nature and culture, but also the predicament of the urban dweller's essential loneliness in the crowd, his social anxieties and identity crisis. There was a sense of the total absurdity of existence. Thrown into the world for no reason, we are somehow here, confronting a hostile and meaningless universe, condemned to make sense of it or perish. The human consciousness inside each of us is a radically different kind of being than all other kinds; it has no given structure, no essence. It is a king of nothingness, a great wind blowing toward objects, a "hole in being." It is wholly free and undetermined, completely unlike physical or objective existence. "I a stranger and afraid,/ In a world I never made"—Housman had caught something of this feeling earlier in the century. When we realize our predicament, we may be overcome with nausea and contemplate suicide—the only serious philosophical question, Camus claimed. If we decide to live, we must do so in full realization that our arbitrary choices and actions endow the universe with its only meaning. Insisting on only integrity, authenticity, and personal commitment, existentialism was a protean philosophy that might be turned in almost any political direction. In the hands of

Camus, who quarreled with Sartre in 1952 on Cold War issues, it was turned in a rather conservative direction, whereas Sartre always remained the embattled and embittered hater of his bourgeois society.

The popular culture of the 1950s featured men in gray flannel suits, young men with crew cuts, girls who dreamed of marrying the right man and settling down to happy domesticity. It was a conservative decade, the time politically of Eisenhower, de Gaulle, Macmillan. The British Labour party withdrew from militant socialism to cautiously pragmatic Gaitskellism; the German Socialists abandoned their socialism; and even in the Soviet Union one might see Khrushchev's ascendancy as a middle-of-the-road compromise between the extremes of Stalinism and total liberation.

This political swing corresponded to the generally successful economic recovery and to the psychology of a generation reacting against the strident ideological battles of the previous decades. There were small currents opposing this main stream—"beat" poets, for example—but even this protest was a quiet one, its adherents fleeing to rural solitudes and cultivating Zen Buddhism. The poetry of the fifties, as represented by Philip Larkin, Donald Davie, and Thom Gunn in England, was a subtle probing of private lives, immensely skillful but wholly nonpolitical. The novels of Graham Greene and François Mauriac and the plays of Friedrich Dürrenmatt caught a deeply religious mood, probing the ultimate human corruptions and sins. Movements of strenuous or violent protest, leading to demonstrations and militant movements, awaited the 1960s. Untroubled by aggressive radicals, the decade of the fifties was later to be accused of apathy and resignation in the face of manifest social evils. On its own view, it had moved beyond superficial social theories to discover the existent individual.

Soviet Communism
After Stalin

13

From Stalin's Death
to the Secret Speech, 1953–1956

Josef Stalin, born Djugashvili, the virtual dictator of Soviet Russia for twenty-five years, was a political genius who built the huge Communist industrial society out of ruins, led Russia to victory in World War II, and was afterwards venerated as a saint. There are stories of his idealized picture hanging alongside Christ's on Italian walls. In his later years he permitted an adulation suggested in Nicholas Virta's 1948 play *Stalingrad*, in which the kindly father of his country is painted as ever-vigilant, ever farsighted (he planned the Stalingrad trap months in advance) yet always ready when time permits for a friendly chat with old comrades. But nothing in Russia could have exceeded the hagiography that emanated from distinguished Western writers. The "myth of Stalin" affected even most Americans, who called him "Uncle Joe" and, like President Harry Truman, attributed difficulties with Russia to evil influences surrounding this essentially amiable person. Millions all over the world mourned his death in 1953 as a blow to world peace and human justice.

There was another Stalin, known to a few earlier but not fully revealed until after 1956, who was a sadistic tyrant and paranoid mass murderer responsible for more deaths than even Adolf Hitler. A careful and scholarly Western account, Robert Conquest's *The Great Terror*, has estimated Stalin's Russian victims, either shot, tortured to death, or sent to a nearly certain early death in prison camps, to be 20 million between 1931 and 1950. Along with the industrial cities rose the slave labor camps, concealed from the view of admiring visitors, with a constantly changing population of several million people. It is an amazing tribute to the power of Soviet propaganda and the gullibility of Western intellectuals that so little was known of this ugly side. Something of the motives may be glimpsed in the great French writer and philosopher Jean-Paul Sartre's view, expressed in the early fifties, that even if these things were true they should not be revealed, lest they damage the Cause.

The "aging god" apparently grew paranoid again, if he had ever stopped, just before his death. Stalin's quarrel with Tito led to a series of public confession trials in the satellite countries. These were staged, as they had been in the thirties. A professor (Kubanin) who wrote that Russia was lagging behind the United States paid with his life; another (Voznesensky) who proved that Western capitalism was writhing in its death agonies did not escape destruction, either. It was dangerous to risk saying anything, and a crowd of toadies desperately tried to read the irritable tyrant's moods in these last years. The brilliant Andrei Zhdanov, who presided over the Soviet Cold War ideology of aggressive anti-Westernism, sternly censoring all "decadent" modernism out of Soviet art and terrorizing writers into producing nothing but propagandistic "socialist realism," lost Stalin's favor evidently because he sympathized with Tito. His death in 1948 may have been from natural causes; but suspicions lingered, especially when in 1949–1950 several thousand of Zhdanov's followers in Leningrad were arrested and many were executed.

Jewish intellectuals were persecuted in 1952–1953 as Stalin discovered the danger of Zionism. Then, just before his death, a "doctors' plot" was announced. Nine prominent Russian physicians and medical professors were arrested and accused of causing the death of Zhdanov and plotting to kill other high Soviet officials. They were said to have been agents of "an international Jewish bourgeois nationalist organization" under the direction of American intelligence (January 1953). They were tortured into confessions, two of them dying in the process. Soviet newspapers and journals began to sound the alarm cry of treason and wrecking, an atmosphere sickeningly reminiscent of the mid-1930s. In his 1956 secret speech, Khrushchev charged that Stalin was preparing a purge of leading party members, just as in 1936–1938 he had gotten rid of every one of the old Bolshevik leaders.

Perhaps he was, and perhaps his death came just in time to save Russia from the horrors of another Terror. Perhaps, some have even speculated, leading party members, aided by the military, actually put Stalin to death or accelerated his demise after an initial illness. They would have had strong and obvious motives for doing so. Perhaps it was Beria who took the lead; Stalin seemed to be feuding with his secret police chief, who moved briefly to the front after Stalin's death only to be deposed within a few months. Rudolf Slansky's spectacular trial in Prague in late 1952 has been seen as a Stalin blow against Beria; the death of Klement Gottwald, who succeeded Slansky as Communist boss in Czechoslovakia, just after attending Stalin's funeral, perhaps was Beria's revenge. Not much imagination is required to reconstruct a scenario in which, convinced that Stalin had gone mad and fearful of their own lives, the Presidium joined forces to dispose of the aging god, let Beria do the dirty work, and then later wiped out their sin and its memory by liquidating the instrument of the crime.

In late February the outcry in the press suddenly ceased; *a few days later*, Stalin was reported to have suffered a stroke, and on March 6 it was announced that he had died the previous evening. The eye witness account published by his daughter, Svetlana, leaves no doubt that such an attack did take place. What remains unclear is whether it was induced or improperly treated. Perhaps the doctors had their revenge. Most authorities, though, are inclined to think that Stalin's death was natural. He was seventy-three, and he had lived—to say the least—a turbulent life.

The death of Stalin was followed by a power struggle, if a somewhat muted one by earlier standards. There was to be little blood let, with the exception of that of L. P. Beria, the secret police boss who was either shot on the spot after a Presidium meeting or executed after a secret trial on December 23, 1953. Other high officials who served under him were also shot. Ironically, Beria not only may have been on Stalin's purge list just before the latter's death, but was associated with liberalization for a while in the months afterward, when he seemed, along with Malenkov, to be one of the heirs apparent. But at the end of June 1953, less than four months after Stalin's demise, Beria was charged with plotting to seize power and accused of all the usual crimes: being an agent of foreign powers, seeking to restore capitalism, sabotaging and wrecking, etc. The abruptness of the change is illustrated by an amusing story: the volume of the Great Soviet Encyclopedia containing Beria's entry had just come out, with a very long article devoted to his career. A letter went out to buyers of this volume requesting them to cut out these pages; replacements would be supplied. When these came they included an exceptionally lengthy treatment of the Bering Straits.

It seems likely that Beria simply knew too much about the bloody past. A holder of his office has yet to survive after leaving office in the USSR. Little more was ever said about the Beria case. The long-time doer of Stalin's dirty work undoubtedly was both feared and hated. The other high Communists joined forces to exterminate him, as a kind of sacrifice on the altar of de-Stalinization. "He was a butcher and an assassin," Khrushchev declared later, accusing Beria also of raping numerous young girls.

The next heir apparent was Malenkov, a rotund and apparently genial long-time Stalin favorite who had quite a reputation as an adroit politician, one with an instinct for survival in the brutal world of Russian politics. Malenkov sought to change the Stalinist policies. He called for more stress on consumer goods and less on heavy industry, an issue that struck close to the heart of de-Stalinization. Mikoyan observed in a speech in October 1953 that, "we have not yet overcome the disproportion between the production of goods and popular consumption, and the saturation of the increasing needs of the masses of the Soviet Union." Orthodox Stalinists still preached the cult of heavy industry's priority.

Agriculture was the other great sore point of the Russian economy. When Malenkov resigned the premiership on February 8, 1955, he mentioned his lack of success in this area. He also preached an extreme version of the "peaceful coexistence" doctrine that Nikita Khrushchev was to stress: war was now unthinkable, because it could only mean the ruin of both sides. Well he might, for by 1955 both the United States and the USSR had succeeded in manufacturing the new and more powerful H-bomb, soon to be carried by long-range missiles.

Nevertheless, veteran Stalin disciple Vyacheslav Molotov attacked Malenkov for the heresy of supposing that in the next war "world civilization" would perish; only the imperialists would go down, he said; socialist society would survive. It appears also that Malenkov was prepared to agree to the unification of Germany under free elections, along with its neutralization, a plan proposed by British Foreign Secretary Anthony Eden in 1954. His fall would seem to have been the result of an excess of de-Stalinizing. The old Stalinists, led by Molotov, joined forces with Khrushchev, who may be thought of as occupying the center, to secure Malenkov's downfall.

For some time the results were unclear, and this uncertainty in the top Soviet leadership is related to the 1956 troubles in Poland and Hungary. Attacks on Molotov broke out in 1955 and 1956, and Khrushchev came to the fore; but he did did not have a firm grip on power (a secure majority in the Presidium) even at the time that he delivered his speech to the Party's Twentieth Congress on February 25, 1956.

The materials for the famous speech had clearly been assembled with care, but Khrushchev may have decided to present them on the spur of the moment. He blurted it all out: Stalin had had "a persecution mania of unbelievable proportions"; he had been arbitrary, capricious, and tyrannical. "Thousands of innocent people fell victims to wilfullness and lawlessness" in the Leningrad affair and on many other occasions. Stalin had threatened to "shorten by a head" his minister of state security if he did not obtain confessions in the doctors' plot, and he had ordered the accused put in chains and beaten. ("Beat, beat, and beat again.") The evidence in this case had been "fabricated from beginning to end." At his death, Stalin was planning to "finish off the old members of the Politburo" including Molotov and Mikoyan.

Releasing copies of Lenin's letter of December 1922, which expressed alarm at Stalin's "immense power" and his "crude" nature, Khrushchev accused the long-time Soviet leader of lacking toleration, patience, and ability to cooperate; Stalin simply imposed his views, demanding "absolute submission." Stalin was admitted to have been right in opposing Trotskyists, Bukharinists, and other deviationists; but in 1935–1938 he had passed beyond the bounds of reason and had obtained confessions "through physical duress against the accused." Mass arrests and mass deportations without trial, Khrushchev went on to say, "created conditions of insecurity, fear and desperation." The meeting surged with indignation, according to the report, when the first secretary revealed that of the 139 members of and candidates for the Central Committee elected in 1934, 98, or 70 percent, had been shot, while of 1,966 delegates to the Party Congress of that year, more than half had been arrested. "Diseased with suspicion," Stalin had grown paranoid and used his unlimited power to stifle all free criticism. Khrushchev did not neglect to point out Stalin's virtual collapse at the beginning of World War II and his uncertain leadership during much of the war.

Why didn't the members of the Politburo assert themselves against the cult of the individual? Well, Khrushchev said, at first Stalin had gained great popularity and support through his vigorous leadership; later he ruled by terror and by guile, and finally he bypassed the Politburo altogether. Khrushchev's attempted explanation of why there had been no resistance to Stalin's tyranny during his lifetime and why his tyranny had not even been mentioned until three years after his death was feeble, but at least he thought an explanation necessary. In 1955, when he had visited Belgrade, Khrushchev had blamed the mishandling of Russian-Yugoslav relations on the conveniently dead Beria, much to Tito's disgust. Now Stalin himself was accused of all manner of crimes.

Not until 1961 would he be removed from Lenin's side in the mausoleum on Red Squire and his name from place names all over the Soviet Union. The speech of February 25, 1956, was given in secret session, though it soon became one of the worst-kept secrets in history. And Stalin was blamed not so much for his policies as for his manner, for his "personality cult."

Since 1956, the USSR has become neither a liberal nor a democratic state. It remains guided by an elite leadership of the only party allowed to exist, the Communist party of the Soviet Union. This leadership, which is not elected by the people, still attempts to control or oversee every aspect of society's and every citizen's life. It still arrests and imprisons or deports dissenters. The press, controlled by this leadership, still systematically distorts and suppresses news. There are no free trade unions. The parliament, the Supreme Soviet, is a farce. It meets for a few days each year to rubber stamp, invariably by a unanimous vote, what it is allowed to approve, including the budget and a few laws. In 1968, as it did in 1956 only a few months after Khrushchev's speech, the Red Army forcibly repressed rebellions designed to secure (within communism) some measure of intellectual and cultural freedom. In 1971, Tibor Szamuely commented that "everything in the USSR, to the smallest detail, is today essentially as Stalin created it. . . . Khrushchev attempted to tinker with the massive edifice— and failed."

Nevertheless 1956 was a turning point, perhaps one of history's greatest ones. Many Stalinist methods were abandoned. Torture, summary execution, and imprisonment in slave labor camps ceased to be the means of government. Leaders might be dismissed, but they were no longer shot. The Terror decree of 1934 was annulled. The population of the labor camps declined sharply, though the camps did not vanish altogether. The system did not much change, but the spirit that informed it slowly altered from unremitting, grim, and brutal to one somewhat more relaxed and humane. After all, those who claimed to be Marxists could not forget that the end product of revolution was supposed to be not perpetual slavery but the good society, in which human nature realizes its fullest creative possibilities.

The immediate result was shock. "For weeks we talked of nothing else," one who was a student at that time recalls. Bierut, the Polish first secretary, died of a heart attack! There was confusion and sometimes anger at Stalin's traducers; had he not been long presented as the hero-leader? Khrushchev says that he argued that one big shock would be better than years of creeping doubt. The truth about Stalin was certain to be known eventually, and it was better to get it out of the Soviet system in one big purgation than to let the poison go on working. In adopting this plan the Soviet leadership showed courage. But it was dangerous to go too far, for this would undermine the very legitimacy of the Soviet order. Stalin had built the system within which Soviet leaders operated. How far could they or should they reform it in basic ways?

There were a number of areas in which reform seemed urgent, including the overcentralized and bureaucratic economic planning structure, which had worked well up to a point but was reaching the limits of its utility. But the most significant task was providing some freedom and democracy for Soviet citizens.

The Khrushchev Era

"De-Stalinization" was a difficult and dangerous process. All the top Soviet leaders had served Stalin, and some had been all too closely involved with his crimes. The Soviet system as it existed was Stalinist, and the legitimacy of the present leaders' rule rested, in the eyes of millions, on their being Stalin's heirs and successors. The secret speech sent a shock and a thrill throughout the Communist world. The Italian Communist leader, P. Togliatti, joined the Hungarian intellectual Marxist George Lukacs in hailing the event and calling for a clean break with the Stalinist past. But very soon the outbreaks in Poland and Hungary revealed the dangers of too precipitous a break. "Despite Khrushchev's repudiation of the Stalinist legacy of terror," as Merle Fainsod writes, "the model he held out for Soviet society was no Liberty Hall where individualism would run rampant." Nagy's democratic communism quickly led to what looked like democracy without communism. This weakened the position of the de-Stalinizers.

There was a brief thaw in the literary and intellectual world, marked by publication of such works critical of Stalinism as Dudintsev's *Not by Bread Alone,* an eloquent attack on the dead hand of bureaucracy. But this thaw was followed almost immediately by a refreeze. The most sensational example of the return to semi-Stalinism in cultural matters was the Pasternak affair, when Soviet Russia's greatest poet was forced to refuse the Nobel Prize awarded him for publication (abroad) of his novel, *Dr. Zhivago.* (This and other matters connected with thought and culture in the USSR are discussed later in this chapter.)

In June 1957, Nikita Khrushchev faced a revolt against his leadership within the normally all-powerful Presidium (as the Politburo was renamed at this time) of the Central Committee of the Communist party. His foes held against the flamboyant Ukrainian not only the rumblings of discontent in the satellites but some ambitious reforms he had undertaken at home, most notably an effort to decentralize the unwieldy government planning bureaucracy. His style and his emergence as a figure rising above the rest of the collective leadership brought such unlikely allies as Molotov, the old Stalinist, and the anti-Stalinist Malenkov together against Krushchev: a case of opposite extremes joining forces. The vote against Khrushchev in the Presidium was 7–4. Instead of accepting the verdict, he appealed, in a manner unprecedented since the 1920s, to the full Central Committee, a body of more than 300. There, on June 29, Khrushchev won a unanimous victory, a tribute not only to his popularity but to his having carefully placed his followers in the lower ranks of the party apparatus. He also had the support of the army.

Molotov, Malenkov, and Kaganovich were dismissed and branded as the "Antiparty" group. Thereafter they were repeatedly assailed as "criminal fractionists," "filthy intriguers and splitters," "political bankrupts," and other choice epithets, which stopped short, however, of charges of treason or heresy. The new style was not to shoot deposed bigwigs nor force them by torture to accuse themselves of gross crimes in stage-managed public trials; they simply ended up managing a power plant in Kazakhstan or something of the sort. They were dismissed from the Central Committee but not expelled from the party. One exception was the execution of Imre Nagy after the Hungarian revolution, and Khrushchev was not above using threats to revert to Stalinist methods in arguments with dissident intellectuals.

It is hard not to think that these veteran Bolsheviks had fallen into a trap cleverly laid by the wilier Khrushchev. He was now the number one man without question, though he never attained—and did not want—the powers Stalin had. In 1964 he was to lose his post in much the same manner as had Molotov and Malenkov; he had introduced a small dose of democracy into the Soviet system. During his years of power he gained world fame and seemed to threaten a new cult of personality, surrounded by adulation as he often was. The launching of the first Sputnik space satellite in October 1957 covered him and his country with enormous prestige. Not all his projects went as well, but he was at least a vigorous, colorful, often unpredictable and exciting participant in the drama of world history for the next seven years.

Energy Khrushchev did not lack. He tried to make basic reforms in the Russian order, though he did not succeed. He threw himself behind such grandiose projects as the "virgin lands" scheme to open up to cultivation a huge acreage in Kazahkstan: a plan based to some extent on the mystical scientific views of the quack Lysenko, whom

Khrushchev supported. T. D. Lysenko claimed that Lamarckian principles of species development were superior to Darwinian because they were more Marxist. Environmental changes could alter heredity; scientists could develop seeds with the ability to grow in the cold and dry climate of the steppes of eastern Russia and Siberia by freezing many generations of them and thus genetically accustoming them to the climate. This, of course, turned out to be untrue, but Lysenko terrorized respectable Russian academic biologists under both Stalin and Khrushchev for many years.

In 1959 and 1963 the expensive virgin lands project got in serious trouble, as disaster struck the crops. Other Khrushchev plans, including the consolidation and increasing proletarianization of the collective farms, did not do much to improve a nagging Soviet problem, the inefficiency of its agriculture.

Khrushchev's most visible activities, however, were on the international scene. He traveled almost incessantly, visiting virtually every country in the world. In 1959 he came to the United States, accompanied by a huge entourage, for a long, much-publicized tour—the first time ever for a visit to the land of capitalism by the ranking leader of the first Communist state. During his visit he conferred at length with President Eisenhower. Enthusiastic, ebullient, and good-natured, the earthy Khrushchev and his wife made a hit. He seemed to want to open a dialogue between the West and Russia, which had long been secluded from the world in suspicious isolation. He was capable of acknowledging that Communists had much to learn from the enemy— these slaves of capitalism live pretty well, he was heard to murmur in Iowa. And he proclaimed that, "the ice of the cold war has begun to melt."

At the same time, under pressure from the "hawks" at home, Khrushchev could not push his peaceful coexistence plan too far. While pressing for détente, he could not afford to seem to be doing so from weakness. Sputnik I and Sputnik II had exhibited Russian missile power, which ought to be exploited. So Khrushchev issued threats as well as smiles. In late 1958 he threatened to make a peace treaty with East Germany that would end the occupation status of Berlin and invite the DDR to take over the western zone of that city, thus reviving once again the Berlin Crisis that had erupted in 1948–1949. West Berlin was "a bone in his throat," Khrushchev declared. It was indeed an anomalous leftover from the Cold War, a Western outpost deep in Communist territory. Bonn claimed it as a part of the Federal Republic. East Germany was increasingly embarrassed by the flow of emigrants who fled to the West, mostly via West Berlin—and not only embarrassed but hurt economically. The rising economic boom in West Germany intensified this problem. It is not surprising that Khrushchev hoped to resolve the problem by a combination of threats and blandishments.

On this issue, Charles de Gaulle was obstinate against the Communists, treating Khrushchev's threats with contempt and telling Eisenhower "we will stand by you on this" when the British seemed to be willing to compromise with the Russians. De Gaulle made friends with Konrad Adenauer at this time, the West German Chancellor naturally being anxious not to surrender the former German capital city, the symbol of the 1949 spirit of resistance against tyranny. The illness and death of John Foster Dulles, Eisenhower's secretary of state, resulted in some confusion in American policy in 1959–1960. Khrushchev blustered and threatened, but he allowed the six-month time limit he had placed on securing a German peace treaty to expire, denying that he had delivered an ultimatum.

The world was going through a confusing period. Off stage, largely unobserved by the somewhat obtuse West, the quarrel between Red China and the Soviet Union was about to burst into a shouting match. It did so openly for the first time at the international Communist meeting at Bucharest in June 1960. Perhaps Khrushchev was interested in Berlin because he wanted to settle matters in Europe before dealing with potentially greater trouble in the East; or perhaps he wanted to secure an agreement limiting nuclear weapons in Europe to bolster his case for refusing such weapons to the Chinese. In 1958 and 1959 the Russians were pushing a plan, originally proposed by the Polish foreign minister, Adam Rapacki, to denuclearize central Europe: no atomic weapons or missiles were to be either manufactured or deployed in the two Germanies, Poland, or Czechoslovakia. The West rejected the plan as a maneuver to weaken NATO, though it clearly resembled an idea that had been suggested by Anthony Eden in 1954.

The Chinese later alleged that in 1959 the USSR reneged on an agreement to provide them with aid in making the fusion bomb. This famous rift deserves discussion in more detail a little later. During the crisis of 1960–1962, the West, bemused by the view that all Communists stood together in ideological unity, seems barely to have been aware of it.

At this time, also, decolonization was proceeding rapidly, both the French and the British granting independence to their former African colonies. The Belgian Congo erupted in civil war and became an international trouble spot. The United Nation's secretary-general, the Swede Dag Hammerskjöld, died there in a plane crash in 1961.

A summit conference was scheduled to be held in Paris in May 1960 to decide the Berlin question at last. With American policy in disarray and the Adenauer-de Gaulle bloc intransigent, prospects for a compromise did not look good. Indeed, how *could* one compromise on Berlin? There were suggestions for some sort of international control of the city, but these were scarcely practical and clearly unacceptable to the Russians unless international control was merely a disguise for Sovietization. Having laid down what amounted to an ultimatum, Khrushchev, now beset with Chinese and other problems (the bad harvest of 1959 threatened his agricultural policy), was in a tight spot. There has always been a suspicion that the U-2 incident, which now occurred, was deliberately arranged as an excuse to adjourn the impending summit meeting. This does not seem to be true, but Khrushchev seized upon the occurrence eagerly. Had he gone to Paris and negotiated, he would have had either to back down and face the wrath of the Chinese and his hawkish critics at home, or he would have have had to risk conflict with the united western European powers and the United States and thus contradict the whole course of peaceful coexistence he had embarked upon. It looks very much as though the impulsive Khrushchev had painted himself into a corner.

On May 1, 1960, an American reconnaissance plane (unarmed) was shot down by a Russian rocket over Soviet territory, near the Urals. Its pilot parachuted to safety, was captured, and confessed that he was on a mission to photograph Russian installations. Such espionage activity had been going on for some time, and Khrushchev had certainly known about it. But this was a bolder flight than any in the past, and it was the first time a pilot had been taken alive. On May 5, Khrushchev reported the incident in a speech but omitted the detail that the pilot had been captured. The United States government quickly responded with a "cover" story: the U-2 plane, engaged in purely scientific high-altitude testing, had strayed across the Pakistan border into Russia by mistake. Two days later, Khrushchev disclosed the full details; he had trapped the U.S. in a lie, and he exploded with righteous indignation.

Thus exposed, Washington made the best of a bad situation by a full confession: yes, the United States had to engage in such "distasteful" espionage, but only because Russian secrecy and the needs of Western security forced her to use defensive measures to guard against nuclear attack. Khrushchev was somewhat mollified; he did not doubt his good friend Eisenhower's sincerity and would not call off the impending summit conference. However, upon arriving in Paris on May 16 Khrushchev demanded an apology and punishment for those responsible for the espionage. Eisenhower said that the flights were being suspended but went no further; Khrushchev angrily stormed out, and the conference was wrecked. Nevertheless, Khrushchev took care to announce at the same time that he would again postpone for six to eight months the signing of a separate peace treaty with East Germany.

Whether he contrived it or it happened opportunely, the U-2 incident thus helped Khrushchev escape a dilemma. The American presidential election was approaching, and while Khrushchev moved over to Bucharest to argue with the Chinese, the Democrats nominated John F. Kennedy. They won a narrow victory over the Republican party in the fall of 1960. The new president was young, personable, and confident, but he was inexperienced. Kennedy and Khrushchev met in Vienna in June 1961. Their encounter was not a success. The peasant Khrushchev got on better with the old soldier, Eisenhower, than he did with this glamorous young urban sophisticate. He chose to fulminate and issue threats: his patience had worn thin; there must be a peace treaty ending the Western occupation of Berlin; he intended to sign one before the year was out. And he soon set about erecting the Berlin Wall, barring movement between East and West Germany.

The Cuban Missile Crisis

Perhaps the Russian chief thought Kennedy could be bullied, not only because the American president was inexperienced but because he had so badly mishandled the Cuban situation early in his term of office. When Kennedy assumed the presidency in early 1961, he faced the question of what to do about the revolutionary regime of Fidel Castro, which had taken over the sugar island from its corrupt rulers in 1959. No Marxist, Castro came out of obscurity to lead a nondoctrinaire group of freedom fighters. He simply filled the power vacuum left by the abdication of the confused and discredited Batista regime. He was a revolutionary adventurer, not a Communist; for this reason the rising New Left, marked by a deep mistrust of all ideology, was to make him its hero. But his violent abuse and threats convinced many Americans that Castro was a danger to Caribbean security, and a growing crowd of Cuban refugees who had fled from revolutionary terror were all too ready to return with arms to overthrow him. On April 17, 1961, some 1,500 CIA-trained Cuban refugees landed at the Bay of Pigs, expecting to ignite a national uprising against Castro. The entire operation had been badly bungled, and it failed. While Kennedy was trying to figure out what had gone wrong in Cuba, the Russians were putting the first man in outer space. Small wonder that Khrushchev felt he had the upper hand when the two leaders met several weeks later.

After his unsatisfactory meeting with Kennedy, Khrushchev proceeded to build the Berlin Wall, which caught the West totally by surprise, and to set off a series of hydrogen bombs in a resumption of above-ground testing. For still one more time, however, he refrained from dropping the other shoe on Berlin. The Wall had seemingly taken care of the problem of people fleeing from East Germany, at whatever cost in inhumanity and in admission before the bar of world opinion that people would not stay in Communist countries if they could help it. In October, the 22nd USSR Party Congress met, and instead of threats against the West it produced a barely disguised outbreak of the quarrel with China. The Russians assailed Albania as a substitute for China, that little country having broken away from Moscow's control to side with the Chinese. Meanwhile the Chinese attacked the USSR under cover of assailing Yugoslavia. And at this same time Khrushchev persuaded the party to renew the attack on Stalin, while encouraging another "thaw" in the climate of opinion. The dead dictator's crimes were extended to include his whole regime rather than just the final years. This development may have reflected Khrushchev's fear of renewed criticism of his policies by the old Stalinists.

The year 1962 was to bring the worst international crisis since 1956. The unpredictable Khrushchev now thought he saw a way out of the Berlin impasse by exerting pressure on the United States through Cuba. Castro and Khrushchev first met in 1960 when the Russian leader visited New York, entertaining the public by banging his shoe on the table at the United Nations and embracing Castro in a Harlem hotel. On December 1, 1961, Castro announced himself a convert to Marxism. In the main, Soviet policy since World War II has adhered to the implicit bargain about spheres of influence by avoiding any significant involvement in Latin America, even though the volatile politics of this region, which is flavored with much anti-Americanism, has offered tempting opportunities. But this time the temptation was too great, and Khrushchev was prepared to gamble.

Hints about shipping arms to Cuba from the Soviet Union appeared in June 1962. A large amount of equipment flowed into Cuban ports during July and August, and construction work began at sites that were intended to be nothing less than nuclear missile installations. The missiles themselves, with their nuclear warheads, began to arrive in September. Did Khrushchev expect this to go unobserved? If not, did he expect the Kennedy government (about whose "liberal" weakness he had spoken to visitors in recent weeks) to do nothing about it? If so, he had badly miscalculated. On October 22, President Kennedy announced a blockade, or "quarantine," of Cuba to be in effect until missiles were withdrawn from that country.

This was rather late; by some time in November, it is calculated, the Russians would have completed the missile bases together with their anti-aircraft protection, and, with numerous medium-range and intermediate-range nuclear missiles in place, would have had the major eastern cities of the United States in range. But certain now of the Russians' intentions, which they had tried to conceal by brazen denials, Kennedy no longer hesitated. He called their bluff.

Khrushchev raged that the Americans were headed toward thermonuclear war, warned of "catastrophic consequences," and asserted that "no state concerned with preserving its independence" could accept the American blockade. U.S. forces all over the world were placed on the alert; submarines received radio information on Polaris missile targeting. The world trembled before the prospect of nuclear Armageddon. But Khrushchev quickly retreated. The maneuvers of the next few days (October 23–28) were complicated by some division of opinion within each government. Khrushchev could not act alone in such a grave emergency; he had to consult high members of the Presidium. Among John Kennedy's coterie of advisers, some wanted to launch an immediate attack on and invasion of Cuba; others evidently wished to do nothing except refer the matter to the United Nations. The blockade strategy was something of a compromise between hawks and doves, but it was effective; and Kennedy gained in confidence as he watched the Russians flinch.

Khrushchev, after all, was in a weak position. It was Hungary in reverse: Russia could not possibly defend Cuba from so far away except by unleashing suicidal nuclear war, and the men in the Kremlin had no desire to die amid the ruins of the socialist state just for Fidel Castro, who was not even a very good Communist. Between October 26 and 28 the Russians arrived at a decision to withdraw the missiles in return for an American pledge not to invade Cuba and to call off the quarantine. At one moment Moscow added a demand that the United States liquidate its Turkish bases, but this was dropped. Several days of frantic exchanges worked out an agreement.

The threat of thermonuclear war was perhaps not quite as great as a terrified world imagined, but this was without a doubt the scariest eyeball-to-eyeball confrontation of all time. Although he had been accused by his many critics of practicing "brinksmanship," the recently departed John Foster Dulles had never come close to anything like this. Nevertheless, the episode had some beneficial results. Awed by their nearly fatal collision, the superpowers not only installed a special telephone line and soon reached an agreement on nuclear testing, but they proceeded toward a general détente. After marching up to the brink and looking into the depths, one can only march back and think things over. A grave crisis surmounted almost always leads to an improvement in international relations.

For Khrushchev, however, it was undoubtedly a serious setback. He had precipitated a world crisis by a rash gamble, but his bluff had

In late October, 1962, exactly six years after the Hungarian Revolution/Suez joint crisis (and just six years before the 1968 crises), the Soviet Union's attempt to station long-range nuclear missiles in Cuba brought confrontation between USSR and USA, threatening the war that might end civilization. Here, on October 1, 1962, President John F. Kennedy confers with his brother Robert as they ponder crucial decisions. *Wide World Photos.*

been called. He had sheepishly retreated, bringing home his missiles while the Chinese waxed indignant at this "shameful capitulation to the imperialists." He could claim to have secured a guarantee of Cuban immunity against U.S. attack, but such an attack had clearly not been imminent; and in any event a simple treaty of alliance between Cuba and the USSR could have gained the same end without all the turmoil. The missile crisis condemned U.S.-Cuban relations to many more years of hostility and ensured that Cuba would remain a reluctant ward of the Soviet Union—more of an expensive encumbrance than an asset, especially since Castro was far from happy with such tutelage. Khrushchev's intentions may have been to subject the United States to nuclear blackmail, forcing it at the very least to give up West Berlin. Aware that the USSR was inferior to the US in missile strength, he hoped to bridge the gap.[1] In this he had totally failed. President Kennedy was soon

[1] A decade later, the United States was prepared to concede that equality between the US and the USSR in nuclear arms was the only realistic basis for a treaty limiting and controlling the arms race.

in Berlin being cheered by ecstatic crowds as he told them "I am a Berliner!" Critics accused Kennedy of heating up the conflict with rhetoric, as Truman had done fifteen years earlier; but the American president had proved his courage as a leader.

The Sino-Soviet Clash

Krushchev did not fall from power at the time of the Cuban missile crisis, but it dealt him a blow from which he never recovered. His other major headache in world affairs was, of course, Soviet Russia's row with her supposed Communist brother, Red China.

To most people in the West, obsessed by the idea that world communism was a monolithic entity, the clash between Communist China and Communist Russia came as one of the great surprises of the sixties. In actuality, nothing should have been less surprising. They were in competition for the leadership of world communism, for one thing. The Russians had long been used to being the unquestioned head, whose ideas the other Communist parties of the world, all much smaller and less significant, were expected to endorse without complaint. But now a land of greater population, with an old and proud history, asked for equality if not primacy. This was even more true after Stalin's death. Though there was little love between them, Mao Tse-tung was prepared to defer to Stalin's seniority while the latter lived; he was not ready to kowtow to the upstart Khrushchev. Mao once declared that whereas Stalin was a fallen eagle, Khrushchev was a backyard hen! The veteran Chinese Communist leader expected to be recognized as the number one world Marxist.

Relations between the two communist movements had never been really close. Back in 1927, the urban-based Chinese Communists, under Russian guidance, were wiped out by Chiang Kai-shek's Nationalist party. They regrouped in rural areas, based their strength upon the peasants (quite in contrast to Marxist teaching as interpreted in Russia), and developed ideas and strategies attuned to this backwoods situation. Mao Tse-tung and his fellows thought they were following Marxism-Leninism, but they owed little or nothing to the Russians and developed on their own for many years.

When Mao visited Moscow in 1949, he made the long journey by train and was treated with none of the honors accorded a major visiting head of state; some date his doubts about the USSR from this experience. The treaty he made at that time with the Soviet Union was not marked by an overwhelming generosity on Russia's part, to say the least, and during the Korean War there were indications of a lack of perfect coordination between the communist allies. After Stalin's death, in the atmosphere of general relaxation, the Russians made some gestures of friendship toward Red China, as they did toward Yugoslavia. But this proved to be the lull before the storm.

Against a background of personal jealousies and cultural rivalry, the trouble started chiefly over Khrushchev's peaceful coexistence line. The Chinese were much more warlike. The doctrine of perpetual revolutionary struggle was Mao's chief gift to mankind's store of ideas, and he thought the Russians should practice it, too. When, looking at the prospect of destruction of all they had so painfully built, the Russians backed away from nuclear war with the United States, Mao was disgusted. He astonished the Russians in November 1957 by pointing out to them that if 200 million Chinese were killed in a nuclear war, along with 200 million Americans (and 200 million Russians?) there still would be plenty of Chinese left. "Hit the aggressors on the head!" he cried during the Lebanese-Jordanian crisis of 1958.[2] The sight of Khrushchev hobnobbing with Eisenhower at Camp David in 1959 was the last straw—or, if not that, the Soviet Union's refusal at this time to share nuclear know-how with its ally because it thought Mao too reckless. The Chinese chairman expected Russian support against the United States in his campaign to overthrow Chiang Kai-shek's government on the island of Taiwan, which still claimed to be the true Chinese

The bitter quarrel between Red China and the Soviet Union had already begun at the time of this picture in Peking, October, 1959; signs of it may be read in the faces of Khrushchev and Mao Tse-tung, while Ho Chi Minh seems to want to be peacemaker. *Wide World Photos.*

[2] In the summer of 1958 American and British troops, now in harmony, landed in Lebanon and Jordan after a revolution in Iraq. Iraqi revolutionaries had assassinated the pro-British king of that country and proclaimed a union with Egypt. Egypt, backed by Russia, threatened retaliation; but the crisis cooled off when both sides showed restraint.

government. He was to find that the Russians did not even support him in a boundary dispute with India.

In the late fifties, the Chinese Communists proclaimed the "Great Leap Forward," which was supposed to carry them toward the state of communism by bringing industry, in the form of small-scale manufacturing, to the villages. This notion was wholly at odds with the Russian idea of centralization, abolition of peasant culture, proletarianization, and urbanization of the countryside. The Russians laughed at such ignorant presumption. Khrushchev thought Mao a "lunatic." Each side began to accuse the other of "revisionism" or "petty bourgeois deviationism"—the Chinese pointing to the Kremlin's soft line on capitalism and Russian elitism and rigidity, the Russians ridiculing Chinese agrarian "populist" ideology. The Soviet Union accused Red China of "adventurism" and "anarchism"; Mao blamed the Kremlin for "shameful compromises with imperialism." In July 1960, following the row at Bucharest, the Russians withdrew all their experts from China and began sharply to reduce economic aid to that country. The ideological struggle broke out in earnest.

At stake was preeminence in the world communist movement; the ideological debates occurred at international CP meetings where the two major communist powers competed for the allegiance of the other parties around the world. It annoyed the Kremlin exceedingly that Albania was already openly siding with the Chinese and that other Communists seemed to welcome an opportunity to criticize the Soviet Union, obliquely and cautiously at first but with growing boldness. In 1961 only two-thirds of the world Communist parties supported Moscow on the "Albanian", i.e. Chinese, issue.

Mao, in brief, was playing Martin Luther to the Kremlin's Infallible Chair, sowing dissension, schism, and even heresy among the faithful Marxists of the world. Very like the Protestant prophet more than four centuries earlier, Mao accused the older authoritative establishment of having lost its spirit, of having grown old, conservative, and rigidly dogmatic. There was an activism and radicalism, along with novel ideas, in Chinese communism that appealed to some elements of the New Left just arising throughout the world. The revolutionary struggle in Vietnam was based on Chinese peasant-guerrilla warfare tactics. The Soviet Union stood to lose its long-held leadership in the world Marxist and revolutionary movement to this young and potentially powerful rival. It was not prepared to accept this defeat without a fight.

There was also the uncomfortable fact that China and Russia shared a tremendously long border, stretching for more than 3,500 miles through ill-defined regions. The Chinese claimed that the border was based on unjust seizures in the past, and in 1963 they asked that the borders be changed. Doubtless this could have been resolved had basic good will existed, but once the quarrel began, the boundary dispute, along with the status of such buffer zones as Outer Mongolia and Sinkiang, added fuel to the fire. In fact there were later to be actual armed conflicts at some localities along the border.

In 1964 the polemical battle raged so loudly that throughout the world even the most ill-informed grew aware of it; from being a family quarrel it had become a public scandal. It was to contribute much to Khrushchev's fall. To some extent, Khrushchev's firmness with China pleased conservative, Stalinist elements in his party, for they were marked by a general hawkishness, admiring strength and toughness in foreign policy. They were psychological "hard-liners," who no more favored "appeasement" of the Chinese than of the Americans. Khrushchev himself reacted against the recklessness and violence of the Chinese, seeing in them a threat to peace; his rivals on other matters within the USSR saw China simply as an upstart challenger of Russian supremacy within world communism, a supremacy which was, of course, impeccably Stalinist. Thus the anti-Chinese line united diverse factions within the Soviet Russian ruling group. At the same time, his indiscreet way of conducting the quarrel exposed Khrushchev to criticism.

Reform and Reaction in the USSR
in the Khrushchev Period

Foreign policy, though it tended to become his main preoccupation, was of course by no means the whole of Khrushchev's concern as first secretary of the party's Central Committee and chairman of the Council of Ministers of the USSR. With General de Gaulle, he might legitimately have complained that widespread opinion linked him entirely with international affairs. Certainly his spectacular forays into foreign policy, climaxed by the Cuban crisis and the China quarrel, focused main attention on this aspect of the volatile Ukrainian, whose penchant for world travel was strong, and whose name is as indissolubly linked with peaceful coexistence as it is with de-Stalinization. The paradox was that in each case he followed a bewilderingly zigzag course. ("Peaceful coexistence" did not, in the official Soviet view, mean an end to class struggle between the two rival and irreconcilable systems of capitalism and socialism; it meant only that the war should be waged in a way "which does not threaten wars, dangerous conflicts, and an uncontrolled arms race.")

But Khrushchev's primary goal was to secure the well-being of the USSR and further its interests. In his eyes, this entailed domestic as well as foreign policy changes. In the end, he largely failed in this area too, although he displayed energy and imagination.

Economic growth became a problem for the USSR about the end of the 1960s, as it did in parts of the West. During the 1950s the Soviet economy grew rapidly, at an average annual gross national product (GNP) rate of about 7 percent, an experience it shared with Western Europe. This growth may best be seen as recovery from the devastation of World War II. It began slowing in 1959. The goal of "overtaking and surpassing the United States" receded into the distance, for the USSR was not gaining any ground; and the capitalistic European Community was outgaining both the two superpowers. Between 1962 and 1972 the American GNP slightly more than doubled, the Russian did not quite double, the EEC nearly tripled. The total Soviet GNP remained less than half that of the U.S. and was now substantially less than Western Europe's; on a per capita basis, Soviet production was no more than a third of the American. This is apart from qualitative considerations, which were urgent in the USSR, for the poor quality of many Russian products as compared to Western ones was a notorious weakness of the Soviet system.

All this added up to something less than a satisfactory performance for an economy that, ideology taught, was supposed to "bury" the capitalist world with its superior efficiency. Part of the problem seemed to lie in the clumsiness of the vast centralized bureaucracy, which was the first target of all the dissident writers. Despite Khrushchev's effort to decentralize the bureaucracy into regional planning councils, it remained. The difficulties of attempting to plan everything from Moscow intensified as the country moved toward a more sophisticated consumer-oriented economy, which stressed number and quality of products rather than just basic industrial plant.

The *distribution* of consumer goods was a difficulty. There were persistent shortages, long lines at the state stores, shoddy goods when one did buy them—to the disgust of an increasingly choosy and complaining Soviet citizenry. As the climate of opinion grew milder, consumer protest became less timid. How long must one wait for the promised land of Communist plenty, for which so many painful sacrifices had been made?

Waste, slowness of innovation, and lack of attention to quality were apparent weaknesses. Several experts came forward with plans of reform in the freer post-Stalinist climate. Of these, Evsei Liberman was the best known. About 1962 his name became associated with the idea of allowing a greater role for individual enterprises and for profit incentives. Well might the Chinese growl about a "restoration of capitalism," even though Liberman's ideas were never tried on more than a limited basis; the power of the central bureaucracy and the inertia of the Stalinist system were too strong. Like Liberman, other reformers proposed that individual economic enterprises be allowed to decide some, though not all, of the economic plan, making many of their own decisions about how most efficiently to operate their plant; sales and profits should be used as criteria for measuring an enterprise's success, leading to higher wages for managers and workers in successful ones; to a limited degree, these enterprises should be able to borrow money, paying an interest charge as firms do in the capitalistic money market.

At the extreme, such reformers as the Czech, Ota Sik, proposed a complete "market socialism" in which socially owned firms would compete in the marketplace with a bare minimum of central planning. Such a system would be socialist in that businesses would be jointly owned and managed; but the economy would chiefly rely upon the market, rather than a central planning bureaucracy, for its impetus. "Even in a socialist economy the market, with its real competitive pressures, cannot be replaced with anything else" as a rational means of deciding what, how much, and where to produce, Sik held. Only in deviant Yugoslavia, though, was this model given a thorough testing.

Khrushchev encouraged such critical and innovative thinking, but it ran up against both ideological and practical obstacles. If carried out thoroughly, such ideas might bring Communist economics rather close to planned capitalism of the French type, thus abolishing any great difference between socialism and capitalism; how could this be squared with that faith in the destiny of socialism to defeat and supplant capitalism on which the whole Soviet order rested? And the weight of the Moscow bureaucracy pushed against any idea that would strike at its vested interest.

When Khrushchev turned his attention to the grave problem of Russian agriculture, he encountered similar roadblocks. Any attempt to divert more resources into agriculture or into consumer goods production entailed disputes with the "steel eaters" who wanted economic priority given to heavy industry—a Stalinist dogma. Often the steel eaters joined lobbying forces with the military. Khrushchev's ideas on agricultural reform included abolishing the independent machine tractor stations and merging them into the collective farms; consolidating the collective farms into a smaller number of larger units; first enlarging and then decreasing the size of tracts that peasants were permitted to work on their own, that is, the private sector; supporting the gigantic virgin lands project; crusading for more corn. Though shrewd, none of these ideas proved very successful. Inefficiency, low yields, and failure to keep up with other countries in agriculture led to the need to import foodstuffs and continued to plague Soviet agriculture. To provide more tractors, fertilizers, and help of all kinds to the kolkhozes would cut into resources allotted to heavy industry and military production. A kind of military-industrial complex ruled Russia, as critics said it ruled the United States.

Khrushchev engaged in a complex struggle with the ghost of the man he had dared attack only three years after his death. The potent remnants of Stalin's spirit still stood in the path of reform. The attempt to rehabilitate the victims of Stalin's terror is a good example of the ambiguities of de-Stalinization. By 1964, 65 percent of those purged from the Central Committee after 1934 had been quietly rehabilitated— posthumously, alas, in the vast majority of cases—in the sense that their names were restored to encyclopedias and official histories with no attribution of guilt. But there was no public statement about all this. Nor did rehabilitation go so far as to restore Trotsky to respectability. Political prisoners were released. The power of the secret police (MVD, later KGB) was restricted. Yet laws against criticizing the regime or the party remained. The liberalizing trends brought mutterings from remnants of the old Stalinists and made timid people nervous at the prospect of unleashing anarchy.

All paths led to the ultimate question: in a society built on Marxist dogma but committed in some sense to ultimate liberation, what are the limits of criticism and dissent?

The Growth of Dissent in the USSR, 1953–1962

The Stalinist party's supervision of literature and the arts reached a peak in the Zhdanov era, right after the war. Freud, Einstein, and all "formalism" in the arts were banned, and Zhdanov did not hesitate to rebuke such great Soviet artists as composers Shostakovich and Prokofiev and cinema director Eisenstein. "Formalism" was a term the Soviet ideologists used to embrace much of Western "modernism": nonrealistic art, experimental techniques in the novel and poetry, in fact nearly everything that had been esthetically exciting in the West since late nineteenth-century naturalism. Formalism was denounced as "fanciful innovation which divorced art from the people and made it a possession of a narrow circle of epicure aesthetes." For the writer or artist to express only his own feelings was decadent bourgeois individualism. He must serve the party by praising its policies and damning its enemies. He must, in brief, become a propagandist, under orders from often philistine politicians. "Socialist realism" was the watchword, but it was not supposed to be so realistic as to depict anything unpleasant in the Russian scene; this was "bourgeois objectivism," and constituted treason to the workers' state by showing it in an unfavorable light. As Soviet writer Ilya Ehrenburg put it, "our so-called statesmen . . . lay down the law on what kind of books we are to write and what kind of pictures we are to paint."

There was censorship; anything published had to appear, if it appeared legally, in organs run by the state or party, and indeed it had to be approved for publication by high bureaucrats in the Ministry of Culture (Agitation and Propaganda Department) if it was at all significant. To continue to work, writers had to belong to the Writers' Union, expulsion from which guaranteed nonpublication, membership in which entitled one to rewards. This carrot-and-stick plan, particularly when the stick might be a bludgeon driving one to the firing squad or the prison camp, sufficed to keep most writers, intellectuals, and artists in line.

The first thaw began only a few weeks after Stalin's death. Ehrenburg, a veteran Soviet writer and an apparent pillar of the establishment, led the protest. His wartime writings celebrating the heroism of the Red Army made him well-known in the West. The theme of his group was that "the author is not a piece of machinery" who can be wound up and turned on to write according to formula; he creates well only when he is inspired to do so. Bureaucratic control of literature leads to insincere, uninspired work, all too much in evidence in the Soviet Union. Somewhat sarcastically one writer pointed out that Shakespeare had not been a member of a union. Thirty hacks grinding out propaganda do not equal one Tolstoy, whatever the party leaders may think. Even Mikhail Sholokhov, a prize-winning novelist *(And Quiet Flows the Don)* [3] who was generally loyal to the party line, conceded that "a dreary torrent of colorless, mediocre literature" had flooded the market in recent years in Russia. A few novels and plays critical of Soviet life were allowed to appear in 1953–1954. An orthodox counterattack soon came in force, however, and limited this early spring thaw to a mere trickle.

The next relaxation naturally followed the secret speech of 1956, but it was also fated to a rather brief life. Intense while it lasted ("the year 1956 was a year of passion," an observer wrote), stressing the theme of giving socialism a "human face"—an important and long-

---

[3] Persistent rumors that this unique achievement of Stalinist literature was in fact partly plagiarized from a White cossack officer killed in the Civil War have pursued Sholokhov. The question is still under debate, but it seems likely that he did plagiarize.

lasting slogan—this phase of the thaw centered on Dudintsev's novel *Not by Bread Alone*. The very title was an inspiration; the content revealed a time-serving, dishonest, on-the-make bureaucrat named Drozdov, a name suggesting servility, "Mr. Toady." But in May 1957, Khrushchev threatened these "muckraking" critics of the system. During a tirade at a Writers' Union meeting, he said that shooting a dozen Hungarian writers could have prevented the "counterrevolution" in Hungary. In a confession forced on her according to the customary ritual of self-abasement, Margarita Aliger apologized, among other things, for having "substituted moral and ethical categories for political ones."

This hard line coincided with the partial retreat from de-Stalinization that followed the Hungarian Revolution, but Khrushchev was not basically prepared to revert to Stalinism. The second thaw was stronger than the first, producing a small flood of new writing and even new journals. It never entirely stopped flowing. Despite continuing denunciations of writers who tried to put themselves above the party, Khrushchev permitted some liberal editors to survive. But when the Pasternak case came up in 1958, a freezing wind blew across the stream.

Boris Pasternak was Russia's greatest surviving poet. Aging by this time, he belonged to the brilliant Silver Age generation, most of whose representatives, as we know, had succumbed in one way or another to the difficulties of life under communism. Rather aloof from politics and perhaps too towering a figure to be easily vulnerable even to Stalin, who sometimes showed a curious respect for true genius among his foes, Pasternak had largely refrained from publishing anything for years. He busied himself with translations (including Shakespeare, Goethe, and some Georgian poets, which may have pleased Stalin) and wrote poems only for private circulation. He had long been working on the novel, *Dr. Zhivago*, which in 1956 he decided to submit for publication. It was rejected as too risky even in the climate of the second thaw. He then sent it to an Italian Communist publisher, who published it in late 1957.

A year later the novel, which attracted worldwide attention and was later made into an American movie, received the Nobel Prize in literature. Pasternak first accepted the coveted award of the Swedish Academy but then was forced to refuse it amid an officially inspired chorus of abuse in Russia, which described him as a "moral freak," a filthy pig, a base slanderer. Expelled from the Writers' Union and forced to utter the usual abject apologies, Pasternak died two years later; the great pianist Svyatoslav Richter played at his funeral, but not many dared to attend. Andrei Sinyavsky and Yuli Daniel were pallbearers. The episode disgusted many outside the Soviet Union who had been its friends, and it brought quite a few resignations from Communist parties.

Pasternak had stepped outside the usual bounds of dissidence by having his work published abroad without permission, setting an example many others were to follow in ensuing years. And *Dr. Zhivago* is a study in profound disillusionment, undercutting all the official cacophony of praise for the Revolution and its accomplishments by showing how irrelevant to the spiritual needs of modern man that whole exercise in political violence was. No wonder the Kremlin hated the book. But the storm of protest aroused by this brutal treatment of an internationally revered book and author must have given Khrushchev pause. He is said to have fired the people who advised him on this issue.

The next wave of de-Stalinization came in 1961. Stalin's body was removed from its position next to Lenin's, and Stalingrad was renamed Volgograd, a tribute to Khrushchev's continuing dedication to erase, so far as feasible, the cruel past. Ehrenburg continued to exploit his privileged position in the interests of a cautious liberalization; his 1960 memoirs were very important in Thaw III. Yevgeny Yevtushenko made a sensation with his poem "Babi Yar" about Soviet antisemitism, a charge that struck Khrushchev himself fairly close to home; Yevtushenko was abused, but he survived.

The Ukrainian poet Yevtushenko spoke for a younger generation of Russians, the counterpart of those restless Western students who were about to disrupt campuses from Berlin to Berkeley. The spirit of the sixties was felt almost as much in the Soviet Union as it was in London or Paris; it was in fact a worldwide phenomenon. The youth rebellion was an antibureaucracy rebellion, a vague and restless search for release from the prison of technological society. Youth alienated from the "system" meant, in the USSR, youth alienated from the party, from the mentality of the *apparatchiki*, indeed from the whole communist ethos as represented by the post-1917 generation. The newly published writings of the young Marx provided another and different, more humanistic communist ethos.

Khrushchev, that amazing bundle of crudities, contradictions, and subtleties, continued to alternate between loud abuse and tacit toleration of intellectual novelty. He harangued coarsely against the tiny amount of abstract art that managed to surface briefly in 1962: "pictures painted by jackasses," "dog shit." He stormed in to close down an exhibit by the great sculptor Ernst Neizvestny, who was thereafter denied materials and facilities. This was perhaps more the bourgeois-peasant philistine than the Communist ideologue; Hitler hated abstract, modernist art too, and we can imagine Harry Truman reacting similarly, and perhaps even Ernie Bevin (not Charles de Gaulle). Yet this same year, 1962, was the year of Solzhenitsyn, whose first book, *One Day in the Life of Ivan Denisovich*, perhaps because it dealt solely with Stalin's concentration camps, was not only permitted but showered with official praise. This, needless to say, did not last, either. Thaw and refreeze, thaw and refreeze—in the end, after innumerable cycles, was there a significant decrease in the size of the ice block? Despite the relapses of Khrushchev's successors, the answer seems a clear yes.

It is to Khrushchev's credit that he allowed the thaw to begin. For obvious reasons he had to control it, lest it become a flood that would sweep away the whole society and delegitimize its rulers. One has no right to expect that this essentially simple man (intellectually), brought up under communism and for years a part of it, would repudiate his belief that communism was the light and hope of suffering humanity. He did rather consistently believe that communism should be democratized and humanized, and he tried as best he could—always consistent with stability and security—to move in that direction. Things would get worse, not better, after he left. He was to be overthrown in 1964 by people who feared freedom and feared democracy. They accepted de-Stalinization only to the extent that it meant the removal of complete brutality and illegal methods. Dissidents, that is to say, are no longer shot without trial or hurled into hideous prison camps in the USSR. But they were to be arrested, tried before biased judges, and sent to mental hospitals or regular prisons from 1965 on.

The Other Communist States of Eastern Europe

Quite often the West's perception of the "satellite" or "bloc" states of eastern Europe—the Warsaw Pact countries—conformed to that view of communism as a single hostile monolith. This view blurred people's vision in the Cold War era. All the satellite countries were allegedly totally dominated by and totally submissive to the USSR, which ruled them by terror and forced them to be its puppets.

Such a view requires considerable nuancing. All were indeed communized. Yugoslavia, of course, remained communist; but she broke away from Moscow, was not a member of the Warsaw Pact, and began in the 1950s to develop a mode of "market socialism" that Stalin's heirs regarded as little more than capitalism in disguise. The Yugoslavians regarded it, however, as truer to the spirit of Karl Marx than the despotic "state capitalism" of the USSR. This development, it should be noted, was not a cause of the breach between the two countries; it followed the breach. In 1945 Tito was on a Stalinist path, to which he had long been loyal. He began to collectivize, centralize, and in all respects follow the Russian model. The clash was a political one, basically caused by Yugoslavia's desire to be independent of Moscow and not take orders from the Russians. Once the break had occurred, the Yugoslav leaders felt impelled to prove their distinctiveness. Without abandoning communism, they joined in what was to be a growing trend to rescue Marx, as it were, from the Russians.

This trend could be construed as staying within the Leninist spirit. And indeed the Soviet de-Stalinizers also claimed that Stalinism was a betrayal of Leninism, not a fulfillment of it. The appeal was not to the Lenin who created the terroristic dictatorship but to the Lenin who spoke of the autonomy of the soviets—the rule of the workers themselves, not an elite party or an omnipotent state. Yugoslav communism came to be best known for its industrial "self-management" by which the workers in the factories or farms jointly owned and participated in the management of their enterprises. Centralized state planning was kept to a minimum. Yet Tito, who imprisoned some of his critics, was far from a political liberal.

Russian-Yugoslav relations fluctuated. In 1955 Khrushchev led a delegation to Belgrade seeking reconciliation, though he did not handle the apology well. Tito apparently approved the brutal military action against Hungary in advance. He also approved of Khrushchev's intermittent anti-Stalinist campaigns but was annoyed by the equally persistent backtracking.

The Yugoslav leader tried to make himself a magnet for the "uncommitted" nations of the Third World. In 1961 he assembled two dozen heads of state at Belgrade, including India's distinguished president Jawaharlal Nehru, Egypt's Abdul Nasser, Algerian leader Ben Bella, and "Kwame" Nkrumah of Ghana from black Africa. But apart from the negative feature of being more or less hostile to both sides in the Cold War and desiring to remain neutral, these states had little in common. By no means were all the Asian and African countries uncommitted; at this stage, Indonesia, North Vietnam, and North Korea were accepting Russian and Chinese aid; South Korea, South Vietnam, the Phillippines, and Japan were committed to the West. Moreover, the young states were unstable. Leaders rose and fell. Six years after 1961, Nehru was dead, Bella deposed, Nkrumah in disgrace, Nasser discredited. Attempts to build a bloc in the turbulent world of the emerging Asian-African nations were condemned to frustration.

So between 1962 and 1968 Tito swung back to building bridges to Russia, only to be disgusted again by the 1968 Czech intervention. Yugoslavia opened lines to the West sooner than did other East European countries. Her percentage of trade with the West grew from

50 percent in 1965 to 61 percent in 1969, during which period her trade with Communist countries declined from 35 percent to 27 percent. And she achieved a rather impressive record of economic growth.

Conditions in the other so-called "people's democracies," a term invented by the Politburo to describe their ambivalent status after the war (not yet socialist but presumably about to be, with or without their consent), actually varied somewhat. All of them were forced to submit to one-party rule, suppression of opposition, censorship of the press; but these varied in intensity. The Catholic church, for example, was able to exist in Poland and East Germany but was severely persecuted in Hungary, where in 1951 Cardinal Mindszenty and other leading Catholics were arrested and church establishments broken up. In the 1956 revolution Mindszenty was released from prison to become a hero of the people, then forced to flee when the revolution was repressed, taking refuge in the American embassy where he remained for many years. In later years, he quarreled with the papacy, which preferred accommodations with the communist regimes to severe criticism of them.

Similarly unevenly applied were the other indices of Sovietization: collectivization of agriculture, that is, enticing or forcing of farmers into large cooperatives of which they became paid employees; crash programs for heavy industry; abolition of strikes and conversion of trade unions into tools of the state; centralized economic planning. Polish agriculture was not collectivized; East German was. Hungary, severely repressed in 1956, quietly became the most liberal of the bloc regimes in the ensuing years, as if the Russians were inhibited from repression by the burden of their 1956 guilt. Rumania had a near-Stalinist internal regime, in return for which she became the most outspoken critic of Soviet foreign policies, siding defiantly with the Chinese, the Albanians, the Jews.

In general, the Russian model was not suitable for these countries. They were attracted to the West. The futile rebellions of 1953, 1956, and 1968 showed that they could not escape by open resistance, but they often gained important concessions by stealth and intrigue. Three million East Germans "voted with their feet" by migrating to the Federal Republic, until the Wall put a stop to it. The members of the bloc differed greatly in degree of economic and social development, from fairly backward peasant societies in Bulgaria and Rumania to highly advanced industrial ones in Czechoslovakia and Germany. They varied greatly too in ethnic composition, culture, national characteristics. On the whole, the Stalin model was never applied to these countries as ruthlessly as it had been in Russia, and economic reforms came faster and went further there in the sixties than they did in the USSR.

The application of Liberman ideas might bring "socialism with a bourgeois face."

No fair-minded person could deny all value to the communist rule in these countries. Quite widely, an old pattern of large privately owned agricultural estates worked by landless peasants gave way to a more efficient form of agriculture with better conditions for the masses. Mechanization of agriculture and industrialization brought higher living standards. There was less inequality and more social welfare.

In this area arose the idea of "human socialism," which, as Edda Werfel wrote, "terrifies not only the capitalists but the Stalinists as well." It was the idea that somehow one might combine the best features of both East and West, the economic security of communism with the personal liberty of capitalist democracy. For these peoples, Stalinist communism brought some economic benefits but made a cultural desert. Tito, Imre Nagy, and, subsequently, Alexander Dubcek spoke for the hope of a happier socialism. That this was not achieved is indicated by the wall around East Germany, periodic revolts in Poland, and spring 1968 in Prague. Thirty-two divisions of Soviet troops stationed in the countries of Poland, Hungary, Czechoslovakia and East Germany guaranteed that these revolts could not succeed, if they were overt and violent. But, gradually and silently, and with varying degrees of progress, the movement toward liberalization went on in East Europe.

The Crisis
of the Late 1960s

From 1964 to 1968

One can hardly avoid making some general comments about the world in the period from about 1964 to 1970. It is difficult not to think that during this half-decade the gods were angry. Perhaps they resented humanity's penetration of outer space. It was a time of confusion, during which nearly every people seemed to lose its way, fall into holes, and get badly bruised.

The troubles came from unexpected quarters and were often caused by good intentions. The United States, seeking to go about its normal business of "containing" communism by showing firmness against aggression, got lost in a dark Indochinese tunnel and, after eight agonizing years, emerged demoralized. In western Europe, complacent about economic success and political stability, violent demonstrations suddenly broke out among students who were supposedly at work happily learning in the many new universities, and these demonstrations spread to become nearly a civil war in 1968. At this same time, playing no favorites, fate threw the Chinese into a time of disorder and strife called the Cultural Revolution. In the USSR, the fall of Khrushchev led to troubles with dissidents. After receiving a setback in the Six

Days War of 1967 when its clients, the Arab states, lost to the Israelis, the Soviet Union intervened in Czechoslovakia in 1968, amid protests from all over the communist as well as the noncommunist world. The 1969 world Communist meeting in Moscow was a disaster.

To the long list of unpredictable misfortunes others could be added, such as the eruption of Northern Ireland in 1968 (a problem the British had thought long settled). A Labour government returned to power in Britain but lost its way. Leaders fell. The great alliances were sundered and rent. A New Left arose to challenge the Old Left as well as the Right. Economic growth slowed at the end of the decade. Man reached the moon and found the thrill oddly disappointing.

By no means all was gloom, and one might indeed make out a case for this being a successful era. The disaffected New Leftists typically accused the capitalist order of doing them the cruel injustice of removing all rational grounds for complaints. Turbulence is not failure, and the various uprisings of students could be seen, as their instigators usually wished them to be, as efforts to "raise consciousness." Rising demands for cultural and intellectual freedom in the Soviet Union was an index of its progress. The superpowers continued to avoid a direct clash, and after 1968 there was a serious and significant move toward closer cooperation (detente) between the USA and the USSR. But for everybody, 1968 was at least a sobering year. It was the year of the Tet offensive, the Prague spring, and the Paris May.

Let us try to sum up a few of the main events from 1964 to 1968. Khrushchev was deposed early in October 1964. In a sudden and rather brutal blow, the Presidium compelled him to resign from that body as well as from his posts as first secretary and chairman. Khrushchev attempted to appeal from the Presidium to the full Central Committee but this time, unlike 1957, he found no support there. The top positions were divided, Alexei Kosygin becoming head of the government and Leonid Brezhnev the party secretary. The indictment against Khrushchev spoke of "the cult of personality" and of his "subjectivism," meaning his erratic qualities. No charges were filed against him, and there was no purge of his followers, some of whom, indeed, like Brezhnev and Podgorny, were prominent members of the new team. Khrushchev was allowed to live undisturbed in retirement, and seven years later was buried with no ceremony and little publicity. It was a relatively peaceful and legal change, for the USSR.

Most of Khrushchev's policies were continued, the problem obviously having been more with his manner than with his content. It would seem that his colleagues found him too uncertain a quantity, too much a gambler, too drunken and loquacious, as well as too dangerously reform-minded. He had piled up a formidable list of failures, and he had stepped on many toes, from old Stalinists to steel-eaters and other entrenched bureaucrats. He was conducting a rather intensely personal style of diplomacy and just before his downfall was said to be working on a deal with West Germany. He may have been anticipating that need for Western technological aid that his successors came around to five or six years later.

In late 1963 Khrushchev's old sparring partner, American President John F. Kennedy, had been assassinated in the first of many blows the USA was to suffer in this decade. Khrushchev's fall followed very soon after the American decision, taken by Kennedy's successor Lyndon Johnson, to "take all necessary measures" in Vietnam. Khrushchev seems to have wished to disengage his country from Vietnam. His successors reversed this course, pledging support for the North Vietnamese if attacked by the United States.

These may have been coincidences, but it is tempting to believe that had Kennedy and Khrushchev survived, they might have avoided the subsequent frightful war in Indochina. In another coincidence, the Chinese exploded their first H-bomb on the day of Khrushchev's resignation. Mao Tse-tung also gave Ho Chi Minh vigorous support; the Chinese and Russians, however, managed to carry on their feud even while jointly backing Ho's government against the American "imperialists." In a repetition of the French error, the Americans sent more and more troops to Indochina until they were engaged in a major war, yet 1968 was to show they could not win it.

There was a changing of the political guard in Great Britain also in 1964, as the thirteen-year Tory rule ended in an electoral victory for Labour. Harold Macmillan had resigned the premiership in 1963 amid the odors of scandal touching his government. A member of his government had visited a lady of no great virtue, who kissed and told; he denied this, Macmillan believed him, and when the lie was exposed, the prime minister was accused of poor judgment. The outcry over the whole Profumo-Keeler affair marked the beginning of a "satire craze," an appetite among the alienated for discrediting all established authority.

Macmillan's government had run into serious difficulties, including de Gaulle's rejection of the application for Common Market membership. The death of Hugh Gaitskell came in 1963—a terrible year for world figures. The remarkable Pope John XXIII died, and Konrad Adenauer retired. Gaitskell's death gave the brilliant Harold Wilson a chance to head the new Labour government, but Wilson was to suffer severe deflation in the next six years. He ran into a series of economic disasters, fought with his own trade union supporters, devalued the pound, was again rebuffed by de Gaulle, and came under attack first from the hawks for deserting the empire (the 1968 "east of Suez" pullout) and then from the doves for hanging on to nuclear weapons and for publicly giving loyal support to the American ally in Vietnam. On top of this, the Scots demanded independence, and North Ireland blew up. Nothing contributed more to the alienation of radical students than their disenchantment with Wilson, once seen as a Kennedy-like figure of youth and hope, now a fallen idol through no fault of his own.

General de Gaulle still reigned in Paris; when he was not disrupting the Atlantic alliance and snubbing the British, he was quarreling with the EEC. He was losing popularity prior to 1968, as the presidential election of 1965 and the parliamentary elections of 1967 showed. De Gaulle had clearly failed to achieve that national consensus he so desired. His charisma was fading. Great and unsettling changes had come to France, as it rapidly modernized, urbanized, mechanized. There was a remarkable rise in the standard of living during these years all over Europe and not the least in France, which had one of the highest growth rates in Europe. At the same time came social dislocations and consequent discontents; a massive movement from country to city converted France from a land still about one-third rural in 1945 to less than one-seventh agricultural by 1970. Technological modernization changed the character of farming as well as manufacturing. Ways of life altered, not always for the better. No one regretted the passing of traditional France more than the man under whose presidency much of it had occurred.

Education was one area of rapid change. Third Republic France had given everyone a free education up to the age of fourteen; beyond that, only a small minority, determined by competitive examination,

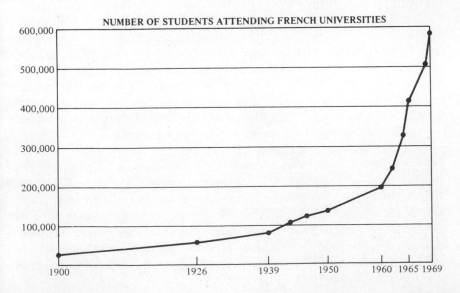

NUMBER OF STUDENTS ATTENDING FRENCH UNIVERSITIES

went on to the luxury of higher education, first in the *lycée* and then in the university. The system was not much different elsewhere in Europe, though France could claim a greater degree of democracy and statism than in England, where far fewer children of working class origin got to the elite public schools and universities. The total pre-World War II French university population was around 60,000; by 1968 the number had increased tenfold. This student explosion occurred all over the Western world.

Charles de Gaulle, writing later about the events of 1968, blamed them on these startling structural changes in French society; France, he said, long content with her ancient ways, had suddenly plunged into the icy waters of modernization, an unavoidable but traumatic experience. "Forced into a mechanized mass existence," living in nondescript houses, herded and regimented, even their leisure now "collective and prescribed," the French people, he thought, took this change less easily than others. (See his *Memoirs of Hope, Renewal and Endeavor*, 1971). Perhaps; but the deep unrest that afflicted young people in the 1960s was a worldwide phenomenon evidently with supranational sources. It spread from California and China to Berlin, Bologna, and London even before lighting on Paris.

The student unrest, the Czechoslovakian 1968 movement (to be described later in this chapter), and the out-of-control war in Vietnam were only some signs of world cataclysm. In 1967 the Middle East erupted in the Six Day War, which reflected an absence of leadership everywhere. The new Soviet leaders, harassed by domestic problems, allowed themselves to be towed in Nasser's wake. They gave rather passive approval to his blockade of the Gulf of Aqaba and encouraged the fanatical Syrian regime. With the United States wholly absorbed in Southeast Asia and the British officially resigning from any world role, the Egyptian leader thought he saw his chance to fulfill his goal of uniting the Arab world to crush Israel and gain revenge for 1948 and 1956. Egypt and Syria were clearly the aggressors in this third round of the Arab-Israeli war, which took place in the first days of June 1967. By their blockade and their demand that United Nations forces be removed, they precipitated the blow that Israel struck.

Losing enormous amounts of war material and the territories of the Sinai, the Golan Heights, and the west bank of the Jordan, the Arab countries (Egypt, Syria, and Jordan) sustained a staggering defeat. The Arabs blamed the Soviet Union for not intervening to save them, but the Russians once again showed restraint when the prospects of an escalation loomed. The Soviet leaders blamed the Arabs for recklessness and incompetence, and in fact had belatedly and ineffectively tried to hold them back. They reequipped the Arab forces but sponsored

Brezhnev and Kosygin, top Soviet leaders, fly to New York, June 16, 1967. The Russians seemed anxious to prevent the Arab-Israeli war from escalating. *United Press International Photo.*

a U.N. ceasefire while Kosygin visited the United States to confer with President Johnson. Since the United States armed Israel to match Soviet weapons in Egypt and Syria, the war did not really end but only diminished for a few years. But the Arabs were disenchanted with their reliance on the Russians, and Nasser, though given a vote of confidence by his people, lived only three years after this defeat.

Two years earlier, the danger of trying to use non-European states as pawns in the power struggle must have forcibly struck the Russians in Indonesia, where they had backed the corrupt dictator Sukarno with massive amounts of aid. A revolution against Sukarno also discharged its strength against the Indonesian Communists, as many as 100,000 of whom were slaughtered in one of the biggest bloodbaths of the decade. Huge debts to the USSR were repudiated, as both Russian and Chinese Communist influence in this populous land came to an abrupt end. It was a defeat almost comparable to that which the Americans were about to suffer in Indochina. Both drove home the lesson that Asia would not be the vassal or the protegé of any Western power.

Less than two years after the immense Kennedy funeral in Washington in November 1963, the world paused in 1965 to mourn the passing of Winston Churchill. Adenauer, having retired in 1963, died in 1967. De Gaulle by then had only a few years left, expiring in the same year as Nasser and a year before Khrushchev. The old figures were passing. A sense of insecurity, of lack of confidence in government, went along with the pronounced generation revolt that burst forth in these years. The year 1968 coincided with the arrival of a generation born after the great war, knowing none of its experiences and sharing few of its values. As Swinburne said, "The old faiths loosen and fall, the new years ruin and rend."

Student Discontent
and the Paris Spring

The rebellion of the French students cannot be placed in isolation, for it was part of an international youth revolt that left few parts of the world untouched in the late sixties and early seventies. The revolt began in Berlin and in Berkeley, California, and spread to London, Paris, Japan, Latin America, even Yugoslavia and behind the iron curtain. Italian and Dutch universities also exploded in revolt. So far as concerns Paris, the most identifiable leader of the uprising was Daniel Cohn-Bendit, a German born in France of parents who had fled from Hitler and then returned to Germany after the war. Another of its heroes was the main personality in an earlier Berlin student riot, Rudi Dutschke.

The uniqueness of the Paris events lay in their magnitude and extent; nowhere else did the "student stirs," as an Oxford professor called them, achieve much more than nuisance value. The French ones spread to the workers and threatened general revolution, and in the long run they caused the fall of de Gaulle's government. Occupation of university buildings, followed perhaps by a pitched battle with police or military, became an all too familiar sequence of events in the universities of the world. But they were nothing like the full-scale war night after night, which left portions of Paris looking as it had in World War II. The French seemed to have decided to continue their long revolutionary tradition by having one more immense émeute.

To some extent the causes of the Paris spring uprising of 1968 were the same as those of the student movement everywhere: boredom with too much pallid conformity, dislike of the technological society, a generation effect among those born after World War II whose world was a wholly different one from their parents'. The drift away from orthodox communism opened the way for a New Left, which celebrated its independence of Marxist orthodoxies by discovering more exciting revolutionary heroes than the old men in the Kremlin: Cuba's Castro and Guevara, China's Mao Tse-tung, Algerian, African, and Vietnamese guerrilla fighters against imperialism. The mixture was complex, but at bottom one found a generation of young people eager for excitement and even violence after a quarter-century of preoccupation with economic growth. They were also bewildered by a society too large to comprehend and usually disgusted with an education that seemed untuned to their needs.

The universities had swollen to enormous size. There were no fewer than 160,000 students in and around Paris. Some thought them spoiled or immature: they had grown up in the new affluence of the consumer society and were, in fact, profiting from its prosperity. In any previous generation most of them would not have been at the university but at work in fields or factories. Typically the leaders of the revolt were moderately well-off children of professional people. There was at times a levity about the revolt, which disgusted real revolutionaries (including the Communists, who were notably cool to it) and justified the joke about Marxism *a la* Harpo, not Karl; it seemed to be a gigantic schoolyard prank. Among the chief complaints at Nanterre, a Paris suburb where it all started, was that there were not enough telephones and TVs. Yet the huge new education mills of which the Fifth Republic was so proud were bleak, isolated, and overcrowded. Students felt processed, computerized, treated as consumers of data that were produced by others in the "knowledge factory." Not for nothing were they reading the young Marx on "alienation," that is, the conversion of human needs into marketable commodities.

Many ideological currents worked to excite the students. A Soviet article in 1973 named all the following as false prophets and "revisionists"; Scheler, Husserl, Unamuno, Heidegger, Jaspers, Camus (all existentialists), Garaudy, Adorno, Horkheimer, Marcuse (Frankfurt School men), and Fromm. In China, the Cultural Revolution, begun in 1965, set an example for an educational takeover by students. The purpose of that tumultuous process, encouraged by Chairman Mao, was to raise the cultural consciousness of the masses so that they need not be guided by any elite but could think for themselves. Beginning with popular discussions of the Chinese-Russian quarrel, the movement soon spread to the universities, where grave professors were dispensing learning, most of it still not extracted from the *Thoughts of Chairman Mao*, to docile pupils much as they had always done in the Celestial Empire. Students demanding an end to this system caused so much turmoil that the universities closed for more than a year.

Mao's Cultural Revolution was probably the main model for student protest in Europe, though students at the University of California might claim priority in educational disruption. The student movement in fact sprang up all over the world at about the same time, the best assumption being that it arose from similar circumstances rather than primarily by diffusion from one central source.

The Vietnam War provided a focus for all the various discontents the young felt, even though no European countries were directly involved in it. De Gaulle did not even verbally support the Americans, though Harold Wilson in Britain and leaders in West Germany did. Even in the United States, student disturbances at Berkeley and elsewhere preceded the time of major American fighting in Vietnam. One might argue that the youthful reaction against this war resulted from a proneness to rebel that was already present. After all, the Korean War of 1950–1953, which was about as bad as Vietnam in terms of damage and casualties, had aroused no such outcry and was generally supported by liberal elements in the United States as containment of Communist aggression. So indeed was Vietnam, at first. Needing some great and manifest evil on which to focus their discontent, university youth found it in the ugly kind of war that steadily expanded in the hills and jungles of Indochina.

A special brutality in police handling of student unrest usually contributed to the spread of the riots in Europe and the United States. Perhaps this reflected a resentment among the uniformed keepers of "law and order" against these spoiled neurotics who broke windows and disrupted classes and meetings for no evident reason. A blue-collar reaction against the students surfaced in some measure almost everywhere. Police brutality gained the students some public sympathy.

In Berlin incidents were common in the universities from 1965 on. A student was shot to death in June 1967, during a demonstration against the Shah of Iran. It was at this time that "Red Rudi" Dutschke emerged as a student leader; in April 1968, the young sociologist was seriously wounded by a right-wing student. But the wide-spread fighting that then broke out in a number of German university cities, including Munich, Hamburg, and Frankfurt as well as Berlin, turned the public against the enraged students. Maddened by the generally liberal *and* conservative viewpoint in Germany—anticommunist, law-and-order, rejecting fanaticism, respecting due processes of law—radical students increasingly turned to violence but found themselves isolated from the main body of German opinion, including the trade unionists.

Radical students at the London School of Economics "sat in" in March 1967, in an atmosphere of general disillusionment with the Labour government that had been elected in 1964 and 1966. "Politics outside the system" in Britain reached back to the massive if relatively sober protest launched in 1959–1961 by the Committee for Nuclear Disarmament, with the objective of getting Britain to withdraw from the arms race and perhaps neutralize herself in the Cold War. The CND mounted huge marches and rallies that were nonviolent and generally orderly. Nowhere was the youth mood of bitter hostility to the "establishment" stronger than in England. It was encouraged by the nonagenarian philosopher Bertrand Russell, celebrated in the songs of such "rock" musicians as the Beatles and the Rolling Stones, and approved by a radical wing of the Labour party who spoke of the "new politics" as one of "direct action" and "confrontation."

Radicalized students added these words to their vocabulary, along with some emanating from Maoism, Castroism, and such New Left theorists as Herbert Marcuse, a German neo-Marxist translated to the heady climate of Southern California, or the embattled Jean-Paul Sartre. The New Left did not lack for ideas and enthusiasm; its prophets were legion and sometimes contradictory. Nevertheless in England as in Germany, student unrest did not seriously threaten to overthrow the existing society. The London *Times* in late summer 1968 wrote editorially of "a collapse of order in English universities." A mob of Cambridge students disrupted a minister's speech. But as in Germany, the English students at this time could not overcome the barrier between themselves and the trade-unionist workers.

Violence broke out in late 1967, also, among Italian university students when about 1,500 students held the Turin university's administration building for a month. Florence, Pisa, Bologna, and Rome all followed suit, featuring battles between police and students, and many other Italian schools experienced similar difficulties in 1968. As elsewhere, there was a pressing need for educational reform, given bad overcrowding and an obsolete university structure, but the students seemed less interested in such reforms than in "overthrowing society." The university revolution was supposed to set off further ones throughout the whole "system." The uprising on the campus would be the detonator of explosions throughout the society. Even the "embourgeoisfied" working class, drugged by material plenty, would perhaps awaken to realize its true oppression when prodded by the students. The universities were only the weakest link in a chain binding the whole people in exploitation; nor could they be reformed without reforming the entire society.

Thus thought the student militants, who, typically hostile to any structure of authority, wanted not to substitute one system for another but to tear down all systems. If they often quoted Marx, Lenin, and Mao, their real interest was much less in overcoming material poverty than in removing alleged shackles of the mind and spirit. Philosophies of "liberation" flourished. The emphasis on action for action's sake, without thought, led some of their friends as well as their enemies to identify the young militants with "left-wing fascism" or simply with childish willfulness. Some of the intellectual leaders who inspired the student revolutionaries recoiled from their violence and occasional mindlessness; at various times Herbert Marcuse, Theodor Adorno, Jürgen Habermas, and other intellectual neo-Marxists expressed their disapproval of what was being done in their names.[1] But to the blue-collar workers, to whom they wished to appeal, the students appeared as bizarre ideologists, speaking all kinds of incomprehensible words: their desire to "demystify bourgeois ideology" was itself a mystification.

In Paris, things almost went otherwise. After a series of incidents beginning in March, Nanterre was ordered closed in early May 1968. Students at the Sorbonne, the main Paris university, rallied in support of their fellow students at a great meeting in the ancient courtyard of this famous university, which is situated in Paris's left-bank Latin Quarter. Police seeking to expel them began clashes between students and *gendarmerie* that were to become a way of life for the next few weeks. Within a few days the battle escalated to a point where it filled much of the university area of the city with overturned and burning automobiles, damaged buildings, and broken or shuttered shop windows. This climaxed on the night of May 10–11, "the night of the barricades," when as many as 25,000 students battled the "flics" all night. Only a few were killed, but many hundreds suffered wounds.

Meanwhile great crowds of students assembled eagerly for speeches and demonstrations in a consciousness-raising imitation of the Chinese. While orthodox communism repudiated the uprising as "left-wing infantilism," which "objectively" played into the hands of the Right, and the students booed Communist spokesmen, the images of Mao, of Cuban guerilla hero Che Guevara, and of Ho Chi Minh were everywhere. Much in evidence, too, were slogans painted on the walls, which became part of the legend of the Paris spring: "Let us be realistic and demand the impossible." Posted over the Odeon theater, which was "liberated" by the students, were the words, "When the National Assembly is a bourgeois theater, bourgeois theaters must become national assemblies." (Or, in halls where students slept, "We fear nothing, we have the Pill.")

On May 13, a one-day general strike signalled the spread of the troubles to the industrial workers. Their motives were not the same as the students' but they joined in, partly out of sympathy with the

---

[1] It is nevertheless true that New Left ideologists had encouraged violence, which is a constant theme in their writings. See, for example, Herbert Marcuse, in *A Critique of Pure Tolerance* (1966); Frantz Fanon in his widely read *Wretched of the Earth* (first English edition, 1964). Jean-Paul Sartre, who deeply influenced Fanon, consistently invoked the need for a violent, purifying, total revolution to destroy bourgeois society.

students and partly because of their own grievances. The revolution spread while the government stood helpless. Baffled by the sudden outbreak of violence in an unexpected place, the government first did nothing and then tried repression, turning to reform only belatedly. By that time the situation was out of hand. Half of France was on strike, and the students basked in their newly discovered power to change the world. "Happenings" proliferated. Jean-Paul Sartre addressed 10,000 students. But the student objectives were vague; they wanted to change society, they wanted to help teach courses, they wanted to make some kind of a revolution; but they were themselves deeply if rather happily divided into anarchists, Maoists, Trotskyites, situationists, and other "groupuscules."

Violence continued into the last week of May. President de Gaulle made a trip to Baden-Baden, Germany, to seek assurance from the French armed forces in Germany. Returning, he showed a determination to restore order. On May 30 he announced that he would hold elections, and reform the universities, but he would tolerate no more violence. That evening an awesome turnout of perhaps 750,000 older people staged a monstrous parade through the streets of Paris (on the right bank), rallying to the government's support. The backlash against student disruptions carried over into the ensuing elections, which were held on June 23. The Left dropped sharply, while the Gaullist UDR gained ninety-four seats. Meanwhile the striking workers received handsome pay raises (13–15 percent) and returned to work. The next months saw work on educational reforms, which included student participation in university governance.

The referendum of April 1969 showed that a majority of the French people thought that de Gaulle had outstayed his time. His longtime prime minister, Georges Pompidou, won a convincing victory in the June presidential election, so that although de Gaulle himself bowed out, Gaullism paradoxically emerged even stronger than it was during his term of office. The great man's death the following year brought tributes to him from all over the world. The last of the European giants of the World War II era, with the single exception of Yugoslavia's Marshall Tito, had passed. Few of the students who helped overthrow him had been alive in 1940 or even in 1945.

Khrushchev's Successors in the Soviet Union

A similar generation effect could be discerned in the USSR. Khrushchev's successors were inclined to be cautious, careful, and prudent. They had overthrown Khrushchev because he was "hare-brained," hasty, and loudmouthed. They would be circumspect, responsible, and discreet. No more swashbuckling diplomatic shootouts, no more games of Russian roulette with thermonuclear weapons. Nor would there be any more drastic changes of the economic and political system at home. The inclination to trust only old Bolsheviks and keep out unsteadier younger sorts, who might perhaps respond to the siren songs of the dissident poets, led the Soviet ruling elite to become a virtual gerontocracy, the oldest governing body in Europe. The average age of the Politburo, as the committee of committees was now again called, soon became well over sixty. Small wonder the Communist party lost touch with European youth, who turned to a New Left in this decade.

The economic reforms initiated by Khrushchev were allowed to go through in 1965, but the experiment was implemented gradually and timidly and in the end amounted to little. The old system was too deeply entrenched. The regime also showed its conservatism by increasing military spending. The effort to close the gap between Soviet and American nuclear missiles was a goal they eventually reached. There was also major stress on building a powerful Soviet navy able to cruise the waters of the world; also a modern fishing fleet. The Soviet air force was enlarged and modernized. This heavy investment in military hardware, which continued to interfere with adequate consumer goods production, indicates the strong role of the military bureaucracy in the post-Khrushchevian balance of power; it also reflects the desire to gain freedom from fear of American military superiority, such as had forced the 1962 humiliation.

This continuation of the relative neglect of consumer goods manufacturing and agriculture, forced to take a back seat to the military and heavy industry (the "steel eaters"), naturally caused continuing economic problems. Amounting to as much as 15 percent of the national product, the resources committed to the defense sector in the second half of the 1960s were a major cause of Soviet economic troubles, Western experts thought.

The Soviet leadership may have held it against Khrushchev that he allowed the quarrel with China to escalate, but if so they did not succeed in reversing his policies. After celebrating Khrushchev's departure in 1964 by exploding a nuclear bomb, the Chinese were soon bickering with his successors. Though the Vietnam War brought them together in common support of the North Vietnamese Communist state against the Americans, it also was a bone of contention between China and the USSR. There were rivalries and differences of opinion about the war. The Soviet Union charged that the Chinese delayed deliveries of Russian supplies to North Vietnam.

China went through the turmoil of the Cultural Revolution between 1965 and 1969. During this time Red Guards blockaded the Soviet embassy in Peking, causing the withdrawal of Russians from China and counterriots against Chinese students in Moscow. The Cultural Revolution had indeed begun with a campaign to debate the Russian-Chinese quarrel as a means of "raising the cultural consciousness of the masses" by showing how backward the Marxism of Moscow was. In return Soviet Russia ridiculed the "infantile" disorders of Mao's attempt at a drastic shake-up of his party and country. Mao hurled insults at the "renegades and scabs" in Moscow. The Chinese called the 1965 Soviet economic reforms "the restoration of capitalism." Rivalry accelerated between the two Communist giants within the other Communist parties of the world and in the Third World as the Chinese entered the field of development diplomacy. (They built a railroad in Tanzania and Zambia.)

The climax to a decade of hostility came with a major battle fought on the Ussuri River in 1969, not the only example of armed border clashes on the Sino-Russian frontier. As massive Soviet troop movements to the east were observed, there was talk of war. It would be tempting, commentaries noted, for the USSR to strike at China before the latter's nuclear delivery system was fully enough developed to ensure effective retaliation. The Chinese dug bomb shelters in their cities. All this fortunately proved mere speculation, but fear of war did widely exist.

Fortunately for the Soviets, the West was in no position to take advantage of any of these troubles. The most serious crisis that faced Russian leaders, and one that they conceivably handled the worst, occurred in 1968 in Czechoslovakia. Postponing for a moment consideration of that significant event, let us take up the story of dissent in the USSR, which continued to be a bothersome problem for the leadership and became a major world news story.

The fall of Khrushchev was the signal for a certain reversal of the uncertain thaw. The conservative oldsters who succeeded Khrushchev were little inclined to continue his experiments in thawing. They did not question the need for party control over intellectual life, though they had no wish to be brutal about it. Their policy might be described as the permanent semifreeze; they engaged in what has been called "hesitant repression." A bureaucracy of 70,000 was keen to uphold the censorship, which is codified in article 70 of the criminal code. It bars "agitation or propaganda carried on for the purpose of subverting or weakening the Soviet regime."

It is an embarrassment to the Russians that such vigilance against anti-Soviet expression continues to be necessary; it ought not to be

Students riot in Paris, May, 1968. *Wide World Photos.*

if the Communist society is as superior as official ideology declares it to be. How could any sane person prefer capitalism to communism? Earlier one could claim that an interim dictatorship had to preside over the period of transition; but after a half-century, the claim's plausibility begins to erode. If leading members of the Soviet society continue to criticize, it must be that they are either crazy, corrupted by foreign capitalist gold, or somehow un-Russian, perhaps Jews owing allegiance to another cause. The only other alternative is that they might be right, a thought scarcely acceptable to those who firmly believe that the custodians of the party (themselves) are in the very nature of things infallible. Of course, "constructive self-criticism" has to be distinguished somehow from "slanders against the Soviet system."

The embarrassment caused by continuing dissidence leads Soviet leaders to belittle it or overlook it. There can be no question of going back to Stalinist terror and illegality. In the Marxist ideology of the Soviet Union, nothing is ever allowed to go back, since history is supposed to have a continuing forward movement. On the other hand, the hesitant repressors were faced with an increasingly bold and determined band of dissenters. Certainly the dissidents have never been more than a very small percentage of the total Soviet population or even of the intellectual community, which is kept reasonably happy by favors and is likely to opt for working within the system. But the later 1960s was a time when some people everywhere got tired of working within the system, and the USSR was no exception. There had been a taste of freedom under Khrushchev, enough to whet an appetite for more and make the retreat from freedom unacceptable. And the very hesitancy or moderation of the new leadership tended to encourage dissent, which was no longer nearly so dangerous as it was in Stalin's time. One now had a trial, with opportunities for some publicity. Punishment was likely to be relatively mild, perhaps a year or two in jail; before, one would have been shot or condemned to a labor camp. Under such circumstances, of course, the leadership might be tempted to return to just a touch of terror. The sometimes sinister device of commitment to mental institutions was tried out.

In late 1965 Andrei Sinyavsky and Yuli Daniel were arrested. Though foreign journalists were excluded from their trial in February 1966, a report got out; they were sentenced to seven and five years respectively of "strict regime corrective labor" for "anti-Soviet agitation and propoganda." Daniel and Sinyavsky, Sinyavsky a well-known Soviet literary critic and his friend Daniel a translator, had published stories in the West under other names. These contained material critical of conditions in Russia, even if in fictional form. The Sinyavsky-Daniel case was clearly intended as a warning to Soviet critics, and it was accompanied by the punishment of a number of other overly bold intellectuals. But it aroused a storm of criticism, as the trial transcript, revealing bullying judges as well as prosecutors, circulated in the West. Among those who denounced it as an outrage was veteran French Communist writer Louis Aragon.

The problem of publication abroad by Soviet authors of works banned in the Soviet Union, which had been initiated with Pasternak's *Dr. Zhivago*, grew to monumental proportions as Moscow became a more cosmopolitan city with many more foreign visitors. The world learned of such bold Soviet dissidents as Vladimir Bukovsky, who at his 1967 trial asked to know why, since we demand the release of Greek political prisoners, can't we ask for the release of our own! And he outraged the judge by calmly comparing Moscow's attitude towards demonstrations with Madrid's (then under the "fascist" Franco.)

Despite his long career as gadfly, during which he was sentenced many times to jail terms, Bukovsky escaped long-term incarceration and bobbed up repeatedly between 1961 and 1974, before finally being deported. (He was exchanged for a Chilean political prisoner.) This seems a sign of the relative moderation of the much-criticized Soviet regime; under Stalin, Bukovsky would not have lasted a week.

At the time of the Soviet invasion of Czechoslovakia, a handful of intellectuals attempted to demonstrate in Moscow and were roughed up by police and antisemitic crowds. They made a literary coup out of the episode. Natalya Gorbanevskaya's *Red Square at Noon* and Pavel Litvinov's *The Demonstration in Pushkin Square* were soon selling at Western bookstores. Litvinov was the son of Stalin's one-time foreign minister. Another dissident, Peter Yakir, was the son of a celebrated hero of the Revolution, later a Stalin victim who was ostentatiously rehabilitated during the first thaw. Such scions of high Soviet gentry presented special difficulties to the harrassed rulers, as did courageous women like Gorbanevskaya and Lydia Chukovskaya.

The midsixties saw the beginning of the *samizdat* ("self-published") privately printed magazines, songs, and books that circulated underground. Typewritten, sometimes photographically copied, such material passed from hand to hand, and some of it found its way out of the country. Purely literary works were supplemented by political reportage, the most famous of *samizdat* publications being the *Chronicle of Current Events*, which appeared bimonthly from 1968 until 1972 when the KGB managed to break it up and arrest a considerable number of people involved in it, Yakir among them. But within eighteen months the *Chronicle* had revived and has since survived numerous arrests of its editors to continue in publication.

The works of the most famous of the dissidents appeared in *samizdat* editions. Unquestionably the two leading figures, presenting the most serious challenge to Soviet orthodoxy, were the brilliant physicist Andrei Sakharov, and the great novelist Alexander Solzhenitsyn. Joining these two giants were others of only slightly less distinction; Roy and Zhores Medvedev, one a historian and the other a biologist, cannot be left off even a short list, nor can the crusading jurist, V. L. Chalidze, a leader of the "democratic movement" that wished to bring legal safeguards of free speech to the USSR. A distinguished biochemist, Zhores Medvedev published an account of the Lysenko affair, along with many essays on the need for freedom and reform in Soviet intellectual life. His twin brother Roy's massively documented history of Stalinism, entitled *Let History Judge*, was published in English in 1971. Together the brothers also wrote a book about Khrushchev, as well as an extraordinary account (*A Question of Madness*) of Zhores' commitment to a mental institution, from which he was finally released in 1970 after an international campaign of protest.

The Medvedevs had long been dedicated Communists and were protected by their scientific prestige. So to an even greater degree was Andrei Sakharov, one of the world's oustanding theoretical physicists and one of the fathers of the Russian nuclear bomb. Lenin and Stalin prize winner, never (like Solzhenitsyn) in a prison camp, he was a privileged member of the Soviet elite and the youngest man ever to become a full member of the USSR Academy of Sciences. In 1958 and 1961 he protested against the scientifically unnecessary nuclear explosions that were set off for political purposes. He fought Lysenkoism, and in 1968 his *Progress, Co-existence and Intellectual Freedom* followed up his support of the dissidents with a ringing statement to the effect that without progress toward full de-Stalinization, freedom of thought, and democracy the USSR was doomed to failure; these things were not simply desirable in themselves but essential to a modernized society. "The division of mankind threatens it with destruction" and "intellectual freedom is essential to human society," he said. Socialism, moreover, will lose to capitalism unless it practices intellectual freedom.

Committed to "the defense of human rights" as the highest social goal and to a "convergence" theory that Soviet and Western societies would come together at some intermediate point, the Soviet scientist clearly was far out of line with official party orthodoxy. He was asking about the same question that got the young historian Amalrik an involuntary journey to Siberia: could the USSR last at all without liberalization? For good measure, Sakharov joined in protests against alleged discrimination against the non-Russian peoples of the USSR and against refusal to allow Jewish emigration. "Freedom to leave . . . is a necessary condition for the spiritual freedom of all." In 1972 he told an American interviewer that he would no longer call himself a Marxist-Leninist, but a liberal. And he spoke out to warn the West that it should not pursue détente with the Soviet Union unless the latter democratized. In brief, his great scientific prestige allowed Sakharov to get by with criticisms it is hard to imagine the authorities tolerating in anyone else. He did not escape the attentions of the KGB or severe attacks in the Soviet press, but he was unintimidated. During the Arab-Israeli war of 1973 he again criticized his country's position, and in 1974 he protested the arrest of Solzhenitsyn.

Solzhenitsyn had served seven years in a concentration camp for no other crime than having been captured by the Germans in World War II. He was released after Stalin's death. In 1962 his remarkable *One Day in the Life of Ivan Denisovich*, about prison camp life, received high praise in the USSR because Khrushchev blessed it, but this was the last time he had any luck publishing in Russia. His most brilliant novel, perhaps, is *The Cancer Ward*; its message, that there is a spiritual cancer at work in the Soviet Union corroding people's souls, was not one likely to appeal to the heads of Soviet society. Another novel, *The First Circle*, displays Solzhenitsyn as the conscious heir of Tolstoy, the chronicler as well as moral critic of an entire society. In it he focuses on a scientific institution that invents devices for helping the KGB trap innocent people—clearly "rabid slander of our social system," the official verdict was.

No Soviet writer had ever been so bold. Solzhenitsyn wrote with the fury of a man possessed by a compulsion to tell the whole ghastly truth and by a fearlessness that sprang from his having been through it all himself. If Sakharov carried conviction because he was so obviously from the highest Soviet intellectual elite, Solzhenitsyn did so because he came out of the concentration camps. All his "novels," down to the *Gulag Archipelago*, which earned him deportation in 1974, are accounts of real people and events. They came from the cancer ward, the first circle of hell, the underground realities of Stalinist life. What made them unacceptable to the guardians of Communist virtue was not so much that they dealt with the Stalinist era, though to do so in any detail was now thought to be in very bad taste; his works radiated a belief that the same poison still works, that Stalinism has not been purged from the system, that the same corruption, materialism, and ideological pettifoggery still exist in the minds of the bureaucrats who run things.

Discouraged by the absence of any popular movement in the USSR, which they attributed to the elimination of dissenting populations by two generations of terror, the dissidents were inclined to look for help abroad. They hoped their appeal to world opinion would have an effect on the Soviet leadership. Undeniably, at times this leadership has been sensitive to foreign criticism, particularly within the Communist party itself. In this respect, however, the worst wounds did not come from the books of Solzhenitsyn and Sakharov. They were self-inflicted, by the military intervention in Czechoslovakia in the summer of 1968.

The Prague Spring and Its Aftermath

The Czechs are not by nature a volatile or a violent people. Their hero is the Good Soldier Schweik, who outwitted the Austrians by cleverness and not by confrontation. (He pretended to be stupid and fouled up every task.) In 1948 Masaryk killed himself, and Benes died of a broken heart; neither thought of leading resistance to Communist rule. As we noted earlier, much good will toward Russia historically existed among both the Czechs and the Slovaks, and the Communist party had a by no means negligible following. By 1968, at one time or another every other satellite in eastern Europe had had a rebellion. The Yugoslavs had defied Stalin himself in 1948 and got away with their independence; Poland, in 1956, and again in 1970, forced the retirement of unpopular leaders and at least some changes. Hungary's wild uprising in 1956 was savagely crushed, but in the ensuing years, unwilling to risk another such encounter, the Russians allowed the Hungarians to get away in practice with more liberties than any other East European satellite. Albania and Rumania used the Chinese issue to express disagreement with Moscow, while retaining completely Communist systems. Bulgaria has been the least restive of the satellites, but even here there were occasional signs of ferment.

Forced collectivization of agriculture and nationalization of private businesses followed the 1948 coup in Czechoslovakia, with the party firmly in control. Beria's man Slansky endured the last of the grand Stalinist purge trials in 1952; Gottwald, who took over as the top leader then, soon died in Moscow after attending Stalin's funeral. The next strong man was Antonin Novotny, a colorless but efficient "little Stalin" who did not de-Stalinize at all until 1961, at which time the Stalin and Gottwald monuments were torn down. All this suggests a substantial degree of submissiveness in the land of Jan Hus, which can partly be explained by the bitter hatred of Germany implanted during World War II, the knowledge of having been betrayed by the West at Munich, and the feeling of having to lean on the Soviet Union for want of alternative. But economic progress was slow, and public opinion polls showed strong anticommunism. Western influences could not easily be kept out of this country, which has borders with Austria and West Germany. Something called the "big beat," an import from Western popular music, became a symbol of anti-Soviet attitudes.

With economic growth continuing to decline, the Czech economist Ota Sik brought forward a Liberman-like plan for market socialism. Tried cautiously in 1965, it did not work because it was not fully applied. Changing just half the economy, Sik noted, was like changing the side of the street on which cars may drive for just half the cars. His was one of the boldest voices calling for economic reforms. The Czechs, a deeply cultured people, also responded to the rising demand for a more humane, democratic, and open type of communism. Some of them knew that Yugoslavia had a decentralized economy and workers' management, that Poland had avoided collectivizing agriculture, that Hungary's economy was flourishing under an experiment in Libermanism.

The Imre Nagy of the Czech 1968 was named Alexander Dubcek. He was a Slovak who had replaced Novotny when the increasingly irritable dictator insulted the Slovaks (whom many Czechs regarded as their cultural inferiors) after a visit to their national museum. This was early in 1968. Dubcek's credentials looked impeccable to Moscow; he had been a faithful *apparatchik* for many years, never disobeying orders or questioning a policy. He had welcomed the coup of 1948, helped with collectivization and nationalization, and accepted the 1950–1954 witch hunts without a murmur. He had spent three years at Moscow attending the Higher Party school (1955–1958). While he was there, the Khrushchev speech threw the school into confusion, and the invasion of Hungary upset him. But in general Dubcek looked like a party hack if ever there was one. His transformation into the democratic hero of the 1968 freedom movement was one of history's major surprises.

The explanation seems to lie in a certain simplicity of mind and character that made this genuine proletarian really believe in communism's promises to lead to a free society. "It is not possible for a small minority to introduce and maintain socialism," Dubcek had come to believe. Under his guidance, or perhaps because he simply followed the public lead, rampant democracy broke out in Czechoslovakia, as it had in Hungary twelve years before. Press censorship was ended, and the newspapers celebrated their independence by indulging in all kinds of criticism, even of the USSR. This and support of the Sik economic reforms were the chief Czech sins. There was no violence, as there had been in the Hungarian revolution. It seemed possible that opposition parties might be permitted. The reforms were all quite legally handled and supported by the vast majority of public opinion. They aimed at curing the economic blight by making party officials responsible to the public—"democratic socialism." The Prague paper *Red Truth* declared that the party should not rule in the name of the workers but must be held accountable to them. It had fallen under the influence of a new breed of "humanist" Marxists.

The wrath of the Kremlin soon turned in Prague's direction. The Russians had had a bad year in 1967. They were coping with Sakharovs and Solzhenitsyns at home, and moreover they could be quite sure that the Americans, hopelessly mired in Vietnam, would not challenge them in eastern Europe. After the Czechs refused to obey a summons to come to Moscow and were unimpressed by the visits of other Communist luminaries including Walter Ulbricht, Brezhnev himself descended on Prague in July, bringing with him almost the entire Presidium. The Czechs were subjected to a tonguelashing, but they stood fast. Dubcek proved a wily and patient negotiator, not losing his temper under abuse and threats and promising to bring the situation under control if given time. He once confided that his tactic was to smile and agree with Brezhnev and then do nothing—a true Good Soldier Schweik. But the Russians' patience neared exhaustion. Dubcek was becoming all too popular in Czechoslovakia. "Socialism with a human face" threatened to spread.

Dubcek's critics allege that he was unrealistic in doing nothing to dampen the euphoria of the Czech and Slovak people but not preparing them for resistance either. On the night of August 20 he was arrested and dragged off to Russia or Poland, along with several of his colleagues. The next day a massive invasion of Czechoslovakia by some 200,000 troops from Russia, Poland, Bulgaria, East Germany, and Hungary began. Dubcek agreed to renounce his ideals and submit. There was no fighting; resistance would have been futile. Dubcek was reinstalled and remained in office for six months, presiding over a return to censorship, purging Dr. Sik, and telling his people, to their dismay, that progress was possible only by bending to the Russian will. He accepted the presence of Soviet troops on Czechoslovak soil.

It was a costly victory for the Soviet Union, for the world Communist movement was completely sundered; the split that began with the Yugoslavian revolt and continued with the Sino-Soviet rift was completed in 1968. It could not be argued that the Czechs had threatened Soviet security, as was the case in Hungary; their only crime was wanting democratic socialism. The Soviet Union stood exposed as a tyrant and a totalitarian state fifteen years after Stalin's death. It was an event that would have shocked the world more had others not been engaged in their own special crimes and insanities: the Americans in Vietnam, the students in Paris and London and Berlin protesting against their own governments and societies. They had as little time to worry about the Czechs as had been the case thirty years before. But for the Communists of western Europe, including Italians, French, and Spanish, it was the watershed; they would never again trust the Brezhnev leadership or accept Russian domination of the communist movement. The affair also brought to a halt a trend toward improvement in Soviet-Yugoslav relations. The Chinese (who claimed that the Americans and Russians were working together against Czechoslovakia) noted with alarm the Russian attack on another communist state.

Manifestations of anti-Soviet sentiment continued in Czechoslovakia for some time. In January 1969, a young man immolated himself; his funeral was attended by 800,000 people, but no violent incidents occurred. On March 28, the Czechs beat the Russians in a hockey game, an event said to have been viewed with delight by six million Czechs on television; crowds then smashed some windows in Russian offices. Dubcek thereupon resigned, and full censorship was imposed. Gustav Husak, replacing Dubcek as first secretary, said the "cheap gestures and slogans about democracy, freedom and humanism and the so-called will of the people" were only "naivete and political romanticism." On the anniversary of August 21, huge crowds fought with police in Prague's Wenceslas Square. Dubcek was dismissed from the

Czech Presidium on September 26. At least, as Husak said, he was not dragged off to be shot; after a short term as ambassador in Turkey he returned to live in the Slovak village where he was born. Party purges and an extreme Stalinist tone in the press marked an abrupt end to socialism with a human face.

Could Dubcek have done better for his people in the Prague spring if he had had more political talent? There have been many verdicts. One thing often noted is that he never tried to mobilize international support. Even had appeal to the West been futile and counterproductive, Rumania, Yugoslavia, and the Western Communist parties, all of whom were furious at this heavy-handed Soviet interference, might have exerted pressure on Moscow. Eighteen Western Communist parties did protest, as did Tito and Rumania's Ceausescu, but Dubcek made no effort to capitalize on this support. He had little guile. But this was exactly the source of his appeal to the Czech and Slovak people—he was a simple, sincere man, asking nothing but freedom and human decency, which he thought socialism and communism ought to bring.

It is interesting to compare this "revolt" with Hungary's in 1956; there were differences as well as similarities. One other similarity may

The Russians invade Czechoslovakia: Prague, August, 1968. *Wide World Photos.*

be noted: in each case the West and world opinion in general was distracted by other crises occurring simultaneously. The role that Suez had played in 1956 was somewhat like that which fell to Vietnam and to the explosion of student and "New Left" demonstrations in Berlin, London, and especially Paris in 1968. The Paris spring and its sequel overlapped the Prague spring. It is true that the radical students were no friends of Soviet communism, and they did not like the August intervention. But their interests were in the main directed elsewhere.[2] Influenced by the Chinese example more than anything in Europe, they had their own revolution to make. Their massive demonstrations and battles with the police reflected their own struggle with what they imagined to be a repressive authority at home; they wished the Czechs well but had little energy to spare on their behalf. By August 21, the main thrust of the French student movement was over, leaving a feeling of exhaustion and disappointment. In any case, Dubcek made no explicit appeal to the West for help, as Nagy had done in 1956. The United States, of course, was mesmerized by Vietnam and in the throes of a presidential election to boot.

The Russian leaders attempted to justify the controversial armed intervention in Czechoslovakia by what became known as the "Brezhnev Doctrine," published on September 28, 1968. Admitting that it was "impossible to ignore the allegations being heard in some places that the actions of the five socialist countries contradict the Marxist-Leninist principle of sovereignty and the right of nations to self-determination," the Soviet secretary-general argued that no Communist party can rightly deviate from basic Marxist-Leninist principles and that, if it does, in the broader interests of socialism as a whole the other socialist states have a right to intervene. "The weakening of any link in the world socialist system has a direct effect on all the socialist countries." In brief, once declared a socialist state, a country has no right to change its mind and will be forcibly prevented from doing so. That they were forcibly compelled to submit to Communist rule in the first place was not, of course, mentioned. In the rigid mental categories of Soviet Communist thought, to change from socialism is not conceivable; this would mean reverting to capitalism. That it might mean going forward to "democratic socialism" or "humane socialism" as opposed to the arbitrary rule of an elite was not considered.

The dilemma exposed by this awkward apology for an act of aggression seems to be as follows: if a Communist country attempts

---

[2] The position of the French Communist party, hostile to both Moscow communism and the New Left, is interesting. Waldeck Rochet, head of the PCF, declared that "hare-brained left-wing youths" were "objectively" collaborators with *both* Gaullism and Stalinism.

to escape from dictatorship by permitting intellectual freedom, accountability of officials, and democratic election of party leaders, it ipso facto reverts to capitalism and bourgeois democracy, ceasing to be a socialist state. If it does not, it must continue to endure no freedom, censorship, repression, and the stultifying rule of an irresponsible bureaucracy. The only escape is hypocrisy, upholding, as in Hungary, a set of official rules that in actuality are circumvented by devious methods.

Results of the 1968 Crises

Both East and West emerged from the scathing events of the late sixties considerably scarred. In 1968 the newly elected Republican administration in the United States began a long and painful process of extrication from Vietnam, which was not completed until 1973. The Vietnamese War had played havoc with the principles on which the postwar foreign policy of the United States had been based. There was talk of neoisolationist withdrawal from world commitments. President Richard Nixon said the United States would stand by NATO while getting out of African and Asian commitments, but some senators talked of making substantial troop cuts in Europe. The credibility of the American "deterrent" was in question.

The year 1969 in western Europe saw the weakening of the Wilson government in Britain, leading to its defeat in 1970 and the return of a Conservative government; the defeat and retirement of de Gaulle; and a change in Germany to a Social Democratic government, which under Chancellor Willi Brandt's leadership embarked on new foreign policies. There were deeper changes, justifying the statement that 1968 marked the end of the postwar era. While the student movement as such utterly failed to bring about the total social revolution of which its militant leaders dreamed, there were significant changes afoot. After 1968 western Europe in general lost the economic buoyancy it had had and began to struggle with the consequences of a reduced rate of growth. The age of growth, it seemed, the postwar period of rapid expansion that had resulted first from the need to repair the damages of the war and then from technological modernization, was over. With a mature economy, the problem was to hold on to what had been gained against the threat of stagnation—accompanied, incongruously, by inflation. People began more and more to talk about the "quality of life" rather than material gains. Allowing for a difference in tone and vocabulary, this is what the students had been saying.

For the USSR, 1968 was a critical moment too. The revolt of the Western Communists at the time of the Czech intervention climaxed the disintegration of world communism under Russian leadership and marked the triumph of polycentrism. In 1969, a long-delayed world Communist conference held in Moscow proved embarrassing to the Russians. Among the ruling parties, China, North Korea, North Vietnam, and Yugoslavia refused to attend, and Cuba sent only an observer. There were no representatives at all from East or Southeast Asian countries. Albania formally withdrew from the Warsaw Pact. Italy's Berlinguer and Rumania's Ceausescu openly criticized the USSR about Czechoslovakia, and the only statement that was satisfactory to most of the parties attending was watered down to the point of meaninglessness; some refused to sign even it. World communism was on the point of being in total disarray.

The collapse of Russian domination opened the way for experiments in other roads to communism. The Italian party led the way in democratizing the Communist outlook, preparing to play a new role in the parliamentary politics of its country.

At the same time, the protests of Solzhenitsyn and Sakharov marked the maturity of Russian dissent, whatever furious resistance the aging Kremlin elite might wage. The iron curtain was disintegrating, and amid their troubles one might discern a common set of problems for the two sides in the erstwhile Cold War. Such problems might bring them closer together in the future. And this was in fact to happen, in some ways, during the next few years, which were dominated by the theme of detente.

Ideological Currents of the 1960s

We already know how many currents of radical social thought motivated the student militants of the 1960s. They typically, or at least very frequently, claimed to be rejecting "ideology," all "programs" and "positioning," sometimes even all intellectual activity. The editor of a compilation of revolutionary materials from this era, which he called BAMN (By Any Means Necessary), noted that the movement "owes more to Marinetti, Dada, Surrealism, Artaud, the Marx Brothers, than to Lenin or Mao," much less to such quaint Victorian intellectuals as Marx and Engels. With affinities to the television generation, it valued a happening far more than a manifesto. The riots, confrontations, bombings reflected this itch for action over thought. If he had heard Goethe's "action is so easy, thought is so difficult," the young street politician of the late sixties would have challenged it: thought, he would have answered, leads nowhere except to endless further thought; action gets something started that may prove useful. Cohn-Bendit's advice was to heave some tomatoes and start a riot, anywhere, for no particular reason.

Behind this alleged total rejection of ideology, though, did lie ideas; one cannot really act without any, and the ideology lurking often unacknowledged behind the activism of the New Leftists was partly provided by neo-Marxism. There was an image of violent revolutionary storms sweeping away entire societies. The mistrust of ideologies and organizations was itself a Nietzschean or existentialist notion of radical personalism and utter "integrity." This idea was also espoused by the earlier Lenin, when he made the Revolution and before he had to organize it into a state tyranny. Prone to hero worship, the young rebels found in Che Guevara, Castro, and many other instant führers of the Third World, or black American activists a model for courage and will—defying the odds, battling the whole society, and perhaps, as in a TV cartoon, miraculously winning. Guevara became the object of a religious cult. His friend Regis Debray's book sold a million copies, and so did West Indian psychiatrist-turned-revolutionary Frantz Fanon's.

At the end of the fifties many new ideas impatiently demanded an end to apathy and noncommitment. "Angry young men" appeared, determined, as one of the German "angries" said, to be sand rather than oil in the world's machinery. This vague anger directed at all establishments, striking at anything within range with a biting satire, reflected a profound but inexplicable alienation. Affluence itself came in for attack. There was too much stupid prosperity! The most identifiable targets were power, bureaucracy, structures of authority, the "technological society," the vastness and impersonality of an order that compelled individuals to adjust to its demand for cogs in the machine. The diagnosis of Max Weber, that magic had vanished from a disenchanted world, or of Émile Durkheim, that dissolution of ancestral authority by the acids of modernity left young people bewildered and valueless, seem closest to the point. Magic was sought in a host of occultisms, while strange religious cults flourished. But in their prevailing mood, radical youth still preferred Marx. The trouble with Marx was that he had been appropriated by the Stalinists. That was remedied by recourse to other interpretations of Marx.

The new Marx was born not only of disenchantment with Soviet Marxism but from his youthful writings heretofore scarcely known. They were first published in the USSR in the early thirties, but the director of the Marx-Engels Institute who was responsible for their publication was soon liquidated; it was too dangerous to go about publishing Marx indiscriminately. These writings talked about "alienation" more than "exploitation," the individual more than social classes, the plight of the human person in an intractable social world more than the necessary advance of history toward an ideal society. The discovery and the interpretation of Marx's early writings, impelled by a desire to rescue him from sterility, was a complicated process to which many minds contributed. Some of them congregated at the Institute for Social Research in Frankfurt in the early thirties and then fled from Hitler to the United States. The best known of these was Herbert Marcuse. The Hungarian George Lukacs, who took part in the Hungarian revolution of 1956 at a ripe age and lived to return in 1968 to Budapest University before his death at the age of 85, had attacked "mechanical materialism" as early as 1923. He proposed a more truly dialectical Marxism. Because Marxism was "dying of boredom," French professors also infused it with new ideas.

Such a Marxism should lead to a democratic socialism, seeking first to elevate proletarian class consciousness rather than seize political power; it should escape the bureaucratic state, that cold monster of dehumanization, by relying on the workers organized in soviets to run the factories and farms themselves. Freeing Marxism from a deterministic system freed the critical mind to reject the *whole* society, rather than making it the prisoner of social forces; it also restored the autonomy of the so-called "superstructure" of ideas, which are not automatically dependent on the economic system.

In 1960 Sartre attempted a marriage between existentialism and Marxism in his *Critique of Dialectical Reason*. Criticizing "official," or Soviet, Marxism for ossifying into a dead dogma with "total loss of the sense of what man is," he proposed not to reject Marxism but to "recapture man in the heart of Marxism" with the aid of existentialism and perhaps Sigmund Freud. Such attempts to add a psychology and human values to the sociological structure of Marxism may not have been altogether successful, but they greatly interested the leftist mind at this time. The goal was a radical critique of existing society in the name of human liberation. The underlying assumption—a dubious one, conservatives might say, but who was listening to them?—was that human nature, freed from external oppressions, mystifications, and alienations, is basically good.

Chinese communism fitted somewhere into this picture. In many ways the Marxism of Mao Tse-tung resembled that of the critical or Lukacsian Western Marxists. Mao stressed the superiority of dialectical over mechanical Marxism; mind can affect material things as well as vice versa. The important goal is to raise mass cultural consciousness. The rule of an elite cut off from the masses and rigidifying into an authoritarian structure is a danger to be struggled against constantly. The whole Cultural Revolution was intended to extend ideological consciousness and chasten the elite party and intelligentsia.

Chinese experiments in industrialism in the village, and subsequent attempts at deurbanization, also relate not only to the peasant basis of the Chinese Communist movement but to the fear of a powerful centralized bureaucracy, which in Mao's view had blighted Russian communism. The Russians had erred in assuming that the superstructure of consciousness automatically follows the transformation of the economic foundation. This simple mechanical model had led them into the trap of elitism, bureaucracy, and dictatorship. They should have kept superstructure and substructure in step, paying as much attention to the former as to the latter. Instead they had built a bureaucratic industrialism at the price of alienating the masses, a situation that led their party elite ever deeper into the morass of oppression and false ideologies of domination—in brief, back to the same horrors from which the revolution was supposed to have escaped.

In the Soviet view, of course, Mao was never a real Marxist but a peasant anarchist, whose effort to build a modern industrial society through backyard blast furnaces was ridiculous and whose so-called dialectical Marxism was really a reversion to "subjective idealism." It was the more irritating that Mao and most of the new Marxists appealed to Lenin, whom they thought Stalin had corrupted. But Moscow was out of step in the sixties, in more ways than one. The Kremlin, condemning rock music and long hair as bourgeois decadence, or "hooliganism," shocked by drug taking and sexual liberation, looked very old-fashioned indeed to university youth.

The campus New Left trafficked in obscenity, sexual promiscuity, LSD experiments, Rolling Stones concerts. Easily disillusioned when the miracle of total revolution failed to transpire overnight, the "new politics" soon passed into the "counterculture," the revolution became the Age of Aquarius.

Perhaps the most fundamental contradiction of the New Left was this: as a self-defined revolt of the totally alienated, the utterly unassimilated, negating the whole existing society, how could the New Left possibly interact with or make any contact with that society? It was hard to credit claims to represent "the people" or engage the masses in "participatory" democracy when these came from a tiny minority of defiant outsiders. If the proletariat has been engulfed by capitalism, how is a true revolution possible? Such a revolution would have to be the dictatorship of a small elite, ruling by force; yet New Left theorists usually rejected such a thing. The *reductio ad absurdum* of this position was Che Guevara refusing to have anything to do with the peasants his revolutionary band had come to liberate.

Despite such manifest inconsistencies, the explosion of radical ideology in the 1960s was clearly most significant. Through its social disguises one could discern an intense personalism, registering a cry of pain from modern consciousness trapped in a bureaucratic and technological society. And when the utopian fantasies of revolutionary creation of a totally new society withered away, the individual tended to retreat to a world of private values. Art, music, and literature were never so plentiful; artists and writers profited from the very processes of a mass production that they hated. Electronic equipment brought symphony orchestras into everyone's home. A stunning variety of popular musical groups provided the modern equivalent of Roman circuses for the masses. Worldcup football or the Olympic games reached hundreds of millions via television. The age of the masses is the age of the mass media; but it is also, paradoxically, the era of the most intense privatization, when each emancipated ego creates its own cultural world in its own house or room.

Social institutions reflected this generalization. Despite much theorizing about the obsolescence of the family in contemporary urban society—both its socializing and its economic functions withering away—the number of marriages steadily increased through the postwar decades. The number of children decreased, and at least in most places families became "nucleated" rather than "extended," that is, they became relatively isolated from the wife's and husband's kinfolk. Disturbed though it might be by intrusions of the outer world, which led to high divorce rates, the family group of marital pair plus one or two children was a refuge against the terrible loneliness of mass society. This was as true in the USSR as the British Isles—a common denominator in the urban, industrial, bureaucratic societies of both Western capitalism and Eastern socialism.

Yet the relentless "neophilia" of contemporary intellectual life—to borrow a term coined by one cultural historian—condemned every fashion in ideas to a short reign and brought forth constantly new criticisms.[3] In sharp reaction against Existential subjectivism and individualism, the later 1960s veered toward a new outlook called structuralism. Put on the map by the Jewish-French anthropologist Claude Lévi-Strauss, structuralism drew on linguistic theory for a mathematical rationalism that declared human consciousness to be the helpless victim of objective structures, chiefly those implicit in the laws of language syntax. Lévi-Strauss attacked Sartre and tried to prove that all human myths derive by inevitable logical progression from a few primeval ones. Structuralist analysis was applied to literature, to popular culture,

---

[3] Especially was this true in the visual arts, where even the museum directors and most critics surrendered to a succession of eccentric fads. Leadership of the art world passed from Paris to New York.

to psychoanalysis, everywhere positing objective laws of the mind—linguistic "deep structures" lying behind the surface phenomena—that impose themselves on our consciousness and, in brief, compel us all to think in certain ways. Formally, human culture is an endless repetition of the same configurations.

Combinations of advanced Marxism and structuralism, mixed perhaps with a flavoring of Freudianism, were possible and fashionable. Such sophisticated academic concoctions were light years away from the simple eschatological faith of the early Marxists. Yet in Paris thousands of people, at the height of the student fever of the sixties, attended debates among Jean-Paul Sartre, Jacques Lacan, Louis Althusser, Michel Foucault, and other high priests of the now arcane science of society on such subjects as the meaning and nature of the Marxian dialectic.

Marxism, after all, could not possibly be what it had been. Capitalism, even if called "state monopoly capitalism," was an economic success. Socialism, in the USSR, was a moral failure. The world communist movement was a scene of disunity. The bureaucratic structures that frustrated human nature were much the same wherever industrial society existed. There was no longer a traditional working class. Revolution was a futile shibboleth. A new criticism of society was needed. Dissent, like everything else, had to be brought up to date in a changing world. Intellectuals clung to traditional systems of thought while trying to adapt these to an obviously different situation. The result was a bewildering but exciting array of ideological positions and controversies. The 1960s were electrifyingly alive. The gods, perhaps, were not so angry after all.

Europe and the World
in the 1970s

15

Relaxing East-West Tensions

In 1969 the new West German Social Democratic government began discussions about a new relationship with the Soviet bloc. In a way, the Czech intervention might be given credit for this; shocking though it was, it made crystal clear that the Soviet Union would not surrender control of its satellites, nor would the West challenge such control. Chancellor Willi Brandt's government entered into negotiations with Poland, then the USSR, and finally with the DDR with the purpose of recognizing the Polish-DDR borders (the Oder-Neisse line), signing nonaggression pacts, and recognizing the sovereignty of the DDR. The blow was softened by a formal four-power agreement finally securing rights of access to West Berlin.

Thus the long-smoldering Berlin problem was settled at the cost of Bonn's virtually giving up its hopes for a united Germany. All this went on from 1969 to 1972, and not without controversy. Critics of Brandt's *Ostpolitik* wondered just what morality or indeed advantage there was in granting recognition to the Soviet empire in the East, and the several treaties were ratified only after stormy debates in the Federal Republic's Bundestag. These treaties constituted as close to a

German peace treaty, formally ending World War II, as there has ever been; it had taken twenty-seven years.

These agreements were arranged in an atmosphere of accelerating detente between the United States and the Soviet Union. Detente flourished because the mood on both sides of the perhaps disintegrating iron curtain was somewhat chastened: the Russians were sobered by Prague, the Americans by Vietnam, Europe by the student revolt, all by economic problems. In addition, the Soviets stood in increasing need of American or West European technological aid, while western Europe, the Europe of the growing Economic Community, worried because its security was dependent on an apparently unreliable United States. Depressed by Vietnam, American legislators muttered about lowering the risks in Europe. A Senate resolution calling for a 50 percent reduction of American troops in Europe, though it was eventually defeated, attracted much support in 1971.

At this time, also, a quarrel between Greece and Turkey over Cyprus weakened the southern flank of NATO. The island, which was shared by hostile communities of Greeks and Turks, exploded in violence in 1964. The violence subsided with the presence of a United Nations peace-keeping force only to reignite in 1971. The strife engendered bitterness between Greece and Turkey, supposed NATO allies, and placed their fellow allies in an awkward spot. The result was that *both* countries threatened noncooperation with NATO. Following the Turkish invasion of Cyprus in 1974, Congress placed an embargo on military aid to Turkey. In 1975, Turkey closed her American bases. In partial compensation for this disarray in NATO ranks, de Gaulle's successors quietly resumed a friendlier French attitude toward the Western military alliance.

The USSR grew ever more estranged from China, and an American move toward China, culminating in President Richard Nixon's visit to Peking in 1972, perhaps prodded the Russians to seek American friendship. Such trends formed the background for a European Security Conference, along with parallel negotiations towards arms reduction. The strategic arms limitations talks (SALT) between the United States and the Soviet Union began at Helsinki, Finland, in 1969 and, proceeding slowly, reached a first-stage agreement in 1972.

The SALT talks were facilitated because the USSR had approached numerical arms equality with the USA, so that the Russians could negotiate from strength rather than be frozen in arms inferiority. In fact, the Soviets now had more intercontinental ballistics missiles (ICBMs) than the United States, a fact that caused the U.S. Congress to hesitate before approving the Helsinki accords. This Russian advantage was balanced by the United States having bomber bases near the USSR and qualitatively better weapons.

In May 1972, at the time of President Nixon's visit to Moscow, an agreement was announced that declared a freeze on numbers of ICBMs and submarine-launched missiles, as well as the nuclear-powered subs that carried them. There was also a limitation on antimissile defenses, which threatened stabilization of mutual deterrence. Each side was permitted two zones for the antimissile defenses, with limits on the number of launchers, interceptor missiles, and radar systems. The agreement was to last for five years. It certainly left much out of account, but it was a hopeful start. Also announced at this same time were a grain purchase agreement and an American oil company arrangement to help develop Soviet oil. Brezhnev spoke of Russian aid in bringing the Vietnam War to its conclusion, which happened early in 1973 in Paris.

Early in 1973, also, seven NATO countries and five Warsaw Pact countries began discussions on mutual force reductions. The Soviet leadership mentioned the possibility of cooperation between COMECON and EEC, the rival economic unions of East and West Europe. Nixon was well received at Moscow, as he had been at Peking. The American president, unfortunately soon to become ensnared in the Watergate scandal that eventually destroyed him, joined his brilliant secretary of state, Henry Kissinger, in talking about a multipolar world, balanced between a number of centers of political if not military power: USA, USSR, Europe, Japan, China. These regional powers would cooperate as well as compete with the hope of stabilizing a world marked by continuing but ever converging nationalism. The affluent, "developed" countries would collaborate to aid the developing peoples and to conserve world resources. Such was the vision. The United States, in particular, would seek friendly understanding with both China and the USSR.

The weakness of the Sino-American detente, if such it may be called, was revealed in late 1971. India, supporting a rebellion in the East Pakistan region of Bangladesh, recognized the independence of this region. She sent in troops to throw out the Pakistani government. As her ally, Soviet Russia gave strong diplomatic support to India, while neither China nor the United States, supposedly committed to Pakistan, did anything to help her. (Pakistan soon withdrew from both the British Commonwealth and SEATO.) Further deterioration of the American position might perhaps be seen in the Middle East. The Six Day War of 1967 had been a stunning victory for the Israelis and a sharp setback for the Arab states of Egypt and Syria and for their backer, the USSR. But Brezhnev and the other Russian leaders did not give up; they continued to supply arms to the Arabs and added Iraq to their circle of allies in 1972. In 1973 the fourth Arab-Israeli War saw initial Arab successes and ended in something like a draw—better by far than the Arabs had ever done against the Israelis.

But the Arab peoples wanted no part of Soviet-style socialism and grew increasingly suspicious of Soviet motives. Detente with the United States was an obstacle. Did the USSR really want to help Egypt and Syria regain land from Israel, or did she want to dampen down the Mideast fires in order to ease US-USSR tensions? Prior to the 1973 war, Egypt's President Anwar Sadat demanded the withdrawal from his country of Soviet military advisers, estimated to be as many as 17,000. Two years later, after the 1973 war, which had ended in a stalemate, Sadat decided to adopt a position of neutrality between the superpowers. He had become convinced that Soviet interests did not dictate complete support of the Arab cause. Better opportunities lay in playing off the two powers against each other. To become the client of one was to put oneself in its power and to become helpless.

The 1973 war, the so-called Yom Kippur War that lasted from October 6 to 25, was longer, closer, and more bitterly fought than the easy Israeli victories of the first three Arab-Israeli wars. The joint Egyptian-Syrian attack achieved initial successes in the Sinai Peninsula and the Golan Heights areas occupied by Israel in 1967, but Israeli counterattacks drove them back. The Arab oil-producing countries applied an oil embargo against the United States and other pro-Israeli states, forcing a severe "energy crisis." The United States put pressure on the Soviet Union, warning it that by disregarding the principles of detente it was "imperilling its entire relationship with the United States," with possibly "incalculable consequences." Both superpowers began airlifting military supplies to their respective allies. Soviet Premier Kosygin visited Cairo; Henry Kissinger went to Moscow and then to Tel Aviv. Clearly the two giants wished to bring the fighting to an end if they could do so without excessive loss of face. In the United Nations Security Council, they joined in calling for a cease-fire. But as the entangled armies continued to struggle, there were further difficulties, which at one point (October 24–25) seemed to threaten a 1962 confrontation with worldwide alerts and threats of direct intervention in the war. On the Sinai peninsula, more tanks were in combat than in any battle of World War II!

But, as in 1956, a United Nations force was used to rescue the situation, and the two armies were disengaged; negotiations between the Arabs and the Israelis soon began under joint US-USSR sponsorship. These negotiations were to go on (and off) during the next several years, perennially threatening breakdown and another war. But the two great powers seemed to be in closer communication than before, and they were determined to prevent being dragged into nuclear holocaust by the small powers of the Middle East. Each great power was somewhat disillusioned with its ally. As in 1962, detente received an assist; after a sobering approach to the brink of the apocalypse, there was a natural drawing back. Unfortunately at just this time the United States began to endure the long agony of the Watergate crisis, which puzzled the USSR (they appear to have thought it was some kind of a diplomatic trick!) and convulsed the American political scene. Yet with Secretary of State Kissinger's high reputation unimpaired and even enhanced by President Nixon's unprecedented disgrace, detente continued to make progress.

That the Soviet Union placed good relations with the United States above possible communist revolution in far places was indicated when Chile's Salvador Allende visited Moscow in 1972, accompanied by Castro. He went to seek aid for his experiment in Andean socialism, which was in desperate financial straits. Having both nationalized American properties without compensation and embarked on a sweeping program of agrarian reform, Allende had lost financial support from the World Bank and other Western sources, and he faced three-digit inflation. Allende received very little Russian help. The Soviet Union did not wish to be stuck with another Cuba at the cost of American ill-will; the Kremlin could well have echoed the famous remark, "Another victory like that and we are undone." It silently watched the subsequent overthrow of Allende in an American-backed coup d'état. Soviet journals criticized the Allende economic policies. Evidently the Russians were still prepared to respect the Western Hemisphere as an American zone of influence.

The Soviets had their own problems. Led by Solzhenitsyn, the dissidents grew ever bolder, with Solzhenitsyn publishing *Gulag Archipelago* and calling for nothing less than repudiation of Marxism, dismantling of controls over the satellites, and decollectivization of agriculture. Perhaps more important, the economy continued to present serious problems. The Soviet growth rate sank to less than 4 percent in 1972. Agriculture continued to lag far behind the West in efficiency. Both 1972 and 1973 were years of bad harvests in Russia, necessitating imports of American grain. One notable change in the attitude of the Soviet leadership in the early 1970s was a stress on foreign trade. In order "to ensure that the Soviet people live better tomorrow than they do today," in Brezhnev's words, there must be technological cooperation between the Soviet Union and Western peoples. During his call on the German Federal Republic in 1973, the Soviet leader signed agreements involving extensive purchase of West German technological aid, for example in building steel works at Kursk. (Oil and natural gas were the bait for the Germans.) Already the Italian firm, Fiat, had begun building mass-production automobile factories in the USSR. Even more vital from the Soviet point of view was American computer and deep oil-drilling technology.

Soviet leaders also showed some inclination to agree that the world energy and environmental crisis transcended politics and could only be tackled by joining East-West resources. In 1974, some further agreements were reached at the SALT talks. Underground nuclear tests above 150 kilotons were banned, completing the 1963 Partial Test Ban agreement; the 1972 agreement limiting antiballistic missile systems was extended; progress was made toward banning environmental and chemical warfare; negotiations attempting to limit offensive nuclear weapons continued. A June agreement on economic, industrial, and technological cooperation (accompanying another presidential visit to Moscow) impressed Brezhnev as a "massive landmark in the history of the relations between the United States and the Soviet Union."

This was also the year of Solzhenitsyn's exile. In the previous year, 1973, an American Senate committee torpedoed a trade agreement with the USSR in protest against Soviet restrictions on Jewish emigration and dissidents. The path to cooperation between the superpowers, or between communism and capitalism in general, was not much smoother than were the sad affairs of a disordered world in the rather cheerless years 1973 and 1974, whose highlights included an energy crisis, world inflation, Watergate, war in the Middle East, and a world food crisis.

The Changing of the Guard

In 1974 and 1975, there was a considerable turnover in world leadership. President Richard Nixon became the first American president in history ever to resign, as a culmination of the Watergate scandal. He was replaced by Gerald Ford in the summer of 1974. In this year of the locust, plagued by the energy crisis, "stagflation," and an Arab oil boycott, Prime Minister Heath was also a political victim, as Harold Wilson returned to power with another Labour government. President Georges Pompidou died suddenly, leading to a lively and somewhat confusing presidential election in France. In Germany, Chancellor Brandt also resigned, giving way to Helmut Schmidt. An obviously sinking Chairman Mao presided over a country already maneuvering for the succession; both Mao and Chou En-lai were to die in 1976.

In Russia, the old guard was still firmly entrenched but aging, and there were rumors that either Brezhnev or Kosygin was nearing the end. The world wondered who the Soviet successor would be, for there was no apparent heir on the horizon; all the other Politburo members of any prominence (Suslov, Grechko, Podgorny, Kirilenki) were as old as or older than Brezhnev and Kosygin. Would the passing of the last figures left over from the Stalin era and the emergence of new Soviet leadership spell an end to the increasingly uncertain Russian hold over the East European countries?

The last remaining grand figure of the World War II era, President Tito, reached the age of eighty-three, and people wondered whether the somewhat precarious Yugoslav confederacy, recently shaken by Serb-Croat clashes, could survive his passing. This was a time, too, in which the death of Portugal's long-time dictator, Salazar, brought political and economic turmoil to a long quiescent little country. Her larger Iberian neighbor prepared for the death of General Francisco Franco, which came late in 1975, amid fears that this succession too would be marked by strife. As it happened, it was not. The government of the Greek colonels fell, and democracy returned. Among other old men who passed from the scene in 1975 were Chiang Kai-shek; Haile Selassie, the Ethiopian emperor; and Cardinal Mindszenty, embattled to the end—now at odds with the Vatican, which found him an obstacle to its plans for better relations with the softening East European dictatorships! Franco, Selassie, Chiang, Mao, Mindszenty—how much of the twentieth century's stormy history these men had helped make.[1]

The sudden death of French President Pompidou in April 1974 forced an unexpected election. The Gaullists split on the first ballot, on which there were no fewer than twelve presidential candidates. (Anyone can run for president in France if he or she can find one hundred notable people to sign a petition and if he or she is willing to put out a fairly small sum of money as a deposit, which is lost if he or she gets less than 5 percent of the vote.) The more orthodox Gaullist and the more conservative candidate was Jacques Chaban-Delmas, who had been Pompidou's prime minister (as Pompidou had been de Gaulle's.) But he was challenged by Valery Giscard d'Estaing, an Independent Republican. On the first ballot Chaban received only 15 percent of the vote, Giscard 35 percent; the Socialist François Mitterand, supported by all the Left parties, led the poll with 43 percent. The runoff election

---

[1] Eamon de Valera also died in 1975; in 1919–1920 he had led "the first significant guerrilla war of liberation of the 20th century," had then become the respected leader of Free Ireland, and was president of the League of Nations Assembly in the 1930s. He, too, had helped make a bit of history.

of the two highest vote-getters resulted in a narrow victory for Giscard, 50.8 to 49.2 percent. He was to repeat this four years later.

The results suggested that French politics were moderating. Giscard was a man of the center, Mitterand a moderate of the Left; between the two there was not a great deal of distance. Mitterand, supported by the Communists, did not repudiate the Atlantic Alliance nor the *force de frappe*. Giscard, backed by the Right, spoke of increasing social services and reducing inequalities of income. Both were loyal Europeanists. There were some areas of disagreement, of course, but no gulf separating haves and have-nots, impoverished proletarians and rich capitalists. Thirty percent of the working class voted for the Gaullist candidates, while a great many middle-class professional people preferred Mitterand. If a movement of the right to the left was discernible, in that both Gaullist candidates talked of change, reform, worker participation in industrial management, and so on, a movement of the left to the right was equally in evidence, for neither Communists nor Socialists used the language of revolutionary millenarianism. French politics appeared to have stabilized around a basically two-party (or coalition of parties) structure, a moderate Right and a moderate Left of almost equal strength.

For all the noise they had made in 1968, the parties of the extreme Left, themselves split, polled less than 3 percent of the vote. A Trotsky-ite candidate named Arlette Laguiller, the only woman to run, got most of these. Eighty-four percent of the eligible voters went to the polls, an impressive number. In a year not marked by serenity, this was a per-formance suggesting Fifth Republic stability and workability.

A similar pattern of political stability seemed to be emerging in post-Franco Spain. Much had changed since 1939. To the surprise of many, Franco followed de Gaulle in choosing the path of modernization for the country he ruled, which for so long had been backward by the standards of the industrialized regions. Spain's growth rate rivalled that of the EEC in the 1960s; industry grew, agriculture was modernized, and urban life expanded in an echo of France's and Italy's experiences. Standing guard against the anarchy that had brought on the civil war, Franco's military-backed regime refused to allow political opposition, trade unions, or free expression of opinion. Many feared that because a lid had held them down so long, these volatile people were bound to explode when the ponderous weight of the generalissimo was re-moved. That this did not happen was due in good part to the unexpected skill of Franco's designated successor, Juan Carlos, prince of the former royal house who became king after Franco's death. He guided Spain on a path that led to a democratic constitution. As if to mock all the stereotypes about the violent, uncompromising Spanish character, almost everybody seemed to behave moderately; attempts by both extreme Right and extreme Left to foment trouble attracted minimal followings in 1976–1977.

The Western Communist Parties

Contributing to this stabilization was the most remarkable political development of the seventies: the increasing participation in parliamentary processes by the Communist parties of the Western democracies. We have already mentioned the Italian CP's leadership in this direction. Hastening this trend was Communist estrangement from the Soviet Union from 1965 on, in disputes over treatment of dissidents and especially over the 1968 military action against Czechoslovakia. The tradition of total unity within international communism was shattered by the heated rivalry of Peking and Moscow; and the philosophic revisions of Marxism that we have mentioned opened up new horizons. But the most important cause was unquestionably the evolution of society. The working class had in fact been given a stake in society. Moreover, in the modernized technological societies, the traditional unskilled or semiskilled proletariat declined in numbers.

Just after the war the French Communist party had had a membership of four million people, and its newspaper, *L'Humanité*, boasted almost three million circulation at its peak in 1947. The party proceeded to forfeit this advantage by tying its policies to Moscow's. Opposition to the Marshall Plan, NATO, and EEC cost it support, for these were all popular measures. The Communists had to defend the attack on Yugoslavia, the Prague coup of 1948, the suppression of the Hungarian revolt in 1956, and other unpopular actions. Then they had to swallow Moscow's friendship with its enemies, watching the Soviets woo de Gaulle, the Greek colonels, and even Franco. The French party submitted to a number of internal purges, as those who gagged at swallowing all this were excommunicated on orders from Moscow—André Marty, Marcel Servin, Laurent Casanova, finally Roger Garaudy for showing too much interest in dialogue with Christians. The Communists lost support among both youth and women, whose causes they failed to adopt; the 1968 students treated them as old fogies.

It is amazing that the Western Communists waited so long to rebel; but habit died hard, and they had to unlearn the tradition of looking to the land of the first great Workers' Revolution for leadership —land of the great Lenin, of the Ten Days That Shook the World. Their membership and newspaper readership dropped sharply. Yet the party retained a hard core of deeply loyal followers; it continued to win around 20 percent of the popular vote in France; and gradually it began to shake off the yoke of the Kremlin and build itself a democratic and pro-French image.

There were two chief remnants of Stalinism or Leninism that were obstacles to the democratization of the Western Communist parties. These were the advocacy of violent revolution, and belief in the dictatorship of the Communist Party as surrogate for the proletariat. Tactically, these policies dictated refusal to form coalitions with other parties, that is, to play the game of democratic ("bourgeois") politics, unless with the ulterior purpose of using democracy to destroy itself. Western Communists were also plagued by the suspicion of intellectuals and "bourgeois" members, the traditional claim to be a party only of the working class, and the demand for total submission of personal views to the policies decided on by the party (which too often had meant those decided on by the Russians). To become a party like other parties in a pluralistic democracy had to be a long and painful process, filled with many twistings and turnings.

The Italian Communists' "historic compromise," so-called, was an acceptance of other political parties, including the Socialists and the Christian Democrats, as equals. The dialogue with Catholicism survived the deaths of Pope John in 1963 and of Togliatti in 1964, though the next pope was to prove far more conservative. A Left-Center coalition of Christian Democrats and Socialists governed Italy between 1963 and 1968. When communism gained in the elections of 1968, a period of cabinet instability began. But in 1976 the PCI agreed not to oppose the government on key issues, thus in effect becoming a member of a governing coalition for the first time since the onset of the Cold War.[2] The Italian Communists had evidently abjured forever the doctrines of violent revolution, revolutionary dictatorship, and one-party rule. In 1975 the French Communist party also formally repudiated "the dictatorship of the proletariat."

The Italian Communists in fact had long ruled in some regions and cities of Italy, especially in the north-central area of Emilio-Romagna. (By 1970 Italy had carried out a plan of regional decentralization, which had passed Parliament in 1960.) In this capacity they featured honest government, town planning, educational improvements, and other social welfare reforms, rather than anything a Russian Bolshevik might have thought of as "Communist." Curiously, the Italian Communists func-

---

[2] Communists participated not only in parliaments but in governments for a brief time after the war (1945–1946) in France, Italy, Belgium, and other West European countries. But this was a purely tactical maneuver, which scarcely reflected any genuine conversion to "class collaboration."

tioned for many people as a kind of bulwark of old-fashioned virtue and discipline against the tide of modernism!

Estimates of Communist performance varied. There were skeptics. In France in 1976, a widely discussed book, written by a socialist, claimed that the leopard cannot change its spots; no Communist party can really accept the rules of democracy. What if a Communist government was voted out after being voted in—would it relinquish power? In power, could it be trusted to hold regular elections and to maintain the rules of freedom to oppose and criticize, or would it try to use its power to end "bourgeois democracy"? On the other side, disillusioned extremists thought that the party had been coopted and corrupted. Leading a splinter-group secession from it, a former member of the Norwegian Communist party said that the party "has become bourgeois and is dying."

Perhaps the large Communist parties of France and Italy had paid the price of success by becoming respectable. Like the proletariat in Marcuse's theory, they had been "embourgeoisified." Another sociological law tells us that the larger and more successful a political party becomes, the more it loses its ideological purity and grows prone to compromise. To be a Communist, it was no longer necessary to be a Marxist or a worker, much less a believer in revolution, dictatorship, or the abolition of private property.

The corruption or maturation of the Communist parties—call it what you will—reflected economic success. Desperate poverty had ended, and the erstwhile "nothing to lose but their chains" element was put in a situation where it *did* have much to lose and to defend. French workers wished to improve on what they had gained, but they desired no revolutionary adventures. At the same time the change in Communist parties left an opening to the Left, which was filled only feebly by the intellectual-led "gauchistes." Those who disliked the "system"— and there were some—might try to demolish it by desperate deeds of "urban guerrilla warfare" or reverting to nineteenth-century anarchism, but more typically they quietly dropped out or withdrew to some counterculture.

Eurocommunism of the Italian variety attracted some of the Warsaw Pact countries. Once considered to be mere tools of Russia, they had by hook or by crook managed to pry themselves loose from that grip in some degree. Riots in Polish cities in 1970 brought threats of Russian intervention, but in the aftermath of 1968 the Kremlin preferred instead to sacrifice veteran Polish Communist chief Gomulka, replacing him with Edward Gierek. Gierek granted some reforms, including greater power for the workers' councils, a move in the direction of Yugoslav self-management. At the same time, Hungary gradually achieved what it had failed to gain in the heroic uprising of 1956; there seemed to be an unwritten agreement by which, if they promised not to repeat those embarrassing events, the Hungarians would in return get privileges from the Russians under the table, so to speak. Cynicism and corruption prevailed, according to some of the old freedom fighters, but so did prosperity under an almost capitalistic economy; Budapest struck its many visitors as the most relaxed and affluent of all the Eastern European capitals. Janos Kadar, the Hungarian leader, expressed interest in Italo-communism. So did Yugoslavia and Rumania. The East European Communists increasingly saw themselves as a bridge between Euro-communism of the Franco-Italian variety and Moscow.

At Helsinki in 1975 there was a conference on European security attended by eastern and western European countries. In 1976 and 1977, stimulated by the agreements signed there, movements emerged for freedom of speech and other human rights in Poland, Hungary, and Czechoslovakia. Most of the Western Communist parties supported these movements, which were subjected to intermittent harassment. This latest wave in the attempted humanization of communism threatened further splits among Communists and perhaps a new crisis.

Convergence?

Those who argue that in the end, after more than half a century, the allegedly antithetical and hostile systems of Soviet communism and Western capitalism will merge to form a single modernized society can point to much persuasive evidence. At the economic level, the Communists seem to be moving slowly toward a market economy replete with profit motives and competition; meanwhile capitalists have been driven to try worker participation in industrial management, the welfare state, and some degree of national planning. Yugoslavia provides a model for something in between. Reluctant though they may be to abandon ideological positions, both sides must adjust to realities. Neither the command economy nor the anarchic one works. The clear optimum for any mature industrial society is a mixed economy, providing freedom within a plan.

To take a concrete example: To meet its acute housing shortage the USSR has been forced to supplement public by private enterprise; the reverse happened in the West. There is no advanced economy today that is either purely socialist or purely capitalist. If we define *capitalism* as essentially (1) private property in the means of production, (2) competitive economic individualism, and (3) a market economy with

(4) little state guidance, and *communism* as the opposite of these, we could conclude that most communist and most capitalist countries accept about half of the four.

Moreover, the logic of a globally intertwined economy pulls the two together. Soviet acceptance of the need for trade and aid in recent years has been accompanied by a growing Western interest in helping Russia develop. According to some, the region around which detente revolves is Siberia. This gigantic area, larger than all Europe or the United States, contains fantastic natural resources beneath its frozen soil: vast supplies of oil, natural gas, coal, copper, iron, lead, zinc, uranium, and other valuable minerals, as well as half the world's resources of coniferous wood and mighty rivers with latent power to produce billions of kilowatts of electricity. The thick permafrost, brutally cold temperatures, and transportation difficulties have defied Soviet efforts to populate and develop this region despite much talk about doing so. Only the combined efforts of all advanced technologies, including those of the United States and Japan, will suffice for the job of conquering this last great frontier.

Negotiations have not thus far proved fruitful. But the pressing problem of world energy needs, largely transcending national boundaries, might pull the world's industrial powers together. They also face the need to look in the direction of the underdeveloped tropics, which also possess immense potential resources requiring all the skills of technology and scientific knowledge the world can muster.

Social factors also suggest convergence. Over this century, the long-term trend in Western societies has been toward greater equality of income, wealth, and opportunity. This process has by no means gone far enough for some, but whether in the form of a guaranteed minimum standard of living, less inequality of weath, greater educational opportunities for all, access to culture, or other indexes, the extremely stratified class society still present at the beginning of the century has slowly changed into a more nearly classless society. No people has attained a condition of perfect equality, and it is doubtful whether such a condition is possible or desirable. The communist societies do not approach such a condition; there is significant inequality of income and even more of privilege in the Soviet Union, though less than in the West European countries. A recent rating of the major nations of the world (by the World Bank) found that the most nearly classless society was capitalist Australia, with Hungary second. Given the commitment that seems to exist in capitalist societies to wipe out gross inequalities, it is reasonable to expect a convergence here, too.

In Great Britain, the wealthiest 10 percent owned 92 percent of the personal wealth in 1913. In 1971, they owned only 75 percent and earned just 25.3 percent of the national income. The trend has been slowly but steadily toward more equality in all the indexes. In 1970, the bottom 50 percent got 29 percent of the income, compared to 23.7 percent in 1955 and probably about 10 percent in 1900. In Denmark, the poorest 10 percent receive 8 percent of the income. The percentage of French workers owning autos and television sets was *larger* than the average for the country as a whole in 1973 (68 percent as compared to 61.6 percent, 83 percent compared to 79 percent), according to the French official statistics. Though there has been some slowing down in this trend toward equality in recent years, the overall pattern remains impressive.

Politically, the USSR stubbornly refuses to contemplate installing what the West thinks of as democracy: free elections and electoral accountability of state officials, freedom of expression, a free press, the right to form opposition parties and to criticize the government. But as we know, the Soviet power elite is under severe criticism from many of its own distinguished citizens for failing to do so, and some of the other communist countries have tried to move in a democratic direction. It is unlikely that such demands can be resisted indefinitely. A growing consensus of world Marxists agrees that the goal of true Marxism is human freedom and self-government, not elite rule and a leviathan state. The aging relics of Stalin's era now grimly holding on to power in the Soviet Union may be the last dam in the way of this tide, and they have not long to survive.

The West can take lessons itself from the more liberal of the Communist regimes, such as that of Yugoslavia, about meaningful democracy in economic life. The conversion of the Western Communist parties to democratic ways is a concrete manifestation of convergence at this political level. It is possible that convergence will take the form of less traditional "democracy" in the Western countries; a modern urban, technological society may demand more specialized direction than is consistent with conventional democratic theory. "Meritocracies," rather than elected officials, may have to guide and plan Western economies.

Ideas, tastes, and styles seem to be irresistibly international. Russian attempts to keep out blue jeans and rock music, however commendable, are destined to fail, just as were its now discredited efforts to mark off a Marxist realm of knowledge different from bourgeois culture. Observers of the Soviet Russian academic community consistently report a trend toward convergence; areas of knowledge ranging from the sciences to philosophy and the social sciences show less isolation and dogmatism than characterized Soviet thought in Stalin's time. Whether it is a question of ethics or esthetics, mathematics or biology, Soviet scholarly work has begun to lose its sectarian character and adopt concepts and methods similar to those of the West.

Increasing communication and travel between Russia and the West also encourages cultural blending. Clearly old Mother Russia is becoming more sophisticated as she urbanizes and modernizes. A cartoon in *Krokodil*, the Soviet satirical journal, in the mid-70s showed some old-fashioned Russian women in their drab garments eyeing their daughters, who were slinking by in slacks and sunglasses. No ideological dikes can prevent the seepage into modernized Russia of all these "decadences" from the rest of the urban, democratic, cosmopolitan world—like it or not. The only other major government attempting thus to quarantine its people from outside cultural contamination is Communist China, which Moscow, committed to urbanism, ridicules for its peasant-rural backwardness. (In 1978 this seemed to be changing rapidly as China's post-Mao leaders moved to modernize their huge country.) And the USSR possesses, among other things, one of the finest school systems in the world, technically speaking. Is it possible to educate while confining the mind to one dimension? It will take more than the 70,000 censors said to be assigned to that job, now that Stalinist terror has vanished and a structure of law is taking shape.

A common interest between East and West Europe may exist in their dialogue with the developing nations, the no-longer so *jeunes états* of the Asian-African Third World (or perhaps now Fourth World). Though Moscow might theorize that it stood with these victims of capitalistic imperialism against their former masters, much evidence suggests that non-Europeans perceive all Europeans—including Russians—as belonging in the opposing camp.

There is certainly no tight cohesiveness among the states of Asia and Africa. Most, but not all, are new; no fewer than a hundred have emerged to about triple the world's total of sovereignties, mostly since 1959. By 1975 they were divided into rich and poor, capitalist and socialist, developed and developing and undeveloped, those aspiring to become great powers and those resigned to being sturdy dwarfs. It is enough to note that the non-European states ranged from Uganda and Burundi to India, China, and Japan; from Paraguay and Peru to Saudi Arabia and Iran—vastly different in size, wealth, level of culture, religion, ideology, and almost any other index one might think of.

They are part of a growingly complex world of political relationships. In 1969 Henry Kissinger spoke of "a world which is bipolar militarily but multipolar politically." In this multipolar world, where such states as Japan, India, Indonesia, Iran, Saudi Arabia, Nigeria, and Brazil lack nuclear clout but are certain to play powerful regional roles economically and politically, there can be no question of a simple

European–non-European opposition. Yet such a disjunction is one important aspect of the political universe; and in this respect the interests of the USSR and the U.S.-West Europe group often coincide.

The interests of Europe are not necessarily the same as those of the U.S., needless to say. Although bound together by the most basic interests, the trans-Atlantic partners have bickered often enough. Europe might be happy to stay under the American nuclear umbrella, but France at least has mistrusted it enough to want to develop her own atomic shield, however small. Gradually organizing herself into a European community for economic purposes, Europe welcomed Great Britain and others into this club at long last in the seventies. Threats by Labour to undo, or "renegotiate," the agreement cast some doubt on the permanence of British entry into the Common Market until 1975, when after the Labour victory in the 1974 general election a referendum finally confirmed the Marketeers' victory. In 1976 the prominent Labourite Roy Jenkins, as if to underscore the British commitment, became chief of the European communities at Brussels. But two years later British complaints again were heard about EEC membership, along with threats to withdraw.

The European Community was a union the Americans had once encouraged but that now looks to some of them rather like a cuckoo in the nest—a source of potent economic competition. Europeans complained of excessive investment by American corporations in Europe. The American threat to buy up Europe is the theme of one of the most widely read books of the sixties in France, Jacques Servan-Schreiber's *The American Challenge.* Certain advanced industries, such as computers, are almost completely American-owned. "Americanization" is often an epithet describing what is plainly happening but hardly greeted with universal joy: supermarkets, freeways, raucous music, Coca-Cola. Again, Europe looked with some suspicion on the tête-à-têtes held by the Russians and Americans, who pursued their detente bilaterally without consulting Europe.

Perhaps under such circumstances both Western and Eastern Europe might function as a bridge between the two poles of Soviet communism and American capitalism. This would be a return to an image many Europeans had had at the end of World War II. Convergence would then center on Europe as a whole, the mediator between the two rival social and economic systems represented by the USSR and the USA.

Doubters of the convergence idea have some arguments, too, including the fairly basic one that a "mixed" economy doesn't really work. It can just as well provide the worst of both worlds as the best. Either straight capitalism or straight socialism (an administered, or "command," economy) can work; a mixture is fatal, like half the cars driving on the right side of the road and half on the left. Capitalism gets in trouble when statism inhibits profits and clogs up the free market.

As for other modes of convergence, is there any sign that the massive Soviet bureaucracy and party apparatus is prepared to give up its power? Or that the mammoth private corporations of the West will do so? The two systems really are different; doubtless each has some advantages and some disadvantages, but they are not compatible. Even if they are in theory, powerful vested interests stand in the way of change. No doubt there are similarities; any human society has *something* in common with any other, but capitalism and socialism remain different in important ways. What gives vitality and legitimacy to each is its ideology.

Only the future can reveal which argument is correct. This is one live question the present is posing for the future. Healing the breach that had opened with the breakdown of order in 1914 and led to the Russian Revolution of 1917 might be one of the twentieth century's appointed tasks.

Some Special Problems of Europe Today

Since 1900, and particularly since 1945, Europe has made extraordinary material progress. If we take Great Britain as an example—and it seems a conservative one, since in 1900 it was just about the wealthiest country in Europe, whereas today it is not—we can cite numerous statistics to prove the gains in living standards. Expectation of longevity at birth rose from around fifty years at the beginning of the century to seventy-three in 1971. It had been forty in the middle of the nineteenth century. (With a life expectancy of seventy and a generally excellent public health system, the Soviet Union compares favorably with the West in this area.) Seebohm Rowntree, who had estimated that in the 1900s, 28 percent of the population lived in poverty, found that by the same criteria this number had sunk to 2 percent in the 1950s, and today it is virtually nonexistent; poverty as the Edwardians defined it has been eliminated.

Hours of work, which averaged sixty-seventy per week in the nineteenth century and fifty-three in 1910, have gone down to forty. The percentage of unskilled and semi-skilled workers in the population —the classical "proletariat"—has greatly declined; allowing some margin for error because of problems of definition, it would seem to have sunk from about 70 percent of the population in 1900 to about

30 percent today in Great Britain. Welfare has, of course, been greatly extended; payments from National Insurance and other benefits just about doubled between 1938 and 1971. (France belatedly arrived at a comprehensive social security system in the 1960s, as it urbanized and modernized.) Needless to say, many such products as electric refrigerators, automobiles, and TVs, which had been nonexistent or owned by a very few before 1914, have become commonplace. Four out of five households had a television set and better than 60 percent an automobile by 1973.

In 1900 only a fraction of 1 percent could expect to receive a higher education, a number that was over 17 percent by 1970. In 1900, indeed, only about 1 percent of the working class even reached secondary school. Now a secondary education is universal, and university grants on a merit basis are widely available. Such statistics, indicative of a startlingly improved standard of life, could be cited almost endlessly.

Were there an objection, especially by members of the recent generation, that such affluence has come at the cost of the environment, the reply might be that London's air is immeasurably cleaner today than it was in 1900, that sanitation is better, that diet has improved. If by environmental concerns, one means less contact with nature, this appears to be true. In the nineteenth century, the farm, the village, the craftsman, the countryside still remained close even after considerable urbanization. "A morning's walk from the largest city and you were in the midst of it," Alan Everitt remarks of the late nineteenth century, "it" being a traditional society where one might meet shoemakers, saddlers, millers, and farmers come to market. Today agriculture is in sight of vanishing in England. Only 3 percent of the population earn their living by agriculture, and these are machine tenders—factory workers on the land, as it were. The urban megalopolis has swallowed up virtually every other kind of social environment.

By the 1970s there were forty cities in Europe and the USSR with a population, counting the entire metropolitan area, of over a million people. In 1970, 17 percent of the people lived in such cities; 48 percent lived in cities over 100,000.

The numbers in Table 15–1 do not entirely tell the story of hyperurbanization, but they suggest it. A collection of Dutch cities with five million inhabitants or so has merged into one continuous megalopolis, something almost true of the German Ruhr. Nearly a quarter of the French populace lives in and around Paris. The amazing urbanization of the Soviet Union must be seen against its heavily rural character as late as the 1920s. But urbanization can be striking even when the figures are not in the millions. Consider, for example, the case

TABLE 15–1   Approximate Population of Major European Cities, by Country, in 1970s

Country	City	Population	
	LONDON†	7,165,000*	
	Birmingham	1,090,000	
Great Britain	Leeds	750,000	
	Liverpool	575,000	(1,500,000*)
Scotland	Glasgow	1,725,000*	
Ireland	DUBLIN	650,000*	
France	PARIS	9,860,000*	
	Lyon	1,075,000*	
	Marseille	965,000*	
	Lille	880,000*	
West Germany	Berlin	2,905,000	
	Hamburg	1,720,000	
	Munich	1,315,000	
	Cologne	1,015,000	
	Frankfurt, Essen, Dortmund, Stuttgart	600–700,000	
East Germany	Berlin	1,100,000	
	Leipzig	570,000*	
	Dresden	510,000*	
USSR	MOSCOW	7,735,000*	
	Leningrad	4,370,000*	
	Kiev	2,015,000	
	Tashkent	1,640,000	
	Baku	1,405,000	
	Kharkov	1,305,000	
	Gorki	1,305,000	
	Minsk	1,190,000*	
	Kuibyshev	1,185,000	
	Sverdlosk	1,170,000	
	Donetsk, Dneprpetrovsk, Volgograd, Rostov, Perm, Tbilisi, Ufa	900,000–1,000,000	
Austria	VIENNA	1,615,000	
Belgium	BRUSSELS	1,055,000*	
Bulgaria	SOFIA	962,000	
Czechoslovakia	PRAGUE	1,100,000	
Denmark	COPENHAGEN	1,325,000*	
Greece	ATHENS	2,100,000*	
Hungary	BUDAPEST	2,065,000	
Italy	ROME	2,870,000	
	Milan	1,730,000	
	Naples	1,225,000	
	Torino	1,200,000	
Finland	HELSINKI	853,000*	
Netherlands	Amsterdam	990,000*	
	Rotterdam	1,030,000*	

TABLE 15–1 (cont.)

Country	City	Population
Norway	OSLO	645,000*
Poland	WARSAW	1,450,000
	Lodz	805,000
	Krakow	695,000
Portugal	LISBON	1,610,000*
	Porto	1,315,000*
Rumania	BUCHAREST	1,565,000
Spain	MADRID	3,520,000*
	Barcelona	1,810,000*
	Valencia	715,000*
Sweden	STOCKHOLM	1,360,000*
	Goteborg	690,000*
Switzerland	Zurich	715,000*
Yugoslavia	BELGRADE	775,000*

* Entire metropolitan area counted.
† Capital letters indicate capital cities.

of Toulouse, now the fifth or sixth city of France and growing rapidly. This is an example of a once sleepy backwater dreaming of medieval glories, a place for tourists. It has become the aeronautical and space capital, almost, of the West: Concorde, Caravelle, and Airbus were built here; the ancient university is known as a center of advanced scientific research; and in 1960 Toulouse undertook one of Europe's most ambitious planned suburban communities, the Mirail, which is intended to house 100,000 people near their employment, parks, and recreational and shopping facilities.

Impressive as it is, the Mirail of Toulouse is architecturally almost indistinguishable from other such urban "developments" in Birmingham, Stockholm, Zurich, Milan, or scores of other European cities. (There are about 120 European and Soviet Russian cities with a population greater than 400,000, which was Toulouse's approximate population in 1975.) The capital of the Midi, boasting supermarkets, bowling alleys, parking lots, and multinational corporations, might as well be Milwaukee or Manchester, except for a very small portion. In Rome, the old city of the Caesars and the popes still exists, but it is a tiny island surrounded by a vast sea of apartment towers and freeways much more reminiscent of Los Angeles. The cultural center of this new Rome, as is the case with other big cities, is probably the sports arena where crowds dwarfing even American ones watch soccer matches.

All this may provide a clue to the apparent mystery of why this impressive material advance has not brought an increase in happiness.

The New Urban Environment. (a) The Farsta Center, near Stockholm, Sweden; (b) The Mirail, suburban Toulouse, France. Planned community developments of this sort, where people live, work, and play, are a creative feature of contemporary Europe. Candilis, architect of the Mirail, is a disciple of Le Corbusier. Can urban man really make himself at home here? *Huys Priviits, The American Swedish News Exchange* and *Yan*.

The evidences of unhappiness are equally impressive. They range from rising suicide rates to opinion polls showing absymally low public confidence in all manner of political and social institutions. A London *Times* poll of this sort in 1974 indicated that those who had "a great deal of confidence" in various institutions were: the press, 19 percent; religion, 22 percent; Parliament, 27 percent; business, 27 percent; nationalized industries, 11 percent; trade unions, 15 percent; education, 33 percent; science, 40 percent; television, 22 percent. The police led the field with a 68 percent vote of confidence, probably a uniquely British situation.[3]

The evidence that ours is an age of anxiety includes a recent German report indicating that 10 to 12 percent of all inhabitants of the Federal Republic will at some time during their lives require the services of a psychiatrist. Hard drugs have come to Europe, though not as yet on the American scale. So have dropouts, commune-formers, and other seekers of an "alternative reality" from the intolerable mainstream one. Inside Copenhagen, which emerged incongruously in the late sixties as the "porn" capital of the world, a "free city" swarming with "unconventionals" became a scandal to respectable Danes in 1975.

Evidence of the profound malaise eating at the heart of this apparently successful society is indicated by the search for spiritual meaning. This often takes the form of a bizarre search for substitute religions: the vogue for the occult, strange religious cults, modern mysticism, witchcraft, astrology. The star-gazing Mme. Soleil became a French institution, *Planete* one of the most popular magazines; a computer named Astroflash near the Champs d'Elysée will grind out your horoscope!

A glance at its literature confirms the spiritual unease of Europe. Violent rage against "society," people going mad or committing murders, on drugs, and so on are par for this course. In a typical novel of the early seventies West German Günter Herburger's *Die Messe (The Fair)*, the hero squirts acid at exhibits in a furniture fair; a middle-class dropout, he is haunted by the obsession that his dead father was a concentration camp commander and, seeking a father substitute, finds one in an ex-concentration camp inmate. With him he forms a homosexual relationship, and he tries to mate him with his mother (the inevitable overtones of Freud.) He also dreams of landing on the moon. Much of Herburger's style is stream-of-consciousness. In Roger Simon's *Heir*, the leading character, having accidently killed his girl with an overdose of heroin, nails her into his harpsichord. These events are recorded in a diary, which also reveals his circuit from analysis to drugs to sexual orgies; he goes insane in the last section, as words wander crazily up and down the page.

[3] April 30, 1974.

In renowned leftist cinema director Jean-Luc Godard's *Weekend* (1968), a married couple butchers the wife's mother before the husband kills and then eats the wife; "it is necessary to surpass the horror of the bourgeoisie by still more horror," Sartre's friend Godard explained. Many other movies of this sort, featuring sadism and cruelty mixed with pornography, come from fashionable filmmakers whose reply to any criticism is the same: we're just trying to wake you up. On the London stage, which was vibrantly interesting in the early seventies, one representative attraction exhibited men burned and kicked to death (Charles Wood's *Dingo*); another, a baby stoned to death (Edward Bond's *Saved*). Absurdity, pornography, and other emblems of total disgust are not missing from the works of those acknowledged to be the greatest writers of this period, for example, Germany's Günter Grass (*The Tin Drum, The Dog Years*) and the American Norman Mailer. The author of a book about the recent American novel entitled it *The Landscape of Nightmare*, which seems appropriate enough.

Such examples are selected rather at random from the teeming supply of books, films, and plays of a cultural hemorrhage. Sheer numbers testify to an immense vitality as well as an unquenchable anger. And we are talking about only the more serious works of art, beneath which a huge quantity of popular writing, music, and art sometimes mirrored the themes of "high culture." No social history of the times could leave out the Beatles or the Rolling Stones, whose 1969 concert was attended by nearly half a million young people. A study of youth literature in 1976 found that it had changed sharply from a familiar happy optimism to preoccupations with "flawed development and psychic catastrophes, violence, injustice, unmerited destruction." [4] To say that this is because of the terrible threat of nuclear extermination lying over the world invites the reply that such a black mood was not nearly so present in the 1950s, when there was probably more danger of an accident or a miscalculation upsetting the balance of terror. There was indeed a good deal of quiet gloom, for example in the existentialist manner of Samuel Beckett or the historical manner of Arnold Toynbee; but there was less raging anger and hatred then.

Fear of ecological or environmental disaster often seems inflated by the mood of pessimism. Whether the industrial world is running out of resources to feed its gargantuan appetite, eventually forcing all the advanced economic societies to retreat somehow to a bucolic past, is a matter of opinion; there is certainly much exaggeration of the problem. In response to such doomsday allegations, one team of experts from the Hudson Institute presented evidence to show that the world has scarcely begun to develop its potential resources of soil, minerals,

---

[4] Walter Scherf, "Trends in der Jugendliteratur," *Stimmen der Zeit*, November, 1976, p. 767.

and technologies, which would suffice for a possibly spectacular growth over the next two hundred years.[5] The bright side is there, if one prefers to see it. Rejection of technology and growth and continued economic development is rooted in ethical choice rather than scientific fact; it reflects a weariness with the Faustian soul of the West, a nostalgia for simpler communities of the past, now unfortunately no longer available. Rich as it is in material goods, the consumer society seems humanly unendurable.

Other Problems

On October 9, 1976, an Italian rented an airplane and dropped a million and a half lire over Rome's Piazza Venezia; he was desperately trying to get the government's attention to obtain information about the death of his son a year and a half earlier in an air accident. The Air Ministry was supposedly investigating it. The War Damages Bureau of the Italian Treasury Department had not yet finished with claims from World War II, which the French and Germans had completed years ago. With two million pending court cases, Italy was worse off in this area than even the United States. Tax collecting was still carried out partly by private collectors, as in pre-1789 France. Bureaucracy is a problem for every modern nation. It is a "convergence" headache cutting across barriers of ideology, for the Russian Communist state suffers from it as severely as anyone. It seems worse in Italy than elsewhere. With much of Italian industry nationalized and millions dependent on government welfare checks (there were perennial scandals about the Italian postal service), administrative disorders are no laughing matter.

The bureaucratized society is a part of the fate of our times. In recent decades Italy has undergone a rapid process of social change and technological modernization. But its government represents a cultural lag. Habits of efficiency, of "rationalization," in Max Weber's term, are cultural growths that generally accompany capitalism and industrialism, but they may lag behind. Northern Italians allege that the bureaucracy is colonized by southerners who, coming from a premodern society, bring to their office a different set of values than those shaped by the ethos of rational efficiency. An attempt to solve the problem

---

[5] See Herman Kahn, William Brown and Leon Martel, *The Next 200 Years: A Scenario for America and the World* (New York: Morrow, 1976). Cf. The Club of Rome, *The Limits of Growth* (Donnella Hagar Meadows and others) (New York: Universe Books, 1972). Or compare Barry Commoner, *The Closing Circle* (London, 1972) with John Maddox, *The Doomsday Syndrome* (London, 1972).

by decentralization did not succeed; it only added another layer of bad government. As we have already noted, the success of the Communist party is at least partly due to its ability to supply competent administration—not so much the classless society as the honest bureaucracy.

French, German, and British administration excels the Italian, but each country might be said to have its Achilles heel. There was much discussion of "the English disease" in the early 1970s when the British economy lagged behind the rest of Western Europe. One charge was that the English have ceased to want to work very hard. This, however, seems true of all the peoples of West Europe. To do the menial, unpleasant, and more arduous chores, France and Germany have imported Algerians, Turks, and other people accustomed to a lower standard of life. The mature economies, having achieved a certain level of affluence, breed a natural disinclination to drive ahead at back-breaking pace to win new rewards. A reaction against the "work ethic" sets in; leisure is valued more than extra money. Stress on the "quality of life" is reflected in the fact that the French have a government department bearing this name.

The rejection of work and technology per se is not confined to the West. East German writers have grown bold enough to question the gospel of the "new socialist man" who is supposed to be happy tending the machines because in theory he owns them. Can tending a machine be other than dehumanizing under any circumstances? was the question raised by writers such as Christa Wolf.[6] In Britain, the petty strikes, often unauthorized by trade union leadership, that plague the economy relate less to wage demands than to human frustrations in a boring work environment.

The welfare state itself comes in for criticism. According to a Danish Marxist, Jorgen Dich, the bureaucrats of the welfare state are the new ruling class, whom he scolds for their grim determination to shower the maximum of largesse on everybody, thus crippling their initiative. Such an analysis is reminiscent of the rich literature discussing the "new class" of the Soviet Union, whose status is no less powerful for being based on political rather than economic monopoly. In Great Britain the silver anniversary of the famed cradle-to-grave system brought it much criticism. Some pronounced it a failure, and everyone agreed on the need for a thorough overhauling.

In the age of bureaucracy and statism, a cry for radical freedom

---

[6] Even in the USSR, the popularity of such a person as the writer and film maker Vasily Shukshin, a curiously tolerated antiestablishment figure, testifies to a yearning for the peace of a simpler, pastoral society. Shukshin's vision of the modern Soviet city as a corruption emanating from the West is not far from Solzhenitsyn's.

goes up from the articulate sector; the message of fashionable social thought is that every institution represses; every system or organization is an enemy of the individual, who must be totally free to realize his hidden promise. The message spreads through society in the form of "permissiveness," the rise of sexual promiscuity, easy divorce, free abortions. The end of censorship, the result of a process substantially beginning in the 1950s, has led to a flood of pornography—a fierce revolution that has swept aside barriers and tabus on language, behavior, and artistic representation that have stood for centuries. There had always been a scandalous minority of rakes, prostitutes, "dirty" books and pictures, and language used in the back room; but it remained distinctively separate from and condemned by respectable society, which considered it immoral or illegal. In premodern times, it appears that the masses outside civilized society, whether peasants or workmen, lived quite immorally, or, better, amorally, but this was a buried subculture. Now it has become the mainstream. Whether this is wholesome release from hypocrisy, or, as British author and educator David Holbrook cried in 1972, "a horrible epidemic . . . that threatens our country's psychic health" or, as spectators of X-rated motion pictures might feel, a threat of the extinction of all art in a wave of pornographic boredom, is rather beside the point; it cannot be stopped; there is no way of bringing back censorship. Even the Yugoslavs are making porn movies.

The cry for radical freedom with an end to all institutions and rules is strangely accompanied, however, by a desperate search for new religions and communities. The Unification Church, the Children of God, scientology, blendings of Eastern and Western religion, "pop" religions of all sorts swarming out of the communes and "hippie" quarters tell of a rejection of tradition along with a quest for new faiths. In Yeats' imagery, the rough beast slouches toward Bethlehem. The old churches have had to change their ceremonies and rituals if they wished to compete. They have introduced rock music, translated the Bible into "street" talk, taken up left-wing social causes.

Radical feminism, perhaps the most striking of all the liberation movements, has brought release from women's traditional role of homemaking to lead, in some cases, to new anxieties, as women join men in the quest for success in the competitive career world. The liberated society is certainly a more anxious one; drugs, psychiatry, astrology, occultisms, new religions are signs of this as much as are various revolts and the tinge of violence in literature, films, and television. Books about living with stress, medical guides to coping, the widespread use of tranquilizing drugs by perfectly respectable citizens are signs of the times. In the United States, the suicide rate increased markedly from 1965 to 1974, rising about 66 percent in the twenty to twenty-four age group. A 1970 questionnaire discovered that almost half of American college students felt that their society was not "satisfactory for the development and expression of your own particular abilities and wishes."[7]

Crime has also climbed spectacularly in the United States; if official statistics are to be believed, it more than doubled in the decade of the 1960s. In this respect Europe is more fortunate, having in general a far lower rate of major crime than either the United States or the Soviet Union, which, though it conceals the extent, is thought by experts to have a really serious crime problem. The French thought they had a crime wave in 1970, but when Americans saw their statistics, they thought the number of crimes must have been daily rather than annual! "There are more murders in New York City in a year than the combined totals of Britain, the Netherlands, Ireland, Switzerland, Spain, Sweden, Norway, Denmark and Luxemburg," someone observed in 1971. There are about 30,000 inmates in French prisons (a reformed prison system much praised for its enlightenment), compared to a total in American prisons of some 200,000—about 1 in 1,700 in France, 1 in 950 in the U.S.

Europeans fear that "Americanization," that is, modernization, will bring them the same social evils more evident across the Atlantic. French President Pompidou declared that "the very foundations of social life stand in danger," pointing to the dissolution of the family, the church, ancient institutions. In 1978 a wave of "urban guerrilla" terrorism stunned Germany and Italy with shootings and kidnappings.

The causes of this profound disturbance in the fabric of human relations, amid all the apparent successes, might be traced to the joint operation of personal liberation and social constraints, squeezing the individual in an evertightening vise. What Max Weber called the "iron cage" of bureaucracy, systemization, "rationalization" of life are operating to force people into a social mold determined by the requirements of a specialized, technological society. On the other hand, the individual ego has steadily been emancipated from all kinds of social control, for modernization works to dissolve traditions, break down ancestral ways, weaken authority. Modern education and communications open up to increased numbers of people realms of feeling and value via literature and art; modern philosophers and social theorists tell them they should realize their unique selves. On the one hand total freedom, on the other increased enslavement—total freedom leading as often as not to total bewilderment, in a normless community, and the economic organization

[7] Charles Morris, "Changes in the Conception of the Good Life by American Students 1950 to 1970," *Journal of Personal and Social Psychology*, XX, 254–260.

of society compelling acceptance of certain occupations and conditions of work not freely chosen by the individual.

What one distinguished German social theorist, Jürgen Habermas, called the "legitimation crisis" has thus resulted: a questioning of all institutions and authorities. One can trace the beginnings of dissolution back to the nineteenth century, when bourgeois and industrial revolutions ruthlessly dismantled customs, community, and stability and set up a society based solely on interests that were essentially egoistic and utilitarian. The decay of society has thus been a long, slow process, which has been going on remorselessly for at least two centuries and now has finally eaten through the fabric that holds people together. One can, for example, find all the emancipations—including the sexual —in the intellectual-literary elite of Edwardian times at the beginning of the century, in the era of Shaw and the Bloomsbury Circle, the pioneer modern artists, the Nietzschean generation. They had announced the death of religion, practiced free love, ridiculed all bourgeois institutions, dabbled in socialism, lived highly unconventional lives, and cultivated their private sensibilities. But at the time these habits were confined to a small coterie, an intellectual elite that was usually supported by the remaining fortunes of an aristocratic or upper bourgeois class. Now these attitudes have spread to reach all classes, and they continue to spread.

Pessimists speak of "the end of the modern world" in a tide of decadence and anarchy, invoking the analogy of the decline and fall of the ancient world and other decays. On this view one can only wait for the barbarians—where are they?—to begin all over again on the ruins of civilization. Optimists speak of a unique opportunity for the first time in history to create a society with opportunity for all. The sense of impending utopia is about as strong as the sense of impending collapse. One can only wonder, without knowing, what the future might bring, being sure only that the unstable present cannot last.

If the West has indeed built a society that provides a relative abundance of material goods at the cost of an intolerably inhuman organization of life and labor (given the expectations this society's culture arouses for total individual fulfillment), then it will have to find a way to alter the organization. It must be more humanly tolerable, but it may not decrease the output of goods and services to an unacceptable extent, or society will have to dampen expectations, a task with poor prospects for success. The goal seems clear. Whether it can be attained is another, and unanswered, question.

Conclusion

The "conclusion" of a work of history that terminates in the "present" is a contradiction, for history does not conclude; it flows on. Even as we write or read, it is probably engaged in undoing our work by arriving at some unexpected denouement or totally reversing a recent trend. The student will have to keep the story going by writing his own postscript to this book.

All one can do by way of taking leave of humanity at a certain moment is to reflect on some possible meanings of the recent past and draw some tentative conclusions. And this is not easy, for paradoxes abound. For example, many would choose to describe the present century as does the title of a recent novel (repeating T.S. Eliot's poem of more than half a century ago): *The Age of Death*. Its outstanding features have been the two awful world wars, which killed millions upon millions of people, and the Nazi and Communist dictatorships, which specialized in the extermination of whole races and classes. It may well be remembered as the century of Hiroshima and Auschwitz, of Stalin and Hitler, unless its remaining decades are reserved for still more terrible holocausts.[1] Death on a scale as yet unknown lies sealed in the

---

[1] Stories of a 1975 holocaust in Cambodia, whose leftist dictators sought to wipe out a whole Westernized urban culture, were greeted as skeptically as were those from Nazi Germany in 1943. They may very well be just as true.

thousands of nuclear warheads that intercontinental missiles are prepared to launch against the enemy at a moment's notice, each one capable of destroying an entire city. Like Macbeth, this century has
"supped full of horrors"; no direness can any longer startle it.

And yet the twentieth century has kept far more people alive than
ever before. In sheer quantitative terms, it outweighs all the rest of
human history. We might as aptly describe it as the Age of Life. More
human life-years have existed in this century than in all previous history. One of this century's critics' prime complaints, indeed, is that it
has *over*populated the world. One of its greatest problems is a super-
abundance of everything, knowledge and manufactured products as well
as human beings. So far as Europe is concerned, increasing average life
expectancy from around fifty to over seventy years has obviously added
the equivalent of more than a third to the total of human life-years, in
effect further increasing population by about 200 million. This would
more than double the population of Europe between 1900 and 1980.
And all these people have been kept alive at a higher standard of living
as well as a richer content of consciousness.

The twentieth century is not yet over. Its last quarter shows signs
of developing new problems and separate interests, thus constituting a
third distinctive segment. Broadly speaking, the 1914-1945 period, fea-

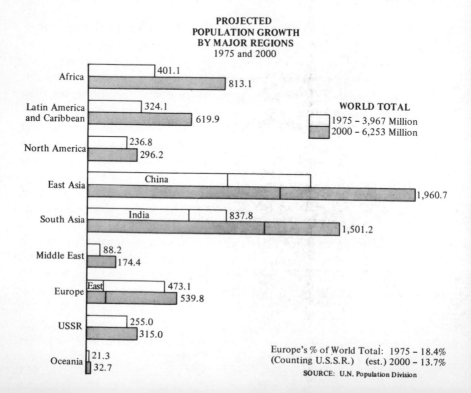

**PROJECTED
POPULATION GROWTH
BY MAJOR REGIONS**
1975 and 2000

Africa — 401.1 / 813.1

Latin America and Caribbean — 324.1 / 619.9

North America — 236.8 / 296.2

East Asia (China) — 1,960.7

South Asia (India) — 837.8 / 1,501.2

Middle East — 88.2 / 174.4

Europe (East) — 473.1 / 539.8

USSR — 255.0 / 315.0

Oceania — 21.3 / 32.7

WORLD TOTAL
1975 – 3,967 Million
2000 – 6,253 Million

Europe's % of World Total: 1975 – 18.4%
(Counting U.S.S.R.)   (est.) 2000 – 13.7%

SOURCE: U.N. Population Division

turing dreadful wars, depressions, revolutions, and dictatorships, was a tragic era signalling an enormous crisis in the Western social order. Then in the next generation Europe achieved an amazing recovery, seemed to solve its economic problems, avoided war, and found considerable political stability. It by no means healed all the damage done earlier but was evidently on the way to doing so. There were hopes of transcending national selfishness and repairing the East-West split, as well as of absorbing the masses politically and economically into an egalitarian society.

The sequel to this interlude has been a return to pessimism, encompassing an end to economic growth, critical problems of energy and resources, and a radical restiveness in social thought reflecting severe psycho-spiritual troubles with the modernized society. There is also a stagnation in those processes directed towards European integration, convergence of the communist and capitalist worlds, ideological and military appeasement. Leadership everywhere looks uninspiring; the affluent economy is a precarious bore, art and literature are at a low ebb. Signs of moral and social disintegration multiply. Even protest, no longer capable of great revolutionary movements such as the Communist and Nazi ones, degenerates into petty acts of terrorism. The confused and desperate student revolt of the late sixties looked like the final flicker of more or less organized protest. As the Third World, now without Mao and Ho, increasingly fell into the hands of practical men rather than revolutionary heroes, it looked far less attractive in the late 70's to radical idealists. If the first act of the century was grandiose and the second hopeful, the last act looks simply tired and bedraggled.

Such an analysis is plainly an oversimplification, as any brief statement must be. The world sits on the edge of many a volcano that might erupt into devastating destruction, whether nuclear war or technological disaster or political breakdown. It also glimpses possibilities of new scientific and technological breakthroughs arising from the challenge of energy shortage; perhaps there will be a cultural renaissance. Nothing is excluded from the range of contemporary possibility.

All the problems identified by a series of twentieth-century social and cultural theorists remain without assured solution: the bureaucratization and disenchantment of modern life; dehumanization in a technological and commodity-market economy; the fragmentation of culture and thought via hyperspecialization, professionalization, "reification"; gaps between high and low culture, between generations, between classes, between sexes; loss of contact with nature in a heavily urbanized world; destruction of traditional values by pervasive skepticism and overly rapid change; collapse of organic relationships and primary social institutions into anomie and the "lonely crowd"; psychic individualism on a collision course with social regimentation; and others, all connected with the question of the individual in a mass, urban, technological culture.

Marxists and neo-Marxists, Max Weber, Émile Durkheim, Freud and Jung, Ortega y Gasset, the existentialists, along with many followers of these giants and a brilliant array of poets and novelists, all addressed these issues—no lack of diagnosticians for the diseases of modern man—too many, indeed, creating a babel of rather discordant voices. The complexity of these controversies then slips away from the average person's comprehension, as coteries of hyperintellectuals further complicate the difficulty of communication. A wild profusion of charlatans offering advice astrological, occult, pseudoscientific, and neosuperstitious testifies to the perplexities of modern life.

To Eastern Europeans, these problems connected with a "free" society look like utopia compared to the forcible suppression that confronts them. But in the communist world, too, revolt seems less likely than a weary skepticism, as courageous dissidents seek in vain to build a mass movement of liberation. The ghost of Stalin will yield, if at all, not to a democratic revolution but to a slow evolution. There is a widespread feeling that the USSR and Eastern Europe are on the eve of great changes, to come when the aging leadership of the Brezhnev-Kosygin-Podgorny team passes. The thirst for personal liberty, more consumer goods, a better distribution system, better quality goods, a life style released from the puritanical style of the old Marxists, a knowledge unimpeded by old dogmas, a freer literature and art—all this seems certain in some way to come, and indeed it is coming. Nevertheless, the huge Soviet bureaucratic machine constitutes a formidable obstacle to change. Protest, as Solzhenitsyn noted in dismay, is the gesture of contempt made inside one's pocket. In the USSR as well as in the West, the individual gives up his discouraging fight against the machine.

Does this portend the end, as so many twentieth-century sages and seers have announced, or is it a lull before Western civilization—which has known such temporary setbacks before, sometimes lasting a century or more—takes off on another stage of that Faustian dynamism it has always shown? No one can say. The twentieth century has thus far defied all the prophets, so there is no reason to think it will not continue to do so. At its beginning, people forecast perpetual peace and got the worst wars of all time. Socialists predicted the doom of capitalism, but it has survived wars and depressions. Virtually no one foresaw World War I, the Russian Revolution, the Nazi dictatorship, atomic energy.

Then in 1945, predicting the past, most experts expected a gloomy time for the war-shattered continent, only to see it make a miraculous recovery. And the catalogue of surprises continued, in small matters as well as great: the student revolt of 1967–1968 was as unexpected as Khrushchev's "secret speech" had been or Watergate would be. Most observer's thought Charles de Gaulle securely on his perch in 1968. In 1972, veteran international commentators thought nothing less likely than another Arab-Israeli war. This catalogue could go on and on. The most bizarre literary imagination could not have invented Hitler, Stalin, Churchill, de Gaulle, or Khrushchev.

So we may anticipate anything, and we will probably get the opposite. It is reasonably clear that the last decades of the twentieth century will find answers, if there are any, in different places than formerly. John Maynard Keynes' economic theory, reigning over the forties and fifties, has now become obsolete.[2] There is a reaction against bureaucratic welfare state regulation. Russian-style Marxism (Leninist or Stalinist) is now outmoded within Marxist circles, which have moved toward the heritage of George Lukacs, the Frankfurt School, or existentialized Marxism, all of which stress culture and consciousness rather than production and institutional change. These are examples of a sharp shift in ideas taking place, promising to bathe this *fin de siècle* in a new atmosphere.

While change takes place, there is also continuity. Long-term processes move slowly under the surface of events. We noted at the beginning of this book that those who peered into the future at the end of the nineteenth century marked as a leading goal a more equitable distribution of the fruits of mechanized industry. As the decades rolled on toward the end of the twentieth century, it became possible to argue that this goal had almost been reached. Interrupted by wars and depression, long-term economic progress nonetheless brought the great majority of Europeans a standard of living enjoyed by only a few prior to 1914.

Many of the early-century prophets, also, had thought that some kind of socialist modification of the capitalist order would have to secure this distribution of material abundance; and in the broadest sense this has come to pass. A massive growth of the public sector, national economic planning, guarantees of minimum welfare via state welfare programs—all the advanced societies, whatever they call themselves, have had to develop in this direction. But the economic formula for maximum success that was painfully worked out over the decades was one that combined capitalism with socialism. If capitalism is forced to take the workers into partnership and provide them with the protection of state-administered welfare, communism must pay its respects to managerial autonomy and the market economy. Stalin's command econ-

[2] See, for example, Robert Skidelsky, ed., *The End of the Keynesian Era* (London: Macmillan, 1978).

omy was as obsolete by 1975 as was unregulated free enterprise. In this convergence of two extremes Western Europe led the way.

Those who tried to chart the course of the coming century in 1901 usually failed to see the danger of war, supposing that this relic of barbarism was about to disappear. They were woefully wrong, and they were condemned to watch in dismay as ghastly slaughter almost took over what was supposed to be a century of peace and progress. No fact was more responsible for the pessimism that pervaded the age's thought. And those who sought an easy villain first in capitalism and then in communism were forced to concede that the roots of conflict are laid deeply within the human condition, a product of human pride and will to independence as well as greed and fear. So this nineteenth-century hope for the twentieth, the hope of eternal peace, has not been realized and seems almost as far away as ever. If a third major holocaust has been avoided, thanks to the balance of terror, this has not prevented many smaller but cruelly destructive wars on the fringe of Europe, in Asia, Africa, and the Middle East, nor has it removed the fear of an eventual upsetting of the precarious nuclear balance, which could mean only universal and total destruction. And in this terrible game of chance, Europe proper is almost helpless, since the two superpowers, Russia and the United States, still hold virtually all the chips in the form of strategic nuclear arms.

On the other hand, nuclear confrontation has become less likely in many ways. The economic revival of Western Europe, the disintegration of the power blocs, trends in the Soviet satellite countries toward greater autonomy (if uneven and uncertain), the crumbling of the hard crust of ideological dogmatism in the USSR itself, and (one hopes) the greater maturity of American diplomacy have all helped. "Brother enemies," the United States and the Soviet Union are bound together by their dangerous rivalry, as they have increasingly realized. They have developed considerable skill in avoiding confrontations that might lead to war, seeing to it that the foe is not pushed too far and is allowed an escape

Whatever its fate in dealing with those problems of economic scarcity and political conflict that have plagued humanity throughout its history, the twentieth century cannot be denied a rich contribution to humanity's store of ideas, its art and literature, its knowledge and practical skills. Among the things too much left out of this "history," which has necessarily had to leave much out, are the advances in those technical arts that make our lives more comfortable, from ways of having a tooth filled or an operation performed to writing on a typewriter, listening to music on the stereo, looking up something in the library, or taking an airplane trip. "Progress" is least deniable in this

Caravelles over the Pyrenees.
Photos Reportage Yan, Jean Dieuzaide.

area, and even those who complain of too many gadgets and the tyranny of technology are hardly ever found denying themselves the benefits of such facilities. A recent historian of medicine notes that "In the first three quarters of the twentieth century more specific remedies and preventives were devised for the control of infectious diseases than during the entire history of mankind before that time."[3] The quality of the music people listen to or the books they read, the reasons for the trips they take, may form an incongruous contrast to the means they employ, but at least they have the opportunity; and technology cannot reasonably be blamed for the misuse of its services. The twentieth century has abundantly provided us with cultural opportunities never before matched.

It has also provided us with cultural instruments, in the form of literature, art, music, philosophy. A reviewer of an edition of the poems of Osip Mandelstam, the martyred Russian literary giant, observed in 1978 that, "It is a miracle that the worst of times produced the best of poets." This might be said of the whole century. If we agree that the twentieth century has brought forth some of humanity's worst times, it has also produced great quantities of excellent poetry, music, and all other forms of art and thought. It is our prerogative, if we choose to exercise it, to reject the century's dismal side and build on its proud achievements.

[3] Harry F. Dowling, *Fighting Infection* (Harvard U. Press, 1977), p. 228.

Recommended Additional Reading

The following list of books, usually confined to twenty-five or thirty titles per chapter, is severely selective; in all of the areas, there is a huge literature, and even when we eliminate the ephemeral or inconsequential we are left with an amount of publication that would quickly overflow our space limitations. The student who wants to do substantial research will be led to other sources as he consults the writings listed below. He should also seek counsel from his instructor. And he should make the acquaintance of scholarly periodicals, where much of the important research in twentieth-century European history is published and where he will find book reviews. Among the most important in English are *Journal of Modern History, Journal of Contemporary History, Journal of Social History, Journal of Central European History, East European Quarterly, Soviet Studies, French Historical Studies,* and *American Historical Review.* Printed as an adjunct to the last named periodical, *Recently Published Articles* can guide the student to other journal articles. The bibliography here attempts to mix useful surveys of relatively large areas with selected specific studies that can put some meat on the bare bones of historical analysis. It is confined to English language works and, for the most part, to books published in the last twenty-five years.

Chapter 1

Anderson, R. D. *France, 1870–1914: Politics and Society.* Boston: Routledge & Kegan Paul, 1977.

Crankshaw, Edward. *The Fall of the House of Habsburg.* New York: Viking Press, 1963.

Curtis, Michael. *Three against the Third Republic.* Princeton: Princeton University Press, 1959.

Evans, Richard J., ed. *Society and Politics in Wilhelmine Germany.* London: Croom Helm, 1978.

Freeden, Michael. *The New Liberalism: An Ideology of Social Reform.* Oxford: Clarendon Press, 1977.

Goldberg, Harvey. *Life of Jean Jaurès.* Madison: University of Wisconsin Press, 1962.

Haimson, L. H. *Russian Marxists and the Origins of Bolshevism.* Boston: Beacon Press, 1955.

Healy, Ann E. *The Russian Autocracy in Crisis 1905–1907.* Hamden, Conn.: Archon Books, 1976.

Hughes, H. Stuart. *Consciousness and Society: European Social Thought 1890–1930.* New York: Alfred A. Knopf, 1958.

Hynes, Samuel. *The Edwardian Turn of Mind.* Princeton: Princeton University Press, 1968.

Janik, Allan and Stephen Toulmin. *Wittgenstein's Vienna.* New York: Simon and Schuster, 1973.

Lees, Andrew and Lyon, eds. *The Urbanization of European Society in the Nineteenth Century.* Lexington, Mass.: D. C. Heath and Co., 1976.

MacKenzie, Norman and Jeanne. *The Fabians.* New York: Simon & Schuster, 1977.

McGrath, William J. *Dionysian Art and Populist Politics in Austria.* New Haven: Yale University Press, 1974.

Meacham, Standish. *A Life Apart: The English Working Class 1870–1914.* Cambridge, Mass.: Harvard University Press, 1977.

Nettl, J. P. *Rosa Luxemburg.* Vol. 1. New York: Oxford University Press, 1966.

Pascal, Roy. *From Naturalism to Expressionism: German Literature and Society 1880–1918.* New York: Basic Books, 1973.

Poirier, Philip. *The Advent of the Labour Party.* New York: Columbia University Press, 1958.

Rosen, Andrew. *Rise Up, Women: The Militant Campaign of the Women's Social and Political Union, 1903–1914.* Boston: Routledge & Kegan Paul, 1974.

Ross, Ronald J. *Beleaguered Tower: The Dilemma of Political Catholicism in Wilhelmine Germany.* Notre Dame: University of Notre Dame Press, 1976.

Sablinsky, Walter. *The Road to Bloody Sunday.* Princeton: Princeton University Press, 1977.

Salomone, A. W. *Italian Democracy in the Making, 1900–1914.* Philadelphia: University of Pennsylvania Press, 1960.

Schorske, Carl. *German Social Democracy 1905–1917.* Cambridge, Mass.: Harvard University Press, 1955.

Thompson, Paul R. *The Edwardians: The Remaking of British Society.* London: Weidenfeld & Nicolson, 1975.

Thomson, David. *Democracy in France since 1870.* New York: Oxford University Press, 1969.

Treadgold, Donald. *Lenin and His Rivals: The Struggle for Russia's Future 1898–1906.* New York: Frederick A. Praeger, 1955.

Von Laue, Theodore. *Sergei Witte and the Industrialization of Russia.* New York: Columbia University Press, 1963.

Weber, Eugen. *The Nationalist Revival in France, 1905–1914.* Berkeley: University of California Press, 1959.

——— *Peasants into Frenchmen: The Modernization of Rural France 1870–1914.* Stanford: Stanford University Press, 1977.

Zeldin, Theodore. *France 1848–1945.* 2 vols. Oxford: Clarendon Press, 1973, 1977.

Chapter 2

Albertini, Luigi. *The Origins of the War of 1914.* 3 vols. New York: Oxford University Press, 1952–1957.

Andrew, Christopher. *Théophile Delcassé and the Making of the Entente Cordiale.* London: Macmillan, 1968.

Bergbahn, V. L. *Germany and the Approach of War in 1914.* New York: St. Martin's Press, 1973.

Dedijer, Vladimir. *The Road to Sarajevo.* New York: Simon & Schuster, 1966.

Ellis, Jack D. *The French Socialists and the Problem of Peace 1904–1914.* Chicago: Loyola University Press, 1966.

Eubank, Keith. *Paul Cambon, Master Diplomatist.* Norman: University of Oklahoma Press, 1960.

Fischer, Fritz. *War of Illusions: German Policies from 1911 to 1914.* New York: W. W. Norton, 1975.

Gooch, G. P. *Studies in Diplomacy and Statecraft.* London: Longman, Green & Co., 1942.

Haupt, Georges. *Socialism and the Great War: The Collapse of the Second International.* Oxford: Clarendon Press, 1972.

Hazelhurst, Cameron. *Politicians at War.* New York: Knopf, 1971.

Helmreich, E. C. *The Diplomacy of the Balkan Wars 1912–1913.* New York: Russell and Russell, 1969 (1938).

Koch, H. W., ed. *The Origins of the First World War.* New York: Taplinger Publishing Co., 1972.

Lafore, Lawrence. *The Long Fuse.* Philadelphia: J. B. Lippincott, 1965.

Laqueur, Walter. *Young Germany.* New York: Basic Books, 1962.

Morris, Anthony A. J. *Radicalism against War, 1906–1914.* Totowa, N.J.: Rowman and Littlefield, 1974.
Remak, Joachim. *Sarajevo, the Story of a Political Murder.* New York: Criterion Books, 1959.
Rich, Norman. *Holstein.* Cambridge: Cambridge University Press, 1965.
Ritter, Gerhart. *The Schlieffen Plan.* New York: Praeger, 1958.
Silverman, Dan P. *Reluctant Union: Alsace-Lorraine and Imperial Germany 1871–1918.* State College, Pa.: Pennsylvania State University Press, 1972.
Tuchman, Barbara. *The Guns of August.* New York: Macmillan, 1962.
Vucinich, Wayne. *Serbia between East and West, 1903–1908.* Stanford: Stanford University Press, 1954.
Williamson, Samuel R. *The Politics of Grand Strategy: Britain and France Prepare for War 1904–1914.* Cambridge, Mass.: Harvard University Press, 1969.

Chapter 3

Adams, R. J. Q. *Arms and the Wizard: Lloyd George and the Ministry of Munitions 1915–1916.* London: Cassell, 1978.
Barnett, Corelli. *The Swordbearers.* New York: Morrow, 1964.
Bergonzi, Bernard. *Heroes' Twilight: A Study of the Literature of the Great War.* London: Constable, 1965.
Chapman, Guy, ed. *Vain Glory.* London: Cassell, 1968.
Falls, Cyril. *The Great War 1914–1918.* New York: Capricorn Books, 1959.
Ferro, Marc. *The Great War, 1914–1918.* London: Routledge & Kegan Paul, 1973.
Fischer, Fritz. *World Power or Decline: The Controversy over Germany's Aims in the First World War.* New York: Norton, 1974.
——— *Germany's Aims in the First World War.* New York: Norton, 1967.
Gardner, Brian. *The Big Push.* New York: Morrow, 1963.
———, ed. *Up the Line to Death.* London: Methuen, 1964.
Gatzke, Hans W. *Germany's Drive to the West: A Study of Germany's Western War Aims during the First World War.* Baltimore: Johns Hopkins University Press, 1950.
Guinn, Paul. *British Strategy and Politics 1914–1918.* Oxford: Clarendon Press, 1965.
Hardach, Gerd. *The First World War.* Berkeley: University of California Press, 1977. (History of the World Economy in the Twentieth Century)
Horn, Daniel. *The German Naval Mutinies of World War I.* New Brunswick, N.J.: Rutgers University Press, 1969.
Horne, Alistair. *The Price of Glory: Verdun 1916.* New York: St. Martin's, 1963.
James, Robert Rhodes. *Gallipoli.* London: B. T. Batsford, 1965.
King, Jere C. *Generals and Politicians.* Berkeley: University of California Press, 1951.

Kitchen, Martin. *The Silent Dictatorship: Politics of the German High Command under Hindenburg and Ludendorff 1916–1918.* New York: Holmes & Meier, 1976.

Marder, Arthur J. *From the Dreadnought to Scapa Flow: The Royal Navy in the Fisher Era 1904–1919.* 3 vols. New York: Oxford University Press, 1961–1966.

Marwick, Arthur. *The Deluge: British Society and the First World War.* Boston: Little, Brown & Co., 1965.

———— *Women at War, 1914–1918.* London: Croom Helm, 1977.

Panichas, George, ed. *Promise of Greatness.* New York: John Day Co., 1968.

Rothwell, Victor H. *British War Aims and Peace Diplomacy 1914–1918.* Oxford: Clarendon Press, 1971.

Stein, Leonard. *The Balfour Declaration.* New York: Simon & Schuster, 1961.

Terraine, John. *The Western Front 1914–1918.* London: Hutchinson, 1964.

Watt, Richard M. *Dare Call It Treason.* New York: Simon & Schuster, 1963.

Williams, John. *The Home Fronts.* London: Constable, 1972.

Woodward, Ernest Llewellyn. *Great Britain and the War of 1914–1918.* New York: Barnes & Noble, 1967.

Zeman, Z. A. B. *Diplomatic History of the First World War.* London: Weidenfeld & Nicolson, 1971.

———— *The Breakup of the Hapsburg Empire.* New York: Oxford University Press, 1961.

Chapter 4

Anweiler, Oskar. *The Soviets.* New York: Pantheon Books, 1975.

Avrich, Peter. *The Russian Anarchists.* Princeton: Princeton University Press, 1967.

———— *Kronstadt 1921.* Princeton: Princeton University Press, 1970.

Bonsal, Stephen. *Suitors and Suppliants: The Little Nations at Versailles.* Englewood Cliffs: Prentice-Hall, 1946.

Bradley, John F. N. *Civil War in Russia 1917–1920.* London: Batsford, 1975.

———— *Allied Intervention in Russia.* New York: Basic Books, 1968.

Carr, Edward H. *The October Revolution, before and after.* New York: Macmillan, 1969.

Carsten, F. L. *Revolution in Central Europe, 1918–1919.* London: Temple Smith, 1972.

Clark, Martin. *Antonio Gramsci and the Revolution That Failed.* New Haven: Yale University Press, 1977.

Daniels, Robert V. *Red October.* New York: Charles Scribner's Sons, 1967.

Gruber, Helmut, ed. *International Communism in the Era of Lenin.* Ithaca, N.Y.: Cornell University Press, 1967.

Helmreich, Paul C. *From Paris to Sèvres: The Partition of the Ottoman Empire at the Peace Conference of 1919–1920.* Columbus: Ohio State University Press, 1974.

Keep, John H. L. *The Russian Revolution: A Study in Mass Mobilization.* New York: Norton, 1977.

Kendall, Walter. *The Revolutionary Movement in Great Britain 1900–1921.* London: Weidenfeld & Nicolson, 1969.

King, Jere C. *Foch versus Clemenceau.* Cambridge, Mass.: Harvard University Press, 1960.

Lindemann, Albert S. *The Red Years: European Socialism versus Bolshevism 1918–1920.* Berkeley: University of California Press, 1974.

Mayer, Arno W. *Political Origins of the New Diplomacy.* New Haven: Yale University Press, 1959.

———— *Politics and Diplomacy of Peacemaking.* New York: Knopf, 1967.

Nettl, J. P. *Rosa Luxemburg.* Vol. 2. New York: Oxford University Press, 1966.

Nicolson, Harold. *Peacemaking 1919.* Boston: Houghton Mifflin, 1933.

Pipes, Richard. *The Formation of the Soviet Union.* Cambridge, Mass.: Harvard University Press, 1964.

————, ed. *Revolutionary Russia.* Cambridge, Mass.: Harvard University Press, 1967.

Rabinowitch, Alexander. *Prelude to Revolution.* Bloomington: Indiana University Press, 1968.

———— *The Bolsheviks Come to Power.* New York: Norton, 1976.

Radkey, O. H. *The Sickle under the Hammer.* New York: Columbia University Press, 1963.

Schapiro, Leonard and Peter Reddaway, eds. *Lenin: The Man, the Theorist, the Leader.* New York: Praeger, 1967.

Thompson, John M. *Russia, Bolshevism and the Versailles Peace.* Princeton: Princeton University Press, 1966.

Tillman, Seth P. *Anglo-American Relations at the Paris Peace Conference of 1919.* Princeton: Princeton University Press, 1961.

Williams, Desmond, ed. *The Irish Struggle, 1919–1926.* London: Routledge & Kegan Paul, 1966.

Chapter 5

Angress, Werner T. *The Stillborn Revolution: The Communist Bid for Power in Germany 1918–1923.* Princeton: Princeton University Press, 1963.

Campbell, F. Gregory. *Confrontation in Central Europe: Weimar Germany and Czechoslovakia.* Chicago: University of Chicago Press, 1975.

Carr, Edward H. *A History of Soviet Russia.* Vols. 4–9. New York: Macmillan, 1954–1971.

Cassels, Alan. *Fascist Italy.* New York: Thomas Y. Crowell, 1968.

Cohen, Stephen F. *Bukharin and the Bolshevist Revolution.* New York: Knopf, 1973.

Day, Richard B. *Leon Trotsky and the Politics of Economic Isolation.* Cambridge: Cambridge University Press, 1973.

Deutscher, Isaac. *Trotsky: The Prophet Unarmed, 1921–1929.* New York: Oxford University Press, 1959.

Dorpalen, Andreas. *Hindenburg and the Weimar Republic.* Princeton: Princeton University Press, 1964.

Erlich, Alexander. *The Soviet Industrialization Debate, 1924–1928.* Cambridge, Mass.: Harvard University Press, 1961.

——— *Soviet Economists of the 1920s.* Cambridge: Cambridge University Press, 1972.

Gatzke, Hans W. *Stresemann and the Rearmament of Germany.* Baltimore: Johns Hopkins University Press, 1954.

Glynn, Sean. *Interwar Britain: Social and Economic History.* London: Allen & Unwin, 1976.

Gordon, Harold J. *Hitler and the Beer Hall Putsch.* Princeton: Princeton University Press, 1972.

Jacobson, Jon. *Locarno Diplomacy: Germany and the West 1925–1929.* Princeton: Princeton University Press, 1972.

Lyttelton, Adrian. *The Seizure of Power: Fascism in Italy 1919–1929.* New York: Scribner's, 1973.

Maier, Charles S. *Recasting Bourgeois Europe: Stabilization in France, Germany and Italy in the Decade after World War I.* Princeton: Princeton University Press, 1975.

Marks, Sally. *The Illusion of Peace: International Relations in Europe 1918–1923.* New York: St. Martin's, 1976.

Middlemas, Keith. *Baldwin, a Biography.* New York: Macmillan, 1970.

Nolte, Ernst. *Three Faces of Fascism.* New York: Holt, Rinehart, & Winston, 1966.

Phillips, G. A. *The General Strike: The Politics of Industrial Conflict.* London: Weidenfeld & Nicolson, 1976.

Raymond, John, ed. *The Baldwin Age.* London: Eyre & Spottiswoode, 1960.

Ringer, Fritz, ed. *The German Inflation of 1923.* New York: Oxford University Press, 1969.

Schuker, Stephen A. *The End of French Predominance in Europe: The Financial Crisis of 1924 and the Adoption of the Dawes Plan.* Chapel Hill: University of North Carolina Press, 1977.

Seton-Watson, Christopher. *Italy from Liberalism to Fascism, 1870–1925.* London: Methuen, 1967.

Turner, Henry A. *Stresemann and the Politics of the Weimar Republic.* Princeton: Princeton University Press, 1963.

Ulam, Adam B. *Stalin: The Man and his Era.* New York: Viking Press, 1973.

Waite, R. G. L. *The Free Corps Movement, 1918–1923.* Cambridge, Mass.: Harvard University Press, 1951.

Chapter 6

Balthasar, Hans Urs von. *The Theology of Karl Barth.* New York: Holt Rinehart, & Winston, 1971.

Bell, Quentin. *Bloomsbury.* London: Futura Publications, 1974.

Blake, Peter. *The Master Builders.* New York: Norton, 1976.

Bree, Germaine and Margaret Guiton. *The French Novel from Gide to Camus.* New York: Harcourt, Brace and World, 1962.

Brennan, Joseph G. *Three Philosophical Novelists.* New York: Macmillan, 1964.

Brown, Edward J. *Mayakovsky: A Poet in the Revolution.* Princeton: Princeton University Press, 1973.

Bullivant, Keith, ed. *Culture and Society in the Weimar Republic.* Manchester: Manchester University Press, 1978.

Copleston, Frederick. *Contemporary Philosophy.* London: Search Press, 1972.

Deak, Istvan. *Weimar Germany's Leftwing Intellectuals.* Berkeley: University of California Press, 1968.

Gamow, George. *Thirty Years That Shook Physics.* Garden City: Doubleday & Co., 1966.

Gay, Peter. *Weimar Culture.* New York: Harper & Row, 1970.

Gershman, Herbert S. *The Surrealist Revolution in France.* Ann Arbor: University of Michigan Press, 1968.

Graves, Robert and Alan Hodge. *The Long Week End: A Social History of Great Britain 1918–1939.* New York: Macmillan, 1941.

Hofmann, Werner. *Turning Points in Twentieth Century Art.* New York: G. Braziller, 1969.

Kenner, Hugh. *The Pound Era.* Berkeley: University of California Press, 1971.

Lanczos, Cornelius. *The Einstein Decade.* London: Elek, 1974.

Laqueur, Walter and George L. Mosse, eds. *International Fascism 1920–1945.* New York: Harper & Row, 1966.

Maguire, Robert A. *Red Virgin Soil: Soviet Literature in the 1920s.* Princeton: Princeton University Press, 1968.

Mandelstam, Nadezhda. *Hope against Hope.* New York: Atheneum, 1970.

Mellers, Wilfrid. *Caliban Reborn: Renewal in Twentieth Century Music.* New York: Harper & Row, 1967.

Monaco, Paul. *Cinema and Society: France and Germany during the Twenties.* New York: Elsevier, 1976.

Poor, Harold L. *Kurt Tucholvsky and the Ordeal of Germany 1914–1935.* New York: Scribner's, 1968.

Press, John. *A Map of Modern English Verse.* London: Oxford University Press, 1969.

Rosengarten, Frank. *The Italian Anti-Fascist Press, 1919–1945.* Cleveland: Case Western Reserve Press, 1968.

Stade, George, ed. *Six Modern British Novelists.* New York: Columbia University Press, 1974.

Struve, Walter. *Elites against Democracy.* Princeton: Princeton University Press, 1973.

Wagar, W. Warren. *Good Tidings: The Belief in Progress from Darwin to Marcuse.* Bloomington: Indiana University Press, 1972.

Williams, L. Pearce, ed. *Relativity Theory: Its Origin and Impact on Modern Thought.* New York: John Wiley, 1968.

Wollheim, Richard. *Sigmund Freud.* New York: Viking Press, 1971.

Chapter 7

Allen, William Sheridan. *Nazi Seizure of Power: The Experience of a Single Town 1930–1935.* Chicago: Quadrangle Books, 1965.

Bassett, Reginald. *1931: Political Crisis.* New York: St. Martin's, 1958.

Brower, Daniel E. *The New Jacobins: The French Communist Party and the Popular Front.* Ithaca, N.Y.: Cornell University Press, 1968.

Carsten, F. L. *The Reichswehr and Politics, 1918–1933.* Oxford: Clarendon Press, 1966.

Caute, David. *The Fellow Travellers.* New York: Macmillan, 1973.

———— *Communism and the French Intellectuals.* New York: Macmillan, 1964.

Colton, Joel. *Leon Blum: Humanist in Politics.* New York: Knopf, 1966.

Eschenburg, Theodor, et al. *The Path to Dictatorship 1918–1933.* Garden City: Doubleday & Co., 1966.

Fest, Joachim C. *Hitler.* New York: Random House, 1975.

Greene, Nathaniel. *Crisis and Decline: The French Socialist Party in the Popular Front Era.* Ithaca: Cornell University Press, 1969.

Heberle, Rudolf. *From Democracy to Nazism.* Baton Rouge: Louisiana State University Press, 1945.

Holborn, Hajo, ed. *Republic to Reich: The Making of the Nazi Revolution.* New York: Pantheon Books, 1972.

Jäckel, Eberhard. *Hitler's Weltanschauung: A Blueprint for Power.* Middletown, Conn.: Wesleyan University Press, 1972.

Jay, Martin. *The Dialectical Imagination: A History of the Frankfurt School, 1923–1950.* Boston: Little, Brown, 1973.

Kele, Max. *The Nazis and the Workers.* Chapel Hill: University of North Carolina Press, 1972.

Kindleberger, Charles P. *The World in Depression, 1929–1939.* London: Allen Lane, 1973.

Larmour, Peter. *The French Radical Party in the 1930s.* Stanford: Stanford University Press, 1964.

Lewis, W. Arthur. *Economic Survey 1919–1939.* London: Allen & Unwin, 1949.

Marcus, John T. *French Socialism in the Crisis Years, 1933–1936.* New York: Praeger, 1963.

Marquand, David. *Ramsay MacDonald.* London: Jonathan Cape, 1977.

Maser, Werner. *Hitler: Legend, Myth and Reality.* New York: Harper & Row, 1973.

Merkl, Peter H. *Political Violence under the Swastika: 581 Early Nazis.* Princeton: Princeton University Press, 1975.

Pimlott, Ben. *Labour and the Left in the 1930s.* London: Cambridge University Press, 1978.

Pridham, Geoffrey. *Hitler's Rise to Power: The Nazi Movement in Bavaria 1928–1933.* London: Hart-Davis MacGibbon, 1973.

Richardson, H. W. *Economic Recovery in Britain 1932–1939.* London: Weidenfeld & Nicolson, 1967.

Schweitzer, Arthur. *Big Business and the Third Reich*. Bloomington: Indiana University Press, 1977.

Shackle, G. L. S. *The Years of High Theory*. Cambridge: Cambridge University Press, 1967.

Stevenson, John and Chris Cook. *Social Conditions in Britain between the Wars*. Harmondsworth: Penguin Books, 1977.

Stewart, Michael. *Keynes and After*. Harmondsworth: Penguin Books, 1972.

Symons, Julian. *The Thirties*. London: Faber, 1975.

Wood, Neal. *Communism and British Intellectuals*. New York: Columbia University Press, 1959.

Chapter 8

Arendt, Hannah. *Origins of Totalitarianism*. New York: Harcourt, Brace & World, 1966.

Benson, Frederick R. *Writers in Arms: The Literary Impact of the Spanish Civil War*. New York: New York University Press, 1967.

Beyerchen, Alan D. *Scientists under Hitler*. New Haven: Yale University Press, 1977.

Bracher, Karl D. *The German Dictatorship*. New York: Praeger, 1970.

Conquest, Robert. *The Great Terror*. Harmondsworth: Penguin, 1971.

────── *Kolyma: The Arctic Death Camps*. New York: Vikings, 1978.

Coverdale, John F. *Italian Intervention in the Spanish Civil War*. Princeton: Princeton University Press, 1975.

Deutsch, Harold C. *Hitler and His Generals: The Crisis of January-June, 1938*. Minneapolis: University of Minnesota Press, 1974.

Dunham, Vera. *In Stalin's Time: Middle Class Values in Soviet Fiction*. New York: Cambridge University Press, 1976.

Farquharson, J. E. *The Plough and the Swastika*. Beverly Hills: Sage Publications, 1977.

Felice, Renzo de. *Interpretations of Fascism*. Cambridge, Mass.: Harvard University Press, 1977.

Fest, J. C. *The Face of the Third Reich*. New York: Random House, 1970.

Gallo, Max. *The Night of the Long Knives*. New York: Harper & Row, 1972.

Gregory, Paul R. and Robert C. Stuart. *Soviet Economic Structure and Performance*. New York: Harper & Row, 1974.

Hale, Oron J. *The Captive Press in the Third Reich*. Princeton: Princeton University Press, 1964.

Hingley, Ronald. *Stalin: Man and Legend*. New York: McGraw-Hill, 1974.

Jackson, Gabriel. *The Spanish Republic and the Civil War 1931–1939*. Princeton: Princeton University Press, 1965.

Medvedev, Roy. *Let History Judge: The Origins and Consequences of Stalinism*. New York: Knopf, 1972.

Mosse, George L., ed. *Nazi Culture*. New York: Grosset & Dunlap, 1966.

O'Neill, Robert J. *The German Army and the Nazi Party 1933–1939*. London: Cassell, 1966.

Payne, Stanley G. *The Spanish Revolution*. New York: Norton, 1970.

Peterson, Edward N. *The Limits of Hitler's Power*. Princeton: Princeton University Press, 1969.

Schleunes, Karl A. *The Twisted Road to Auschwitz: Nazi Policy toward German Jews 1933–1939*. Urbana: University of Illinois Press, 1970.

Schoenbaum, David. *Hitler's Social Revolution*. Garden City: Doubleday, 1966.

Soucy, Robert. *Fascism in France: The Case of Maurice Barrès*. Berkeley: University of California Press, 1972.

Stephenson, Jill. *Women in Nazi Society*. New York: Barnes & Noble, 1975.

Sutton, Anthony C. *Western Technology and Soviet Economic Development, 1930–1945*. Stanford: Stanford University Press, 1972.

Swianiewicz, S. *Forced Labour and Economic Development: An Enquiry into the Experience of Soviet Industrialization*. London: Oxford University Press, 1965.

Thomas, Hugh. *The Spanish Civil War*. New York: Harper & Row, 1977.

Weintraub, Stanley. *The Last Great Cause: The Intellectuals and the Spanish Civil War*. New York: Weybright and Talley, 1968.

Chapter 9

Adamthwaite, Anthony. *France and the Coming of the Second World War 1936–1939*. London: Frank Cass, 1977.

Baer, George W. *The Coming of the Italian-Ethiopian War*. Cambridge, Mass.: Harvard University Press, 1967.

———— *Test Case: Italy, Ethiopia and the League of Nations*. Stanford: Stanford University Press, 1976.

Bruegel, J. W. *Czechoslovakia before Munich*. Cambridge: Cambridge University Press, 1973.

Ciencala, Anna M. *Poland and the Western Powers, 1938–1939*. Toronto: University of Toronto Press, 1968.

Cowling, Maurice. *The Impact of Hitler: British Politics and British Foreign Policy 1933–1940*. Cambridge: Cambridge University Press, 1975.

Deakin, F. W. *The Brutal Friendship: Hitler and Mussolini*. New York: Harper & Row, 1962.

Documents on German Foreign Policy, 1918–1945. Series C. vols. I-IV, 1933–1936; Series D. vols. I-VII, 1937–1939. Washington: Government Printing Office, 1949–1966.

Emmerson, J. T. *The Rhineland Crisis*. Ames, Ia.: Iowa State University Press, 1977.

Eubank, Keith. *Munich*. Norman: University of Oklahoma Press, 1963.

Gatzke, Hans W., ed. *European Diplomacy between Two Wars, 1919–1939*. Chicago: Quadrangle Books, 1972.

Gehl, Jurgen. *Austria, Germany and the Anschluss*. London: Oxford University Press, 1963.

Gibbs, N. H. *Grand Strategy*. Vol. 1: *Rearmament Strategy 1933 to September 1939*. London: Her Majesty's Stationery Office, 1977.

Gilbert, Martin. *The Roots of Appeasement*. London: Weidenfeld & Nicolson, 1966.

Korbel, Joseph. *Poland between East and West: Soviet and German Diplomacy toward Poland 1933–1939*. Princeton: Princeton University Press, 1963.

Micaud, Charles A. *The French Right and Nazi Germany, 1933–1939*. Durham, N.C.: Duke University Press, 1943.

Remak, Joachim. *The Origins of the Second World War*. Englewood Cliffs: Prentice-Hall, Inc., 1976.

Robbins, Keith. *Munich 1938*. London: Cassell, 1968.

Thorne, Christopher. *The Approach of War 1938–1939*. New York: St. Martin's, 1967.

Watt, Donald C. *Too Serious a Business: European Armies and the Approach of the Second World War*. Berkeley: University of California Press, 1975.

Weinberg, Gerhard. *The Foreign Policy of Hitler's Germany: Diplomatic Revolution in Europe 1933–1936*. Chicago: University of Chicago Press, 1970.

Chapter 10

Andrews, Allen. *Air Marshals: The Air War in Western Europe*. New York: Morrow, 1970.

Armstrong, John A., ed. *Soviet Partisans in World War II*. Madison: University of Wisconsin Press, 1964.

Baldwin, Hanson W. *The Crucial Years: The World at War, 1939–1941*. New York: Harper & Row, 1976.

Barker, Elisabeth. *British Policy in Southeast Europe in the Second World War*. London: Macmillan, 1976.

Bruce, George. *The Warsaw Uprising, 1 August-2 October 1944*. London: Hart-Davis, 1972.

Carsten, F. L. *The German Resistance to Hitler*. Berkeley: University of California Press, 1970.

Cave Brown, Anthony. *Bodyguard of Lies*. New York: Harper & Row, 1975.

Churchill, Winston. *The Second World War*. 6 vols. Boston: Houghton & Mifflin, 1948–1954.

Clark, Alan. *Barbarossa: The Russian-German Conflict 1941–1945*. New York: Morrow, 1965.

Conquest, Robert. *The Nation Killers: Soviet Deportation of Nationalities*. London: Macmillan, 1970.

Dallin, Alexander. *German Rule in Russia, 1941–1945*. New York: St. Martin's, 1957.

Dawidowicz, Lucy S., ed. *A Holocaust Reader*. New York: Behrman House, 1976.

Deakin, F. W. *The Embattled Mountain.* New York: Oxford University Press, 1971.

Deighton, Len. *Fighter: The True Story of the Battle of Britain.* London: J. Cape, 1977.

Delzell, Charles F. *Mussolini's Enemies: The Italian Anti-Fascist Resistance.* Princeton: Princeton University Press, 1961.

Dulles, Allen. *The Secret Surrender.* London: Weidenfeld & Nicolson, 1967.

Feis, Herbert. *Churchill, Roosevelt, Stalin.* Princeton: Princeton University Press, 1957.

Fenyo, Mario D. *Hitler, Horthy, and Hungary: German-Hungarian Relations 1941–1944.* New Haven: Yale University Press, 1973.

Gowing, Margaret. *Britain and Atomic Energy 1939–1945.* London: Macmillan, 1965.

Hilberg, Raul. *The Destruction of the European Jews.* Chicago: Quadrangle Books, 1961.

Irving, David. *Hitler's War.* New York: Viking, 1977.

—— *The German Atomic Bomb.* New York: Simon & Schuster, 1967.

—— *The Trail of the Fox.* New York: Dutton, 1977.

Jackson, W. G. F. *Overlord.* London: Batsford, 1978.

—— *The Battle for Italy.* New York: Harper & Row, 1967.

Jones, R. V. *The Wizard War: British Scientific Intelligence 1939–1945.* New York: Coward, McCann & Geoghegan, 1978. (British title: *The Most Secret War.*)

Jungk, Robert. *Brighter than a Thousand Suns.* New York: Harcourt Brace Jovanovich, 1958.

Lewin, Ronald. *The Life and Death of the Afrika Corps.* London: Batsford, 1977.

Masterman, John C. *The Double Cross System.* New Haven: Yale University Press, 1972.

Michel, Henri. *The Shadow War: European Resistance 1939–1945.* New York: Harper & Row, 1972.

Milward, Alan S. *War, Economy and Society 1939–1945.* Berkeley: University of California Press, 1977.

Montague, Ewen. *Beyond Top Secret U.* London: P. Davies, 1977.

Osgood, Samuel M., ed. *The Fall of France, 1940: Causes and Responsibilities.* Lexington, Mass.: D. C. Heath, 1972.

Paxton, Robert O. *Vichy France, 1940–1944.* New York: Knopf, 1972.

Roberts, Walter S. *Tito, Mihailovich and the Allies 1941–1945.* New Brunswick, N.J.: Rutgers University Press, 1973.

Rozek, Edward J. *Allied Wartime Diplomacy: A Pattern in Poland.* New York: Wiley, 1958.

Rupp, Leila J. *Mobilizing Women for War, 1939–1945.* Princeton: Princeton University Press, 1977.

Speer, Albert. *Inside the Third Reich: Memoirs of Albert Speer.* New York: Macmillan, 1970.

Stein, George H. *The Waffen SS: Hitler's Elite Guard at War 1939–1945.* Ithaca: Cornell University Press, 1966.

Strik-Strikfeldt, Wilfrid. *Against Stalin and Hitler: Memoirs of the Russian Liberation Movement, 1941–1945*. London: Macmillan, 1970.

Sweets, John F. *The Politics of Resistance: France 1940–1944*. De Kalb: Northern Illinois University Press, 1976.

Tolstoy, Nikolai. *Victims of Yalta*. London: Hodder & Stoughton, 1978.

Viorst, Milton. *Hostile Allies: FDR and Charles de Gaulle*. New York: Macmillan, 1965.

Woodward, E. Llewellyn. *British Foreign Policy in World War II*. London: H. M. S. O., 1970.

Wright, Gordon. *The Ordeal of Total War, 1939–1945*. New York: Harper & Row, 1968.

Chapter 11

Bader, William B. *Austria between East and West, 1945–1955*. Stanford: Stanford University Press, 1966.

Barber, Noel. *Seven Days of Freedom: The Hungarian Uprising, 1956*. London: Macmillan, 1974.

Baring, Arnulf. *Uprising in East Germany, June 17, 1953*. Ithaca: Cornell University Press, 1972.

Clay, Lucius. *Decision in Germany*. Garden City: Doubleday, 1950.

Davidson, Eugene. *The Death and Life of Germany: An Account of the American Occupation*. New York: Knopf, 1961.

Davis, Lynn E. *The Cold War Begins*. Princeton: Princeton University Press, 1974.

Dedijer, Valdimir. *The Battle Stalin Lost: Memoirs of Yugoslavia 1948–1953*. New York: Viking, 1971.

Eden, Anthony. *The Suez Crisis of 1956*. Boston: Beacon Press, 1960.

Gaddis, John L. *The United States and the Origins of the Cold War, 1941–1947*. New York: Columbia University Press, 1972.

Gimbel, John. *The Origins of the Marshall Plan*. Stanford: Stanford University Press, 1976.

———— *The American Occupation of Germany*. Stanford: Stanford University Press, 1968.

Hammond, Paul F. *Cold War and Détente*. New York: Harcourt Brace Jovanovich, 1975.

Kennan, George F. *Memoirs, 1925–1950*. Boston: Little, Brown, 1967.

LaFeber, Walter. *America, Russia and the Cold War, 1945–1966*. New York: Wiley, 1976.

Petrov, Vladimir. *A Study in Diplomacy: The Story of Arthur Bliss Lane*. Chicago: Regnery, 1971.

Radvanyi, Janos. *Hungary and Superpowers: The 1956 Revolution and Realpolitik*. Stanford: Stanford University Press, 1972.

Rusinow, Dennison. *The Yugoslav Experiment, 1948–1974*. Berkeley: University of California Press, 1977.

Sharp, Tony. *The Wartime Alliance and the Zonal Division of Germany.* Oxford: Clarendon Press, 1975.

Smith, Bradley F. *Reaching Judgment at Nuremberg.* New York: Basic Books, 1977.

Thomas, Hugh. *The Suez Affair.* Harmondsworth: Penguin, 1970.

Ulam, Adam B. *The Rivals: America and Russia since World War II.* New York: Viking, 1971.

Willis, F. Roy. *The French in Germany, 1945–1949.* Stanford: Stanford University Press, 1962.

Woodhouse, C. M. *The Struggle for Greece 1941–1949.* London: Hart-Davis MacGibbon, 1976.

Zinner, Paul E. *Communist Strategy and Tactics in Czechoslovakia, 1918–1948.* New York: Praeger, 1963.

Chapter 12

Armes, Roy. *French Cinema since 1946.* London: Zwemmer, 1970.

Aron, Raymond. *France: Steadfast and Changing.* Cambridge: Harvard University Press, 1960.

Bartlett, C. J. *A History of Postwar Britain.* New York: Longman, Inc., 1977.

Bell, Daniel. *The End of Ideology.* Glencoe, Ill.: Free Press, 1960.

Bogdanor, Vernon and Robert Skidelsky, eds. *The Age of Affluence, 1951–1964.* London: Macmillan, 1970.

Booker, Christopher. *The Neophiliacs.* London: Collins, 1970.

Bromberger, Merry and Serge. *Jean Monnet and the United States of Europe.* New York: Coward-McCann, 1969.

Butler, David E. *Political Change in Britain.* London: Macmillan, 1974.

Cox, C. B. and A. E. Dyson, eds. *The Twentieth Century Mind.* Vol. 3, *1945–1965.* London: Oxford University Press, 1972.

Denton, Geoffrey, Murray Forsyth and Malcolm Maclennan. *Economic Planning and Policies in Britain, France, and Germany.* New York: Praeger, 1968.

Gallo, Max. *Spain under Franco.* New York: Dutton, 1974.

Grosser, Alfred. *French Foreign Policy under de Gaulle.* Boston: Little, Brown, 1967.

——— *Germany in Our Times: A Political History of the Postwar Years.* New York: Praeger, 1971.

Haseler, Stephen. *The Gaitskellites.* London: Macmillan, 1969.

Hoffman, John D. *The Conservative Party in Opposition 1946–1952.* London: MacGibbon & Kee, 1964.

Horne, Alistair. *A Savage War of Peace: Algeria 1954–1962.* London: Macmillan, 1977.

Kogan, Norman. *A Political History of Postwar Italy.* New York: Praeger, 1966.

Lieberman, Sima. *The Growth of European Mixed Economies 1945–1970.* New York: Wiley, 1977.

MacRae, Duncan. *Parliament, Parties and Society in France, 1946–1958.* New York: St. Martin's Press, 1967.

Maier, Charles S. and Don S. White, eds. *The 13th of May: The Advent of de Gaulle's Republic.* New York: Oxford University Press, 1968.

Mayne, Richard. *The Recovery of Europe, 1945–1973.* Garden City: Doubleday, 1973.

McClelland, Charles E. and Steven P. Scher, eds. *Postwar German Culture.* New York: E. P. Dutton, 1974.

Morgan, Roger P. *West European Politics since 1945: The Shaping of the European Community.* London: Batsford, 1972.

Pattison de Ménil, Lois. *Who Speaks for Europe? The Vision of Charles de Gaulle.* London: Weidenfeld & Nicolson, 1977.

Phillips, G. A. *Growth of the British Economy, 1918–1968.* London: Allen & Unwin, 1973.

Pryce, Roy. *The Politics of the European Community.* Totowa, N.J.: Rowman & Littlefield, 1973.

Schellenger, H. K. *The SPD in the Bonn Republic.* The Hague: M. Nijhoff, 1968.

Shonfield, Andrew. *Modern Capitalism.* New York and London: Oxford University Press, 1965.

Sontheimer, Kurt. *The Government and Politics of West Germany.* New York: Praeger, 1973

Stromberg, Roland N. *After Everything: European Intellectual History since 1945.* New York: St. Martin's Press, 1975.

Williams, Philip M. and Martin Harrison. *Politics and Society in de Gaulle's Republic.* London: Longman, 1971.

Willis, F. Roy. *Italy Chooses Europe.* New York: Oxford University Press, 1971.

Chapter 13

Armstrong, John A. *Ideology, Politics and Government in the Soviet Union.* New York: Praeger, 1967.

Bortoli, Georges. *The Death of Stalin.* New York: Praeger, 1975.

The Chronicle of Current Events. Nos. 1–45. London: Routledge & Kegan Paul, 1978.

Conquest, Robert. *The Pasternak Affair.* Philadelphia: Lippincott, 1962.

———— *The Politics of Ideas in the USSR.* New York: Praeger, 1967.

Crankshaw, Edward. *Khrushchev, a Career.* New York: Viking Press, 1966.

Dinerstein, Herbert G. *The Making of a Missile Crisis.* Baltimore: Johns Hopkins University Press, 1976.

Edmonds, Robin. *Soviet Foreign Policy 1962–1973.* London: Oxford University Press, 1975.

Feiwel, George R. *The Soviet Quest for Economic Efficiency.* New York: Praeger, 1972.

Joravsky, David. *The Lysenko Affair.* Cambridge, Mass.: Harvard University Press, 1970.

Khrushchev, Nikita. *Khrushchev Remembers.* 2 vols. Boston: Little, Brown, 1970, 1974.

Korey, William. *The Soviet Cage: Anti-Semitism in the Soviet Union.* New York: Viking Press, 1972.

McCauley, Martin. *Khrushchev and the Development of Soviet Agriculture.* London: Macmillan, 1976.

Medvedev, Roy and Zhores. *Khrushchev: The Years in Power.* New York: Columbia University Press, 1976.

Nove, Alex. *Stalinism and After.* London: Allen & Unwin, 1975.

Reddaway, Peter, ed. *Uncensored Russia.* New York: American Heritage Press, 1972.

Rothberg, Abraham. *The Heirs of Stalin: Dissidence and the Soviet Regime 1953–1970.* Ithaca: Cornell University Press, 1972.

Sakharov, Andrei. *Progress, Coexistence and Intellectual Freedom.* New York: Norton, 1968.

Schwartz, Harry. *Tsars, Mandarins and Commissars: A History of Chinese-Russian Relations.* Garden City: Doubleday, 1973.

——— *The Soviet Economy since Stalin.* Philadelphia: Lippincott, 1965 .

Slusser, Robert M. *The Berlin Crisis of 1961.* Baltimore: Johns Hopkins University Press, 1973.

Solzhenitsyn, Alexander. *One Day in the Life of Ivan Denisovich; The First Circle; The Cancer Ward; The Gulag Archipelago.* For discussion of translations, see Alexis Klimoff, "Solzhenitsyn in English," in Kathryn Feuer, ed., *Solzhenitsyn: A Collection of Critical Essays.* Englewood Cliffs: Prentice-Hall, 1976.

Steele, Jonathan, ed. *Eastern Europe since Stalin.* Newton Abbot: David & Charles, 1974.

Tokes, Rudolf L. ed. *Dissent in the USSR.* Baltimore: Johns Hopkins University Press, 1975.

Treadgold, Donald, ed. *Soviet and Chinese Communism.* Seattle: University of Washington Press, 1967.

Wolfe, Thomas W. *Soviet Power and Europe, 1945–1970.* Baltimore: Johns Hopkins University Press, 1970.

Wolff, Robert L. *The Balkans in Our Time.* Cambridge, Mass.: Harvard University Press, 1974.

Chapter 14

Ardagh, John. *The New French Revolution.* New York: Harper & Row, 1968.
——— *The New France.* Harmondsworth: Penguin, 1973.
Aron, Raymond. *Progress and Disillusion: The Dialectics of Modern Society.* New York: Praeger, 1968.

Brown, Archie and Michael Kaser, eds. *The Soviet Union since the Fall of Khrushchev.* New York: Free Press, 1975.

Brown, Bernard E. *Protest in Paris: Anatomy of a Revolt.* Morristown, N.J.: General Learning Press, 1974.

Cranston, Maurice, ed. *The New Left: Six Critical Essays.* New York: The Library Press, 1971.

Darby, John. *Conflict in Northern Ireland.* New York: Barnes & Noble, 1976.

Demetz, Peter. *Postwar German Literature.* New York: Pegasus, 1970.

Ellul, Jacques. *The Technological Society.* New York: Knopf, 1964.

Fyvel, T. R. *Intellectuals Today: Problems in a Changing Society.* New York: Schocken Books, 1968.

Golan, Galia. *The Czechoslovakian Reform Movement: Communism in Crisis, 1962–1968.* Cambridge: Cambridge University Press, 1971.

James, Robert R. *Ambitions and Realities: British Politics 1964–1970.* London: Weidenfeld & Nicolson, 1972.

Kusin, Vladimir V. *The Intellectual Origins of the Prague Spring.* Cambridge: Cambridge University Press, 1971.

Leonhard, Wolfgang. *Three Faces of Marxism.* New York: Holt, Rinehart, & Winston, 1974.

McKie, David and Chris Cook, eds. *The Decade of Disillusion: British Politics in the Sixties.* London: Macmillan, 1972.

Mehnert, Klaus. *The Kremlin and the New Left.* Berkeley: University of California Press, 1975.

Monaco, James. *The New Wave.* New York: Oxford University Press, 1976.

Page, Benjamin B. *The Czech Reform Movement, 1963–1968.* Amsterdam: Grüner, 1973.

Poster, Mark. *Marxism and Existentialism in Postwar France.* Princeton: Princeton University Press, 1976.

Sampson, Anthony. *The New Europeans.* London: Hodder & Stoughton, 1968.

Shawcross, William. *Dubcek.* London: Weidenfeld & Nicolson, 1970.

Skilling, H. Gordon. *Czechoslovakia's Interrupted Revolution.* Princeton: Princeton University Press, 1976.

Spender, Stephen. *Year of the Young Rebels.* New York: Random House, 1969.

Statera, Gianni. *Death of a Utopia: Development and Decline of Student Movements in Europe.* New York: Oxford University Press, 1975.

Tatu, Michel. *Power in the Kremlin from Khrushchev to Kosygin.* New York: Viking, 1970.

Touraine, Alain. *The Post-Industrial Society.* New York: Random House, 1971.

——— *The May Movement: Revolt and Reform.* New York: Random House, 1971.

Watson, George. *Politics and Literature in Modern Britain.* London: Macmillan, 1977.

Widgery, David, ed. *The Left in Britain 1956–1968.* Baltimore: Johns Hopkins University Press, 1976.

Chapter 15

Acquaviva, S. S. and M. Santuccio. *Social Structure in Italy: Crisis of a System*. London: Martin Robertson, 1977.

Bell, Daniel. *The Coming of Post-Industrial Society*. New York: Basic Books, 1973.

Bigsby, C. W. E., ed. *Superculture: American Popular Culture and Europe*. Bowling Green, O.: Bowling Green University Press, 1975.

Buchan, Alastair. *The End of the Postwar Era*. London: Weidenfeld & Nicolson, 1974.

Elkins, T. H. *The Urban Explosion*. London: Macmillan, 1973.

Fiegehen, G. C., P. S. Lansley and A. D. Smith. *Poverty and Progress in Britain, 1953–1973*. Cambridge: Cambridge University Press, 1978.

Flower, J. E., ed. *France Today*. London: Methuen, 1973.

Frisling, B. W., ed. *Social Change in Europe*. New York: Humanities Press, 1974.

Geiger, Kent H. *The Family in Soviet Russia*. Cambridge, Mass.: Harvard University Press, 1977.

Giner, Salvador and Margaret Scotford Archer, eds. *Contemporary Europe: Social Structure and Cultural Patterns*. London: Routledge & Kegan Paul, 1978.

Glyn, Andrew and Bob Sutcliffe. *Capitalism in Crisis*. New York: Pantheon Books, 1972.

Graham, Loren. *Science and Philosophy in the Soviet Union*. New York: Knopf, 1972.

Halsey, A. H. *Change in British Society*. London: Oxford University Press, 1978.

Haseler, Stephen. *The Death of British Democracy*. London: Paul Elek, 1976.

King, Richard. *The Party of Eros*. Chapel Hill: University of North Carolina Press, 1972.

Korbel, Joseph. *Detente in Europe: Real or Imaginary?* Princeton: Princeton University Press, 1972.

Lapidus, Gail W. *Women in Soviet Society*. Berkeley: University of California Press, 1978.

McInnes, Neil. *The Western Marxists*. New York: Library Press, 1972.

———— *The Communist Parties of Western Europe*. London: Oxford University Press, 1975.

Meissner, Boris, ed. *Social Change in the Soviet Union*. Notre Dame: University of Notre Dame Press, 1972.

Melly, George. *Revolt into Style: The Pop Arts in Britain*. London: Allen Lane, 1970

Morton, Henry W. and R. L. Tokes, eds. *Soviet Politics and Society in the 1970s*. New York: Free Press, 1974.

Newhouse, John. *Cold Dawn: The Story of SALT*. New York: Holt, Rinehart, & Winston, 1973.

Noble, Trevor. *Modern Britain: Structure and Change*. London: B. T. Batsford, 1975.

Preston, Paul, ed. *Spain in Crisis.* Hassocks, Eng.: Harvester Press, 1976.

Robinson, Paul. *The Modernization of Sex.* New York: Harper & Row, 1976.

Rose, Richard. *Politics in England Today.* Boston: Little, Brown, 1974.

Shanor, Donald. *Soviet Europe.* New York: Harper & Row, 1975.

Sharp, Denis. *A Visual History of Twentieth Century Architecture.* Greenwich, Conn.: New York Graphic Society, 1972.

Sinanian, Sylvia et al. *Eastern Europe in the 1970s.* New York: Praeger, 1972.

Tokes, Rudolph L., ed. *European Communism in the Age of Detente.* New York: New York University Press, 1978.

Warnecke, Steven J., ed. *The European Community in the 1970s.* New York: Praeger, 1972.

Whetten, Lawrence L. *Germany's Ostpolitik.* London: Oxford University Press, 1971.

Williamson, John. *The Failure of World Monetary Reform 1971–1974.* London: Nelson & Sons, 1977.

Wood, David M. *Power and Policy in Western European Democracies.* New York: Wiley, 1978.

Index

A

Acheson, Dean, 326, 335
Adenauer, Konrad, 151, 338, 355–58, 382–83, 407
Adler, Friedrich, 88
Adorno,Theodor, 409, 412
Aerenthal, Lexa von, 53–54, 56, 58–59
Agriculture, 18, 201–2, 214, 368, 405, 450
    in USSR, 236–37, 376, 380–81, 393–94
Akhmatova, Anna, 180
Alain-Fournier, Henry, 91
Albania, 61, 80, 147, 282, 328, 337, 384, 421, 427
Alcala Zamora, Niceto, 244
Alexander, King of Yugoslavia, 163–64, 262
Alfonso XII, King of Spain, 243
Algeciras Conference (1906), 50–51, 59
Algeria, 51
    Algerian War (1954–62), 351–53
Aliger, Margarita, 396
Allende, Salvador, 437
Alsace-Lorraine, 11, 48, 62, 101, 123, 155, 364
Althusser, Louis, 432

Amalrik, Andrei, 419
Anarchism, Anarchists, 37, 45, 64, 114, 244–45, 247, 413
Angell, Norman, 42
Anglo-German Naval Treaty (1935), 255–56, 260, 261
Anti-semitism, 29, 209, 213, 215–17, 230, 305–7, 397
Arabs, 129–130
    Arab-Israeli wars (1948–73), 326, 340, 406–7, 435–37
Aragon, Louis, 222, 417
Architecture, 176–77, 452
Arendt, Hannah, 181
Arlen, Michael, 195
Armand, Inessa, 107
Armenians, massacre of, 94
Art, 24, 156, 176, 431
Asquith, Herbert, 26–27, 52, 73, 80, 87, 140
Atatürk, Kemal, 8, 127
Atomic weapons, 187, 307–8, 313, 333–34, 387, 434–35, 438
Attlee, Clement, 360–61
Auden, W. H., 248
Auschwitz, 233, 306–7, 317, 369, 445
Australia, 445